Human–Computer Interaction Series

Editors-in-Chief

Desney Tan
Microsoft Research, Redmond, WA, USA

Jean Vanderdonckt
Louvain School of Management, Université catholique de Louvain,
Louvain-La-Neuve, Belgium

The Human–Computer Interaction Series, launched in 2004, publishes books that advance the science and technology of developing systems which are effective and satisfying for people in a wide variety of contexts. Titles focus on theoretical perspectives (such as formal approaches drawn from a variety of behavioural sciences), practical approaches (such as techniques for effectively integrating user needs in system development), and social issues (such as the determinants of utility, usability and acceptability).

HCI is a multidisciplinary field and focuses on the human aspects in the development of computer technology. As technology becomes increasingly more pervasive the need to take a human-centred approach in the design and development of computer-based systems becomes ever more important.

Titles published within the Human–Computer Interaction Series are included in Thomson Reuters' Book Citation Index, The DBLP Computer Science Bibliography and The HCI Bibliography.

More information about this series at http://www.springer.com/series/6033

Boris Galitsky

Artificial Intelligence for Customer Relationship Management

Keeping Customers Informed

 Springer

Boris Galitsky
Oracle Labs
Redwood Shores, CA, USA

ISSN 1571-5035 ISSN 2524-4477 (electronic)
Human–Computer Interaction Series
ISBN 978-3-030-52169-1 ISBN 978-3-030-52167-7 (eBook)
https://doi.org/10.1007/978-3-030-52167-7

This Springer imprint is published by the registered company Springer Nature Switzerland AG
The registered company address is: Gewerbestrasse 11, 6330 Cham, Switzerland

Contents

Chapter 1
Introduction to Volume 1 and Volume 2

Abstract This chapter is an Introduction to both volumes of this Artificial Intelligence for Customer Relationship Management book: Volume 1 "Keeping Customers Informed" and Volume 2 "Solving Customer Problems". We analyze AI adoption in Customer Relationship Management (CRM), briefly survey current trends, introduce AI CRM companies and discuss what kind of machine learning (ML) is best to support CRM. We explore where CRM is today and identify a lack of intelligence as a major bottleneck of current CRM systems. A hint to the reader is given on how to navigate this book.

1.1 AI Adoption in CRM

For any company, its customers are the foundation for its success and revenue. Businesses become more aware of the importance of gaining customers' satisfaction. Customer relationship management (CRM) supports marketing by selecting target consumers and creating cost-effective relationships with them. CRM is the process of machine understanding of customer behavior to support an organization to enhance customer acquisition, retention, and profitability (Fig. 1.1). CRM systems leverage business intelligence and analytical models to identify the most profitable group of consumers and target them to maintain higher customer retention rates. Business intelligence models predict customers with a high probability to leave based on analyzing customers' personal, demographic and behavioral data as well as their complaints to provide personalized and customer-oriented marketing campaigns to gain customer satisfaction (Sabbeh 2018). The lifecycle of a business–customer relationship includes four main stages:

(1) *Identification*. This phase, also referred to as *Acquisition*, identifies profitable customers and the ones that are highly probable to become customers. Segmentation and clustering techniques can explore customers' personal and historical data to create segments/cohorts of similar customers.
(2) *Attraction*. Cohorts identified in (1) are analyzed to compute the common features that distinguish customers within this cohort. A variety of marketing

© Springer Nature Switzerland AG 2020

B. Galitsky, *Artificial Intelligence for Customer Relationship Management*,
Human–Computer Interaction Series,
https://doi.org/10.1007/978-3-030-52167-7_1

Fig. 1.1 CRM is about understanding human thinking and human behavior

techniques are used to target different customer cohorts (Brito et al. 2015, Chaps. 2–8 Volume 1).

(3) *Retention.* This is the main objective of CRM. Retaining existing customers is five to twenty times more cost-efficient than acquiring new ones (The Chartered Institute of Marketing 2010; Shaw 2013). Customer retention includes all actions taken by a company to guarantee customer loyalty and reduce customer churn. Customer churn refers to customers moving to a competitive organization or service provider. Churns can occur for better quality of products elsewhere, offers, benefits or better customer service. A churn rate is a key indicator that all businesses minimize (Chaps. 7–9 Volume 2).

(4) *Customer development* increases the number of transactions for more profitability. To achieve this, market basket analysis, customer lifetime value, up/cross-selling techniques are employed. Market basket analysis tries to analyze customers' behavior patterns to maximize the intensity of transactions (Jain et al. 2018; Kaur and Kang 2016) Analyzing customers' lifetime values and communicating with them (Chap. 10 Volume 1 and Chaps. 1–5 Volume 2) can help to identify the total net income expected from customers.

Artificial Intelligence (AI) techniques support all of these phases. AI has impacted nearly every aspect of our consumer lives, redefining how we engage with technology and each other. With the convergence of increased computing power, big data and breakthroughs in ML, AI is also poised to transform how people work. While some researchers predict automation driven by AI could impact almost a half of job activities and eliminate around 5 percent of jobs, AI could also augment and increase the productivity of employees, specifically in CRM-related fields (IDC White Paper 2017). From predictive sales lead scoring to service chatbots to personalized marketing campaigns, AI could provide every employee with tools to be more productive and provide smarter, more personalized customer experiences.

According to McKinsey (2017), 2021–2022 will be breakthrough years for AI adoption. About a half of the companies said they would adopt AI within the next two years. By 2021, more than 70% of enterprises will include AI or ML functionality in at least one application. AI-powered CRM activities will cover a large spectrum of use cases and touch almost all facets of an enterprise, including accelerating sales cycles, improving lead generation and qualification, personalizing marketing campaigns and lowering costs of support calls.

"AI is impacting all sectors of the economy and every business. For the CRM market, the fastest-growing category in enterprise software, the impact of AI will be profound, stimulating new levels of productivity for employees and empowering companies to drive even better user experience. For companies embracing AI, it is critical that they create new workforce development programs to ensure employees are prepared for this next wave of innovation" according to Keith Block, vice chairman, president and COO, Salesforce.

CRM Companies Turn to AI to work smarter and more efficiently. AI associated with CRM is estimated to boost global business revenues by $1.1 trillion from the beginning of 2017 to the end of 2021. This revenue boost is expected to be driven primarily by increased productivity ($120 billion+) and lowered expenses due to automation ($260 billion+).

The types of AI and Data Science companies are planning to use range from:

(1) ML (25%)
(2) Voice/speech recognition (30%),
(3) Text analysis (27%) and
(4) Advanced numerical analysis (31%).

New jobs associated with the boost in global business revenues could reach more than 800,000 by 2021, surpassing those jobs lost to automation from AI. Similar to the past technology revolutions, the rise of AI will change the employment landscape as more tasks are automated and new opportunities are created. AI for CRM will soon become a global economic engine for new innovation, business models and jobs such as data scientist (Fig. 1.2).

Natural Language Processing (NLP) analyzes communications in emails, LinkedIn, Sugar and other sources between customer-facing professionals and their contacts to keep their relationships on track, helping the former provide a better customer experience to the latter. These are four ways in how NLP will enhance the customer experience:

(1) *Determine what customers are asking for when they send an email.* This is the most basic use of NLP. NLP gives employees a head start on what a customer is requesting via email. A customer in the financial services space, for example, is using a CRM for their customer service department. Many of the requests their NLP chatbot receives are common: *transfer money from one account to another, replace my debit card, change my address*, etc. An NLP technology can scan email before the user even opens the message and initiates its processing.

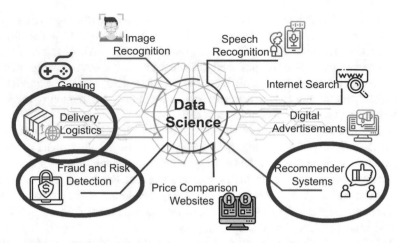

Fig. 1.2 Applications of data science. The domains of data science applicable to CRM are shown in bold blue ovals

(2) *Communicate Urgency.* Scanning for keywords and phrases to determine what the customer is asking for can be done by basic NLP. The next step is to examine an email and determine urgency. Building on the example above, a request for "lost debit card" while "on vacation" is something that is likely urgent. A change of address request, while important, does not reach that level of urgency. NLP can help push the urgent requests to the top of the customer service agent's queue so that they know what task to tackle next.

(3) *Determine customer satisfaction.* Many times customers have been asked to take a brief survey at the end of a support call. Consumers are attacked by a ton of customer surveys and considerate organizations realize that many customers find these surveys annoying and unnecessary. NLP has the capability to examine email correspondence between the employee and the customer and determine how happy, or how unhappy the customer is with his or her experience. Organizations can then step in and reach out to the unhappy customers much faster to rectify the customer's mood.

(4) *Resolve customer problems.* Given that a single bad review can harm a business, how can the business owner mitigate the negative impact? One approach is to improve the business's CRM by raising review complaints to the business's attention and developing an automated real-time complaint response engine.

1.2   What Kind of Learning for CRM

CRM software has always incorporated promising technological developments to produce better, smarter platforms.

CRM came from unassertive beginnings: its roots were in on-premise mainframes for digital storage of analog files. In the early eighties, database marketing emerged to consolidate transactional, analytical, and customer data platforms for marketers to reach out to prospects directly. The late eighties brought us the first contact management software, and booming development in the nineties brought us combined contact, lead, and opportunity management tools and thus CRMs achieved their steady pace.

In the late 1990s, as Salesforce, an enterprise CRM company, switched to the cloud, the rest became history. Modern innovations in ML, data analytics, NLP, and statistics are bringing AI to business applications. These are the technologies that provide the foundation for social CRM. CRM providers are struggling to outperform each other to offer ML capabilities that promise to apply computer cognition to business advantages. Following the 1999 cloud revolution, Deep Learning (DL), copying natural intelligence, made a breakthrough that dramatically affected what is AI today. But is DL good for CRM?

Much of the behavior of natural agents is innate and does not originate from learning. DL scientists would dream of an animal brain modeled as a set of blank slates, equipped with a general-purpose learning algorithm for acquiring any kind of data. Regretfully, this is not the case. There is a strong natural selection mechanism for animals to restrict their learning to just what is needed for their well-being. In AI research and cognitive science the idea that animals are predisposed to learn certain things rapidly is rather "mcta-learning" then "object-level learning" (Chap. 8 Volume 1). This idea is associated with "inductive biases", the assumptions made by the model to learn the target function and to generalize beyond training data.

The importance of innate mechanisms suggests that a neural network solving a new problem should attempt as much as possible to build on the solutions to previous related problems. Indeed, this idea is related to an active area of research in ML and artificial neural networks (ANNs, Chap. 3 Volume 1), Transfer Learning. In this approach, connections are pre-trained in the solution for one recognition task and then are transferred to accelerate learning on a related but different task. For example, a network trained to classify texts into such classes as finance and legal might be used as a starting point for a network that distinguishes legal agreements from offer letters. However, transfer learning differs from the innate mechanisms used in brains in an important way. Whereas in transfer learning the ANN's entire connection matrix (or a significant fraction of it) is typically used as a starting point, in animal brains the amount of information passed from generation to generation is smaller, because it must pass through the bottleneck of the genome.

Unlike ANN, the genome does not represent behaviors directly. The genome encodes much higher-level (meta-level) information such as wiring rules and patterns, which then must instantiate behaviors and representations. It is these wiring rules that are the target of evolution, neither the behaviors nor decision-making together. This suggests wiring topology and network architecture as a target for optimization in artificial systems. Classical ANNs largely ignore this abstraction of network architecture, being led by theoretical results on the universality of fully connected three-layer networks. At present, however, ANNs exploit only a tiny fraction of possible network architectures, raising the possibility that more powerful, cortically inspired architectures still remain to be explored and designed.

It remains unclear and controversial whether further progress in AI will benefit from the study of animal brains, and the other way around. There is a possibility that we have already learned all that we need to from animal brains, to build intelligent machines. As airplanes are very different from birds, most likely we do not need to learn more from birds to build better airplanes. Naturally, intelligent machines would operate by very different principles from those of animals.

A number of computer scientists demand "artificial general intelligence" from intelligent computers. However, such kind of intelligence is not general at all: it is highly constrained to match human capacities so tightly that only a machine structured similarly to a brain can achieve it (Zador 2019). An airplane by some measures is significantly better than a bird. It can fly much faster, at greater altitude, for longer distances, with vastly greater capacity for cargo. However, a plane cannot dive into the grass to catch a grasshopper, or jump silently from a tree to catch a rat. In many aspects, modern computers have already significantly exceeded human computational abilities, such as game playing and navigation, but cannot match humans on the decidedly specialized set of tasks defined as general intelligence. If we want to design a system that can do what we do, we will need to build it according to the same design principles as the brain. Hence it is not obvious that learning for CRM needs to be inspired by natural learning (Fig. 1.3).

The question is what kind of learning is the best for CRM is addressed in all chapters of this book. Humans, unlike statistical learners such as DL, can learn from a very limited dataset, and explain what they learn and what they recognize as a result. We argue that these features are a must for CRM (Fig. 1.3). The key ML areas for CRM are deep, reinforcement, NLP-supporting and large-scale ML (Fig. 1.4). We show the time in years till a technology is adopted from the time the development

Fig. 1.3 Human learning versus neural network learning

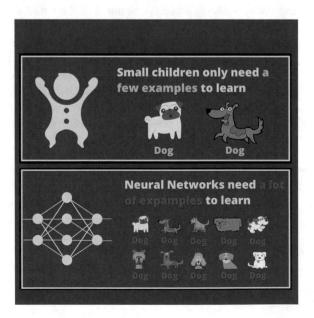

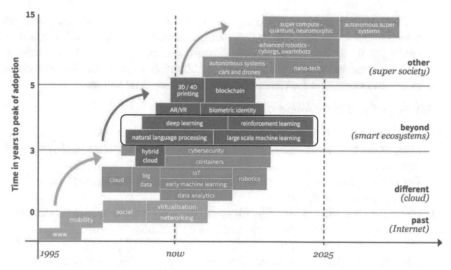

Fig. 1.4 Technology disruption dynamics with the ML suite highlighted

is started as Y-axis. X-axis is the time to exponential breakthrough point. It all started
with World Wide Web (left-bottom) and the time in years till a technology is adopted
for today's AI technologies are 3–5 years.

What can AI provide on top of a conventional algorithmic software? The most-
valuable and most-used outcomes of AI in CRM are:

(1) Predictive scoring. When a CRM system provides a score behind a decision, it
    comes with an insight into how it was arrived at. In a sales domain, predictive
    lead scoring gives each sales lead a score representing the probability that it will
    convert into an opportunity. In these domains, the reasons behind the score are
    the lead source, the industry, or some other essential indicator that a lead will
    or will not convert.
(2) The predictive capabilities of AI are not limited to scoring. An AI-based predic-
    tion can be used to predict the future value of a times series, like a stock portfolio
    or a real estate investment. AI can predict for a sales manager values like quar-
    terly bookings and provide an ahead of time information whether or not a sales
    team is on track to meet its quota.
(3) Recommendations (Fig. 1.5). AI not only makes suggestions for retail purchases
    but also produces smart recommendations for any other product or service cate-
    gory from accounting software to investment consulting to cargo containers. AI
    can also recommend things other than products. For example, AI can suggest
    which white paper a company should email a prospect in order to optimize a
    chance to close a deal. The purpose of this chart (Zhao et al. 2019) is to show
    the complexity of a recommendation system, where distributional semantics
    (Chap. 2 Volume 1) and DL (Chap. 3 Volume 1) need to come into play. A Wide

& Deep model architecture (Cheng 2016) was used that combines the power of a wide linear model alongside a deep neural network. The model will generate a prediction for each of the defined objectives (both engagement and satisfaction). These objectives are grouped in binary classification problems of liking a video or not and regression problems of estimating a rating of a video.

ML helps CRM in the following ways:

(1) For sales, ML can analyze information from email, calendars and CRM data to proactively recommend actions like the best email response to move a deal forward;
(2) For service, ML can automatically classify cases and intelligently route them to the right service agent;
(3) For marketing, ML can intelligently score the likelihood of a customer to open an email, subscribe to a newsletter, or make a purchase.

These are all examples of supervised learning where a training set is used. Unsupervised learning such as clustering users into cohorts does not need a training set (Fig. 1.6). Both types of ML are a must for CRM.

As to natural language processing (NLP), it assists CRM in many ways:

(1) For sales, NLP can "read" the text of emails exchanged with customers to obtain the probability of a potential sale, detect the best possible deals, identify deals a team is at greatest risk of losing and provide recommended actions to improve the sales process.
(2) For service, NLP can help route and more efficiently respond to customer emails by analyzing the written content.
(3) For marketing, NLP performs sentiment analysis on text to understand how customers feel about specific brands and products. If a business receives one more star in overall rating, it can generate a 5 to 9% increase in revenue according to (Luca 2011). However, a single negative review may cost a business 30 future customers, which implies that an unfavorable comment can significantly damage the reputation, profitability and trustworthiness of a business.

1.3   CRM Trends

The use of CRM is growing, and top CRM vendors like Salesforce, Oracle and SAP, have been making improvements in their key CRM functionalities. Each have AI capabilities, and with the ability to improve conversion rates, boost sales, collect important data and improve customer satisfaction, emerging from the crowd is a hard task.

The public will observe an increase in spending on CRM as companies realize the importance of not just knowing but understanding their customers. As technology such as voice and mobile capabilities are used in CRM, it improves not only the customer experience but the user experience as well.

CRM providers are faced with an age-old confusing and difficult problem:

(1) invest in uncertain capabilities, potentially at the expense of a more refined existing platform,
(2) risk missing out on the functionality that might come to define the space.

These providers have placed their bets that might pay off for companies and customers alike quicker than one would think.

Automation of support in financial services. In Fig. 1.7 one can see AI support for investment management, payments, insurance, capital markets and infrastructures, deposits and lending.

Conversational AI-Powered CRM. Combining AI with CRM will fuel the focus on conversational CRM systems and beyond. There are many new developments in the CRM world like text and face recognition, but voice functionalities will lead in the next few years. Just like the voice assistants on smartphone, AI-powered CRM, such as Salesforce's Einstein, enables organizations to get information from simple to complex data by using voice commands. The lesser-known, Zia, from Zoho CRM, is a voice assistant that allows users to easily and quickly query for information and data. In the author's previous book (Galitsky 2019), the poor state of conversational AI has been claimed and a number of solutions proposed. Reliance on DL was cited as a major reason of a limited chatbot performance. Still, the quality of the available dialogue system is well below user expectation (Fig. 1.8).

The use of voice is changing the way we live and work, and integrating it into CRM will only make tasks simpler, allowing for dictation instead of manually typing or to quickly access information through voice commands. There is no doubt that AI is this the future of CRM (Liu 2020):

(1) It is estimated that by 2021, an additional $400 Billion in revenue could be gained from AI adoption in CRM activities in North America;
(2) Of more than a thousand companies worldwide, 28% said they have already adopted AI and another 41% said they would do so within two years.

Internet of Things (IoT) in CRM is fairly trendy now for providing proactive, predictive and prescriptive customer service. IoT in CRM is believed to be the future of customer service (Lee 2019). IoT is believed to be one of the main drivers of CRM as it will give a big boost to CRM in terms of having CRM systems work better for organizations, driving sales and improving customer service and satisfaction. One example of such integration is the ability to analyze information generated from connected devices, and if any issues are reported, even fixing them remotely. As everything is becoming connected to the network, various industries will be transformed and IoT in CRM will be able to handle this transformation by better automation of the customer service to solve problems faster, more efficiently and even before they occur. IoT will significantly impact CRM as the vast amount of valuable data gathered from customers and potential customers will dramatically improve the function of CRM.

About 13 billion installed bases of IoT are in use in the consumer segment. Many believe that the problems related to IoT will be solved in the next few years. Edge processing with AI creates a better IoT experience. IoT device makers know the benefits of edge-based processing, but so far, high cost, performance and security have made it implausible for implementing in consumer-facing products and systems. The shift toward more use of edge processing in conjunction with cloud connectivity has already started and will continue to evolve over the next years. From a consumer view, this trend will result in an IoT experience that is faster, more reliable and more private.

Increase of Mobile CRM usage. Mobile CRM delivers full CRM capabilities on almost any device that can connect to the network. Enabling real-time access at any time and place, it is no surprise that this trend will continue to flourish in 2021. With mobile device usage continuing to grow, it is only natural that the number of CRM users that access their system on smartphones and tablets will continue to grow as well. An increase in mobile CRM usage means increased efficiency, access to more accurate information, improved customer experience, and eliminating the need to learn new software. With more than 90% of small businesses having a CRM system in place, it is important to make sure that these systems are accessible from a range of devices.

Hyper-personalization for unbeatable customer experience (CX). Many companies have years of data in their CRM systems that will enable them to provide customers with an unbeatable hyper-individualized customer experience; a trend that will be evident in 2021. Hyper-personalization provides services where customers feel valued and appreciated because businesses understand them and will know what they want, when and where. "Hyper-Individualization is a key objective for the future of CRM. The ability to have each customer interaction defined by the customer themselves will make Hyper-Individualization possible in the near future. When customers know the business is all about them, they have the potential to become brand ambassadors for your brand". This is according to Stephen Fioretti, VP of Product Management for Oracle Service Cloud. Hyper-personalization will help companies with a competitive edge on CX and engagement. It means gathering the right data as opposed to more data and being able to answer Why-questions instead of What-questions (Chaps. 3–7 Volume 1). These insights will provide more accurate and useful recommendations (Chap. 2 Volume 2), thereby greatly improving the customer experience (Fig. 1.5).

AI will dramatically improve the CX in general. The ability to automatically and instantly collect data from across multiple channels, analyze it and provide actionable insights will enable support agents to more quickly, easily and accurately address customer inquiries and come to highly satisfactory issue resolution (Fig. 1.9).

Digital presence is already more apparent than ever, and more so in the future (Zhang et al 2017). With an increasing amount of information being available, businesses are targeting the right customer, at the right time, and with the timely offers. Having a deep understanding of customers and a strong digital presence will lead to a smooth multi-channel experience, stable customer relations and increased profitability. Companies that transform digitally have customers that are 6 times more likely to try a new product or service from their preferred brand, 4 times more likely to refer to a given brand, and two times more likely to make a purchase with their

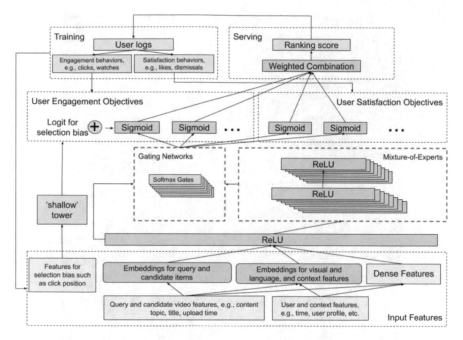

Fig. 1.5 YouTube video recommendation

preferred brand, even when a competitor has something better to offer at a lower price (Lund 2020).

Takeover of jobs by AI. This is haunting most people's dreams. However, many defeat this concern. As opposed to being a cause of job insecurity over the next years, AI will prove to be a crucial tool for improving careers. Through AI, employers will be able to provide enhanced opportunities for their employees and facilitate the diversity of experience they encounter. Thanks to AI, employees will be able to expand and enhance their skill sets and ensure they stay relevant in a rapidly evolving market. Accountability, particularly with respect to explaining results and bias prevention, will continue to go hand-in-hand with AI's development. Figure 1.10 shows the AI domains, with percentages of the people believing that a given possibility is viable.

Marketing Insights. Retailers will increasingly turn to AI as their main source of marketing insights as opposed to surveys and studies. Many retailers, however, will still struggle to turn those insights derived from AI into actionable business rules for their pricing, supply chain and merchandising. AI is becoming more and more mainstream, but not all companies yet realize that using AI technology for data analysis is only the first step into a larger process of true transformation.

Transforming healthcare workflows. AI's main impact in 2020 will be updating healthcare workflows to the benefit of patients and healthcare professionals alike, while at the same time reducing costs. ML and AI will deliver cost savings through greater cloud efficiencies. Achieving this will require the environment or application to understand when it needs more resources and then automatically scaling up those

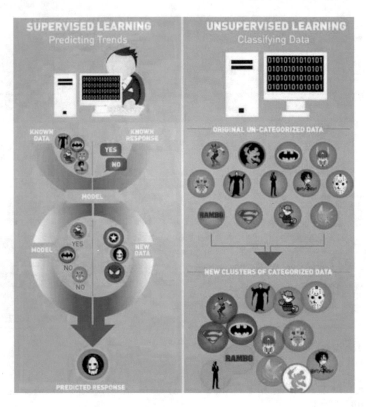

Fig. 1.6 Supervised (on the left) and unsupervised (on the right) ML for CRM

resources to meet the increased demand. Conversely, the technology will need to understand when specific resources are no longer needed and safely turn them off to minimize costs. The ability of this new healthcare workflow to acquire data in real-time from multiple hospital information flows—electronic health records, emergency department admissions, equipment utilization, staffing levels etc.—and to interpret and analyze it in meaningful ways will enable a wide range of efficiency and care enhancing capabilities.

Fairly recently CRM used to be a fragmented and often poorly integrated set of customer functions: sales, marketing, and customer support. Each of these often had their own dedicated systems with limited awareness or connection with the others. In addition, access to these systems was largely mediated by people, typically salespeople, marketing staff, and customer care representatives meaning that one had to call, meet, or otherwise contact a person that these systems in turn supported. Today, CRM is shifting toward systems of engagement, or direct connection with customers, even as it keeps its system of record roots. Hence, customer support and advertisement can be coordinated.

CRM used to rely on highly structured customer data, slow to change, transactional, reliable and stable, with the focus on core record keeping. Therefore, it was

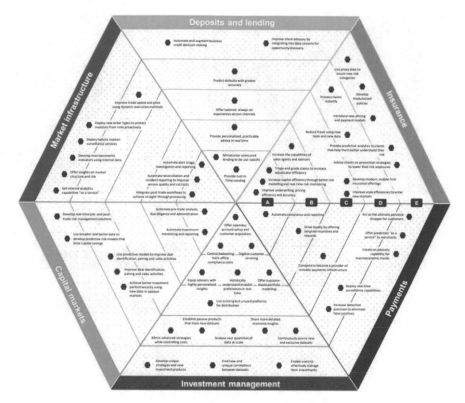

Fig. 1.7 AI assisting in various tasks in Finance

fairly difficult to use. CRM's new paradigm is a big shift is toward loosely structured conversational sessions, easy adaptation to new situations and users, optimization toward collaborating with customers (Fig. 1.11). As a result, modern CRM systems are highly social and easy to use and engage with. The capabilities of a CRM system based on this new paradigm can be leveraged, in particular, by advertising in the course of a CRM conversation session, which is a focus of Sect. 9 Volume 1.

1.4 AI CRM Companies

All the world's tech giants from Salesforce to Amazon are in a race to become the world's leaders in AI. These companies are AI trailblazers and embrace AI to provide next-level products and services. It is widely believed that every company will eventually become an AI company, modernizing their workforce to support innovation. As enterprises learn how to effectively deploy AI-based projects in cloud environments, they will turn their attention toward hiring data analysts and scientists with expertise in AI and DL. The companies comprising AI ecosystem are shown in

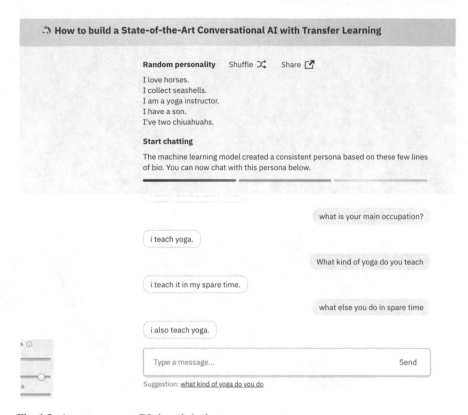

Fig. 1.8 A not very smart DL-based chatbot

Fig. 1.12, split into major categories such as *service/solution providers, technologies and hardware.*

We enumerate the major players in the technology field with the focus on AI and ML:

(1)   *Salesforce* is the largest CRM provider. It was the Salesforce upstart that took to the cloud in 1999 and exploded not only CRM but software distribution as a subscription model (Yonatan 2018). Salesforce by far is the market leader in the CRM space, and they have known which way the wind is blowing. Their AI platform, Einstein, learns from users' data and can predict outcomes, prescribe solutions, and automate tasks. Salesforce offers solutions according to company size, industry, and need. Further, an Einstein iteration exists for each one: there is an Einstein for the Service Cloud, Sales Cloud, Marketing Cloud, Commerce Cloud, App Cloud, Financial Services Cloud (Fig. 1.13). Salesforce recently added features to its Einstein Sales Cloud for high velocity sales: the capability of generating predictive lead scoring, previously accomplished by using data from integrated partners, will now be built-in. In the same update, the Einstein High Velocity Sales Cloud will now automatically capture

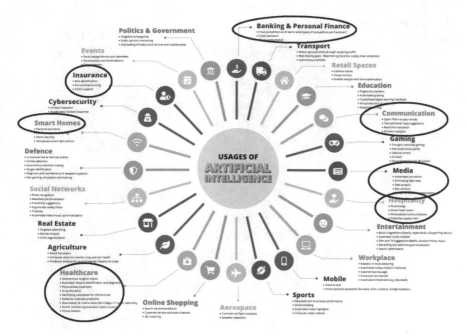

Fig. 1.9   Usages of AI in CRM

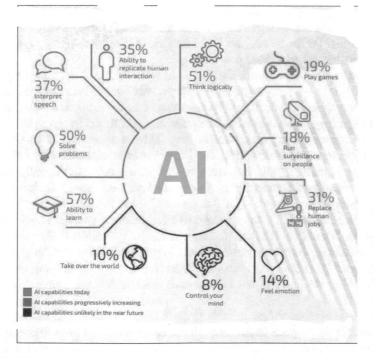

Fig. 1.10   What consumers believe AI can do

Fig. 1.11 CRM paradigm transition

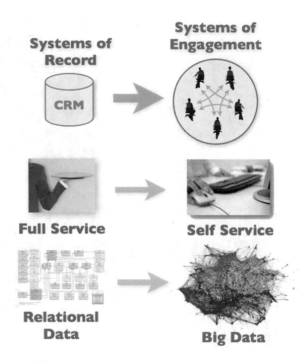

interactions between users and customers through linked email and calendar accounts. Suffice to say, the CRM behemoth keeps its fingers in many pots, but it always keeps those pots stirring.

(2) *Alibaba.* Chinese company Alibaba is the world's largest e-commerce platform that sells more than Amazon and eBay combined. AI is integral in Alibaba's daily operations and is used to predict what customers might want to buy. With natural language processing, the company automatically generates product descriptions for the site. Another way Alibaba uses AI is in its City Brain project to create smart cities. The project uses AI algorithms to help reduce traffic jams by monitoring every vehicle in the city. Additionally, Alibaba, through its cloud computing division called Alibaba Cloud, is helping farmers monitor crops to improve yield and cuts costs with AI.

(3) *Google* indicated its commitment to deep learning when it acquired Deep-Mind. Not only did the system learn how to play 49 different Atari games, the AlphaGo program was the first to beat a professional player at the game of Go. Another AI innovation from Google is Google Duplex. Relying on NLP, an AI voice interface can make phone calls and schedule appointments on behalf of its host.

(4) *Amazon* is in the AI game with its digital voice assistant, Alexa. AI is also a part of many aspects of Amazon's business of shipping things to clients before people even think about buying it. The company collects a lot of data about each person's buying habits and has a high confidence in how the data it collects

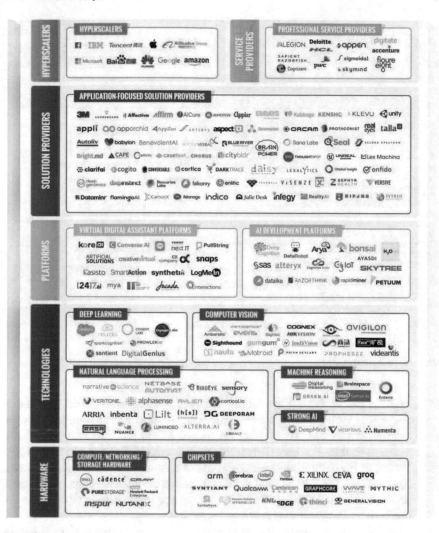

Fig. 1.12 AI Ecosystems

helps them recommend items to its customers. Amazon now predicts what the customers need even before they need it, by using predictive analytics. When many traditional stores are struggling to determine how to stay relevant, the largest electronic retailer in the US offers a new convenience store concept called Amazon Go. Unlike other stores, there is no requirement for checkout. The stores have AI technology that tracks what items a buyer picks up and then automatically charges this buyer for the purchased items through the Amazon Go app on her phone. Since there is no checkout, buyers bring their own bags to fill up with items, and there are cameras watching their every move to recognize each item hey put in their bags to ultimately charge for them.

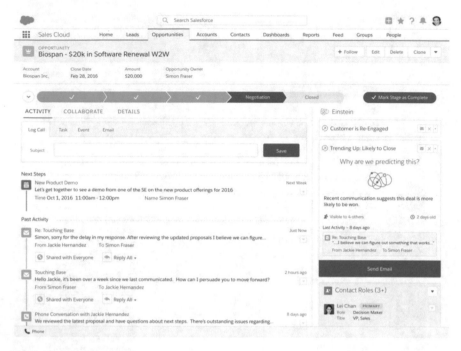

Fig. 1.13 Salesforce CRM

(5) *Apple* is one of the world's largest technology companies, selling consumer electronics such as iPhones and Apple Watches, as well as computer software and online services. Apple relies on AI and ML in products like the iPhone, where it enables the FaceID feature, or in products like the AirPods, Apple Watch, or HomePod smart speakers, where it enables the smart assistant Siri. Apple is also growing its service offering and is using AI to recommend songs on Apple Music, help the users find their photos in the iCloud or navigate the user to his next appointment using Apple Maps.

(6) *Baidu*, the Chinese equivalent of Google, uses AI in many ways. They have a tool called Deep Voice that employs AI and DL that needs less than 4 seconds of audio to clone a voice. Baidu uses this same technology to create a tool that reads books to a user in the author's voice in a fully automated way without a recording studio.

(7) *Facebook.* One of the primary ways Facebook uses AI and DL is to add structure to its unstructured data. They use DeepText, a text understanding engine, to automatically understand and interpret the content and emotional sentiments of the thousands of posts in multiple languages. With DeepFace, the social media giant can automatically identify you in a photo that is shared on their platform. Facebook face recognition algorithm is claimed to be better at facial recognition than humans. The company also uses AI to automatically catch and remove images that are posted on its site as revenge porn.

(8) *IBM* has been at the forefront of AI for years. Over two decades ago IBM's Deep Blue computer became the first to defeat a human world chess champion. The company continued with other man vs. machine competitions, including its Watson computer winning the game show Jeopardy. The latest AI achievement for IBM is Project Debater, a cognitive computing system that provides an adversarial environment against two professional debaters and formulated human-like arguments. IBM also offers Watson Assistant, an AI and NL-driven chatbot designed to allow anyone to deploy a chatbot in an app or website.

(9) *JD.com* is striving to be fully automated. The founder of this Chinese version of Amazon, Richard Liu makes sure their warehouses are fully automated, JD has been making drone deliveries of packages for the last few years. JD's retail infrastructure is driven by AI, big data and robotics.

(10) *Microsoft's* vision statement has AI as its focus. It illustrates the company's target on having intelligent systems to be central to everything they do. Microsoft is embedding intelligent features to all its products and services, including Cortana, Skype, Bing and Office 365. The company is the world's biggest supplier of the cloud-based AI as a Service vendor. Microsoft has invested a lot in its ML capabilities, distributing its Azure ML Studio for designers to develop, test and deploy predictive analytics models. Cortana Intelligence Suite augments Dynamics 365 through Microsoft Flow to provide translation, sentiment analysis, keyword identification and other NLP tasks. These ML features benefit all aspects of CRM, from sales leads, call centers, social customer service and SEO support. Microsoft provides solutions for companies of all sizes, industries and needs. In addition to Azure, Cortana, and Power BI, Microsoft invests heavily in its well known ML technology.

(11) *Tencent* employed AI into its operations as it intends to become the most efficient internet enterprise. Chinese social media company has 1 billion users on its app WeChat and is expanding toward gaming, CRM, mobile infrastructure, cloud computing, live streaming, education, multimedia and even self-driving cars. One of the company's slogans is "AI in all". Tencent processes huge amounts of information about its customers that it processes and takes advantage of.

(12) *Marketo* develops a company-mining (rather than web-mining) technology to identify people with certain roles in an organization. This platform is positioned "by marketers, for marketers" and provides account-based marketing solutions by identifying leads that have the most buying interest and the individuals within the organization with buying authority. Marketo together with Mintigo, a predictive analytics platform founded in 2009, will reduce the time required to estimate high-value leads in a company, better align the marketing and sales teams and improve personalized prospect engagement.

(13) *Base* is a sales automation mobile CRM. This Silicon Valley-based company pursues an ML CRM direction and recently launched the Apollo sales science platform. Base's program is solely focused on sales. Base's platform acquires and analyzes millions of data points in real-time to offer users a live insight feed and recommendations to increase sales, goal tracking, and forecasting. It also

distributes a data repair feature, allowing real-time monitoring of the health of CRM data. Apollo platform computes a percentage of fields completed, quality and the accuracy of data. Up to ten thousand users rely on Apollo; Base is fulfilling multi-million dollar CRM contracts with major players in retail and manufacturing.

(14) *SugarCRM* has introduced two new services: a predictive analytics platform called Sugar Intelligence, and an AI assistant named Candace. An initial goal of the features will be to reduce or remove the need for users to modify contact information on their own. Instead, AI would integrate external data points (including from the IoT) with users' CRM data to update records on its own. Additionally, the assistant would be able to recommend specific inter-actions with customers, help users plan meetings, build deeper connections, and respond to real-time developments as required. Candace would use natural language processing to parse conversations and plan follow-up actions while Sugar Intelligence will be an open platform so developers can add their own features.

(15) *Zoho* is distributing an AI-powered sales assistant. Its name is Zia. Zia aims at detecting anomalies in sales operations to predict whether teams will be able to meet their goals. This works better and predicts earlier than traditional benchmarks. The CRM system predicts the best time for salespeople to reach out to potential buyers by phone or email. Zia learns individual user activities, recommend workflows or macros to automate them, and then set them up for the users. Zia is a part of the Zoho CRM Enterprise plan.

(16) *Zendesk* is a "friendly neighborhood" company. Its helpdesk offers multiple ML capabilities including *Satisfaction Prediction* and *Automatic Answers.* *Satisfaction Prediction* applies predictive analytics to assess the confidence about the particular ticket to be completed with a good or bad satisfaction rating. It incorporates hundreds of features such as text description, number of replies, and total wait time to calculate a satisfaction score. Then agents can prioritize tickets accordingly to produce more positive outcomes and reduce wasted time and efforts. *Satisfaction Prediction* also provides dashboard analytics. *Automatic Answers* adds AI to the customer self-service infrastructure. To reduce a ticket volume, *Automatic Answers* interprets customer questions and directs them to the most relevant knowledge base articles. AI includes a DL model, a fully integrated end user experience, adaptability to user needs, and an assessment for how many users are finding their own answers relying on *Automatic Answers* (Fig. 1.14).

(17) *Gorgias.io* is a helpdesk company that integrates communication with customers across channels including social network messengers. At the same time, Gorgias.io contextualizes each customer by drawing upon a variety of external apps. The technology allows users to create macros that apply to integrated third-party tools and to construct workflows that associates some customers to certain kinds of issues. Gorgias applies ML and semantic analysis to process tickets, recommend pre-formed responses, and to automatically tag incoming tickets, serving e-commerce websites and on-demand startups,

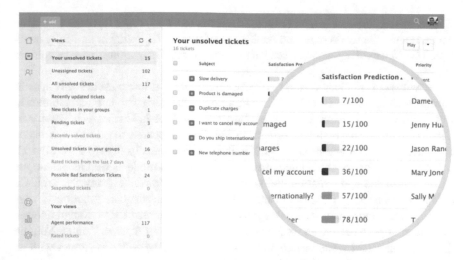

Fig. 1.14 Zendesk CRM

integrating with messenger apps as support channels as well as third-party
analytics tools.

(18) *Tact.ai* delivers a system of workflow for sellers to transform their everyday
sales activities. The system is powered by AI running on edge devices,
providing a smooth way to work with apps. Company's AI platform connects
any application to any device.

1.5 Where CRM is Today

In spite of the huge amount of efforts put into developing technologies for helping
customers in all phases of product and services consumption, in many cases, these
customers are in the worst situation than one or two decades ago. This became
especially evident in the times of COVID 19. Most CRM systems are unable to handle
high call volume, questions and requests beyond basic knowledge and operations.

This book is being completed at COVID-19 times when a total failure of customer
relations was encountered, especially in such industries as travel, finance, healthcare
and retail. Many companies are unable to notify customers about service cancel-
lations even via emails. There is a concern that the quality of customer support is
deteriorating as companies want to reduce cost in call centers, relying on outsourcing
and unreliable or irrelevant automation. It is not unusual to have the main reason for
the customer retention based on the following belief: customers stay with a current
business because they think that other competitive businesses are even worse.

One of the purposes of this book is to automate CRM, make it robust in hostile environments the world may find itself in the future. An intelligent and fully automated CRM would be needed in case of possible world collapse due to one or another reason.

To withstand anticipated issues, a CRM system of the future must not only answer questions about products and services in a comprehensive way but also attempt to solve customer problems. We will explain how to do it in Chaps. 4–6 Volume 1. CRM cannot be successful in providing solutions prepared in advance: it needs to be able to reason and produce such solutions dynamically (Chap. 7 Volume 1). Information exchange should occur in a single question mode as well as a dialogue with clarification and dynamic dialogue management toward solving the problem (Chap. 1 Volume 2). The system must demonstrate an adequate reaction to user concerns and complaints. The users must trust an automated CRM system enough to let it attempt to resolve an issue and handle a complaint (Chaps. 7 and 9 Volume 2). A modern CRM system needs to be capable of dealing with a customer with an issue with personality, or in a bad mood (Fig. 1.15).

Another challenge of modern CRM technologies is a gap between acquisition and retention. As acquisition strategies have become more complex, such as programmatic advertising across major social channels, retention strategies are lagging behind. Usually, customers are buying when they first engage with a business, that knows the least about these customers. The challenge here is to process acquisition data including cookies to maintain growth and retention.

Making behavior-based personalization relevant is another challenge of modern CRM. Targeting is becoming a much-debated topic in advertising and marketing: businesses are admitting they went too broad with its Facebook advertising and their micro-segmented content is of a poor quality (Davis 2016). It is important to differentiate between persona- and behavior-based marketing. It does not matter if the customer is a 55-year-old ex-military based in Natick MA, we should be making decisions based on the fact that she only ever buys childrens clothing with a

Fig. 1.15 Managing customers with a variety in personalities and moods

given retailer. This challenge will be solved via a conversational recommendation in Chaps. 10 and 2 Volume 2. A CRM. Instead of having a random probabilistic hope about what a buyer wants, an efficient CRM needs to derive an information about what she is looking at, how often she comes to the website, across all devices.

CRM content is another area that demands intelligent decisions. Retailers must set rules for a number of customer views for a category or product before a promotional email is sent to him. As to the content of these emails, it should revolve around a category, which includes a browsed product, so it looks like it has been visually merchandised. It can also be a set of categories. The email content should impress the user with the thrill of discovery, like finding something of a high value in a boutique off the high street. Hence the importance of semantic techniques and content quality assessment is crucial (Chap. 3 of Volume 1 and Chaps. 5 and 6 Volume 2).

Overall, a lack of intelligence as a major bottleneck of current CRM systems. Each chapter in this book proposes how to enable a baseline CRM system with predictions, classification, clustering, emotional, truth-discovering, deep understanding of user mood and other kinds of intelligence.

1.6 How to Read This Book (Volumes 1 and 2)

We did not cluster the chapters around the phases of the customer pathway of *identification, attraction, retention* and *customer development*. Instead, we organized the chapters according to the requirements to automate intelligence: *answering, explaining, chatting* and *reasoning*. Hence there are four blocks of chapters:

(1) Answering customer questions. These questions might be hard in terms of finding an answer and also finding a resolution in a complex situation (Chaps. 2–7 Volume 1);
(2) Explaining things to customers. Customers are serious about how companies explain their decisions to them (Chaps. 8–10 Volume 1);
(3) Chatting with customers while solving their problems. They do not want the company's decision and information just thrown on them: customers prefer to have a conversation to solve their problem (Chaps. 1–5 Volume 2);
(4) Reasoning about customer attitudes. To retain customers, one needs to understand them and to do that, one should be capable of reasoning about and simulating them (Chaps. 6–10 Volume 2).

References

Brito PQ, Soares C, Almeida S, Monte A, Byvoet M (2015) Customer segmentation in a large database of an online customized fashion business.". Elsevier, Robotics and Computer-Integrated Manufacturing

Cheng H-T (2016) Wide & deep learning: better together with TensorFlow. https://ai.googleblog.com/2016/06/wide-deep-learning-better-together-with.html

Davis B (2016) 10 key challenges facing CRM marketers. https://econsultancy.com/10-key-challenges-facing-crm-marketers/

Galitsky B (2019) Developing enterprise chatbots: learning linguistic structures. Springer, Cham Switzerland

IDC White Paper (2017) A trillion-dollar boost: the economic impact of ai on customer relationship management. Commissioned by Salesforce

Jain S, Sharma NK, Gupta S, Doohan N (2018) Business strategy prediction system for market basket analysis. In: Kapur P, Kumar U, Verma A (eds) Quality, IT and business operations. Springer proceedings in business and economics. Springer, Singapore

Kaur M, Kang S (2016) Market basket analysis: identify the changing trends of market data using association rule mining. Procedia Comput Sci 85:78–85

Lee S (2019) 4 trends that are transforming CRM in 2019. https://www.fmtconsultants.com/4-trends-that-are-transforming-crm-in-2019/

Liu S (2020) Increased revenue from AI adoption in CRM in the U.S. 2017-2021. https://www.statista.com/statistics/738060/us-increased-revenue-from-ai-in-customer-management-activities/

Luca M (2011) Reviews, reputation, and revenue: the case of Yelp.com. https://www.hbs.edu/faculty/Publication%20Files/12-016_a7e4a5a2-03f9-490d-b093-8f951238dba2.pdf

Lund J (2020) How digital transformation is driving customer experience. https://www.superoffice.com/blog/digital-transformation/

McKinsey (2017) A future that works: automation, employment and productivity, January 2017

Sabbeh S (2018) Machine-Learning techniques for customer retention: a comparative study. Int J Adv Comput Sci Appl (IJACSA) 9(2):273–281

Shaw C (2013) Beyond philosophy, 15 statistics that should change the business world—but haven't, featured in: customer experience

The Chartered Institute of Marketing (2010) Cost of customer acquisition versus customer retention

Yonatan R (2018) 8 machine learning CRMs that are moving the industry forward. https://saaslist.com/blog/machine-learning-crm/

Zador AM (2019) A critique of pure learning and what artificial neural networks can learn from animal brains. Nat Commun 10:3770

Zhang Y, Trusov M, Stephen AT, Jamal Z (2017) Online shopping and social media: friends or foes? J Mark 81(6):24–41

Zhao Z, Hong L, Wei L, Chen J, Nath A, Andrews S, Kumthekar A, Sathiamoorthy M, Yi X, Chi E (2019) Recommending what video to watch next: a multitask ranking system. In Proceedings of the 13th ACM conference on recommender systems (RecSys '19). ACM, New York, NY, USA, pp 43–51

Chapter 2
Distributional Semantics for CRM: Making Word2vec Models Robust by Structurizing Them

Abstract Distributional Semantics has become extremely popular in natural language processing (NLP) and language learning tasks. We subject it to critical evaluation and observe its limitations in expressing semantic relatedness of words. We spot-check representation of meaning by the Distributional Semantics and also obtain an anecdotal evidence about various systems employing it. To overcome the revealed limitations of the Distributional Semantics, we propose to use it on top of a linguistic structure, not in a stand-alone mode. In a phrase similarity task, only when phrases are aligned and syntactic, semantic and entity-based map is established, we assess word2vec similarity between aligned words. We add the Distributional Semantics feature to the results of syntactic, semantic and entity/attribute-based generalizations and observe an improvement in the similarity assessment task. Structurized word2vec improves the similarity assessment task performed by the integrated syntactic, abstract meaning representation (AMR) and entity comparison baseline system by more than 10%.

2.1 Introduction

Distributional models of lexical semantics have recently attracted considerable interest in the NLP community. With the increase in popularity, the issue of evaluation of distributional models is becoming more and more important. Distributional semantics (DS), is a model of meaning, which is based on how words are used in the text; this model characterizes a semantic behavior of words in a corpus of documents. Its main focus is the lexicon: DS is primarily an empirical method for the analysis of lexical meaning. The theoretical foundation of DS has become known as the distributional hypothesis: lexemes with similar linguistic *contexts* have similar meanings. The root of the DS lies in the distributionalism advocated by structural linguists including (Harris 1968). He claimed that a variation of meaning is correlated with a variation in distribution.

It is important to introduce a structure in these contexts. DS offers both a model to represent meaning and computational methods to learn such representations from

© Springer Nature Switzerland AG 2020

B. Galitsky, *Artificial Intelligence for Customer Relationship Management*,
Human–Computer Interaction Series,
https://doi.org/10.1007/978-3-030-52167-7_2

language data. Given the ever-increasing availability of texts, distributional models can rely on huge amounts of empirical evidence to characterize the semantic properties of lexemes (Ruber 2016). It is essential to structure distributional semantics within the traditional semantic frameworks such as logical forms and integrate distributional semantic knowledge with other available forms of domain knowledge such as taxonomy (Galitsky et al. 2011b). After (Mikolov et al. 2013) released the word2vec tool, a corpus of articles followed about word vector representations, including Stanford's GloVe (Pennington et al. 2014) that explained why such algorithms work and reformulated word2vec optimizations as a special kind of factorization for word co-occurrence matrices.

A revolutionary idea that word meaning word could be represented as a point in space was the first expression of the vector semantics models (Osgood et al. 1957, Jurafsky and Martin 2019). Let us see an example illustrating a DS approach. Suppose you did not know what the Russian word *sputnik* meant, but you do see it in the following sentences or contexts:

> *Sputnik is launched and follows an orbit…*
> *Sputnik is used to carry people in space…*
> *Sputnik is driven by jet engines…*

Now let us imagine that the reader have seen many of these context words occurring in contexts like:

> *a satellite is launched and flies along an orbit…*
> *a jet engine of a rocket …*
> *can a rocket carry humans?…*

The fact that *sputnik* occurs with words like *launch* and *jet* and *engine* and *orbit*, as do words like *satellite* and *rocket* might suggest to the reader that *sputnik* is a *satellite* similar to other types of *rockets*.

This form of reasoning can be done computationally by just counting words in the context of *sputnik*; the readers tend to see words like *rocket* and *missile*. The fact that these words and other similar context words also occur around the word *fly* or *follow an orbit* can help the reader to discover the similarity between these words and *sputnik*.

DS thus combines two viewpoints:

(1) the distributionalist viewpoint, defining a word by counting what other words occur in its environment; and

(2) the vector viewpoint, defining the meaning of a word w as a vector, a list of numbers, a point in N-dimensional space. There are various versions of vector semantics, each defining the numbers in the vector somewhat differently, but in each case the numbers are based in some way on counts of neighboring words.

The training objectives for GloVe and word2vec are to produce DS models that encode general semantic relationships and can provide benefit in many downstream tasks. Regular neural networks, in comparison, generally produce task-specific models with limitations in relation to their useability elsewhere. The GloVe algorithm consists of the following steps (Selivanov 2018):

(1) Collect word co-occurrence statistics in a form of word co-occurrence matrix X. Each element X_{ij} of such matrix represents how often word i appears in context of word j. Usually, we scan our corpus in the following manner: for each term, we look for context terms within some area defined by a *window_size* before the term and a *window_size* after the term. Also, we give less weight for more distant words, usually using this formula *decay = 1/offset.*

(2) Soft constraint for each word pair is defined as

$$w_i^T w_j + b_i + b_j = \log(X_{ij})$$

where w_i is a vector for the main word, w_j is a vector for the context word, b_i, b_j are scalar biases for the main and context words.

(3) Optimization cost function is then defined as

$$J = \sum_{i=1}^{V} \sum_{j=1}^{V} f(X_{ij})(w_i^T w_j + b_i + b_j - \log X_{ij})^2$$

Here f is a weighting function which helps to avoid learning only from most common word pairs. The (Pennington et al. 2014) rely on

$$f(X_{ij}) = \begin{cases} \left(\frac{X_{ij}}{X_{\max}}\right)^{\alpha} & \text{if } X_{ij} < X_{\max} \\ 1 & \text{otherwise} \end{cases}.$$

Since the word2vec family of models (Mikolov et al. 2013) is so popular, we are going to spend substantial efforts criticizing them from the resultant accuracy standpoint as well as from the conceptual mutual information standpoint. We start analyzing the accuracy of the model from its visualization (Migdal 2017).

2.2 Spot-Checking of Distributional Semantics Data

In this section, we subject word2vec and GloVe data to critical analysis and observe whether it can be trusted for NLP tasks with decision making and decision support down the line. We select various data points and explore if what we see matches our intuition of meaning of certain words.

Let us first consider a projection of verbs onto gender and verb tense dimensions (Fig. 2.1, Bazińska 2017).

Why are *fail* and *bring* and *destroy* and *play* closer to *he* than to *she*? And why is *swim* closer to *she*? Why do verb tenses deviate so strongly proceeding from *he*

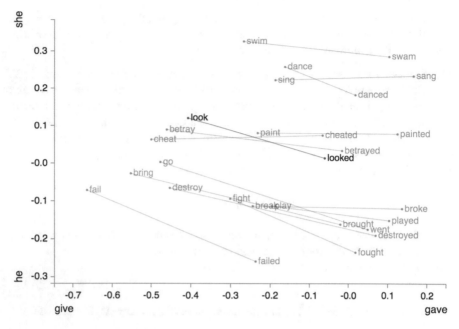

Fig. 2.1 GloVe representation of verbs

to *she*? This is what happens if dimension of logical data is reduced. Why does the past tense tend to be closer associated with *he* than with *she*?

These systematic deviations in meaning representation are expected to be generalized by downstream learning systems and lead to inadequate classification or prediction problems. In most evaluation settings in NLP, where samples in training and testing sets are fairly close to each other, a machine learning system based on compositional semantics can still give high accuracy. However, with real-word data that is more diverse, much more accurate semantic representation is needed and most systems display unsatisfactory performance, such as Deep Learning (DL)-based search engines and chatbots (Galitsky 2019). This is what can be tracked in terms of how GloVe learns. Most of it becomes intractable once DL is build on top of compositional semantics.

To do CRM, one needs a thorough understanding of how people think and behave. People express their behavior in words. Once a system encodes words in such a noisy way, humans will no longer be understood properly (Galitsky 2003).

Figure 2.2 is an ontology of animals with the parameters of size and speed of movement. These values for animals look pretty random. We would expect DS to learn the sizes of animals from their respective Wikipedia entries. But it turns out what has been "learned" is that *crickets* are the *fastest* (well, OK) and also fairly *large* (!). *Snails* have an average *speed, birds* are *large* and have an *average speed*, and so forth. If a real ontology on animals is available, a system definitely should

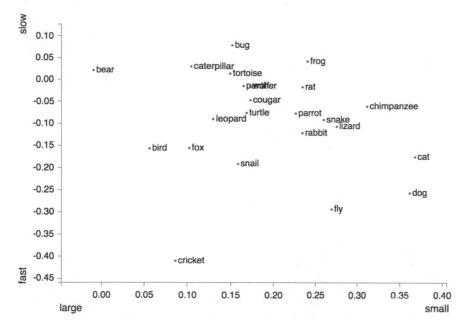

Fig. 2.2 Animals in slow/fast and large/small dimensions

use it instead of word2vec and fall back only when no domain ontology is available, or in a domain-independent NLP task.

Why is being *smart* in some way *faster* than being a *genius* (Fig. 2.3)?

Why is *key* defined by *system/current/performance/concept*? Can a human who deals with a "*key*" on a daily basis infer it from the list of "defining altogether" 10 words. Is it possible to deduce the concept of "key" from them? No, it is not. Even a human brain cannot produce a seed word from a list of word2vec "synononyms". This is also true for a majority of definitions via word2vec. Hence the "meanings" of words in the DS models available actually live in a world totally different from the one with real humans. Who would think this word2vec evaluation would pass a quality assurance of an average software company? Very unlikely. Nevertheless, the systems where word2vec is integrated into, are getting released in many companies.

Any surprises why Facebook recommends baby stuff to bachelors and dating to married moms with 3+ kids? Possibly, this is because in their internal word representations they perhaps use something similar to word2vec and encode *bachelor* and *kid* in as noisy way as the above examples.

In many presentations about word2vec, distributional semantics is presented as a "science" with just a single example. Have the reader encountered an article on word2vec with an example of assertion other than "*king - man + woman = queen*"? If you have please let us know but we doubt it. Some word2vec toolkits cannot reproduce even this assertion (Fig. 2.5, Turbomaze 2019). The system is expected to produce *queen*, but it is not in the list down to the similarity score of 0.39.

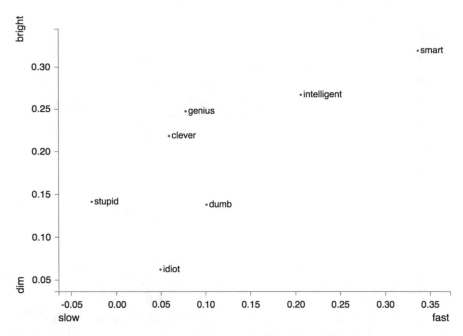

Fig. 2.3 Some approximation of meaning in the space *dim.. bright* and *slow.. fast*

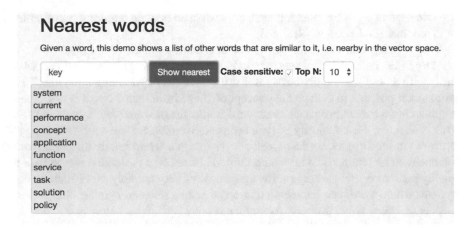

Fig. 2.4 Synonyms of *key*: it is hard to deduce the word from its ordered list of synonyms

Lets try to form a similar example from the words for a *profession*.

We can see that *king* and *lord* and *general* perform *basic* stuff, *doctor, waiter, colonel* and *officer*—*average* in terms of job complexity and *waitress/boss*—professional stuff. One can argue that *general* has a different meaning—why would it be so strongly male then? *Plumber, carpenter, driver* and *soldier* turn out to be gender-independent occupations (this is a dream conjecture for certain audiences!).

Word Algebra

Enter all three words, the first two, or the last two and see the words that result.

| king | + (man | − woman |) = Get result |

king	0.8503608729126318
jackson	0.48038624456486534
prince	0.47813850597769697
brown	0.42256800505150915
clark	0.4175870557909351
lewis	0.41052567552275254
smith	0.4029177092936253
wallace	0.40032982128315686
johnson	0.399872167103048
kings	0.39929417936472633

Fig. 2.5 Word Algebra from Turbomaze (2019), attempting to reproduce a famous word2vec formula

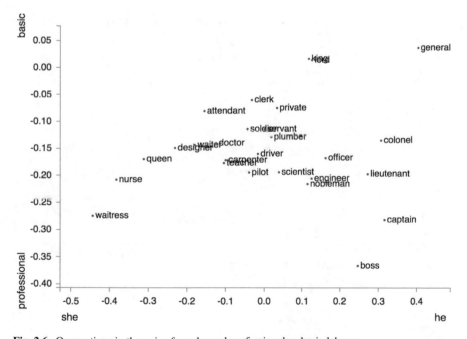

Fig. 2.6 Occupations in the axis of gender and professionals—basic laborers

What the reader sees from this example is that the errors are not individual but there is a systematic bias, so there is no evidence that summing up over all words for occupation would make it less noisy. Can one imagine a job search based on word2vec for computing similarity between a resume and a job description? We are afraid an engineer from a headhunter company can…

One can doubt if information in Fig. 6 can be useful for applications like search. Imagine a query expansion that takes a query about a *pilot* and expand it toward *clerk*, in a query *pilot training = >pilot or clerk training*. The latter query would give at least half meaningless results. In systems employing word2vec for solving problems, it does not lose face just because competitive systems use word2vec as well.

Once word2vec is used for training a linguistic model for something like a dialogue, what kind of performance can one expect? It is not easy to find a chatbot demo based on DL but those which can be found are not impressive at all (Galitsky 2019). It is unclear how in the times of advanced search engine one can demo something like (Fig. 2.7). A user fails to learn what is agent's occupation, one of the

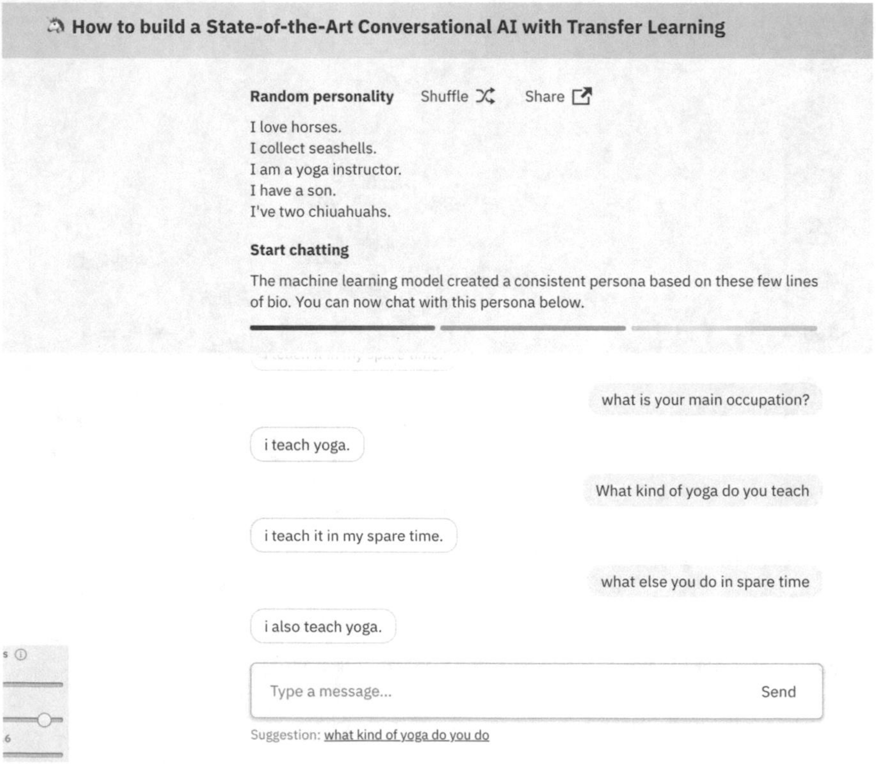

How to build a State-of-the-Art Conversational AI with Transfer Learning

Random personality   Shuffle ⤮   Share ↗

I love horses.
I collect seashells.
I am a yoga instructor.
I have a son.
I've two chiuahuahs.

Start chatting

The machine learning model created a consistent persona based on these few lines of bio. You can now chat with this persona below.

what is your main occupation?

i teach yoga.

What kind of yoga do you teach

i teach it in my spare time.

what else you do in spare time

i also teach yoga.

Type a message…   Send

Suggestion: what kind of yoga do you do

Fig. 2.7 A DL-based chatbot is failing to answer a basic question

Fig. 2.8 Humans should be able to reconstruct the word given its ordered list of word2vec synonyms… because it is supposed to express the meaning of human language

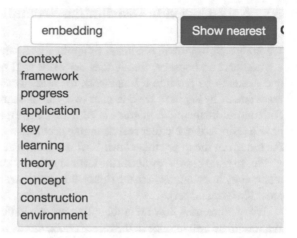

simplest possible answers. It is hard to see what kind of "intelligence" is implemented here other than providing a few unconnected hard-coded answers like "*I do yoga*". This user might be curious about what DL could be used for here?

Word2vec is expected to encode the meaning of words used by humans. So given an ordered list of similar words, a human should be able to reconstruct the original word. Now the reader can try to do it from the example (Fig. 2.8) Obviously, in most cases it is impossible to recognize. This way we can intuitively feel how much information/meaning is lost in the course of word2vec approximation.

It is obvious that a chatbot like this can hardly be used in a customer support (CS) scenario. If a customer is frustrated before starting a conversation, he would get even more frustrated because of a lack of understanding of his problem.

DL for which word2vec is a foundation has been also used in search in so-called machine reading comprehension task. Let us evaluate Google/Bing on the following generalized/semantic query.

[*Who/when/where*]   [*did/wrote   music/wrote   screen-play/produced/filmed/suggested*] on movie [*Titanic 1997/Darkest Hour/Free Solo*].

We find that while the entity (movie name) is recognized properly, the answer is very sensitive to how the query is formulated in terms of the verb used for the creation of an entity such as a movie (write/created/did/ …}.

One can conclude that some meanings of words are indeed captured by distributional semantics but it is hard to see which features are retained, which features are lost and which are reliable. Therefore, we cannot recommend using DS for NLP tasks which would result in a decision, especially if it is a mission-critical. Word2vec and GloVe are suitable for less relevance-critical applications such as data visualization where various kinds of data errors associated with misrepresentation of the meaning of words can be tolerated.

2.3   Spot-Checking Distribution Semantic-Based Systems

We are going to look at a number of applications where distributional semantics is a workhorse and observe that it does not work well as it is, without structurization, and needs to be put into a framework for more systematic and accurate similarity assessment. In Fig. 2.9, we compare two sets of search results for the entity *Dawn Wall* and its attribute *Who-wrote-script,* assuming all entities of the type *movie* should have a scriptwriter. Neither search engine provides a correct value, and Bing ignores the hint from the query that *Dawn Wall* is a movie, not a person.

Not so good search results on the left show limitation in entity extraction/matching technology in comparison to the right where an answer is inferred (might be guessed, most likely incorrect).

We explore now how an ambiguity can be handled by distributional semantics. We formulate two queries in the topic *"character … personal assistant"* (Fig. 2.10). Additional query keywords bring in two contexts: *characters* as letters and *character* as a personality. In the answer on the right, the system correctly recognized the context of character as *organized, highly detailed.* Once a phrase match between an answer and a question is established, word2vec model needs to come into play to associate *character* with *person* (on the right). One first tries to find candidate answers with the maximum phrase match (in this case, multiple answers where *'personal assistant'* matched). Then iterating through these candidates, we attempt to match other answer keywords with that of this query, such as *character* in the query with *person* in the best candidate. This case is a great luck for this search engine.

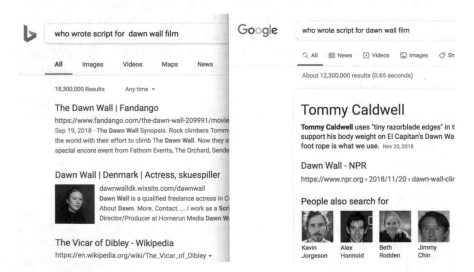

Fig. 2.9 Comparison of search results for a factoid question about an attribute (scriptwriter) of an entity (movie "Dawn Wall")

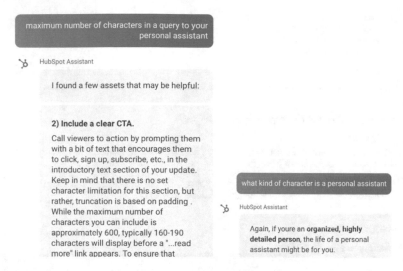

Fig. 2.10 Answering questions requiring disambiguation (Frase 2019)

The other meaning of *character*, a letter, perhaps does not have an answer in this index. The search just found the best match for *maximum number of characters*. If there is a very close synonym substitution in the user query: *maximal* then the result is totally different and totally irrelevant, so less luck there.

We now proceed to a demo of a vertical search based on word2vec and DL from (Deep Pavlov 2019, Fig. 2.11). We first run a query to get some answers and then formulate a query where we know the answer for it does exist.

The first query is answered incorrectly: no answer is related to a termination of *auto insurance* (on the bottom). We consider the third answer, select its fragment

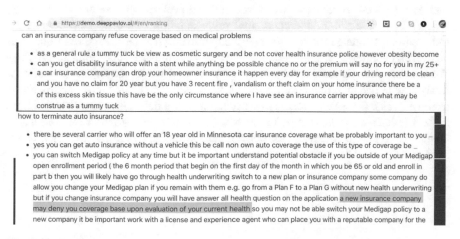

Fig. 2.11 Running a query, selecting an answer and testing the search formulating this answer fragment as a query

Fig. 2.12 Text comprehension based on ELMo DS model: unable to answer a basic question (Peters et al. 2018)

(highlighted) and turn it into a question: "*Can an insurance company refuse coverage based on medical problem?*". The answers for the second query are incorrect again: they are not related to a denial of medical insurance. We will focus on this example in the following sections.

Toward the end of this section we perform a spot-checking of another DS model that is supposed to improve word2vec and GloVe: ELMo (Peters et al. 2018, Fig. 2.11). It is a pre-trained contextual representation of words from large-scale bidirectional language models for many supervised NLP tasks including question answering, coreference, semantic role labeling, classification, and syntactic parsing. We take an example from an annotated corpus of AMR (Chap. 3) and formulate a fairly simple question that requires only a verb matching to find a relevant passage (*to be named*). However, a reading comprehension model uses some other features, believing that *named* is not important in this query but *how, are* and mainly *small* are. Hence the answer is irrelevant: the correct here would be a phrase matching *named*, such as *not give it a name, only a number*.

2.4 Structurizing Compositional Semantics

The notion of word similarity is very useful in larger semantic tasks. Knowing how similar two words are can help in computing how similar the meaning of two phrases or sentences are, a very important component of NLU tasks like question answering, recommendation, paraphrasing, and summarization. One way of getting values for word similarity is to ask humans to judge how similar one word is to another.

The meaning of two words can be related in ways other than relatedness similarity. One such class of connections is called word relatedness (Budanitsky and Hirst 2006), also traditionally called *word association* in psychology. Consider the meanings of the words *coffee* and *cup*. *Coffee* is not similar to *cup*; they share practically no features (*coffee* is a plant or a beverage, while a *cup* is a specific object made by human with a particular shape). But *coffee* and *cup* are clearly related; they are associated by co-participating in an everyday event (the event of drinking *coffee* out of a *cup*). Similarly, the nouns *chef* and *knife* are not similar but are related via a usability event: a *chef* employs a *knife*.

One common kind of relatedness between words is if they belong to the same semantic field. A semantic field is a set of words that cover a particular semantic domain and bear structured relations with each other. For example, words might be related by being in the semantic field of schools (*pupil, teacher, board, lesson*), or restaurants (*waitress, menu, dish, food*).

Regretfully, word2vec and GloVe do not differentiate between similarity and relatedness. In these approaches, similarity and relatedness are expressed by the same "physical units" of similarity. In the spirit of word2vec, weight can be summed up with the electrical current. Similar words play the same semantic role, and related words play complementary roles, such as an adjective and a noun in a noun phrase, a verb and a noun in verb phrases above. Structurization enforces that the measure of relatedness is computed separately from the measure of similarity between the entities.

Just getting a list of related words (related in a variety of ways) is not very useful in applications, and frequently used carelessly. This results in an application producing meaningless responses. Using tools such as (Explosion AI 2019; TurkuNLP 2019; Turbomaze 2019) lets a user get a list of related words. Structurization is required to bring this list into a robust, meaningful context.

To compare meaning of two words, they need to play the same semantic role. For example, to be a second argument of the same verb or a first argument of two different verbs in the same verb group, like *deny* and *reject*. Let us consider a verb phrase: *"gave up what might have been a magnificent career as a painter"*. For example, a semantic representation according to Advanced Meaning Representation (AMR, Banarescu et al. 2013) approach is as follows (Chap. 3):

Fig. 2.13 Word2vec and
GloVe derivatives of *painter*

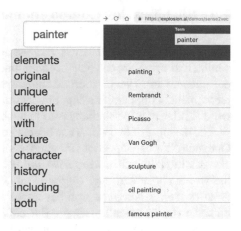

```
:ARG1 (g / give-up-07
        :ARG0 (i / i)
        :ARG1 (c / career
                :mod (m / magnificent)
                :topic (p / person
                        :ARG0-of (p2 / paint-02)))
```

Now let us see which word2vec derivatives of *painter* are appropriate (Fig. 2.13). For *painter*, word2vec does nothing meaningful in terms of profession for both implementations:

Semantic annotation tells us that the query *painter* should be expanded by the members of this list with a noun of the semantic role of human (which turns out to be in the tail of this list: *calligrapher* and *visual artist*). Both of these entries are meaningful synonyms in the context of profession, so the query can be safely expanded accordingly without ruining the precision.

Notice that in AMR a *painter* is defined as a person whose argument is verb *paint*. This way a rather high level of abstraction is achieved (Galitsky et al. 2012).

2.5 Similarity Assessment Algorithm

In this section we build an algorithm that combines the best of the following worlds:

- Word2vec;
- Syntactic, domain-independent analysis;
- Semantic analysis, which requires domain-specific ontology and possibly domain-independent semantic parsing engine;
- Named-entity analysis, which sometimes require domain-specific ontology of entities, attributes and entity–entity, entity-attribute and attribute-attribute (cross entity type) relations.

Word2vec would assist with the representation of meaning of individual words, syntactic analysis would direct word2vec into comparing only comparable words, in appropriate positions and roles.

Semantic analysis would complement word2vec with meaning where knowledge of context is a key, and named-entity analysis extends word2vec in case words name entities instead of having generic meanings. Grasping this structured and integrated text similarity assessment algorithm, the reader would acquire intuitive understanding of why word2vec on its own, without syntactic analysis, is inaccurate, and without semantic and entity analysis is incomplete. The main idea of this chapter is to apply word2vec to an aligned linguistic structure, not to an original text. We will further advance an alignment of linguistic structures in Chap. 3.

Our running example will be a health insurance related query that was failed by a reading comprehension task example in the section above. We expand this query with synonyms and a variety of phrasings:

'Health Insurance May Be Denied/rejected/ not Qualified if/when/due to I Have Problem with My Health/illness/Pre-Existing Condition'

Notice that *pre-existing condition* is equivalent to *bad health* only in the context (phrase) *insurance-denied.* However, without structurization, GloVe associates *pre-existing condition* with *health insurance* directly (which is not surprising, but not useful, according to this example, Fig. 2.14).

In a question-answering setting, we intend to demonstrate that proper meaning similarity assessment would correctly associate an A with a Q:

Q: health coverage is rejected because of bad health;
A: medical insurance is denied due to pre-existing conditions.

Term		Sense	
pre-existing conditions	Q	auto	↕
preexisting conditions ›			**90%**
pre existing conditions ›			**86%**
insurance plans ›			**80%**
preventative care ›			**80%**
insurance coverage ›			**80%**
medical coverage ›			**79%**

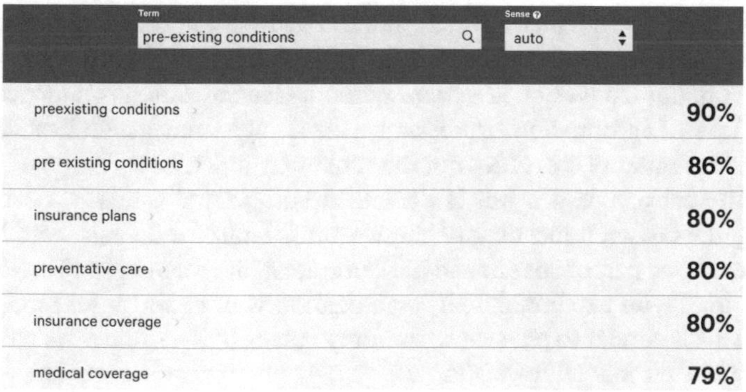

Fig. 2.14 GloVe synonyms for pre-existing conditions

Notice that this Q/A pair is derived from various phrasings of our running example. If these phrases are not identified as semantically identical, search recall would drop.

It is worth mentioning that good search engines know that these texts have the same meaning (give similar search results). In particular, Google knows that these two expressions mean similar things, but most likely obtained this knowledge outside of linguistic means. By accumulating data on what query people input and what was the selected hit, Google figures out that some n-grams of words in these two expressions, Q and A, lead to the same search result related to *health insurance* and its *possible denial of coverage due to pre-existing conditions*. In this section, we explore the linguistic opportunities of relating these expressions in the same semantic class based on syntactic, conventional semantic and entity/ontology-based analyses.

We first try to find a semantic similarity assessment tool on the web that would correctly associate Q and A (Fig. 2.15).

Other APIs from Quora (2019) do not work either.

Notice that if the main entity, *health insurance* is not identified, similarity assessment becomes irrelevant. So texts need to be parsed.

To structurize DS-based similarity assessment, we attach DS similarity to structures built for text: syntactic, semantic and entity/attribute-based (Fig. 2.16).

To do the merge, we add nodes and combine the labels for the nodes where is a one-to-one correspondence. (syntactic_node = *today*, Semantic_mode = *today*, Date-Time = today) = > node of the generalization structure = < today, {syntactic_node, semantic(mod), entity_type(DateTime)}> .

Notice that the structurized word2vec possesses an explainability feature: the system can provide a full log for a similarity assessment, citing all linguistic features that led to it. In a number of applications this log is visualized (Galitsky et al. 2011a).

2.5.1 Syntactic Generalization

To machine-learn meaning of words in a numerical space, one needs to express a numerical relation between them such as *similarity*. To provide a meaningful expression of similarity between two words, numbers are not good enough since poorly interpretable, and we need other words for such expression (Galitsky 2017a).

We refer to this expression as *generalization*. Generalization is intended to minimize the loss of information expressing a meaning: from generalization we can computer the similarity score, but not the other way around.

Similarity between two words is a number, and generalization is a list of words expressing the common meaning of these words. Unlike a default word2vec, only words of the same part of speech and the same semantic role/tag can be generalized, such as animal with another animal, organization with organization, location with location. This is similar to physics where only values of the same physical units can be added, not a current with weight.

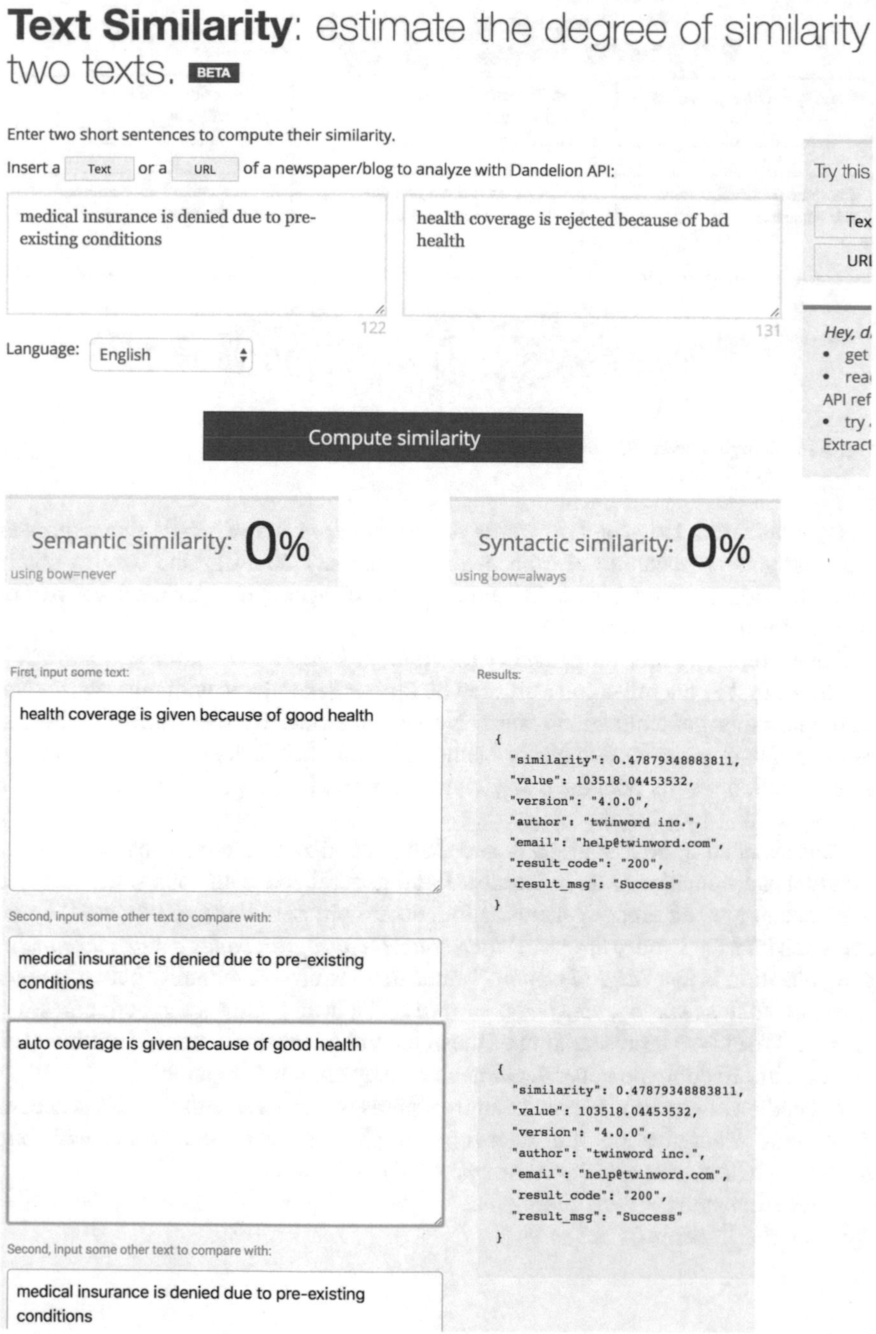

Text Similarity: estimate the degree of similarity two texts. BETA

Enter two short sentences to compute their similarity.

Insert a [Text] or a [URL] of a newspaper/blog to analyze with Dandelion API: Try this

medical insurance is denied due to pre-existing conditions	health coverage is rejected because of bad health
122	131

Tex

URl

Hey, d.
- get
- rea
API ref
- try ,
Extract

Language: [English ▾]

Compute similarity

Semantic similarity: **0%**
using bow=never

Syntactic similarity: **0%**
using bow=always

First, input some text:

health coverage is given because of good health

Results:

{
    "similarity": 0.47879348883811,
    "value": 103518.04453532,
    "version": "4.0.0",
    "author": "twinword inc.",
    "email": "help@twinword.com",
    "result_code": "200",
    "result_msg": "Success"
}

Second, input some other text to compare with:

medical insurance is denied due to pre-existing conditions

auto coverage is given because of good health

{
    "similarity": 0.47879348883811,
    "value": 103518.04453532,
    "version": "4.0.0",
    "author": "twinword inc.",
    "email": "help@twinword.com",
    "result_code": "200",
    "result_msg": "Success"
}

Second, input some other text to compare with:

medical insurance is denied due to pre-existing conditions

Fig. 2.15 Available text similarity assessment tools on the web fail to identify that the meaning of two texts is almost the same

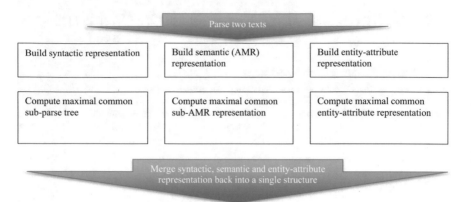

Fig. 2.16 A high—level view of generalizing two texts

Generalization between two words is an unordered list of words that expresses the least general meaning of both of them (Galitsky 2017b). One way to obtain generalization via word2vec is to intersect a list of synonyms (for the same part of speech) for these two words.

For example, *painter ^ architect = {exhibition, idea, student, nature, modernity}*.

Notice that a generalization result can be further generalized with other words and also with other generalization results. Numerical similarity then can be expressed as the relative common number of elements in this list. If w_1 and w_2 are word or generalization results with the lists $\{..., w_{1i},...\}$ and $\{..., w_{2j},...\}$ respectively, then $w_1 \char"005E w_2 = \bigcup_{i,j} (w_{1i} \char"005E w_{2j})$.

Phrases need to be first aligned, and then generalized on a word-by-word basis. Firstly, head nouns need to be extracted and generalized with each other. If these head nouns give an empty generalization, so are phrases. For two phrases "*digital camera with long battery life*" and "*long zoom focus digital camera with viewfinder*" generalization is just "*digital camera*" since there is no commonality between other attributes such as *battery, viewfinder* or *zoom*. The head noun here in both phrases is *camera*. Word2vec representation of these individual attributes should not be taken into account to compute generalization since they are not comparable.

Other then alignment, a normalization of phrases such as *A* with *B* ⇒ *BA* is needed to compute generalization of distinct forms of phrases. "*video camcorder with long zoom*" = > "*long zoom video camcorder*". We then obtain

"*video camcorder with long zoom*" ^ "*short-focus zoom digital camera*" = "*(camcorder ^ camera) with zoom*".

To generalize two expressions, we first generalize their main entities (head nouns in their main noun phrase) and then add a sequence of argument-by-argument generalizations:

$$AMR(Q) \barwedge AMR(A) = E(Q) \barwedge E(A) \cup_n ARGn(Q) \barwedge ARGn(a)$$

Although *similarity(deny, reject)* < *similarity(deny, accept)*, it is still high enough to conclude that *deny* = *reject* for the purpose of generalization.

For syntactic generalization, it is important to generate paraphrases and then compute the maximum common sub parse tree. Generating accurate and diverse paraphrases automatically is still very challenging. Traditional methods (Bolshakov and Gelbukh 2004) exploit how linguistic knowledge can improve the quality of generated paraphrases, including shallow linguistic features (Zhao et al. 2009), and syntactic and semantic information (Ellsworth and Janin 2007; Sidorov et al. 2012). However, they are often domain-specific and hard to scale, or yield inferior results. With the help of growing large data and neural network models, recent studies have shown promising results. A number of DL architectures have been investigated with the goal of generating high-quality paraphrases. One approach is to formulate paraphrase generation as a sequence-to-sequence problem, following experience from machine translation (Cheng et al. 2016).

For parse trees, generalization operation is defined as finding maximal common subgraph (Galitsky et al. 2012, Fig. 2.17).

Generalization at the level of parse trees is shown in Fig. 2.17. One can see that common words remain in the maximum common sub-tree, except *can* which is unique for the second sentence, and modifiers for *lens* which are different in these two sentences (shown as *[NN-focus NN-* NN-lens]*).

As a whole expression, generalization result is *[MD-can, PRP-I, VB-get, NN-focus, NN-lens, IN-for JJ-digital NN-camera]*. At the phrase level, we obtain:

Noun phrases: [[NN-focus NN-*], [JJ-digital NN-camera]]
Verb phrases: [[VB-get NN-focus NN-* NN-lens IN-for JJ-digital NN-camera]].

To get to the application of word2vec, a number of phrase extraction, aggregation and alignment are necessary so that word-to-word comparison is syntactically meaningful (Figs. 2.18 and 2.19). The problem of phrase alignment is connected with natural language inference (NLI) in determining whether a natural-language hypothesis *H* can be reasonably inferred from a given premise text *P*. In order to recognize that *"New CA governor visited LA"* can be inferred from *"California government attended a meeting in Los Angeles"*, one must first recognize the correspondence between *CA* and *California*, and between *visited* and *attended* <an event>. Most current approaches to alignment rely on establishing links between corresponding entities and predicates in *P* and *H*. Glickman et al. (2005) and Jijkoun and de Rijke (2005) have explored approaches based on measuring the degree of lexical overlap

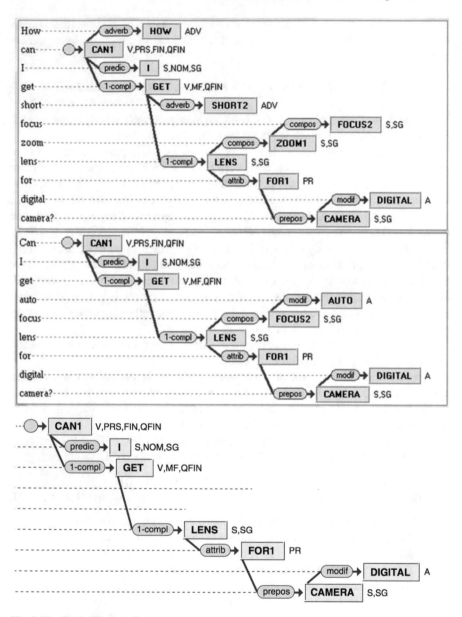

Fig. 2.17 Generalization of two parse trees (on the top and in the middle). The generalization result is shown on the bottom

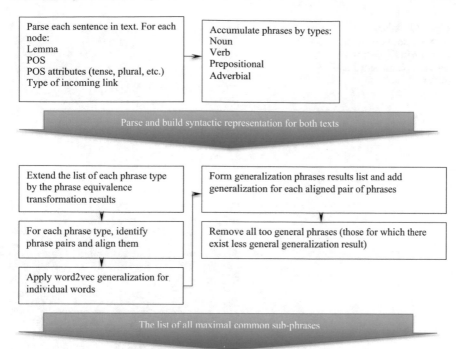

Fig. 2.18 Syntactic generalization component

between bags of words. While ignoring structure, such methods depend on matching each word in H to the word in P with which it is most similar (which is an alignment). Phrase alignment is essential in machine translation. Figure 2.19 shows two aligned parse trees for sentences for Swedish and English. In spite of the difference in tree topology, there is a one-to-one mapping for each part of speech and a complete alignment.

Fig. 2.19 Alignment between parse tree for a sentence in English and Swedish (Arase and Tsujii 2017)

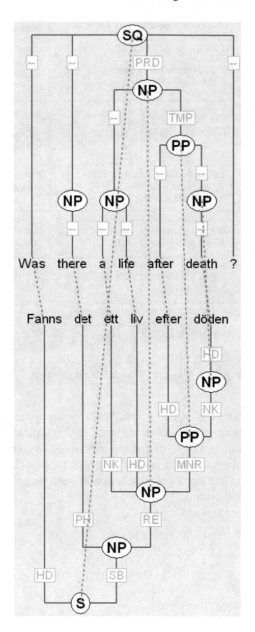

```
AMR(Q): reject-01(
        [:ARG1 (company )fictitious]
        :ARG1-of (coverage
                 :mod (health)
        :ARG2-of (cause-01 (
                 :ARG0 (health
                          :mod (bad))))


AMR(A) deny-01(
        [:ARG1 (company )fictitious]
        :ARG1-of (insurance
                 :mod (medical)
        :ARG2-of (cause-01 (
                 :ARG0 (condition
                            :ARG0 (exist)
                                  :mod (pre))))
AMR(Q)  ^  AMR (A) = deny^reject(
        [:ARG1 (company )fictitious]
        :ARG1-of (insurance^coverage
                 :mod (medical^health)
        :ARG2-of (cause-01 (
                 :ARG0 ("bad health" ^ "pre-existing conditions")))) =
not-acceptance(
        [:ARG1 (company )fictitious]
        :ARG1-of ({medical, plan, regular, deductible, payments}
                 :mod ({wellness, personal, good, bad, physical, wellbeing,
dental, pediatric})
        :ARG2-of (cause-01 (
                 :ARG0({problem, issues, increased, higher, premiums, cost,
deductibles})))) =
```

Fig. 2.20 Example of semantic generalization

2.5.2 Semantic Generalization

Example of semantic generalization for our running example is shown in Fig. 2.20. On the top, semantic structures for each text are shown according to simplified AMR notation conventions. On the bottom, intermediate and final generalization results are shown. The root-level verbs are generalized against each other, as well as each semantic role, one against a corresponding one. Nesting of semantic roles is preserved. Since the semantic structures vary in innermost expression, generalization is reduced to the respective phrases ('*bad health*' ^ 'pre-*existing conditions*') and not their semantic structures.

2.5.3 Attribute-Based Generalization

It is based on available ontology and entity extraction results (Fig. 2.21). Two entities such as *organization, person, location* or *time* can be matched against each other unless there is an entry in the ontology that related two entities of different types, like *Jeff Besos—isCEO—Amazon.*

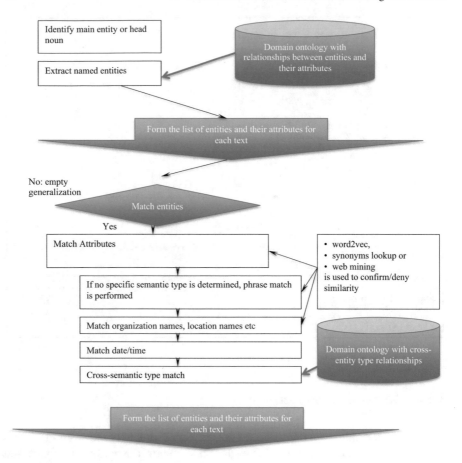

Fig. 2.21 Entity/attribute generalization component

Times and *dates* are generalized as a range the events from both texts occur; generalization is empty if these events are too distant in time (Galitsky and Botros 2015).

Geo locations, addresses, points of interest are generalized into the location range or common properties (if available).

$(Lattutude1, Longtitude1)$ ^ $(Lattutude2, Longitude2)$ = range $[(Lattutude1, Longitude1), (Lattutude2, Longtitude2)]$.

Lattutude, Longtitude ^ *Location name* = range $[(Lattitude, Longitude), (Lattutude_{Loc}, Longitude_{Loc})]$ which includes/covers the Lat/Long of this *Location*, if below certain distance threshold. (Galitsky and Usikov 2008).

Range1 ^ *Range2* = $\cup_{ij} (Range1_j$ ^ $Range2_j)$, computing overlaps of all ranges, for time and space.

If time and space points or ranges are related, they are generalized together with a relation between them occur$_1$ (*Location1, Time1*) ^ occur$_2$ (*Location2, Time2*) = {(occur$_1$ ^ occur$_2$)(*Location1* ^ *Location2, Time1* ^ *Time2*), occur$_1$ (*Location1* ^ *Location2, Time1* ^ *Time2*), occur$_2$ (*Location1* ^ *Location2, Time1* ^ *Time2*),

2.6 Evaluation

We compare the performance of the integrated structurized word2vec with the original word2vec, syntactic + semantic + entity -based analyses, and with the text similarity assessment components available on the web. Original word2vec for text is computed as SentenceToVec, an average of the word vector representations of all the words in the sentence. We use Yahoo! Answers dataset (Webscope 2017), Yahoo Non-Factoid Question Dataset (Yahoo 2019), Stanford Question Answering (Rajpurkar 2019) and (Google Natural Answers 2019) datasets.

We assume the similarity between the question and the correct answer is 1 and between all other answers (to different questions) as 0. We randomly select incorrect answer based on TF*IDF search within the same dataset.

Our assumption is that an abstract ideal (gold standard) similarity assessment system would give 1 for a correct answer and 0 for an incorrect (although containing similar keywords, per its search algorithm). The stronger the deviation of a given similarity assessment system is, the lower is its performance. Hence the accuracy of the similarity assessment is measured as a deviation from the gold standard.

Table 2.1 shows the results of similarity assessment by various methods described or developed in this section.

In the bottom row, we see the relative improvement compared to the baseline (pure sentence2vec). Available similarity assessment systems show the performance below the baseline. Linguistic analysis without word2vec gives 45% boost, followed by the major boost my merging word2vec with syntax. It turns out word2vec and syntactic analysis complement each other in a higher degree than semantic and entity-based components. Nevertheless, all these components together further improve the performance by 10%. Notice that this measure cannot be compared to search F1 measure: this is done by design, to demonstrate how well similarity assessment can classify answers as correct and incorrect.

Table 2.1 Percentages of deviation from the correct similarity measure

Dataset	Original word2vec (SentenceToVec)	Explosion.ai/wv_demo	Syntactic + semantic + entity - based	Syntactic + w2v	Semantic + w2v	entity – based + w2v	Structurized word2vec
Yahoo! Answers	45	37.1/32.7	62.3	68.2	66.2	70.2	75.4
Yahoo! Non-factoid	46.2	31.2/37.9	60.3	70.3	69.7	65.2	72
Stanford SQuAD	43.2	34.5/36.3	65.8	73.1	65.9	63.2	77.9
Google NaturalQuestions	41.1	38.9/40.6	66.2	69.3	70.1	60.7	73.2
Average improvement over baseline			0.45	0.60	0.55	0.48	0.70

2.7 Related Work

Every downstream application of word2vec has its own kind of similarity that needs to be defined. Words are therefore not inherently similar or dissimilar. For example, "good acting" and "cluttered set" are highly dissimilar in terms of the sentiment they express toward a theatrical play. However, they are very similar in the context of detecting news items related to the theatre, as both phrases are highly indicative of theatre-related content. It is often unclear what kind of similarity is useful for a downstream problem in advance. Indeed, it has been shown that being able to learn the notion defined by a particular word similarity task does not necessarily translate to superior extrinsic performance (Schnabel et al. 2015). Depending on the downstream use of a particular clustering (division into clusters), the same clustering can solve a problem or not: the quality of an unsupervised algorithm can therefore only be assessed in the context of an application (Makhalova et al. 2015).

Distributional semantics models even without structurization provide better similarity assessment than Dekang Lin's dependency-based word similarity (Lin 1998) and the measure based on lexical chains in WordNet (Hirst and St-Onge 1998).

2.7.1 Languages Other Than English

Word2vec models can be built for various languages (WordSimilarity 2019). To implement structurization of distributional semantics in languages other English, we need syntactic parsers trained on a given language and some kind of semantic annotation.

A number of methods have been explored to train and align bilingual word embeddings. These methods pursue two objectives: first, similar representations (i.e., spatially close) must be assigned to similar words (i.e., "semantically close") within each language—this is the mono-lingual objective; second, similar representations must be assigned to similar words across languages—this is the cross-lingual objective. The simplest approach consists in separating the mono-lingual optimization task from the cross-lingual optimization task. This is for example the case in (Mikolov et al. 2013). The idea is to separately train two sets of word-embeddings for each language and then to do a parametric estimation of the mapping between word-embeddings across languages. This method was further extended by (Faruqui and Dyer 2014). Even though those algorithms proved to be viable and fast, it is not clear whether or not a simple mapping between whole languages exists. Moreover, they require word alignments which is a rare and expensive resource.

Coulmance et al. (2015) introduce Trans-gram, a simple and computationally efficient method to simultaneously learn and align word embeddings for a variety of languages, using only monolingual data and a smaller set of sentence-aligned data. A new method was used to compute aligned word embeddings for twenty-one languages using English as a pivot language. The authors show that some linguistic features are aligned across languages for which they do not have aligned data, even though those properties do not exist in the pivot language. The authors obtained state -of- the -art results on standard cross-lingual text classification and word translation tasks.

2.8 Conclusions

Word embeddings are considered to be among a small number of successful applications of unsupervised learning at present. The fact that they do not require extensive and expensive annotation work is perhaps their main benefit. Rather, they can be derived from already available unannotated corpora.

We analyzed the weaknesses of distributional semantics and proposed its structurization that significantly improves the performance of word2vec applications based on text similarity. To perform such structurization, we attach the word2vec assessment to a generic tree structure-based operation of generalization. This operation, as a least-general generalization, follows the tradition of logic in data analysis to find a commonality between features to learn a target feature of an object (Galitsky et al. 2010), which is a key in inductive learning.

Structurized word2vec not only complements ontology for applications like search, but also is a tool to build tree-like ontologies (taxonomies), generalizing from data (Galitsky et al. 2011b). As word2vec models are aggregated to the levels of sentences, paragraphs and documents, generalization is defined for these levels too (Galitsky et al. 2013, 2014).

Evaluating DL and distributional semantic-based system, the NLP substantially lowered evaluation standards by relying on smaller and distorted evaluation datasets where both training and testing cases do not represent well the diversity of language patterns used by customers. That is why these systems might perform well in leaderboard assessments and then underperform in real-world usage. In a lot of evaluation settings, performance of DL systems is claimed to approach human performance. However, most of these problems, such as tagging discourse relations and argumentation patterns, are unnatural for human and are not associated with their vital activities. Inter-annotation agreement in these tasks can be low because these problems are not necessarily meaningful and concise for humans.

This can be observed in such tasks as search, conversation, summarization, classification and recommendation. Therefore, unstructured word2vec models are believed not to be a good source of semantic features of words in domain-specific tasks such as CRM. Distributional semantics need to be structurized and augmented with ontologies to perform NLP tasks involving a thorough understanding of user needs and responsible.

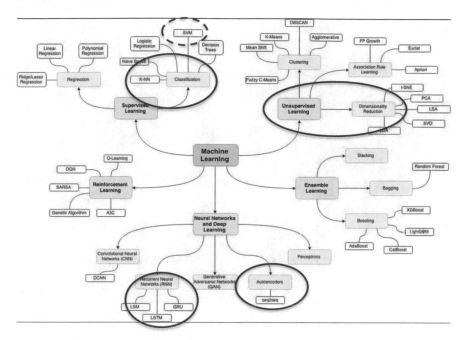

Fig. 2.22 Classes of statistical ML (from heu.ai) and the ones used in this chapter

A task of matching a meaning of two phrases is essentially non-monotonic. A slight change of meaning of a head noun may change the meaning of the whole phrase dramatically.

We conclude this chapter with an outline of which ML methods we used (Fig. 2.22). Relying on RNN, Unsupervised learning with dimensionality reduction and seq2seq supports traditional word2vec and MRC. Nearest-neighbor learning leverages semantic (AMR) and syntactic generalization. The classes of statistical ML are shown in red ovals. We show SVM as a branch of supervised learning in red dotted oval used in many other chapters of this book.

Toward the end of this Chapter we highlight the classes of ML essential for CRM (Fig. 2.23). These classes are shown in blue ovals.

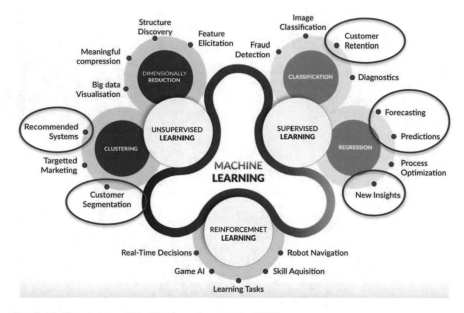

Fig. 2.23 The classes of Machine Learning used in CRM

References

Arase Y, Tsujii J (2017) Monolingual phrase alignment on parse forests. Proceedings of the 2017 Conference on Empirical Methods in Natural Language Processing, 1–11 Copenhagen, Denmark

Banarescu L, Bonial C, Cai S, Georgescu M, Griffitt K, Hermjakob U, Knight K, Koehn P, Palmer M, Schneider N (2013) Abstract meaning representation for Sembanking. In: Proceedings of the 7th linguistic annotation workshop and interoperability with discourse. Sofia, Bulgaria, pp 178–186

Bazińska (2017) Explore word analogies. https://lamyiowce.github.io

Bolshakov IA, Gelbukh A (2004) Synonymous paraphrasing using wordnet and internet. In: International conference on application of natural language to information systems. Springer, pp 312–323

Budanitsky A, Hirst G (2006) Evaluating WordNet—based measures of lexical semantic relatedness. Comput Linguist 32(1):13–47

Cheng Y, Liu Y, Yang Q, Sun M, Xu W (2016) Neural machine translation with pivot languages. arXiv preprint arXiv:1611.04928

Coulmance J, Marty J-M, Wenzek G, Benhalloum A (2015) Trans-gram, fast cross-lingual word-embeddings. EMNLP, Lisbon, Portugal, pp 1109–1113

Deep P (2019) https://deeppavlov.ai/

Ellsworth M, Janin A (2007) Mutaphrase: paraphrasing with FrameNet. In: Proceedings of the ACL-PASCAL workshop on textual entailment and paraphrasing, pp 143–150

Explosion AI (2019) Sense2vec: semantic analysis of the Reddit Hivemind. https://explosion.ai/demos/sense2vec

Faruqui M, Dyer C (2014) Improving vector space word representations using multilingual correlation. ACL

Frase (2019) Frase HubSpot Assistant. https://www.frase.io/?hubspot

Galitsky B (2003) Natural language question answering system: technique of semantic headers. Advanced Knowledge International, Australia

Galitsky B, Usikov D (2008) Programming spatial algorithms in natural language. In: AAAI workshop technical report WS-08–11.Palo Alto, pp 16–24

Galitsky B, Dobrocsi G, De La Rosa JL, Kuznetsov SO (2010) From generalization of syntactic parse trees to conceptual graphs. In: International conference on conceptual structures, pp 185–190

Galitsky B, De la Rosa JL, Dobrocsi G (2011a) Building integrated opinion delivery environment. FLAIRS-24, West Palm Beach FL May 2011

Galitsky B, Dobrocsi G, De la Rosa JL, Kuznetsov SO (2011b) Using generalization of syntactic parse trees for taxonomy capture on the web. ICCS, pp 104–117

Galitsky B, De La Rosa JL, Dobrocsi G (2012) Inferring the semantic properties of sentences by mining syntactic parse trees. Data Knowl Eng 81:21–45

Galitsky B, Kuznetsov SO, Usikov D (2013) Parse thicket representation for multi-sentence search. In: International conference on conceptual structures, pp 153–172

Galitsky B, Ilvovsky DI, Kuznetsov SO (2014) Extending tree kernels towards paragraphs. Int J Comput Linguist Appl 5(1):105–116

Galitsky B, Botros S (2015) Searching for associated events in log data. US Patent 9,171,037

Galitsky B (2017a) Improving relevance in a content pipeline via syntactic generalization. Eng Appl Artif Intell 58:1–26

Galitsky B (2017b) Matching parse thickets for open domain question answering. Data Knowl Eng 107:24–50

Galitsky B (2019) Introduction. In: Developing enterprise chatbots. Springer, Cham

Glickman O, Dagan I, Koppel M (2005) Web based probabilistic textual entailment. In: Proceedings of the PASCAL challenges workshop on recognizing textual entailment

Google Natural Answers (2019) Natural questions. A Benchmark for question answering research. https://ai.google.com/research/NaturalQuestions

Harris Z (1968) Mathematical structures of language. Wiley, New York

Hirst G, St-Onge D (1998) Lexical chains as representations of context for the detection and correction of malapropisms. In: Fellbaum C (ed) WordNet: an electronic lexical database. The MIT Press, Cambridge, MA, pp 305–332

Jijkoun V, Rijke M (2005) Recognizing textual entailment: is word similarity enough? 449–460

Jurafsky D, Martin JH (2019) Speech and language processing, 3rd edn. draft

Lin D (1998) Automatic retrieval and clustering of similar words. In ACL, 768–774, Stroudsburg, PA

Makhalova T, Ilvovsky DI, Galitsky B (2015) Pattern structures for news clustering. FCA4AI@ IJCAI, pp 35–42

Migdal P (2017) King - man + woman is queen; but why? https://lamyiowce.github.io/word2viz/

Mikolov T, Chen K, Corrado G, Dean J (2013) Efficient estimation of word representations in vector space. arXiv Preprint arXiv:1301.3781

Osgood CE, Suci GJ, Tannenbaum PH (1957) The measurement of meaning. University of Illinois Press

Pennington J, Socher R, Manning CD (2014) GloVe: global vectors for word representation. https://nlp.stanford.edu/projects/glove/

Peters M, Neumann M, Iyyer M, Gardner M, Clark C, Lee K, Zettlemoyer L (2018) Deep contextualized word representations. NAACL, pp 2227–2237

Quora (2019) Best tools to know similarity between documents. https://www.quora.com/What-is-the-best-tool-or-API-to-know-the-text-similarity-between-two-documents-in-NLP

Rajpurkar (2019) Rajpurkar P, Jia R, Liang P (2018) Know what you don't know: unanswerable questions for SQuAD. ACL. https://rajpurkar.github.io/SQuAD-explorer/

Ruder S (2016) An overview of word embeddings and their connection to distributional semantic models

Schnabel T, Labutov I, Mimno D, and Joachims T (2015) Evaluation methods for unsupervised word embeddings. EMNLP

Selivanov D (2018) GloVe Word embeddings. https://cran.r-project.org/web/packages/text2vec/vig nettes/glove.html

Sidorov G, Velasquez F, Stamatatos E, Gelbukh A, Chanona-Hernández L (2012) Syntactic N-grams as machine learning features for natural language processing. Expert Syst Appl 41(3):853C860

Turbomaze (2019). https://turbomaze.github.io/word2vecjson/

TurkuNLP (2019) https://bionlp-www.utu.fi/wv_demo/

Webscope (2017) Yahoo! Answers dataset. https://webscope.sandbox.yahoo.com/catalog.php?dat atype=l

WordSimilarity (2019) www.wordsimilarity.com

Yahoo Non-Factoid Question Dataset (2019) https://ciir.cs.umass.edu/downloads/nfL6/

Zhao S, Lan X, Liu T, Li S (2009) Application-driven statistical paraphrase generation. ACL 2:834–842

Chapter 3
Employing Abstract Meaning Representation to Lay the Last-Mile Toward Reading Comprehension

Abstract We propose a Machine reading comprehension (MRC) method based on the Abstract Meaning Representation (AMR) framework and a universal graph alignment algorithm. We combine syntactic, semantic and entity-based graph representations of a question to match it with a combined representation of an answer. The alignment algorithm is applied for combining various representations of the same text as well as for matching (generalization) of two different texts such as a question and an answer. We explore a number of Question Answering (Q/A) configurations and select a scenario where the proposed AMR generalization-based algorithm AMRG detects and rectifies the errors of a traditional neural MRC. When the state-of-the-art neural MRC is applied and delivers the correct answer in almost 90% of cases, the proposed AMRG verifies each answer and if it determines that it is incorrect, attempts to find a correct one. This error-correction scenario boosts the state-of-the-art performance of a neural MRC by at least 4%.

3.1 Introduction

Machine Reading Comprehension (MRC) is a fundamental and long-standing goal of natural language understanding that aims to teach the machine to answer a question automatically according to a given passage (Hermann et al. 2015; Rajpurkar et al. 2018; Burtsev et al. 2018). Multi-choice reading comprehension is a challenging task to select an answer (A) from a set of candidates when given a passage and a question (Q).

In spite of the great success of Deep Learning (DL) in Machine Reading Comprehension (MRC) tasks, a substantial number of simple questions are still answered incorrectly. When semantic roles are ambiguous, multiple instances of attributes of the same semantic types exist, or there is a complex syntactic construction of modifies, the learning-based models are frequently confused. In these cases, a direct assessment of similarity between a Q and A is beneficial, such as a maximal common sub-structure of linguistic representations (Collins and Duffy 2002; Galitsky 2013).

© Springer Nature Switzerland AG 2020
B. Galitsky, *Artificial Intelligence for Customer Relationship Management*,
Human–Computer Interaction Series,
https://doi.org/10.1007/978-3-030-52167-7_3

Answering factoid questions has remained a major challenge in industrial conversational interfaces. The state-of-the-art systems are trained with curated questions and answers by business users. The limitation, however, is that the factoid questions must exist in the training data (a curated set of question–answer (Q/A) pairs) prepared by the enterprise users. Given the range of products and services that large enterprises like banks offer, an extensive number of questions need to be trained to ensure a coverage is adequate. Maintaining an industrial training dataset is a challenge as products, conditions and regulations are constantly updated, which makes it a difficult task to build a search engine and a content management system for a CRM portal (Galitsky 2019b).

At the same time, incorporating knowledge about the target paragraph from such sources as syntactic parse tree and semantic abstract meaning representation (AMR) parsing results can provide systematic means for answering attribute-value questions (Galitsky 2014). Traversing syntactic parse tree and semantic parse in parallel allows for exhaustive coverage of possible question phrasings, given an answer.

To enable a machine to 'truly comprehend' the meaning of a sentence, semantic parsing is applied to map an NL sentence to a certain semantic representation. AMR is one such semantic representation and it is represented as a rooted, directed, acyclic graph with labels on edges (relations) and leaves (entities). AMR comprises a readable sembank of English sentences paired with their whole-sentence, logical meanings, resulting in semantic parsers that are as ubiquitous as syntactic ones. A corpus of over thirty thousand sentences annotated with the AMR representation (Banarescu et al. 2013) is available. The building blocks for the AMR representation are entities and relations between them. Understanding these concepts and their relations is crucial to computing the meaning of a sentence. This work leverages the availability of efficient AMR parsers such as (Damonte et al 2017). The parser of May and Priyadarshi (2017) could have been used as well.

As Deep Learning (DL) does the heavy lifting of answering a high percentage of arbitrary–phrased questions, a deterministic technique can lay the last-mile toward answering all user questions. Firstly, a technique for navigating a semantic graph such as AMR can verify the correctness of a DL answer, involving syntactic and NER tags as well as semantic role information. Secondly, when the DL answer is determined to be incorrect, AMR employs answer-finding means complementary to that of DL and identifies the correct answer within the answer text (context).

We expect that a DL system and a direct syntactic/semantic similarity approach would complement each other since they rely on totally different feature spaces. DL approaches frequently fail because there is a lack of a phrase structure similar to the ones in a training set, or DL does not generalize well enough to cover a given case. A direct syntactic/semantic similarity approach has its own limitations, including a lack of ontology and noise in a semantic parsing. The proposed similarity-based approach fails when a correct Q/A pair is similar in meaning but very different in constructed semantic and syntactic representations. It turns out that these two classifiers mostly make mistakes in different cases.

One can see that usually there is a substantial syntactic similarity between phrasing in a Q and in an A. Once a Wh-word is substituted by a placeholder of a certain

The Stanford Question Answering Dataset

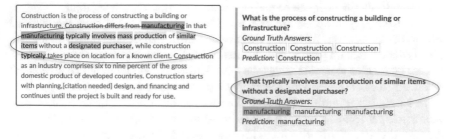

Construction is the process of constructing a building or infrastructure. Construction differs from manufacturing in that manufacturing typically involves mass production of similar items without a designated purchaser, while construction typically takes place on location for a known client. Construction as an industry comprises six to nine percent of the gross domestic product of developed countries. Construction starts with planning,[citation needed] design, and financing and continues until the project is built and ready for use.

What is the process of constructing a building or infrastructure?
Ground Truth Answers:
Construction Construction Construction
Prediction: Construction

What typically involves mass production of similar items without a designated purchaser?
Ground Truth Answers:
manufacturing manufacturing manufacturing
Prediction: manufacturing

Fig. 3.1 A typical question in SQuAD

semantic type (such as noun-entity), a syntactic similarity between a Q and an A can be easily established (Fig. 3.1, shown in red ovals).

In this Chapter, we describe AMR Generalization (AMRG) approach to Q/A, which turns out to be capable of improving a DL-based one in peculiar cases. We explore various modes of integration between AMRG and DL as a combination of two classifiers of candidate answers and discover that they mutually benefit each other in a configuration when DL acts first and then AMRG attempts to identify DL's errors and correct them.

3.2 Deep Learning Models

We briefly outline the internals of a DL used for MRC. It is a multi-layer neural network.

Embedding Layer. The training dataset for the model consists of the context and corresponding questions. Both of these can be broken into individual words and then these words converted into Word Embeddings using pre-trained vector like word2vec. One can also use a hundred-dimensional GloVe word embeddings and tune them during the training process (Dwivedi 2018).

Encoder Layer. The next layer is an RNN-based Encoder layer (Fig. 3.2). Each word in the answer text must be associated with the words before it and after it. A bi-directional GRU/LSTM can help to do that. The output of the RNN is a series of

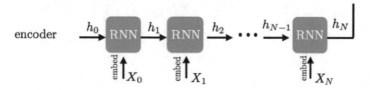

Fig. 3.2 RNN Encoder

hidden vectors in the forward and backward directions and they are concatenated. The same RNN Encoder can be used to create question hidden vectors.

Attention Layer. So far, we have a hidden vector for the context and a hidden vector for the question. To identify the answer, one has to consider these two together. This is done based on what is called "attention". It is the key component of the Q/A system as it helps to decide, given the question, which words in the context should it "attend" to. Let us start with the simplest possible attention model: dot product.

Dot product attention. For each context vector c_i we multiply each question vector q_j to get vectors e_i which are attention scores in Fig. 3.3. A softmax is taken over e_i to get attention distribution a_j. Softmax ensures that the sum of all e_i is 1. Finally, a_i is computed as a product of the attention distribution α_i and the corresponding question vector that is attention output. Dot product attention is computed as:

$$e^i = \left[c_i^T q_1, \ldots, c_i^T q_M\right] \in R^M$$
$$a^i = \operatorname{soft\,max}\left(e^i\right) \in R^M$$

$$a_i = \sum_{j=1}^{M} \alpha_j^i q_j \in R^{2h}$$

Fig. 3.3 A basic attention

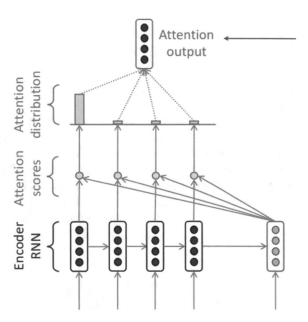

3.3 A Bi-LSTM-Based Reading Comprehension Algorithm

Neural algorithms for MRC are given a question q consisting of l tokens $q_1,...,q_l$ and a passage p of m tokens $p_1,..., p_m$. For each token p_i we compute:

(1) the probability $p_{start}(i)$ that p_i is the start of the answer span;
(2) the probability $p_{end}(i)$ that p_i is the end of the answer span.

A Bi-LSTM architecture is shown in Fig. 3.4. We build an embedding for the question, build an embedding for each token in the passage, compute a similarity function between the question and each passage word in context, and then use the question-passage similarity scores to decide where the answer span starts and ends. The question is represented by a single embedding $\boldsymbol{q}$, which is a weighted sum of representations for each question word q_i. It is computed by passing the series of embeddings $PE(q_1),...,E(q_l)$ of question words through a bi-LSTM network. The resulting hidden representations $\{\boldsymbol{q}_1,...,\boldsymbol{q}_l\}$ are combined by a weighted sum

$$q = \sum_j b_j q_j$$

The weight b_j is a measure of the relevance of each question word, and relies on a learned weight vector $\mathbf{w}$:

$$b_j = \frac{\exp(w \cdot q_j)}{\sum_j \exp(w \cdot q_j^{xxx})}$$

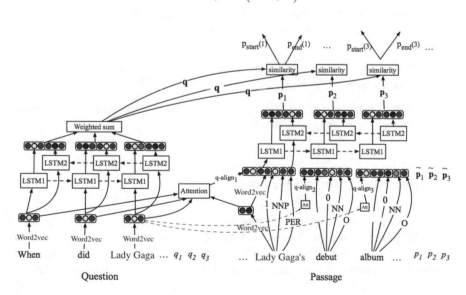

Fig. 3.4 A Bi-LSTM Architecture for MRC

To compute the passage embedding $\{\boldsymbol{p}_1,...,\boldsymbol{p}_m\}$, we first form an input representation $p^\sim = \{\boldsymbol{p}^\sim_1,...,\boldsymbol{p}^\sim_m\}$ by combining four sources:

(1)   An embedding for each word $\boldsymbol{E}(p_i)$ such as word2vec or GLoVE;
(2)   Token features like POS, or the NE tag of p_i obtained from POS or NER taggers;
(3)   Exact match features representing whether the passage word p_i occurred in the question (1 if $p_i \in q$) = and 0 otherwise). Separate exact match features might be used for lemmatized or lower-cased versions of the tokens;
(4)   Aligned question embedding. An attention mechanism to give a more sophisticated model of similarity between the passage and question words, such as low-similarity words like *childhood* and *education*. A weighted similarity $\sum_j a_{i,j} E(q_j)$ can be used, where the attention weight $a_{i,j}$ encodes the similarity between p_i and each question word q_j. This attention weight can be computed as the dot product between functions α of the word embeddings of the question and passage:

$$q_{i,j} = \frac{\exp\big(\alpha(E(p_i)) \cdot \alpha\big(E\big(q_j\big)\big)\big)}{\sum_{j'} \exp\big(\alpha(E(p_i)) \cdot \alpha\big(E\big(q'_j\big)\big)\big)}$$

$\alpha(\cdot)$ can be a simple feed-forward network.

$p^\sim$ is passed through a biLSTM: $\{\boldsymbol{p}_i,...,\boldsymbol{p}_m\} = \mathrm{RNN}(\{\boldsymbol{p}^\sim_1,...\boldsymbol{p}^\sim_m\})$. We now have a single question embedding q and a representation for each word in the passage $\{\boldsymbol{p}_i,...,\boldsymbol{p}_m\}$. To find the answer span, one can train two separate classifiers, the first to compute for each p_i the probability $p_{start}(i)$ that p_i is the start of the answer span, and the second to compute the probability $p_{end}(i)$. These classifiers could rely on dot product between the passage and question embeddings as input. However, it turns out we would rather learn a more sophisticated similarity function, like a bilinear attention layer W:

$p_{start}(i) \propto \exp(p_i W_s q)$;
$p_{end}(i) \propto \exp(p_i W_e q)$.

These neural network-based MRC systems can be trained end-to-end by using datasets where spans are tagged, like SQuAD.

3.4   An Answer and Its Questions

Let us look at semantic representation of an answer text (People.cn 2019, Fig. 3.5):

As of Monday morning, there have been 21 people from Nghe An suspected of missing in Britain, head of Nghe An police Nguyen Huu Cau told local media on the sidelines of the ongoing biannual meeting of the country's top legislature. This is Abstract Meaning Representation (AMR) of text which forms a basis for our AMRG approach. Figure 3.5 shows a semantic representation as a logic form, and Fig. 3.6

Fig. 3.5 An AMR
expression for the answer
text. The respective graph
representation of the same
text is shown in Fig. 6

```
(tell-01
  :ARG0 (v11 / person
    :name (v12 / name
      :op1 "Nguyen"
      :op2 "Huu"
      :op3 "Cau")
    :wiki "Nguyen_Huu_Cau")
  :ARG2 (v15 / media
    :ARG1-of (v14 / local-02))
  :ARG1 (v16 / sideline
    :mod (v17 / meet-03
      :time "biannual"
      :ARG0 (v20 / legislate-01
        :mod (v19 / top)
        :ARG0 (v18 / country))))
  :ARG0 (v3 / person
    :quant 21
    :time (v2 / morning
      :mod (v1 / monday))
    :ARG2-of (v4 / suspect-01
      :ARG1 (v5 / miss-01
        :location (v6 / country
          :name (v7 / name
            :op1 "Britain")
          :wiki "United_Kingdom")))
    :ARG0-of (v8 / head-01
      :ARG1 (v10 / police
        :name (v9 / name
          :op1 "Nghe"
          :op2 "An")))))
```

shows a graph-based representation of an answer, a question and association between
the selected nodes.

In Fig. 3.5, indentations denote the order entities occur as arguments of other
entities. The rook entity is tell-01(ARG0, ARG1, ARG2), where ARG0 is a *telling
person*, ARG1 is meeting circumstances (*sideline*) and ARG2 is a *telling means*. Each
node of an AMR has a label for the word lemma and a node ID, such as 'v9/name'.
Further details about AMR are in consecutive Chaps. 5 and 7.

We implement a procedure of an assessment of a match between a candidate
answer and a question as a traversal of the answer AMR graph. Certain question features, such as a Wh-expression, need different kinds of AMR traversal. We
illustrate a number of examples for questions, starting from:

Q: < *What happened* > on Monday morning?
AMR traversal:

(1)   identify path "Monday – morning"
(2)   traverse up to the node whose argument is "Monday – morning": < person >
(3)   Get the full verb phrase from the node

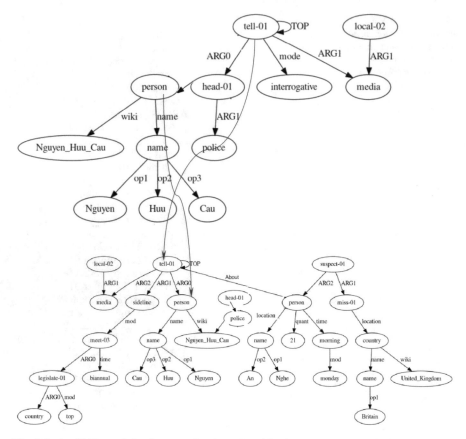

Fig. 3.6 An AMR graph for the query (on the top) and for the answer text (on the bottom)

A correspondence between the question Q (on the top) and its answer (on the bottom) is shown in Fig. 3.6. In this case, *person* node is an argument of both *head* and *suspect* (that is a wrong semantic parsing result). Syntactically, *person* (mapped into *people*) is related to *suspect* and not *head,* so we navigate upwards to *suspect* and return the whole verb phrase for *suspect* in the answer: *"suspected of missing in Britain".*

Questions with wrong answers given by the DL approach are marked with 'Q*'. Below we present more questions and the respective AMR graph traversals steps required to answer them.

Q: < *When/Where/How many* > *were the suspect report missing?*
AMR traversal:

(1) Identify the path for the expression *"suspect report missing"* as *suspect-miss*;
(2) Traverse down from *suspect* through all branches until we hit edge label *time/location/quan[tity]*;
(3) Return the value from the target node of this edge.

Notice the difference between the location of the event being described (in *Britain*) and the location of agents being described (in Vietnam). DL approach cannot figure out this difference.

Q*: < *Who* > < *told/informed/shared information* > *that the suspects were missing?*
AMR traversal:

(1) Identify path "*suspects were missing*": *suspects-miss*;
(2) Traverse up or down till we hit the next level predicate: *tell*;
(3) Traverse down till we hit the edge with label *person:*;
(4) Return the value from the target node of this edge.

Q: < *Who is/are/were* > / < *Tell me/provide information about* > *missing suspects?*
AMR traversal:

(1) Identify path "*missing suspects*": *suspects-miss*;
(2) Go to other nodes connected to this graph path from upward or at the same level;
(3) Get all values from these nodes and return all these values as an unordered set.

Q*: < *Where/From where/Which place* > *21 missing people* < *live/come/travel* > *?*
AMR traversal:

(1) Identify path "*21 missing people*": *suspects-miss*;
(2) Identify the top level node connected with this path;
(3) Traverse down for the edge labeled location, return its value.

Q*: < *How* > did *local media learn about missing people?*
AMR traversal:

(1) Extract a mental action from the query: learn;
(2) Split the query with identified mental actions into two parts/phrases;
(3) Identify paths for phrases in the query: *local-media, missing-person*;
(4) Identify a verb in the sentence logically associated with the extracted mental action:

> *If a Tells B About F then B Learns F: Tell*

(5) Return all arguments of *tell* other than those in the query.

Q*: < *What* > *did head of police Nguyen Huu Cau tell/say/inform/shared with/let know to local media?* (Fig. 5).
AMR traversal:

> < *At What* > *organization/venue/place Did the Head of Police Nguyen Huu Cau Tell to Local Media?*
> Extract a mental action from the query: *tell*
> Split the query with identified mental actions into two parts/phrases;

dentify paths for phrases in the query: *head-of-police-Nguyen-Huu-Cau, local-media*;
Return all arguments of *tell* other than those in the query.

Concluding this subsection, we enumerate the other questions most of which are handled properly by DL:

> *< How > often/frequent/regular is Meeting of the country's Top Legislature Organized/held?*
> *What Was the Agenda of the country's Top Legislature Meeting?*
> *What Official/officer/who Shared Information on the country's Top Legislature Meeting?*
> *When Police Officer Spoke on the country's Top Legislature Meeting?*
> *When Did Police Officer Report at country's Top Legislature Meeting?*

One can observe that semantic representation allows us to provide much broader associations between questions and answers, then a syntactic one, or a pure data-driven one.

3.5   Selecting AMR Over Other Structured Knowledge Representations

An open-domain Q/A can rely on organization of the world's facts and storing them in a structured database, large scale Knowledge Bases (KB) like DBPedia (Auer et al. 2007), Freebase (Bollacker et al. 2008) and Yago (Suchanek et al. 2007). These KBs have become important resources for supporting open-domain Q/A. A typical KB consists of a collection of subject-predicate-object triples (s, r, t) where $s, t \in E$ are entities and $r \in R$ is a predicate or relation. A KB in this form is often called a Knowledge Graph due to its graphical representation, i.e., the entities are nodes and the relations the directed edges that link the nodes. A Knowledge Graph in the form of taxonomy can be automatically learned from the web (Galitsky et al. 2011). Note that this KB contains just a very limited subset of relations in comparison to what AMR can capture from text (Galitsky 2019a).

Yih et al. (2015) attempt to make the search more efficient by focusing on the promising areas of KBs that most likely lead to the correct query graph, before the full parse is determined. For example, after linking *Family Guy* in the question *'Who first voiced Meg on Family Guy?'* to *Family Guy* (the TV show) in the knowledge base, the procedure of alignment between a KB graph and query representation graph needs only to examine the predicates that can be applied to *FamilyGuy* instead of all the predicates in the KB. Resolving other entities also becomes easy, as given the context, it is clear that *Meg* refers to *Meg Griffin* (the character in *Family Guy*). Hence this node would serve as the alignment seed. (Yih et al. 2015) divide this semantic parsing problem into several subtasks, such as *entity linking* and *relation matching*. With this integrated framework, best solutions to each subtask can be easily combined to produce the correct semantic parse. For instance, an advanced entity linking system that is employed by the authors outputs candidate entities for each question with high accuracy. Also, by leveraging a recently developed semantic matching framework based on convolutional networks, the authors improve their relation matching models using continuous-space representations instead of pure lexical matching.

Notice that the KB in Fig. 3.7. (Yih et al. 2015a) can support answering only questions which have entities available in KB, unlike the AMR which supports all entities and their attributes available in textual descriptions, which are always richer than KBs built from them.

One can also learn low-dimensional vector embeddings of words appearing in questions and of entities and relation types of a KB so that the representations of

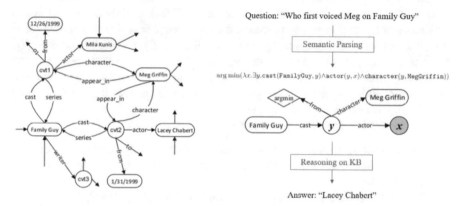

Fig. 3.7 An example of a semantic parsing for KB-QA. (Left) A subgraph of Freebase related to the TV show Family Guy. (Right) A question, its logical form in λ-calculus and query graph, and the answer

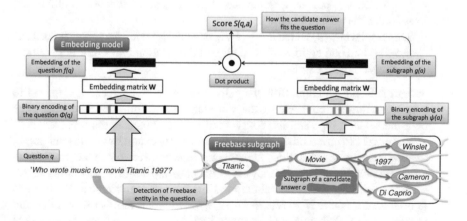

Fig. 3.8 Illustration of the subgraph embedding model scoring a candidate answer

questions and of their corresponding answers are close to each other in the joint embedding space. Learning embeddings is achieved by learning a scoring function $S(Q, A)$, so that S generates a high score if A is the correct answer to the question Q, and a low score otherwise. Note that both Q and A are represented as a combination of the embeddings of their individual words and/or symbols; hence, learning S essentially involves learning these embeddings. In the model of (Bordes et al. 2014), the form of the scoring function is:

$$S(Q,\ A)\ =\ f(Q)^T g(A).$$

Let $\mathbf{W}$ be a matrix of $R^{k \times N}$, where k is the dimension of the embedding space which is fixed a-priori, and N is the dictionary of embeddings to be learned. Let N_W denote the total number of words and N_S the total number of entities and relation types. With $N = N_W + N_S$, the i-th column of W is the embedding of the i-th element (word, entity or relation type) in the dictionary. Function $f(.)$, which maps the questions into the embedding space R^k is defined as $f(Q) = W_\varphi(Q)$, where $\varphi(Q) \in N^N$ is a sparse vector indicating the number of times each word appears in the question Q (usually 0 or 1). Likewise the function $g(.)$ which maps the answer into the same embedding space R^k as the questions, is given by $g(A) = W_\psi(A)$. Here $\psi(A) \in N^N$ is a sparse vector representation of the answer A.

Each answer is represented in the following way:

(1)   **Single Entity.** The answer is represented as a single entity from Freebase: $\psi(a)$ is a 1-of-NS coded vector with 1 corresponding to the entity of the answer, and 0 elsewhere.

(2)   **Path Representation.** The answer is represented as a path from the entity mentioned in the question to the answer entity. Usually, 1- or 2-step paths (1 or 2 edges to traverse correspondingly) are considered:

   - (*"bill clinton"*, people.person.place of birth, *hope*) is a 1-hop path; and
   - (*"bill clinton"*, people.person.place of birth, location. location.containedby, *arkansas*) is a 2-hops path.
     This results in $\psi(a)$ which is a 3-of-N_S or 4-of-N_S coded vector that expresses the start and end entities of the path and the relation types (but not entities) in between these entities.

(3)   **Subgraph Representation.** Both the path representation from (2), and the entire subgraph of entities connected to the candidate answer entity are encoded. Hence both the relation type and the entity itself are combined in the representation $\psi(a)$. In order to differentiate between the answer path and its vicinity subgraph, the dictionary size for entities is extended in two directions. One embedding representation is employed if they are in the path and another embedding representation—if they are in the subgraph. Thus the parameter matrix $R_{k \times N}$ needs to be learned, where $N = N_W + 2N_S$ (N_S is the total number of entities and relation types). If there are C connected entities with D relation types to the

candidate answer, its representation depends on the path length and is a $3 + C + D$ or $4 + C + D$-of- N_S coded vector.

We show the chart of subgraph embedding in Fig. 8 (Bordes et al. 2014). The following steps are performed:

(1) Locate entity in the question;
(2) Compute path from entity to answer;
(3) Represent A as path plus all connected entities to the answer (the subgraph);
(4) Embed both the Q and the A subgraph separately using the learned embedding vectors, and score the match via their dot product.

Note the difference between the similarity of Q to A expressed in a vector space versus expressed as a maximum common sub-graph, obtained via generalization (Galitsky 2012).

3.6 Syntactic Generalization

We show examples of mappings between a parse tree for a question and a parse tree for an answer. Further details on finding maximal common sub-graph for linguistic structures are available in Chap. 2.

This is an entity-relation view for a fragment of the answer text (Fig. 3.10).

Here we show how the parse tree for Q can be aligned with the parse tree for A (Figs. 3.9 and 3.10, Galitsky et al. 2012). We also show an alignment between the two entity graphs. Establishing of entities is fairly noisy: whereas we can associate local media as an entity, we cannot do that for the person name.

Further details on syntactic generalization are available in Chap. 2. Semantic parsing frameworks which leverage the knowledge base to a high degree when forming the semantic parse for an input question are proposed in (Yao and Van Durme 2014; Bao et al. 2014, Yih et al. 2015).

3.7 Alignment for AMR Graph, Syntactic Tree and Query Representation

In this section, we describe the graph alignment algorithm that is a foundation for AMRG. The purpose of alignment is two-fold: combine structural information about a text (such as a question) and assess its similarity of meaning to another text, such as an answer. We first define a query graph that can be straightforwardly mapped to a logical form in λ-calculus and is semantically closely related to λ-dependency-based compositional semantics (DCS, Liang 2013). For expression, *"citizens who live in Boston"* the regular λ- calculus gives $\lambda x.\exists e.PlacesLive(x, e) \wedge Location(e,$

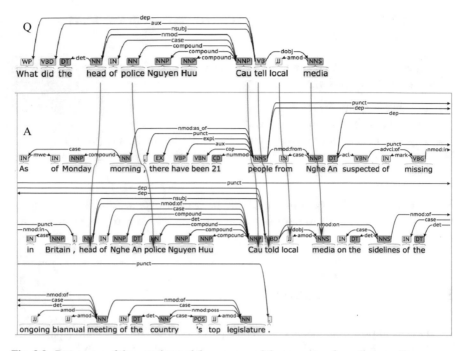

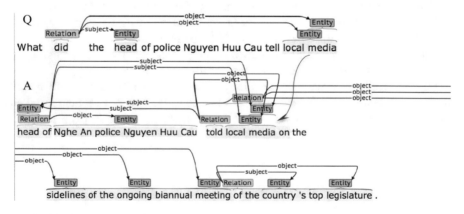

Fig. 3.9 Parse trees of the question and the answer and the mapping of question words

Fig. 3.10 Mapping between entity graphs for Q and A

Boston) and λ-DCS gives *PlacesLive.Location.Boston*. Hence DCS attempts to remove explicit use of variables; it makes it similar in flavor to dependency-based compositional semantics.

Matching semantic parse for Q against that of for A is formulated as a query graph generation in the form of the state transitions from a seed alignment toward a full alignment. Each state is a candidate mapping between parses such as *AMR(Q) →*

Fig. 3.11 Alignment between a sentence and its AMR representation

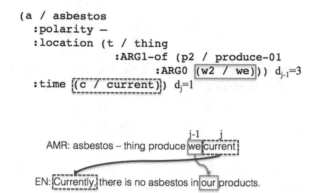

AMR(A) in the query graph representation and each action defines a way to grow the alignment. The representation power of the alignment of a pair of semantic parses is thus controlled by the set of allowed alignment actions applicable to each state. In particular, the actions are split into three main steps: locating the topic entity in the question, finding the main relationship between the answer and the topic entity, and expanding the query graph with additional constraints that describe properties the answer needs to have, or relationships between the answer and other entities in the question.

When aligning an $AMR(V,E)$ against syntactic dependency parse tree $T(U,F)$ or another AMR graph, we first compute the costs of aligning each node v in AMR with each node n in T. The cost of aligning two nodes takes into account the *graphlet degree signature similarity* between them, modified to reduce the cost as the degrees of both nodes increase, since higher degree nodes with similar signatures provide a tighter constraint than correspondingly similar low degree nodes. In this way, we align the densest parts of the AMR graph first.

Let us define graphlets as *small connected non-isomorphic induced subgraphs* of a large graph such as an AMR graph. We now introduce *graphlet degree vectors* (signatures) and signature similarities to support graph alignment procedure. This measure generalizes the degree of a node, which counts the number of edges that the node touches, into the vector of graphlet degrees, or graphlet degree signature, counting the number of graphlets that the node touches at a particular orbit, for all graphlets on 2 to 5 nodes. The resulting vector of seventy-three coordinates is the signature of a node that describes the topology of this node's neighborhood and captures its interconnectivity out to a distance of 4 (see Milenković and Pržulj (2008) for details). The graphlet degree signature of a node provides a highly constraining measure of local topology in its vicinity and comparing the signatures of two nodes provides a highly constraining measure of local topological similarity between them.

The *signature similarity* is computed as follows. For a node u in graph G, u_i denotes the ith coordinate of its signature vector, i.e., u_i is the number of times node u is touched by an orbit i in G. The distance $D_i(u,v)$ between the ith orbits of nodes u and v is defined as:

$$D_i(u, v) = w_i \times \frac{|\log(u_i + 1) - \log(v_i + 1)|}{\log(\max\{u_i + v_i\} + 2)}$$

where w_i is the weight of orbit i that accounts for dependencies between orbits. The total distance $D(u,v)$ between nodes u and v is defined as:

$$D(u, v) = \frac{\sum_{i=0}^{T2} D_i}{\sum_{i=0}^{T2} w_i}$$

The distance $D(u,v)$ is in $[0, 1)$, where distance 0 means that signatures of nodes u and v are identical. Finally, the signature similarity, $S(u,v)$, between nodes u and v is:

$$S(u, v) = 1 - D(u, v).$$

Clearly, a higher signature similarity between two nodes corresponds to a higher topological similarity between their extended neighborhoods up to the distance of four. The number four corresponds to a typical maximum number of arguments of a verb node of an AMR graph.

Let $deg(v)$ be the degree of a node v in AMR, let $max_{deg(AMR)}$ be the maximum degree of nodes in AMR, and let $S(v, u)$ be the graphlet degree signature similarity of nodes v and u, and let α be a parameter in $[0, 1]$ that controls the contribution of the node signature similarity to the cost function (that is, $1-\alpha$ is the parameter that controls the contribution of node degrees to the cost function), then the cost of aligning nodes v and u is computed as:

$$C(v, u) = 2 - \left((1 - \alpha) \times \frac{deg(v) + deg(u)}{\max_{deg(G)} + \max_{deg(H)}} + \alpha \times S(v, u) \right).$$

A cost of 0 corresponds to a pair of topologically identical nodes v and u, while a cost close to 2 corresponds to a pair of topologically different nodes.

The graph alignment algorithm chooses (as the initial seed) a pair of nodes v and u from AMR and T which $v \in V$ have the smallest cost. The ties are broken randomly. Once the seed is found, we build the spheres of all possible radii around nodes v and u. A sphere of radius r around node v is the set of nodes $S_{AMR}(v, r) = \{x \in AMR: d(v, x) = r\}$ that are at distance r from v, where the distance $d(v, x)$ is the length of the shortest path from v to x. Spheres of the same radius in two networks are then greedily aligned together by searching for the pairs (v', u'): $v' \in S_{AMR}(v, r)$ and $u' \in S_T(u, r)$ that are not already aligned and that can be aligned with the minimal cost.

When all spheres around the initial seed (v',u') have been aligned, other nodes in both AMR and T are still unaligned. We repeat the same algorithm on a pair of graphs (AMR^p, T^p) for $p = 1.3$ and 3 attempt to identify a new seed again, if necessary. The graph AMR^p is defined as a new *graph* $AMR^p = (V, E^p)$ having the same set of nodes as AMR and having $(v,x) \in E^p$ if and only if the distance between nodes v and x in AMR is less than or equal to p. In other words $d_{AMR}(v, x) \leq p$. AMR^1

$= AMR$. Using AMR^p ($p > 1$) lets us align a path of length p in one graph to a single edge in another graph, which is analogous to allowing "insertions" or "deletions" in a sequence alignment. We stop alignment procedure when each node from AMR is aligned to exactly one node in T.

Such a feature of AMR parsing as *abstraction* is associated with alignment between words and their semantic representations (not a graph alignment). This feature is closely related to how we extract concepts from AMR and build mappings between word's surface form and its semantic meaning. (Wang 2018) proposes to tackle it with a novel graph-based aligner designed specifically for word-to-concept scenario and show that better alignment result could improve AMR parsing result. Building the alignment between a word and an AMR concept is often conducted as a preprocessing step. As a result, accurate concept identification crucially depends on the word-to-(AMR concept) alignment. Since there is no manual alignment in AMR annotation, typically either a rule-based or unsupervised aligner is applied to the training data to extract the mapping between words and concepts. This mapping will then be used as reference data to train concept identification models. The JAMR aligner (Flanigan et al. 2014) greedily aligns a span of words to a graph fragment using a set of heuristic rules. While it can easily incorporate information from additional linguistic sources such as WordNet, it is not adaptable to other domains. Unsupervised aligners borrow techniques from Machine Translation and treat sentence-to-AMR alignment as a word alignment problem between a source sentence and its linearized AMR graph (Pourdamghani et al. 2014). Wang (2018) proposes a Hidden Markov Model (HMM)-based sentence-to-AMR alignment method with a graph distance distortion model to leverage the structural information in AMR.

The alignment needs to be capable of tackling distortion in the order of words (Fig. 3.11). The concept *we* in AMR list of tokens is mapped into English word *our,* and AMR *current* into *Currently*. Hence the alignment is essentially non-monotonic.

We have two kinds of graph alignment-based operations: *enrichment* and *generalization*. Enrichment of two graphs aligns them and retains all information. In this work, we enrich a semantic graph by a syntactic one and add named entity labels; other linguistic sources can enrich such representation as well. A discourse-level information for representations of longer texts can be also added (Galitsky and Ilvovsky 2019). Once we obtain an enriched representation for a question Q and candidate answers A_n (e.g. all sentences and longer phrases in text), we find a generalization between them to estimate similarity as an indication of an A correctness for Q. Notice that DL-based approaches assess Q to answer passage similarity as well, relying on a totally different set of features and entirely distinct learning settings.

The "Enrich and generalize" methodology for AMRG is illustrated in Fig. 3.12. We first obtain as rich graph representation for each text such as a Q or a candidate answer A_n as possible. We take this greedy approach for enrichment since we do not know in advance which features are shared by Q and A_n so we involve as much node labels as possible. This is to make sure that if there is a commonality in meaning between a Q and an A, it would be captured by a generalization operation. Hence once we aligned all source representations for each text, we can generalize these representations against each other, aligning them, but only retaining the maximal common subgraphs for A_{best}.

Enriching alignment:

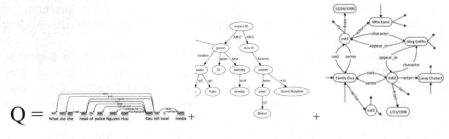

Generalizing alignment:

$$\frac{Q^{\wedge}A_1 \dots Q^{\wedge}A_n}{Q \rightarrow A_{best} \text{ (largest graph overlap)}}$$

Fig. 3.12 Enrich and Generalize methodology for Q/A

3.8 Correcting the DL Answer

We take a question and substitute the identified answer into the Wh-expression denoted by " $< + \dots + >$ "(Fig. 3.13):

Q = "What happened with Beyonce after 1990?" →
Q + A = "Their hiatus saw the release of Beyonce's debut album, Dangerously in Love" $< +$ "with Beyonce after 1990" $+ >$
In Q + A, we show the mandatory part in $< + \dots + >$ (since it is specified in the Q), preceded by the optional part, identified by the answer.
Now if we generalize (Q + A) with each sentence of context:
(Q + A) ˆ *context1*, *context1* = "Beyonce Giselle …" (sentence 1);
(Q + A) ˆ *context2*, *context2* = "Born and raised in Houston …" (sentence 2);
… then the mandatory part will not be retained in each generalization result, which indicates that the answer is incorrect.
(After 1990)ˆ1990s = 1990s.

Passage Context

Beyonce Giselle Knowles-Carter (born September 4, 1981) is an American singer, songwriter, ´ record producer and actress. Born and raised in Houston, Texas, she performed in various singing and dancing competitions as a child, and rose to fame in the late 1990s as lead singer of R&B girl-group Destiny's Child. Managed by her father, Mathew Knowles, the group became one of the world's best-selling girl groups of all time. Their hiatus saw the release of Beyonce's ´ debut album, Dangerously in Love (2003), which established her as a solo artist worldwide, earned five Grammy Awards and featured the Billboard Hot 100 number-one singles "Crazy in Love" and "Baby Boy"

Question

What happened with Beyonce after 1990?

Fig. 3.13 An incorrect answer that can be detected

Hence the generalization of this incorrect answer does not retain *"after 1990"* part. At the same time, generalization of this query with another expression, *"rose to fame in the late 1990s"* retains all constraint keywords from the Q, hence this A is the correct one.

3.9 Identifying the Correct Answer by Generalization

Once AMRG detects that the answer is incorrect, it performs its own search for a sentence or a phrase that has the largest generalization (the set of sub-graph with the maximum number of nodes). To do that, we first form a syntactic template to be generalized with each sentence, to be converted from a question to a statement template. For example, *"What time is it?"* is converted into {Time-NN is-VBZ *-CD, Time-NN is-VBZ *-NER = *date_time*}. In this template, the last token is for an expression for time, either as a number or an entity with NER type recognized as *date_time*.

Once we formed a template, we generalize it with each sentence and each verb phrase to get the one with the largest sub-graph. In our running example, the template is.

[*-VP Beyonce- "NE = PERSON" after-IN 1990s-{NNS, Date}] as making

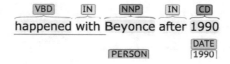

as general as possible to cover a broad range of phrasings in a candidate answer. "*-VP" here is an arbitrary verb phrase. Hence the intersection with the phrase '*rose to fame in the late 1990s as lead singer*'.

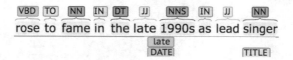

is [she-PRP rose-VBD, to-TO, fame-NN, 1990-DATE] which is a sufficient evidence that this phrase is a suitable answer. Intersections with other sentences and phrases are insignificant, so it is the only answer.

So far, we have described the generalization algorithm based on syntactic and entity-based graph nodes. In real life, the syntactic trees with addition named entity labels are first enriched by aligning with AMR graphs and then generalized between questions and candidate answers to identify the correct one.

3.10   System Architecture

A high-level architecture of a graph representation matching for MRC is shown in
Fig. 3.14. Both the question and text from which an answer is to be extracted is subject
to both syntactic and semantic parsing such as AMR. Additionally, other tagging
pipelines are applied including NER, sentiment, emotion and others (Manning et al.
2014). At the next step, all available representation for Q are aligned with each other,
and all representation for answer text (context) are aligned with each other as well.
Finally, a search of the answer is an alignment of a hybrid (aligned) representation
for the Q against that of the A (Galitsky et al. 2015). An answer fragment is a result
of a maximal common subgraph between the aligned Q and the aligned A (Galitsky
2017b).

An architecture of a hybrid DL + AMRG system that achieves the best performance is shown in Fig. 3.15. First, the DL module works as in a traditional neural
MRC. Once an answer A is obtained, the meta-agent of the AMRG components
with architecture shown in Fig. 3.12 above comes into play verifying that the answer
is linguistically and semantically fit. To do that, it substitutes it into the question and performs syntactic and semantic matching with the answer text (context).
Parse thicket is an ordered set of parse trees with additional inter-sentence arcs for
coreferences, discourse and other relations (Galitsky et al. 2013; Galitsky 2017a).

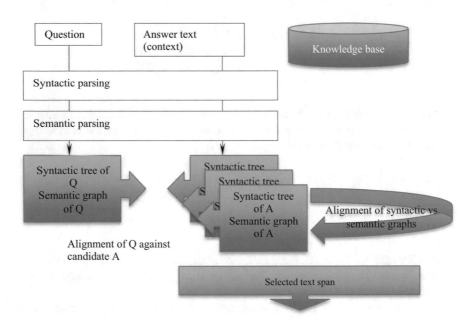

Fig. 3.14 AMRG architecture for finding an answer to a question by respective graph alignment

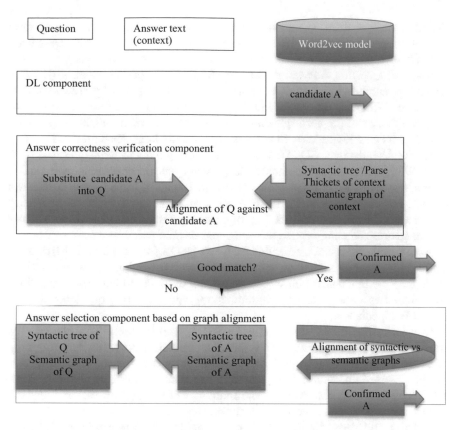

Fig. 3.15 Error identification and answer selection scenario of hybrid DL and AMRG system. It is implemented as a meta-agent

3.11 Evaluation

We evaluate the AMRG-based Reading Comprehension in the following settings:

- A stand-alone Q/A;
- Error correction Q/A of DL, where each question is handled by DL and then by AMR attempts to verify/correct it;
- Hybrid approach where both DL and AMR produces answers and a meta-agent then decides on which answer to choose.

Also, we evaluate the search of the same queries against an index that includes the totality of all documents. Not only a position within a document but a relevant document itself needs to be found. The purpose of this evaluation is to compare the developed AMRG-based Q/A technique with a conventional search engine. In addition to search F1 measure, we use a normalized Discounted Cumulative Gain

(NDCG, Wang, et al. 2013), measuring the top five search results. Full corpus search is implemented integrating MRC component with a conventional TF*IDF search which finds candidate documents subject to MRC on a one-by-one basis.

Stanford Question Answering Dataset (SQuAD, Rajpurkar, et al. 2018) is a reading comprehension dataset, consisting of questions posed by crowd-workers on a set of Wikipedia articles, where the answer to every question is a segment of text, or span, from the corresponding reading passage. With 100,000+ question–answer pairs on 500+ articles, SQuAD is significantly larger than previous reading comprehension datasets. SQuAD was built by having humans write questions for a given Wikipedia passage and choose the answer span. Other datasets used similar techniques; the NewsQA dataset also consists of 100,000 Q/A pairs from CNN news articles. For other datasets like WikiQA the span is the entire sentence containing the answer (Yang et al. 2015); the task of choosing a sentence rather than a smaller answer span is sometimes called the *sentence selection* task.

As to the other datasets, we mention the NarrativeQA (Kocisky et al. 2018) dataset-that includes questions based on entire long documents like books or movie scripts, while the Q/A in Context (QuAC) dataset (Choi et al. 2018) has 100 K questions created by two crowd workers who are asking and answering questions about a hidden Wikipedia text.

Our performance of a stand-alone AMRG system is shown in Table 3.1. We employ both SQuAD 1.1 and 2.0 test data for evaluation. As we switch from only syntactic to only semantic level (without any alignment), to the one with alignment, we gain 5–6% in accuracy. Joint syntactic and semantic systems with alignment delivers further 3–4% improvement, and enabling word2vec (Chap. 2) into the hybrid aligned syntactic-semantic graph further boosts performance by 5% (shown in bolded row). This is still 8% below the DL state-of-the art (the bottom row in the last column).

We observe in Table 3.2 that the preferred Q/A setting is an answering by DL first and error correction by AMRG as the second step, as we described in detail in previous sections. This optimal configuration is (three rows on the top with the third row bolded):

Table 3.1 Performance of the stand-alone AMR system

	SQuAD 1.1 test			SQuAD 2.0 test		
	P	R	F1	P	R	F1
Only syntactic parse trees	71.6	72.9	72.24	67.2	68.3	67.75
Only AMR graphs	75.4	78.3	76.82	74.2	73.5	73.85
Aligned syntactic parse trees and AMR graphs	83.0	78.7	80.79	78.8	75.8	77.27
Aligned syntactic parse trees and AMR graphs + word2vec	**85.3**	**86.3**	**85.80**	**83.4**	**84.1**	**83.75**
ALBERT (Lan et al. 2019)	–	–	–	–	–	92.2

Table 3.2 Performance of a hybrid DL + AMR system on SQuAD 2.0 Test set

	P	R	F1
Stand-alone AMRG	83.3	84.1	83.70
Stand-alone end-to-end DL	88.2	87.4	87.80
DL + AMRG correcting DL's errors	**92.7**	**92.3**	**92.50**
DL versus AMRG as selected by meta-agent	83.1	85.0	84.04
AMR Errors identification rate	76.8	77.2	77.0
AMR Errors correction rate	70.2	72.1	71.1

(1) 4.5% above DL only;
(2) About 9% above the hybrid stand-alone AMRG and a stand-alone DL, so that the answers are selected by a meta-agent. This meta-agent takes DL score and maximal common subgraph score and decides on which answer to choose. As this configuration is not optimal, we do not describe it in detail;
(3) About 9% above the stand-alone AMRG.

Two rows on the bottom provide further details on the optimal hybrid system. The false-positive rate of AMRG component is noticeable so some correct answers are classified as incorrect and then a wrong answer is delivered. However, it happens less frequently than the other way around, so overall impact of AMRG component is positive and more answers are turned from incorrect to correct, than vice versa. This is due to a totally different nature and sources of information of AMRG Q/A in comparison with neural, ML-based Q/A. Error-correction rate is lower than the overall performance because DL makes most mistakes in complicated cases.

Notice that AMR parsing is in turn done by a neural mechanism and is itself much noisier than MRC learning. However, because of the alignment with reliable syntactic parse, the resultant AMR representation serves as a reliable source for MRC.

We perform a case study on what kinds of errors are produced by each method. It turns out that these kinds of errors are fairly different:

(1) AMRG makes errors where syntactic similarity is low, or important phrases are spread apart in the sentence;
(2) DL makes errors where it is hard to form a meaning of a multiword.

We observed that an overlap between the AMRG and DL errors is about 34.6%.

We proceed with our evaluation of the full-corpus search of an index of Wikipedia pages (Table 3.3). One can see from Table 3.3 that for a conventional search relying on DL and AMR, error correction scenario is also beneficial in comparison to a hybrid or stand-alone systems, similar to what we observed in Table 3.2. This is reflected in both F1 measure of the first search result and also NDCG measure for top five search results. A performance of a TF*IDF component that finds the candidate documents does not affect significantly the overall search accuracy.

Table 3.3 Full Index search accuracy

	P	R	F1	NDCG @ 5 hits
Stand alone AMR	61.1	56.3	58.60	0.331
Stand-alone end-to-end DL	64.7	62.4	63.53	0.358
DL + AMR correcting DL's errors	**66.2**	**63.3**	64.72	0.410
DL versus AMR as selected by meta-agent	63.0	65.4	64.18	0.342

Fig. 3.16 Sample sentence in Little Prince (Chinese translation)

```
# ::en And there is sweetness in the laughter of all the stars .
# ::snt 这时，所有 的 星星 都 在 柔情 地 轻声 笑 着 。
(x1 / 笑-01 laugh
    :arg0  (x2 / 星星 star
        :mod  (x3 / 所有 all))
    :time  (x4 / 这时 now)
    :manner  (x5 / 柔情 sweetness)
    :manner  (x6 / 轻声 soft sound))
```

3.12 MRC in Languages Beyond English

Both DL and AMRG components can be implemented in languages for which word2vec models and semantic annotations are available. (Damonte and Cohen 2018) released AMR parsers for German, Italian and Spanish. Chinese AMR is available (Li et al. 2016; Xue 2019). In Fig. 3.16 one can see an AMR representation for a sentence in English and Chinese where each node also annotates in each of these languages. Distributional semantic models have been built for major natural languages as well. Hence the proposed technique of MRC enhancement can be applied in a number of languages: this is a subject of our future studies.

Nguyen et al. (2020) introduce ViMMRC, a MRC corpus with almost 3 thousand multiple-choice questions, intended for research on the machine comprehension of Vietnamese text. Answering questions from this corpus demands reasoning abilities beyond a simple word matching.

3.13 Conclusions

In this Chapter, we demonstrated that a DL-based end-to-end approach can be systematically improved by an "old-fashioned" compartmental Q/A based on semantic and syntactic parsing.

The recent surge in NLP model complexity has outstripped Moore's law (Peters et al. 2018; Devlin et al. 2019; Narasimhan 2019). A complexity and length of queries have significantly risen (Ilvovsky 2014, Galitsky 2017b). Deeply stacked layers of transformers (including BERT, RoBERTa (Liu et al. 2019), XLNet (Yang et al. 2019), and ALBERT (Lan et al. 2019)) have greatly improved state-of-the-art accuracies across a variety of NLP tasks, but the computational intensity has dramatically increased.

We outline the main advantages of AMRG-based Q/A over the DL family of approaches:

- The path to answers is deterministic so can be fully explained;
- How an answer is related to a question can also be fully explained;
- A structured data points with known semantic roles are returned as an answer, such as a list of values, instead of a text fragment;
- Questions can be automatically generated for given complexity (entity—single attribute, entity—multiple attributes, multiple entities);
- Q/A performance can be automatically assessed since the similarity between Q and A can be automatically computed and it is interpretable by a human;
- The class of questions answered properly can be circumscribed and the users can acquire intuition on what can be answered and how to formulate questions;
- When a DL system answers questions randomly, it is hard for a user to learn how to cooperate better with the Q/A system and formulate questions in the way optimal for accurate answering.

According to (Narasimhan 2019), possessing language superpower brains, humans are capable of recognizing both nuance and broader meaning of language as they communicate. With the arrival of massive Transformer-based language models like BERT (Bidirectional Encoder Representations from Transformer), and 1 billion-plus parameter GPT-2 (Generative Pretrained Transformer 2) models, DL research community is seeing rapid progress on difficult language understanding tasks. We believe a different English word from "understanding" is required to select a proper part of a sentence out of five-eight sentences in a text context. A new English word for separating a few items by means of billions of computing units is badly needed, and "understanding" in double quotes is not necessarily expressive enough to refer to this operation. A neural network is supposed to perform generalization, and imagine a size of generalization from hundred thousand samples which involve billions of memory units. We would refer to what this network in MRC context is doing an "anti-generalization", or just storing all samples without generalizing from them. Even if the last layer only stores generalization results, it impresses a conventional machine learning scientist with an overkill of computing power.

Thinking about the hard computational problem of identifying one sentence out of three-five in an average short text, we recall (Saltykov-Shchedrin 1870) who introduced this expression into everyday life, describing in his work the stupid adventures of people who could not only *get lost in three pines*, but also wear smoke with a sieve, mix up their legs under the table, and forget whether the person had a head or not. "The History of a Town" is a fictional chronicle by Saltykov-Shchedrin regarded as the major satirical Russian novel of the nineteenth century (Fig. 3.17, top-right). It is well known that Reading Comprehension is not always easy for human, even

Fig. 3.17 Humans doing reading comprehension. Top-right: a Q/A system got lost trying to find an answer out of three passages. We follow the idiom "To get lost in three pines"

for adults. Figure 3.17 depicts a movie where criminals undergo a reading-based rehabilitation program.

Abstract semantic approach allows formulation of an exhaustive set of questions for an entity and its attributes. Also, this approach allows systematic testing and identifying problems with answer selection. AMR-based Q/A is an example of explainable, responsible Q/A well suited for CRM applications (Sidorov et al. 2019).

SQuAD ranking is not necessarily a reflection of the effectiveness of the real world deployment of the developed Q/A technology. SQuAD is an easier task than the real world problem because one needs to process a lot more content for any practical application in conversational interfaces, which makes the ability to select candidate paragraphs from tens and hundreds of thousands paragraphs very important. An ability to understand structured embedded content like tables is also essential.

Understanding open-domain text is one of the primary challenges in NLP. Machine comprehension benchmarks evaluate the system's ability to understand text based on the text content only. A number of studies investigate machine comprehension on MCTest, a Q/A benchmark. While prior work is mainly based on feature engineering approaches, a convolutional neural network (Fig. 3.18) is capable of addressing this task without any manually designed features. Learning-based approaches associate

Fig. 3.18 CNN, Convolutional Neural Networks (and news network) perform a non-binary decision on answer correctness

answers to questions via the score, not a binary correct/incorrect decisions (on the right).

Most traditional approaches for semantic parsing are largely decoupled from the knowledge base and thus are associated with substantial difficulties when adapted to applications like Q/A. For instance, a generic meaning representation may have the ontology matching problem when the logical form uses predicates that differ from those defined in the KB (Kwiatkowski et al. 2013). Even when the representation language is closely related to the knowledge base schema, finding the correct predicates from the large vocabulary in the KB to relations described in the utterance remains a difficult problem (Berant and Liang 2014). In this Chapter, we analyzed the support of abstract semantic representation for MRC in a broader setting, with or without a KB.

Note that general-purpose MRC systems are still extractive in nature. They can only answer questions for which the answers are present directly in the content they were trained on. A skill to infer new facts from multiple parts of the content (unavailable via training) and formulate a response to a user query is significantly more difficult (Chap. 6). Answering almost all customer questions correctly and concisely is essential for CRM. The state-of-the-art neural MRC is applied and delivers correct answer in almost 90% of cases. The proposed framework based on AMR and graph alignment verifies each answer attempts to find a proper one, if DL results are classified as incorrect. This error-correction hybrid architecture boosts the state-of-the-art performance by more than 4%. AMR leverages additional abstract-level data accumulated in the course of AMR annotation that is not available for DL-based MRC system, therefore the former nicely complements that latter.

References

Auer S, Bizer C, Kobilarov G, Lehmann J, Cyganiak R, Ives Z (2007) DBpedia: a nucleus for a web of open data. In: The semantic web, pp 722–735. Springer

Banarescu L, Bonial C, Cai S, Georgesc M, Griffitt K, Hermjakob U, Knight K, Koehn P, Palmer M, Schneider N (2013) Abstract meaning representation for sembanking. In: Proceedings of the 7th linguistic annotation workshop and interoperability with discourse

Bao J, Nan D, Ming Z, Tiejun Z (2014) Knowledge-based question answering as machine translation. In: ACL, pp 967–976

Bollacker K, Evans C, Paritosh P, Sturge T, Taylor J (2008) Freebase: a collaboratively created graph database for structuring human knowledge. In: Proceedings of the 2008 ACM SIGMOD international conference on management of data. ACM, pp 1247–1250

Bordes A, Sumit C, Jason W (2014) Question answering with subgraph embeddings. In: EMNLP, pp 615–620

Burtsev M, Seliverstov A, Airapetyan R, Arkhipov M, Baymurzina D, Bushkov N, Gureenkova O, Khakhulin T, Kuratov Y, Kuznetsov D, Litinsky A, Logacheva V, Lymar A, Malykh V, Petrov M, Polulyakh V, Pugachev L, Sorokin A, Vikhreva M, Zaynutdinov M (2018) DeepPavlov: open-source library for dialogue systems. In: ACL-system demonstrations, pp 122–127

Choi E, He H, Mohit I, Mark Y, Wen-tau Y, Yejin C, Percy L, Luke Z (2018) QuAC: question answering in context. In: EMNLP, pp 2174–2184

Collins M, Duffy N (2002) Convolution kernels for natural language. In: Proceedings of NIPS, pp 625–632

Damonte M, Shay B. Cohen (2018) Cross-lingual abstract meaning representation parsing. In: Proceedings of NAACL

Damonte M, Shay B, Cohen and Giorgio Satta (2017) An incremental parser for abstract meaning representation. In: Proceedings of EACL

Devlin J, Chang MW, Lee K, Toutanova K (2019) BERT: pre-training of deep bidirectional transformers for language understanding. NAACL V1

Dwivedi P (2018) NLP—building a question answering model. https://towardsdatascience.com/nlp-building-a-question-answering-model-ed0529a68c54

Flanigan J, Thomson S, Carbonell J, Dyer C, Smith NA (2014) A discriminative graph-based parser for the abstract meaning representation. ACL 1426–1436

Galitsky B (2014) Learning parse structure of paragraphs and its applications in search. Eng Appl Artif Intell 32:160–184

Galitsky B (2017) Matching parse thickets for open domain question answering. Data Knowl Eng 107:24–50

Galitsky B (2017a) Improving relevance in a content pipeline via syntactic generalization. Eng Appl Artif Intell 58:1–26

Galitsky B (2019a) Building Chatbot Thesaurus, in *Developing Enterprise Chatbots*. Springer, Cham

Galitsky B (2019b) Assuring Chatbot Relevance at Syntactic Level, in *Developing Enterprise Chatbots*. Springer, Cham

Galitsky B (2012) Machine learning of syntactic parse trees for search and classification of text. Eng Appl AI 26(3):1072–1091

Galitsky B (2013) Transfer learning of syntactic structures for building taxonomies for search engines. Eng Appl Artif Intell 26(10):2504–2515

Galitsky B, Ilvovsky D (2019) Discourse-based approach to involvement of background knowledge for question answering. Recent advances in natural language processing, pp 373–381, Varna, Bulgaria, Sep 2–4

Galitsky B, Dobrocsi G, de la Rosa JL, Kuznetsov SO (2011) Using generalization of syntactic parse trees for taxonomy capture on the web. Int Conf Concept Structures, pp 104–117

Galitsky B, Dobrocsi G, de la Rosa JL (2012) Inferring semantic properties of sentences mining syntactic parse trees. Data Knowl Eng 81:21–45

Galitsky B, Ilvovsky D, Strok F, Kuznetsov SO (2013) Improving text retrieval efficiency with pattern structures on parse thickets. In: Proceedings of FCAIR, pp 6–21

Galitsky B, Ilvovsky D, Kuznetsov SO (2015) Rhetoric map of an answer to compound queries. ACL, Beijing, pp 681–686

Hermann KM, Kociský T, Grefenstette E, Espeholt L, Kay W, Suleyman M and Blunsom P (2015) Teaching machines to read and comprehend. https://arxiv.org/abs/1506.03340.

Ilvovsky D (2014) Using semantically connected parse trees to answer multi-sentence queries. Automatic Documentation and Mathematical Linguistics 48:33–41

Kočiský T, Jonathan S, Phil B, Chris D, Karl Moritz H, Gábor M, Edward G. The NarrativeQA reading comprehension challenge. Transactions of the Association for Computational Linguistics, Volume 6, 317–328

Kwiatkowski T, Eunsol C, Yoav A, Luke Z (2013) Scaling semantic parsers with on-the-fly ontology matching. In: EMNLP, pp 1545–1556, Seattle, Washington, USA

Lan Z, Chen M, Goodman S, Gimpel K, Sharma P, Soricut R (2019) ALBERT: a lite bert for self-supervised learning of language representations. ArXiv, abs/1909.11942

Liang P (2013) Lambda dependency-based compositional semantics. Technical report, arXiv

Li B, Wen Y, Lijun B, Weiguang Q, Nianwen X (2016) Annotating the little prince with Chinese AMRs. LAW-2016, Berlin, Germany

Liu Y, Myle O, Naman G, Jingfei D, Mandar J, Danqi C, Omer L, Mike L, Luke Z, Veselin S (2019) Roberta: a robustly optimized BERT pretraining approach. CoRR, https://arxiv.org/abs/1907.11692

Manning CD, Surdeanu M, Bauer J, Finkel J, Bethard SJ, McClosky (2014) The stanford CoreNLP natural language processing toolkit. Proceedings of 52nd Annual Meeting of the Association for Computational Linguistics: System Demonstrations, pp 55–60, Baltimore, Maryland USA, June 23–24

May J, Priyadarshi J (2017) SemEval-2017 Task 9: Abstract meaning representation parsing and generation. In: Proceedings of the 11th international workshop on semantic evaluation (SemEval-2017), pp 536–545

Milenkovic T, Pržulj N (2008) Uncovering biological network function via graphlet degree signatures. Cancer Inform 6:257–273

Narasimhan S (2019) Nvidia clocks worlds fastest BERT training time and largest transformer based model, paving path for advanced conversational AI. https://devblogs.nvidia.com/training-bert-with-gpus/

Nguyen K, Tran K, Luu S, Nguyen A, Nguyen N (2020). A pilot study on multiple choice machine reading comprehension for vietnamese texts

People.cn (2019) Vietnamese police detain 8 suspects in connection with illegal immigration organizing. https://en.people.cn/n3/2019/1104/c90000-9629296.html

Peters ME, Mark N, Mohit I, Matt G, Christopher C, Kenton L, Luke Z (2018) Deep contextualized word representations. NAACL

Pourdamghani N, Gao Y, Hermjakob U, Knight K (2014) Aligning English strings with abstract meaning representation graphs. In: EMNLP, pp 425–429

Rajpurkar P, Jia R, Liang P (2018) Know what you don't know: unanswerable questions for SQuAD. ACL

Saltykov-Shchedrin M (1870) The history of a town (In Russian) Otechestvennye Zapiski, Saint Petersburg Russia

Sidorov G, Markov, Ilia & Kolesnikova, Olga & Chanona-Hernández, Liliana (2019) Human interaction with shopping assistant robot in natural language. Journal of Intelligent and Fuzzy Systems. 36. 4889–4899. 10.3233/JIFS-179036

Suchanek FM, Kasneci G, Weikum G (2007) YAGO: a core of semantic knowledge. In: Proceedings of the 16th international conference on World Wide Web. ACM, pp 697–706

Wang Y, Liwei Wang, Yuanzhi Li, Di He, Wei Chen, Tie-Yan Liu (2013) A theoretical analysis of normalized discounted cumulative gain (NDCG) ranking measures. In: Proceedings of the 26th annual conference on learning theory (COLT 2013)

Xue N (2019) Chinese abstract meaning representation. https://www.cs.brandeis.edu/~clp/camr/camr.html

Yao X, Benjamin Van Durme (2014) Information extraction over structured data: question answering with Freebase. In: Proceedings of the 52nd ACL, pp 956–966

Yih W.-T, Chang M.-W, He X, and Gao J (2015) Semantic parsing via staged query graph generation: Question answering with knowledge base. In: ACL, pp 1321–1331

Chapter 4
Summarized Logical Forms
for Controlled Question Answering

Abstract Providing a high-end question answering (Q/A) requires a special knowledge representation technique, which is based on phrasing-independent partial formalization of the essential information contained in domain answers. We introduce Summarized Logical forms (SLFs), the formalized expressions which contain the most important knowledge extracted from answers to be queried. Instead of indexing the whole answer, we index only its SLFs as a set of expressions for most important topics in this answer. By doing that, we achieve substantially higher Q/A precision since foreign answers will not be triggered. We also introduce Linked SLFs connected by entries of a domain-specific ontology to increase the coverage of a knowledge domain. A methodology of constructing SLFs and Linked SLFs is outlined and the achieved Q/A accuracy is evaluated. Meta-programming issues of matching query representations (QRs) against SLFs and domain taxonomy are addressed as well.

4.1 Introduction: Why Manual Text Preparation for Q/A Is Necessary in the Epoch of Successful Reading Comprehension?

The task of textual question answering (Q/A), where a system injects a corpus of documents and answers questions about them, is an important and challenging problem in natural language processing (NLP). In recent years, the interest in Q/A research community has shifted from logical and information-extraction based toward learning-based, especially based on neural systems. Recent progress in performance of machine learning-based Q/A models has been largely due to the variety of available Q/A datasets. However, an accuracy of an end-to-end pure learning Q/A system in a real-world, extensive corpus of documents is fairly low (Chap. 3). Q/A sessions based on numerical ranking of search results relying on statistical or deep ML technique do not guarantee an exact answer for an important user question. A user of a fuzzy, non-deterministic search system may encounter an irrelevant answer, advice or recommendation and turn away from the business providing this answer.

© Springer Nature Switzerland AG 2020   87
B. Galitsky, *Artificial Intelligence for Customer Relationship Management*,
Human–Computer Interaction Series,
https://doi.org/10.1007/978-3-030-52167-7_4

To maintain a systematic customer retention, a Q/A needs to provide answers in a systematic way, relying on strict logical rules rather than on a statistical system optimized for performance for an average query (Galitsky 2001; Galitsky and Grudin 2001). Although statistical ML-based Q/A helps in knowledge exploration in general, it does not provide an efficient and effective means of a fast arrival to the exact answer, as a deterministic system does.

In many non-professional, exploratory, entertainment domains, users can tolerate a situation when they do not arrive to the exact expected answer right away. However, in a CRM domain, for questions related to product usability, service benefits, recommendations and problem resolutions, exact answers need to be delivered immediately. A Q/A technique for CRM does not have to handle millions of documents in most cases but needs to provide high-quality content in a timely and appropriate manner (Galitsky 2016b) so that the users can act on it and solve their problems. Therefore, CRM requires a high-end, expensive Q/A with significantly more manual contributions than other Q/A domains.

In this chapter, we develop a manually crafted technique of *controlled* Q/A, so that the answer for frequent, important customer question is properly associated with its question at a high-level abstraction and phrase-independence. Conceptually, an association between a question and an answer is designed as a logical system, where a formal representation of a question is derived from formal representations of its answers.

Recent tendencies in machine reading comprehension (MRC) shifted the focus of Q/A to less abstract, more concrete questions that are syntactically closer to answers. The strongest deviation in phrasings between Q and A tolerated under MRC is synonymy covered by word2vec models. Neural models for Q/A over documents have achieved significant performance improvements. These models do not scale to large corpora due to their complex modeling of interactions between the document and the question. Another disadvantage of the neural MRC is their sensitivity to adversarial inputs (Min et al 2018). In CRM applications, the focus is on *understanding of customer knowledge acquiring intent*, not just on a specific entity and its attribute to extract from the text. In this respect, CRM applications require much higher level of abstraction than typical MRC settings provide.

Since professionals spend substantial efforts writing content to address important customer issues such as *"why is a product so expensive?"* or *"why is it missing features wanted badly"*, we would expect these professionals to also invest a fair share of time to turn their content into a form ready for a controlled Q/A. Not only content creation itself requires a certain level of intelligence, but also making it accessible via Q/A. CRM applications frequently require a Mercedes-class of Q/A systems that cannot be achieved yet by a fully automated end-to-end learning. The controlled Q/A technique we propose in this chapter belongs to the class of expensive approaches with a fair amount of manual labor to achieve a high level of abstraction and robustness.

While an enormous amount of information is encoded in the vast amount of texts on the web, some information also exists in more structured forms. We use the term *knowledge-based* Q/A for answering an NL question by mapping it to a query over a structured database (Chap. 7). Like the text-based paradigm for Q/A, this approach dates back to the earliest days of NLP, with systems like BASEBALL (Green et al. 1961) that answered questions from a structured database of baseball games and stats. In this chapter, we attempt to reduce the unstructured text search to a structured database by annotating texts SLFs.

4.1.1   Turning Documents into Answers

The technique of summarized logical forms (SLF) is proposed to solve the problem of converting an abstract textual document into Q/A-accessible form. There are two opposing approaches to this problem.

1. Assuming that complete formal representation of any textual document is possible, so matching a Q with A should occur as a logical inference of logical forms;
2. Assuming that a textual information is too tightly linked to natural language to be satisfactorily represented without it, so so matching a Q with A should occur as a keyword match.

The first approach brings the advantage of fully formalized understanding, based on the full range of reasoning capabilities (Galitsky 2016c), which is not always plausible. Moreover, the first approach requires NL generation that introduces additional deviation of relevance. Attempts to provide an exact answer, inherent in the fully formalized approach, would narrow down the overlap between a query and existing answers. At the same time, keyword match is not very expressive; keyword statistics ranging from TF*IDF to word2vec does not always assure good relevance.

Hence we select an intermediate approach: under the SLF technique, query understanding is posed as a recognition problem of how to find the most relevant A for a given Q, even if there is no direct A. The SLF technique is an intermediate one in respect to the degree of knowledge formalization. The SLF approach is intended for the NLP system that is a combination of information extraction and NL understanding systems (Fig. 4.1). In information extraction, only a fraction of the text is relevant; information is represented by a predefined, fully formalized, relatively simple (in respect to the original text) structure (e.g., logical expressions or a database). Only the data, which can be explicitly mentioned in a potential query, occurs in SLFs. The rest of the information, which is unlikely to occur in a question but can potentially form the relevant answer, does not have to be formalized. Under the SLF technique, a formal representation of a query (QR) is matched against one or many SLFs.

Pattern recognition methodology has a significant influence on how we treat the answers. When we say that a document (or its fragment) serves as an answer to a question we mean that for this either of the following holds:

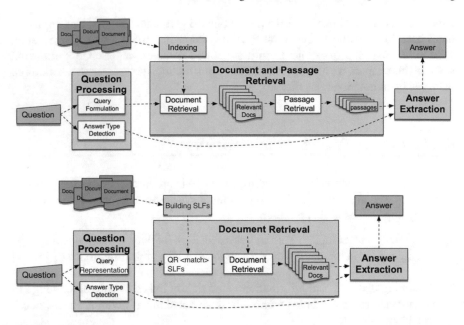

Fig. 4.1 The difference between a factoid retrieval-based Q/A (on the top) and SLF-based Q/A (on the bottom)

(1) The information contained in the document matches the subject of this question; or

(2) The fragment is marginally related to the question, but the other fragments have even lower correlation with the question (assuming the question is indeed related to the given domain).

The SLF technique is based on logic programming, taking advantage of its convenient handling of semantic rules on one hand, and explicit implementation of the domain commonsense reasoning on the other hand. The declarative nature of coding semantic rules, domain knowledge and generalized candidate query representations (QRs) make logic programming a reasonable tool for Q/A (Gazdar and Mellish 1989; Tarau et al. 1999; Abramson and Dahl 1989). Although some approximation of SLF technique can be implemented via conventional inverse-index search, we do an introduction to Logic Programming to make Q/A via reasoning more explicit and familiarize the reader with the concept.

The key advantage of a logic programming-based approach is that a high Q/A performance can be achieved for *each* identified problematic case, not for an average query. This feature is essential for CRM Q/A where we can guarantee that each question can be answered properly. We share a conversation between the author of this book and his peers concerning the systematic incapability of Google NLP system to handle a manifold of cases (Fig. 4.2).

Various viewpoints exist on the value of end-to-end learning that does not require feature engineering (Fig. 4.2). Its key limitation is that it is hard to repair particular

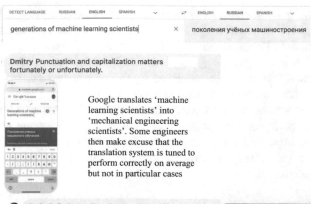

Dmitry Punctuation and capitalization matters fortunately or unfortunately.

Google translates 'machine learning scientists' into 'mechanical engineering scientists'. Some engineers then make excuse that the translation system is tuned to perform correctly on average but not in particular cases

Boris Galitsky It tells us how random and irresponsible the whole approach is. This failure of a basic phrase indicates there are not going to be monotonic improvements of translation quality. The translation system by now should figure out that just word alignment by a neural network does not work. You cannot say in Russian 'ученые машинного обучения', it should be 'ученые ЗАНИМАЮЩИЕСЯ … '. And to achieve this, throw away end-to-end deep learning and start learning language grammar.

Ilya The suggested solution to throw away E2E DL is of course, a reflection of Boris's opinion, but his criticism is valid, IMHO. I mean it's hard to brush off the issues when the models fail. And our only tool as DL priests ..err … practitioners is to feed the the God … I'm sorry, the Model ever more data and pray 😊

Dmitry Ilya Model robustness is an issue. It is the price of on-average higher translation quality. 'A' and 'a' are simply different inputs to the model, no relationship whatsoever, and German 'A' and English 'A' are sometimes the same. You can make model robust to such changes, in fact previous model generations did it. But there's a _huge_ quality price. Anecdotal failure to translate a sentence tells nothing about the on-average quality and human perception of what's "easy" to translate is misleading.

Boris Galitsky It is not anecdotal failure, it is a systematic failure to handle phrases. Forget about sentences. We talk about basic translation stuff. Translate 'Chemical [Engineering/Computing/ …] scientist' into Russian. The system just fails on handling modifiers. It always translates like Ученый-химик so modifiers are just thrown away. It should not even be called a translation. I suspect my examples are not covered by training set and DL can only handle cases very similar to a training set

Dmitry Boris, one can easily make current system better at "phrase" or single-word translation, at the cost of loosing quality across the board. You have to understand that there's a notion of target domain, e.g. what are you trying to accomplish with a model. People who define the product define the model domain indirectly. Model focused on a specific domain will always outperform generic one.

You can always make model do multiple things (multiple tasks or losses), at the cost of suboptimal performance for a main task, e.g. grammatical sentence translation.

And in general, if you have training data, end-to-end approach will always be better than pipelined (multi-step), or one using intermediate representation (semantics).

Fig. 4.2   A conversation on the methodology of machine translation

cases wanted badly by the users. The discussion shows two camps: one believes in component-based development and feature engineering, and the second camp—in an end-to-end approach. The argument of the former camp is that unless a non-working phrase translation is working the system is stuck. The latter camp cites the scoring system and claims that any errors observed by the user are acceptable as long as overall performance improves, according to these scores.

In this chapter, we design a Q/A system that can assure that each individual question can be answered properly, rather than guarantee high answering performance on average. It is important for domains of responsible Q/A where certain critical questions need to be under full control and should be answered exactly as designed by the content managers.

4.2   Brief Introduction to Logic Programming as a Tool for Q/A

Programs are written in the language of some logic. Execution of a logic program is a theorem proving. Answering a question is formulated as a search of inference for a logical representation of this question, where available answers are associated with some axioms (expressing meanings of these answers). The axioms which are employed to infer the question are associated with *correct* answers for this question. Hence a set of answers along with their logical representations is a logic program.

An execution of a logic program is a theorem proving process; that is, computation is done by logic process. Prolog is a representative logic language. For a Q/A use of a logic program is peculiar, so we start with a simple example of a logic program. A Prolog program is a collection of clauses of the form $A \vdash B_1, B_2, ..., B_n$ where A and B_i's are atoms. '$\vdash$' replaces the logic implication.

Given information about who is a mother/father of whom, one can define a grand mother/father relationship. Answers are in format "text : *LF*".

A1: Joe is father of Mary: *father(joe, mary)*
A2: Kathy is mother of Mary: *mother(kathy, mary)*
A3: Mary is mother of Bill: *mother(mary, bill)*
A4: Ken is father of Karen : *father(ken, karen)*
Q: Who are grand parents of Joe?

In this simple case, LFs are *atoms*. Capital letters denote variables, quantified by ∀ (for any). A predicate's variables (arguments) can be instantiated (have values) or uninstantiated (remain a variable). For example, the first argument is uninstantiated and the second is instantiated in *father(F, karen)*.

We define the meaning of the predicated involved in answers: *grandparent(X,Z) :- parent(Y,Z parent(Y,Z)*.

parent(X,Y):-father(X,Y); mother(X,Y).

Having above definitions as a logic program for answers, we can formulate questions:

Q: ?-*grandparent(joe, bill)* – "*is Joe a grand parent of Bill?*". A: Yes
Q: ?- *grandparent(Q, karen)* –"*Who is a grand parent of Karen?*", A: No
Q:- ?- grandparent(Q, *bill*) – "*Who is a grand parent of Bill?*", A: Q = *joe* ; Q = *kathy*.

Above are regular predicates whose variables range over objects like people. Metapredicates are predicates whose variables range over atoms and clauses.

4.3 Introducing Summarized Logical Forms

Let us consider the *Internet Auction* domain, which includes the description of bidding rules and various types of auctions:

Restricted-Access Auctions. This separate category makes it easy for you to find or avoid adult-only merchandise. To view and bid on adult-only items, buyers need to have a credit card on file with eBay. Your card will not be charged. Sellers must also have credit card verification. Items listed in the Adult-Only category are not included in the New Items page or the Hot Items section, and currently, are not available by any title search.

We follow the concept of inverse index and formulate a problem of organizing answers first and then considering which questions they would answer. What is this paragraph about and how to answer it in a *controlled* way? It introduces the "Restricted-Access" auction as a specific class of auction, explains how to search for, or avoid, selected categories of products, presents the credit card rules and describes the relations between this class of auctions and the highlighted sections of the Internet auction site. We do not change the paragraph to adjust it to the potential questions; instead, we consider all the possible questions this paragraph can serve as an answer to by enumerating the respective SLFs. What kind of questions can this paragraph serve as an answer to?

(1) *What is the restricted-access auction?* This question is raised when a customer knows the name of the specific class of auction and wants to get more details about it.
(2) *What kind of auctions sell adult-only items? How is my son accessing adult-rated products? How do you sell adult items?* These are similar questions, but the class of auctions is specified implicitly via the key attribute *adult-only*. With this question, the customer expects to receive something similar to the previous question.
(3) *When does a buyer need a credit card on file? Who needs to have a credit card on file? Why does a seller need credit card verification?* These are more specific questions about what kind of auction requires having credit cards on file, and what the difference is in credit card processing for the auction buyer/seller. The paragraph above serves as an answer to these questions as well, and since we are

not dividing the paragraph into smaller fragments, the question addressee will get more information than he has directly requested. However, this additional information is related to that request.

Below is the list of SLFs for the answer above. These summarized logical forms constitute a part of the knowledge base such that the formalized input question is queried against it (Sect. 4.6).

```
auction(restricted_access,_):-restrictedAuction.
product(adult,_):-restrictedAuction.
seller(credit_card(verification,_),_):-restrictedAuction.
credit_card(verification,_)):-restrictedAuction.
sell(credit_card(reject(_,_),_),_):-restrictedAuction.
bidder(credit_card(_,_),_):-restrictedAuction.
seller(credit_card(_,_),_):-restrictedAuction.
what_is(auction(restricted_access,_),_):-restrictedAuction.
```

The second SLF above can be read *if the query is about product(adult,_) then retrieve restrictedAuction.* The term *restrictedAuction* is used to index the paragraph above. If the call to the query representation (QR) of an input query initiates any of the summarized logical forms (clauses) above then, in turn, the call to *restrictedAuction* adds the paragraph above to the resultant answer.

Usually there are ten semantically different questions per answer, subject to coding as summarized logical forms. Each of these questions may be phrased differently, so additional summarized logical forms and domain-specific synonym substitution are required. The 10:1 question/answer ratio is typical for financial and legal domains. Other domains, associated with less formal human activity (e.g., advising on medical and psychological matters) require 20:1 and even 30:1 semantically different questions per answer 1–6 paragraphs each (Galitsky 2004). The size of an answer is motivated by the factors traditional for the pattern recognition problems. The shorter the answer, the higher is its attraction to the customer (answers precision), but the lower the probability of obtaining the correct answer. We choose 2–4 paragraphs as the optimal answer size.

Under the SLF technique, domain coding starts with the set of answers (the content). Canonical (potential) questions are then formed, taking into account the other answers. In particular, building-specific questions for an answer containing an entity is useless, if this entity is irrelevant for the other answers (just mentioning this entity is sufficient). As another example, we consider an answer from the *Tax* domain:

When we say that a document (or its fragment) serves as an answer to a question, we mean that for this question (related to domains) either (or) holds:

(1)   the fragments contain the information that is the subject of this question;
(2)   the fragment is marginally related to the question, but the other fragments have even lower correlation with the question (assuming the question indeed related to the given domain).

The timing of your divorce could have a significant effect on the amount of federal income tax you will pay this year. If both spouses earn about the same amount of money, getting a divorce before the year ends will save taxes by eliminating the marriage penalty. However, if one spouse earns a significant amount more than the other, waiting until January will save taxes by taking advantage of the married filing jointly status for one last year.

When we form the canonical questions, we start with the answers phrasing. Then, we try to compose more general questions using words that are not necessarily present in the answer. If we have a complex sentence as a canonical query, its components must be canonical queries as well (some of them, possibly, for another answer).

> *What are the tax issues of divorce?*
> *How can the timing of my divorce save a lot of federal income tax?*
> *I am recently divorced; how should I file so I do not have a net tax liability?*
> *Can I avoid a marriage penalty?*
> *How can I take advantage of the married filing jointly status when I am getting divorced?*

Below is the list of SLF for the answer above. Note that the third canonical query is represented by a single term (not a conjunctive member) because the first part of the question is semantically insignificant (just *divorce* is important; *recently* is irrelevant here).

> *divorce(tax(_,_,_),_):-divorceTax.*
> *divorce(tax(_,_,_), time):-divorceTax.*
> *divorce(tax(file(_),liability,_), _):-*
> *penalty(marriage,_):- divorceTax.*
> *divorce(file(joint),_):-divorceTax.*

A query is expected to trigger any of the clause heads. Then the call to *divorceTax* in turn delivers the answer above. In addition to the previous example, a predicate is substituted into another predicate to form an SLF which includes a pair of entities. One of these entities is more general for a given domain (*tax*), and another (*divorce*, that is substituted) is more specific. It is also worth mentioning an example of a query representation: *divorce(file(joint), self_employment)*, that will initiate the last clause above when called.

The reader may ask what would happen for the query representations *divorce(file(separate),_)* or *divorce(file(_),_)*; these issues are the essence of SLF coding which we start considering in the following subsection.

4.3.1 A Generic Set of Summarized Logical Forms

From a simple introductory example of SLFs we proceed to the way they appear in a real-world domain. A generic set of SLFs for an entity e, its attributes $c_1, c_2, ...,$ *variables ranging over them* C, C_1, other involved entities $e_1,...,$ and the resultant answer with *id* (and respective variable *Id*) looks like the following:

e(A):-var(A), answer(id). This is a very general answer, introducing (defining) the entity *e.* It is not always appropriate to provide a general answer (e.g. to answer *What is tax?*), so the system may ask a user to be more specific:

e(A):-var(A), clarify([c₁, c₂, …]). If the attribute of *e* is unknown, a clarification procedure is initiated, suggesting the choice of an attribute from the list $c_1, c_2,…$ to have a specific answer about $e(c_i)$ instead of just for *e(_).*

e(A):-nonvar(A), A = c₁ , answer(id). The attribute is determined and the system outputs the answer associated with the entity and its attribute (*id* is the answer identificator).

e(e₁(A)):-nonvar(A), A= c₁ , e₁(A).

e(e₁(A),e₂):-nonvar(A), A≠ c₁ , e₂(_). Depending on the existence and values of attributes, an embedded expression is reduced to its innermost entity that calls another SLF.

e(A,id). This (dead-end) SLF serves as a constraint for the representation of a complex query, $e_1(A,id)$, $e_2(B,id)$, to deliver just an *answer(id)* instead of all pairs for e_1 and e_2. It works in the situation where neither e_1 nor e_2 can be substituted (into each other).

Note that *var/1* and *nonvar/1* are the built-in Prolog metapredicates that obtain the respective status of variables. A SLF template is applicable if:

1)   An entity expresses a series of meanings;
2)   These meanings are associated with distinct answers.

Otherwise, there is no need to have multiple SLFs for an entity; furthermore, multiple entities and respective meanings may correspond to the same answer.

The method of *dead-end* SLFs comes into play when a QR contains two or more conjunctive members (last case in the template) and we do not want the union of answers for each of these terms, as a general case would deliver. Assuming QR is $e_1(c_1,Id)$ & $e_2(c_2,Id)$, the following pair of SLFs is designed to handle it properly:

e₁(c₁,id)).
e₂(c₂,Id)) :- nonvar(c₂), c₂=c_{attribute}, nonvar(Id), Id=id, answer(id).

Here we take advantage of the reserved last argument of a SLF predicate that ranges over answer identifiers *id* (denoted as # above). The first SLF is called dead-end because it does not lead to an answer. Indeed, the answer is determined by the second SLF that verifies that the dead-end SLF has yielded a proper *id.* As a result, we obtain just the answer for e_2, which is supposed to be more specific than the answers for both e_1 and e_2, assuming e_1 is more general. This method will become clearer for the reader when we deal with more examples below.

The template above demonstrates that a series of meanings for an entity that is expressible by summarized logical forms is not as rich as NL would provide; however, it is sufficient to separate the answers. We put forward the following statements:

Statement 3.1 As many answers as possible can be separated by the SLF template given that there are distinguishing NL queries for these answers.

Statement 3.2 The template set of SLFs assures a completeness, consistency and coverage of the possible spectrum of meanings by a formalized entity.

If a domain entity has less SLFs than the template set, it means that more answers can be added (and successfully separated) by the system. A richer set of SLFs may lead to inconsistency: unexpected SLFs can be matched. Besides, the degree to which domains entities fill a template, characterizes the domain coverage by this entity. Such a parameter indicates whether or not there is a combination of entities and attributes (that is meaningful in a domain) which may potentially match either none or wrong SLFs. However, in practice, there may be a wider variety of SLFs included in the template; this is determined by the domain structure and the skills of a knowledge engineer or an automated annotation engine.

From the perspective of logic, the choice of an SLF to be matched against a query representation corresponds to the search for a proof of this query representation, considering SLFs as axioms (Galitsky 2003). It is quite natural from the perspective of mathematical logics, starting from the 1960s, to consider Q/A as an initiator for automatic theorem proving (Black 1964; Chang and Lee 1973; Darlington 1969). The system searches for as many proofs as possible: the totality of answers, associated with all involved axioms, is considered relevant to the query (here, the theorem being proved). If no proof exists then either the system is unable to find it (a query with unfamiliar phrasing) or, the system does not have the axioms being queried (no relevant answers). We conclude the section with a brief definition of what SLFs are.

Definition 3.1 SLFs of an answer are the formal syntactically generalized (Chap. 2) representations of potential questions, obtained from an answer. SLFs contain the essential information of answers and serve to separate them, being matched with formal representations of questions. SLFs are built taking into account:

(1) The set of other semantically close answers.
(2) The totality of relevant questions, semantically similar to generic questions above.

4.4   Linked Summarized Logical Forms of an Answer

4.4.1   Motivations

Domain-specific ontologies are an important component of Q/A bots. While the keyword search and open domain Q/A target horizontal domains, handling relatively simple, factoid questions containing an entity and its attribute, this is not the case for a legal, financial or business Q/A (Sidorov et al 2012, Galitsky 2017). Representation of the above knowledge, oriented to the general audience, is much less structured and requires much richer set of entities than an NL interface to SQL databases (Maybury 2000, Popescu et al. 2003, Galitsky 2003, Chap. 7). Furthermore, the structure of links between these entities is significantly more complex in such domains.

Domain-specific ontologies for Q/A must be designed in a way to deliver answers which:

(1) are adjusted to a given question;
(2) are linked to additional resources if they are necessary;
(3) indicate its position in the taxonomy of a given Q/A domain (Galitsky 2016a);

(4) are consistent with other answers and provides uniform coverage of this Q/A domain.

Earlier studies of the design of NL-based and expert systems showed that adequate commonsense reasoning is essential for answering complex questions (Winograd 1972, Galitsky et al. 2013c). A number of studies have shown how an application of advanced reasoning is helpful to compensate for a lack of linguistic or domain-dependent knowledge answering questions in poorly structured domains (Ng et al. 2001; Moldovan et al. 2002; Pasca 2003; Rus and Moldovan 2002; Baral et al. 2004; Galitsky 2004; Sidorov et al 2013).

In our earlier studies, we have explored what forms of reasoning can overcome the bottleneck of limited accuracy of delivered answers. Default logic has been shown to provide significant assistance disambiguating questions formed by a domain non-expert (Galitsky 2005). An architecture for merging vertical search ontologies has been proposed in (Galitsky and Pampapathi 2005). Parse thicket-based knowledge representation assists in answering complex, multi-sentence questions (Galitsky et al 2014). In this chapter, we continue our development of the knowledge representation and reasoning technique for building sharable reusable ontologies for answering complex questions.

Evidently, a set of SLFs represents an associated answer with a loss of information. What kind of information can be saved given the formal language that supports SLFs? When we extract the answer identifying information and construct a set of SLFs for it, we intentionally lose the commonsense links between the entities and objects used. This happens for the sole purpose of building the most robust and compact expressions for matching with the query representations. Nevertheless, it seems reasonable to retain the answer information which is not directly connected with potential questions, but useful for completeness of knowledge being queried. A Linked SLF can be considered as a combination of SLFs with *mutual explanations* of how they are related to each other from the answer's perspective.

4.4.2   Virtual SLFs

Linked SLFs serve the purpose of handling the queries not directly related to the informational content of the answers, represented by SLFs. For an answer and a set of SLFs, a linked SLF (LSLF) derives an additional set of *virtual SLF*s to cover those questions which require a deductive step to be associated with this answer. In other words, a linked SLF extends a set of questions that are covered by existing SLFs toward the superset of questions, deductively connected with the existing SLFs. It happens during a Q/A session, unlike the creation of regular SLFs which are built in the course of domain construction (Galitsky 2006).

Yielding virtual SLFs can be written as $\forall a\ LSLF : \{SLF(a)\} \rightarrow \{vSLF(a)\}$, where $\{SLF(a)\}$ is the set of original SLFs for answer a, and $\{vSLF(a)\}$ is the set of virtual SLFs derived from LSLF for an answer a. A virtual summarized logical form (vSLF)

Fig. 4.3 Illustration for the idea of linked SLFs

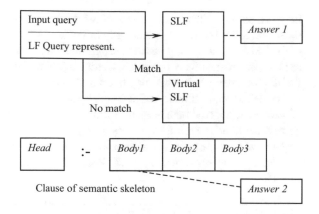

can be yielded by multiple answers. However, a vSLF cannot be a regular SLF for another answer (note that two SLFs for different answers are allowed to be deductively linked): $\forall a,a'$ $vSLF(a) \cap SLF(a')=\emptyset$. Hence, a vSLF for a query is an expression that occurs in a clause of a Linked SLF and can be matched with the query representation or its conjunctive component. In the latter case, the terms of these clauses must not match with the negations of the (conjunctive) components of that query representation. LSLFs = SLFs + vSLFs.

The idea of an LSLF is depicted in Fig. 4.3. The input query is converted into QR and matched against the virtual summarized logical forms if there is no appropriate regular summarized logical form to match with. Virtual summarized logical forms are obtained given the terms of LSLF clauses. The SLFs are assigned to answers directly. However, vSLFs are assigned to answers via clauses. Both *Answer1* and *Answer2* may have other assigned regular and virtual summarized logical forms.

For example, imagine a SLF *tax(income)* that is intended to handle questions about *tax brackets* in the *Tax* domain: how the *tax* amount depends on *income*. Evidently, this answer would be a relevant one to the question *"What would my tax be if I lost my job last year"*? Since *"losing a job"* is not directly related to *tax* (the former is deductively linked to the latter via *income, job(lost)→ not income(_)*), it would be unreasonable to have a special SLF to link *tax* and *job-lost*. Therefore, the expression *job(lost)* serves as a virtual SLF in the Tax domain, being generated dynamically from the clause *job(lost)→ not income(_)*, instead of being a regular one. If we do not use the regular SLF instead of the virtual one for the entities which are neither deductively nor syntactically linked in a query, it would damage the domain structure and lead to an excess number of SLFs. Indeed, this happened in domain knowledge engineering before the concept of the LSLF was introduced.

At the same time, in the IRA domain the *"loosing job"* scenario is under special consideration, and expressions *ira(tax(income))* and *ira(job(lost))* are expected to be the SLFs for different answers; one for calculating *tax* on *IRA distribution amount* that depends on *income*, and the other for the special case of *tax* on *IRA distribution* under *employment termination*. Thus a pair (triple, etc.) of entities may form a vSLF that requires a LSLF-clause that would yield, generally speaking, multiple links between entities. This LSLF-clause may form a regular SLF, depending on whether these entities are directly semantically or syntactically linked in a query. The clauses of the LSLF are not *directly* used to separate answers, so they can be built as complete as possible irrespectively on the knowledge contained in other answers. Furthermore, LSLFs for a pair of answers may overlap, having the common clauses.

As well as approximation of meaning by semantic herders, linked SLF are capable of involving approximate semantic links. For example, various *forms of payment* questions are addressed to the *Internet retailer* domain that usually has an answer about *credit card payment*. How should we handle the questions mentioning *payment by check, money order, wiring* etc.? "Pure" SLF technique requires enumeration of SLFs:

```
payment(check):-credit_card_payment_answer.
payment(money_order) :-credit_card_payment_answer.
payment(wiring) :-credit_card_payment_answer.
payment(credit_card) :-credit_card_payment_answer.
```

However, using a LSLF clause:

payment(X):-member(X, [check, money_order, wiring, credit_card]),

one can use the fourth SLF above as a regular SLF and the first three ones as virtual SLFs, involving the clause about the forms of payment. The advantages of using a LSLF are the lower number of SLFs to code, clearer semantic structure of a domain and reusability of encoded commonsense knowledge for similar domains.

We proceed to another example of a Linked SLF. Again, the SLFs need to be deductively linked via the clauses, involving the entities from these SLFs and other ones. The clauses below present the explanation of how a term *divorce* is linked to the terms *marriage, tax, file, separate,* and *joint*. The first clause, completing the set of SLFs above, introduces the commonsense fact that being *divorced* is an opposite entity to being *married*. The second clause is saying that if a couple was filing a *joint tax return* before the *divorce*, they are *filing separate tax returns* afterwards. Enumeration of terms within a clause may be used to express the temporal relationship of a sequence in time (read *file(joint)* then *divorce(_)*).

```
divorce(_):- not marriage(_).
tax(file(separate)):- file(joint),  divorce(_).
single(_):-divorce(_);not marriage(_).
```

Using just the SLFs, we can answer the *divorce* questions without knowing that *divorce* ends *marriage*! Surprisingly, one does not need to know that fact to separate answers about *divorce*. Intuitively, a speaker would definitely need some basic commonsense facts to *talk* about a topic, but an agent can answer questions about a topic, including rather specific and deep questions, without these facts. Linked SLFs come into play, in particular, to semantically link the basic domain entities. LSLF is the *least* knowledge required to have all the entities linked.

Note that the predicates we use to describe the tax issues of marriage to occur in an SLF for Q/A are different from the ones we would use to better formalize the domain itself. The SLF-oriented predicate *divorce* ranges over its attributes, which are reduced to a single argument, and an *extended* predicate *divorce* in a logic program would have two arguments ranging over the divorce parties and other arguments for the various circumstances of the *divorce* action. Extended predicates for verbs are the entries of verb ontologies such as VerbNet and FrameNet (Palmer 2009). Evidently, extended predicates better fit the traditions of computational semantics, specifying the *roles* of their arguments. Frequently, extended predicates are required to form the Linked SLF; analogous SLF predicates should then be mutually expressed via the extended ones. These definitions do not usually bring in constraints for the arguments of SLF predicates.

Below is the LSLF (the set of clauses of the form *extended_predicate ↔ SLF_predicate*) for the sample answer above. The first argument of the extended predicate *tax* ranges over the formulas for *taxpayer's states*; therefore, *tax* is a metapredicate. Note that these clauses need to work both ways (right to left and left to right) to deploy the capability of the vSLFs, yielded by the LSLF.

A particular case of what we call a non-direct link between entities is the temporal one. If a pair of answers describe two consecutive states or actions, and a given query addresses a state before, in between, or after these states (actions), the clauses of the Linked SLF are expected to link the latter states with the former ones and to provide a relevant (though possibly indirect) answer.

---

divorce(Husband, Wife, Date, Place, ...) ↔ divorce(_).
marriage(Husband, Wife, Date, Place, ...) ↔ marriage(_).
tax((pay(Husband)&pay(Wife)), file (separate), _) ↔ tax(file(separate))).
tax((pay(Husband)&pay(Wife)), file (joint), _) ↔ tax(file(joint)).
divorce(Husband, Wife, Date, Place) ↔ not marriage(Husband, Wife, Date1, Place1)
tax((pay(Husband)&pay(Wife)), file (separate), _) ↔
  tax((pay(Husband)&pay(Wife)), file (joint), _), divorce(Husband, Wife, Date, Place).

For a scenario, the Linked SLF may include alternating sequences of states, interchanging with actions intermediate states (we assume no branching plans for simplicity). States and actions can be merged into the same sequence from the perspective of being explicitly assigned with an answer. The set of these states and actions falls into subsets corresponding to the answers (based on the expressions for these states and actions which are in turn SLFs as well). It can naturally happen that answers are not ordered by this sequence; they may be assigned by the SLF expressions for alternating states and actions. Then, if a question addresses some *unassigned states* or *actions*, those *answers* should be *chosen* which are assigned to the *previous* and *following* elements of the sequence.

4.4.3 LSLF and Event Calculus

For the sequences being considered, we do not require their elements to be *deductively* linked: their enumeration is sufficient. We follow the same idea of information approximation as when constructing summarized logical forms. To deductively link states and actions (more precisely, situations) in a real-world domain, it would be necessary to define all the entities used and to provide a large number of details (preconditions and successor state expressions) irrelevant to querying a domain. However, we take advantage of some analogy to the frame axiom. There is a way to optimize the representation of knowledge such that only the objects affected by actions change their states.

The frame axiom (Shanahan 1997, Fig. 4.4) is applicable to our considerations while choosing an optimal SLF in the case of a direct match.

Event calculus can be a base for a number of reasoning tasks such as deduction, abduction and induction.

In a *deduction task*, the input is *what happens when* and *what actions do* and the output is *what is true when*. A deductive task can produce a prediction for the outcome of a known sequence of actions.

Abduction task inputs *what actions do* and *what is true when* and outputs *what happens when*. Abduction produces a sequence of actions that leads to a specified outcome. Abduction gives a temporal explanation, diagnosis and planning.

The task of induction inputs *what is true when* and *what happens when* and produces a generalization *what actions do*. Induction yields a set of rules, a formal theory of the effects of actions, based on observed data. Induction is a foundation of an explainable machine learning.

If an action is mentioned in a query and there is a set of answers that characterize the states, only the states, which are possibly *affected* by the mentioned action may be relevant.

We present the state-action sequence for the *tax return preparation* scenario:

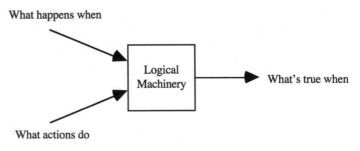

Fig. 4.4 Machinery of event calculus

```
file(tax(return)):- tax(minimize(speculate), _),            % state
        collect(receipts), calculate(deduction),            % action
        collect(form(_)), consult(accountant),              % action
        fill(form(_)),                                      % action
        calculate(tax(property )),                          % action
        calculate(tax(income)),                             % action
        estimate(tax(value)),                               % state
        send(form),                                         % action
        tax(return(_), expect(_)).                          % state
```

4.4.4 LSLFs' Handling of Complex Questions

LSLFs are helpful for queries with query representation as conjunctions of multiple terms. This happens for complex queries consisting of two or more components, for example *Can I qualify for a 15-year loan if I filed bankruptcy two years ago with my partner?* → *loan(qualify)& bankruptcy(file, 2 years))*. If a term is either matched against none of the SLFs or delivers too many of them, then this term can serve as a virtual one. In Table 4.1 we analyze various cases of the satisfaction (matching) of a query representation with two terms against regular and virtual SLFs.

We continue development of the method of dead-end SLFs and extend it to the case of vSLF. In the complex sentence, we distinguish two parts: *kernel* and *satellite*. These parts are frequently correlated with the syntactic components of a sentence. In accordance with our informational model of a complex question, the principal part is usually more general than the dependent part. One of the canonical examples of a complex query is as follows: *How can I do this **Action** with that **Attribute**, if I am **AdditionalAttribute1** of / by / with / from/and **AdditionalAttribute2**.* We enumerate the properties of our informational model above as follows:

(1) *Action and its Attribute are more important (and more general) than AdditionalAttribute1 and AdditionalAttribute2; they are more likely to point to a specific topic (group of answers).*
(2) *AdditionalAttribute1 or AdditionalAttribute2 are more specific and more likely to point to an exact answer.*

Therefore, if we mishandle the leading part, we would probably dissatisfy the assisting one and find ourselves with a totally irrelevant answer. Conversely, if the assisting part is mishandled when the leading part has been matched, we frequently find ourselves in the situation where we have either a marginally relevant answer or too many answers. In general, the variety of assisting components is much higher than that of the leading ones. Therefore, it is reasonable to represent them as virtual SLFs. Proper coding is intended to achieve the coverage of all leading components, so most of them are represented by SLFs.

There are a few additional models for complex questions. When the questions obey neither informational model, SLFs and LSLFs can be individually built to

Table 4.1 Various cases of matching (disagreements) for the nucleus and satellite components of a compound query. First and second columns enumerate matching possibilities for the nucleus and satellite components

Nucleus term	Satellite term	Resultant answer and comments
Matches with multiple SLFs	Matches with a single SLF(a)	The case for a "dead end" SLF for an assisting term, which reduces the number of matched SLFs for the first term, having the common variable (answer Id). Answer a is chosen in this situation which had required special preparation
Matches with a single SLF(a)	Matches with multiple SLFs	Answer a from the leading term is taking over the multiple ones delivered by the assisting term. The confidence of that right decision would grow if the assisting term matches with a vSLF of a; otherwise, we conclude that the assisting component is unknown
Matches with a single SLF(a) or only vSLF(a)	Matches with a single SLF(a) or only vSLF(a)	The answer is a. Higher confidence in the proper decision would be established if the leading term matches with SLF and the assisting one with vSLF
Matches with a set of SLF(a), $a \in A$	Matches with a single SLF(a)	The answer is a. The assisting term matches against a single summarized logical form and therefore reduces the answers yielded by the leading term
Matches with a set of SLF(a), $a \in A$	Matches with a vSLF(a) only	All answers from A. The fact that the assisting term matches against a virtual summarized logical form is insufficient evidence to reduce the answers yield by the leading term
Matches with a set of vSLF(a), $a \in A$	Matches with a single SLF(a)	The answer is a. The assisting term contributes to that decision, consistent with the match of the leading term

(continued)

Table 4.1   (continued)

Nucleus term	Satellite term	Resultant answer and comments
Matches with a set of vSLF(a), $a \in A$	Matches with a vSLF(a) only	All answers from A. The resultant confidence level is rather low and there is insufficient evidence to reduce the answers yielded by the set of vSLF of the leading term
Matches with a single SLF(a)	Matches with a virtual SLF(a') only	The answers are both a and a' except in the case when the first term matches with virtual SLF(a') and the answer is just a
Matches with a virtual SLF(a) only	Matches with a virtual SLF(a') only	All answers which are yielded by vSLF(a). The question is far from being covered by SLF, so it is safer to provide all answers, deductively linked to the leading term and ignore the assisting term
Matches with a set of vSLF(a): $a \in A$	Matches with a set of vSLF(a'): $a' \in A'$	We find the answer which delivers most of vSLF in {vSLF(a)$\cap$ vSLF(a'): $a \in A$, $a' \in A'$ }

handle particular asking schema. However, if no special means have been designed for the deviated (semantically) questions, the resultant answers may be irrelevant.

To estimate the results of matching procedure without a LSLF, the reader may hypothetically replace matching with a virtual SLF by "no match" and track the number of situations with the lack of proper handling where LSLFs are not in use. Assuming that the complete (linking all entities) LSLF is built, we approach the Table 4.1.

Proposition 4.4.1 The rules (Table 4.1) for matching a query representation as a conjunction with virtual SLFs deliver the highest resultant accuracy, averaging through the respective set of queries (complex sentences).

It is very important for observing the optimal domain structure that the LSLF clauses "fill the gaps" in between the SLFs, which enforce the domain taxonomy. Hence, building LSLFs should follow the construction of the SLF domain and the verification of its taxonomy, set by the answers.

LSLF approach adds the advanced reasoning capabilities to the SLF technique. The LSLF technique brings in the deductive links between the SLFs, completing the commonsense knowledge representation on the one hand and keeping the convenience of SLF domain coding, on the other hand. Deductive links between the SLFs improve the content and query phrasing coverage of a domain, providing a more powerful way to associate a QR with the existing SLFs.

The key requirement to a knowledge representation system for Q/A is easy extension capability. The normal procedure for building a knowledge base is its continuous update with new answers and new links between existing entities, attributes and objects. Therefore, the set of SLFs and LSLFs of a domain must be able to naturally accept whatever needs to be done to properly handle a new query. It is clear, for example, that it may not be straightforward to add a new axiom to a (complete) axiomatic system.

Indeed, the set of SLFs is far from being complete in the sense that it stops separating answers way in advance, before approaching a state of being a complete axiomatic system.

At the same time, the set of LSLFs is approaching the coverage of all possible questions that we can call the *coverage completeness*. Therefore, the logical system for Q/A must be incomplete as the axiomatic system but complete in terms of handling all potential queries.

Proposition 4.4.2 Any LSLF system is logically incomplete but possesses potential coverage completeness. The latter means that for any new query it is possible to add a SLF, readjust the other ones in accordance to certain rules, add a vSLF clause or modify the existing vSLF clauses in accordance with these rules such that it will be properly handled, along with the other ones of the original system.

The proposition above is based on the existence of SLF *modifications rules* and *vSLF modification rules* under domain update. Existence of such rules means that to add a new SLF only a limited subset of the totality of SLFs should be modified to obey the original separation of answers. Indeed, if a new SLF introduces a new entity, there is no potential conflict with the other SLFs. If a new object or attribute is added with an existing entity, all the SLFs for this entity must undergo a possible modification of instantiation states of arguments and verification of possible exception for the mentioned object or attribute is necessary.

4.4.5   Evaluation of Relevance Improvement Due to LSLF

A series of tax return assisting, investment, mortgage and financial companies have been using the Q/A system being presented with LSLF-based knowledge representation. LSLF-based Q/A system can replace human agents, automatically answering tax questions in up to 85% of all cases. Human agents were ready to get involved in the Q/A process in case of a failure of the automatic system.

In particular, the suite of legal (family law) domain has been created, which covers sufficient information for the general audience of using about 1000 answers in the main and accompanying domains. This domain includes more than 240 entities and more than 2000 of their parameters in these sub-domains. More than 3000 LSLFs were designed to provide an access to these answers. During the beta testing, the Family Law advisor was subject to evaluation by a few hundred users. Customers

had the options to provide feedback to the system concerning a particular answer if
they were dissatisfied or not fully satisfied with it (too long, non-relevant, partially
relevant, etc.). With the answer size not to exceed 6 paragraphs, the system correctly
answers more than 70% of all queries, in accordance to the analysis of the Q/A log
by the experts. Even with 82% resultant accuracy (Table 4.2), which is relatively
low for traditional pattern recognition systems, over 95% of customers and quality
assurance personnel agreed that the legal advisor is the preferable way of accessing
information for non-professional users.

Usually, customers tried to rephrase questions in case of the system's misunderstanding or failure to provide a response. Reiteration (rephrasing the question) was
almost always sufficient to obtain the required information. At the beginning of the
evaluation period, the number of misunderstood question was significantly exceeded
by the number of answers not known by the system. This situation was reversed later:
a number of misunderstood questions was monotonically decreasing in spite of an
increase in overall represented knowledge.

Table 4.2 The progress of question answering enhancement at consecutive steps of domain
development (%). LSLF step is shown in bold. *Commonsense domain knowledge* helps to yield
questions which were not encoded during initial phase of domain development, but are nevertheless
relevant

Development step	Source of questions	Correct answer	No knowledge	No understanding	Misunderstanding
Initial coding	Initially designed (expert) questions for SH	47	0	35	18
Testing and reviewing of initial coding	Initially designed and accompanying questions	52	18	21	9
Adjustment to testers' questions	Additional and reformulated and rephrased testers' questions	60	15	10	15
Adding LSLFs without Table 4.1 rules	Domain-specific knowledge	63	17	7	13
Adding LSLFs with Table 4.1 rules	**Domain-specific knowledge**	**67**	**17**	**4**	**12**
Adjustment to content providers' questions	More questions, reflecting a different viewpoint	74	8	4	14
Adjustment to users' questions	No additional questions	82	4	4	10

The use of LSLF allowed increasing the percentage of correctly answered questions from 60 to 67 (Table 4.2): about 7% of questions are indirect and require to apply commonsense reasoning to link these questions to formalized answer components. In 2% of cases, vSHs were built but they derived multiple inconsistent SHs because of a lack of specific knowledge (which has been added later). As one would expect, applying LSLF technique, the decrease of cases with a lack of understanding (6%) was higher than (twice as much as) the decrease of cases with misunderstanding (3%). To estimate the results of matching procedure without a LSLF, the reader may hypothetically replace matching with a virtual SH by "no match" and track the number of situations with the lack of proper handling where LSLFs are not in use.

4.5 Building Summarized Logical Forms

We have introduced the SLF technique and explained how they work for the representation of semi-structured knowledge. In this Section, we outline the methodology of SLF construction.

4.5.1 Entity and Its Attribute (Object)

It is important for a semantic model to distinguish the roles of an entity and an object. Though the distinction has a fuzzy boundary and varies between approaches to NLP, we present the most essential differences:

(1) Typically, the number of entities is much lower than the number of objects in a vertical domain;
(2) To relate a query to a sub-domain, it is sufficient to analyze the query words, which refer to entities rather than to objects;
(3) In the first order logic, the simplest representation of the NL semantics, entities are represented by predicates and objects are represented by their arguments;
(4) The arguments of a predicate have semantic types (e.g., person, country, city, product). The structure of all semantic types is a tree with directed edges which denote the relations of semantic types inclusion (e.g., *person* → *leader of* … → *president*);
(5) To express the semantic link between predicates we unify their arguments, which have a compatible semantic type;
(6) Typically, there are reasonable subdomains of vertical domains where the following approximation holds: predicates and metapredicates correspond to verbs and objects/attributes correspond to nouns in the canonical questions to these subdomains.

There are certain linguistic findings that the first-order language and its extension with metapredicates corresponds to both the syntax and semantics of NL

(Montague 1974; Partee et al 1990); in particular, the grammatical principle of a single subject-predicate relation (Redey 1999). Any syntactical relation such as complement forming, other than copulative conjunction or coordination, is repeatedly derivable from the subject-predicate relation. There exists a grammatical model of the NL sentence structure describing the non-coordinate relations among its constituents as predicative, objective, determinative, attributive, etc. Grammatical constituents corresponding to these relation types are not distinct in a logical sense; the roles of these constituents can be interchanged (what was an object can be a subject further on), hence all other differences can be neglected. In other words, the functional sentence model can be based on one single generalized subject-predicate relation.

The peculiarities of the *entity/object* division introduce the general framework for the deployment of ML both for semantic representation of a *query* and for the SLFs of an *answer*. To match a semantic representation of a query with a summarized logical form, a naïve approach would be to calculate the weighted sum of the number of different predicates and the number of different corresponding arguments for the predicates, which occur in both query and template. However, experiments show that more robust Q/A can be achieved by the straight unification of the query representation with the SLF, as is traditional for logic programming (see, for example, Apt (1997) and Bramer (2013) for more details).

We outline certain criteria a potential SLF should meet. Articles, prepositions, auxiliary verbs, etc. should never be used in SLFs. Consider the query *Does the lender have any additional responsibilities?* It would be a mistake to represent this semantically as *lender(responsibility(additional,_),have,_)*. The verb *have* in this sentence is almost semantically empty, its function is mainly syntactic. It is evident that *responsibility* is confined to a certain person, namely the *lender*; the verb *have* here is a part of the meaning of the word *responsibility* and for this reason the SLF should be reduced to *lender(responsibility(additional,_))*.

Secondly, SLFs for each query should not be derived from a surface language form of a question but instead formed from some kind of semantic representation. We should form logical predicates from the words with general meanings which are the elements of the semantic language. Otherwise, we risk getting complicated expressions with embedded predicates even for simple queries. For example, there is no need to represent the query *"What should I look for when walking through a home?"* as *home(walking_through, look_for,_)*, since in fact it is a question about the criteria of home evaluation and we can choose *home(esteem)* as a SLF for it. This is true if there is no separate information block (answer) in the domain related to *esteem* or, if it is necessary to distinguish such actions as *"walking through"* and *"looking for"*. Similarly, the question *"How large a down payment do I need?"* does not require the complicated and cumbersome representation *need(down_payment, large,_,_)*, but instead can be reduced to *down_payment(amount)*. Modal verbs should participate in SLFs (answer separation) as little as possible. Also, the qualitative characteristics of *amount* should be avoided, because they can be chosen randomly and do not reflect the content of a potential answer in most cases.

4.5.2 Semantic Types of Arguments

In this Section, we discuss how to manage semantic roles for an SLF predicates' arguments. To estimate the set of words which form the totality of specific meanings for an entity in a domain, one needs to observe all the answers whose SLFs involve this entity. The SLF technique requires forming as many meanings by means of adding the attributes to an entity as necessary to distinguish between answers in a given set. The SLF approach is based on a thorough linguistic analysis of involved entities to separate the answers in the given domain. This is in contrast to the traditional linguistic analysis systems, which usually do their best to form complete semantic representations from a full parse tree.

Fully formalized domains usually allow for a choice of semantic types covering a uniform set of objects or attributes. Semantic types may correspond to entity types like *country, organization, position, time*. For example, a geography domain uses the semantic types of *xcity, xcountry, xcapital, xpresident*, etc., each of which ranges over similar kinds of objects. In the fully formalized domain, the semantic types serve to express the semantic link between a pair of predicates: two predicates are linked if they have a common variable. Only variables of the same semantic types can be set equal for a pair of predicates. To represent a query from the geographical domain *Which capital does the country with president named Blair have?* we involve two predicates, *capital(xcountry, xcity)* and *president(xcountry, xperson)* in the query representation *capital(C, Xcity), president(C, blair)*. The semantic link between these predicates is expressed via the common variable over countries *xcountry*.

On the contrary, in SLF domains semantic types *range over all attributes* required to *separate the answers*. Semantically linked predicates are substituted into each other in accordance to the intuitive "importance" parameter and/or their classes which are assigned a common variable. For example, the expression *"to invest in stock"* gives us the query representation *invest(stock(_))*. Both entities are expressed via predicates: *invest(xinvest), stock(xamoney)*. The semantic type *xinvest* includes *stock* as a value to specify the substitution. Both these entities can be used independently, however, to form the meaning for a particular answer, one does not need additional explicit variables. So in SLF domains we just substitute one predicate into another. This choice is based on a one-to-many mapping: one can *invest* in *stock, mutual_fund, IRA, 401k*, etc. Notice that the opposite choice can be motivated by a set of actions applicable to the *options*: to *invest*, to *sell*, to *buy*, to *analyze*, etc. The reader may take into account the fact that even more specific meanings can be expressed by substituting an attribute into the internal predicate.

For example, the query *"How efficient can investment in stocks be?"* is represented using the attribute *efficient* (which belongs to semantic type *xamoney)*: *invest(stock(efficient)), signature(stock(xamoney))*.

A *signature* of a predicate is an ordered list of the semantic types of its arguments. The name of semantic type *xamoney* may initially seem to the reader to be unrelated to the term *efficient*; other semantic types can include *efficient* or *inefficient* as well. Working with domains, a knowledge engineer quickly stops perceiving this way of coding semantic types as unnatural. Families of SLFs for the given set of answers are formed based on the necessity to separate these answers; therefore *efficient* could potentially be a value for multiple semantic types. However, in a given domain it is the case only for a limited number of semantic types.

One may argue that the term *invest(stock(efficient)* does not properly express the syntactic relation between *invest* and *efficient*. Furthermore, the representation of the query *"How to make an efficient investment in bonds?"* would motivate a knowledge engineer to choose an additional argument in the predicate *invest* to range over *investment types*. In addition, the Wh-argument (distinguishing *what...* from *when...* etc., questions) may be necessary to distinguish the queries *"when to invest"* from *"where to invest"*.

How many arguments should a predicate have? If we have a reasonable query, where more than one word needs to be substituted into a predicate, then its signature should include semantic types for both these words (constants or predicates). For example, when we have a query *"Can I deduct expenses on my house repair if I am head of a household?"* we conclude that predicate *deduct* needs to have at least two arguments which will range over the *deduction items* and the *category of deducting individual*. Additional Wh-arguments are required to distinguish *"How to report..."*, *"What to report ..."*, *"When to obtain..."*, etc., kind of questions, which we call the *focus of question*. Finally, we derive the following signature: *signature(deduct(xdeduct, xcategory, xquest, xscore))*. The last argument is reserved for the answer identification number and serves as a means to link two predicates.

A good example of the choice of arguments appears in the child psychology domain. The basic predicates are the psychological/behavioral states. The first argument of these predicates is substituted by the predicates for reaction of a teaching agent (e.g., a *parent*) to that state. It is very important to separate the *states* of the agents (*teachers, parents* and their *children*) from the reactions (actions), which are advised to follow these states. In the financial domains, the division of predicates into state and action is not essential; the former can be an attribute of the latter and vice versa. The query *"Should I appeal an audit decision if it requires me to pay more tax than I owe?"* can be represented as *audit (appeal(_), tax(pay(_), more))*. In the psychological domains, special arguments for states and actions are essential and improve the overall domain structure.

How many semantic types does a domain need? Usually, a knowledge engineer chooses the basic entities of a domain and derives the semantic types to separate the answers relying on these entities. The motivation for the basic entities to have the distinguishing semantic types is that if a sentence includes two or more of these predicates and a common attribute, a conflict will arise as to which predicate should be substituted. Additional predicates acquire new semantic types to avoid this kind of conflict.

For example, the predicate *file(xafile, xquest)* is the basis for derivation of the following eight meanings in accordance with the values of semantic type *xafile*: *disclosure, april15, on_time, safe, fast, electronic, tele, credit_card*. Note that these attributes are far from being uniform: they include the legal actions, specific dates, adverbs, ways of filing, and payment. A natural approach to semantic types of an action like *file* would be:

1. agent, performing filing.
2. subject of filing (document).
3. temporal attribute of filing (*on_time, delay*, etc.).
4. general attribute of filing (additional information on filing).

However, this approach is inefficient for encoding the SLFs in a real-world domain.

The number of documents that are supposed to be distinguished based on the attributes of a predicate is limited. Our experiments of the building of SLF domains show that less than a thousand documents are sufficient to cover a vertical domain for an average user. Therefore, the number of attributes to separate the answers for a predicate is far below a hundred.

A division of attributes in accordance with semantically uniform subsets would make the domain encoding rather inefficient. So we merge the semantic types proposed above into *xafile*, specific for the particular predicate. Furthermore, we add the specific semantic type *xquest* to distinguish between the answers for *"what is…"*, *"how to calculate…"*, *"how to respond…"*, *"where to report…"*, *"when to report…"*, etc. As a result, we get *signature(file(xafile, xquest))*, see the second row from the bottom in Table 4.3.

Let us consider the critical cases of the ratios between the number of semantic types and the number of predicates. Since we do not need to have the same semantic types for different predicates, each predicate can be assigned a unique semantic type. The more semantic types we choose for a domain, the easier it will be to avoid conflicts substituting a constant into either predicate if two predicates, each having the same semantic type, occurs in a query. At the same time, a high number of semantic types for a domain leads to the repetition of the same value for multiple semantic types. In turn, it implies the worsening of the structure of the domain classification tree (such as depicted in Fig. 4.5). The exhaustive search of argument substitution becomes less efficient.

If we minimize the number of semantic types and try to achieve a situation where a constant occurs only in a single semantic type, the number of substitution conflicts will rise dramatically. Our experiments in the creation of the suite of financial domains showed that it is impossible to avoid the repetition of a constant in a vertical SLF domain.

We present an extensive example of entities and their attributes to show that each semantic type contains the words with a high variety of meanings and different parts of speech (Table 4.3). It is evident that if one wanted to divide each semantic type into intuitively uniform components and create additional arguments correspondingly, then the instantiation would be very sparse and the coding be inefficient.

Table 4.3 Semantic types and predicates with arguments of these semantic types

Semantic_type([list of objects of this type])	Predicates with the argument of that type
xamoney([ira, home, protect, safe, creditor, back, IRS, retirement, fee, home_equity, mortgage, personal, cash, non_cash, property, carryover, recover, distribution, income, capital_gain, self_employment, donate, charity, growth, file, discharge, allocate, uncollect, report])	money, loan, lien, charity_contribution, cost, compensation, commission, lump_sum, foreign, stock, bond, CD, MMA, bankruptcy, funds, mutual_fund, saving, tip, alimony
xlegal([period, audit, collection, passive, involve, bankruptcy, resolve, notice, appeal, convert, eira, ira, tax_credit, advance_tax_credit, taxpayer, totalization, separation, eligible, education, clearance, depart, lost, adjusted_basis])	limitations, dispute, tax_court, proof, right, agreement, bluff, request, spy, institution, record
xatax([work, foreign, alien, convert, benefit, ira, resident, avoid, decrease, capital_gain, partnership, owe, over_withhold, social_security, medicare, form, estimate, sole_proprietor, contractor, wage, bank, report, calculate, business, interest, dividend, claim, test, home, non_deductible, abusive, collection])	tax, levy, affedavit, self_employment_tax, preparer, dependent, income_tax xcategory, property_tax, transfer_tax, stamp_tax, tax_shelter
xatransaction([deduct, deduction, property_tax, form, additional, return, pay, auditor, audit, collect, collection, bankruptcy, examination, accept, spouse, cash, problem, alien, income])	force, challenge, appeal, company, prevent, offer_in_compromise, disclose, relief, extension, complete, winning, resolve, depart, defer, search
xaira([open, flexibility, candidate, collateral, non_deductible, college, penalize, roth, annuity, group, spouse, marriage, mix, inheritance, death, widow, simple_plan, traditional, more, medical_insurance])	ira, educational_ira, rollover_ira
xasell([stock, property, hobby, stamp, coin, collection, home, long_term, short_term, car, computer, boat, medical_insurance, ira])	sell, trade, buy, installment_sell
xafile([disclosure, april15, on_time, safe, fast, electronic, tele, credit_card])	File
xincome([sell, installment_sell, trade, home, withdraw, bad_debt, determine, long_term, decrease, hobby, short_term, future, self_employment, net, distribution, current, commission, foreign, tax_deferred, nontaxable, award, property, less, illegal_income, debt, gift, meal, lodging, expense, severance_pay, lump_sum, benefit, pay, wage, winning, lottery, tip, alimony, farming, business, sole_proprietor, director, contractor, church, rent, fishing, partnership, interest, dividend, carrier, official]	capital_gain, capital_loss, gain, loss, taxable_earned_income, earned_income, gross_income, taxable_income, self_employment_income

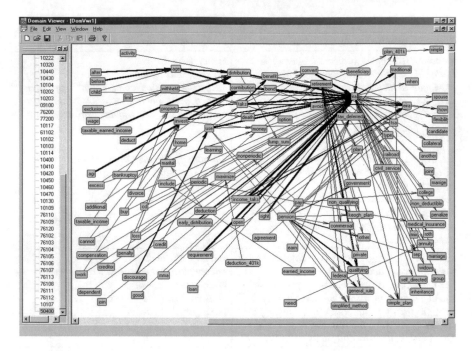

Fig. 4.5 UI for the domain visualization

4.5.3 Family of Summarized Logical Forms for an Answer

An SLF is intended to express the semantic link between a sequence (pair, triple) of entities, inherent to a given portion of information in an answer rather than to introduce a specific way of asking about it. So the number of SLFs is supposed to be significantly lower than the number of ways of asking about this answer. In other words, the following assertion holds:

# of SLFs < # of ways of asking with the same superficial semantics < # of syntactically different ways of asking

A construction of the family of SLFs for an answer combines the following goals:

(1) To represent the answer content from the perspective of potential querying;
(2) To provide the answer accessibility for as many ways of asking as possible.

Let us consider the following example for the answer #50400. A screen-shot of our domain visualization and restructuring tool is shown in Fig. 4.5 (Galitsky 2002). On the right, the classification graph is displayed; the nodes are assigned with predicates and edges and their mutual substitution to SLFs. The thicker the edge, the more times the different paths for the whole domain (here, IRA) contain this edge. In other words, the edge thickness visualizes how many times the corresponding sub-formula occurs in the totality of SLF for the whole domain. Evidently, the majority of edges converge into the predicate *ira(...)*.

On the left, the answers are enumerated. The paths for the given answer are shown in lighter gray. In particular, answer # 50400 has the paths (a single edge) *wage-withheld-tax*, *ira-railroad* and *excess-credit* (not shown). Judging by these entities, one can roughly reconstruct the meaning of the answer, encoded using the respective SLFs. Figure 4.6 contains the SLFs for this answer.

Frequently, encoding an answer by the SLF family loses the logical links between various issues, addressed in this answer. Since the expression of interconnections between the paragraphs in an answer is outside of the scope of formalization, the

---

```
pay(tax(social_security,_,_),50400):-do(50400).
tax(social_security,_,50400):-do(50400).
```
This is the answer about *social security tax*, in particular, about "paying" it.
```
information(social_security,50400):-do(50400), do(10240).
```
This SLF is less specific and involves another answer. So, if one is interested in the social security issues in general, both answers #50400 and #10240 are relevant (and useful). If the question just addresses social security in connection with the tax issues, then #50400 is supposed to be sufficient.
```
retirement(railroad,50400):-do(50400).
```
This is another narrow topic the answer raises.
```
wage(withheld(X,_),50400):-nonvar(X), X=tax(Y,_,_), nonvar(Y),
  Y=retirement(railroad,_), do(50400).
```
withholding tax from wage for retirement of railroad employees is the third topic of the answer #50400. The sequence of constraints is represented by the simplified formula
wage(withhold(tax(retirement(railroad))))   which cannot serve as a   SLF, because it should neither match, for example, with QR *wage(withhold(_))* nor with QR *wage(withhold(tax(_)))*, because the other unrelated answers will be initiated in addition. Therefore, built-in predicate `nonvar` is required to filter out the unrelated answers.
```
withheld(tax(X,_,_),50400):-nonvar(X),
  (X=retirement(railroad,_);X=social_security), do(50400),!.
```
This is similar way of asking about the same as above, but without mentioning "wage". If this SLF is satisfied, the search for other possibly related answers is terminated (by *cut*, '!').
```
excess(credit(_,_),50400):-do(50400).
```
Above is the third item this answer addresses.

Fig. 4.6 Enumeration of SLFs for the answer #50400

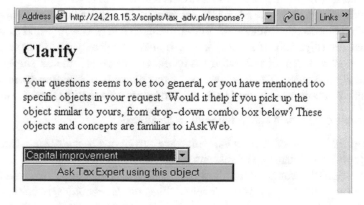

Fig. 4.7 Interactive clarification

members of the SLF family for an answer are not always formally correlated with each other.

SLF technique requires the answers to be present at the beginning stages of the domain development. If the answers are absent, then just an initial approximation of SLFs for a domain can be designed, because all the machinery of answer separation cannot be applied. Without the answers, SLFs do not have sufficient information to include the inter-SLF controls like *var/nonvar*, cuts, etc. Therefore, textual answers and not questions are the primary domain sources under the SLF approach.

4.5.4 Summarized Logical Forms for an Entity

How can an entity be represented by a family of SLFs? How do SLFs express the spectrum of meanings for an entity that is significant for a given domain? It is done by means of the attributes of the selected semantic type, substituted into the predicate for this entity. A constant, as well as a term with the outermost predicate of this semantic type, may serve the role of such attributes. Various meanings of an entity are expressed via combinations of the various parts of speech which form that semantic type. Usually, it is insufficient to use only the attributes of the same part of speech for an entity, even for a very narrow domain.

A user interface of the domain visualization/restructuring tool, the software for knowledge engineers, experts and domain testers is shown in Fig. 4.5. The highlighted answer #50400 is as follows:

> Most employers must withhold social security tax from your wages. Certain government employers (some federal, state, and local governments) do not have to withhold social security tax. If you work for a railroad employer, that employer must withhold… You can claim the excess as a credit against your income tax…

Enumeration of all SLFs for this answer is shown in Fig. 4.6.

The following needs to be taken into account to distinguish answers involving the same entity. One needs as many SLFs containing an entity as is required to separate these answers (Fig. 4.8). If there is a single answer, introducing or explaining an entity as well as semantically linking it to the other entities, then a single SLF is sufficient for a domain. There is a series of mechanisms of building more specific SLFs when multiple answers are characterized by the same entity (Figs. 4.7 and 4.8).

- Attributes of the main entity, inherent to an answer.

    - Logical links to other entities, which vary from one to another answer within a highlighted manifold of answers.
    - Question Wh-words, which allow distinguishing, for example, *where* and *when* answers (*Where to send tax returns? / When are tax refunds sent back?*). As we have mentioned, the special semantic type *xquest* is introduced to recognize these kinds of questions.

```
gain(X,_,_):-var(X),clarify([home,remainder_interest,       trade,       transfer,
installement_sale ]), !, fail.
```
If a query contains gain without parameters (or with unknown parameters), the customer is suggested to clarify (to choose from the drop-down combo box), Fig. 7. *Fail* is required to let the system know that clarification is provided instead of an answer. Cut eliminates the attempts to try the other clauses of summarized logical forms.
```
gain(sell(P,_),_,77114):- nonvar(P), sell(P,77114).
```
The line above reduces one SLF to another. Document about the gain on a sale is the same document, containing general information about sales. Argument of the predicate *sale* should be instantiated.
```
gain(sell(home(X,_,_),_),how(calculate,_),82103):-var(X), do(82103).
gain(sell(home(X,_,_),_),how(calculate,_),82107):- nonvar(X), home(X,_,82107).
```
If we speak about calculation of the gain for a sale of home, the situation depends on the attribute of this home.

If there is no attribute (var(X)), then the answer *To figure the gain (or loss) on the sale of your main home…* is initiated. If there is a specific home attribute (a word forming a specific meaning together with the entity *home*) such as *remainder_interest, improvement, inheritance, temporary, condominium, selling_price*, the answer is different.

In contrast to the previous SLF above, the *gain-sell-home is* reduced to *home* and not to *sell*; in addition, instantiated argument of *home* is required to obtain the answer about *Foreclosure or repossession / Ordinary income*.
```
gain(sell(home(_,_,_),_),_,82116).
```
The SLF above is required when we build a query representation with two or more conjunctive members with the common answer id (here, 82116). This SLF is design to be matched against one of these members; this match will not occur if another answer id will be generated (verified) by the previous (following) conjunctive member (in the query representation).

For example, the query *How to estimate the gain from sale of my house if I have used it for business* is represented as
```
  gain(sell(home(_,_,_),_),_,Id), business(use(home(_,_,_),_),_,Id).
```
The SLF for the second conjunctive member contains the reference to the answer (do(82116)) and the first conjunctive member introduces the constraint via the answer id (SLF above).
```
gain(sell(home(_,_,_),_),when,82121):- do(82121).
gain(sell(home(_,_,_),_),how(report,_),82122):do(82122),
do(82125).gain(sell(home(_,_,_),_),example,82125):- do(82125).
```
These SLFs introduce the difference between the questions *When to do something?* and *How to report something?*
```
gain(sell(home(X,_,_),_),_,82128):-nonvar(X), X=remainder_interest, do(82128).
```
The particular case of the family of SLF above for *remainder_interest*.
```
gain(trade(home(_,_,_),_),how(calculate,_),82106):-do(82106).
```
We have different answers for *sale* and *trade*, though their occurrence is symmetric.
```
gain(home(X,_,_),_,82107):- nonvar(X), home(X,_,82107).
```
Gain for a home is the same as *gain for a sale of home*, if the predicate *home* is instantiated.
```
gain(home(transfer,_,_),_,82108):-do(82108).
gain(home(spouse,_),_,82108):-do(82108).
```
This SLF is employed when the *home* is associated with *spouse*. Intuitively, it is hard to imagine the meaning for the pair *home-spouse*, which is indeed *transferring home to a spouse*. Since multiple synonyms may occur instead of *transferring*, we would like not to add an entity or attribute for this kind of action. It is motivated by the fact that we currently do not need to distinguish *to transfer, to gain, to change ownership* to separate answers about gain.

Fig. 4.8 Representation of an entity *gain*. See the examples of the queries for each answer in Fig. 4.9

- Defining one SLF via another SLF, adding/eliminating entities or even substituting foreign ones.
- Using the procedure "Clarify" to encourage a customer to replace with / add attribute already known to the system to obtain a more specific answer instead of the general one (Fig. 4.7).

How the SLF technique supports a dialog is shown in Fig. 4.7. A customer is asked to clarify the situation where the system understood the general entity in a query, but it is unable to capture a parameter for this entity. When a customer asks whether it

82103	How to figure gain (loss) on sale of my home?
82106	How to figure gain (loss) when I trade home?
82107	How to figure gain in the case of home foreclosure (repossession)?
82107	How to figure gain if I abandon my home?
82108	How to figure gain (loss) when I transfer home to spouse?
82116	How about ownership (use) test if I used my home for business (rental) purpose?
82121	Do I need to report gain (on my tax return) if I sold my house?
82122	How do I report gain on sale of my house?
82123	What is an installment sale?
82124	How to fill in tax return when I had installment sale of home?
82125	Give an example of reporting gain on selling a home?
77114	What should I do if I sell stamps from my collection?
45400	How can classify current losses to produce future gains?

Fig. 4.9 Examples of the queries involving the entity *gain* for each answer in Fig. 4.8

is possible to *deduct a roof repair*, the system understands that the question is about a *deduction* of some object unknown to it. Therefore, the system is suggesting a list of objects, which are supposed to be relevant or to cover as a category what has been asked.

4.5.5 Combining the Meanings of Entities

Throughout the text, we frequently use the phrase "meaning of an entity (keyword, atom)". In this Section, we present its definition in the SLF environment and compare it with speculations in linguistic semantics, where the "meaning" by itself can only be approached approximately, but the combination of meanings to form a new one is explored in detail. Evidently, construction of an SLF from the atoms is the combination of meaning of the corresponding words. This is one of the fundamental problems in linguistics, how to form a meaning of NL expression combining the meaning of its lexical units. In contrast to traditional linguistic studies (see for example, (Partee et al. 1990; Boguslavsky 1996), addressing the issues of the semantic sphere), the theory of SLFs provides a strict background for this issue because the meaning of an atom is relative and the role an atom serves is solely to separate the answers. Meaning in SLF theory has a "relative to domain" nature: the meaning of an atom is a set of answers this atom is in use to separate from the other answers. The meaning of a predicate (for an entity) is expressed via the set of all SLFs including this predicate and only this set. Roughly, meaning of a predicate is the set of these answers. A constant does not have a separate meaning by itself, it forms a meaning when it is substituted into a particular predicate, reducing the set of answers.

Other authors support using answers in a Q/A system to formally define the meaning of an NL expression. The Q/A setting allows defining the meaning of a sentence as being encoded in the questions it can answer. Semantic complexity of NL (Bunt et al 2014) can be defined accordingly based on Kolmogorov complexity, widely used in theoretical computer science.

Having Q as a set of questions, *Q-complexity* of a set of sentences *S* can be defined as the size of the simplest model scheme M_S (Turing machine, a logic program, UML specification, etc.) such that:

(1) For any sentence $s \in S$ its meaning is given by *M(s)*.
(2) *M(s)*correctly answers all questions about *s* contained in *Q*.

M can be thought of as a Turing machine that computes the meaning of the sentence in *S*. The size of this machine is measured as the product (# of states) × (# of symbols). To define the concept of *meaning automation*, we treat each question as a partial function from sentences *S* to a set of answers *A q: S→A*. Informally, *M* implements examination by *q* of each sentence for a piece of relevant information. Then, the meaning of a sentence (or respective ML expression) is determined by a set of answers (instead of its truth condition or denotation): ‖s‖ = { <q, q(s)> : q ∈ Q }. Now the *meaning automation* is the function *M: S × Q→A* which satisfies the constraint *M(s,q)=q(s)* of giving a correct answer to every question.

A *lemma* is a word that stands at the head of a definition in a dictionary. All the headwords in a dictionary are lemmas. A *lexeme* is a unit of meaning, and can be more than one word. A lexeme is the set of all forms that have the same meaning, while lemma refers to the particular form that is chosen by convention to represent the lexeme. For example, *get* is the lemma and *get, gets, getter* and *getting* are forms of the same lexeme.

We usually merge the forms of the same lexeme into a single entity predicate. To compensate for the lost part-of-speech information, we employ logical means to better analyze the context of the query. In other words, sacrificing knowledge about the form of the word, we establish its meaning by taking into account the other significant words in building the translation. The rules, i.e., how to involve the other syntactically dependent words in the determination of the meaning (translation) of the given one must be very flexible; therefore, the default logic comes into play (Chap. 6). For example, we represent the meaning of the words *tax* and *taxable* by the same entity *tax*, because there is no other entity (attribute) *E* in our domains such that *tax(E)* and *taxable(E)* (or *E(tax)* and *E(taxable)*) would be assigned to different answers.

Sometimes it is important to form distinguishing predicates for different parts of speech with the same root, for example, *deduct* and *deduction* in the Tax domain, where these words are sometimes associated with different answers. Entities *deduct* and *deduction* are so important for the Tax domain that there are multiple situations involving *deduct* (as an action of a participating agent) and *deduction* (as a complex relation between *expenses*), which must be distinguished. At the same time, for the rest of the answers *deduct* and *deduction* are fully synonymous, so the corresponding pairs of SLFs are required. In the course of developing an arbitrary domain, a knowledge engineer may need to split a predicate (entity) in accordance with different parts-of-speech or even forms of the same parts of speech, when a new set of answers with respective meanings requires separation. Note that *deductible* ⇒ (means) "appropriate for" *deduction* rather than *deductible* ⇒ "appropriate to" *deduct* in our domain, because semantically in our domain *possibly can be deducted*

⇒ *deduction* is closer to a relation then to an action: usually *deductible* is related to *expense*.

To derive a meaning, expressed by a query representation, we combine up to four entities (the number of attributes is limited to a lesser degree). Usually, a sentence with a higher number of entities can be split into two consecutive queries, and a user is encouraged to do so. To handle unreasonably complex sentences with more than four entities we would need to extend the number of arguments for predicates, which leads to rather inefficient and cumbersome domain coding. Obtained predicate expressions with more than four levels may mean that some syntactically separate entities are mistakenly involved, though the system may still perform robustly if some additional instantiation of arguments does not affect the choice of the answer. Indeed, building SLFs in a way independent from the eventual instantiation of arguments is a good style of domain design.

As an example, in Table 4.4 we present the NL expression, combined from the set of words *deduction, itemize, decrease, increase, reduce, business, expense, tax, income, property* and their derivatives. A family of meanings can be expressed on this basis; syntactic relationship between these words helps to build the QRs for each case. Based on the set of words we could derive a much larger set of combinations using various forms of these words. However, to separate the documents, it is sufficient for SLF technique to use just the normalized forms of words.

Table 4.4 shows how multiple meanings are derived given limited numbers of entities and their attributes. This analysis of the typical combinations of meanings of entities helps to choose the proper semantic types and an interdependence between the predicates. For example, to choose whether to substitute *deduct* into *tax* or vice versa, one needs to consider the meaning of the words *to deduct* as *to subtract* and their roles in domain taxonomy. If to assume that the role of *deduct* in the domain taxonomy is higher than that of *tax*, then the latter is substituted into the former: *deduct(_,tax(_))*. To act properly within the above set, the predicate *deduct* needs to have an active and a passive pair of arguments (*deduction* needs two arguments for the object of *deduction* and the attribute of *deduction*). Note that this table is simplified in terms of semantic types in respect to Table 4.3 for the totality of semantic types for the Tax domain.

A certain portion of subsets of our set represents a unique meaning in terms of potential answer separation (*reduce business expense, deduct tax from income,* amongst others). This is frequently true for the greater part of domains and their entities. In these cases, the meanings of NL expressions can be represented just by unordered enumerations of entities (keywords). Such the technique, developed here, allows an estimation of the portion of meanings (>50% in Tax domain) which is lost when a knowledge engineer uses keywords with synonyms and normalization for Q/A instead of SLF.

In the left hand column of Table 4.4, we present the expressions, consisting of the set of words above and reasonable in our domain. In the middle column, the reader can see the chains of respective syntactic structures (pairs or triads of *predicate-object* relation chains). Each row contains one or two of these chains. Synonym

Table 4.4 Deriving the meanings from the combination of entities and their attributes

N	Expression from a query	Fragments of syntactic representation for selected words	Query representation
1	*Decrease itemized deduction*	*decrease – deduction - itemize*	*deduction(decrease, itemize)*
2	*Deduct business expenses*	*deduct-expense- business*	*deduct(expense(_, business),_)*
3	*Itemize expenses*	*expense-itemize*	*expense(_,itemize)*
3	*Reduce business expenses*	*decrease- business- expense*	*expense(decrease, business)*
4	*Decrease tax deduction*	*decrease-deduction-tax*	*deduction(decrease, tax(_))*
5	*Decrease tax*	*decrease – tax*	*tax(decrease)*
6	*Deduct tax from income*	*deduct - tax, deduct - income*	*deduct(tax(_), income(_))*
7	*Deduct employee expenses from income*	*deduct –employee- expense, deduct – income*	*deduct(expense(employee), income(_))*
8	*Taxable income*	*tax – income*	*tax(income)*
9	*Deductible income*	*deduct- income*	*deduct(_, income(_))*
10	*Deduct property tax from income tax*	*deduct – tax - property, deduct – tax - income*	*deduct(tax(property), tax(income(_)))*
11	*How expensive is (to file) tax deduction*	*tax-deduction-expense*	*deduction(expense(_,_), tax(_))*
12	*Increase income because of increased deduction*	*income-increase, deduction-increase*	*deduction(increase, income(increase))*
13	*Deduction of income tax*	*deduction-tax-income*	*deduction(_, tax(income(_)))*
14	*Increase income by reducing expenses*	*increase-income, decrease-expense*	*income(increase), expense(reduce,_)*
15	*Increase income from property*	*increase - income, reduce - expense*	*income(increase, property)*

substitution is applied: for example, in this domain it is sufficient to suppose that *reduce ⟹ decrease* to separate the answers.

The right hand column presents the predicate language encoding of these expressions (QRs), where some of the words from our set are mapped into entities, expressed by the predicates, and the rest of the words are mapped into their arguments, which in turn can be predicates as well. For simplicity, some arguments are not shown.

Note that the order of the (normalized) words in the middle column follows the syntactic dependence between these words. However, the occurrence of the corresponding atoms in the right hand column is determined by the dependence between the entities for the whole domain. The latter is implied by the structure of a domain: how these entities contribute to the recognition of documents (answers) for this domain. Representation of predicates is more complex in a real-world domain; the additional semantic type *xquest* is sometimes required to distinguish answers. The reader should take into account that this sort of QRs is appropriate for SLF-domains and not for the fully formalized ones.

Our representation language L turns the entities with a wide spectrum of meanings in use into *metapredicates*. This way they are capable of expressing a higher number of meanings, having arbitrary formulas, which are constructed from other predicates and constants as their arguments. The reader may easily estimate that given the fixed number of predicates and constants, much higher number of meanings can be formed using arbitrary formulas instead of just having the constants as arguments. Besides, taking advantage of the expressive power of L, we do not intend to use its metalanguage deductive capabilities, which suffer from inference search (incompleteness) problems.

For our analysis, parts of speech tagging is required to obtain the links between the words; further coding loses this information as far as the context has been established. In that respect, our approach can be referred to as the reduction of the general syntactic analysis to keyword extraction. However, advanced deductive means are involved to compensate for the loss of syntactic information; the rules of semantic processing take advantage of knowledge of interconnection between the words in a query. Therefore, SLF approach is positioned between the full syntactic analysis and pure keyword extraction in terms of the query processing but, requires rather sophisticated semantic means to derive the query representation.

4.6 Matching Query Representation with SLF

Matching the query representation (QR) with a SLF is a key step of Q/A, where the recognized meaning of a question is compared with the pre-encoded meaning of an answer. The totality of SLFs establishes the axiomatic environment that serves as a basis to produce the inference link to a query. Those summarized logical forms involved in the resultant link are considered to be associated with the relevant answers. Matching the query representation (formal query representation) with SLFs is therefore the central operation, which follows NLP (Fig. 4.10).

Match of QR against SLF implements the following functionality:

(1) Answer generality/specificity control (Galitsky 1999). Since we match a predicate formula and not the list of keywords, we take advantage of the formula unification under logic programming. For instantiated QR, the system gives the specific answer, determined by the instantiation arguments; for uninstantiated QR, the system gives all answers for the QR predicates;

(2) Invariant properties in respect to morphological and syntactical specificity of query phrasing;

(3) Working in the non-uniformly encoded domain; some answers are assigned more complex SLFs (areas with higher completeness within a domain) and

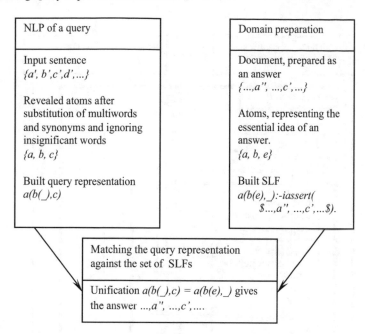

Fig. 4.10 The information flow under the SLF technique. The input query is subject to NLP (on the left). The document is subject to the procedure of SLF construction, performed during preparation of the Q/A domain. The essence of finding an answer is the unification of query representation with all SLFs of the domain. However, the unification of the standard PROLOG is insufficiently flexible to search for semantically close headers. a', a" are the synonyms that are mapped into atom *a*

    other answers are assigned with a single predicate formula (lower completeness sub-domains);

(4) SLFs have the full capability to express content. Some predicates may be synonymous in the context of a specific answer, but may have distinct meanings which must be separated to properly handle the other answers (for example, *cost()* and *expenses()* are synonyms in the context of *education*, but have different sense when one speaks about *deduction*).

    If there is no SLF that a given QR can be matched against, then a QR can be subject to *attenuation* that can lead to an approximately related answer in the case there is no exact one or the proper SLF is absent.

    Use of metapredicates in QR and SLF is not only implied by the language expressiveness requirements. Since QR~SLF match is based on the satisfaction call to QR (and not the direct unification) in logic programming, we match the metapredicate expression $p(q(s))$ rather than the conjunction $(p(q), q(s))$. The latter would be matched with two SLFs assigned to two different answers, which is not what we usually want. Therefore, we define p to range over arbitrary formulas, which specify its meaning. Note that the satisfaction call to $(p(q), q(s))$ will first match $p(q)$, and

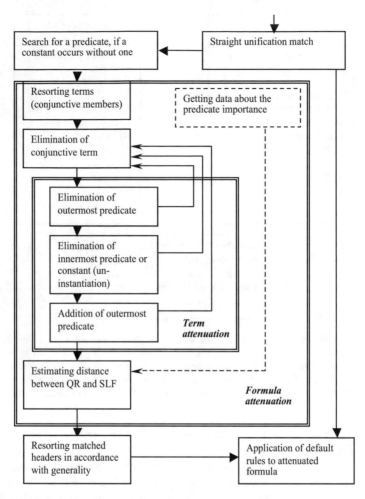

Fig. 4.11 The extended match

then match $q(s)$; matching results can depend on the order. QR~SLF match implementation based on a built-in satisfaction call is more computationally efficient and convenient than a unification with a set of expression we would need to explicitly program.

We proceed to the attenuation algorithm while matching QR against SLF. There are two ways to achieve a situation where each possible QR can be matched:

(1) SLFs are designed to include all well-written formulas of a given complexity (ignoring *var/nonvar* constraints), and, there is no approximation of QR. In this case, the problem of separation of answers arises because QR for general questions would create too many answers.
(2) SLFs are intact, and QR should be sequentially approximated by attenuated QRs till unification occurs.

QR attenuation procedure by means of predicate approx (_,_) is defined as the syntactic modification of formula, implying minimal semantic impact on its meaning. The following transformations are allowed (from weak to strong):

(1) Resorting of terms in the QR;
(2) Elimination of conjunctive terms in the QR.

For each of the terms, the following transformations are applied:

(1) Elimination of outer term (for example, *approx((..., p(q(a)),...) , (..., q(a),...)))*.
(2) Addition of outermost atom (for example, *approx((..., p(q(a)),...) , (..., q(a),...)))*.
(3) Replacement of constants (attributes) (for example, *approx((..., p(q(a)),...) , (..., p(q(b)),...)))*.
(4) Uninstantiation of inner constant (turning into a variable, for example, *approx((..., p(q(a)),...) , (..., p(q(A)),...)))*. This makes a difference with (2) for SLF clauses, using the metaprogramming tricks).

These transformations are obtained empirically based on the experiments in the domains with statistically significant numbers of SLFs. However, the attenuation procedure obeys the monotonicity property. This property can be formulated based on the numerical estimate of the transformation as a distance between QR candidates. A distance between a QR and an SLF is defined as the number of transformations applied to this QR to achieve unification with an SLF, deriving SLF^{approx} (by definition, $d(QR, SLF) = d(SLF, SLF^{approx})$). Note, that approximation of QR can match with multiple SLFs, and the following *monotonicity property* holds:

Propositon 6.1.1 *For any QR, if one obtains two approximations QR_1 and QR_2 such that $d(QR_1, SLF_1) < d(QR_2, SLF_2)$, then cardinality($\{SLF_1: QR_1 \sim SLF_1\}$) < cardinality($\{SLF_2: QR_2 \sim SLF_2\}$).*

Cardinality here is the number of elements in the set (of SLFs).

We sketch the Prolog implementations of some attenuation steps (Table 4.5 and Fig. 4.12). The metaprogramming technique is illustrated. For attenuation, a clause needs to be represented by a list, then some list modifications are applied, followed by the conversion back into a clause to verify its satisfaction. We comment on the *service* metapredicates (as opposed to the domain representation ones), which implement the attenuation. The service predicate *change_char* replaces a character to convert the implementation-specific representation of a variable into the representation of a canonical constant. *findall* is a built-in Prolog metapredicate, which obtains the list of values (the third argument) for an expression (the second argument) given its parameter (the first argument). The service predicate *member* verifies or yields a member of a list. *"Operator = .."* converts a term into a list.

The chart for extended match of the query representation with SLFs is shown in Fig. 4.11. In the case of a failure of the direct call to the QR, it is subject to sequential attenuation (the next step is applied if the current one does not deliver the match of

Table 4.5 Attenuation of terms

Eliminating outer atom	```modyTranslTerm(QueElim,Ques):-
	    QueElim=[Que], (Que=..[Extern, FullC|_]),
	                    var_const(FullV, FullC),
	call(FullV), Ques=[FullC].```

Substituting attribute	```modyTranslTerm(QueElim,Ques):- QueElim=[Que],
	(Que=..[Pred, FirstArg |Args]),
	    signature(Full), Full=..[Pred|ArgsFL],
	    clause_list(ArgsF, ArgsFL),
	    change_char('x','_', any(ArgsF), any(ArgsVC)),
	    clause_list(ArgsVC, ArgsV), FullV=..[Pred |
	ArgsV],
	    findall(ArgsV, call(FullV), ArgsVs),
	
	    findall(FArg, member(([FArg, _,_]), ArgsVs),
	Vs),
	    Vs=[First|_], Qu=..[Pred, First| Args],
	Ques=[Qu].```

Eliminate upper and enforcing uninstantiation of inner variable	```modyTranslTerm(QueElim,Ques):-
	    QueElim=[Que], (Que=..[Extern, RestOfFull|_]),
	      (RestOfFull=..[Pred, FirstArg |Args]),
	      signature(Full), Full=..[Pred|ArgsFL],
	      clause_list(ArgsF, ArgsFL),
	      change_char('x','_',any(ArgsF), any(ArgsVC)) ,
	      clause_list(ArgsVC, ArgsV), FullV=..[Pred |
	ArgsV],
	      findall((ArgsV), call(FullV), ArgsVs),
	
	      findall(FArg, member(([FArg, _,_]), ArgsVs),
	Vs),
	      Vs=[First|_], Qu=..[Pred, First| Args],
	QuesV=[Qu],
	      var_const(QuesV, Ques).```

Addition of outer predicate	```modyTranslTerm(QueElim,Ques):-
	    QueElim=[Que], (Que=..[Pred| OldArgs]),
	    signature(ExternFull),
	    ExternFull=..[ExternPred, Arg|ExternArgs],
	VRun=..[Arg, Values],
	    call(VRun), member(Pred, Values),
	NewExternC=..[ExternPred,Que|ExternArgs],
	    var_const(NewExternVC, NewExternC),
	    change_char('x','_', NewExternVC,NewExternV),
	
	var_var(NewExternV,NewExternVV),call(NewExternVV),
	    var_const(NewExternV,NewExternVCC).```

```
%Straight (no modification)
modyTranslFormula(QueElim,Ques):- var_list(Que,QueElim), var_var(Que,QueCheck),
call(QueCheck), Ques=QueElim,!.
Reversing of terms
modyTranslFormula(QueElim,Ques):- nrev(QueElim, QueR), var_list(Que,QueR),
var_var(Que,QueCheck), call(QueCheck), Ques=QueR ,!.

%Attenuating each term
modyTranslFormula(QueElim,Ques):-  len(QueElim,L),L>0,
  findall( NewTerm, ( member(Term, QueElim), var_const(TermV, Term),
  [!((call(TermV),NewTerm=Term ); ( [! modyTranslTerm([Term],[NewTerm])!]
  )) !]), QuesD), QuesD\=[], remove_duplicates(QuesD, Ques), len(Ques, L).
```

Fig. 4.12 Attenuation of formulas

the QR against the SLF). Attenuated unification match is followed by application of default rules, which are intended to eliminate the conjunctive members in despite that they may be satisfied. Extension of this unification is presented in Fig. 4.12.

4.6.1 Introduction to Metaprogramming Technique

We present four basic service predicates, which are required to implement the semantic processing of query representation (Table 4.6).

Transition from the strict to attenuated match is one of the issues of domain development strategy. At the *debug* stage, the approximate match is turned off such that the system can be verified to provide exact answers for all questions, designed a priori. Knowledge engineers are required to achieve the proper answering of all

Table 4.6 Service predicates of clause/list conversion

Predicate	Comments	Example
var_const	Converts all the occurrences of the variables in an expression into the canonical constants such that for each pair of occurrences of the same variables the resultant corresponding constants are equal. A formula is subject to syntactic transformation, when all arguments are actual or canonical constants	var_const(p(V1,V2,V1), p(v1,v2,v1))
var_var	Converts all the occurrences of the variables in an expression into the variables with other names such that for each pair of occurrences of the same variables the resultant corresponding constants are equal. This predicate is required to make a copy of a formula to check its satisfiability, not affecting the values of the variables of the original formula	var_var(p(V1,V2,V1), p(U1,U2,U1)), call(p(U1,U2,U1))
clause_ list	Converts a clause into a list	clause_list((p(V1),q(V2,V1)), [p(V1), q(V2,V1)]
change_ char	Replaces a character of a string representation of a formula. Particularly used to replace the initial character of a constant into '_' and back to convert it into variable (canonical constant)	change_char('x','_', any(xV1), any(_V1)). xV1-constant, _V1-variable.

questions by exact match. The extended match serves as a basis for the *release* version; when an unexpected question is tackled with the full power of approximation machinery.

4.6.2 Classification Graph of Q/A Domain

NL understanding problem can be reduced to a classification problem, if the cardinality of the document set is much lower than that of the set of all possible semantic representations of input queries (Galitsky et al 2015). The latter set of all semantic representations, which depends on the problem domain coverage by the particular semantic model, is in its turn much smaller than the original set of all possible queries in NL. The decision, whether a given domain with the particular semantic model falls into the *classification* or *understanding* model approach for Q/A, should be made given the ratio:

# of possible semantic representations : # of all documents,

(but not the ratio *# of possible NL questions : # all documents)*. If this ratio is low, then the Q/A domain is subject to *classification*. If it is of the magnitude of 100–1000, then the NL *understanding* approach should come into play, where an answer is obtained as a value of predicate's parameter.

Classification of a real Q/A domain is far from ideal; there are common sub-nodes for two different classification nodes of the graph (Fig. 4.13). In the other words, the classification graph cannot be reduced to a tree if we ignore the direction of edges.

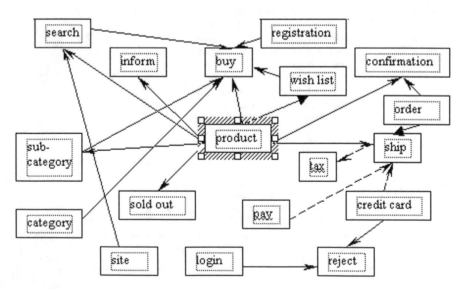

Fig. 4.13 The graph of domain predicates (e-commerce retailer domain)

In particular, there are common subclasses (*car, student*) for the classes *deduct* and *sale* (Fig. 4.14). Furthermore, there are links between the nodes for classes and sub-subclasses. There is a common sub-subclass *business* for the class *sale* and subclass *car*.

The arcs in the domain predicate graph (Fig. 4.13) denote SLFs where one predicate is substituted into another predicate. For example, the SLF *login(reject(_,_),_)* is associated with an answer to the question *"What should I do if my login is rejected?"*. Note that since there are multiple SLFs for an answer, there can be more than one node associated with this answer. For example, three SLFs: *pay(ship(_,_),_), credit_card(ship(free,_),_) and ship(tax(_,_),_)* are associated with the answer *"Shipping is always free"* for the questions: *"How to pay for delivery?"*, *"Can I use credit card to pay for shipping?"* and *"Is tax included in shipping?"*

Figure 4.14 introduces the classification graph for the fragment of a financial domain. The essential entities are chosen to divide the set of all answers *D* into three classes: about *deduction*, about *sale* and about *expenses*. The following subclasses are revealed: *car, student, home, filing*. Three of these subclasses are further divided into sub-subclasses *{business, owner},{loan},{repair, rent, property_tax}* correspondingly.

The nodes of the graph are assigned by a predicate; there is a single node for each predicate. The directed edge denotes the substitution of one predicate into another (arrow side). A given SLF is associated with a sub-graph of classification graph; in particular, for unary predicates, the SLF is associated with a path of the classification graph. For example, the SLF *deduct(car(business()))* is associated with the path *deduct-car-business* of the classification graph (shown as a bold dotted line). The answer is assigned by two SLFs: *deduct(car(business()))* and *car(business())*.

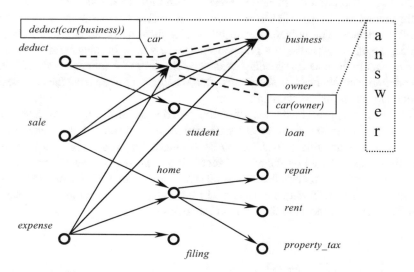

Fig. 4.14 Classification graph for the fragment of a financial domain

Note that the division of entities into class-determining ones reflects neither parts of speech nor general meaning of the words. Inversely, the position of an entity p in the classification tree is determined by the semantic role p plays to separate its answer from others, given a subset of documents p occurs in SLFs for.

We address the important issue of whether the predicates for a verb or a noun should be at a higher level in a domain classification. It actually depends on the ratio

other_nouns : other_verbs,
where *other_nouns* $=\{V \mid noun(V)\}$ *and other_verbs* $=\{N \mid verb(N)\}$.

Naturally, the number of predicates $\#p$ is lower than the number of the constants or predicates the arguments of p range over. In other words, the deeper the level of classification, the larger the number of nodes for the classification graph. For example, if a domain contains a few actions with products and thousands of these products, the actions will range over products. On the other hand, if a manifold of operations can be applied to a small number of products, the situation is reversed. The predicates or objects for actions will be substituted into the predicates for product names.

Our SLF technique introduces a hierarchical structure on the portions of data for a domain. The hierarchical structure of the domain is expressed via the set of links between a predicate and its argument. Let us pose a problem of document classification based on SLFs. To divide a totality of all documents of a domain into classes, we choose the class-determining predicates. Their arguments will be the other predicates and objects which determine subclasses. Those subclasses, which are assigned by predicates, are split into sub-subclasses, and so forth. The terminal classification nodes are assigned by objects (not predicates).

Achieving certain classification criteria determines the division of the set of all terms (keywords) into predicates and objects, as well as the hierarchy within the set of all predicates. The universal criterion of classification of an arbitrary nature is the degree of the classification graph similarity to a tree. In other words, different classes should have as few subclasses as possible, different subclasses should have the minimum number of sub-subclasses, etc. (see Fig. 4.15 to observe the complexity of domain graph for Tax domain).

In the SLF approach, the classification criteria match the question answering quality: the better the structure of classification, the "cleaner" the answer (in the sense of fewer documents from a foreign sub-unit for an answer). To prepare a domain for Q/A, based on the answer recognition, the set of answer documents is subject to hierarchical classification. A classification of an arbitrary nature is based on the chosen set of features of objects. In our case, we choose the most essential entities of the documents to divide them into classes.

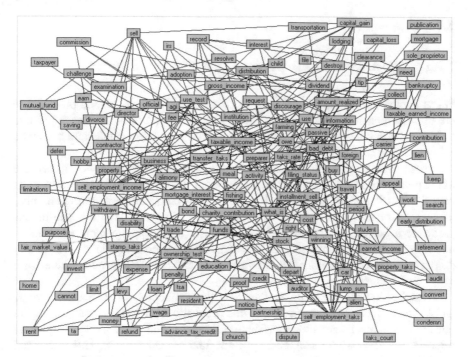

Fig. 4.15 Visualization of the domain taxonomy (personal income tax). The entities are randomly distributed to show the complexity of interconnections in accordance to existing summarized logical forms. For example, edge *audit-appeal* visualizes the summarized logical form ...*(audit (appeal(...,....),...),...*

For example, we divide the Internet retailer domain into documents about products, about order processing, about shipping, and about navigating the site. This occurs based on the predicates *product(_), order(_), ship(_), site(_).* Evidently other divisions are possible, they are based on an alternative choice of the essential entities. Each class can be divided into subclasses, which are determined by a predicate or an object. For example, the documents about shipping are divided into documents about returns, about the geography of shipping, about length of shipping, about the duration of shipping, and about the price of shipping. The SLFs for these documents are: *ship(return(_)), ship(overseas), ship(duration), ship(pay(_)).* Subclasses are subject to further division into sub-subclasses, if they are determined by a predicate (not by an object). The subclass of documents about shipping is further divided into sub-subclasses.

Our approach to classification graphs can be considered from the perspective of conceptual clustering. It is an unsupervised learning procedure, which builds a discrimination net given a set of input parameters. A *discrimination net* is a mechanism for allocating an input data item to its class by applying successive tests for different individual predicates. The terminal nodes of the net represent the results to be returned for the various possible sequences of predicates.

4.7 SLF Space

4.7.1 The Measure of Importance for Domain Entities

When coding a domain, it is necessary to distinguish the role of each predicate in the domain representation. When we extend the match procedure between QR and SLF, elimination/addition of a predicate into a formula needs to take into account a *relative importance* of a predicate.

To estimate the importance, we compute the symmetric difference of occurrence of the predicates in a SLF family of the pairs of answers and then perform averaging over the set of all pairs. Intuitively, if a predicate is associated with a small number of answers or occurs in the SLFs for almost every answer, then the role of this predicate in answer classification (and therefore in the domain representation) is not very significant. Conversely, if an occurrence of a predicate in an SLF family dramatically affects the assigned answers, this predicate is rather important for a given Q/A domain.

Therefore for each predicate, we calculate the number of pairs of answers, where an SLF family for one answer contains this predicate and that of the second answer does not. The results are shown in Table 4.7 where each predicate is assigned an importance index. As we see, the most important are entities *distribution, tax* and *contribution*. This means that if we analyze a query for the occurrence of each of these words, we will filter out approximately half of the set of answers as inappropriate. If we use the terms from the lower right part of the table (minimum importance), the absence of these predicates would mean that we have crossed out just an insignificant portion of the set of answers.

Table 4.7 Entities and their importance

distribution	780	sep	222	loan	150	wage	76
tax	726	deduct	222	invest	150	rollover_ira	76
contribution	670	widow	150	inheritance	150	rmd	76
age	670	tax_deferred	150	flexibility	150	railroad	76
convert	490	simplified_method	150	earned_income	150	periodic	76
requirement	426	self_directed	150	discourage	150	penalize	76
income_tax	426	roth	150	death	150	other	76
educational ira	426	qualifying	150	collateral	150	option	76
early_distribution	360	property	150	child	150	nonperiodic	76

4.7.2 SLF as Approximation Means

One of the important features of the SLF approach is that it approximates the meaning of an answer to make efficient and plausible its match with the question via QR. Modeling the representation of answer meanings by SLFs, we use the term *approximation* to show the reduction from the fully formalized answer (assuming it is possible) to its essential content, represented by means of an SLF. We use the idealization of the *fully formalized answer* as the potential capability of representing each sentence and interlinks between the terms for the whole answer in our formal language L.

More precisely, *approximation* is the *transformation of a set of formulas* (SLFs) for an answer into another set, *ignoring a given predicate*. This transformation follows the intuitive procedure of declaring this predicate *unknown*. The approximation transformation therefore eliminates each occurrence of this predicate in the set of SLFs for an answer. Modeling the process of approximation is important to understand the mechanism of SLF creation and to properly handle the issues of domain update.

Syntactically, if the predicate to be eliminated is the innermost in a formula, it is replaced by a variable; more than a single occurrence is replaced by the same variable. For expression $p(q(t(...)))$, we obtain

$p(Q, t(...))$, so the arity of p is decreased by one. The new variable is the same for each occurrence of q in a formula.

To sum up, we write the definition and properties of our approximation operator $approx_q$ which eliminates q:

(1) $approx_q(q(...))$ gives an empty formula (the formula is eliminated from the set);
(2) $approx_q(p(q(...)))= p(Q)$;
(3) $approx_q(p(q(t(...))))= p(Q,t(...))$;

Generally speaking, approximation is not commutative:

(4) $approx_q(approx_p(\varphi)) \neq approx_p(approx_q(\varphi))$.

Ideally, one would want to have the following feature for the approximation: if a QR matches with a SLF, then this QR will match with any prototype of the SLF under approximation (totality of SLF_1 which can be approximated into SLF):

5) *Approximation monotonicity:*
   $(QR \approx SLF) \Longrightarrow (\forall p (QR \approx SLF_1 \& approx_p (SLF_1, SLF)))$.

Since this does not always hold, we do need to apply approximation to the fully formalized answer representation: when we build it, the focus is on more complete representation of the content rather than on the representation appropriate for Q/A. Therefore, the formal approximations are intended to convert the former into the latter. From the Q/A perspective, approximation of the set of SLFs is actually an improvement of it in terms of decreasing the ambiguity of $QR \approx SLF$ match in the case of full formalization.

(6) As a property, complimentary to approximation monotonicity, we consider the
     separation monotonicity property:
     $((QR \approx SLF)$ & $\neg(QR_1 \approx SLF)) \Longrightarrow (\forall p(QR \approx SLF_1)$ & $approx_p(SLF_1, SLF$
     $)$ & $\neg(QR_1 \approx SLF_1))$.

This property states that if two SLFs are separated by any query representation
then all the approximation prototypes are separated by this query representation as
well.

Furthermore, extended match for QR brings in additional constraints on the
distance conservation under approximation:

(7) *Distance monotonicity* property:
     $(d(QR, SLF) < d(QR_1, SLF)) \Longrightarrow$

$$(\forall p (approx_p(SLF_1, SLF) \& (d(QR, SLF_1) < d(QR_1, SLF_1)))).$$

In a real domain these properties are desirable but not always achievable. For a
domain and a given answer the set of SLFs can be optimized, with respect to the
portion of knowledge formalization of an answer.

Proposition 7.2.1 *If conditions (1)–(7) above hold for a domain, then there exists
an optimal sequence of approximation operators (of the predicates to be eliminated)
for this domain.*

Formal approximation of a set of summarized logical forms can be performed via
anti-unification of formulas in logic programming (Pfenning 1991, Amiridze and
Kutsia 2018). Similarity of two formulas in a domain (particularly two SLFs) can
be expressed as an anti-unification of two formulas (not a numerical value). Anti-
unification of two SLFs is the least general formula that can be instantiated into
these two SLFs. We present a declarative definition for the procedure of forming the
anti-unification of two summarized logical forms (ignoring the body of the clause of
an SLF), Fig. 4.16. We refer the reader to (Vo and Popescu 2016, 2019) proposal for
a four-layer system that leverages word alignment, sentence structure and semantic
word similarities for relevance assessment.

4.7.3 Approximation Subgraph

We have introduced the approximation operation on the set of SLF for a domain.
Since the classification graph fully represents the domain structure (interconnection
between its entities), it seems natural to define a domain approximation as a graph
reduction operation.

The approximation operation is applied to a *node*; it is identified with all nodes
it has a directed edge to. This operation is not allowed to distort the original paths
except ones consisting solely of the edges to be eliminated. Only answers which are
assigned to the latter edges can become inaccessible as a result of approximation.

```
antiUnify(T1, T2, Tv):- var_const( (T1,T2), (T1c,T2c)),
   antiUnifyConst(T1c, T2c, T),
                 %converts formulas' variables into canonical constants
   var_const(Tv, T).
antiUnifyConst(Term1, Term2,Term):-
   Term1=..[Pred0|Args1],   len(Args1, LA),
   Term2=..[Pred0|Args2],   len(Args2, LA),
   findall( Var, ( member(N, [0,1,2,3,4,5,6,7 ]),
   [! sublist(N, 1, Args1, [VarN1]), %loop through arguments
   sublist(N, 1, Args2, [VarN2]),
   string_term(Nstr, N), VarN1=..[Name|_],
   string_term(Tstr, Name),concat(['z',Nstr,Tstr],ZNstr),
   atom_string(ZN, ZNstr) !],
   %building a canonical argument to create a variable as a result of anti-unification
                   ifthenelse( not (VarN1=VarN2),
                      ifthenelse((  VarN1=..[Pred,_|_],VarN2=..[Pred,_|_]),
       ifthenelse( antiUnifyConst(VarN1, VarN2, VarN12),
            %  going deeper into a subterm when an argument is a term
                      (Var=VarN12  ),
              Var=ZNstr) ),
   %  various cases: variable vs variable, or vs constant, or constant vs constant
                      Var=ZNstr),Var=VarN1)
          ), Args),              Term=..[Pred0|Args].
```

Fig. 4.16 Anti-unification algorithm

The operation of graph modification $gapprox^n$ that acts on the node n of graph G gives G^n as a result. Acting on a path $path$ such that n belongs to it, $gapprox^n(path)$ gives the resultant path.

$gapprox^n: (n, G) \rightarrow (n', G^n), n \rightarrow n',$
$\forall n_1\ edge(n_1, n)\ n_1 \rightarrow n',$
$\forall path_1 \forall path_2 (\ gapprox^n(path_1\ )=gapprox^n\ (path_2\ ) \implies \exists\ n_1 \exists\ n_2\ (path_1 = edge(n_1, n)\ \&\ path_2 = edge(n_2, n)))$

The graph monotonicity property looks as follows:

$\{SLFs\}$	$\rightarrow$	G	
$\downarrow$		$\downarrow\ gapprox^n_1, gapprox^n_2,...$	
$\{SLFs^{approx}\}$	$\rightarrow$	G-subgraph	

An approximate domain classification graph (Fig. 4.17) is obtained as a reduction by means of eliminating the predicate $car()$. The node car of the original graph (Fig. 4.14) is merged with either node it has a directed edge to (here for example, the node for the constant $business$). The ends of all edges, directed to the node to be eliminated, are transferred forward along the edge that is coming out from the node to be eliminated. Assuming there is a single such node, it is designed in a way to retain the original paths. For example, the path $sale$-car-$owner$ is reduced to the single-edge path $sale(W, business)$. The new argument appears to represent the "unknown" predicate we have just eliminated.

This chart is a commutative diagram: for any domain classification graph and its approximation subgraph there is a corresponding pair of the SLF sets, one of which is an approximation of the other. The same approximation subgraph can be obtained in one of two ways:

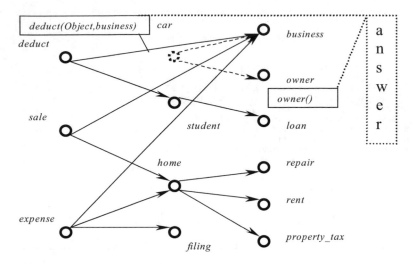

Fig. 4.17 The domain classification graph

(1) Building the classification graph, followed by the construction of its approximation subgraph, or
(2) First deriving approximation SLF set and then building its classification graph.

   If retraction of a node eliminates the single-edge path which is assigned with an answer, this answer (possibly ambiguously) becomes assigned to another path ending in the merged node. Note that the node elimination operation can lead to a non-deterministic merge of answers.

4.7.4 Modifying SLF Domain to Achieve Optimality

In this section, we focus on domain optimality and achieve it by means of SLF. Cleary, the less non-adequate information an average query delivers, the better the Q/A system is. A quality of domain representation can be measured by the minimal number of SLFs delivering the marginally related answers. The following should be stated to clarify the domain *quality criterion*:

(1) We fix the overall domain knowledge and vary our access to it. For SLF domains we keep the totality of textual documents, but can vary their division into answers to provide the most accurate ones.
(2) Furthermore, we fix the formalization degree: all the facts of the under-threshold importance are ignored; only the combinations of important facts to form SLFs are varied. In addition, we fix the QR-SLF matching machinery.
(3) The definition of optimality criteria is based on the totality of formalized (not NL) queries, which is defined as the set of well-written formulas in the language

L (derived from the original set of keywords K). Note that we distinguish between instantiated and non-instantiated formulas since they can form different SLFs.

Generally speaking, increasing the answer size would improve the probability of providing the correct answer but decrease the answer precision: the lower portion of an answer becomes relevant. We call the corresponding parameters answer *accessibility a* and *precision p*. In addition, separation criterion s characterizes the difference between the answers, expressed via SLFs: how many queries deliver both answers.

The accessibility of an answer is defined as a number of queries delivering this answer, normalized to the total number of queries. The domain accessibility is then derived by averaging through the accessibilities of all answers: $a=<\#q_a/\#q>_{answers}$. This criterion tends to increase the number of SLFs per answer and is in conflict with the *separation* criterion. The latter is defined for a domain as a portion of "ambiguous" queries which are matched with more than one SLF from different answers. Note that frequently the drop of separation is a desired property for general questions. Numerically, $s=<1- \#ambiguous\ q>_{answers}$.

The precision of an answer for a query is based on the number q_a of other queries that deliver this answer. Generally speaking, precision p is determined by the number of SLFs per answer (the more topics an answer contains, the more SLFs it will be assigned to and therefore the less precise it will be). For a domain, the precision definition is based on the averaging through all queries: $p = 1/(1 + <q_a>_{answers})$. The reader can verify the boundary values when we have a single answer per individual query $(p=1, a\rightarrow0, s=1)$ or, a single answer $(p\rightarrow0, a\rightarrow1, s\rightarrow0)$. Now we can define the domain optimality as $pas \rightarrow max$. To compare two domains when different portions of q can be matched, one needs to introduce additional criteria of domain completeness: $c =<\#q_{match}/\#q>_{answers}$, where $\#q_{match}$ is the successfully answered portion of the total number of real-world questions $\#q$ per answer. Then $pasc\rightarrow max$ would serve as the optimality criterion, if one were allowed to add new SLFs.

Therefore, one uses pas-optimality to estimate the results of the modification of a domain when taken separately, and $pasc$-optimality to compare the quality of different domains.

The following domain modifications affect the optimality criteria pas:

(1) Dividing an answer a_{div} into two answers, a_1 and a_2, based on the division of the SLF family into two sub-families. The domain precision will increase because the average number of queries per answer decreases. Averaged a decreases by $((a_{div}/\#answer)- (a_{div}/(\#answer+1)))$. s can decrease if there are queries which were addressing the SLF corresponding to a_1 and a_2

(2) Merging of answers has the inverse effect on the values of optimality criteria.

(3) Merging or splitting SLFs for an answer does not affect the optimality.

4) Adding SLFs to an answer will directly affect c criteria, decrease p and s criteria, and increase a.

(5) Adding a more specific new answer to an existing (general) answer, splitting existing SLFs, affects optimality similarly to (1) except that p increases more strongly.

(6) Replacement of an existing (more general) answer by a new specific answer, merging and/or eliminating existing SLFs increases p more strongly than (5), increases s and decreases a more strongly than (1).
(7) Operations, which are the inverse to (5) and (6) affect the optimality correspondingly.
(8) Approximating summarized logical forms increases a and decreases s.

Each of the operations (1), (2) and (4)–(8) could increase or decrease pas, so one needs to explicitly estimate the parameters to choose domain modification properly. Optimality criterion can be in conflict with some additional domain-specific requirements (for example, how the answers should be formed), so the resultant optimality may have more complex expression or it might be hard to estimate it.

We proceed to the operations accompanying the process of achieving domain optimality.

(a) Operations while *adding new answers:*

   (1) Introduction of a predicate;
   (2) Introduction of a new constant;
   (3) Adding a constant to a semantic type.

(b) Operations while *domain re-evaluation.* If a term is not required to distinguish between the current set of answers, this term is eliminated. There are two methods of elimination with respect to information loss:

   • Eliminating a predicate by approximation;
   • Eliminating a predicate by expressing it via the other predicates in all the SLFs it occurs in.

(c) Solving *equations with respect to a predicate.* A *meaning* of a predicate is its capability to separate answers based on the questions, having the families of SLFs for each answer fixed. For knowledge representation in a Q/A domain *expression* of a predicate means the following: which words should replace the given one to conserve the capability of accessing the same number of answers. We need to obtain the expression formula for a predicate to reconstruct the set of words which need to occur in a query instead of the word for a predicate being hypothetically eliminated. Required machinery is a subject of our future study.

4.7.5   Conceptual Graph and Semantic Network

Knowledge representation under the SLF technique is strongly correlated with the conceptual graph formalism, which is a variant of semantic networks (Sowa 1992). A conceptual graph is a structure of concepts and conceptual relations linked with edges, where every edge connects a conceptual relation to an entity. The types of the entities and these relations form entity-hierarchies and relation-hierarchies (lattices).

A graph can be embedded in another graph by means of the context mechanism. The default existential quantifier and the possibility to negate contexts give conceptual graphs an equivalent expressiveness power to classical predicate calculus. Concept graphs have definitional mechanisms that can support extensions to the core in a controlled, systematic way. Because conceptual graphs can be mapped to classical predicate calculus (or order-sorted logic), they can be seen as a graphical notation for logic. However, it is the topological nature of formulas that conceptual grammar makes clear, and which can be exploited in reasoning and processing. Concept graphs are intuitive because they allow humans to exploit their powerful pattern matching abilities to a larger extent than does the classical notation. Therefore, conceptual graphs are particularly useful for the interchange of knowledge between humans and computers. Conceptual graphs can be viewed as an attempt to build a unified modeling language and reasoning tool. They can model data, functional and dynamic aspects of systems. They form a unified diagrammatic tool that can integrate entity-relationship diagrams, finite-state machines, Petri nets and dataflow diagrams. Conceptual graphs have found wide application in systems for IR, database design, expert systems, conceptual modeling and NLP. SLF technique is based on a special reduced version of conceptual graphs.

Semantic networks (Lehmann 1992) are a means for the large scale organization of knowledge emphasizing the *multiple association of individual entities* (which is the case in SLF technique). Concepts, objects, entities, etc., are represented as nodes in a linked graph and relationships between these are represented as labeled edges. The range of possible network structure types is very wide. Semantic networks should be properly based on definitions of this network structure, i.e., the syntax and semantics of nodes and links and their configurations. Also important are the definitions of network operations, in particular, syntax and semantics of node-node transitions. Semantic networks have been found to be an attractive descriptive means, but the systematic graph processing algorithm (for selective writing or reading at nodes) is hard to construct. The emphasis on concept association introduces difficulties in representing any partitioning or grouping of net elements, for example to represent quantified propositions, clusters of similar entities, etc. There are means of enhancing the organizational and expressive power of semantic nets through the grouping of nodes and links, which may occur in one or more "spaces". These spaces in turn may be bundled into the higher-level super-spaces, which could be explored autonomously and structured hierarchically. The efficient encoding of logical statements involving connectives and quantifiers is an important motivation for such partitioning, but its mechanism is sufficiently correct, general and powerful to support the dynamic representation of a wide range of language and domain representations. The reader should be aware of the difference between the domain classification graph and the semantic network for domain entities.

4.8 Handling Situations with a Lack of a Direct Answer

In Sect. 4.6, we presented the mechanism of attenuation of a query representation when there is no direct answer (no SLF can match it). Attenuation of query representation serves as the main mechanism of the search for an appropriate answer in case the direct answer is absent in the system (Fig. 4.18). In the bottom left corner, reduction of the attenuation procedure (Fig. 4.10) is depicted.

If no entity is found in a query, the exact answer is not expected but a close one can be obtained if the system finds a predicate, which is satisfied, instantiated by a constant from the input query (top middle units). In particular, *what_is* predicate is verified to be satisfied with that constant. If there are too many predicates that can be potentially satisfied with the attributes from a query, it is very unlikely that a proper one will be chosen. Therefore, it is preferable for the system to give no answer or try a keyword search, especially in multiagent environment (Galitsky and Pampapathi

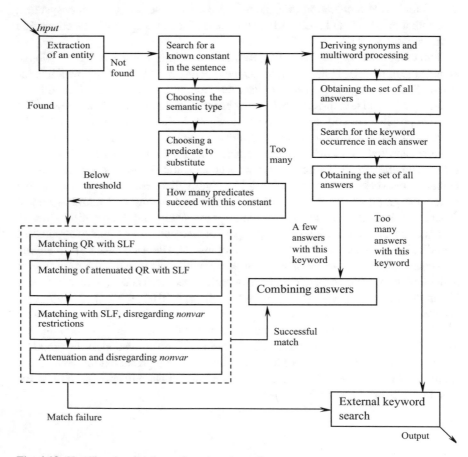

Fig. 4.18 Handling the situations where there is no direct answer

2005), where another agent may have an answer with a higher confidence level. For each identified constant, we look for all the predicates and try to substitute that constant into each argument of those predicates with the proper semantic type. As an output, we merge the answers for each predicate if their total number is below a threshold.

If no potential constant has been extracted from a query the *internal keyword search* (through the stored answers) is launched. Only the keywords, found in just a few answers, are considered adequate, and these answers form an output one. An external keyword search is initiated if the Q/A agents have failed to:

(1) Satisfy a query representation by existing SLFs;
(2) Attenuate a query representation to satisfy, not exceeding a threshold number of answers;
(3) Find a predicate to form a query representation with a constant which occurs in a query, not exceeding the number above;
4) Run an internal keyword search, not exceeding the number above.

This enumeration presents the cases with decreasing confidence level (expected relevance) of the resultant answers.

The *combining answers* unit merges the answers, which are yielded either by multiple predicates found for a constant or, multiple occurrences of a constant in the stored answers.

4.9 A Sample Run

We present the log of answering a relatively complex query *"Should I appeal if the audit requires me to pay more tax than I owe?"*. In addition to the domain-independent semantic analysis, transformation *applyDefault* eliminates from the query representation the least instantiated terms. The predicate *audit(_,_)* is eliminated because it would initiate all answers about the *audit* but it should not, because the expected answer is about *appeal*, not *audit*. Indeed, the word combination [*pay,more,tax,than,owe*] expresses the central meaning using the term *pay(tax(owe(more,_),_,_),_,_)*. If we do not eliminate *audit(_,_)*, too many foreign answers would appear. The variables (e.g., *_39AC*) and respective constants (e.g., *z339AC*) are shown in accordance to a specific Prolog implementation.

In the log of the QR processing steps Fig. 4.19, identifying the *signatures* of predicates is followed by the substitution verification, implemented by the service predicate *related_to_check*. Constant substitution is followed by the metapredicate substitution, and the results are subject to elimination of the (most) uninstantiated predicate, if the QR is a conjunction. The resultant QR cannot be satisfied by a SLF, so attenuation is required. The term *appeal(more,z36324)* requires the addition of an external predicate; *more* is substituted into *appeal* because it belongs to the semantic type *xatransaction*.

```
[should,i,appeal,if,the,audit,requires,to,pay,more,tax,than,i,owe]
% Initial query
replace_abbrev([should,i,appeal,if,the,audit,requires,to,pay,more,tax,than,i,ow
e])   % synonyms/multiword substitution
signature(appeal(xatransaction,xscore))    %        signature for appeal
related_to_check(appeal,more) % more is substituted into appeal
signature(audit(xcontrol,xscore))
signature(pay(xmoneyaction,xcategory,xscore))
related_to_check(pay,tax)      %     tax is substituted into pay
signature(tax(xatax,xcategory,xscore))
related_to_check(tax,owe)      %     owe is substituted into tax
signature(owe(xdebt,xscore))
related_to_check(owe,more)     %    more is substituted into owe
[appeal(more,_33908),audit(_33928,_3393C),pay(tax,_33958,_3396C),
tax(owe,_33990,_339AC), owe(more,_339D0)]
%      flat (before substitution into metapredicate) query representation
metapred_subst([appeal(more,z33908),audit(z33928,z3393C),pay(tax(owe(more,z339D
0),z33990,z339AC),z33958,z3396C)])       % the results of substitution into the metapredicates
applyDefault([appeal(more,z33908),audit(z33928,z3393C),pay(tax(owe(more,z339D0)
,z33990,z339AC),
z33958,z3396C)],[appeal(more,z33908),pay(tax(owe(more,z339D0),z33990,z339AC),z3
3958,z3396C)])
   % Predicate audit is eliminated because it is uninstantiated.
   % It is indeed semantically redundant.
addition of external predicate :
modyTranslTerm([appeal(more,z33908)],[right(appeal(more,z36324),z36344)])
attenuate each term:
modyTranslFormula([appeal(more,z33908),pay(tax(owe(more,z339D0),z33990,z39AC),z
33958,z3396C],
[right(appeal(more,z36324),z36344),pay(tax(owe(more,z339D0),z33990,z339AC),z339
58,z3396C)])
%Neither straight nor reordered call succeeded, so attenuation was initiated
```

For various reasons, you may not be able to pay your federal individual income tax in full. Do **not** delay filing your tax return because you are unable to pay in full. If your tax return is not filed on time, you may have to pay a late filing penalty, in addition to a late payment penalty, and interest…

It is important not to ignore an IRS notice. If you neglect or refuse to make payment or other arrangements to satisfy your obligation in full, we may take enforced collection action (filing a notice of federal tax lien, serving a notice of levy or offset of a tax refund). When doubt exists as to whether you owe the liability or whether you have the ability to make full payment on the amount owed, the IRS may be able to settle your unpaid tax balance for less than the amount owed. See Topic 204, Offers in Compromise, for more information. If you would like more information on "your rights as a taxpayer," how to make arrangements to pay your bill, enter into an installment agreement, and to inquire about the implications when you take no action to pay, download Publication 594, and … etc. The IRS has an appeals system for people who do not agree with the results of an examination of their tax returns or with other adjustments to their tax liability. For further information on the appeals process and information on …. Publication 1660 This publication explains … etc.

Fig. 4.19 A log of Q/A session and delivered answers

A combination *right-appeal* has not been set at indexing time, therefore, the system needs to compensate for the lack of the necessary prepared SLF. The predicate *right* comes into play to form the satisfied term *right(appeal(more,z36324),z36344)])*.

We show the answers the resultant QR delivers. We see that the first conjunctive member (which has actually been attenuated) delivered a more relevant answer than the second conjunctive member, *pay(tax(owe(more(…)…)…)…)*. Note that the answer components appear in the inverse order. Indeed, the first answer is about *owing tax*, and the second one is about the *IRS appeal procedures*.

4.10 Conclusions

In a domain that requires a concise and authoritative answer, one should rely on mature reasoning-based techniques of *controlled* Q/A. For a convincing recommendation or fast problem resolution, a CRM customer needs a high-accuracy, immediate, exact answer. In a CRM environment, not so high Q/A standards like in the machine reading comprehension (MRC) setting would drop a customers' confidence in company's capabilities to provide required information in a timely manner and to resolve issues. We now proceed to informal, entertaining analysis of competitive approaches to Q/A.

4.10.1 Deep Leaning and the Clever Hans

When an end-to-end learning happening for Q/A, it is hard to confirm that the system learns semantically essential features and not syntactic cues that happen to correlate with correct classes. Most research in DL does not concern which features are used for decision as long as the evaluation shows a good performance. Hence the model is tightly connected with a training dataset, and it is hard to observe if it learns significant semantic features that could be used in other domains and other datasets. There is a great analogy between a DL methodology and training animals such as Clever Hans horse trained to solve numerical problems. Clever Hans the horse learned to use his hoof to tap out numbers written on a blackboard. Clever Hans's abilities impress the public and were sought to be explained (Bellows 2007, Fig. 4.20).

Observing the humans interacting with Hans, it was noticed that each questioner's breathing, posture, and facial expression involuntarily changed each time the hoof tapped, showing ever-so-slight increases in tension. Once the "correct" tap was made, that subtle underlying tension suddenly disappeared from the person's face, which Hans apparently took as the cue to stop tapping. This tension was not present when the questioner was unaware of the correct answer, which left Clever Hans without the necessary feedback.

As DL system nowadays, Clever Hans was not dipping into a reservoir of intellect to work out the answers. Instead, the horse was merely being receptive to the subtle, unconscious cues which were universally present in his human questioners. Similarly, DL can employ features weakly correlated with a target phenomenon but provided by human annotators.

Many neural Q/A models have been proposed for the datasets such as SQuAD, NewsQA, TriviaQA and SQuAD-Open. The highest-performance models employ co-attention or bidirectional attention mechanisms that build codependent representations of the document and the question (Seo et al. 2017). Yet, learning the full context over the document is challenging and inefficient. In particular, when the model is given a long document, or multiple documents, learning the full context is intractably slow and hence difficult to scale to large corpora. Also, Jia and Liang

Fig. 4.20 Illustration for the Clever Hans house capable of performing basic math, capturing visual cues from the person asking the question

(2017) show that, given adversarial inputs, such models tend to focus on wrong parts of the context and produce incorrect answers. There is a concerning observation that these models can be easily perturbed by a simple adversarial example added

Lee et al. (2019) propose a diagnosing tool, for troubleshooting the performance of DL Q/A systems. The tool can reveal a lower than expected accuracy due to a biased training to certain types of questions or texts. Also, the tool can help identify wrong words for question or text understanding, or a suitability of an embedding for the given task. The QADiver tool may support system to identify various vulnerabilities of their models (Fig. 4.21).

We now return to anecdotal analysis of the main topic of this chapter. There are usually multiple SLFs per answer (shown as texts in Fig. 4.22). SLFs do not necessarily represent sentences or phrases from an answer as long as they are logically linked with it. SLFs need to represent a diversity of possible questions or claims…

4.10.2   Performance of Controlled Q/A

Application of the LSLF technique to Q/A system showed the following. There is a superior performance over the knowledge systems based on the syntactic matching of NL queries with the previously prepared NL representation of canonical queries, and the knowledge systems based on fully formalized knowledge. Moreover, the domain coverage of LSLF is better than that of SH (Galitsky 2003) because a new question can be reduced to existing pre-coded ones by means of commonsense reasoning.

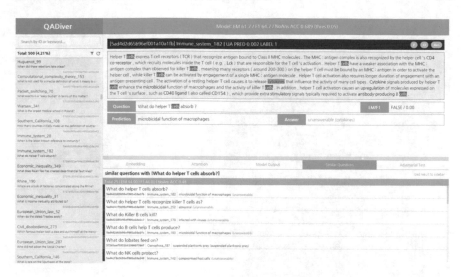

Fig. 4.21 A screen-shot of a diagnostic system for DL-based Q/A from (Lee et al. 2019)

LSLF can potentially include richer syntactic information; extended syntactic representation for n-gram analysis helps in a number of NLP tasks (Sidorov 2014). LSLF is also helpful in an answer triggering feature, enabling a Q/A systems to detect whether there exists at least one valid answer in the set of candidate sentences for the question; and if yes, select one of the valid answer sentences from the candidate sentence set (Acheampong et al. 2016). A reduced version of LSLF representation can be automatically learned from the web (Galitsky and Kovalerchuk 2014). LSLF can be an alternative to soft computing and computing with words, which operate with uncertain NL statements to make them more exact (Kovalerchuk and Smigaj 2015), in particular, for matching questions and answers. The proposed approach can be extended beyond the consumer search toward a log search (Galitsky and Botros 2015).

The LSLF approach to knowledge representation for Q/A gives a higher precision in answers than the SH and syntactic matching-based ones because it involves semantic information in higher degree. The LSLF technique gives more complete answers, possesses higher consistency to context deviation and is more efficient than a fully formalized thesaurus-based approach such as (Galitsky et al 2010) because all information in answers does not have to be obtained via reasoning.

The achieved accuracy of providing an advice in response to a NL question is much higher than an alternative approach to advising in a vertical domain would provide, including open-domain question answering, an expert system on its own, a keyword search, statistical or syntactic pattern matcher (Galitsky et al. 2013a; Galitsky 2019). Indeed, LSLF technique approaches the accuracy of a Q/A in a fully-formalized domain, assuming the knowledge representation machinery obeys the features outlined in this chapter. However, for fairly long, complex, multi-sentence

Fig. 4.22 Four SLFs (on the top-left) and an answer (on the right). On the bottom: an answer needs an SLF to be matched with a question (cartoonbank 2020)

queries, SLFs are not working well and paragraph-level Q/A is required (Galitsky et al. 2013b).

In this chapter, we described the design of a single controlled Q/A domain. To merge multiple vertical domains to form a horizontal one, we suggest a multiagent question answering approach, where each domain is represented by an agent that tries to answer questions taking into account its specific knowledge. The meta-agent controls the cooperation between question answering agents and chooses the most relevant answer(s). Back in 2000s (Galitsky and Pampapathi 2005), we argued that the multiagent question answering is optimal in terms of access to business and financial

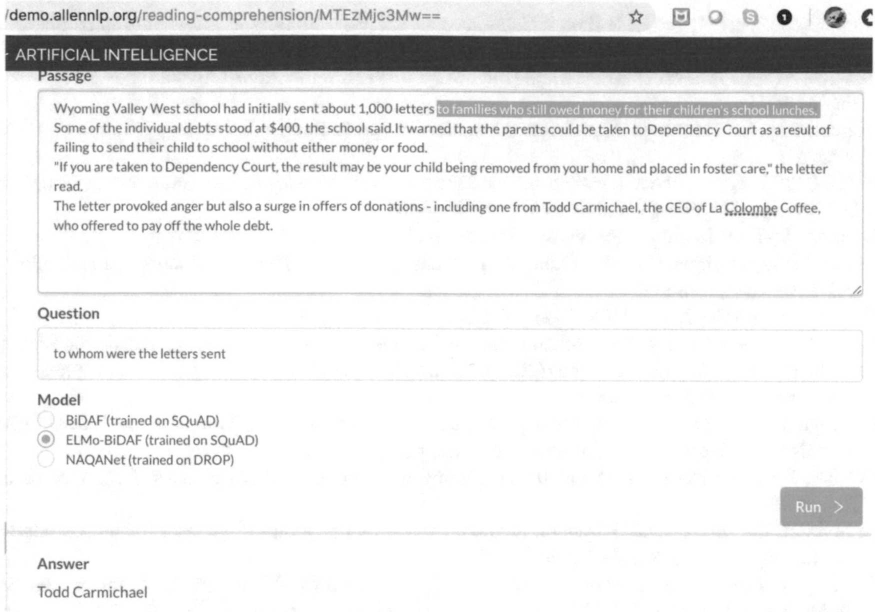

Fig. 4.23 A deep learning-based Q/A reading comprehension system. The correct answer is highlighted on the top, and the system answer is given on the bottom. The system correctly identified semantic type but incorrectly selected the value

knowledge, flexibility in query phrasing, and efficiency and usability of advice. These days, multi-agent Q/A such as Amazon Alexa Skills is a widely accepted chatbot architecture (Galitsky et al 2019).

In recent years, Q/A based on deep learning from a vast set of Q/A pairs became popular (Rajpurkar 2016, Chen et al 2017). However, complexity of questions being evaluated is way below that one of a real user asking questions in the domains of the current study (Fig. 4.23). Factoid, Wikipedia-targeted questions usually have fewer entities and simpler links between entities than the ones where LSLF technique is necessary. At the same time, neural network-based approach requires a huge training set of Q/A pairs that are rarely available in industrial Q/A domains.

References

Abramson H, Dahl V (1989) Logic grammars. Springer, New York, Berlin, Heidelberg
Acheampong KN, Pan Z-H, Zhou E-Q, Li X-Y (2016) Answer triggering of factoid questions: a cognitive approach. In: 13th international computer conference on wavelet active media technology and information processing (ICCWAMTIP)
Amiridze N, Kutsia T (2018) Anti-unification and natural language processing fifth workshop on natural language and computer science. NLCS'18, EasyChair Preprint no. 203
Apt KR (1997) From logic programming to PROLOG. Prentice Hall, London

Baral C, Gelfond M, Scherl R (2004) Using answer set programming to answer complex queries. In: Workshop on pragmatics of question answering at HLT-NAAC2004

Bellows A (2007) Clever Hans the Math Horse. https://www.damninteresting.com/clever-hans-the-math-horse/

Boguslavsky IM (1996) The sphere of action for lexical units, Studia philologica. Moscow (In Russian)

Black F (1964) A deductive question-answering system. In: Minsky M (ed) Semantic Information Processing. MIT Press, Cambridge MA, pp 354–402

Bramer M (2013) Logic programming with Prolog. Switzerland, Springer, Cham

Bunt H, Bos J, Pulman S (2014) Computing meaning. In: Text, speech and language technology vol 4. Springer, London

Cartoonbank (2020) http://cartoonbank.ru/?page_id=29&category=5

Chang C-L, Lee RC-T (1973) Symbolic logic and mechanical theorem proving. Academic Press

Chen D, A Fisch, J Weston, A Bordes (2017) Reading Wikipedia to answer open-domain questions. https://arxiv.org/abs/1704.00051

Darlington JL (1969). Theorem proving and information retrieval. In: Meltzer B, Michie D (eds) Machine intelligence, vol 4. American Elsevier, pp 173–181

Galitsky B (1999) Natural language understanding with the generality feedback. DIMACS Tech. Report 99

Galitsky B, Grudin M (2001) System, method, and computer program product for responding to natural language queries. US Patent App 09756722

Galitsky B (2001) Semi-structured knowledge representation for the automated financial advisor. In: Monostori L, Váncza J, Ali M (eds) Engineering of intelligent systems. IEA/AIE 2001. Lecture notes in computer science, vol 2070. Springer, Berlin, Heidelberg

Galitsky B (2002) A tool for extension and restructuring natural language question answering domains. In: International conference on industrial, engineering and other applications of applied intelligent systems

Galitsky B (2003) Natural language question answering system: technique of semantic headers. Adv Knowl Int, Australia

Galitsky B (2004) Question answering system for teaching autistic children to reason about mental states. DIMACS Technical Report 2000-24

Galitsky B, Pampapathi R. (2005) Can many agents answer questions better than one? First Monday vol 10, no 1. http://firstmonday.org/issues/issue10_1/galitsky/index.html

Galitsky B (2005) Disambiguation via default reasoning for answering complex questions. Intl J AI Tools N1-2:157–175

Galitsky B (2006) Building a repository of background knowledge using semantic skeletons. In: AAAI spring symposium series

Galitsky B, Dobrocsi G, De La Rosa JL, Kuznetsov SO (2010) From generalization of syntactic parse trees to conceptual graphs. In: International conference on conceptual structures, pp 185–190

Galitsky B, Ilvovsky D, Strok F, Kuznetsov SO (2013a) Improving text retrieval efficiency with pattern structures on parse thickets. In: Proceedings of FCAIR@IJCAI, pp 6–21

Galitsky B, Kuznetsov SO, Usikov D (2013b) Parse thicket representation for multi-sentence search. In: International conference on conceptual structures, pp 153–172

Galitsky B, Ilvovsky D, Kuznetsov SO, Strok F (2013c) Matching sets of parse trees for answering multi-sentence questions. In: Proceedings of the recent advances in natural language processing, RANLP 2013. Shoumen, Bulgaria, pp 285–294

Galitsky B, Ilvovsky D, Kuznetsov SO, Strok F (2014) Finding maximal common sub-parse thickets for multi-sentence search. In: Graph structures for knowledge representation and reasoning, IJCAI Workshop, pp 39–57

Galitsky B, Botros S (2015) Searching for associated events in log data. US Patent 8,306,967

Galitsky B, Ilvovsky D, Kuznetsov SO (2015) Rhetoric map of an answer to compound queries. In: Proceedings of the 53rd annual meeting of the association for computational linguistics and the 7th international joint conference on natural language processing, vol 2, pp 681–686

Galitsky B, Kovalerchuk B (2014) Improving web search relevance with learning structure of domain concepts. Clust Order Trees Methods Appl: 341–376

Galitsky B (2016a) Generalization of parse trees for iterative taxonomy learning. Inf Sci 329:125–143

Galitsky B (2016b) A tool for efficient content compilation. In: Proceedings of COLING

Galitsky B (2016c) Reasoning beyond the mental world. In: Computational autism, pp 215–244

Galitsky B (2017) Matching parse thickets for open domain question answering. Data Knowl Eng 107:24–50

Galitsky B (2019) Learning discourse-level structures for question answering. Developing enterprise chatbots. Springer, Cham, Switzerland, pp 177–219

Galitsky B, Ilvovsky D, Goncharova E (2019) On a chatbot providing virtual dialogues. In: Proceedings of the international conference on recent advances in natural language processing (RANLP), pp 382–387

Gazdar G, Mellish C (1989) Natural language processing in Prolog: an introduction to computational linguistics. Addison-Wesley, Wokingham

Green BF, Wolf AK, Chomsky C, Laughery K (1961) Baseball: an automatic question-answerer. IRE-AIEE-ACM western joint computer conference

Jia R, Liang P (2017) Adversarial examples for evaluating reading comprehension systems. In: EMNLP, 2021–2031

Kovalerchuk B, Smigaj A (2015) Computing with words beyond quantitative words: incongruity modeling. In: 2015 annual conference of the North American Fuzzy Information Processing Society (NAFIPS), Redmond, WA, USA

Lee G, Kim S, Hwang S (2019) QADiver: interactive framework for diagnosing QA models. AAAI

Lehmann F (1992) Semantic networks, Computers & Mathematics with Applications 23(2–5):1–50

Maybury MT (2000) Adaptive multimedia information access—ask questions, get answers. In: First international conference on adaptive hypertext AH 00. Trento, Italy

Min S, Zhong V, Socher R, Xiong C (2018) Efficient and robust question answering from minimal context over documents. ACL 1725–1735

Moldovan D, Pasca M, Harabagiu S, Surdeanu M (2002) Performance issues and error analysis in an open-domain question answering system. In: ACL-2002

Montague R (1974) Formal philosophy. Yale University Press, New Haven

Ng HT, Lai Pheng Kwan J, Xia Y (2001) Question answering using a large text database: a machine learning approach. In: Proceedings of the 2001 conference on empirical methods in natural language processing. EMNLP 2001. Pittsburgh, PA

Palmer M (2009) Semlink: linking PropBank, VerbNet and FrameNet. In: Proceedings of the generative lexicon conference, September 2009, Pisa, Italy, GenLex-09

Partee BH, ter Meulen A, Wall RE (1990) Mathematical methods in linguistics. Kluwer, Dordrecht

Pasca M (2003) Open-domain question answering from large text collections. CSLI Publication series

Pfenning F (1991) Unification and anti-unification in the calculus of constructions. In: Proceedings, sixth annual IEEE symposium on logic in computer science, Amsterdam, The Netherlands, 15–18 July. IEEE Computer Society Press, pp 74–85

Popescu A-M, Etzioni O, Kautz H (2003) Towards a theory of natural language interfaces to databases. Intelligent User Interface

Rajpurkar P, Zhang J, Lopyrev K, Liang P (2016) Squad: 100,000 questions for machine comprehension of text. https://arxiv.org/abs/1606.05250

Redey G (1999) iCTRL: intensional conformal text representation language. Artif Intell 109:33–70

Rus V, Moldovan D (2002). High precision logic form transformation. Intl J AI Tools 11(3)

Seo M, Kembhavi A, Farhadi A, Hajishirzi. H (2017) Bidirectional attention flow for machine comprehension. In: ICLR, p 755

Shanahan M (1997) Solving the frame problem. The MIT Press, Cambridge, Massachusetts, London, England

Sidorov G (2014) Should syntactic N-grams contain names of syntactic relations? Int J Comput Linguist Appl 5(1):139–158

Sidorov G, Velasquez F, Stamatatos E, Gelbukh A, Chanona-Hernández L (2012) Syntactic dependency-based N-grams as classification features. LNAI 7630:1–11

Sidorov G, Velasquez F, Stamatatos E, Gelbukh A, Chanona-Hernández L (2013) Syntactic N-grams as machine learning features for natural language processing. Expert Syst Appl 41(3):853–860

Sowa J (1992) Conceptual graphs summary. In: Nagle TE, Nagle JA, Gerholz LL, Eklund PW (eds) Conceptual structures: current research and practice. Ellis Horwood, Chichester, pp 3–51

Tarau P, De Boschere K, Dahl V, Rochefort S (1999) LogiMOO: an extensible multi-user virtual world with natural language control. J Logic Program 38(3):331–353

Vo NPA, Popescu O (2016) A multi-layer system for semantic textual similarity. In: 8th international conference on knowledge discovery and information retrieval, vol 1, pp 56–67

Vo NPA, Popescu O (2019) Multi-layer and co-learning systems for semantic textual similarity, semantic relatedness and recognizing textual entailment. In: 8th international joint conference, IC3K 2016, Porto, Portugal, November 9–11, 2016, Revised selected papers, pp 54–77

Winograd T (1972) Understanding natural language. Academic Press, New York

Chapter 5
Summarized Logical Forms Based on Abstract Meaning Representation and Discourse Trees

Abstract We propose a way to build summarized logical forms (SLFs) automatically relying on semantic and discourse parsers, as well as syntactic and semantic generalization. Summarized logical forms represent the main topic and the essential part of answer content and are designed to be matched with a logical representation of a question. We explore the possibilities of building SLFs from Abstract Meaning Representation (AMR) of sentences supposed to be the most important, by selecting the AMR subgraphs. In parallel, we leverage discourse analysis of answer paragraphs to highlight more important elementary discourse units (EDUs) to convert into SLFs (less important EDUs are not converted into SLFs). The third source of SLFs is a pair-wise generalization of answers with each other. Proposed methodology is designed to improve question answering (Q/A) precision to avoid matching questions with less important, uninformative parts of a given answer (to avoid delivering foreign answers). A stand-alone evaluation of each of the three sources of SLFs is conducted as well as an assessment of a hybrid SLF generation system. We conclude that indexing the most important text fragments of an answer such as SLF instead of the whole answer improves the Q/A precision by almost 10% as measured by F1 and 8% as measured by NDCG.

5.1 Introduction

In the previous Chapter, we outlined the technique of summarized logical forms (SLF). Instead of indexing the whole answer for search, we index its summary via a logical form. In this Chapter, we explore how this can be implemented relying on abstract semantic representation, discourse and syntactic generalization.

Much online content is available via question–answer pairs such as frequently-asked questions stored on customer portals or internal company portals. Question–answer pairs can be an efficient manner to familiarize a user with content. In some cases, autonomous agents (chatbots) can import such question–answer pairs in order to answer user questions.

© Springer Nature Switzerland AG 2020

B. Galitsky, *Artificial Intelligence for Customer Relationship Management*,
Human–Computer Interaction Series,
https://doi.org/10.1007/978-3-030-52167-7_5

But such question–answer pairs can contain content that is not central to a topic of an answer. For example, a content can include a text that is irrelevant or misleading, non-responsive to the particular question, or is neutral and not helpful. If irrelevant text is indexed by a keyword-based search engine, the precision of the search engine is lowered. Moreover, an autonomous agent attempting to answer a user question based on erroneously indexed text may answer the question incorrectly, resulting in lowered user confidence in the agent. Despite the fact that standard relevance techniques such as ontology, the keyword frequency models and some individual features obtained from discourse analysis (Chali et al. 2009; Jansen et al. 2014; Jacobs and Tschötschel 2019) can be applied to solve this problem, a solution is needed for identifying informative parts in a whole answer text.

Today, it is hard to overestimate the usability of search engines and question answering, especially in CRM. A high number of distributed computing frameworks have been proposed for big data. They provide scalable storage and efficient retrieval, capable of collecting data from various sources, fast-moving and fairly diverse. Modern open source big data search and exploration systems like SOLR and ElasticSearch are broadly used for access and analysis of big data. However, intelligence features such as search relevance and adequate analysis, retrieval and exploration of large quantities of natural language texts are still lacking. Therefore, for a CRM chatbot or a search engine it is still hard to rely on available statistical-based or machine learning-based relevance to yield a high volume of meaningful responses. Modern search engines and libraries still treat a query as a bag of words with their statistics (Galitsky 2017). Recently proposed deep learning (DL)-based approaches have strong accuracy limitations as well. In spite of the extensive capabilities of natural language parsing, they are still not leveraged by most search engines.

In this Chapter, we propose a way to build summarized logical forms (SLFs) automatically relying on semantic and discourse parsers, as well as syntactic and semantic generalization. Summarized logical forms represent the main topic and the essential part of answer content and are designed to be matched with questions. We explore the possibilities of building SLFs from Abstract Meaning Representation (AMR) of sentences by selecting the subgraphs supposed to be the most important. In parallel, we leverage discourse analysis of answer paragraphs to highlight more important elementary discourse units (EDUs) to convert into SLFs and avoid less important EDUs which are not converted into SLFs. The third source of SLFs is a pair-wise generalization of answers. SLF technique is a development of the Semantic Header approach developed two decades ago (Galitsky 2003).

In this Chapter, we also build SLFs for more complex questions requiring multiple merged answers. It is often hard for users who are new to a domain to pick proper keywords. Also, frequently novice users of search engines experience difficulties formulating their queries, especially when these queries are long compound sentences (Galitsky et al. 2015). Even for advanced users, exploring data via querying, including web queries, it is usually hard to estimate proper generality/specificity of a query being formulated. Obtaining SLFs by intersecting answers turns out to be an efficient way to tackle complex queries. Maintaining multiple intersections as an ordered set (a lattice) makes it easier for a broad range of user and data exploration tasks to formulate the query: given a few examples, it formulates the query automatically (Greene et al. 2015). This approach also helps with cases where the words people use to formulate questions significantly deviate from the words a content is written in: only more common words are retained in the intersection results.

In search engineering, selecting keywords or parts of the answer to be indexed and included into a search index is an issue of utmost importance. In a default approach, where the whole documents are indexed, search precision is frequently low because the keywords, which are not indicative of the content of an answer, might be matched with the query. If too few words from a document are indexed, a search recall is low since for many queries this document will not be triggered as an answer.

Given a set of documents or texts, different techniques can be applied to select phrases, sentences or text fragments that should form SLFs. Then at search time, more specific SLFs should be matched with query representation first, followed by less specific SLFs until the match is successful. In Fig. 5.1, we show the search scenario with three iterations. Three following technics of various levels of linguistic analysis are used:

(1) The first technique is based on semantic analysis, trying to select most "informative" parts of a semantic representation;
(2) The second technique is based on discourse analysis, identifying preferred text fragments (nucleus elementary discourse units (EDUs) in a discourse tree (DT) of an answer.

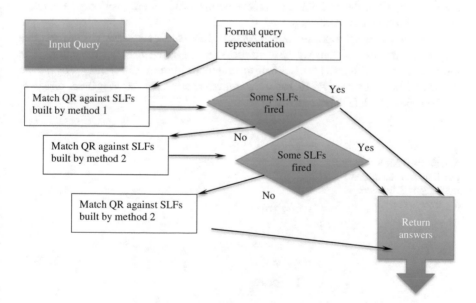

Fig. 5.1 Iterative procedure for matching with SLFs obtained by different methods

(3) The third technique takes two or more text fragments and generalizes their syntactic (Galitsky et al. 2012; Sidorov 2014), semantic (Kamp and Reyle 1993) or discourse-level representations, producing a partially ordered set of generalization results.

5.2   Forming SLFs from AMR

In this subsection, we focus on a special case of SLFs built automatically based on sematic parsing and discourse analysis of answer texts. The former helps with selecting phrases determined to be more important by generalizing individual sentences. The latter provides cues on which sentences or sentence fragments are suitable to form questions based on logical organization of text, as obtained via discourse analysis.

Abstract Meaning Representation (AMR, Banarescu et al. 2013) was proposed as a general-purpose meaning representation language for broad-coverage text, and work is ongoing to study its use for a variety of applications such as machine translation (Jones et al. 2012) and summarization.

AMR meaning bank provides a large new corpus that enables computational linguists to study the problem of grammar induction for broad-coverage semantic parsing (Artzi et al. 2015). However, it also presents significant challenges for existing algorithms, including much longer sentences, more complex syntactic phenomena (Eremeev and Vorontsov 2019) and increased use of non-compositional semantics, such as within-sentence coreference.

Abstract meaning representation (AMR) aims to abstract away from various syntactic phrasings so that we have fewer SLFs covering broader meanings. The motivation is to assign the same AMR to sentences phrased differently which have the same basic meaning. AMR has a tree representation format as rooted, directed, edge-labeled and leaf-labeled trees.

Fig. 5.2 An AMR directed graph for representing the meaning of *"The clerk prepares to leave"*

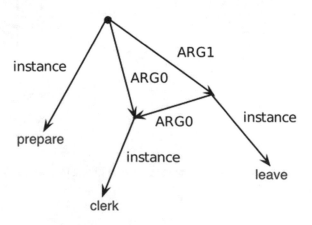

Figure 5.2 shows a graph representation. A conventional AMR representation is

> *(w / prepare*
> *:arg0 (b / clerk)*
> *:arg1 (g / leave*
> *:arg0 b))*

For the logical representations, we differentiate between semantic types and the instances. In our further examples, we skip the instance notation where it does not introduce ambiguity. As a logical forms (LF), this reads as:

> *∃ w, b, g: instance(w, prepare) ∧ instance(g, leave)*
> *∧ instance(b, clerk) ∧ arg0(w, b)*
> *∧ arg1(w, g) ∧ arg0(g, b)*

AMR relies on PropBank framesets to abstract away from English syntax. For example, the frameset *associate-01* has three pre-defined slots:

:arg0 is the agent doing association,
:arg1 is the thing being associated with, and
:arg2 is an association thing.

> *(associate-01*
> *:arg0 (teacher)*
> *:arg1 (m2 / apple)*
> *:arg2 (d / ball))*

AMR has multiple syntactic relations: *'The manager spoke to the client as she walked in from the street'.*

> *(speak*
> *:arg0 (manager)*
> *:beneficiary (client)*
> *:time (walk*
> *:arg0 (client)*
> *:source (street)))*

This structure covers various phrasings: *"While the client was walking in from the street, a manager spoke to her. The client walked in, and had the manager spoke to her. As the client walk in, there was a manager speaking to her. She walking in from the street; the manager was speaking to her".*

AMR authors separate annotations for named entities, co-reference, semantic relations, discourse connectives, temporal entities, etc. Each annotation is evaluated separately, and training data is split across many resources. Since there is a lack of a simple readable semantic bank of English sentences paired with their whole-sentence, logical meanings, an extensive semantic bank promises a new work in natural language understanding (NLU), resulting in semantic parsers that are as ubiquitous as syntactic ones. AMR also supports natural language generation (NLG) by providing a logical semantic input.

The motivations for AMR are as follows:

(1) It is represented as rooted, labeled graphs rather than trees that can be subject to traversal;
(2) It expresses an abstraction away from syntactic idiosyncrasies. The same AMR are assigned to sentences that have the identical meaning;
(3) It heavily relies on PropBank Framesets (Kingsbury and Palmer 2002; Palmer 2009);
(4) It is agnostic about how we might want to derive meanings from lexical units, or other way around. In translating sentences to AMR, we do not dictate a particular sequence of rule applications or provide alignments that reflect such rule sequences. This makes semantic banking very fast, and it allows researchers to explore their own ideas about how strings are related to meanings;
(5) It is heavily biased toward English.

AMR has gained substantial popularity in computational linguistics (Werling et al. 2015). This is due to the simple tree structure of AMRs, showing the connections between concepts and events, make them easy to read. Also, because AMRs can simply be expressed as directed acyclic graphs, machine-generated output can be evaluated in a standard way by computing precision and recall on triples of gold-standard AMRs (Cai and Knight 2013). Moreover, AMRs are arguably easier to produce manually than traditional formal meaning representations, and, as a result, there are now corpora with gold-standard AMRs available (Banarescu et al. 2015).

How to form SLFs given an AMR? In each answer sentence, we need to identify more important parts and build SLFs from them, and ignore less important parts. These parts are:

- Definitions;
- Main parts of compound queries;
- Facts;
- Actions over main entities;
- Domain-specific information.

The phrases to be excluded are frequently related to

- Opinionated expressions;
- Clarifying, explaining, motivating expressions;
- Auxiliary attributes of main entities.

Discourse analysis allows better classification of discourse units into informative (from which SLFs are formed) and uninformative parts. However, AMRs allow for better control of generalization level, selecting more general phrases for SLFs and ignoring too specific information.

The subgraphs for the phrases which express an essential meaning of a sentence are on the top of the AMR, attached to the root node. The paths of AMR for the phrases which are supposed to be less important are located closer to the leaves of AMR. Other criteria of importance are also necessary since semantic parsing is unreliable and produces noisy AMRs.

Once texts or AMR fragments are selected, they are translated from graphs to a logical form (a native representation for AMR).

5.2.1 AMR of an Answer and Its Subgraphs for SLFs

We now show an example of how to build SLFs from AMR. Let us look at our earlier example (Chap. 4) of an answer about a specific auction:

> *"Restricted-Access Auctions. This separate category makes it easy for you to find or avoid adult-only merchandise. To view and bid on adult-only items, buyers need to have a credit card on file with eBay. Your card will not be charged. Sellers must also have credit card verification. Items listed in the Adult-Only category are not included in the New Items page or the Hot Items section, and currently, are not available by any title search. "*

We first make sure there is a continuous flow of information by means of building a discourse tree and verifying that all rhetorical relations are *Elaborations*. Then we want to form a canonical question for each chunk of information introduced by each new sentence.

```
elaboration
 elaboration
  TEXT:Restricted-Access Auctions .
  elaboration
   elaboration
    TEXT:This separate category makes it easy for you to find or avoid adult-only merchandise .
    elaboration
     enablement (RightToLeft)
      TEXT:To view and bid on adult-only items ,
      TEXT:buyers need to have a credit card on file with eBay .
     TEXT:Your card will not be charged .
   TEXT:Sellers must also have credit card verification .
 same-unit
  TEXT:Items
  joint
   TEXT:listed in the Adult-Only category are not included in the New Items page or the Hot Items section
   TEXT:and currently , are not available by any title search .
```

For rhetorical relation of *Enablement*, we expect the question on "*<What to do to achieve> bid on…*", but not "*<What I achieve if I do> this and that …*".

How to derive canonical questions given these two AMR graphs (Fig. 5.3)? Firstly, we find the common subgraph which gives us "*<What-is> adult-only [item/merchandise]*". The common subgraph gives us the *main_entity* for the whole paragraph that can be added to canonical questions obtained by other means *main_entity* = "*adult-only [item/merchandise]*".

Then we identify subgraphs that are unique for each sentence. For the first, we select

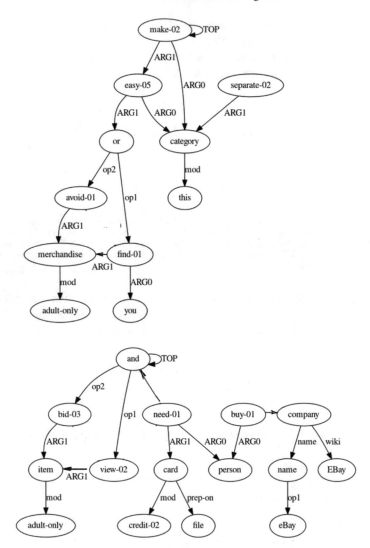

Fig. 5.3 AMR graph for two sentences from the answer text

"<how-To/why/when/where> [Avoid/find] <main_entity>". Another question relates to the remainder of the AMR graph: *"Why/what / Reason for Separate Category for < main_entity]"*.

For the second, we start with the root *need* and form questions *"<What you/he/she> need to [bid/view] <main_entity>"*.

"<Why/what for you/he/she> need a credit card". Rhetorical relation of *Enablement* gives us an idea for questions: one for *what is enabled*, and another *"what enables"*.

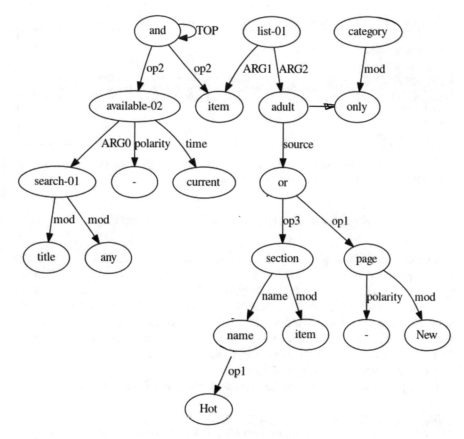

Fig. 5.4 AMR graph for complex sentence with negations and named entities confusing the parser

The last sentence is more complex and contains named entities confusing for semantic parsers (Fig. 5.4). This sentence also has the *main_entity*.

The questions including the root node of AMR are as follows:

"<How/where/can is/be Main_entity> listed/shown/identified"

Notice that without SLFs, based on DL, search results are frequently random (Fig. 5.5).

Having looked at examples of AMRs for answer sentences, we observed that the closer the phrase as a path in AMR is located to the root of AMR, the higher is the chance of its inclusion as an SLF.

Notice that without SLFs, based on DL, search results are frequently random (Fig. 5)

Answer

Restricted-Access Auctions

Passage Context

Restricted-Access Auctions . This separate category makes it easy for you to find or avoid adult-only merchandise. To view and bid on adult-only items, buyers need to have a credit card on file with eBay. Your card will not be charged. Sellers must also have credit card verification. Items listed in the Adult-Only category are not included in the New Items page or the Hot Items section, and currently, are not available by any title search.

Question

how to find adult only merchandise

Fig. 5.5 A Machine Reading Comprehension answers questions given the answer text. The red oval shows the correct phrase to answer the question

5.2.2 AMR Representation in Specialized Domains

In a highly specialized domain such as finance, legal, medical, Q/A works well as long as questions name the correct terms. As a deviation between the proper domain-specific terms and the ones used by a non-specialist user is possible, a Q/A system is frequently confused. It needs to establish a context-dependent synonymy not only between the noun phrases used to refer to certain entities, but also between the verbs applied to domain-specific entities. In a CRM domain, one can expect a strong deviation between how questions are formulated from how the content is written by a product producer or service provider.

Let us proceed to another example of an answer and AMR graphs for its sentences:

> *'If you do not pay your tax through withholding, or do not pay enough tax that way, you might have to pay estimated tax. People who are in business for themselves generally will have to pay their tax this way. You may have to pay estimated tax if you receive income such as dividends, interest, capital gains, rents, and royalties. Estimated tax is used to pay not only income tax, but other taxes such as self-employment tax and alternative minimum tax.'*

It is not hard to answer a Q formulated with the verb *use* from the A such as "*How are estimated taxes used?*". However, once a Q verb is deviated, the Q/A system is lost (Fig. 5.6). A MRC system finds a high similarity between the question "*What for is estimated tax **used**?*" and the correct passage but not for "*What for is estimated tax **spent**?*" because in general context, word2vec does not give high enough similarity for *spend* and *use*.

One way to associate *use* and *spend* is to rely on a verb ontology. Another is to consider association of phrases "*use tax*" and "*spend tax*" (Fig. 5.7).

To discover if the verbs *spend* and u*se* are synonymous or imply one another in the context of *tax*, we formulate a query and collect web document snippets which include a sentence or a paragraph that contains both of these phrases, indicating an association between them. Further details are available in Chap. 7.

We now proceed to inventing questions from AMR trees rather than trying to formulate them from text. For each sentence, we show the graph and the generalized questions beneath it. For the first sentence (Fig. 5.8) there is a conditional (IF) part that

Answer

If you do not pay your tax through withholding, or do not pay enough tax that way, you might have to pay estimated tax. People who are in business for themselves generally will have to pay their tax this way. You may have to pay estimated tax if you receive income such as dividends, interest, capital gains, rents, and royalties. Estimated tax is used to pay not only income tax

Passage Context

If you do not pay your tax through withholding, or do not pay enough tax that way, you might have to pay estimated tax. People who are in business for themselves generally will have to pay their tax this way. You may have to pay estimated tax if you receive income such as dividends, interest, capital gains, rents, and royalties. Estimated tax is used to pay not only income tax, but other taxes such as self-employment tax and alternative minimum tax.

Question

Where is an estimated tax spent?

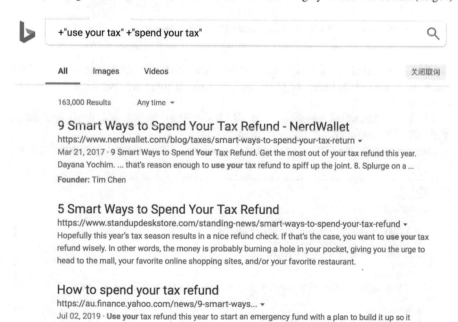

Fig. 5.6 A DL system is given a passage opposite to what it should have been given (shown in red oval, on the top). A web search engine does not provide a good answer to its question either (on the bottom), taking into account that the correct answer exists in a highly-ranked web domain (irs.gov)

+"use your tax" +"spend your tax"

All   Images   Videos   关闭取词

163,000 Results   Any time ▾

9 Smart Ways to Spend Your Tax Refund - NerdWallet
https://www.nerdwallet.com/blog/taxes/smart-ways-to-spend-your-tax-return ▾
Mar 21, 2017 · 9 Smart Ways to Spend Your Tax Refund. Get the most out of your tax refund this year. Dayana Yochim. ... that's reason enough to **use your** tax refund to spiff up the joint. 8. Splurge on a ...
Founder: Tim Chen

5 Smart Ways to Spend Your Tax Refund
https://www.standupdeskstore.com/standing-news/smart-ways-to-spend-your-tax-refund ▾
Hopefully this year's tax season results in a nice refund check. If that's the case, you want to **use your** tax refund wisely. In other words, the money is probably burning a hole in your pocket, giving you the urge to head to the mall, your favorite online shopping sites, and/or your favorite restaurant.

How to spend your tax refund
https://au.finance.yahoo.com/news/9-smart-ways... ▾
Jul 02, 2019 · **Use your** tax refund this year to start an emergency fund with a plan to build it up so it covers six months expenses for those rainy days. #9 How to spend **your** tax refund: Put in ...

Fig. 5.7 Web mining to confirm or reject an association between two phrases

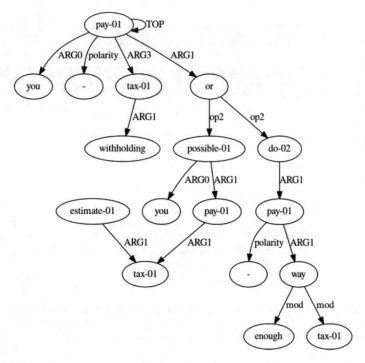

Fig. 5.8 AMR for an answer in financial domain (the first sentence)

should be excluded from the question generation. It can be established by building a discourse tree of this answer paragraph and identifying the rhetorical relation of *Condition.*

We build canonical questions for SLFs for the second and third sentences (Fig. 5.9). The main entity is shown in bold.

Below we show the discourse tree for the answer with canonical questions bolded:

---

elaboration
 elaboration
  condition
   joint
    TEXT:If you do not pay your tax through withholding ,
    TEXT:or do not pay enough tax that way ,
   TEXT:**you might have to pay estimated tax** .
  attribution
   TEXT:People
   TEXT:who are **in business for themselves generally will have to pay their tax** this way .
 elaboration
  condition
   TEXT:You may have to pay estimated tax
   TEXT:if you **receive income such as dividends , interest , capital gains , rents , and royalties** .
  TEXT:Estimated tax is used to pay not only income tax , but other taxes such as self-employment tax and alternative minimum tax .

---

*'What happens when **I pay not enough tax**'*
*'How is it possible that I have to **pay estimated tax**'*
*'How can **I estimate** my **tax**'*

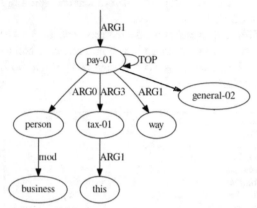

'When/how/ do/am I have/must/should/required to pay business tax'

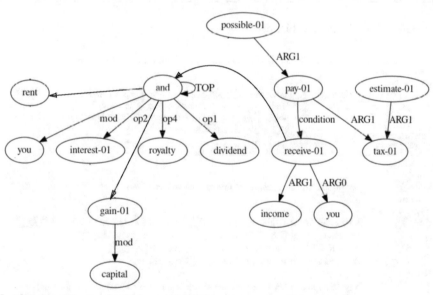

In what circumstances should I pay estimated tax
How to pay tax if I receive income from rent/interest/royalty/dividend/gain

Fig. 5.9 AMR for an answer in financial domain (the second and the third sentence) and canonical questions

5.2.3   Extending AMR with Verb Ontologies

To systematically treat synonyms of verbs, one needs a special verb-oriented ontology such as FrameNet or VerbNet (Palmer 2009).

If a verb such as *use* has two different event noun derivatives, and they have different meanings that are also found in the verb, that verb should be described as polysemous. Below we have verbs *adhere, observe, commit* and *deliver* and verb phrases for them to set a context (in bold):

adhere to a belief:	***adherence***
adhere to your skin:	***adhesion***
observe a rule:	***observance***
observe the kids:	***observation***
commit to a cause:	***commitment***
commit to an asylum:	***commitment***
commit a crime:	***commission***
deliver a package:	***delivery***
deliver somebody from danger:	***deliverance***

Here's a frame for *use* (Fig. 5.10).

Using_resource
Definition:
An Agent has access to a finite amount of some Resource and uses it in some way to complete a Purpose. The specific Portion of the Resource may be stated, and after the Resource is spent, it is no longer available to the Agent. The Means by which the Resource is used may be mentioned, but it is often implied by the stated Purpose or understood based on what the Resource is.
I USED half of the bag of dirt to plant the roses.
She just SPENDS all her time sitting in front of the television.
Frame Elements:
Core:
Agent []   The person who depletes a Resource to achieve some Goal
Semantic
Type: Sentient
Means []   A more specific description of how the Purpose is achieved by spending the Resource.
Portion []   The amount of the Resource that the Agent uses to achieve the Purpose.
Purpose []   What the Agent is attempting to achieve by using the Resource.
Resource []   The exhaustible commodity that the Agent has access to.
Non-Core:
Manner []   Any description of the intentional act which is not covered by more specific FEs,
                              including secondary effects (quietly, loudly), and general descriptions comparing events
                              (the same way). In addition, it may indicate salient characteristics of an Agent that also
                              affect the action (deliberately, eagerly, carefully).
Place []   The physical location where the Resource is used.
Time []   The time at which the Resource is used.
Lexical Units: *spend.v, use.v* (meanings of these words as *verbs*)

Fig. 5.10 Entry for the frame *use resources*

5.3   Forming SLF from Discourse Trees

In this Section, we propose a new discourse-based approach to determine informative parts of an answer. This approach accesses a body of text and creates a searchable index including multiple entries, each entry corresponding to a selected fragment of this text. Splitting into fragments occurs based on the discourse operation of segmentation, taking into account discourse cue words like *however, since, due*. We propose two different methods of fragment selection based on rules and classification model, respectively.

Discourse analysis has been proved to be useful in different aspects of question-answering: answer extraction (Zong et al. 2011), modeling rationale in design questions (Kim et al. 2004), query expansion based on relations between sequential questions (Sun and Chai 2007), etc.

Discourse trees (DT) originate from Rhetorical Structure Theory (RST, Mann and Thompson 1988). RST models a logical organization of text, relying on relations between parts of text. RST simulates text coherence (Hobbs 1985) by forming a hierarchical, connected structure of texts via discourse trees. Rhetoric relations are split into the classes of coordinate and subordinate; these relations hold across two or more text spans and therefore implement coherence. These text spans are called elementary discourse units (EDUs). The leaves of a discourse tree correspond to EDUs, the contiguous atomic text spans. Adjacent EDUs are connected by coherence relations (e.g., attribution, sequence), forming higher-level discourse units.

The term "nuclearity" in RST refers to which text segment, fragment, or span, is more central to an author's purpose. A "*nucleus*" refers to a span of text that is more central to an author's purpose than a "*satellite*", which is less central to the topic. We use the determined EDUs of a discourse tree for a body of text and the relations between the EDUs to determine which EDUs should be indexed for search. Different rhetorical relations (e.g., *Elaboration, Contrast*, etc.) can employ different rules. In general, we hypothesize that a satellite may express a detail of information that is unlikely to be explicitly queried by a user (Galitsky et al. 2015; Jasinskaja and Karagjosova 2017).

5.3.1   Example of DT Analysis

Let's illustrate our analysis with a question–answer pair and a discourse tree for an answer.

Q: *How should I plan to pay for taxes resulting from converting to a Roth IRA?*

A: *To help maximize your retirement savings, it's generally a good idea to consider not using the proceeds from the conversion to pay the resulting tax costs. Instead, you should consider using cash or other savings held in nonretirement accounts. Using retirement account funds to pay the taxes will reduce the amount you would have available to potentially grow tax-free in your new Roth IRA. Additionally, if you are*

under 59½, using funds from your retirement account could result in an additional
10% tax penalty, which may significantly reduce the potential benefit of conversion.

The discourse tree for the answer is shown in Fig. 5.11 and elementary discourse
units (EDUs) selected for indexing are circled in green.

The answer could be obtained from a source such as a Frequently Asked Questions
(FAQ) database, or a question–answer index (Galitsky 2019b). A question–answer
index can include multiple questions and corresponding answers. But some fragments
in each answer are more informative to answering the corresponding question than
other fragments. For example, the phrase *"it is generally a good idea"* adds little
to the answer, whereas *"consider not using the proceeds from the conversion"* is

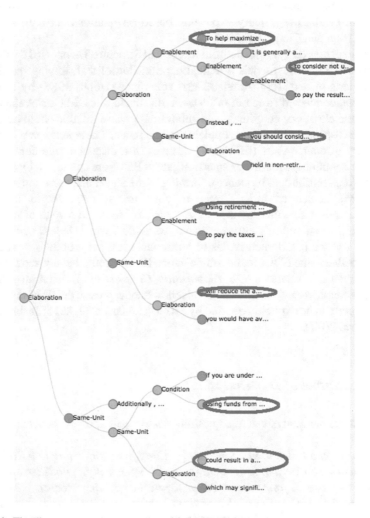

Fig. 5.11 The discourse tree for an answer with the EDUs selected for indexing

Table 5.1 Indexing rules for rhetorical relations

Relation	Example	SLF selection rule
Elaboration	To achieve some state [nucleus] I *do this and that* [satellite]	Nucleus
Enablement	A query may be of the form *"how to achieve some state?"* but less likely be of the form *"what can I achieve doing this and that?"*	Nucleus
Condition	A query may be of the form *"how to achieve some state?"* but less likely of the form *"what can I achieve doing this and that?"*	When the question is of the type **"when/where/under what condition** ...", select the *if* part (the satellite)
Contrast	Select the nucleus. The satellite includes facts which are unusual, unexpected, unanticipated	
Same-Unit, Joint	Select both nucleus and satellite because of the symmetric relationship of Same-unit	

informative to the user who posed the original question. Each answer in the question–answer index may provide additional insight in terms of additional questions that can be answered, which are in turn indexed, increasing the usefulness of the data. For example, *"at what age do I pay a penalty for using retirement funds?"* could be answered by the text (e.g., *"age 59 ½"*). We can determine informative text from a body of text and such additional questions that can be answered from the body of text.

The above hypothesis that only EDUs that are *nucleus* of rhetoric relations should be indexed and all *satellite* EDUs should not be selected for indexing is illustrated by the *Elaboration* relationship where the nucleus expresses more important information than the satellite. But the general rule described above can be subject to certain exceptions. For example, under certain conditions, *Contrast* relation can require a selection of the satellite rather than the nucleus. Additionally, for the *Same-unit* and *Joint* relations, both the nucleus and the satellite are selected for the SLFs. Different rhetorical relations can have different rules, as shown in Table 5.1.

5.3.2 Search Scenario for SLF from DT

Two forms of SLF construction is plausible:

(1) Rule-based. We take question–answer pairs and create, for each answer, a discourse tree using RST-parser (Surdeanu et al. 2015; Joty et al. 2013). For each non-terminal node in each answer, we then identify a rhetorical relationship associated with the non-terminal node and label each terminal node associated with the non-terminal node as either a *nucleus* or a *satellite*. Then we apply a set of rules (see Table 5.1) associated with the rhetorical relationships and select,

based on the rules, one or more of the fragment associated with the nucleus or the fragment associated with the satellite.

(2) Classification-based. We use machine learning to learn rules such as those depicted in Table 5.1. A machine learning problem is formulated as a classification task that classifies EDUs into a first class that is suitable for indexing (i.e., *informative*) and forming alternative questions for an answer and a second class that is not suitable for indexing (i.e., *not informative*).

We elaborate more on the latter SLF construction mode. To accumulate training question–answer pairs with marked answers, we ran selection of queries against short texts. Because longer queries are necessary to assure a corresponding match is nontrivial, we used public question–answer Yahoo! Answers dataset (Webscope 2017). More specifically, questions from this dataset were formed from the first sentence of the question and executed as queries by Bing Search engine API. Search results which are short texts (4–6 sentences) were selected as suitable for parsing and discourse analysis.

Matched fragments of these texts were taken as elements of the training set. Such fragments from the top ten or more pages of search result formed a positive dataset, i.e., informative fragments. For the negative dataset, fragments with matched keywords from the set of lower ranked (100–1000+) search results pages were taken, as these results are assumed to be significantly less relevant.

We applied SVM tree kernel learning (Moschitti 2006; Severyn and Moschitti 2012) to train the model since this algorithm is capable of learning directly on a parse tree structure. Once a text fragment to form an SLF is selected, actual SLF is built from the AMR representation (sub-graph) for this fragment.

In terms of search engineering, SLF construction can be viewed as building a search inverse index. Once our method constructs the indexes, we can build the online search algorithm which combines default functionality provided by the Lucene search engine and syntactic similarity between answer and a query. Search results candidate are selected by Lucene and then matched with the query via finding a maximal common sub tree which is a combination of semantic (AMR) and syntactic parse trees (Galitsky 2017).

5.4 Text Generalization Lattice

When we build canonical questions and/or SLFs, we do not know in advance which level or degree of generalization is optimal. If an SLF for a given answer is too general, it can trigger this answer to answer questions it should not, so precision would drop. If a canonical question is too specific, recall would deteriorate (Galitsky 2019a). A solution here is to maintain multiple generalization results and match the query with each canonical question in real time, trying to find the least general. To treat multiple generalizations systematically, we chose a lattice to order them according to how each pair-wise generalization of texts iteratively converges to the default non-informative (empty) generalization. We refer to this proposal as lattice SLF ($SLF_{lattice}$): multiple generalizations of two or more answers are stored. It is then decided in search time instead of indexing time, going from least general to more general, which generalization of answers to match with the query representation. When a given $SLF_{lattice}$ fires, all texts which yielded this $SLF_{lattice}$ are returned as an answer. $SLF_{lattice}$ are designed to be applied when all available SLF_{AMR} and SLF_{DT} have failed to fire.

Lattice querying also supports a proactive querying mode, when a Q/A system finds information for its human host automatically (Galitsky 2015b). Lattice querying automatically forms a query from a set of text samples provided by a user by generalizing them from the respective parse trees. Also, the system produces search results by matching parse trees of this query with that of candidate answers. Lattice queries allow an increase in big data exploration efficiency since they form multiple *hypotheses* concerning user intent and explore data from multiple angles (generalizations).

Exploring data, mostly keyword query and phrase queries are popular, as well as natural language-like ones. Users of search engines also appreciate "fuzzy match" queries, which help to explore new areas where knowledge of exact keywords is lacking. Using synonyms, taxonomies, ontologies and query expansions helps to substitute user keywords with the domain-specific ones to find what the system believes users are looking for (Ourioupina and Galitsky 2001; Galitsky 2003). Lattice queries increase the usability of search, proceeding from expressions in user terms toward queries against available data sources.

The concept of lattice generalization is illustrated in Fig. 5.12. Instead of a user formulating a query exploring a dataset, he provides a few samples (expressions of interest) so that the system formulates a query as an overlap (generalization) of these samples, applied in the form of a lattice (whose nodes are shown in bold on the bottom).

Fig. 5.12 A set of queries obtained by lattice generalization in comparison with a regular search query

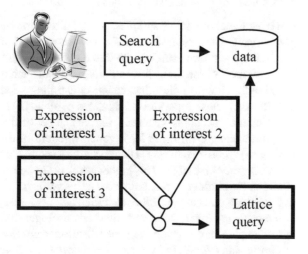

Proceeding from a keyword query to regular expressions or fuzzy one allows making search more general, flexible, assists in exploration of a new domain, as a set of document with unknown vocabulary. We introduce lattice queries, based on NL expressions that are generalized (Chaps. 2 and 4 Volume 2) into an actual query.

Nowadays, search engines ranging from open source to enterprise offer a broad range of queries with string character-based similarity. They include Boolean queries, span queries which restrict the distances between keywords in a document, regular expressions queries which allow a range of characters at certain positions, fuzzy match queries and more-like-this which allow substitution of certain characters based on string distances. Other kinds of queries allow expressing constraints in a particular dimension, such as geo-shape query. Proceeding from a keyword query to regular expression or fuzzy one allows making search more general, flexible, assists in exploration of a new domain, such as a set of document with unknown vocabulary. Lattice queries are a further step in this direction. Instead of getting search results similar to a given expression (done by "more like this" query), we first build the commonality expression between all or subsets of the given sample expressions, and then use it as a query. A lattice query includes words as well as attributes such as entity types and verb attributes. Forming lattice queries is based on Generalization operation introduced in Chap. 2.

5.4.1 Sentence-Based Lattice Generalization

Let us start with an employee search example; imagine a company looking for the following individuals:

- *A junior sale engineer expert travels to customers on site;*
- *A junior design expert goes to customer companies;*
- *A junior software engineer rushes to customer sites.*

Given the above set of samples, we need to form a job-search query that would give us candidates somewhat similar to what we are looking for. A trivial approach would be to just turn each sample into a query and attempt to find an exact match. However most of the times it would not work, so such queries need to release some constraints. How to determine which constraints need to be dropped and which keywords are most important (Makhalova et al. 2019)?

To do that, we apply generalization to the set of these samples. For the entities and attributes, we form the least general generalization. The seniority of the job (adjective) "*junior*" will stay. The job activity (noun phrase) varies, so we generalize them into <*job-activity*>. The higher-level reference to the job is "*expert*" and is common for all three cases, so it stays. The verbs for *job responsibility* vary, so we use <*action*> that can be further specified as

<*moving_action*> , using verb-focused ontologies like VerbNet. To generalize the last noun phrase, we obtain the generalization <*customer, NP*>:

Junior <any Job Activity> expert <action> customer-NP.

This is a lattice query, which is expected to be run against *job descriptions* index and find the cases which are supposed to be most desired, according to the set of samples.

In terms of parse trees of the potential sentences to be matched with the lattice query, we rewrite it as

JJ-Junior NP-* NN-Expert VP-* NN-Customer NP-*

The lattice query is as follows: *find me a junior something expert doing-something-with customer of-something.*

Now we show how this template can be applied to accept/reject a candidate answer *Cisco junior sale representative expert flew to customers' data centers.*

We represent the lattice query as a conjunction of noun phrases (NP) and verb phrases (VP) set:

[[NP [DT-A JJ-Junior NN-* NN-*], NP [NN*-Customers]], [VP [VB-* TO-To NN*-Customers]]]

The first NP covers the beginning of the lattice query above, and the second NP covers the end. VP covers the second half of the lattice query starting from *doing-something.*

The generalization between the lattice query and a candidate answer is

[[NP [JJ-Junior NN-* NN-*], NP [NN*-Customers]], [VP [VB-* TO-To NN*-Customers]]]

```
[[<1>NP'A':DT, <2>NP'junior':JJ, <3>NP'sale':NN, <4>NP'engineer':NN,
<5>NP'expert':NN], [<6>VP'travels':VBZ, <7>VP'to':TO, <8>VP'customers':NNS,
<9>VP'on':IN, <10>VP'site':NN], [<7>PP'to':TO, <8>PP'customers':NNS,
<9>PP'on':IN, <10>PP'site':NN], [<8>NP'customers':NNS, <9>NP'on':IN,
<10>NP'site':NN], [<8>NP'customers':NNS], [<9>PP'on':IN, <10>PP'site':NN],
[<10>NP'site':NN]]

[[<1>NP'A':DT, <2>NP'junior':JJ, <3>NP'design':NN, <4>NP'expert':NN],
[<5>VP'goes':VBZ, <6>VP'to':TO, <7>VP'customer':NN, <8>VP'companies':NNS],
[<6>PP'to':TO, <7>PP'customer':NN, <8>PP'companies':NNS], [<7>NP'customer':NN,
<8>NP'companies':NNS]]

[[<1>NP'A':DT, <2>NP'junior':JJ, <3>NP'software':NN, <4>NP'engineer':NN],
[<5>VP'rushes':VBZ, <6>VP'to':TO, <7>VP'customer':NN, <8>VP'sites':NNS],
[<6>PP'to':TO, <7>PP'customer':NN, <8>PP'sites':NNS], [<7>NP'customer':NN,
<8>NP'sites':NNS]]
```

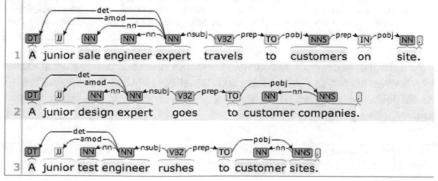

Fig. 5.13 Parse trees and phrase representation for three samples to form a lattice query

One can see that the NP part is partially satisfied (the article a does not occur in the candidate answer) and VP part is fully satisfied.

The parse trees for three samples are shown in Fig. 5.13.

Generalizing these three expressions, we obtain the query to run against a hypothetical dataset:

[[NP [DT-A JJ-Junior NN-* NN-*], NP [NN*-Customers]], [VP [VB-* TO-To NN*-Customers]]]

One can see that using a lattice of queries, one can be very sensitive in selecting search results. Searching for a token followed by a word with certain POS instead of just a single token gives a control over false-positive rate. Automated derivation of such constraint allows a user to focus on cases instead of making efforts to generate a query which would keep expected search results in and unwanted out.

Definition: a lattice query Q is satisfied by a sentence S, if $Q\hat{\ }S = S$.

In practice a weak satisfaction is acceptable, where

$Q\hat{\ }S \in S$, but there are constraints on the parts of the lattice query:

- A number of parts in $Q\hat{\ }S$ should be the same as in Q;
- All words (not POS-* placeholders) from Q should also be in $Q\hat{\ }S$.

5.4.2   Paragraph-Level Lattice Queries

Text samples to form a lattice query can be typed, but also can be taken from an existing text. To expand the dimensionality of content exploration, samples can be paragraph-size texts (Galitsky 2014).

Let us consider an example of a safety-related exploration task, where a researcher attempts to find a potential reason for an accident. Let us have the following texts as incidents descriptions. These descriptions should be generalized into a lattice query to be run against a corpus of texts for the purpose of finding a root cause of a situation being described.

Crossing the snow slope was dangerous. They informed in the blog that an ice axe should be used. However, I am reporting that crossing the snow field in the late afternoon I had to use crampons. I could not cross the snow creek since it was dangerous. This was because the previous hiker reported that ice axe should be used in late afternoon. To inform the fellow hikers, I had to use crampons going across the show field in the late afternoon.

As a result of generalization from two above cases, we will obtain a set of expressions for various ways of formulating commonalities between these cases. We will use the following snapshot of a corpus of text to illustrate how a lattice query is matched with a paragraph:

I had to use crampons to cross snow slopes without an ice axe in late afternoon this spring. However in summer I do not feel it was dangerous crossing the snow.

We link two phrases in different sentences since they are connected by a rhetoric relation based on *However ...*

```
rel: <sent=1-word=1..inform> ===> <sent=2-word=4..report>
From [<1>NP'They':PRP]
TO  [<4>NP'am':VBP,  NP'reporting':VBG, <8>NP'the':DT, <9>NP'snow':NN,
<10>NP'field':NN,   <11>NP'in':IN,   <12>NP'the':DT,  <13>NP'late':JJ,
<14>NP'afternoon':NN, <15>NP'I':PRP, <16>NP'had':VBD,  <17>NP'to':TO,
<18>NP'use':VB, <19>NP'crampons':NNS]
```

We are also linking phrases of different sentences based on communicative actions:

```
rel: <sent=1-word=6..report> ===> <sent=2-word=1..inform>
From [<4>NP'the':DT, <5>NP'previous':JJ, <6>NP'hiker':NN]
TO  [<1>NP'To':TO,  <2>NP'inform':VB, <3>NP'the':DT,  <4>NP'fellow':JJ,
<5>NP'hikers':NNS]
```

As a result of generalizing two paragraphs, we obtain the lattice query:

```
[[NP [NN-ice NN-axe ], NP [DT-the NN-snow NN-* ], NP [PRP-i ], NP [NNS-
crampons ], NP [DT-the TO-to VB-* ], NP [VB-* DT-the NN-* NN-field IN-
in DT-the JJ-late NN-afternoon (TIME) ]], [VP [VB-was JJ-dangerous ],
VP [VB-* IN-* DT-the NN-* VB-* ], VP [VB-* IN-* DT-the IN-that NN-ice
NN-axe MD-should VB-be VB-used ], VP [VB-* NN-* VB-use ], VP [DT-the
IN-in ], VP [VB-reporting IN-in JJ-late NN-afternoon (TIME) ], VP [VB-*
NN*-* NN-* NN*-* ], VP [VB-crossing DT-the NN-snow NN-* IN-* ], VP [DT-
the NN-* NN-field IN-in DT-the JJ-late NN-afternoon (TIME) ], VP [VB-
had TO-to VB-use NNS-crampons ]]]
```

Notice that potential safety-related "issues" are *ice-axe, snow, crampons, being at a ... field during later afternoon, being dangerous, necessity to use ice-axe, crossing the snow,* and others. These issues occur in both samples, so that are of a potential interest. Now we can run the formed lattice query against the corpus and observe which issues extracted above are confirmed. A simple way to look at it is as a Boolean OR query: find me the conditions from the list which are satisfied by the corpus. The generalization for the lattice query and the paragraph above turns out to be satisfactory:

```
[[NP [NN-ice NN-axe ], NP [NN-snow NN*-* ], NP [DT-the NN-snow ], NP [PRP-i ],
NP [NNS-crampons ], NP [NN-* NN-* IN-in JJ-late NN-afternoon (TIME) ]], [VP
[VB-was JJ-dangerous ], VP [VB-* VB-use ], VP [VB-* NN*-* IN-* ], VP [VB-
crossing NN-snow NN*-* IN-* ], VP [VB-crossing DT-the NN-snow ], VP [VB-had TO-
to VB-use NNS-crampons ], VP [TO-to VB-* NN*-* ]]] => matched
```

Hence we got the confirmation from the corpus that the above hypotheses, encoded into this lattice query, are true. Notice that forming a data exploration queries from the original paragraphs would contain too many keywords and would produce too much marginally relevant results.

We conclude this subsection with another example of lattice generalization.

We have three seeds:

---

1) *Mr. Bean is a British sitcom created by Rowan Atkinson and Richard Curtis, produced by Tiger Aspect Productions and starring Atkinson as the title character. Mr. Bean, described by Atkinson as "a child in a grown man's body", as he solves various problems presented by everyday tasks and often causes disruption in the process*

2) *Mr. Bean is a fictional character from the British comedy television program, Mr. Bean, its animated spin-off, and two live-action feature films. He was created and is portrayed by Rowan Atkinson and made his first appearance on television in the pilot episode which first aired on January 1, 1990.*

3) *Mr. Bean is childish, selfish character and brings various unusual schemes and contrivances to everyday tasks. He rarely speaks, and when he does, it is generally only a few mumbled words which are in a comically low-pitched voice. He also does not like people taking his things. Mr. Bean often seems unaware of basic aspects of the way the world works, and the program usually features his attempts at what would normally be considered simple activities, such as going swimming, using a television set, redecorating or going to church. The humor largely comes from his original (and often absurd) solutions to problems - usually self-inflicted - and his total disregard for others when solving them, his pettiness and occasional malevolence.*

1^2 gives 'Mr Bean British Atkinson'.
2^3 gives 'Mr Bean Programme Television'.
1^3 gives 'Mr Bean child character'.

All these queries need to be run to obtain a broader set of candidate answers.

5.4.3   Evaluation of Web Mining with Lattice Query Generalizations

To abstract away from an implementation of Q/A, we experiment with knowledge exploration scenarios for a lattice of generalization of samples using a search engine API such as Bing. Instead of formulating a single complex question and submitting it to Q/A, a user is required to express her interest step-by-step, via portions of text (Galitsky 2015a). Then the lattice generalization would formulate a number of hypotheses for questions in which some terms are important and other terms are not. Then the search engine API will search the web with these questions and automatically filter out results that are not covered by the generalization lattice. This filtering is done as a generalization of each candidate search results with each question from the generalization lattice and rejection of the ones not covered (producing empty generalization).

Let us have an example of a customer support CRM Q/A system where users share hew experience with healthcare providers:

This year I purchased my anthem blue cross insurance through my employer. what is the maximum out-of-pocket expense for a family of two in case of emergency?

Last year I acquired my individual kaiser health insurance for emergency cases only. how much would be my out of pocket expense within a year for emergency services for my wife and kids?

Q/A system finds a commonality between these paragraphs and forms the generalization lattice, so that the search results are as close to this set of queries as possible. An alternative approach is to derive a set of queries, varying generalization results, and to provide those search results which are covered the best with one of the queries from this set (not evaluated here).

We show NDCG @ 5 hits, depending on how queries are formed, in Table 5.2. We ran 20 queries for each evaluation setting and considered first 20 results for each. We use Bing search engine API for these experiments.

One can see that for the sentence-level analysis, there is 18% improvement proceeding from keyword overlap to parse structures delivering phrases for web search, and further 1% improvement leveraging lattice queries derived from a pair of sentences. For the paragraphs, there are respective 13 and 25% improvement, since web search engines do not do well with paragraph-sized queries. If the number of keywords in a query is high, it is hard for a search engine to select which keywords are important, and term frequency becomes the major ranking factor. Also, for such queries, a search engine cannot rely on learned user selections from previous querying, therefore, the quality of web search results are so low.

An importance of a generalization lattice is that it produces common features that are hypothesized to cause a target feature (Galitsky and Goldberg 2019). It is extremely important to control which features are used in a prediction task, otherwise a model (such as DL model where it is hard to control features) cannot be generalized or applied to similar domains.

An example here is relying on DL to achieve an impressive result on a relatively obscure natural language understanding benchmark called the argument reasoning comprehension task. The authors found out that BERT was picking up on superficial patterns the sample text was formulated with. Indeed, after re-analyzing their training data, the authors found ample evidence of spurious cues. For example, simply choosing a sample with the word "not" in it led to correct answers 61% of the time. After these patterns were removed from the data, BERT's (Devlin et al. 2019) score dropped from 77 to 53 (this is almost equivalent to random guessing).

Lattice of generalization is an underlying technique for an ML system that scores well on a given test set by relying on heuristics that are effective for frequent example types but can fail in more difficult tasks. (McCoy et al. 2019) study this issue solving the task of natural language inference. The authors propose that statistical models may be subject to learning three following rules it should not learn: a lexical overlap, a subsequence and a constituent. A controlled evaluation set is introduced that contains many examples where these rules fail. DL models trained do not do well on this dataset, suggesting that they have indeed adopted these *wrong* rules. A generalization lattice is a systematic framework to select and accept/reject such rules in an explicit form (that is unavailable in statistical learning).

Table 5.2 Evaluation of web mining

Method task	Forming generalization lattice as keyword overlap for two sentences	Forming generalization lattice via an intersection of parse structures of a sentence	Semantic-level AMR generalization lattice	Forming generalization lattice query as keyword overlap for paragraphs	Forming generalization lattice as a parse structure (parse thicket, Galitsky 2017, Chap. 4 Volume 2) for paragraphs	Lattice queries for two paragraphs
Legal research	0.344	0.373	0.393	0.305	0.287	0.403
Marketing research	0.354	0.452	0.430	0.282	0.318	0.403
Health research	0.331	0.390	0.442	0.316	0.381	0.406
Technology research	0.383	0.436	0.440	0.266	0.293	0.435
History research	0.350	0.442	0.410	0.257	0.335	0.369

5.5 Implementation of SLF-Based Q/A

We relied on semantic parsers (Damonte et al. 2017 and Damonte and Cohen 2018), discourse parsers of (Surdeanu et al. 2015; Joty et al. 2013) and syntactic generalization of (Galitsky et al. 2012) for building three components for SLF sources. SLF technique itself is presented in Chap. 4.

5.5.1 Evaluation of SLF_{AMR}

We used four datasets to evaluate the contribution of our methodology to search quality (Table 5.3):

- **Yahoo! Answer** (Webscope 2017) subset of question–answer pairs with broad topics where main question is a single sentence (possibly, compound) with ten-fifteen keywords. The dataset includes various domains, and domain knowledge coverage is shallow.
- **Financial questions** scraped from Fidelity.com (2018). This dataset demonstrates how search relevance improvement may occur in a vertical domain with reasonable coverage.
- **Car repair conversations** selected from www.2carpros.com (CarPros 2018) including car problem descriptions and recommendation on how to rectify them. These pairs were extracted from dialogues as first and second utterances.
- **SQuAD dataset** for factoid questions against well-organized sources like Wikipedia.

As a baseline, we chose an improved version of TF*IDF search typical for industrial search engines. Entity-based queries are represented with the help phrase search, distance between words are taken into account, stop words and tokenization settings are set to default (Ingersoll et al. 2012).

Table 5.3 Dataset statistics

Dataset	Question/Answer	Total #	Avg # words
Yahoo! Answers	Q	3700	12.3
	A	3700	124.1
Fidelity	Q	500	6.2
	A	500	118.0
Car repair	Q	10,000	5.5
	A	10,000	141.3
SQuAD	Q	18,000	5.3
	A	6000	563

5.5.2   Evaluation of Individual SLF Builders

Notice again that SLFs are designed to differentiate between the keywords which *must* occur in a query to trigger a given answer, and other keywords in this answer which do not necessarily trigger it. By avoiding false positives, providing the answers caused by the latter class of keywords, precision is expected to increase and recall stay unaffected.

For each search session of the stand-alone evaluation, we only consider the first results and reject the others. For all these datasets we assume that there is only one correct answer (from the Q/A pair) and the rest of answers are incorrect. Hence the evaluation framework for the algorithm contribution is straightforward: each query either succeeds or fails. We track if precision increases and recall stays about the same or deviates insignificantly after our indexing procedure is applied. The same baseline is used for all three stand-alone evaluations. The relevance of the baseline system is determined by many factors and is therefore not very insightful, so we focus at the change in precision (ΔP) and also make sure there is no substantial deterioration of recall (ΔR).

Evaluation results for the proposed SLF_{AMR} methodology are presented in Table 5.4. One can see a 4–5% improvement in Q/A precision and $\pm 2\%$ deviation in recall for full AMR SLFs. Therefore, we choose the methodology of AMR paths selected as most important (bolded) that delivers 4–6% precision improvement with $-0.5...2.0$ change in recall. The latter methodology is advantageous since it helps to avoid too specific keyword matches leading to distantly relevant answers.

SLF_{DT} delivers about 4% improvements in precision having recall almost unaffected, for the Nucleus/Satellite rules (Table 5.5). There is a further 1.5% improvement by using the automated classifier of EDUs. Since the deployment of such classifier in a domain-dependent manner is associated with substantial efforts, it is not necessarily recommended when this 1.5% improvement in search accuracy is not critical. Hence in the hybrid system we rely on the rule-based approach.

We also compare the performance of the proposed SLF_{DT} search on the extended framework derived from SQuAD 2.0 dataset and applied to *why?* and *how-to?* Wikipedia questions. Instead of addressing a question to a single Wikipedia text as standard evaluations do, we run them against all texts. We use SLF_{DT} vs neural

Table 5.4 Search relevance improvement by the stand-alone SLF_{AMR}

Dataset/Method	Baseline		Full AMR		AMR paths selected as most important	
	P	R	ΔP, %	ΔR, %	ΔP,%	ΔR, %
Yahoo! Answers	79.2	74.3	+4.5	+1.7	**+5.7**	−0.5
Fidelity	77.0	80.2	+5.7	−1.6	**+5.9**	+1.8
Car repair	78.7	81.4	+3.4	+0.2	**+4.3**	+0.4
SQuAD	68.3	71.4	+4.0	+2.0	**+5.2**	+1.1

Table 5.5 Search relevance improvement by stand-alone SLF_{DT}

Dataset/Method	Baseline		Nucleus/Satellite rules, improvement		Classification-based, improvement	
	P	R	ΔP, %	ΔR, %	ΔP,%	ΔR, %
Yahoo! Answers	79.2	74.3	+3.4	+1.1	4.4	−0.1
Fidelity	77.0	80.2	+3.3	−0.8	4.9	+1.3
Car repair	78.7	81.4	+4.3	+1.2	4.8	+0.3
SQuAD	68.3	71.4	+5.1	−2.0	5.3	−1.2

Table 5.6 Search relevance improvement by stand-alone $SLF_{lattice}$

Dataset/Method	Baseline		Generalizing 2–3 answers		Generalizing 3 + answers	
	P	R	ΔP, %	ΔR, %	ΔP, %	ΔR, %
Yahoo! Answers	79.2	74.3	2.5	+0.1	2.2	−0.4
Fidelity	77.0	80.2	4.3	−0.6	2.8	+1.8
Car repair	78.7	81.4	3.2	+0.02	2.3	−1.3
SQuAD	68.3	71.4	4.2	−0.09	3.2	+0.2

extractive reading comprehension one and exceed F1 of Allen AI (Gardner et al. 2018) and iPavlov (Burtsev et al. 2018) by at least 6% with the search engine trained on our corpus.

Lattices work well for questions that must be covered by multiple answers (Table 5.6). This set of SLFs does not trigger sets of answers frequently, but when it does, the improvement is valuable for users. Based on our analysis, we retain both 2–3 answers and 3+ answers generalizations since they complement each other and are both valuable.

5.5.3   Evaluating the Hybrid Performance

One can observe that the more sources of SLFs are employed, the better is the search accuracy (Table 5.7). SLF_{AMR}'s contribution is the highest, followed by SLF_{DT}. $SLF_{lattice}$ has the lowest contribution among these three sources, but each source mostly tackles its own class of questions. Therefore, SLFs of all these three sources complement each other and all of them are required.

The accuracy of search with an exhaustive set of manually built SLFs still has the highest accuracy as a result of incremental development: most cases with a lack or precision or recall can be tackled by adding constraints to an SLF or adding an SLF, respectively. A hybrid automated SLF system is ten percent less accurate than manual, so there is still room for new sources of automated SLFs.

Table 5.7 Hybrid performance of Auto-SLF approach

Method	Accuracy			
	R	P	F1	NDCG @ 5 hits
Baseline	75.8	76.8	76.3	0.316
SLF_{AMR}	82.1	82.9	82.5	0.332
SLF_{DT}	79.9	81.6	80.7	0.324
$SLF_{lattice}$	77.4	78.4	77.9	0.320
$SLF_{AMR} + SLF_{DT}$	84.5	84.5	84.5	0.336
$SLF_{AMR} + SLF_{lattice}$	83.0	83.6	83.3	0.338
$SLF_{AMR} + SLF_{DT} + SLF_{lattice}$	**85.7**	**85.9**	**85.8**	**0.345**
Manual SLF	93.2	98.0	95.5	0.446

In the right column, we evaluate search sessions from the standpoint of multiple answers (NDCG measure), obtained, for example, for not-factoid questions. We can observe a monotonic improvement of search accuracy proceeding from less effective to more effective SLF sources and then to the hybrid SLF formation architecture.

5.5.4 Overall Q/A Architecture

The developed methodology of the AMR, DT-based and Lattice-based analyses of answers is going to be applied in the following way, given an index of Q/A pairs:

1. Run a default query to shortlist candidate answers;
2. Search a user query against the SLF_{AMR} index and the shortlist of answers;
3. If no or too few answers search only SLF_{DT} index and the shortlist of answers;
4. If still no or too few results, search $SLF_{lattice}$ index and the shortlist of answers;
5. If still no or too few results, search the combined $SLF_{AMR} + SLF_{DT} + SLF_{lattice}$;
6. If still no or too few results, run default search against original answers and rank according to available facets (location, popularity, etc.).

This order is based on step-by-step release of constraints for the search query. These steps can also be done in parallel and a meta-search agent can choose the search result with the strongest constraint.

We now proceed to a generic architecture of an industrial search where the proposed technique can naturally fit (Fig. 5.14).

In addition to returning search results links, web search Q/A generates a direct answer to a user query by reading the passages retrieved by the web search engine using machine reading comprehension (MRC) models, as illustrated in Fig. 5.14.

The web Q/A task is far more challenging than most of the academic MRC tasks. One dimension of complexity is the scale and quality of the text collection. In MRC settings, it is assumed that SQuAD includes an answer as a text span in a passage which is a well-readable text section from a Wikipedia page. On the contrary, web Q/A

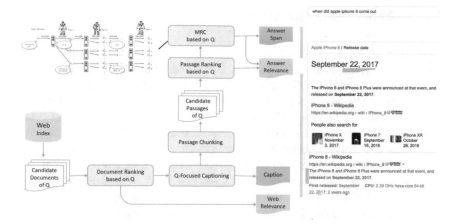

Fig. 5.14 Architecture of a web search Q/A system

has to identify an answer from billions of web documents which consist of trillions of noisy passages that often contain contradictory, wrong, obsolete information due to the dynamic nature of arbitrary content.

Another difficulty is runtime latency. In an academic setting, an MRC model might take seconds to read and re-read documents to generate an answer, while in the Q/A setting the MRC part (implemented via reinforcement learning, top-left corner of Fig. 5.14) is required to add no more than a tenth of a second to the whole search session processing time.

User experience requirements for industrial-level and CRM-level Q/A are much more advanced. While an academic setting MRC models provide a text span as an answer, CRM Q/A needs to provide different user experiences depending on different devices where the answer is shown (such as Search Engine Result Page). Figure 5.14 (on the right) shows an example of the search engine result page which includes not only the answers presented as a highlighted text span, but also various supporting evidence and related web search results (i.e., captions of retrieved documents, passages, audios and videos) that are consistent with the answer.

As a result, a commercial Web Q/A agent such as Bing or Google often incorporates a MRC module as a post-web component on top of its Web search engine stack. Given a question, a set of candidate documents are retrieved from the inverse index via a fast, primary ranker. Then the Document Ranking component is used to assign relevance scores for these documents. The top-ranked relevant documents are presented with their captions generated from a Query-Focused Captioning module. The Passage Chunking module segments the top documents into a set of candidate passages, which are further ranked by the Passage Ranking module based on another passage-level boosted trees ranker. Finally, the MRC module finds the answer span *"September 22, 2017"* from the top-ranked passages.

5.5.5 CCG Semantic Parsing with AMR

The task of building SLFs from text is a special case of semantic parsing. In this Section, we do a dive into the AMR parsing. (Artzi et al. 2015) introduce a new, scalable Combinatory Categorial Grammar (CCG; Steedman 2000) induction approach that solves these challenges with a learned joint model of both compositional and non-compositional semantics, and achieves state-of-the-art performance on AMR Bank parsing. Sentences are mapped into AMR structures. CCG is used to construct a lambda-calculus representation of the compositional aspects of AMR. CCG is designed to capture a wide range of linguistic phenomena, such as coordination and long-distance dependencies, and has been used extensively for semantic parsing. To use CCG for AMR parsing, the authors define a simple encoding for AMRs in lambda calculus, for example, as seen with the logical form z and AMR a in Fig. 5.15 for the sentence *"Target team confirm their participation"*. Using CCG to construct such logical forms requires a new mechanism for non-compositional reasoning, for example, to model the long-range anaphoric dependency introduced by *their* in Fig. 5.15.

In this Fig, we have AMR (a), underspecified logical form (u), which contains underspecified constants in bold that are mapped to AMR relations to generate the fully specified logical form (z).

Fig. 5.15 Conversion from a sentence to AMR (**a**) and then on to a logical form

```
a:
  (d/confirm-01
        :ARG0 (p/person
                    :ARG0-of (h/have-org-role-91 :
                          ARG1 (c/organization
                                      : name (n/name :op1"Target"))
                          :ARG2(o/team)))
        :ARG1 (i/participate-01 :ARG1 p))
```

```
u:
  A₁(λd.confirm-01 (d) ∧
        ARG0(d,  A₂ (λp.person(p) ∧
              REL-of(p, A₃ ,  (λh/have-org-role-91(h) ∧
                    ARG1 (h, A₄ (λc.organization(c) ∧
                          name (c, A₅ (λn.name(n) ∧
                                op1(n, Target))))) ∧
                    REL(h, A₆ (λo/team(o)))))) ∧
        ARG1(d, A₇ (λn.participate-01(n) ∧
              ARG1 (I, R(ID))))))
```

```
z:
  A₁(λd.confirm-01 (d) ∧
        ARG0(d,  A₂ (λp.person(p) ∧
              ARG0-of(p, A₃ ,  (λh/have-org-role-91(h) ∧
                    ARG1 (h, A₄ (λc.organization(c) ∧
                          name (c, A₅ (λn.name(n) ∧
                                op1(n, Target))))) ∧
                    ARG2(h, A₆ (λo/team(o)))))) ∧
        ARG1(d,  A₇ (λn.participate-01(n) ∧
              ARG1 (I, R(2))))))
```

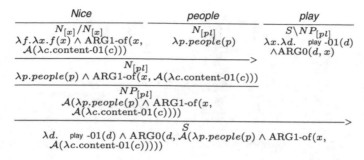

Fig. 5.16 Example CCG tree

Figure 5.15 shows an underspecified logical form u that would be constructed by the grammar with the bolded placeholder token indicating an anaphoric link that is unresolved. These placeholders are resolved by a factor graph model. It is applied to the output logical form such as SLF and models which part of SLF they refer to. This is needed, for example, to find the referent for a pronoun.

A CCG grammar induction algorithm first attempts to use a set of templates to hypothesize about new lexical entries. It then attempts to combine bottom-up parsing with top-down recursive splitting to select the best entries and learn new templates for complex syntactic and semantic phenomena, which are re-used in later sentences to hypothesize about new entries.

Combinatory Categorial Grammar CCG is a semantic representation supporting a transition from syntax to semantics (Steedman 2000). In CCG trees, each node is a category (Fig. 5.16). For example, $S\backslash NP_{[pl]}$: $\lambda x.\lambda d.dance\text{-}01(d)$ & ARG0(d, x) is a category for an intransitive verb phrase. The syntactic type $S\backslash NP_{[pl]}$ indicates that a noun phrase type of argument (NP[pl]) is to follow. The returned syntactic type will be S. \ and/shows an argument on the left or right, respectively. The syntactic attribute pl specifies that the argument must be plural.

Attribute variables spell out an agreement between syntactic attributes. In particular, adjectives are assigned the syntax $N_{[x]}/N_{[x]}$, where x is used to indicate that the attribute of the argument will determine the attribute of the returned category. The simply typed lambda calculus encodes a semantic meaning relying on types such as entity e, truth value t, functional types $<e, t>$ for a function from e to t.

In Fig. 5.16, *category, $\lambda x.\lambda d.play\text{-}01(d)$ & ARG0(d, x)* is a $<e, <e, t>>$-typed function expecting an ARG0 argument, and the conjunction specifies the roles of the *play-01* frame.

Example CCG tree has three lexical entries, two forward applications (>) and type-shifting of a plural noun to a noun phrase.

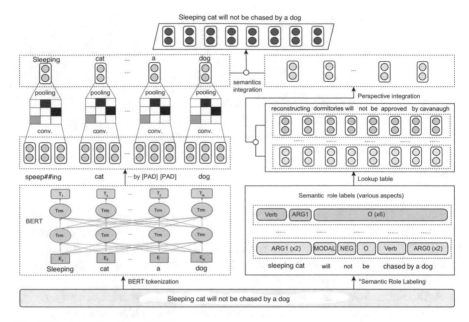

Fig. 5.17 Semantics-aware BERT

5.6   Pre-Trained Language Models and Their Semantic Extensions

Distributed representations have been widely used as a standard part of NLP models due to the ability to capture the local co-occurrence of words from large scale unlabeled text (Mikolov et al. 2013). However, these approaches for learning word vectors only involve a single, context independent representation for each word with little consideration of contextual encoding in sentence level. Thus recently introduced contextual language models including ELMo (Peters et al. 2018), GPT, BERT and XLNet fill the gap by strengthening the contextual sentence modeling for better representation, among which BERT uses a different pre-training objective, masked language model, which allows capturing both sides of context, left and right. Besides, BERT also introduces a next sentence prediction task that jointly pre-trains text-pair representations. Recent studies show that contextual language models are powerful and convenient for downstream NLU tasks.

However, a number of studies have found DL models might not really understand the NL queries (Mudrakarta et al. 2018) and vulnerably suffer from adversarial attacks (Jia and Liang 2017). Frequently, DL models pay great attention to nonsignificant words and ignore important ones; current NLU models suffer from insufficient contextual semantic representation and learning. (Zhang et al. 2020) proposed to enable BERT with semantic role labeling (SRL), and in Chap. 3 of this book we combine DL with semantically rich approaches. Semantics-aware BERT with explicit contextual semantic clues learns the representation in a fine grained, combing the strengths of BERT on plain context representation and an explicit semantic analysis for deeper meaning representation.

Semantic BERT is intended to handle multiple sequence inputs. In semantic BERT, words in the input sequence are passed to SRL to obtain multiple predicate-derived structures to form a semantic embedding. In parallel, the input sequence is segmented to subwords (if any) by BERT word-piece tokenizer, then the subword representation is transformed back to word level via a convolutional layer to obtain the contextual word representations. Finally, the word representations and semantic embedding are concatenated to form the joint representation.

For the text, {*Sleeping cat will not be chased by a dog*}, it is tokenized to a subword-level sequence, {

Sleep, ##ing, cat, will, not, be, chas, ##ed, by, a, dog}

As to the word-level semantic structures, they are as follows: [ARG1: sleeping cat] [ARGM-MOD: will] [ARGM-NEG: not] be [V: chased] [ARG0: by a dog]

[V: sleeping] [ARG1: cat] will not be chased by a dog

5.6.1 Encoding and Alignment with BERT

The raw text sequences and semantic role label sequences are firstly represented as embedding vectors to feed a pretrained BERT. The input sentence $X = \{x_1, ..., x_n\}$ is a sequence of words of length n, which is first tokenized to subword tokens. Then the transformer encoder captures the contextual information for each token via self-attention and produces a sequence of contextual embeddings.

For m label sequences related to each predicate, $T = \{ t_1, ..., t_m \}$ where t_i contains n labels denoted as $\{label_1^i, label_2^i, ..., label_n^i\}$. Since these labels are in the level of words, the length is equal to the original sentence length n of X. Semantic roles are also encoded as embeddings via a mapping of these labels into vectors $\{ v_1^i, v_2^i, ..., v_n^i \}$ and feed a BiGRU layer to obtain the label representations for m label sequences in the latent space, $e(t_i) = \text{BiGRU}(v_1^i, v_2^i, ..., v_n^i)$ where $0 < i < m$.

Gated recurrent units (GRUs) are a gating mechanism in recurrent neural networks, The GRU is like a long short-term memory (LSTM) with forget gate but has fewer parameters than LSTM, as it lacks an output gate. BiGRU is a Bidirectional GRU. Each time step the BiGRU gets as input a word vector. Afterward, an attention layer is applied over each hidden state h_t. The attention weights are learned using the concatenation of the current hidden state of the BiGRU and the past hidden state in the second BiGRU layer.

For m label sequences, let L_i denote the label sequences for token x_i, so that we have $e(L_i) = \{e(t_1), ..., e(t_m)\}$. We concatenate the m sequences of label representation and feed them to a fully connected layer to obtain the refined joint representation e t in dimension d:

$$e'(L_i) = W_2[e(t_1), ..., e(t_m)] + b_2,$$
$$e^t = \{ e'(L_1), ..., e'(L_n) = \},$$

where W_2 and b_2 are trainable parameters.

The integration must merge the lexical text embedding and label representations. As the original pre-trained BERT is based on a sequence of subwords, while the semantic representation labels the words, it is necessary to align these sequences of different sizes. Thus we group the subwords for each word and use convolutional neural network (CNN) with a max pooling to obtain a word-level representation.

We now show how the merge works on the level of an individual word. Let us select word x_i that consists of a sequence of subwords $[s_1, s_2,..., s_l]$, where l is the number of subwords for word x_i. Denoting the representation of subword s_j from BERT as $e(s_j)$, we first utilize a Convolutional layer,

$e_i' = W_1 [e(s_i), e(s_{i+1}),..., e(s_{i+k-1})] + b_1$, where W_1 and b_1 are trainable parameters and k is the kernel size. Then ReLU (rectified linear unit $y = max(0, x)$) and max pooling are applied to the output embedding sequence for x_i:

$e_i^* = ReLU(e_i')$ and

$e(x_i) = \text{MaxPooling}(e_1^*, ..., e_{l-k+1}^*)$.

Hence the overall representation for the word sequence X is

$e^w = \{ e(x_1), ..., e(x_n)\} \in R^{n \times dw}$ where d_w is the dimension of word embedding.

The aligned word embedding and encoded semantic embeddings are then merged by a fusion function

$h = concatenation(e_w, e_t)$

The experimental results that BERT can be easily improved in many domains by addition of some limited semantic information defeats the paradigm of an end-to-end system. This experiment demonstrates that split into components each of which solves its own task guarantees improvement over an end-to-end system.

5.7 Conclusions

Having explored the possibility of manual construction of the summarized logical forms for Q/A, in this chapter we focused on automated building of SLFs, relying on semantic, discourse, and syntactic generalization, to abstract away from particular phrasing of possible questions. Summarized logical forms are designed to represent the main issues of an answer which can be queried explicitly and avoid miscellaneous topics and details which should not be taken into account associating this answer with a potential question.

We explored the possibilities of building SLFs from Abstract Meaning Representation (AMR) of sentences by selecting the subgraphs supposed to be the most important. We looked at examples showing that the closer the phrase as a path in AMR is located to the root of AMR, the higher is the score of the inclusion of this phrase as an SLF. SLF based on AMR is a particular method of *semantic search* (Zelevinsky et al. 2017).

In parallel, we leverage discourse analysis of answer paragraphs to highlight more important elementary discourse units (EDUs) to convert in SLFs and less important EDUs which are not converted into SLFs. The third source of SLFs is a pair-wise generalization of answers. Proposed methodology is designed to improve question answering Q/A precision to avoid matching questions with less important, uninformative parts of a given answer so that some other answer is delivered instead. A stand-alone evaluation of each of three sources of SLFs is conducted as long as an assessment of a hybrid SLF generation system. We conclude that indexing of the most important text fragments of an answer instead of the whole answer improves the Q/A precision by almost 10% as measured by F1 and 8% as measured by NDCG.

The proposed generalization lattice technique seems to be an adequate solution for cross-sentence alignment (MacCartney et al. 2008). One application of this problem is automated solving of numerical equations formulated as algebra word problems (Kushman et al. 2014). To form a representation for an elementary algebra problem *text*, we would use a training set of pairs *textT—equationT* and produce an alignment of *text* and *textT* by means of generalization *text ^ text* (Chap. 5) that is an expression to be converted into a numerical expression. The capability to "solve" an algebraic problem is based on the completeness of a training set: for each type of equation, there should be a textual algebraic problem for it. Also, the problem of phrase alignment for such areas as machine translation has been explored in (Jiang and Conrath 1997).

Let us consider an algebra problem.

An amusement park sells adult tickets for $3 and kids tickets for $2, and got the revenue $500 yesterday.

We attempt to find a problem from our training set, such as:

A certified trainer conducts training for adult customers for $30 per hour and kid customer for $20 per hour, and got the revenue $1000 today.

Generalization looks like the following, including the placeholders for the values

```
[[NP [JJ-adult NNS-* IN-for $-$ CD-3 CC-and NN*-kids NN*-* ], NP
[IN-* NN*-* ], NP [DT-the NN-revenue $-$ CD-* ]],
[VP [NN-* IN-for $-$ CD-3 ,-, CC-and VB-got DT-the NN-revenue $-
$ CD-* NN-* (DATE) ], VP [CC-and NN*-kids NN*-* IN-for $-$ CD-2 CC-
and VB-got DT-the NN-revenue $-$ CD-* NN-* (DATE) ], VP [NN*-* IN-
for $-$ CD-3 CC-and NN*-kids NN*-* IN-for $-$ CD-2 ]]].
```

The space of possible equations can be defined by a set of equation templates, induced from training examples. Each equation template has a set of placeholders, CD-placeholders are matched with numbers from the text, and unknown placeholders are matched with nouns. (Kushman et al. 2014) define a joint log-linear distribution over the system of equations with certain completeness properties. The authors learned from varied supervision, including question answers and equation systems, obtained from annotators. Features used are unigrams and bigrams, question object/sentence, word lemma nearby constant, what dependency path contains (word or another dependency path), and others, as well as equation features.

Fig. 5.18 SLFs are designed for a controlled Q/A as an opposite approach to what an end-to-end learning provides

On the contrary, we rely on linguistic discourse (parse trees and their connecting arcs) to find the matching element in the training set. It is expected to shed the light on the linguistic properties of how a sentence can be converted into a part of an algebra equation.

We conclude this chapter with the claim that SLF-based search engine with automated SLF construction is designed for domains where a thorough semantic representation of questions and answers is essential. In such domains a CRM, a fully automated end-to-end learning without human feature engineering and interpretable intermediate representations is not very plausible (Fig. 5.18).

References

Artzi Y, Lee K, Zettlemoyer L (2015) Broad-coverage CCG semantic parsing with AMR. In: Empirical Methods in Natural Language Processing. Lisbon, Portugal, pp 1699–1710

Banarescu L, Bonial C, Cai S, Georgescu M, Griffitt K, Hermjakob U, Knight K, Koehn P, Palmer M, Schneider N (2013) Abstract Meaning Representation for Sembanking. In: Proceedings of the 7th linguistic annotation workshop and interoperability with discourse. pp 178–186

Burtsev M, Seliverstov A, Airapetyan R, Arkhipov M, Baymurzina D, Bushkov N, Gureenkova O, Khakhulin T, Kuratov Y, Kuznetsov D, Litinsky A, Logacheva V, Lymar A, Malykh V, Petrov

M, Polulyakh V, Pugachev L, Sorokin A, Vikhreva M, Zaynutdinov M (2018) DeepPavlov: open-source library for dialogue systems. In: ACL-system demonstrations, pp 122–127

Cai S, Knight K (2013) Smatch: an evaluation metric for semantic feature structures. In: Proceedings of the 51st annual meeting of the association for computational linguistics (Volume 2: Short Papers). Sofia, pp 748–752

CarPros   (2018)   https://github.com/bgalitsky/relevance-based-on-parse-trees/blob/master/exa mples/CarRepairData_AnswerAnatomyDataset2.csv.zip

Chali Y, Joty SR, Hasan SA (2009) Complex question answering: unsupervised learning approaches and experiments. J Artif Int Res 35(1):1–47

Damonte M, Cohen SB (2018) Cross-lingual abstract meaning representation parsing. In: Proceedings of NAACL

Damonte M, Cohen SB, Satta G (2017) An incremental parser for abstract meaning representation. In: Proceedings of EACL

Devlin J, Chang MW, Lee K, Toutanova K (2019) BERT: pre-training of deep bidirectional transformers for language understanding. NAACL V1

Eremeev M, Vorontsov K (2019) Semantic-based text complexity measure. RANLP

Fidelity   (2018)   https://github.com/bgalitsky/relevance-based-on-parse-trees/blob/master/exa mples/Fidelity_FAQs_AnswerAnatomyDataset1.csv.zip

Galitsky B (2003) Natural language question answering system: technique of semantic headers. Advanced Knowledge International, Australia

Galitsky B (2014) Learning parse structure of paragraphs and its applications in search. Eng Appl Artif Intell 32, 160–184

Galitsky B (2015a) Finding a lattice of needles in a haystack: forming a query from a set of items of interest. LNCS 1430, FCA4AI@IJCAI 99–106

Galitsky, B (2015b) Lattice queries for search and data exploration. In: The Twenty-Eighth international flairs conference flairs. The track on Semantic, Logics, Information Extraction, and AI

Galitsky B (2017) Matching parse thickets for open domain question answering. Data Knowl Eng 107:24–50

Galitsky B (2019a). A social promotion chatbot. Developing Enterprise Chatbots. Springer, Cham

Galitsky B (2019b) A content management system for chatbots. Developing Enterprise Chatbots. Springer, Cham

Galitsky B, Goldberg S (2019) Explainable machine learning for chatbots. Developing Enterprise Chatbots, Springer Cham

Galitsky B, Dobrocsi G, de la Rosa JL (2012) Inferring semantic properties of sentences mining syntactic parse trees. Data Knowl Eng 81:21–45

Galitsky B, Ilvovsky D, Kuznetsov SO (2015) Rhetorical map of an answer to compound queries. ACL-2 681–686

Gardner M, Grus J, Neumann M,Tafjord O, Dasigi P, Liu N, Peters M, Schmitz M, Zettlemoyer L (2018) AllenNLP: A deep semantic natural language processing platform. https://arxiv.org/abs/ 1803.07640

Greene GJ, Dunaiski M, Fischer B, Ilvovsky D, Kuznetsov SO (2015) Browsing publication data using tag clouds over concept lattices constructed by key-phrase extraction. RuZA Workshop. In: Proceedings of Russian and South African workshop on knowledge discovery techniques based on formal concept analysis (RuZA) pp 10–22

Hobbs JR (1985) On the coherence and structure of discourse. Tech. Rep. CSLI-85–37, Center for the Study of Language and Information, Stanford University

Ingersoll GS, Morton TS, Farris AL (2012) Taming text. How to find, organize, and manipulate it. Manning Publ., Shelter, Island, NY

Jacobs T, Tschötschel R (2019) Topic models meet discourse analysis: a quantitative tool for a qualitative approach. Int J Soc Res Methodol 22(5):469–485

Jansen P, Surdeanu M, Clark P (2014) Discourse complements lexical semantics for nonfactoid answer reranking. ACL

Jasinskaja K, Karagjosova E (2017) Rhetorical relations: the companion to semantics. Wiley, Oxford

Jia R, Liang P (2017) Adversarial examples for evaluating reading comprehension systems. EMNLP

Jiang JJ, Conrath DW (1997) Semantic similarity based on corpus statistics and lexical taxonomy. In: Proceedings of the international conference on research in computational linguistics, Taiwan

Jones B, Andreas J, Bauer D, Hermann KM, Knight K (2012) Semantics-based machine translation with hyperedge replacement grammars. In: Proceedings COLING

Joty SR, Carenini G, Ng RT, Mehdad Y (2013) Combining intra-and multi- sentential rhetorical parsing for document-level discourse analysis. ACL 1:486–496

Kamp H, Reyle U (1993) From discourse to logic; an introduction to modeltheoretic semantics of natural language. Formal Logic and DRT, Kluwer, Dordrecht

Kim S, Bracewell R, Wallace K (2004). From discourse analysis to answering design questions. In: International workshop on the application of language and semantic technologies to support knowledge management processes (EKAW 2004). At: Whittlebury Hall, Northamptonshire, UK

Kingsbury P, Palmer M (2002) From treebank to propbank. In: LREC. pp 1989–1993

Kushman N, Artzi Y, Zettlemoyer L, Barzilay R (2014) Learning to automatically solve algebra word problems. ACL 2014

MacCartney B, Galley M, Manning CD (2008) A phrase-based alignment model for natural language inference. EMNLP, 802–811

Makhalova T, Ilvovsky D, Galitsky B (2019) Information Retrieval Chatbots Based on Conceptual Models. In: International Conference on Conceptual Structures. pp 230–238

Mann W, Thompson S (1988) Rhetorical structure theory: towards a functional theory of text organization Text. Interdisc J Study Discourse 8(3):243–281

McCoy T, Pavlick E, Linzen T (2019) Right for the wrong reasons: diagnosing syntactic heuristics in natural language inference. ACL 3428–3448

Mikolov T, Sutskever I, Chen K, Corrado GS, Dean J (2013) Distributed representations of words and phrases and their compositionality. NIPS

Moschitti A (2006) Efficient Convolution Kernels for Dependency and Constituent Syntactic Trees. In: Proceedings of the 17th European conference on machine learning, Berlin, Germany

Mudrakarta PK, Taly A, Sundararajan M, Dhamdhere K (2018) Did the model understand the question? ACL

Ourioupina O, Galitsky B (2001) Application of default reasoning to semantic processing under question-answering. DIMACS Tech Report 16

Palmer M (2009) Semlink: Linking propbank, verbnet and framenet. In: Proceedings of the generative lexicon conference. Pisa, Italy, pp 9–15

Peters ME, Neumann M, Iyyer M, Gardner M, Clark C, Lee K, Zettlemoyer L (2018) Deep contextualized word representations. NAACL-HLT

Rajpurkar P, Jia R, Liang P (2018) Know what you don't know: unanswerable questions for SQuAD. ACL

Severyn A, Moschitti A (2012) Fast support vector machines for convolution tree kernels. Data Min-Ing Knowl Discov 25:325–357

Sidorov G (2014) Should syntactic N-grams contain names of syntactic relations? Int J Comput Linguist Appl 5(1):139–158

Steedman M (2000) The syntactic process. The MIT Press

Sun M, Chai JY (2007) Discourse processing for context question answering based on linguistic knowledge. Knowl. Based Syst. 20(6):511–526

Surdeanu M, Hicks T, Valenzuela-Escarcega MA (2015) Two practical rhetorical structure theory parsers. In: Proceedings of the Conference of the north american chapter of the association for computational linguistics—human language technologies: software demonstrations (NAACL HLT), 2015

Webscope (2017) Yahoo! answers dataset. https://webscope.sandbox.yahoo.com/catalog.php?dat atype=l

Werling K, Angeli G, Manning CD (2015) Robust subgraph generation improves abstract meaning representation parsing. In: Proceedings of the 53rd annual meeting of the ACL. Beijing, pp 982–991

Zelevinsky V, Dashevsky Y, Diana YE (2017) Semantic text search US Patent 9836,529

Zhang Z, Wu Y, Zhao H, Li Z, Zhang S, Zhou X, Zhou X (2020) Semantics-aware BERT for language understanding. AAAI

Zong H, Yu Z, Guo J, Xian, Y., Li, J. (2011) An answer extraction method based on discourse structure and rank learning. In: 7th International conference on natural language processing and knowledge engineering (NLP-KE)

Chapter 6
Acquiring New Definitions of Entities

Abstract We focus on understanding natural language (NL) definitions of new entities via the ones available in the current version of an ontology. Once a definition is acquired from a user or from documents, this and other users can rely on the newly defined entity to formulate new questions. We first explore how to automatically build a taxonomy from a corpus of documents or from the web, and use this taxonomy to filter out irrelevant answers. We then develop a logical form approach to building definitions from text and outline an algorithm to build a step-by-step definition representation that is consistent with the current ontology. A nonmonotonic reasoning-based method is also proposed to correct semantic representations of a query. In addition, we focus on a special case of definitions such as NL descriptions of algorithm for the NL programming paradigm. Finally, search relevance improvement is evaluated based on acquired taxonomy and ontology.

6.1 Introduction

In the previous chapter, we explored how a Question Answering (Q/A) system can automatically form definitions of new entities and associate existing entities from a training corpus of texts. In this chapter, we will build a system to *acquire new definitions* of entities from a user and the web. Formulating definitions, the user can select a term she would like to use and let other users use while asking questions. This flexibility feature is essential for the user to teach the system "new stuff" including novel entities, facts and assertions expressed in these entities. This feature is lacking by not only major search engines but also by virtual assistants as well. Historically, even Eliza (Weizenbaum 1976) chatbot attempted to imitate understanding of human definitions but since then no dialogue system approached a robust understanding. Users of modern virtual assistants like Microsoft Cortana, Google Home and Amazon Alexa desire to teach them definitions of entities important for them, but this capability is not supported by the underlying data-driven technologies popular these days (Higashinaka et al. 2014).

© Springer Nature Switzerland AG 2020 193
B. Galitsky, *Artificial Intelligence for Customer Relationship Management*,
Human–Computer Interaction Series,
https://doi.org/10.1007/978-3-030-52167-7_6

The focus of this chapter is a definition understanding system, built on top of a conventional ontology-based Q/A (a question understanding system). We refer to it as a DU system. A special case of a question understanding system is a summarized logical form (SLF) one, where a set of SLFs can be extended by a definition supplied by a user.

A human skill in acquiring new definition is an important step in brain development (Fig. 6.1, Piaget and Cook 1952). On the top: a boy acquires a definition of an airplane as a version of bird (which he already knows) such that people travel in it. As a result, the boy can recognize airplanes and answer questions about them. In this Chapter, we enable a Q/A system with this skill. This is a deductive reasoning approach. On the contrary, on the bottom there is a girl learning to recognize a dog not via a definition,

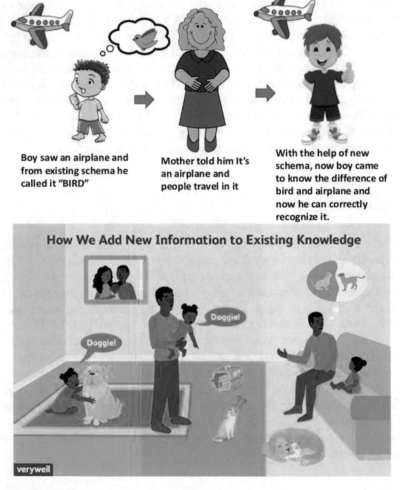

Fig. 6.1 Acquisition of definitions via deductive (on the top) and inductive (on the bottom) ways

but by means of distinguishing between dogs and cats (inductive approach, frequently referred to as data-driven).

A certain knowledge of logic programming technique is required in this chapter, as it was in the previous chapters on SLF - based Q/A.

6.1.1 Knowledge Acquisition

The problem of knowledge acquisition lies at the core of NLP. In recent decades, there is massive exploitation of collaborative, semi-structured information as the ideal middle ground between high-quality, fully-structured resources and the larger amount of cheaper (but noisy) unstructured text (Hovy et al. 2013).

The usefulness of domain ontologies in various fields is well established. Indeed, they are a pivotal piece when dealing with heterogeneity or complex semantic issues (Berners-Lee et al 2001; Boukharu et al. 2012). Building ontologies is a difficult and time-consuming task that usually requires to combine the knowledge of domain experts with the skills of ontology engineers into a single effort. This bottleneck currently constitutes a real obstacle for the adoption of semantic technologies into industrial applications such as CRM (Galitsky and de la Rosa 2011).

NL lexical definitions of terms can be used as a source of knowledge in a number of semantic tasks, such as Question Answering, Information Extraction and Text Entailment. While formal, structured resources such as ontologies are still scarce and usually target a very specific domain, a large number of linguistic resources gathering dictionary definitions is available not only for particular domains but also addressing wide-coverage commonsense knowledge. However, in order to make the most of those resources, it is necessary to capture the semantic shape of NL definitions and structure them in a way that favors both the information extraction process and the subsequent information retrieval. This process should be allowing an effective construction of semantic models from these data sources while keeping the resulting model easily searchable and interpretable. Furthermore, by using these models, Q/A systems can increase their own interpretability, benefiting from the structured data for performing traceable reasoning and generating explanations. These are the features that are essential for Explainable AI (Holzinger et al. 2017) and are valuable for CRM.

A broad corpus of research addresses improving available semi-structured resources such as Freebase (Bollacker et al. 2008) and Wikidata (Vrandecic 2012), taxonomies (Ponzetto and Strube 2011), ontologies (Mahdisoltani et al. 2015) and semantic networks (Nastase and Strube 2013) with a limited set of relations. Such direction of research as Open Information Extraction (IE) (Etzioni et al. 2008) is focused on the unconstrained extraction of a large number of relations from massive unstructured corpora such as the web. It has been implemented in systems like TEXTRUNNER and REVERB (Fader et al. 2011). An ultimate goal of these explorations is a domain-independent knowledge acquisition to support such tasks as Machine Reading Comprehension.

In this Chapter, we propose a methodology for automatically building and extending commonsense knowledge bases given NL definitions provided by users or extracted from a textual resource. Relying on a conceptual model based on a set of semantic roles for definitions, we classify each fragment of a defining part according to its relation to the entity being defined (definiendum), and convert the classified data into a logic representation. A user's ability to define new entity or fact so that other users and herself can then use this definition and access this fact is a badly needed feature of a Q/A system and a conversational agent (Volker et al. 2007).

Although recent years have seen an explosion in the Q/A technology, there is still a lack of systems satisfactorily providing answers in the domains which are logically complex, poorly structured, hardly formalized and subject to extension by users (Galitsky 2001b). To approach such domains, designers of every Q/A system must find a compromise between a *full-featured NLP* system oriented for complex domains, *advanced reasoning* for semantic processing, knowledge representation and extension and *shallow online processing for queries* to assure fast replies.

In spite of the high number of commercial Q/A systems, functioning in a wide spectrum of domains, it is still unclear which NLP component is essential to achieve satisfactory answer accuracy, high performance and efficient domain preparation. Clearly, an increase of the (logical) complexity of queries to be understood can be accomplished by involving more sophisticated reasoning. Let us enumerate the potential components of an abstract rule-based Q/A system, considering them from the practical reasoning viewpoint. The reader should bear in mind that a particular implementation is based on a selected subset of these components (Galitsky 2003):

(1) Rule-based system for *morphological and syntactic* analysis that reveals the interconnections between the words;
(2) Rule-based *semantic* analysis, obtaining the query representation (QR) with the optimal generality after the maximum possible number of rules have been applied (Diefenbach et al. 2018);
(3) Inference-based *pragmatic* analysis, transforming query representation in accordance with the answer knowledge base;
(4) Answer knowledge base, obeying the efficient reasoning-based properties of consistency, completeness, easy update and restructuring;
(5) Reasoning-accented *information extraction* (Etzioni et al. 2008);
(6) Reasoning-accented textual annotation;
(7) Interactive Q/A domain development tools (Galitsky 2002a).

The component (3), pragmatic analysis, usually attracts the least attention in comparison to the other items above, perhaps because it is based on heuristics rather than on a firm linguistic or logical base. Pragmatic component may implement the verification of compatibility between the formal representation of a query and the knowledge base. In particular, our study of generality control (Sect. 6.5.2) suggests the feedback mechanism of sorting out the invalid query representations. Therefore, pragmatic analysis filters out the hypotheses of syntactic and semantic representations of input query, inconsistent with domain representation (Galitsky 2001a). We will focus on pragmatic analysis in Sect. 6.6.

Ontology-based data access is a popular approach in knowledge representation and reasoning (Poggi et al. 2008; Navigli and Velardi 2004), supporting querying access to possibly heterogeneous and incomplete data sources based on a logical theory. This is achieved via an ontology that enriches the user query, typically a union of conjunctive queries, with commonsense knowledge. In this framework, the ontology and the user query are viewed as two components of one composite query.

6.2 Related Work

Silva et al. (2018) process the whole noun and verb databases of WordNet (Fellbaum 1998) and build the WordNetGraph, and then use this knowledge graph to recognize text entailments in an interpretable way, providing concise justifications for the entailment decisions. Bovi et al. (2015) went beyond the word-level representation, being able to identify multiword expressions. They perform a syntactic-semantic analysis of textual definitions for Open Information Extraction (OIE). Although they generate a syntactic-semantic graph representation of the definitions, the resulting graphs are used only as an intermediary resource for the final goal of extracting semantic relations between the entities present in the definition. Casu and Tacchella (2011) build a system that translates NL definitions into logical forms and then perform a partial translation from first-order formulas into Description Logics.

Noraset et al. (2017) investigate RNN models that learn to define word embeddings by training on examples of dictionary definitions. The authors explore a possibility to utilize distributional semantics to generate dictionary definitions of words, performing definition modeling, the task of generating a definition for a given word and its embedding. The results show that a model that controls dependencies between the definiendum word and the definition words perform significantly better, and that a character-level convolution layer designed to leverage morphology can complement word-level embeddings.

Emani et al. (2019) propose to enrich an ontology automatically by obtaining logical expressions of concepts, providing an OWL DL (Web Ontology Language Description Logics) expression of a concept from two inputs:

(1) An NL definition of the concept;
(2) An ontology for the domain of this concept.

NALDO uses as much as possible entities provided by the domain ontology, however, it can suggest, when needed, new entities, covering values, cardinality restrictions, subsumption and equivalence (Fig. 6.2). The following processing steps are used:

(1) Splitting;
(2) Lemmatization + Syntactic Pruning;
(3) Semantic Pruning;
(4) Concepts Identification;

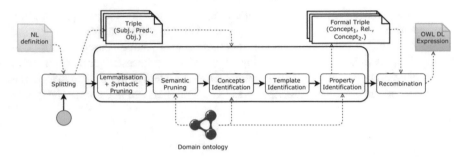

Fig. 6.2   Architecture of NL to OWL DL converter

(5)   Template Identification;
(6)   Property Identification;
(7)   Recombination (combining a set of formal triples to obtain a single resultant OWL DL expression.

Given a large corpus of definitions, (Bovi et al. 2015) leverage syntactic dependencies to reduce data sparsity, then disambiguate the arguments and content words of the relation strings and leverage the resulting information to organize the acquired relations hierarchically. It results in a high-quality knowledge base consisting of millions of automatically acquired semantic relations. The syntactic-semantic graph construction from a textual definition is depicted in (Fig. 6.3). The semantics of the relations follows along the lines of BabelNet (Navigli and Ponzetto 2010), a wide-coverage multilingual semantic network obtained from the automatic integration of WordNet, Wikipedia and other resources. For each relation instance t extracted, both a_i, a_j and the content words appearing in r are linked to the BabelNet inventory. $band_{bn}^{N}$ refers to the i-th BabelNet sense for the English word *band*.

More recent work in the area of open domain IE is focused on deeper language understanding at the level of both syntax and semantics (Nakashole et al. 2012) and tackles challenging linguistic phenomena like synonymy and polysemy. However, these issues have not yet been fully addressed. Relation strings are still bound to surface text, lacking actual semantic content. Furthermore, most open-domain IE systems do not have a clear and unified ontological structure and require additional processing steps, such as statistical inference mappings (Dutta et al. 2014), graph-based alignments of relational phrases (Grycner and Weikum 2014), or knowledge base unification procedures (Bovi et al. 2015), in order for their potential to be exploitable in industrial applications such as CRM.

6.2.1   Grammars for Semantic Representation

A number of different grammars for semantic parsers are used in Q/A: Gramatical Framework grammars used by (Marginean 2017), feature-based context-free

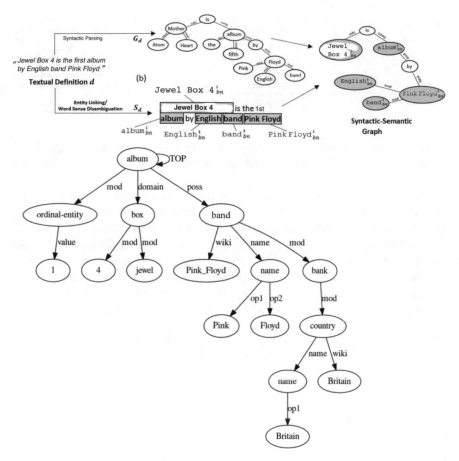

Fig. 6.3 On the top, joint syntactic and semantic representation for a definitional sentence. On the bottom, AMR graph for this sentence

grammar (FCFG, Song et al. 2015), Combinatory Categorial Grammar (CCG) used by (Hakimov et al. 2015) and lexical tree-adjoint grammars used in (Unger et al. 2012).

As to an example of using the CCG grammar, let us represent a sentence *"Bill Clinton is married to Hillary Clinton"*. To parse the sentence, the following grammar rules are needed (Table 6.1).

The main syntactic categories here are noun phrase (NP) and sentence and combinations of them (S). The syntactic category (S\NP)..N P, for example, indicates that it can be combined with a NP on the left and on the right to get S. The phrase *married-to* is semantically mapped into a binary predicate that takes two arguments. The semantic representation of *Hillary Clinton* is a constant which in DBpedia is *dbr : Hillary Clinton*. Hence we obtain representation.

$\lambda y.\lambda x.dbo : spouse$ (dbr : *Bill_Clinton*, dbr : *Michelle_Obama*).

Table 6.1 Categorial grammar representation example

Lexical item	Syntactic category	Semantic representation
Bill Clinton	NP	dbr : *Bill_Clinton*
is	(S\NP)..(S\NP)	$\lambda f.\lambda x.f(x)$
married to	(S\NP)..NP	$\lambda y.\lambda x.dbo : spouse(x, y)$
Hillary Clinton	NP	dbr : *Hillary_Clinton*

At the same time, Abstract Meaning Representation (AMR) of a simple fact is as follows (Fig. 6.4). Introduction and further details about AMR are available in previous Chaps. 3–5.

The main advantage of this approach is that one can directly get a semantic representation of a question, which also covers the superlative and comparative phrasings of it. A disadvantage is that the questions have to be well formulated, CCG is not robust with respect to malformed questions. The main disadvantage is that one needs to have for each lexical item a corresponding semantic representation. To generate the semantic representations, (Hakimov et al. 2015) relied on the approach of (Zettlemoyer and Collins 2012) that generates a semantic representation from a learning corpus of pairs of questions and the corresponding answers. Regretfully, many lexical items do not appear in the training corpus; that leads to a low recall. To address this problem, one can generate candidate semantic representations of unknown lexical items based on their POS tags. In the example of Table 6.1, if the

```
(v3 / marry-01
  :ARG1 (v1 / person
    :name (v2 / name
      :op1 "Bill"
      :op2 "Clinton")
    :wiki "Bill_Clinton")
  :ARG2 (v4 / person
    :name (v5 / name
      :op1 "Hillary"
      :op2 "Clinton")
    :wiki "Hillary_Clinton"))
```

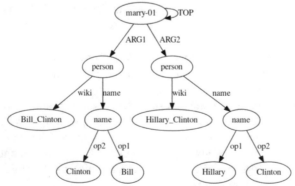

Fig. 6.4 AMR representation: on the top, as a logical form; on the bottom, as a graph

"applied machine learning" "prepare data"

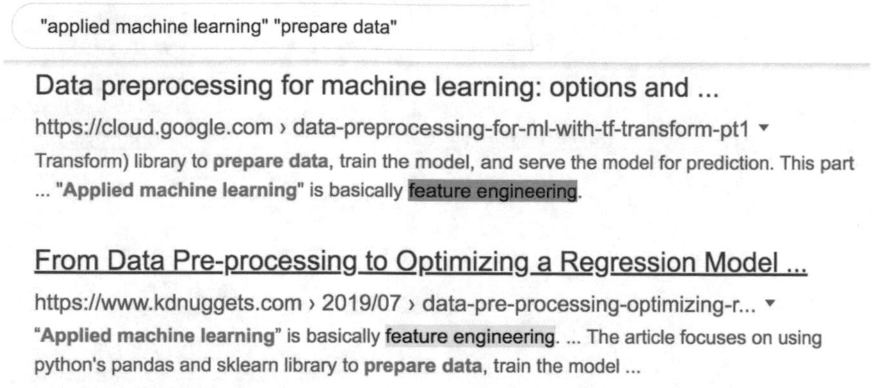

Data preprocessing for machine learning: options and ...

https://cloud.google.com › data-preprocessing-for-ml-with-tf-transform-pt1 ▾

Transform) library to **prepare data**, train the model, and serve the model for prediction. This part
... "**Applied machine learning**" is basically feature engineering.

From Data Pre-processing to Optimizing a Regression Model ...

https://www.kdnuggets.com › 2019/07 › data-pre-processing-optimizing-r... ▾

"**Applied machine learning**" is basically feature engineering. ... The article focuses on using
python's pandas and sklearn library to **prepare data**, train the model ...

Fig. 6.5 Mining for a value for next taxonomy node

lexical item *married-to* is unknown, then possible interpretations are generated (such
as two binary functions with the arguments x and y exchanged). Since there is no
knowledge that exists about the fact that *married-to* has to be mapped to the property
dbo: spouse, some templates are generated. Hence the parser is able to parse the
question, but a binary property corresponding to *married-to* still needs to be found.
Alternatively, one can leverage verb signatures from VerbNet (Kipper et al. 2008,
Chaps. 1 and 4 Volume 2) or web mining (Figs. 6.5 and 6.6).

6.2.2 Difficulties in Understanding Definitions

Getting automatically a correct expression from a given natural language (NL) definition, toward a domain ontology, requires to deal with many issues. A formal representation of definition expression is correct if it is accepted by domain experts as
it is. The main issues while tackling the problem of automatic formalization of NL
definitions are enumerated below.

(1) Identification of single definitions in a sentence multiple definitions. In practice,
a sentence may contain more than one definition. So, when one wants to enrich
automatically an ontology using definitions in texts, a first challenge is to identify
automatically these definitions. For instance, the sentence "*An italian pizza is
a pizza which has toppings of tomato and a souvlaki pizza is the one done with
Tzatziki sauce*" contains two distinct definitions.

(2) Identification of the defined concept and its definition. The same definition
can have multiple wordings. The challenge here is to identify the concept that
is defined and the phrases that give the definition itself. For example, all the
following sentences define what is "*cell space*".

- *A cell space is an anatomical space that is part of a healthy cell;*
- *An anatomical space that is part of a healthy cell is a cell space;*

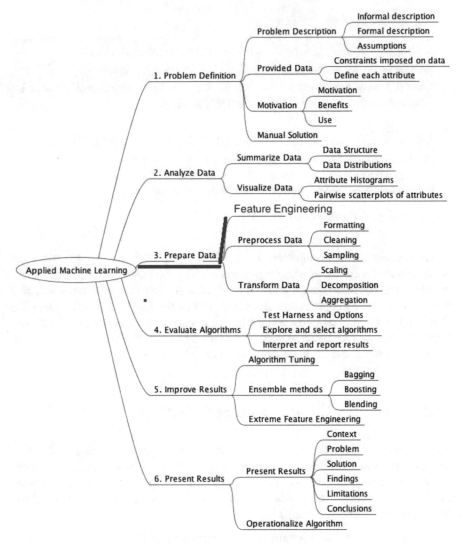

Fig. 6.6 A Machine Learning taxonomy. Web mining is used for computing a new node (shown in bold red)

- *If an anatomical space is part of a healthy cell then it is a cell space.*

(3) Entity linking (Galitsky et al. 2010). The formalization task requires building a formal expression of concepts using entities provided in the domain ontology. Hence, a challenge consists of linking the terms of the definition with the corresponding entities in the ontology. This linking can be:

- *Default,* which means that there are some similarities between the surface form of the term of the definition and the one of the ontology's entity. For example, when the definition *"An american pizza is a pizza which has toppings of tomato"* is formalized, against the pizza ontology, as *italian-Pizza(p) :- pizza(p) & ∃ Topping topping(p, cheeseTopping)*, we consider the linking of the entity *cheese* to *cheeseTopping* as default. Formally, default linking can be defined as: Given a string *s*, an ontology *O*, identify entity *e* ∈ *O* so that *s* refers to *e*. In this task, *s* and labels of *e* share the common stem.

- *Strong*, to denote linking where there is no similarity between the term of the definition and its formal correspondence in the ontology. When the definition *"AGreek pizza is a pizza made with meet such as lamb"* is formalized within the *pizza* ontology, as

  greekPizza(p) :- pizza(p) & ∃ lambTopping topping(p, lambTopping) & meat(lambTopping)

  we associate *lamb* as meat as a strong entity linking. Formally, a strong linking can be defined for string s and an ontology O as an identification of entity *e* ∈ *O* so that *s* refers to a hypothetical entity *e*, not found in *O*, but semantically related to *e*.

(4) Pruning. When we transform an NL definition of a concept into a formal expression, some terms of the definition are redundant. The formalization procedure needs to remove these phrases. Domain experts, who validate the formalization, assume that those terms are meaningless for this definition. For example, when the definition "A cell space is an anatomical space that is part of a healthy cell" is formalized as *cellSpace(X) :- AnatomicalSpace (X) & cell(Cell) & ∃ part of(X, Cell)*, the word *healthy* is pruned. Formally, pruning can be defined as: Given a string *s*, an ontology *O*, discard all the words in *s* so that the intended matching of *s* to entity *e* can be done correctly without these words.

6.3 Building a Taxonomy by Web Mining

Our main hypotheses for automated learning taxonomies on the web is that common expressions between search results for a given set of entities give us *parameters* of these entities (Galitsky et al. 2011). Formation of the taxonomy follows an unsupervised learning style, once the set of seed taxonomy entities is given. This approach can be viewed as a human development process, where a baby explores a new environment and forms new rules. The initial set of rules is set genetically, and the learning process adjusts these rules to a specific habituation environment to make the rules more sensitive (and therefore allows more beneficial decision making). As new rules are being accepted or rejected during their application process, exposure to new environments facilitates formation of new specific rules. After the new, more complex rules are evaluated and some portion of these newly formed rules is accepted, the complexity of the rules grows further, to adapt to additional peculiarities of the environment.

We learn new entities to extend our taxonomy in a similar learning setting (Galitsky 2013). The taxonomy learning process is iterative: at each new learning step, we add new edges to the nodes that are currently terminal. We start with the seed taxonomy, which enumerates a few of the main entities of a given domain and the relations of these entities with a few domain-determining entities. For example, the seed for the tax domain will include the relationships

$$tax - deduct \quad tax - on - income \quad tax - on - property,$$

where *tax* is a domain-determining entity and {*deduct, income, property*} are the main entities in this domain. The objective of taxonomy learning is to acquire further parameters of existing entities such as *tax-deduct*. In the next iteration of learning, these parameters will be turned into entities, to enable a new set of parameters to be learned, such as *sales-tax, 401k* (Fig. 6.7).

Each learning iteration is based on web mining. To find parameters for a given set of tree leaves (current entities), we go to the web and try to obtain common expressions between the search results (snippets) for the query formed for the current tree paths (Galitsky and Kovalerchuk 2014). For the example above, we search for *tax-deduct, tax-on-income,* and *tax-on-property* and extract words and expressions that are **common** among the search results (Fig. 6.8). Common words are single verbs, nouns, adjectives and even adverbs, prepositional phrases or multi-words in addition to prepositional, noun and verb phrases, which occur in **multiple** search results.

After such common words and multi-words are identified, they are added as new entities to the list of existing entities. For example, for the path *tax-deduct* newly learned entities can be

$$tax - deduct \rightarrow decrease - by \qquad tax - deduct \rightarrow of - income$$
$$tax - deduct \rightarrow property - of \qquad tax - deduct \rightarrow business$$
$$tax - deduct \rightarrow medical - expense.$$

The format here is *existing_entity → its parameter (to become a new_entity);*

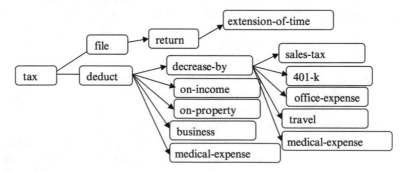

Fig. 6.7 A taxonomy for Tax domain

1. TurboTax® - **Tax Deduction** Wisdom - Should You Itemize?
   turbotax.intuit.com › Tax Calculators & Tips - Cached
   **Learn whether itemizing your deductions makes sense, or if you should simply take 1
   no-questions-asked standard deduction. The standard deduction is ....**

2. 10 big **deductions** too many of us miss - **tax** preparation - MSN Money
   money.msn.com/**taxes**/10-big-**deductions**-too-many-of-us-miss-schn... - Cached
   A lot of taxpayers don't know they can save thousands of dollars with these **tax** break
   Did you forget about any of these **deductions** and credits?

3. The Most-**Overlooked** Tax Deductions
   www.kiplinger.com/.../the-mostoverlooked-tax-deductions.html - Cached
   Every year, the IRS dutifully reports the most common blunders that taxpayers make
   their returns. And every year, at or near the top of the "oops" list ...

4. **Tax** Credits and **Deductions**
   taxes.about.com/od/deductionscredits/Deductions_Credits.htm - Cached
   Lower your **tax** bill by taking advantage of **deductions** and **tax** credits. Tips for
   preparing your**taxes**.

5. **Tax** Topics - Topic 503 **Deductible Taxes**
   www.irs.gov/**taxtopics**/tc503.html - Cached
   Feb 7, 2011 – To be **deductible**, the **tax** must be imposed on you and must have bee
   paid during your **tax** year. However, tables are available to determine ...

6. **Tax** - **Tax Deductions** - H&R Block
   www.hrblock.com/**taxes**/tax.../deductions.../overlooked_deductions... - Cached
   Find information on **tax deductions** from H&R Block.

7. What is a **Tax Deduction**?
   www.wisegeek.com/what-is-a-tax-deduction.htm - Cached
   May 13, 2011 – A **tax deduction** reduces the taxes a person must pay by a certain
   percentage. **Tax deductions** are different from **tax** credits, which...

Fig. 6.8 The first step of thesaurus learning, given the seed tax-deduct. We highlight the terms that
occur in more than one answer and consider them to be parameters

where "→" here is an unlabeled edge of the taxonomy extension at the current
learning step.

Next, from the path in the taxonomy tree *tax-deduct,* we obtain five new paths.
The next step is to collect the parameters for each path in the new set of leaves for
the taxonomy tree. In our example, we run five queries and extract parameters for
each of them. The results will resemble the following:

$$tax - deduct - decrease - by \rightarrow sales$$
$$tax - deduct - decrease - by \rightarrow 401 - K$$
$$tax - deduct - decrease - by \rightarrow medical$$

$$tax - deduct - of - income \rightarrow rental$$
$$tax - deduct - of - income \rightarrow itemized$$
$$tax - deduct - of - income \rightarrow mutual - funds$$

For example, searching the web for *tax-deduct-decrease* allows the discovery of
an entity *sales-tax,* which is associated with a *decrease in a tax deduction,* usually

with the meaning "*sales tax*". The commonality between snippets shows that the *sales tax* should be accounted for while calculating *tax deduction* (and not doing something that would *decrease* it).

Hence, the taxonomy is built via inductive learning from web search results. We start with the taxonomy seed nodes, and then we find web search results for all of the currently available graph paths. Next, for each commonality found in these search results, we augment each of the taxonomy paths by adding respective leaf nodes. In other words, for each iteration, we discover the list of parameters for each set of currently available entities, and then, we turn these parameters into entities for the next iteration (Galitsky et al. 2010).

The taxonomy seed is formed manually or can be compiled from available domain-specific resources. Seed taxonomy should contain at least 2–3 nodes, to enable the taxonomy growth process to have a meaningful start. A taxonomy seed can include, for example, a glossary of a specific knowledge domain, readily available for a given vertical domain, such as (Investopedia 2019) for tax entities.

Figure 6.6 shows a machine learning taxonomy. To form its current node, we search the web or a corpus of documents on machine learning for the labels of the previous node and the root node and generalize from search results (Fig. 6.5). This way we obtain the node "feature engineering".

6.4   Improving Q/A Relevance by a Taxonomy

Logical properties of sets of keywords and logical forms that express meanings of queries are explored in (Galitsky 2003). There is a systematic way to treat the relative importance of keywords via default reasoning (Galitsky 2005); multiple meanings of keyword combinations are represented via operational semantics of default logic.

Achieving relevancy using a taxonomy is based on a totally different mechanism compared with a conventional TF*IDF- based search. In the latter, the importance of the terms is based on the frequency of occurrence. For an NL query (not a Boolean query), any term can be omitted in the search result if the remaining terms give an acceptable relevancy score. In the case of a Boolean query, this statement is true for each of its conjunctive members. In a taxonomy-based search, we know which terms *should* occur in the answer and which terms *must* occur there; otherwise, the search result becomes irrelevant.

6.4.1   Ranking Based on Taxonomies

To use a taxonomy to filter out irrelevant answers, we search for a taxonomy path (down to a leaf node, if possible) that is the closest to the given question in terms of the number of entities from this question. Then, this path and leaf node most accurately specifies the meaning of the question, and constrains which entities *must* occur and which *should* occur in the answer, to be considered relevant. If the n-th node entity from the question occurs in the answer, then all k < n entities should occur in it as well.

For a taxonomy-supported search, we use two conditions:

- *Acceptability* condition. It verifies that all of the essential words from the query that exist in a taxonomy path are also in the answer.
- *Maximum relevance* condition. It finds words from the query that exist in a taxonomy path and are in the answer. It then computes the score based on the number of found essential and other keywords.

For the majority of search applications, the *acceptability* condition is easier to apply than the *Maximum relevance* condition: An answer $a_i \in A$ is acceptable if it includes *all of the essential* (according to is_about) keywords from question Q, as found in the taxonomy path $T_p \in T$. For any taxonomy path T_p that covers the question q (the intersections of their keywords is not empty), these intersection keywords *must be* in the acceptable answer a_i.

$$\forall T_p \in T: \quad T_p \cap q \neq \emptyset \Rightarrow a_i \supseteq T_p \cap q$$

For the best answer (most accurate) we write
$a_{best} : \exists\, T_p\, max(cardinality\, (a_i \cap (T_p \cap q))$

A taxonomy-based relevance score can be defined as the value of the *cardinality* $(a_i \cap (T_p \cap q)$, which is computed for all T_p that cover q. Then, the best answer score $a_{best} = max\, \{a_i\, \}_{Tp}\, (cardinality\, (a_i \cap (T_p \cap q)))$ is found among the scores for all of the answers A. The taxonomy-based score can be combined with the other scores such as the TF*IDF, popularity, the temporal/decay parameter, location distance, pricing, linguistic similarity, and other scores for the resultant ranking, depending on the search engine architecture. In our evaluation, we will be combining this score with the linguistic similarity score.

For a sentence (a set of keywords) s and a taxonomy path T_p, $s \cap T_p$ is the operation of finding a set of keywords that are the labels of a path T_p in taxonomy T. In general, there are taxonomy paths that cover a given question q, and each result of $s \cap T_p$ must be intersected with a question. Having multiple paths that cover a given query q means that this query has multiple meanings in this domain; for each such meaning a separate set of acceptable answers is expected.

Hence, the reader can see that the taxonomies are designed to support computing the is_about relation. Given a query q and a taxonomy T, we find the path T_p in such a way that is_about$(q, T_p \cap q)$.

Let us consider the taxonomy example in Fig. 6.7 for the query *"How can tax deduction be decreased by ignoring office expenses"*, $q =$ {*how, can, tax, deduct(ion), decreas(ed)-by, ignor(ing), office, expense*} and $A =$ {

a1 = {*deduct, tax, business, expense, while, decreas(ing), holiday, travel, away, from, office*},

a2 = {*pay, decreas(ed), sales-tax, return, trip, from, office, to, holiday, no, deduct(ion)*},
a3 = {*when, file, tax, return, deduct, decrease-by, not, calculate, office, expense, and, employee, expense*}}.

We will not consider tokenization and word form normalization issues in our examples, and we will show endings in brackets for convenience. Note that, in terms of keyword overlap, a1, a2 and a3 all look like good answers.

For *q*, we have this query covered by T_p = {<tax>-<deduct>-<decrease-by>-<office-expense>}. Let us calculate the taxonomy score for each answer:

$$score(a1) = cardinality(a_1 \cap (T_p \cap q)) = cardinality(\{tax, deduct\}) = 2;$$

$$score(a2) = cardinality(\{tax, deduct, sales\_tax\}) = 3;$$

socre(a3) = cardinality({*tax, deduct, decrease-by, office-expense*}) = 3; Note that this answer is the only answer that passes the acceptability criterion.

Our next example concerns the disambiguation problem. For a question

q = "*When can I file an extension for the time for my tax return?*"

let us imagine two answers:

a1 = "*You must file form 1234 to request a 4 month extension of time to file your tax return*"

a2 = "*You must download a file with the extension 'pdf', complete it, and print it to do your taxes*".

We expect the closest taxonomy path to be:

$$T_p = \{<tax>-<file>-<return>-<extension-of-time>\}$$

Here, *tax* is a main entity, *file* and *return* we expect to be in the seed, and *extension-of-time* would be the learned entity; as a result, *a1* will match with taxonomy and is an acceptable answer, and *a2* is not.

Another way to represent taxonomy is not to enforce it to be a tree (least general) but to allow only single node for each label instead (Fig. 6.7).

Further details on building taxonomies and thesauri are available in (Galitsky 2019).

6.4.2 Taxonomy-Based Relevance Verification Algorithm

We now outline the algorithm, which takes a query q, runs a search (outside of this algorithm), obtains a set of candidate answers a and finds the best acceptable answer according to the definitions that we introduced in the previous section.

The input: query q
The output: the best answer a_{best}

---

1) For a query q, obtain a set of candidate answers A by the available means (using keywords, using an internal index, or using an external index of search engine APIs);
2) Find a path in taxonomy T_p that covers maximal terms in q, along with other paths that cover q, to form a set $P = \{ T_p \}$.
   Unless an acceptable answer is found:
   3) Compute the set $T_p \cap q$.
   For each answer $a_i \in A$
      4) compute $a_i \cap (T_p \cap q))$ and apply an acceptability criterion.
      5) compute the score for each a_i.
      6) compute the best answer a_{best} and the set of acceptable answers A_a.
If no acceptable answer is found, then return to 2) for the next path from P.
   7) Return a_{best} and the set of acceptable answers A_a if available.

6.4.3 Evaluation of Taxonomy-Based Q/A

We evaluate the constructed taxonomy in the financial domain (Galitsky 2001a) answering questions from the Fidelity (2018) dataset. This dataset of 500 financial questions is scraped from Fidelity.com and demonstrates how search relevance improvement may occur in a vertical domain with a reasonable coverage. An example of a question, and answer and the taxonomy for Fidelity financial domain is shown in Fig. 6.9. The question dataset was also extended by 200 more complex questions related to investment from Yahoo! Answers (Webscope 2017),

Taxonomies are frequently assessed manually by experts or researches themselves, or via comparison with existing ontologies like WordNet. Some evaluation metrics have been defined for triplets produced by unsupervised web miner (Grefenstette 1994, Reinberger and Spyns 2005). Instead, in this Chapter, we perform an evaluation of the Q/A enabled with taxonomy.

We measure normalized Discounted Cumulative Gain (NDCG, Wang et al. 2013), assessing the top five search results (Table 6.2).

Q: '*Can I still contribute to my IRAs while taking Minimum Required Distributions?*'
Topic: '*Beneficiaries and Stretching Tax Advantages of Assets*'
A: '*You can contribute to a Roth IRA after age 70½ as long as you have compensation and meet the income eligibility requirements. Otherwise, you generally cannot contribute to any other kind of IRA in the year you turn age 70½ or any year thereafter.*'

[11] Technical Support	[12] Account Security
	[14] Username and Password
	[15] Other Personal Information
	[30] Customers Outside US
[19] Positions	[20] Balances
	[21] Activity History
	[22] Activity Orders
[31] Stocks	[32] Mutual Funds
	[33] Order Execution
	[36] Basket Trading
	[37] How Margin Works
[35] Advanced	[39] Portfolio Margin
	[40] Limited Margin for IRAs
	[42] Cash Account Trading And Free Ride Restrictions

Fig. 6.9 A question, an answer and the taxonomy in Fidelity financial domain

Table 6.2 Evaluation of taxonomy-enabled search

Query	Phrase sub-type	Baseline TF*IDF search	Taxonomy-based relevance	The suite of Q/A techniques including syntactic and semantic components	The suite + Taxonomy-based
3–4 word phrases	Noun phrase	0.264	0.290	0.313	0.318
	Verb phrase	0.271	0.296	0.309	0.323
	How-to expression	0.260	0.286	0.297	0.312
5–10 word phrases	Noun phrase	0.248	0.278	0.290	0.309
	Verb phrase	0.251	0.270	0.295	0.316
	How-to expression	0.245	0.262	0.286	0.307
2–3 sentences	One verb one noun phrases	0.201	0.223	0.238	0.261
	Both verb phrases	0.212	0.218	0.230	0.243
	One sent of how-to type	0.193	0.221	0.224	0.236

The baseline is just a TF*IDF search, employed in a majority of search engine libraries such as SOLR, ElasticSearch and Google Cloud Search. The Integrated search system included the following components, described in Chaps. 2 and 3:

(1) Structurized word2vec for the treatment of domain-independent synonyms;
(2) Deep Learning-based reading comprehension for factoid value-based questions. This component is good at finding an exact vales (and its location in text) for an attribute in question, given an entity;
(3) Syntactic generalization (Galitsky 2014). This component thoroughly treats the phrase structure for an entity in question and answer. It is leveraged in longer queries for matching multiwords and complicated structure of attributes for multiple entities.

To observe how taxonomies help various kinds of questions, we varied the question type in terms of the linguistic phrase (NP, VP, Why/How-to) and question complexity, ranging from a single phrase to a compound sentence up to multiple sentences in a query (the case of Yahoo! Answers).

We track whether the performance improves relative to a simple baseline and also relative to a complex integrated system but without a domain-specific taxonomy (Table 6.2). We observe that the average performance is improved by using this taxonomy by 9% compared to the TF*IDG baseline and 6% compared to integrated system baseline. This integrated system on its own yields 14% improvement over the TF*IDF baseline without taxonomies. Improvement for simpler queries (rows 2–5) is stronger for TF*IDF baseline (10%) and weaker over the integrated system baseline (only 4%).

6.5 Acquiring Definitions of New Entities in NL

A processing of NL definitions of new entities (predicates) is associated with significantly more difficulties of both a syntactical and logical nature than a query processing. It is hard not only for a machine but for a human as well to formulate a definition of an entity that can be usable in multiple contexts. Users of a CRM Q/A would appreciate the capability of teaching a system a new entity, so that their peers and themselves can rely on it in formulating their further questions (Galitsky 2003, Fig. 6.10). Domain designers update the domain knowledge directly, and via domain extension and restructuring tools. New definitions are introduced manually by users and knowledge engineers. In addition to asking questions, customers may define new objects and entities (using the same input areas for questions and definitions), as well as introduce new facts, recommendations and advices. AMR of a definition is shown in Fig. 6.11.

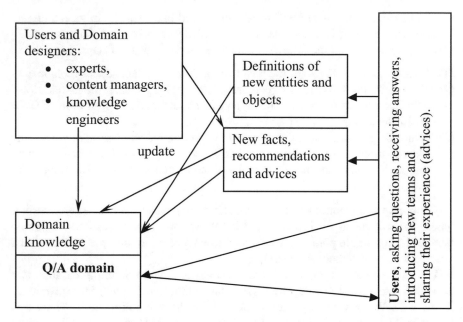

Fig. 6.10 Information flow while extending NL Q/A ontology by definition of new entities

Fig. 6.11 AMR
representation of a definition.
Definiendum is shown with a
red oval, and the rest of the
the graph is a defining part

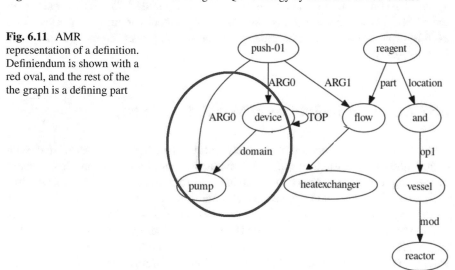

The task of the definition understanding system is not only to translate a definition
from NL to a logical form properly. In addition, the DU system needs to model the
current predicate structure (which a user might not be aware of) and to identify a
position for the new entity or its new instance in the domain ontology.

6.5.1 Syntactic Template of a Definition

We assume that an NL definition consists of two parts of a compound sentence, one of which contains a definiendum predicate, and the second part begins from *if*, *when*, *as only as* and includes the defining predicates. To properly recognize the definitions, we use the *syntactic templates*, including the above components and the words with special functions within a definition (Fig. 6.12). As the practice shows, a rather limited number of syntactic templates cover the majority of ways customers formulate the definitions of entities they feel it is necessary to use in various domains. Other studies have addressed the issue of analyzing NL definitions, using pattern matching (Chodorow et al. 1985), and special definition-oriented parsers (Wilks et al. 1996).

Below we present a series of examples of how a definition can be phrased. Meanings of variables (their semantic types, Chap. 4) are expected to be clear given their denotations; defining predicates are assumed to exist in the Q/A ontology. In the defining part, we highlight the *main defining predicate*: the one whose arguments are inherited by the definiendum predicate.

(1) *Pump is a device that pushes the flows of reagents through the reactor vessels and heatexchangers:*
pump(Xapp, Xflow):- push(Xapp, Xflow), (reactor(Xapp, Xflow); heatexchanger(Xapp, Xflow)).
This is an introduction of the entity *pump* as a device *Xapp* (entity, expressed by a unary predicate such that the DU system is supposed to be already familiar with it) with certain properties and/or functions. Note that *and* in the definition has the meaning of "*either...or*". This can be deduced since the predicates *reactor* and *heatexchanger* are symmetric with respect to the transmission of instantiated variables *Xapp* and *Xflow* from predicate *push*. Translating *and* into conjunction in this sentence would violate this property of being symmetric.

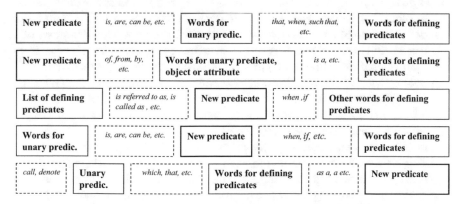

Fig. 6.12 Selected syntactic templates of definitions, formed for their recognition. Words which map into predicates are shown in bold: the words from the definiendum, the unary predicates, the predicates naming the introduced object, and the defining predicates. Some examples of linking words are presented

(2) *Maximum pressure of a pump is such pressure value that a flow stops flowing:*
     pressure(Xpump, Xvalue, maximum):- pump(Xpump, Xflow), pressure(Xpump,
     Xvalue), flow(Xflow, stop).
     In our model, a *pressure* "becomes *maximum*" if the *flow stops*. Newly built pred-
     icate *pressure* needs to have an argument for a device *Xpump*, an argument over
     the pressure value *Xvalue* and an argument for the attribute which is substituted
     right away with the constant from the definiendum: *XAttr = maximum.*
     There is a possibility of translating this definition into summarized logical
     form (Chap. 4), to represent this definition as an additional instance of
     pressure(maximum).
(3) *Stopping the engine under excessive temperature is referred to as its emergency*
     shut-off when the valve is being closed:
     shut_off(Xapp, emergency):- engine(Xapp, stop), temperature(Xapp, Xflow,
     Xtemp), excessive(Xtemp), valve(Xapp, close). In this definition *engine(_)*, is the
     unary predicate that characterizes a device to be *shut_off* and *temperature(_,_,_)*
     may serve as a main defining predicate.
(4) *A pump is not operational if it cannot start when it is necessary to increase the*
     pressure
     not_operational(Xpump):- pump(Xpump), not start(Xpump), pressure(Xpump,
     increase, _). It is not just the negation as a failure paradigm that keeps us
     from defining the negation of *operational.* Instead of defining the negation of a
     predicate, we form a new one for the "negative" state and then define it via the
     positive one explicitly *not_operational(Xpump):- not operational(Xpump).*
(5) *We call a device that exchanges energy between the flows as a heatexchanger.*
     heatexchanger(Xapp, Xflow):- device(Xapp), temperature(Xapp, Xflow, Xtemp),
     flow(Xflow).
     We take into account that *energy* and *temperature* are synonyms here and ignore
     plural for *flows*, attempting to approximate the real world in our definition.
(6) *A person informs another person about a subject if he wants the other person*
     to know that subject, believes that he does not know the subject yet and also
     believes that the other person want to know the subject. This definition of a
     mental entity has neither unary nor main defining predicates, also, it consists of
     the metapredicates (the last argument ranges over the arbitrary formula):
     inform(Who, Whom, What):-want(Who, know(Whom, What)), believe(Who, not
     know(Whom, What)), believe(Who, want(Whom, know(Whom, What))).
(7) *SEP IRA is a retirement plan for self-employed individuals without becoming*
     involved in more complex retirement plans.
     ira(sep):- retirement(plan, self_employed), not retirement(plan, complex).
     This is the SLF-type definition for semi-structured domains, where knowledge
     is not fully formalized. This definition introduces a new clause, linking existing
     entities or introducing a new one to grow the formalized component of domain
     representation. Note that variables are absent in this definition that introduces a
     clause for a virtual SLF (Chaps. 4 and 5). The constants (objects and attributes)

are supposed to occur in other definitions, including definitions of other retirement plans. At the same time, this definition obeys both the syntactic and semantic structures of the definitions (1)–(6) from the fully formalized domains.

Using placeholders for objects and attributes, explicit variables, etc. instead of entity names and pronouns decreases the complexity of the syntactic analysis of a definition, as well as the formation of the resultant clause. For example, if in the definition (6) above we use X and Y for the denotation of the mentioned persons, that would make the definition structure clearer and easier to understand for both humans and computers: "*a person X informs another person Y about a subject S if A wants X to know S, believes that he does not know S yet and also believes that Y want to know S*".

Also, a propagation of variables from defining part to the definiendum while processing the definitions becomes more transparent.

Usually, the defining part starts with the unary predicate and includes the words for defining predicates from one or two sentence parts. Creation of arguments for a new predicate is not directly linked to the definition construction; the rules of building a new predicate are domain dependent rather than phrasing dependent. The main semantic criterion for the defining part of clauses is that it should constitute a meaningful query (assuming the existence of all objects and attributes). It is a good style to introduce a definition to specify the new object via existing properties first. For example, to introduce the definition of *operational(xpump)* above, domain knowledge is supposed to already contain sufficient number of *pumps* to satisfy a newly defined predicate.

6.5.2   Generality Control of a Query Representation

Generality control is a pragmatic context-dependent approach to building accurate logical representation of an NL query. It is based on our observations of the query misunderstanding situations: if a particular query representation hypothesis is wrong then either zero or too many tuples of objects satisfy this representation hypothesis (Galitsky 1999). Therefore, verification of the compatibility of query representation with domain serves as a strong criterion of the correctness of current representation hypothesis.

The existence of the *best generality* of a query representation (QR) has computational rather than analytical (linguistic or cognitive) nature. Compatibility of a query representation with domain representation implements the feedback in the understanding procedure. Control of the generality of a QR is intended to compensate for the disagreements in the syntactic pre-processing and the application of semantic rules in abnormal situations. Our heuristics are based on observations that a query is usually expected to yield a rather limited number of answers. Thus, if that is not the case, we conclude that the QR is wrong rather than that a large set of answers is wanted. In terms of the understanding algorithm, the query has to become more constrained if it yields too many answers, and should be attenuated in the opposite situation with no answers. Generality of a QR serves as a criterion of its correctness and determines the direction of its modification. The major portion of the semantic rules is specifically designed to be parameterized to control the QR (Fig. 6.13).

Let us consider a family of the hypotheses for the query representation for "*What is the export to the country that has the coal agreement with China?*" (Fig. 6.14):

As we see, representation (6) is correct, in the representations (1), (2), (3), (8) constraints are too strong, and in (4), (7), (9) the constraints are too loose. Representation (5) is incorrect because the query mentions *export to the country such that...* and not *export from the country such that...* Representation (1) is incorrect because it is not always true that the same product is necessarily the subject of both *export* and *agreement*. Representation (2) is incorrect as well because it is the partial case (less general) than (1): variable *Xproduct* is instantiated by *coal*.

Representation (3) is stronger than the actual query because it says that the same pair of countries is linked with both *export* and *agreement*. In the representation (4) *XcountryWith* is supposed to be substituted with *china*. The problem of representation (7) is that two conjunctive terms are not connected via any variable (continuity rule has not been applied) and therefore it can potentially yield too many answers. We note that all combinations for the object tuples for each term if they were satisfiable, would form these answers. Hence the generality analysis, taken separately, is capable of selecting the correct QR and rejecting both too general and too specific representations (assuming the latter would lead to no answers).

Units involved in generality control are shown in Fig. 6.13. Feedback is based on the backtracking mechanism, inherent to our logic programming implementation. We describe the generality control units in the direct order (of the query modification). To achieve the optimum query representation, the DU system firstly chooses the predicates signatures, delivering the smallest positive number of answers. Returning to the earlier processing units, the DU system releases some syntactic QR constraints.

Then the Q/A performs attenuation by means of the argument "propagation through formula", turning two equal arguments of the pair of predicates into the different values such that the other predicates are not affected. Formula modification (constraint release) is implemented using the metapredicate *approx(Orig, Attenuated)* (see Chap. 4, Sect. 4.6). After that, the DU system returns to the argument substitution unit and uninstantiates an argument, assuming that the corresponding object was wrongly related to a predicate by syntactic analysis.

Our computational experiments (Galitsky 2003) showed that *the best* query understanding *corresponds* to the representation with the *minimum number of answers* (Fig. 6.15). We take advantage of the fact that typically the query author expects to obtain rather limited data (set of answers). If this is not the case, the understanding system switches to *interactive* mode, requesting certain clarifications (Chap. 1, Volume 2). Alternatively, once the DU system makes decisions about the optimality of the particular representation, it outputs the resultant data together with comments concerning the level of generality. A user can then explicitly raise or drop that level, reformulating the question in more general or concrete terms. Finally, the DU system translates the reformulated query and finds the intersection of the representation

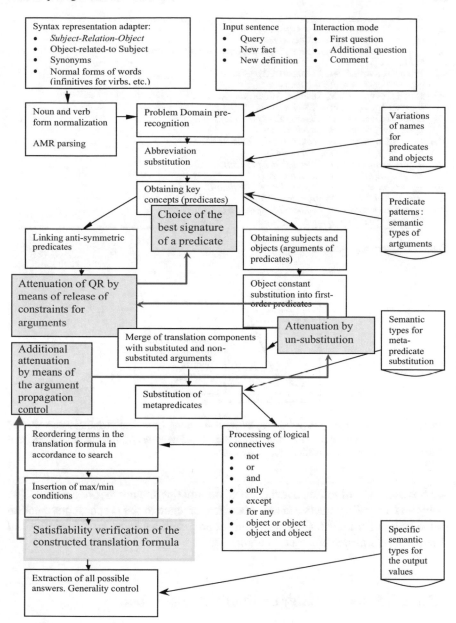

Fig. 6.13 Feedback (backtracking) mechanism for building query representation with optimal generality

1) *export(XcountryFrom, XcountryTo, Xproduct),*
    agreement(XcountryTo, china, Xproduct).
2) *export(XcountryFrom, XcountryTo, coal), agreement(XcountryTo,*
    china, coal).
3) *export(XcountryFrom, XcountryTo, Xproduct),*
    agreement(XcountryTo, XcountryFrom, coal).
4) *export(XcountryFrom, XcountryTo, Xproduct),*
    agreement(XcountryTo, XcountryWith, coal).
5) *export(XcountryFrom, XcountryTo, Xproduct),*
    agreement(XcountryFrom, china, coal).
6) *export(XcountryFrom, XcountryTo, Xproduct),*
    agreement(XcountryTo, china, coal).
7) *export(XcountryFrom, XcountryTo, Xproduct),*
    agreement(XcountryWith, china, coal).
8) *export(XcountryFrom, XcountryFrom, Xproduct),*
    agreement(XcountryFrom, china, coal).
9) *export(XcountryFrom, XcountryTo, Xproduct),*
    agreement(XcountryWith, china, coal).

Fig. 6.14 Query representations

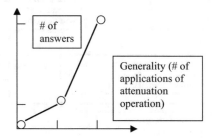

Fig. 6.15 *Generality versus the number of answers* graph for the typical situation. Application of attenuation once brings the situation from "no answer" to "a few answers". Just one more application of attenuation delivers the situation "too many answers"

sets for original and reformulated queries, minimizing the number of answers. The query understanding practice showed fast convergence to the proper representation (three or less iterations). Generality control approach achieves *high flexibility and domain-independence* processing definitions.

6.5.3   Defining an Entity and Introducing a Fact

Usually a domain cannot be significantly extended via NL definitions. As we acquire definitions with specific parameters individually, multiple definitions of the same entity with various parameter values can easily make a domain inconsistent and/or corrupt it. The majority of definitions cannot be expressed in the NL in a single sentence: specification of parameters and additional comments frequently require multiple sentences to introduce a definition. Therefore, specific-usage entities rather than common, general domain-usage entities are introduced by means of acquiring new definitions in NL.

To form a new definition, an NL expression is checked to establish whether it brings new information to the DU system (Fig. 6.16). If this expression is a compound sentence that contains parts linked with *when, where, if, is a,* etc., we proceed, hypothesizing that the left part contains the definiendum entity (being defined), and the right part includes the defining predicates. For example, in the sentences below, the first one introduces the object *Minsk* and the fact that *Minsk is the capital of Belarus,* the second and third sentences introduce only the fact itself, assuming the DU system knows *Minsk: capital(minsk, belarus).*

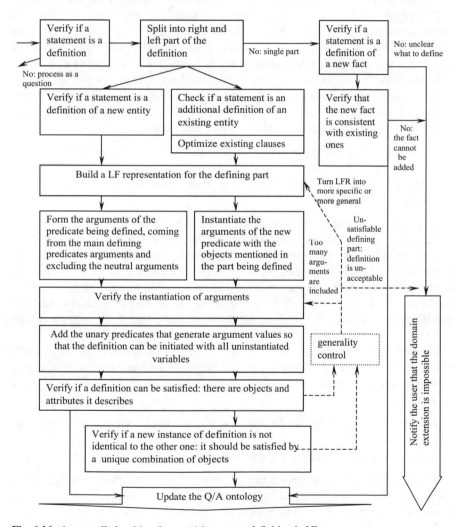

Fig. 6.16 An overall algorithm for acquiring a new definition in NL

Minsk is the city; it is the capital of Belarus.
Minsk is the capital of Belarus.
The capital of Belarus is such city as Minsk.

Also, a sentence may introduce the signature for a predicate without specifying its meaning:

$$Delivery\ from\ country\ to\ country\ of\ a\ product\ in\ year \rightarrow$$
$$deliver(xcountryFrom, xcountryTo, xproduct, xyear).$$

To recognize what kind of definition the DU system is dealing with, it is important to properly determine the boundary between the part sentence with the definiendum entity (including words referencing its attributes) and the defining part. The definition may introduce a new entity as well as a new definition of an existing one. Also, in specifying a new entity, a definition may introduce a new link between existing objects and also a new object (or a set of objects) as an argument of this entity.

An example of the former kind of definition may be as follows: *President's residence is a capital of the country where its president lives.* The query representation for this definition of *president_residence* we intend to obtain is:

president_residence(Person, City):- capital(City, Country), president(Person, Country) or
president_residence(Person, Country, City):- capital(City, Country), president(Person, Country).

The entities in the defining part are supposed to be linked by arguments of predicates (in a similar way to how entities are represented by predicates in a QR). The *linking* variables may (*City*) or may not (*Country* in the top definition) go into the arguments of the newly created predicate (as in the clauses above). To form the arguments of the newly created predicate, variables need to connect two or more predicates in the defining part. In the example above, *Country* is the linking variable that links the predicates *president* and *capital* with their respective arguments *Person* and *City*.

Now let us imagine that one wants to introduce a specific instance for a president's residence in case *"the president has to live abroad"* for some reason: *President's residence is a city abroad if the city he lives is not the capital of the president's country,*

president_residence(Person, City_abroad):- capital(City, Country), live(Person, City_abroad),
president(Person, Country), City\= City_abroad.

In this case, the DU system needs to introduce constraints for the same pair of arguments as it has done for the first instance of the definition of *president_residence*. However, there are different predicates from the defining component, which now includes *live*. The expression *city is not the capital* is translated into *capital(City, Country), City\= City_abroad*. As in the previous definition, variable *Country* links the predicates *capital* and *president,* and variable *Person* links predicates *live* and *president,* so all three defining predicates are linked. Both variables *City* and *City_abroad* would be present as arguments of *president_residence,* in addition to *Person,* if it were the first instance of the definition. Since we have already formed the binary predicate *president_residence* and want to keep its semantics, when adding definition instances, we attempt not add the variable *City_abroad* to the list of arguments.

We proceed to the example of the introduction of a new object via a predicate. Let us imagine that a domain needs a definition of *NATO block* and we just need to know that it is a *place of gathering the presidents from Europe and US.* For us defining an entity means establishing its links with the other entities: *NATO block* is linked to *gathering* of *presidents.* Imagine also that we are not using other *blocks* except *NATO,* so the predicate targets the introduction of a single object *NATO.*

> *block(nato, Country):- gather(Person, City, Country), president(Person, Country), (belong(Country, europe); Country = us).*

Country here means the countries which are members of *NATO* (and not the *NATO* location that is not mentioned in the defining part). This definition would be more efficient if we consider the list of countries, but it is too hard for a definition understanding system to build clauses in terms of lists. Note that a presentation of information from a limited perspective is acceptable for a Q/A domain ontology: representing and storing a complete domain knowledge is not a viable option.

6.5.4 An Algorithm of Acquiring a New Definition

We now proceed to the general algorithm of processing all types of acquiring new definitions, considered above. The blocks of the definition understanding algorithms are depicted in Fig. 6.16. An input NL expression for a definition is first recognized with respect to being a definition of an entity (new or existing) "*A circle is a set of points each of which has a fixed distance from the center (a given point))*", a fact "*Circle c has radius 4*", or neither "*What is the radius of circle d?*", based on syntactic properties of this expression. If there is a failure in the consecutive steps of recognition or in the forming of a definition, the user is notified about the DU system's inability to understand his definition. Such a situation may be caused by an unclear phrasing, system's unfamiliarity with mentioned lexical units, or a lack of knowledge of the proper synonyms, as well as the incompatibility of suggested definition with the domain.

Split component identifies the defining part (on the right, "*a set of points each of which has a fixed distance from the center*") and definiendum (on the left, "*a circle is*"). If the split fails, we further check that the input is a fact to add to an ontology ("*circle c has radius 4*"). If this input text is not recognized as a fact, the DU process stops. Otherwise, we check if circle *c* has radius 4 represented as *radius(c, 4)* that does not contradict to any formalized fact such as *radius(c, 5).* This step is based on a rule specific to predicate *radius* stating that it is a single value, not a list or multiple values.

If we are on a definition of a new entity path, we verify that this entity has not been defined yet, or multiple definitions are allowed: *circle(C):- ...* does not exist. If such a definition already exists then we might need to update an existing one together with the new one:

New*: circle(A, Center):- point(P), distance(P, Center, D).*
Already defined: *circle(A, Center, Diameter)):- point(P), distance(P, Center, Diameter).* Here we used *Diameter* instead of *Radius* we are going to use in the new definition.
Modification for already defined: Add Prolog statement for fining all such points: *circle(A, Center, Radius, Points)):- findAll(P, (point(P), distance(P, Center, Radius)), Points).*
As a result, the component Build a LF representation for the defining part will produce:
findAll(P, (point(_), distance(_, _, _)), Points).
Where *distance(P, Center, Radius))* is an existing predicate, and
findAll(P, Condition, Points) is a built-in Prolog predicate
Now the components *Form the argument ...* and *Instantiate the argument ...* will yield:
findAll(P, (point(P), distance(P, Center, Radius)), Points),
turning anonymous variables '_' into *P, Center, Radius.*
Add the unary predicate component will add
point(P), findAll(P, (point(P), distance(P, Center, Radius)), Points),
Verification component will run the clause
circle(A, Center, Radius, Points)) :- point(P), findAll(P, (point(P), distance(P, Center, Radius)), Points)
given *Center* and *Radius,* and producing the set of *Points*
Finally, once verified, this definition will be added to the ontology.
Other components are related to generality control. Let us imagine we have a candidate defining part represented as
point(P1), findAll(P2, (point(P), distance(P3, Center, Radius)), Points)
It would produce too many points P1 since there is only constraint for P3, not P1. If we make such mistake in building LF, the clause would produce too many (all available points P1) that would indicate that the definition is wrong. We come back and set:
P1 = P2
P2 = P3
And come to the correct definition.
Conversely, if we have representation:
point(P), findAll(P, (point(P), distance(P, P, Radius)), Points)
it would produce zero results since the first and the second argument in *distance(P, P, Radius)* are identical. We need to turn the second argument into a new variable such as *Center.*

The chart Fig. 6.13 does exactly that but for a query representation. A query can be *"What are the points locating at a distance Radius from center?"*. QR can be an incorrect form, such as the expression above. Turning *distance(P, P, Radius)* into *distance(P, Center, Radius)* is made by *Attenuation by un-substitution* component. *Choice of the best signature* component will try both

distance(P, Center, Radius),

distance(P, Center, Diameter), diameter(Diameter)

distance(P, Center, Radius), radius(Radius)

signatures and pick the one that successfully yields results.

We enumerate the groups of rules for definition processing. These rules work on top of the question representation rules (Chap. 4).

(1)   Identifying the variables that link the predicates in the defining part;
(2)   Identifying the *main defining predicate* that yields the (initial approximation of) signature of a newly defined predicate;
(3)   Identifying the variables that constitute the arguments of the definiendum;
(4)   Assigning the *neutral* roles to the rest of the variables. This neutrality is in respect to forming the arguments of the new predicate;
(5)   Conversion of the QR of the defining part into the definiendum part of the clause.

We enumerate the most frequent instances for these groups of rules (Fig. 6.17). If the DU system encounters a contradiction, more complex or domain-specific rules could potentially be required.

(1)   As for a query, we initially apply discontinuity and independence rules, assuming that all the variables of the same semantic types are equal (excluding the arguments of anti-symmetric predicates). Then the principle of generality control is applied in the direction of generality increase, starting with TF (right part of the definition) satisfaction with the lowest number of object tuples.
(2)   The *main defining* predicate is usually the one with the highest number of arguments; it links the other predicates (between each other) in the highest degree (taking into account the number of variables). In the other words, for the main defining predicate, the number of arguments it has in common with the rest of the predicates is maximum in comparison with the other predicates of defining part. For example, the main defining predicate in definition (5) from Fig. 6.17 is *temperature(Xapp, Xflow, Xtemp)*. In other sample definitions, either predicate in the defining part may serve as the main one. Also, the main predicate is supposed to verify the value of an argument, yielded by a unary predicate that is syntactically linked with the definiendum predicate.
(3)   The set of variables that constitute the arguments of the definiendum predicate is a subset of all variables participating in the defining part, and the superset of the arguments of the main defining predicate that do not occur in the other defining predicates.
(4)   *Neutral* are the variables that are the means to link the defining predicates, but not to denote the objects of attributes such that a new predicate introduces a relation

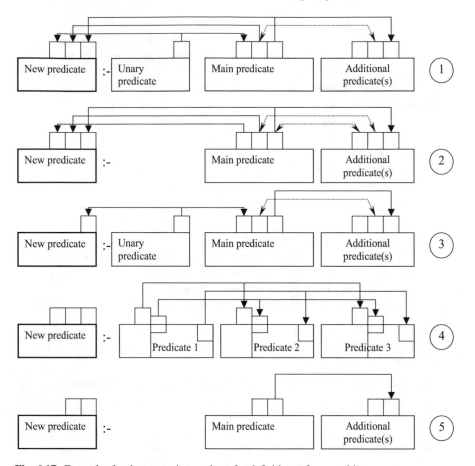

Fig. 6.17 Examples for the semantic templates for definitions of new entities

between them. Neutral are usually the variables, yielded by one predicate and verified by the other one.

(5) To be turned into the defining part of a clause, the query representation of the defining part must properly handle the totality of instantiation states for its predicates (or the totality of instantiation states for a new predicate). Therefore, for each argument, there should be a predicate that yields its value (added if necessary). Also the predicates, which neither bring in constraints nor yield values, are eliminated from the defining part.

Further steps of the formation of the left part (definiendum) of the definition clause are presented in detail in Fig. 6.16. The left column plots the required steps for a first entity definition, and the middle column for additional definition of an existing entity. Before QR is constructed, the latter requires optimization of existing clauses in case of partially-structured domains (Chap. 4) so that the new clause becomes compatible with existing ones. An old signature is used when all the objects which occur in the left part can be substituted. Conversely, a new signature with an additional semantic type (with respect to existing signature) is created and further verified for satisfiability. Also, a new instance of a definition needs verification with respect to its novelty.

To create the arguments of a novel predicate (the left column), the Q/A system takes the arguments of the main defining predicate and excludes the neutral arguments. Also, the arguments for the objects, which are mentioned in the defining part, are included with respective semantic types (analogously to the case above). It will be revealed further on whether these objects or variables of respective semantic types serve as the arguments in the resultant clause.

Generality control acquires additional functionality in comparison to handling a query. Generality control is initiated by either satisfaction failure or a failure to derive an original definition. In addition to the controlled units of the left part (QR) processing analogous to the one depicted in Fig. 6.13, the hypotheses concerning the instantiation state of the new predicate are evaluated to achieve optimal generality.

The main semantic rules of definition processing are developed based on the typical semantic patterns (clause templates) of definitions, some of which are depicted in Fig. 6.17. The reader can observe that there is a weak correlation between the syntactic definition templates and semantic ones, mainly concerned with the formation of arguments of the new predicate and the links between the defining predicates. Once the whole definition is parsed by the AMR parsing, we can form the template directly from the AMR representation.

In Fig. 6.17, the rectangles depict the predicates and the squares above depict their arguments. An arrow from the square (variable) of one predicate to the square (variable) of another predicate depicts the equality of corresponding values such that the first variable generates its value and the second verifies it. Bi-directional dotted arrow paths mean that backtracking is assumed when the definition clause is initiated. The most typical definition templates for the fully formalized domains are (1) and (3). The differences between templates are mainly determined by the interaction between the unary predicate, by the way of phrasing the definiendum entity, and by the features of the main defining predicate, which inherits the arguments to the definiendum predicate. The other predicates just implement the additional constraints on the variables of the main predicate and do not make the structure of the definiendum more sophisticated. Frequently, these additional predicates initiate backtracking of the main one. A particular definition deviates from a template by the number of arguments for the main and additional predicates, and by the instantiation state (whether these arguments generate values or verify the relationship between instantiated arguments).

The templates may become quite different for the definitions in the other kinds of domains. In the mental states one, multiple mental metapredicates simultaneously inherit the arguments to the new predicate (4). In the weakly formalized domains, where the predicates arguments serve the purpose of separating answers (Chap. 4), the arguments of the definiendum predicate are instantiated by the objects or attributes from the left part (5).

6.5.5   Defining New Entities in a Vertical Domain

Usually, there are two general ways the definitions may be interpreted. The first way to introduce a new entity is to shorten NL expressions, which contain the defining entities. Also, new entities may add certain knowledge to the DU system. For example, in a process control domain, a derived entity can make the allowed NL command brief; at the same time, a definiendum may be a new control rule for a process.

We proceed to the examples of such definitions and their representations. Let us introduce the definition of term *engaging a pump* that is currently new for the DU system, assuming the system is already familiar with the entities *pump, flow, transformation, cool*, etc.

A pump, from which a reagent follows to an absorber, is engaged, if the result of its transformation must be cooled down.

There are two ways to interpret this definition. The first way is to introduce the concept of *engaging* given the instance of a *pump* with *absorber* and reagent transformation. The main purpose is to shorten the above phrasing by the entity *engage*. However, this does not seem natural. One needs to distinguish the definitions *It is necessary to engage a pump, when…* and *To engage a pump means, that… .* Thus the definition above is indeed the introduction of a *new control algorithm* (Fig. 6.18).

The most correct representation is:

> *engage_pump(Xreag1, Xapp, absorb) :- pump(Xapp),*
> *   flow(Xreag1, Xapp, absorb),*
> *   % reagent Xreag1 flows from Xapp towards absorber absorb*
> *   transform(Xreag1, Xreag2, absorb),*
> *   % reagent Xreag1 is transformed into reagent Xreag2*
> *   cool(Xdegree, Xreag2, Xapp2).*
> *   % reagent Xreag2 is cooled down by xdegree in device (heat exchanger) Xapp2).*

Note that this definition is designed specifically for *engaging* a *pump* for an *absorber*, then for an arbitrary device, therefore, the third argument is instantiated by the constant *absorb*. Using this example, we present a typical semantic rules for definition processing. The following instances of semantic rules are applied:

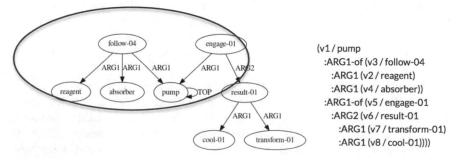

```
(v1 / pump
  :ARG1-of (v3 / follow-04
    :ARG1 (v2 / reagent)
    :ARG1 (v4 / absorber))
  :ARG1-of (v5 / engage-01
    :ARG2 (v6 / result-01
      :ARG1 (v7 / transform-01)
      :ARG1 (v8 / cool-01))))
```

Fig. 6.18 AMR representation of a definition (the graph and the LF). The definiendum is shown with a red oval

(1) If a unary predicate has the argument of the same semantic type as the one following in QR of the right part, then the latter predicate is determined to be the main defining predicate, and the mentioned argument should occur in the predicate being defined. *Xreag1 flows* from *pump Xapp*. First (unary) and second predicates have the common variable *Xapp*.

(2) For each predicate after the main one in the QR (of the right, defining part), variables (with the same semantic type) propagate from right to left from predicate to predicate. The same reagent *Xreag1 flows* and is being *transformed*. *Xreag1* is the common variable for the second and third predicates.

(3) Reagent *Xreag2*, being the result of transformation of *Xreag1*, is cooled. If the Q/A system misses the hypothesis that the *transformation* process precedes the *cooling* one, the system exceeds the generality parameter, not taking into account the restrictions of the predicate *transform(_, _, _)*.

Now we can ask the DU system a question, containing the new entity *to engage a pump*. For example, *'How many degrees warmer would the acid get in those heat exchangers which are affected by the engaged pumps?'* gives us the following QR:

pump(Xpump), engage_pump(Xreag, Xpump, Xapp1), Xapp1 = absorb, affect(Xapp1, Xreag, Xapp2), heat(Xvalue, acid, Xapp2).

Variable *Xreag* may be instantiated by *acid* (the name of the flow), and therefore, the predicates *affect* and *heat* would share two arguments *Xreag* and *Xapp3* (of the same semantic types). However, in accordance with the default independence rule, it is too strong for the given domain. There are no such objects, therefore *Xreag* $\neq$ *acid*. The semantics of *affect(Xapp1, Xreag, Xapp3)* is as follows: in the device *Xapp1*, reagent *Xreag affects Xapp2* (via some parameters). In the given domain, the hypothesis that *Xreag* in *Xapp1* = *absorb* affects a device *Xapp2* so that the *acid* is *heated* there, contains the strongest constraint, but nevertheless is compatible with the domain.

To conclude the Section we note that the above definition understanding methodology is applicable to both fully and partially formalized domains. The former needs the means to introduce the formalized facts, and the latter should be capable of accepting textual answers, database links, or parameterized queries. Concerning the processing of definitions of new terms, it happens irrespectively of the degree of formalization.

6.6 Nonmonotonic Reasoning for Handling Ambiguity in Queries and Definitions

In this Section, we introduce a nonmonotonic reasoning technique that allows developers of Q/A systems to use nonmonotonic reasoning for making a semantic representation of an input query more precise, resolving ambiguities. Using nonmonotonic reasoning for Q/A was first suggested in (Ourioupina and Galitsky 2001) and further developed in (Galitsky 2004; 2005). The aim of these studies was not to achieve a semantic representation which is more precise, but to make the given representation better fit the formal domain representation. This was achieved by the application of the default logic machinery.

Default rules can naturally appear in the domain representation itself. Note that the use of default rules for the transformation of query representation is independent of the degree of knowledge formalization: it helps from fully to partially formalized domains. However, one needs to distinguish the default rules for query transformation and for domain representation: the former are linked to NL, and the latter are supposed to be language-independent. Though the default reasoning technique is applicable to a variety of semantic analysis approaches, the particular set of default rules is domain-specific.

The *contribution* of this section is to build a general query rewriting framework based on default logic and to adjust it to the Summarized Logical form technique developed in Chap. 4. Due to the substantial development of NLP techniques for query processing including syntactic and semantic parsing on one hand and the advancement of scalable search engineering on the other hand, nonmonotonic reasoning can further benefit Q/A, being applied after the query is enriched with available syntactic and semantic knowledge. We build upon our exploration of the possibility to index a summary of an answer as a summarized logical form (SLF, Galitsky 2000b, 2003) instead of indexing the whole answer, as a traditional search engineering does.

Nonmonotonic logics cover a family of formal frameworks devised to capture and represent defeasible inference. Reasoners draw conclusions defeasibly when they reserve the right to retract them in the light of further information. Nonmonotonic logics occur in everyday reasoning, in expert reasoning such as legal verdicts or medical diagnoses, and in scientific reasoning, ranging from inductive generalizations to reasoning to the best explanation to inferences on the basis of expert opinions (Galitsky and Ilvovsky 2019). Defeasible reasoning follows along the lines of deductive reasoning and can follow complex patterns which are beyond reach for classical, intuitionistic or other kind of logic from the deductive family since they do not allow for a retraction of inferences (Ginsberg 1987).

6.6.1 Disambiguation

One source of ambiguity in Q/A pipeline is *entity linking*. We represent the concept 'Bill Clinton' by a unique identifier of a Wikipedia page. If this subject string is not associated with a unique page on Wikipedia, we can disambiguate which page is being sought, for example by using the cosine distance between the triple string (*"Bill Clinton was born in 1946"*) and each candidate Wikipedia page. Date strings like "1946" can be normalized by using a standard tool for temporal normalization such as SUTime (Chang and Manning, 2012) that is a part of Stanford NLP.

When the question analysis step is performed, *chunking, segmentation* and *establishing dependencies* between the segments produce multiple versions possibly with similar confidence. For example, in the question *"List all South-Asian countries"*, the segmentation can group or not the expression *"South-Asian countries"* or *"Asian countries"*, leading to two possibilities.

The third source of ambiguity is in the phrase mapping step that returns multiple possible resources for one phrase. In the example above, *Asian* could be mapped to different contexts such as geographical, political or cultural.

Because of these ambiguities in online query processing and offline index construction, Q/A systems generate many possible interpretations. To select the most plausible version, mainly two approaches are used:

(1) String, syntactic or semantic similarity of the label of the resource and the corresponding phrase;
(2) Type consistency check between the properties and their arguments.

(1) is used to rank the possible interpretations and (2) is used to exclude some. Only the consistency between the two resources that are directly related is checked, that is easy, fast and effective. A main shortcoming is that actual knowledge bases (KBs) often do not contain domain and range information of a property of an entity so that the type consistency cannot be done.

Consider, for example, the question *"Who is the director of Gone with the Wind?"*. In this case, *"Gone with the Wind"* is clearly referring to the film and not to the book. If the property corresponding to director has no domain/range information, then this strategy would not allow to decide if *"Gone with the Wind"* is a book or a film. The interpretation as a *book* can only be excluded later by querying the knowledge base (KB).

In this Section, we focus on the distinct source of ambiguity associated not with the processing but the meanings of words and phrases. We refer the reader to Creary and Pollard (1985) and Hirst (1988) for discussions on the disambiguation problem.

6.6.2 Introduction to Default Reasoning for Q/A

A branch of nonmonotonic reasoning, Default Logic, seems to be well suited to represent the semantic rules which process the ambiguous terms. In a horizontal domain, a term may have a set of meanings such that each of them is important and needs separate consideration. For a vertical Q/A domain, an ambiguous term usually has one common meaning and multiple infrequent meanings which still have to be formally represented. The DU system may assume the default meaning of this term unless it is inconsistent to do so. This inconsistency can be determined based on the occurrence of some words in a sentence, or some terms in the query representation.

The proposed technique for nonmonotonic reasoning for query rewrite can be combined with Summarized Logical forms (Chap. 4) and other approaches to formal semantic analyses, achieving a certain level of formalization.

From the perspective of nonmonotonic reasoning, linking the semantic representation of a query with that of answers, additional (lexical) data in a query may switch the resultant pattern (answer). Such nonmonotonicity would be considered a non-desired property in the standard (statistical or structural) pattern recognition settings: discovering an additional feature of an input stimulus is not supposed to alter the resultant pattern. This is not the case for the pattern recognition under Q/A: an occurrence of an additional word which may seem insignificant on its own may cause a totally different answer for a query. We believe explicit nonmonotonic reasoning machinery is an appropriate means to handle this phenomenon by an NL-based recognition system.

A default logic as formulated by Reiter (1980) distinguishes between two kinds of knowledge:

(1)   usual predicate logical formulas (axioms, facts); and
(2)   "rules of thumb" (defaults).

Default theory (Brewka et al. 1995; Bochman 2001) includes a set of facts which represent certain, but usually incomplete, information about the world (a query, in our case); and a set of defaults which cause plausible but not necessarily true conclusions (for example, because of NL ambiguity in queries). In the case of textual knowledge representation, some of these conclusions have to be revised when additional context information becomes available.

This split of knowledge about the world into the fixed (facts) and flexible (rules) components may serve as a good means to simulate a meaning of a text, taken apart from its context. Some texts are context-independent and have a single meaning, other texts have context-dependent meanings that can be determined after the context is established, and a third group of texts is those ambiguous even in a fixed context. Nonmonotonic reasoning helps to compute the range meaning in the third case. A system of default rules can modify the formal representation of a question and/or an answer to better associate them with each other (rather than to obtain their absolute best meaning representation).

Let us consider the traditional example quoted in the literature on nonmonotonic reasoning:

$$\frac{human(X) : can\ speak(X)}{can\ speak(X)}$$

One reads it as *If X is a human and it is consistent to assume that X can speak, then conclude that X can speak (and does not have a mental disease preventing him from speaking)*. As a Q/A matching rule default, it reads as follows: If the query is about a *human, and it is consistent to assume that there can be a word in this query with the meaning of speaking*, then conclude that the query is about *speaking*. If nothing contradictory can be derived from the other words of the query, it is natural to assume that this query is about the *a human speaking* and not about, for example, issues requiring a *speech therapy*.

A classical example of a default rule express ambiguity in the activity associated with a bird: it usually flies (meaning 1) but sometimes it does not (meaning 2):

$$\frac{bird(X) : fly(X)}{fly(X)}$$

As a traditional default, we obtain the assumption *Usually (typically) birds fly*. Given the information that *"Tweety is a bird"* (in accordance with the history of nonmonotonic reasoning) we may conclude that it flies (meaning 1). But if we learn later that it cannot fly, for example, because he is a *penguin*, then the default becomes inapplicable (meaning 2).

The nonmonotonic reasoning technique helps us to provide the proper Q/A in this situation. Imagine that we have a set of documents answering questions about birds. Let us imagine there is a general answer, which presents information that *birds fly*, and which contains common remarks. Besides, there is also a specific answer *"there is a bird Tweety, who is a penguin, lives at the South Pole, swims, but does not fly"*.

If nonmonotonic reasoning about query representation is absent, then the explicit restriction for the semantic representation for a query is necessary, which does not scale well. We have to check for each query, if it does not match a list of exceptions:

Do birds fly?, Tell me about birds, Which animals fly?, Do seagulls fly?, What do you know about eagle birds?, Is Tweety a bird?, Does Tweety fly?, Is Tweety a penguin?; they will cause the same answer that birds fly, unless we mention the *bird Tweety*.

bird(X), not(X−Tweety) ⇒ *answer(birds fly)*.

fly(X), not(X=Tweety) ⇒ *answer(birds fly)*.

bird(Tweety) ⇒ *answer('there is a bird Tweety, which is a penguin, lives at the South Pole, swims, but does not fly')*.

fly(Tweety) ⇒ *answer('there is a bird Tweety, which is a penguin, lives at the South Pole, swims, but does not fly')*.

The problem with this approach is that it requires explicit enumeration of constraints in a knowledge base. Each exceptional object has to be enumerated in the representation, which includes the properties of normal, typical objects. When default rules come into play to modify the query representation, this complication is avoided. The first answer does not have to contain explicit constraints that X *is not Tweety* or some other object; it will be reached if it is consistent to assume that *fly(X)*. The latter is verified using the default rule above and the clause that *Tweety does not fly*.

We proceed to a formal definition of a default rule, as proposed in Antoniou (1997). A default δ has the form:

$$\delta = \frac{\varphi : \psi_1 \ldots \psi_n}{\chi}$$

where $\varphi, \psi_1, \ldots, \psi_n, \chi$ are closed predicate formula and $n > 0$. The formula φ is called the prerequisite, $\psi_1, \ldots, \psi_n$ the justification, and χ the consequent of δ $(pre(\delta), just(\delta)$

and *cons(δ)* correspondingly). A default $δ$ is applicable to a deductively closed set of formulae E iff $φ∈E$ and $¬ψ_1 ∉ E, ..., ¬ψ_n ∉ E$.

Defaults can be used to model situations in various domains. Below there are several examples:

(1) Legal reasoning and justice:

$$\frac{accused(X) : innocent(X)}{innocent(X)}$$

This rule models the presumption of the innocence principle: if there is no evidence to the contrary, we assume the accused to be innocent.

(2) Databases and logic programming:

$$\frac{true : not\ X}{not\ X}$$

This rule formalizes the *Closed World Assumption* (Reiter 1978) According to it, a ground fact is taken to be false if it doesn't follow from the axioms or cannot be found in the database. For example, if there is no 10:30 train from Glasgow central station in the schedule, then there is also no such train in the real world.

(3) Every-day life:

$$\frac{go\_to\_work(X) : use\_bus(X)}{use\_bus(X)}$$

This rule describes usual morning behavior: if nothing contradicts it, people go to work by bus. Following such rules of thumb, I should go to the bus station and, most probably, take a bus. But it can turn out that the drivers are on strike, I am late or I want to go on foot, because the weather is fine. In those cases, I definitely know that I cannot (or don't want to) use the bus and the rule becomes inapplicable. Let us now imagine that one follows the classical logic rule:

$$go\_to\_work(X) \& not(strike) \& not(late(X)) \& not(fine\_weather) \& ... → use\_bus(X).$$

In this case, she has to list all the possible obstacles: *strike, hurry, fine_weather,* and so on. Then she has to obtain a lot of information to establish whether all the preconditions are true. Therefore she finally arrives at work in the afternoon. In other words, it is inefficient to encode the rules for typical and non-typical situations on the same level of their potential application. Instead, all abnormalities should be merged and linked with the negation of justification of the default rule. The prerequisite of this rule should include typical conditions.

6.6.3 Handling Conflicting Default Rules

In an abstract rule-based DU system, the inference (or recognition) result depends on the order of rule applications. The operational semantics of default logic come into play to handle the possible order of application of the conflicting default rules. In this Subsection, we propose an informal description of operational semantics for default reasoning. Formal definitions, theorems and proofs can be found, for example, in Antoniou (1997).

The main goal of applying default rules is to make all the possible conclusions from the given set of facts. If we apply only one default, we can simply add its consequent to our knowledge base. The situation becomes more complicated if we have a set of defaults because, for example, the rules can have consequents contradicting each other or, a consequent of one rule can contradict the justification of another one. In order to provide an accurate solution, we have to introduce the notion of *extensions*: current knowledge bases, satisfying some specific conditions.

Suppose D is a set of defaults and W is a set of facts (our initial knowledge base). Let Δ be an ordered subset of D without multiple occurrences (it is useless to apply the default twice because it would add no information). We denote a deductive closure (in terms of classical logic) of Δ by $Accepted(\Delta)$: $W \cup \{cons(\delta)|\delta \in \Delta\}$. We also denote by $Rejected(\Delta)$ the set $\{\neg\psi | \psi \in just(\delta),\ \delta \in \Delta\}$. We call $\Delta = \{\delta_0, \delta_1,...\}$ a *process* iff for every k δ_k is applicable to $Accepted(\Delta_k)$, where Δ_k is the initial part of Δ of the length k.

Given a process Δ, we can determine whether it is successful and closed. A process Δ is called successful iff $Accepted(\Delta) \cap Rejected(\Delta) = \emptyset$. A process Δ is called closed if Δ already contains all the defaults from D, applicable to $Accepted(\Delta)$.

Now we can define extensions. A set of formulae $E \supset W$ is an extension of the default theory $<D, W>$ iff there is some process Δ so that it is successful, closed, and $E = Accepted(\Delta)$.

Let us consider an example (Antoniou, 1997). Suppose for example that W is empty and D is the set of

$$\delta_1 \quad \frac{true : not\ tax\_fraud(X)}{not\ tax\_fraud(X)}$$

$$\delta_2 \quad \frac{true : tax\_fraud(X)}{check(tax\_police, X)}$$

These rules describe a situation when people are normally not assumed to commit tax frauds but, if it's consistent to suspect someone of tax fraud, then the tax police look more thoroughly at his bills. This kind of reasoning is required when answering questions like *How can I avoid tax audit if I have significant deduction this year?* from the *tax* domain.

After we have applied the first rule, we extend our knowledge base by *not tax_fraud(X)*:

$$Accepted(\{\delta_1\}) = \{not\ tax\_fraud(X)\},$$
$$Rejected(\{\delta_1\}) = \{tax\_fraud(X)\}.$$

The second rule is not applicable to $Accepted(\{\delta_1\})$. Therefore the process $\Delta = \{\delta_1\}$ is closed. It is also successful, so $Accepted(\{\delta_1\})$ is an extension. Suppose now we now apply δ_1 first:

$$Accepted(\{\delta_2\}) = \{check(tax\_police, X)\},$$
$$Rejected(\{\delta_2\}) = \{\ not\ tax\_fraud(X)\}.$$

The rule δ_1 is still applicable now, so $\{\delta_2\}$ process is not closed. Let us apply δ_1 to $Accepted(\{\delta_2\})$:

$$Accepted(\{\delta_2, \delta_1\}) = \{check(tax\_police, X), not\ tax\_fraud(X)\},$$
$$Rejected(\{\delta_2, \delta_1\}) = \{\ not\ tax\_fraud(X), tax\_fraud(X)\}.$$

Now $Accepted(\{\delta_2, \delta_1\}) \cap Rejected(\{\delta_2, \delta_1\}) \neq \emptyset$ so $\{\delta_2, \delta_1\}$ is not successful and $\{check(tax\_police, X), not\ tax\_fraud(X)\ \}$ is not an extension. This comes in accordance with our intuitive expectations, because if we accept the later statement to be a possible knowledge base, then we conjecture that the tax police check thoroughly the tax bills of all people, not only the suspicious ones.

The next example (life insurance domain, Galitsky 2001a) shows that there can be multiple extensions for one set of facts and default rules:

$$\delta_1 \quad \frac{dangerous\_job(X) : insure\_life(X)}{insure\_life(X)}$$

$$\delta_2 \quad \frac{young(X) : not\ insure\_life(X)}{not\ insure\_life(X)}$$

These rules explain that people with dangerous jobs usually insure their lives and young people usually do not insure their lives. This is knowledge required to answer, for example, the question "*Should I have a life insurance as a university graduate?*" Let us suppose that we want to conclude something about a young man who has a dangerous job: $W = \{dangerous\_job(X), young(X)\}$. After the application of each default, the other one becomes inapplicable. So, both $\{\delta_1\}$ and $\{\delta_1\}$ are closed and successful processes. Thus, both *{dangerous_job(X), young(X), insure_life(X)}* and *{dangerous_job(X), young(X), not(insure_life(X))}* are two extensions which are mutually inconsistent.

6.6.4   Query Rewrite with the Help of Default Rules

Suppose S is a semantic representation of a query. Our intention is to transform S into another well-formed semantic representation, $@S$ (about S), which fits our virtical domain better because it takes into account default domain knowledge. Note that the latter is not necessarily explicitly mentioned in a NL query, so the transformation above is required. To perform it, the following algorithm is proposed: using a set of facts like *word X is used in S* and *word X is not used in S* as an initial knowledge base, we can apply default rules (created manually by knowledge engineers) to obtain all the possible extensions. These extensions contain facts about elements of $@S$ (as well as initial statements). After doing that we can use the extensions to build up the $@S$ representation. It includes the n-conjunction of initial facts (word occurrences in a query X_i) and their specific meanings $@X_j$:

$$@S = \underset{i,j<n}{\&} \left(X_i, @X_j, \right)$$

Note that S (and not $@S$) is indeed the most precise representation of the query meaning, taken separately. However, S needs to be transformed to point to the desired answer with higher accuracy. This transformation is intended to eliminate the least important entities so as not to interfere with the most important ones, as well as to add the implicitly assumed elements.

There are two possible ways to use default systems to modify semantic representations:

- Application of defaults in the fixed order. This can be used when there are no conflicts in the consequents of the default rules.
- Building extensions for conflicting defaults. We employ the operational semantics of default logic in more complex situation, for example, when we have multiple ambiguous terms in a query (Fig. 6.19, Galitsky 2003).

If we do not want to modify initial representation at all ($S = @S$), we can apply trivial defaults to each element of S:

$$\frac{X \ is \ used \ in \ S \ : \ X \ is \ used \ in \ @S}{X \ is \ used \ in \ @S}$$

All the facts in our knowledge base are about the element occurrence: it is either used in the representation or not. Accepted our rules we can write X instead of *X is used in S* and $@X$ instead of *X is used in $@S$,* not causing any confusion. Sometimes we will speak about entities X and Y connected semantically or syntactically. In that case, we would write $X(Y)$, which means that *X is used in S, Y is used in S* and *X and Y are connected by semantic or syntactic link*. In this form trivial rules look like:

$$\frac{X \ : \ @X}{@X}$$

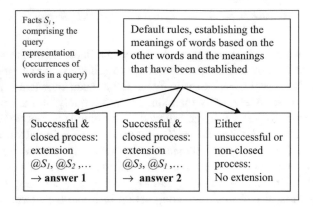

Fig. 6.19 Processing a question as a set of facts in the default theory. For a given domain, default system includes the fixed set of default rules D, determining the meaning of the terms, and the set of facts about the word occurrence, specific to each query. Multiple processes are constructed in real time. If the process is successful and closed, it is associated with an answer via @S. Modified representations are formed by the obtained extensions of the default theory

We can use these defaults not only when we want to have S unmodified. In fact we should apply trivial rules to every representation. Elements that are not affected by nontrivial defaults are simply moved from S to @S. As far as other elements are concerned, trivial and nontrivial rules can interact with each other, leading to specific extensions.

6.6.5 Ambiguous Entities in Query

Ambiguous elements correspond to multiple default rules. Let us consider an example from an insurance domain. The word *company* is ambiguous: it can refer either to *insurance company* or to *company where the customer works*. In default form it looks like:

$$\delta : \frac{company() : @insurance\_company(), not\,@place\_of\_work}{@insurance\_company()}$$

$$\varepsilon : \frac{company() : not@insurance\_company(), @place\_of\_work}{@place\_of\_work}$$

If we have no other entities in the query which can help us to make a decision on what *company* is meant, both rules (δ and ε) can lead to an extension. As a result, we have two representations $@S_{\delta}$ and $@S_{\varepsilon}$, and two respective answers.

However, if the query contains some words incompatible with one of the meanings proposed, then one of the rules does not lead to an extension. For example, if the query is about companies' ratings (*What is the best company?*) then it is about *insurance_company* rather than about *place_of_work*. Note that this rule of thumb holds for the virtical domain on insurance. If a person looks for a job-related domain, the Q/A system's decision should be the opposite one. And in the everything-about-the-world domain we cannot create such rules at all. As a default rule, it looks like the following:

$$\alpha : \frac{company(rating) : @insurance\_company()}{@insurance\_company(rating)}$$

Consequent of α contradicts a justification of ε. That is why there can be no extension created by means of ε: ε is inapplicable after α, α is still applicable after ε, but it makes the process unsuccessful.

Let us now consider a more complicated example from the Tax domain. In Table 6.3 below some questions concerning *rent* are listed. They refer either to a situation when someone rents out a property (*rent1*), or to a situation when someone rents a property for business (*rent2*). In reality, the first one is more frequent, because *renting for business* has no cffcct on individual taxes. Nevertheless, both situations may appear in a question, so we need to propose the proper disambiguation here.

We propose a set of defaults to analyze the concept *rent*. The following defaults lead to two extensions when no specific words are used in the query.

$$\alpha_1 : \frac{rent : @rent1, not @rent2}{@rent1}$$

Table 6.3 Two meanings of questions about *tax* and *rent*

Questions about a person who rents out his/her property (landlord) and may have maintenance expenses	Questions about a person who rents a property to conduct his/her business (renter) and may consider it as a business expense
How to deduct rental expense?	
How to deduct rental expenses from my taxes?	
Can I include my rent expense in the itemized deduction?	
How to deduct rental expenses from my rent income?	*How to deduct rent expense from my business income?*
How much tax should I pay on my rental income?	*How to calculate my expenses when renting a property for my business?*
My business is to rent out my property. How about taxes?	*If I need to rent a property from the property management business, what are the tax issues?*
How much tax do I pay when I rent out my property?	*How to deduct rental expenses from the income of my business?*
How can I deduct what I paid for repair from the income of my rental business	*How to deduct rent from my salary?*

$$\alpha_2 : \frac{rent \,:\, @rent2, \, not\, @rent1}{@rent2}$$

The second group consists of rules that block α_2 default. They are used when a query contains some concepts, helping us to conclude, that it is actually about renting out a property:

$$\delta_1 : \frac{(rent\&\_out) \,:\, @rent1}{@rent1(\_out)} \qquad \delta_2 : \frac{income(rent) \,:\, @rent1}{@income(rent1)}$$

$$\delta_3 : \frac{repair(rent) \,:\, @rent1}{@repair(rent1)} \qquad \delta_4 : \frac{business(rent) \,:\, @rent1}{@business(rent1)}$$

Note that in our examples we simplify the arguments of predicates relatively to their occurrence in semantic headers (Galitsky 2000a) or semantic skeletons.

The third group consists of rules that block α_2 default. They are used when a query contains some concepts, helping us to conclude, that it is actually about renting something for business:

$$\varepsilon_1 : \frac{(salary\&rent) \,:\, @rent2}{@rent2}$$

$$\varepsilon_2 : \frac{(rent\&business(Activity)\&Activity \neq rent) \,:\, @rent2}{@rent2}$$

Note that the rules (ε_2, δ_2, δ_4) use information not only about words in a query, but also about their semantic and syntactic connections.

Below we describe how some queries can be analyzed with the help of proposed rules.

(1) *How to deduct rental expense?*

The initial representation for this query is *deduct(expense(rent()))*. Only α_1 and α_2 defaults are applicable to it:

$$Accepted(\{\alpha_1\}) = \{deduct, expense, rent, @rent1\},$$

$$Accepted(\{\alpha_2\}) = \{deduct, expense, rent, @rent2\}.$$

After the application of α_1, the α_2 rule becomes inapplicable and vice versa. So, both {*deduct,expense,rent,@rent1*} and {*deduct,expense,rent,@rent2*} are extensions. Therefore, the system will give both answers to the question *How to deduct rental expense?*, about *rent1* and about *rent2*. Indeed, it is impossible to disambiguate these meanings given the question (1).

(2) *How to deduct my rental expenses from my rental income?*

The initial representation for this query is *deduct(expense(rent()), income(rent()))*. The rules α_1, α_2 and δ_2 are applicable to it. The only successful and closed processes

Fig. 6.20 AMR parse for the query. The read oval shows the question focus

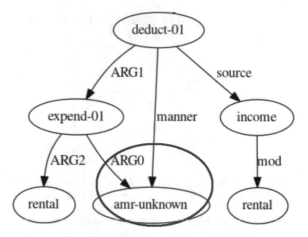

are $\{\alpha_1,\delta_2\}$ and $\{\delta_2,\ \alpha_1\ \}$. They lead to the extension {*deduct, expense, rent, income(rent), @income(rent1)*}. The AMR graph is shown in Fig. 6.20 and process tree for this query is depicted in Fig. 6.21.

Hence if the query contains no information which can help us to perform the query disambiguation, default rules lead to multiple extensions, corresponding to multiple meanings of ambiguous elements. If the query contains some specific concepts, our rules lead to single extension and the system proposes a single answer. We believe that the optimal solution for a Q/A system is to provide multiple answers in case of multiple extensions (i.e., in case there are no words indicating the particular meaning).

Default rules can help us to add new elements to semantic representation, using the basics of commonsense knowledge. Frequently, it is necessary to insert an entity that links the specific attribute with the more general concept occurring in a query. For example, if the query contains word *school* it is likely to be about education. So *Can I deduct my school expenses?* should be interpreted as *deduct(expense(education(school())))*. We propose the following default rule:

$$\frac{school() : @education()}{@education(school())}$$

This rule should be accompanied by the clause presenting situations of justification inconsistency. If we have a query *Can I deduct my donation to a catholic school?*, it is about a donation rather than about education. The following clause provides the proper solution:

$$@education : -deduct(Attribute), not(Attribute = expense).$$

The rule above expresses the fact that if there are attributes of *deduct* in a query, then the query is likely about these attributes (*donation, construction, moving*, etc.).

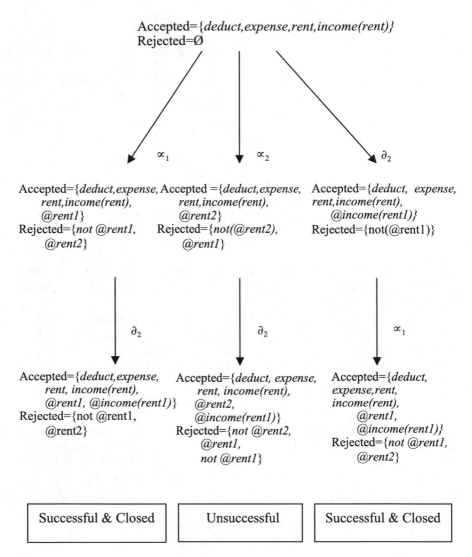

Fig. 6.21 Process tree for *How to deduct my rental expenses from my rental income?*

If *Attribute* is rather general (*expense*), then the clause fails and justification stays consistent.

Let us consider another example when we add an entity (*donation*) to the query representation to link the specific word (*church*) to a general concept (*deduct*): *Can I deduct what I gave to church?* We have similar default rule:

$$\frac{church() : @donation()}{@donation(church())}$$

Furthermore, what would happen if we have more than one specific word potentially connected with the general concept, as in a query *Can I deduct my church school expenses?* Occurrence of multiple attributes may require analysis of conflicting defaults (operational semantics). If the justification failure clause for *@donation* is similar to that proposed above, we have two extensions for this query - {..., *@donation*} and {...,*@education*}. But if we consider *education* to be more general than *donation*, the justification failure clause looks like

@donation:-

$$deduct(Attribute), not(Attribute = expense), not(Attribute = education),$$

and the only possible extension is *{..., @donation}.*

The default technique indeed brings in significant advantages in the processing of poorly structured (NL) knowledge representation. If we do not want to use default technique for our *school* example then, either we are not able to substitute *school()* in the formula at all or, we have to use

deduct(expense(school())) representation. In the first case, we lose important information and obtain a wrong answer. In the second case we have to provide the possibility to substitute *university, college, institute*, and other terms in *expense()* as well. As a result, the domain becomes less structured and query processing loses efficiency.

As we have seen, default rules can help us to improve domain hierarchy. It affects not only the performance but also the quality of query processing. Let us imagine that we have no information about *school expenses*. Instead, we know how to treat *educational expenses* in general. If the system cannot connect *school* with *education*, users get wrong answers because the formula *deduct(expense(school()))* is interpreted literally.

Semantic representation can contain more or less specific entities. The most general parts can lead to vague answers. For example, the query *How to file time extension for my tax return?* has a representation *tax(return)&extension(file)*. It leads to two answers: about *tax returns* in general and about *extension of time for filing*. It is obvious that the first part is superfluous and must be eliminated. In fact, in *tax* domain we can interpret *extension* only as *extension of time to file*, and not for example, as *extension of computer file*. Therefore, *tax(return)* can be deleted from the formula without loss of information. We first present the naïve stand-alone rule:

$$\frac{extension(time) : tax}{@extension()}$$

This rule can be read as follows: if a query mentions *extension of time* and it is consistent to assume that it is about *tax*, then the query is indeed only about *extension*. Although this rule follows our intuition better, it is not appropriate for interaction with other rules, because it does not actually eliminate *tax* from the current knowledge base. Therefore, we suggest the following rule instead:

$$\delta : \frac{extension() : not\,@tax()}{not\,@tax()}$$

It is read as follows: if a query contains the word *extension,* then *tax* should be eliminated. Note that the elimination of superfluous elements is connected with the disambiguation problem. If we have no idea about the topic of the query, both meanings (*filing time extension* and *computer file extension*) are probable, so we need an additional information to apply our analysis to. However, if we provide the Q/A for a narrow domain, only one meaning is expected and the other is exceptional. That is why this additional information becomes superfluous.

To comment on the rule δ, we present the simplified default "without *extension*", which would mean that we can always eliminate *tax* from a query.

$$\frac{\perp : not\,@tax()}{not\,@tax}$$

However, this rule would misinterpret the queries *What is tax?, Can I deduct the tax I paid last year?,* and others.

Depending on the order in which rules of eliminating superfluous parts and trivial rules are used, we can obtain several extensions containing more or less elements of the initial structure, because these two types of defaults make each other inapplicable. If we begin with trivial rules, the representation remains unmodified. Otherwise, some entities are eliminated. The order in which defaults are applied can be chosen by knowledge engineers depending on the task specifics.

6.6.6 Using Nonmonotonic Pragmatics for Summarized Logical Forms

Usually, using pure keyword analysis for Q/A is considered a rather primitive approach. Representing a query as a Boolean combination of keywords is insufficiently expressive if there are more than two entities (with attributes) in a query. To obtain high Q/A accuracy under the shallow syntactic processing, it is necessary to apply some pragmatic machinery to sort out improper query representation hypotheses (Grishman 1997; Ng et al. 1997; Boros et al. 1998). We use the default logic to build a set of keywords for an answer such that these keywords will be directly matched against the query keywords, providing satisfactory accuracy. In this Section, we show that the use of nonmonotonic reasoning versus pure Boolean keyword expressions can compensate for sophisticated semantic machinery and perform a proper Q/A for queries with multiple entities.

In this Section, the technique of SLFs (Chap. 4) is reduced to the keywords SLFs, consisting of the list of entities and their attributes, corresponding to the atoms of the expressions for standard SLFs. Under the SLF technique, the Q/A problem is posed as finding the most relevant class (answer) for a query, using the pre-built set of the canonical queries. We reformulate this problem as a *separation* of answers, using the representation of these canonical queries as keyword lists (keyword SLFs). In contrast to the above presentation of default reasoning for NLP, appropriate for a generic semantic analysis, this Section introduces the default reasoning approach, oriented to the keyword SLF technique.

Below we will present two answers and propose a way to distinguish them. Then we demonstrate how default rules are used to transform an input NL query into a form that can be matched against the keyword summarized logical form of an answer. Building default rules is followed by their verification, given the set of semantically diverse queries, and construction of the clauses for checking their justifications. Further on we show how to perform the automatic annotation of new answers, where the constructed default rules build the keyword SLFs for these answers, together with the new defaults for them.

6.6.7 Annotating Answers with Unique Keywords

As an example, let us have the following two answers that need to be annotated by the set of keywords that is unique for this answer

> *You can get the information about your tax return from the IRS website. The documents are available for download as the files with extension *.pdf. From time to time, the website may experience technical difficulties.*
>
> *Everyone is encouraged to file the tax return on time. If you experience financial difficulties, you can file an extension of time for your tax return. Detailed information is available for download at the IRS website.*

In terms of the keywords, these paragraphs are almost identical, but the topics they express are quite different. Such situations occur frequently when a Q/A system goes deeper into details within a vertical domain trying to separate the answers consisting of the same keywords.

We ignore the information about syntactic relations between words in sentences and consider the full list of keywords for these paragraphs. As a result, we see that they are different by domain-invariant words only (*need, encourage, technical*), so they should be used to annotate these answers.

> {*download, tax, return , irs, website, file, extension, time, experience, technical, difficulty*},
>
> {*encourage, file, tax , return, time, experience, financial, difficulty, file, extension, time, tax, return, information, irs, website*}.

It is evident that although the paragraphs above have similar keywords there is a critical difference in their importance for the meanings of these paragraphs. The main question of this section is how to properly annotate these paragraphs, based on the most important keywords and ignoring the least important ones. For the first paragraph, one of the expected annotating sets of keywords (summarized logical form) is *information, tax, return*. For the second one, we have *file, extension, time, tax, return*.

A pure keyword extraction system would not be able to distinguish between these answers. The suggested application of the default reasoning is based on the specific model of how the textual information is distributed through the sentences in a paragraph.

Keyword-based default rules are intended to link the approximate, deviated meaning, expressed by a *prerequisite*, to the exact meaning, expressed by *consequent*:

$$\frac{prerequisite : justifications}{consequent}$$

where *prerequisite, justifications and consequent* are the lists of keywords. *Prerequisite* includes the list of keywords that may occur in a sentence, *justification* specifies the wider topic (context of this sentence) which is evaluated by processing the current and the other sentences in a paragraph. *Consequent* contains the combination of keywords which is the best representation of meaning of a portion of text (sentence in an answer or a query). Intuitively, an arbitrary way of asking about a topic is expressed (potentially matched) with the prerequisite, and the exact topic is expressed by the consequent.

One of the natural ways to distinguish the answers is to assign different justifications to the keyword pair *file, extension*, which will serve as a prerequisite to the pair of default rules:

$$\frac{file, extension : download}{file, download, tax}$$

$$\frac{file, extension : time}{extension, time, tax, information}$$

Consequences of the first and second rules present the essential idea of the respective answers. These defaults are natural from the perspective of the domain knowledge representation, but they are not helpful to link a possible question with the most relevant canonical one.

6.6.8 Using Defaults to Transform a Query into a Summarized Logical Form

To obtain an answer given a question, we would expect to employ the default rules in the following way. A question corresponds to prerequisite and justification, and an answer is associated with the keyword summarized logical form (list of keywords) of the consequence:

$$\frac{question}{SH \ of \ answer}$$

How can a question be divided into prerequisite and justification? The prerequisite includes the keywords, unique for the answer, and the justification contains the rest of the words. We call the default alien if there are no common keywords in its prerequisite and consequence.

Let us consider the first sentences of the answers and build the templates of the default rules:

$$\frac{download, information, tax, return, irs, website}{file, download, tax, information}$$

$$\frac{encourage, \ file, tax, return, time}{extension, time, tax}$$

To construct the default rules from their templates, we form the justification from the keywords, not participating in the separation between answers (i.e., not occurring in summarized logical forms). These words are simultaneously frequent and essential for a given Q/A domain.

$$\frac{download, information, website, irs : tax, return}{file, download, tax, information}$$

$$\frac{time, encourage : file, tax, return}{extension, time, tax}$$

Since the words *tax, return, file* occur in both answers, they do not have to be matched against an input query to provide a specific answer. However, these words are necessary to obtain evidence of the proper context (sub-domain) for the words from the prerequisite. In other words, prerequisite performs the answer separation on the lower (specific) level, and justification does the same on the higher (general) level.

The learning stage of automatic annotation consists of building the default rules given the pre-composed SLFs associated with an answer. A template of a default rule is built for each SLF and for each sentence in an answer. A template is convertible into a default rule if there is at least a single common word in prerequisite and in consequent. Evidently, if we allow an overlap just between justification and consequent, it would mean that we let a very general answer to be activated which can cause a potential conflict with the other more specific answers. The procedure of conversion of a template to default rules is based on the intuition that a potential question can be close to an answer sentence, however, not all the answer sentences need to be represented by SLFs.

Template of default rule	default rule
answer sentence	*prerequisite (unique words) : justification (assumed words)*
SLF $\rightarrow$	*words of the existing SLF*

How do defaults convert an input query into a summarized logical form? For a given query, the system looks through SLFs to match the maximal number of words, and through default rules to match the maximal number of words against their prerequisite and verifies the consistency of justification. If the number of matched keywords of a default rule prerequisite is higher than that of an SLF, the former is chosen. Note that multiple answers can be delivered. We present the algorithm of matching the keywords of an input query against SLF and default rules (DR) in accordance to the following expression, where *cardinality* means the number of keywords:

$$query \leftrightarrow keywords : max\{cardinality(\{keywords\}) : keywords \in SLF \cup ($$
$$keywords \in (prerequisite(DR) : justification(DR) \, holds)\}$$

A *query* is mapped into the set of *keywords* such that this set delivers the highest number of matched words for the totality of all SLFs and default rules with consistent justifications.

To improve relevance of these computations, we suggest taking into account the number of unmatched keywords in an SLF and the default rule justification as well. The lower the number of unmatched keywords, the higher is the evidence of relevance between a query and a keyword SLF.

To discover that the justifications of default rules are consistent, the system needs to verify the following:

(1) While processing a query: a clause, expressing the justification inconsistency, fails;
(2) While processing a sentence within an answer, subject to annotation

   (a) justification words are present in a given sentence or preceding or following sentences in an answer;
   (b) there are no explicit negations of the justification atoms obtained by other default rules which have been applied to the other sentences in an answer;
   (c) a clause, expressing the justification inconsistency, fails.

For example, the query *"Does IRS encourage taxpayers to timely respond to the audit notice?"* should not activate the second default rule above. In the *tax* domain, the most common action is *filing a tax return*, which is assumed by default in the rule. If one speaks about such action as *responding to an audit*, it is legitimate but not most common, therefore, the justification is exptected to be inconsistent. We need to add the clause in accordance with the following scheme:

justification_inconsistent(tax) :- [tax, Action], Action $\neq$ file.

This means that the rule is about *encouraging to file tax on time* and not about encouraging to perform some other, less frequent action on time.

The predicate *justification_inconsistent* is called for each keyword in justification. If there is no special clause for a keyword, this predicate fails:

justification_inconsistent(A) :- fail.

A negation may appear in a prerequisite in the following situation. Let us have a pair of answers, one is for an entity *e* and the set of its attributes, and another for this entity *e* and a particular attribute *a*. Then the first answer can be assigned by a default with prerequisite containing this entity and the justification containing the negation of this particular attribute. The second default will not have such constraints in its justification:

$$\frac{e,\ldots:\ not\ a,\ \ldots}{\ldots}, \quad \frac{e,\ldots:\ \ldots}{\ldots}$$

For example, if we have a general answer about the *deduction of everything except mortgages*, and a specific one about *mortgage deduction*, the following rules will be in use:

$$\frac{deduct,\ not\ (\ mortgage):\ tax}{general\_deduct}, \quad \frac{deduct,\ mortgage,\ \ldots:tax}{deduct,\ mortgage}$$

6.6.9 Constructing SLFs for a New Answer, Based on the Available Default Rules

An answer which is subject to annotation is considered as a set of sentences, each of which can serve as a template for canonical questions to this answer. For each sentence in an answer, we search for the most adequate pre-built default rule in the sense of the best match of this sentence and the consequent. An SLF is constructed with a new default rule assigned to the annotated answer. We use the correspondence diagram between the existing and new defaults to show how they are interrelated:

$$\frac{prerequisite:\ justification}{consequent} \rightarrow \frac{answer\ sentence:\ justification}{canonical\ question}$$

Unmatched words in the answer sentence can participate in the formation of semantics as well, if the structure of the semantic link between the pair of matched-unmatched words in the answer sentence is similar to that of two words in a consequent of the used default rule. We can plot the correspondence diagram, taking into account replacement of *unmatched* by *newTerm*, if *matched* is an entity, and *unmatched* together with *newTerm* are its attributes:

$$matched, unmatched, ... : justification \qquad matched, newTerm, ... : justification$$
$$\overline{\qquad\qquad\qquad\qquad\qquad} \rightarrow \overline{\qquad\qquad\qquad\qquad\qquad}$$
$$matched, unmatched, ... \qquad\qquad\qquad matched, newTerm, ...$$

As an example, we construct an SLF with default rule for the answer, containing the following sentence:

... You can obtain information about filing your tax return by calling IRS 1-800- ⋯
download, information, website, irs: tax, return   call, information, irs: tax, return
————————————————— → ————————————
file, download, tax, information   file, call, tax, information

We replace *download* by *call,* because both *download* and *call* are the attributes (actions) of the entity *information* which is essential for the answer.

Evidently, we need a sufficient number of pre-built default rules to adequately annotate the new answer in the same domain, consisting mostly of known terms. Therefore, the annotation training needs to provide reasonable coverage of the domain and its terms to prepare it for automatic annotation.

To conclude the Subsection, we outline the semantic features of the suggested technique. Generally speaking, default rules are used to convert a query representation in case it does not match existing summarized logical forms. Analogously to virtual SLFs (Chap. 4), default rules are designed to cover the space of queries not directly represented by SLFs. As we explained while introducing the SLF technique, an individual SLF covers the totality of semantically similar, but syntactically different queries. The set of default rules with the consequence that matches an SLF covers semantically different, but pragmatically similar questions.

One of the motivations of our study of default reasoning for Q/A is a lack of convincing, from our viewpoint, examples of practical default reasoning, and especially the operational semantics of default reasoning (Galitsky 2003). The verbal description highlights "usual" (default) and "unusual" circumstances, but, once the data is formalized and there are conflicting rules while computing the extensions, intuitive perception of being and unusual is gone. Only thorough considerations of NL scenarios, presented within a vertical domain, may serve as a satisfactory illustration of practical nonmonotonic reasoning. Nontrivial extensions induced by a query appear when this query has multiple ambiguities. In particular, the situations where two words or multi-words have double possible meanings each such that the sentence has at least three overall meanings, are relatively rare.

Reasoning with exceptions is an inherent feature of natural language. Domain-independent semantic analysis skips the exceptions, and therefore the matching unit becomes the essential one to handle the domain-specific deviations of the meanings of the concepts.

We implement the machinery of default logic to handle exceptions. Default reasoning is a convenient means of programming the data analysis rules, presented separately for typical and special situations. Typical rules are applied first, and the rules for unusual situations are called only upon request. Thus, default logic serves as a reasonable structure on the set of rules in terms of software coding styles, when a knowledge engineer represents the frequently and infrequently accessed pieces of knowledge separately. As a result, modifications of the latter component (enumeration of the exceptions) do not affect the main body of domain code.

6.6.10 Evaluation of Non-monotonic Pragmatic Reasoning

We use the same evaluation framework, dataset and Q/A components as for the evaluation of taxonomy-based search (Sect. 4.3). The taxonomy-filtered search results are subject to 218 manually constructed default rules in the financial domain (the taxonomy itself is used in default rule construction). We measure normalized Discounted Cumulative Gain (NDCG, Wang et al. 2013), assessing the top five search results. Table 6.4 shows the improvement of search where the manually developed default rules are applied to query rewrite.

The third column contains the results obtained by the suite of components including the taxonomy. The improvement for all cases due to default rules is 4.6% (ranging from 3.5% for simpler queries to 7% for complex queries (bottom three rows)).

Table 6.4 Improvement of Q? A due to the default rules used to transform the formal representation of input query

Query	Phrase sub-type	The suite + Taxonomy-based, NDCG	The suite + Taxonomy-based + domain-dependent default rules, NDCG
3–4 word phrases	Noun phrase	0.318	0.329
	Verb phrase	0.323	0.330
	How-to expression	0.312	0.328
5–10 word phrases	Noun phrase	0.309	0.318
	Verb phrase	0.316	0.327
	How-to expression	0.307	0.322
2–3 sentences	One verb one noun phrases	0.261	0.282
	Both verb phrases	0.243	0.259
	One sent of how-to type	0.236	0.251

6.6.11 General Question Rewriting Considerations

Given a question q, potentially ill-formed, the question rewriting task is to convert it to a well-formed natural language question q_w while preserving its semantics and intention. Following Faruqui and Das (2018), we define a well-formed question as one satisfying the following constraints:

(1) The question is grammatically correct. Common grammatical errors include misuse of third person singular or verb tense.
(2) The question does not contain spelling errors. Spelling errors refer specifically to typos and other misspellings, but not to grammatical errors such as third person singular or tense misuse in verbs.
(3) The question is explicit. A well-formed question must be explicit and end with a question mark. A command or search query-like fragment is not well-formed.

Sometimes query rewriting is performed for sponsored search (Zhang et al. 2007; Zhang and Jones 2007). This work differs from our goal as we rewrite ill-formed questions to be well-formed. Some studies rewrite queries by searching through a database of query logs to find a semantically similar query to replace the original query. De Bona et al. (2010) compute query similarities for query ranking based on user click information. Dong et al. (2017) learn paraphrases of questions to improve question answering systems. Kumar et al (2018) translate queries from search engines into natural language questions, relying on Microsoft Cognitive Services' search logs and their corresponding clicked question page as a dataset that maps queries into questions. Also, rewriting questions on demand with reinforcement learning has been shown to improve Q/A (Buck et al. 2018).

Paraphrase generation has been used in several applications. Cho et al (2019) use paraphrase generation as a data augmentation technique to train NLU. Iyyer et al. (2018) and Ribeiro et al. (2018) compose adversarial paraphrases, varying the resultant phrasing to assess and enhance the model accuracy. Wieting and Gimpel (2018) build paraphrases using machine translation on parallel text and use the resulting sentential paraphrase pairs to learn sentence embeddings for semantic textual similarity.

Forward + inverse machine translation is an effective approach for question or sentence paraphrasing (Mallinson et al. 2017; Iyyer et al. 2018). It first translates a sentence to another pivot language, then translates it back to the original language. (Chu et al. 2020) used both German and French.

6.7   Acquiring Instructions on How to Do Stuff

In recent years, there has been much work in the area of program synthesis from natural language, examples or a mixture of such approaches. Many computing domains have documentation in NL describing the capabilities and dynamics of the domain. Correct interpretation of this text can provide a formal high-level description of the structure of the domain. These formal descriptions can be used by a low-level planner to help constrain the search process it performs during program synthesis (Kushman 2015).

NL learning approaches have implemented the translation of sentences to meaning representations such as database queries (Chap. 7), navigation plans (Chen and Mooney 2011), semantic frames (Das and Smith 2011) and string manipulation expressions (Manshadi et al., 2013; Kushman and Barzilay, 2013, Lutcev 2015). The limitation of these approaches are due to ambiguity issues in NL, domain-specific training phase, language learning supervision, a necessity to reduce the amount of examples required for this supervised training and a lack of required detailed domain-specific ontology.

On the contrary, (Raza et al 2015) do not apply any NL learning techniques commonly used in programming in NL approaches, but instead only utilize the NL decomposition to enable compositional input in the form of constituent examples.

An arlgebra for string transformation to convert NL into code is shown in Fig. 6.22. The start symbol is f, the terminal symbols k, n, c and s represent literal values of type integer, natural number, character and string, respectively, and w is an integer variable. An example of a generated program is shown in Fig. 6.23.

Lei et al. (2013) proposes an automatic construction of input parsers from English specifications of input file formats. A Bayesian generative model translates an English specification into a specification tree, which is then translated into a C programming language input parser, relying on semantic role labeling. The methods are based on two sources of information:

(1)   The correlation between the text and the specification tree;
(2)   Noisy supervision as determined by the success of the generated C parser in reading input examples.

```
String f := SubStr(p, p) | SubStr2(r , i) | ConstStr(s) | ConstChar(c) | Filter(r ) | Replace(r , s) |
Remove(p) | Loop(w, f ) | cnd | Concat(f , f )
String condition := IfThen(b, f ) | IfThenElse(b, f , f )
bool b := Match(r , n) | Not(b) | And(b, b) | Or(b, b)
int p := CPos(k) | Pos(r , r , i)
record r := EmptyTok | StartTok | EndTok | StrTok(s) | CharTok(c) | chCl | Neg(chCl) | ConcatTok(r , r
) | Interval(r , n, n) | Interval(r , n) | Optional(r ) | KleenePlus(r ) | KleeneStar(r ) | DisjTok(r , r ) |
LkBehind(r ) | LkAhead(r ) | IncludeWS(r )
record chCl := AnyChar | NumChar | LowerChar | UpperChar | LiteralChar(c) | Union(chCl, chCl)
int i := k | k ∗ w   k
```

Fig. 6.22 Algebra for string transformations

	Ex 1	Ex 2
Input	Class (4) 1m5f Good	2 2 3 5M2Fxyz 3
Output	1m5f	5M2F
"a digit"	1	5
"the letter"	m	M
"a digit"	5	2
"the letter"	f	F

```
SubStr2(
  ConcatTok(
    NumChar,
    ConcatTok(
      DisjTok(CharTok('m'), CharTok('M')),
      ConcatTok(NumChar, DisjTok(CharTok('f'), CharTok('F'))))
  )
  ),
  0
)
```

Fig. 6.23 Sample tasks in programming Excel macros: the original task descriptions, the examples given to the system and the synthesized programs

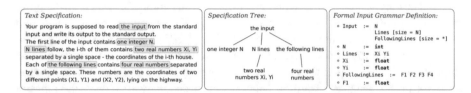

Fig. 6.24 From input specification to code

An example of generating input parser code from text is shown in (Fig. 6.24). On the left, there is an NL input specification; in the middle, there is a specification tree representing the input format structure (the background phrases in this tree are skipped). On the right, there is a formal definition of the input format constructed from the specification tree, represented as a context-free grammar.

In this Section, we provide an example of how an NL description of an algorithm can be translated into a code with the support of semantic and discourse analyses. This is another example for how one can build a cohesive formal representation of text leveraging DTs.

The ability to map natural language to a formal query or command language is critical to developing more user-friendly interfaces to many computing systems such as databases. However, relatively little research has addressed the problem of learning such semantic parsers from corpora of sentences paired with their formal-language equivalents (Kate et al. 2005). Furthermore, to the best of our knowledge, no such research was conducted at discourse level. By learning to transform an NL into a complete formal language, NL interfaces to complex computing and AI systems can be more easily developed.

6.7.1 AMR-Based Programming in NL

NL descriptions of programs is an area where a detailed semantic parsing is essential (Galitsky and Usikov 2008). In this Section, we explore the possibility of using AMR for parsing NL descriptions of programs. We will look at a common rhetorical representation and also a domain-specific representation that maps algorithm description into software code.

Fig. 6.25 Abstract meaning representation (AMR) tree of a second command

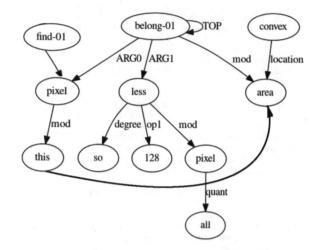

We have the following text and its AMR representation (Fig. 6.25):

(1) *Find a random pixel p1.*
(2) *Find a convex area a_off this pixel p1 belongs so that all pixels are less than 128.*
(3) *Verify that the border of the selected area has all pixels above 128.*
(4) *If the above verification succeeds, stop with positive result. Otherwise, add all pixels which are below 128 to the a_off.*
(5) *Check that the size of a_off is below the threshold. Then go to 2. Otherwise, stop with negative result.*

Figure 6.25 shows the semantic representation of the second line of code instruction taken without variable names. We now demonstrate how to convert a particular sentence into logical form and then to software code representation. Certain rhetorical relations help to combine statements obtained as a result of translation of individual sentences (Fig. 6.26).

6.7.2 Reinforcement Learning Planning Approach

In order to take advantage of NL documents to help solve the computation problems in planning, two issues must be addressed:

(1) Mismatch in Abstraction: There is a mismatch between the typical abstraction level of human language and the granularity of planning primitives. While the text provides a high-level description of world dynamics, it does not provide sufficient details for successful plan execution.

Verify that the border of the selected area has all pixels above 128.
1-1) We express in predicate with arguments as sequence of NL expressions

```
Verify:Verb  border -of- area   border -have- pixel   pixel above 128
```

1-2) And now code it as predicates

```
epistemic_action(verify)  & border(area)  & border(pixel)& above(pixel,
128)
```

1-3) Convert constants into variables with proper generality control

```
epistemic_action(verify) & border(Area) & border(Pixel) & above(Pixel, 128)
```

Converting all constants into variables, we attempt to minimize the number of free variables, and not over-constrain the expression at the same time. Coupled (linked by the edge) arrows show that the same constant values (pixel) are mapped into equal variables (Pixel), following the conventions of logic programming. To achieve this, we add (unary) predicates which need to constrain free variables.

1-4) Adding predicates which constrain free variables

```
epistemic_action(verify)    &    border(Area)    &    border(Pixel)    &
above(Pixel, 128) & area(Area)
```

Now we need to build an explicit expression for quantification **all.** In this particular case it will not be in use, since we use a loop structure anyway

1-5) Quantification

```
epistemic_action(verify) & border(Area) & not ( border(Pixel) & not
above(Pixel, 128)) & area(Area)
```

2-1) Next step is to map predicates and their arguments into the objects, their methods and arguments:

```
Loop  =>   Pixel.next()                      border.belong(Pixel)  &&
Pixel.above(128)){
```

Finally, the expression can be transformed into a loop, since epistemic_action is 'verify'. We have the following template for it.

2-2) Finding code template for specified epistemic action

```
Bool bOn=true;
while (!(ObjectToTest.next()==null)){
if !(Conditions){
bOn=false;
      break;}
} Return bOn;
```

Finally, we have

2-3) Resultant code fragment

```
while (!(Pixel.next()==null)) {
if !(border.belong(Pixel) && Pixel.above(128)){
bOn=false;
      break;
      }
}
Return bOn;
```

Fig. 6.26 Steps of transition from NL instructions into code

(2) Lack of Labeled Training Data: The main goal of an ML system is to avoid the need to manually generate domain-specific heuristics or action hierarchies. Instead, one should leverage existing NL documents. However, traditional NL grounding techniques rely on domain-specific labeled training data which is typically generated manually (Tellex et al. 2011). If it is necessary to generate such resources for every domain of interest, then it is better to focus on developing domain-specific planning systems, rather than annotating a NL corpus.

To handle a disagreement in abstraction, a learning system must take advantage of the fact that NL domain documents typically describe the set of available actions one can perform, and how those actions relate to each other. Thus, a solution is expected to ground these linguistic relations in abstract precondition relations between states in the underlying domain. It sounds more promising than to ground directly in the entities of the domain. To avoid the need for extensive labeled training data, it makes sense to leverage the ability of the underlying system to compute execution outcomes. The validity of precondition relations extracted from text can be assessed by the execution of a low-level planner. For example, if a planner can find a plan to successfully compute an edge after identifying a round area in an image, then a round image area is likely a precondition for an edge. Conversely, if a planner generates a plan to identify an edge without first identifying a round area, then it is likely not a precondition. This feedback can enable one to acquire a skill to correctly ground NL relations without annotated training data. Also, one can use the acquired relations to navigate a high level planner and ultimately improve planning performance.

Given a text document describing an environment, (Branavan et al. 2012) extract a set of precondition/effect relations implied by the text. Also, the authors use these induced relations to determine an action sequence for completing a given task. This is formalized as follows (Fig. 6.27). Input is a world defined by the tuple $<S, A, T>$, where S is the set of possible world states, A is the set of possible actions and T is a deterministic state transition function. Executing action a in state s causes a jump to a new state s' according to $T(s' \mid s, a)$. States are represented using propositional logic predicates $x_i \in X$, where each state is simply a set of such predicates, i.e. $s \subset X$. The objective of the NLP is to automatically extract a set of valid precondition/effect relationships from a document d. Given our definition of the world state, preconditions and effects are unary predicates, x_i, in this world state. We assume that we are given a seed mapping between a predicate x_i, and the word types in the

Fig. 6.27 A high-level plan showing two subgoals in a relation of precondition

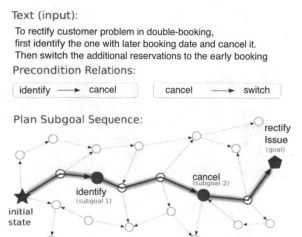

Text (input):

To rectify customer problem in double-booking,
first identify the one with later booking date and cancel it.
Then switch the additional reservations to the early booking

Precondition Relations:

identify ⟶ cancel   cancel ⟶ switch

Plan Subgoal Sequence:

document that reference it. For each predicate pair $< x_k, x_l >$ and a given text, it is possible predict whether x_k is a precondition for x_l. For example, from the text in Fig. 6.27, one can to predict that *identifying a later booking date* is a precondition for *canceling a flight before making a new reservation.*

6.8 Conclusions

A number of previous chapters addressed a broad spectrum of issues of controlled, robust, reliable and responsible answering questions to educate a customer to resolve her problems. With this Chapter, we conclude the Q/A series based on SLFs and proceed to other areas where AI helps CRM.

We learned to acquire new definition of entities such as a *cow* and extend a knowledge base with it (Fig. 6.28). From the standpoint of child development, this is called accommodation, a term developed by (Piaget and Cook 1952) to describe the process in which we modify existing cognitive schemas in order to include new information. Instead of making new information fit into an existing schema, humans change the schema in order to accommodate the new information. However, it is not plausible for machines, so for Q/A we do the other way around, rewrite query and definitions to fit the available knowledge base.

In conclusion, we comment on how the nonmonotonic reasoning for query rewrite is positioned in Logical AI. Generally speaking, default rules are used to convert a formal representation of an NL question in the form that is adequate as a knowledge base query. Such a conversion is required even for a semantically correct representation of a given query. The set of default rules with consequents that correspond to a single knowledge base query covers semantically different, but pragmatically similar questions. Syntactically different questions are handled on the earlier stage

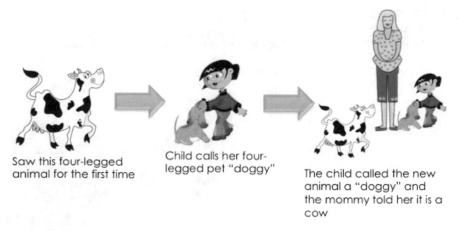

Saw this four-legged animal for the first time

Child calls her four-legged pet "doggy"

The child called the new animal a "doggy" and the mommy told her it is a cow

Fig. 6.28 Extending knowledge domain

(at a lower level with respect to a knowledge base); however, application of default rule is capable of correcting a wrong syntactic or semantic processing.

The nonmonotonic means for modeling the NL semantics have raised a substantial interest over last two decades. A version of nonmonotonic circumscription provides an explicit formalism for dealing with atypical situations (Lifschitz 1988). Circumscription is based on second-order logic, and it can be generalized toward intensional logic (Thomason 1990), following Montague (1969) approach. The associated philosophico-local issues of NL, formalizing commonsense have been addressed as well (Thomason 1991). Also, a method to extract norms (typical cases) from text has been proposed: narrative texts generally do not describe a norm, but rather present the discrepancies between what actually happened, and the corresponding normal sequence of events (Kayser and Nouioua 2004). Advanced theoretical investigations have been carried out in order to build the formal background for nonmonotonic intuition and a series of counter-examples (Pascu and Carpentier 2002). Answers about the causes of an event often reveal the implicit norms. Ourioupina and Galitsky (2001) have applied the default reasoning to pragmatics of Q/A; this direction is further developed in this chapter.

We have chosen the particular default system to suite the needs of question answering. We cannot restrict ourselves to the normal defaults (a single conjunctive member in the justification of a default rule) if we intend to match the expressiveness of semantic representation language, set by the query complexity. Having the logic programming implementation of semantic and pragmatic processing, as well as domain knowledge, we are not concerned with the decidability issues (Pascu and Carpentier 2002) associated with non-normal defaults in this chapter.

NLP offers unique possibilities to apply nonmonotonic reasoning to a domain which is sufficiently complex in terms of knowledge structure on one hand and possess the intrinsic feature of having a typical and atypical meanings on the other hand. However, the number of practical applications of nonmonotonic reasoning is far below the number of the theoretical results and their value. We believe that this chapter contributes to restoration of the balance between theoretical and applied issues of default reasoning (Galitsky 2002b).

In this Chapter, we explored the structure of definitions that are expressed as clauses with the head H and bodies $B_1, ..., B_n$ (Fig. 6.29). To acquire a definition, its text needs to be split into the definiendum H and the defining part $B_1, ..., B_n$, and the propagation of variable values from left to right needs to be established based on the syntactic clues from text and the existing ontology structure.

The use of nonmonotonic reasoning to handle rules with exceptions is shown in Fig. 6.30. We first provide a main rule, followed by enumeration of exceptions. Then the default rules assume there the case being applied to does not constitute an exception, unless we encounter this case in our list of exceptions.

In this chapter, we have demonstrated how an advanced reasoning assists Q/A in fully formalized or partially formalized domains where establishing additional deductive links between the domain facts in search time is necessary. The nonmonotonic reasoning technique can help to perform pragmatic analysis in processing a NL query and therefore improve the Q/A quality for virtical domains. Several

Fig. 6.29   Illustration for the structure of definition as clauses in Logic Programming. On the right : a definition (rule) and an example of its application

Fig. 6.30   Default reasoning methodology and handling exceptions

types of defaults are proposed which can be used in reasoning for Q/A in order to process ambiguous concepts, apply commonsense knowledge, and eliminate super-fluous terms. A disadvantage of traditional reasoning to represent the semantic and pragmatic rules is that it symmetrically handles frequent and infrequent situations. Instead, the nonmonotonic system always assumes that the typical situation occurs, unless it is not consistent for a variety of reasons to apply this assumption. A consid-eration of these "reasons" requires much more detailed domain analysis. Hence, application of default reasoning helps us to structure the domain representation, firstly considering the main rules, and then forming the additional ones.

More than 40 years ago (Dijkstra 1965), a Dutch computer scientist who invented the concept of structured programming, wrote: "I suspect that machines to be programmed in our native tongues –be it Dutch, English, American, French, German, or Swahili– are as damned difficult to make as they would be to use". The visionary was definitely right—the specialization and the high accuracy of programming languages are what made possible the tremendous progress in computing and computers as well. Dijkstra compares the invention of programming languages with invention of mathematical symbolism. In his words "Instead of regarding the obligation to use formal symbols as a burden, we should regard the convenience of using them as a privilege: thanks to them, school children can learn to do what in earlier days only genius could achieve". But four decades later we keep hitting a wall with the amount of code sitting in a typical industry applications. A large software project (tens and hundred of millions lines of code) is a nightmare to support and develop. The idiom *"The code itself is the best description"* became the kind of a bad joke. Hence we proposed a machinery to convert an NL description into a code.

References

Antoniou G (1997) Nonmonotonic reasoning. MIT Press Cambridge, MA London England

Berners-Lee T, Hendler J, Lassila O (2001) The semantic web. Sci Am 284(5):28–37

Bochman A (2001) A logical theory of nonmonotonic inference and belief change. Springer Verlag

Bollacker K, Evans C, Paritosh P, Sturge T, Taylor J (2008) Freebase: a collaboratively created graph database for structuring human knowledge. In: Proceedings of SIGMOD, pp 1247–1250

Boros E, Kantor PB, Lee JJ, Ng KB, Zhao D (1998) Application of logical analysis of data to TREC6 routing task. In: Text Retrieval Conference-6, NIST Special Publication

Boukhari I, Bellatreche L, Jean S (2012) An ontological pivot model to interoperate heterogeneous user requirements. In: International symposium on leveraging applications of formal methods, verification and validation. Springer, pp 344–358

Bovi CD, Telesca L, Navigli R (2015) Large-scale information extraction from textual definitions through deep syntactic and semantic analysis. Trans Assoc Comput Linguist 3:529–543

Branavan SRK, Kushman N, Lei T, Barzilay R (2012) Learning High-Level Planning from Text . ACL, pages 126–135

Brewka G, Dix J, Konolige K (1995) Nonmonotonic reasoning: an overview. CSLI Lecture Notes 73

Buck C, Bulian J, Ciaramita M, Gajewski W, Gesmundo A, Houlsby N, Wang W (2018) Ask the right questions: active question reformulation with reinforcement learning. ICLR

Casu M, Tacchella A (2011) From natural language definitions to knowledge bases axioms. In: Pirrone R, Sorbello F (eds) AI*IA 2011: artificial intelligence around man and beyond. AI*IA 2011. Lecture Notes in Computer Science, vol 6934. Springer, Berlin, Heidelberg

Chang AX. and Manning CD (2012) SUTime: A library for recognizing and normalizing time expressions.. In LREC-12, 3735–3740

Chen DL and Mooney RJ (2001) Learning to interpret natural language navigation instructions from observations. AAAI

Cho E, Xie H and Campbell WM (2019) Paraphrase generation for semi-supervised learning in NLU. In Proceedings of the Workshop on Methods for Optimizing and Evaluating Neural Language Generation

Chu Z, Chen M, Chen, Wang JM, Gimpel K, Faruqui M, Si X (2020) How to Ask Better Questions? A Large-Scale Multi-Domain Dataset for Rewriting Ill-Formed Questions. in AAAI

Chodorow MS, Byrd RJ, Heidorn GE (1985) Extracting Semantic Hierarchies from a Large On-Line Dictionary. In Proceedings 23 rd Annual Meetings of the Assoc Comp Linguistics, pp. 299–304, Chicago IL

Creary, L.G. & Pollard, C.J. (1985). A computational semantics for natural language. In Proc ACM-85 pp. 172–179

Denny Vrandecic (2012) Wikidata: A New Platform for Collaborative Data Collection. In Proceedings of WWW, pages 1063–1064

De Bona F, Riezler S, Hall K, Ciaramita M, Herdadelen A and Holmqvist M (2010) Learning dense models of query similarity from user click logs. In Proc. of NAACL

Diefenbach D, Lopez V, Singh K, Maret P (2018) Core techniques of question answering systems over knowledge bases: a survey. Knowl Inf Syst 55:529–569

Dijkstra EW (1965) Programming considered as a human activity. In: Proceedings of the IFIP Congress, pp 213–217

Dong L, Mallinson J, Reddy S and Lapata M (2017) Learning to paraphrase for question answering. In Proc. of EMNLP

Dutta A, Meilicke C and Ponzetto SP. (2014) A Probabilistic Approach for Integrating Heterogeneous Knowledge Sources. In ESWC, pp 286–301

Emani CK, Catarina Ferreira da Silva, Bruno Fies, Parisa Ghodous (2019) NALDO: From natural language definitions to OWL expressions. Data and Knowledge Engineering, Elsevier, pp. 29

Etzioni O, Banko M, Soderland S, Weld DS (2008) Open Information Extraction from the Web. Commun ACM 51(12):68–74

Fader A, Soderland S and Etzioni O(2011) Identifying Relations for Open Information Extraction. In Proceedings of EMNLP, pages 1535– 1545

Fellbaum C (1998) A semantic network of english: the mother of all wordnets. Comput Humanit 32, 209–220

Fidelity   (2018)   https://github.com/bgalitsky/relevance-based-on-parse-trees/blob/master/exa mples/ Fidelity_FAQs_AnswerAnatomyDataset1.csv.zip

Galitsky B (2002b). On the training of mental reasoning: searching the works of literature. FLAIRS – 02, Pensacola Beach, FL, May 2002, pp. 113–118

Galitsky B (2003) Natural language question answering system: technique of semantic headers. Advanced Knowledge International Adelaide Australia

Galitsky B (2004) Use of Default Reasoning for Disambiguation Under Question Answering. FLAIRS conference, 496–501

Galitsky B (2013) Transfer learning of syntactic structures for building taxonomies for search engines. Eng Appl Artif Intell 26(10):2504–2515

Galitsky B (2014) Learning parse structure of paragraphs and its applications in search. Eng Appl of AI 32:160–184

Galitsky B, de la Rosa JL (2011) Concept-based learning of human behavior for customer relationship management. Inf Sci 181(10):2016–2035

Galitsky B, Dobrocsi G, de la Rosa JL (2010) Inverting semantic structure under open domain opinion mining. Twenty-third international FLAIRS conference

Galitsky B, Dobrocsi G, de la Rosa JL, Kuznetsov SO (2011) Using generalization of syntactic parse trees for taxonomy capture on the web. In: International conference on conceptual structures, pp 104–117

Galitsky B, Kovalerchuk B (2014) Improving web search relevance with learning structure of domain concepts. In: Clusters, orders, and trees: methods and applications, pp 341–376

Galitsky B, Usikov D (2008) Programming Spatial Algorithms in Natural Language. AAAI Workshop Technical Report WS-08–11.–Palo Alto CA

Galitsky B (1999). Natural Language Understanding with the Generality Feedback DIMACS Technical Report 99–32, Rutgers University

Galitsky B (2005) Disambiguation via default rules under answering complex questions. Int J Artif Intell Tools 14 (01n02), 157–175

Galitsky B (2000a) Technique of semantic headers for answering questions in Tax domain. Proc. IASTED Conf. on Law & Technology, San Francisco CA, pp 117–123

Galitsky B (2000b). Technique of semantic headers: a manual for knowledge engineers. DIMACS Tech. Report #2000–29, Rutgers University

Galitsky B (2001a) Financial advisor: technique of semantic headers. Workshop on Inference in Computational Semantics, Sienna, Italy, p 2001

Galitsky, B (2001b). Semi-structured knowledge representation for the automated financial advisor. In Monostori et al, (Eds.) Engineering of Intelligent Systems, LNAI 2070: 14 th IEA/AIE Conference, p. 874–879

Galitsky, B (2002a) A tool for extension and restructuring natural language question answering domains, In Hendtlass, T., Ali, M. (Eds.) Developments in Applied Artificial Intelligence 15th IEA/AIE 2002, Cairns, Australia, LNCS 2358, Springer, pp. 482–492

Galitsky B,Ilvovsky D (2019) Least General Generalization of the Linguistic Structures. FCA4A workshop at IJCAI. CEUR-WS 2529

Ginsberg ML (1987) Readings in nonmonotonic reasoning. Morgan Kaufmann, San Francisco

Grefenstette G (1994) Explorations in automatic thesaurus discovery. Kluwer Academic, Boston/London/Dordrecht

Grishman R (1997) Information extraction: Techniques and challenges. In Pazienza, M.T. (ed.) Information extraction: a multidisciplinary approach to an emerging technology. Springer-Verlag, p. 18

Grigori Sidorov G(2019) Syntactic n-grams in Computational Linguistics

Grycner A and Weikum G. (2014) HARPY: Hypernyms and Alignment of Relational Paraphrases. In COLING, pp 2195–2204

Hakimov S, Unger C, Walter S, Cimiano P (2015) Applying semantic parsing to question answering over linked data: addressing the lexical gap. In: Natural language processing and information systems, Springer

Higashinaka R, Imamura K, Meguro T, Miyazaki C, Kobayashi N, Sugiyama H, Hirano T, Makino T, and Matsuo Y (2014) Towards an open-domain conversational system fully based on natural language processing. In: COLING

Hirst G (1988) Semantic interpretation and ambiguity Artificial Intelligence 34(2):131–177

Holzinger, A., Biemann, C., Pattichis, C.S., & Kell, D.B. (2017). What do we need to build explainable AI systems for the medical domain? ArXiv, abs/1712.09923

Hovy E, Navigli R, Ponzetto SP (2013) Collaboratively built semi-structured content and Artificial Intelligence: the story so far. Artif Intell 194:2–27

Investopedia (2019) http://www.investopedia.com/categories/taxes.asp

Iyyer M, Wieting J, Gimpel K and Zettlemoyer L (2018) Adversarial example generation with syntactically controlled paraphrase networks. In Proc. of NAACL, 1875–1885

Kate R, Wong YW, Mooney R (2005) Learning to transform natural to formal languages. Proc Natl Conf Artif Intell 20:1062–1068

Kayser D and Nouioua F (2004) About Norms and Causes. FLAIRS Conference, Miami Beach FL AAAI Press

Kipper K, Korhonen A, Ryant N, Palmer M (2008) A large-scale classification of English verbs. Language Resources and Evaluation Journal 42:21–40

Kumar A, Dandapat S and Chordia S (2018) Translating web search queries into natural language questions. In Proc. of LREC

Kushman N and Barzilay N (2013) Using semantic unification to generate regular expressions from natural language. In HLT-NAACL, 826–836

Kushman N (2015) Generating Computer Programs from Natural Language Descriptions. MIT PhD Thesis 940573214

Lifschitz V (1988) Circumscriptive theories: A logic-based framework for knowledge representation. Journal of Philosophical Logic 17(3):391–441

Lutcev EG (2015) Programming in Languages similar to Natural: A survey paper. Informatics N2:39–45

Mahdisoltani F, Biega J, and Suchanek FM (2015) YAGO3: A Knowledge Base from Multilingual Wikipedias. In CIDR

Manshadi MH, Gildea D and Allen JF (2013) Integrating programming by example and natural language programming. In AAAI

Marginean A (2017) Question answering over biomedical linked data with grammatical framework. Semant Web 8(4):565–580

Montague R (1969) On the nature of certain philosophical entities. The Monist 53:159–194

Mallinson J, Sennrich R and Lapata M (2017) Paraphrasing revisited with neural machine translation. In Proc. of EACL

Navigli R, Ponzetto S (2010) BabelNet: building a very large multilingual semantic network. 216–225

Navigli R, Velardi P (2004) Learning domain ontologies from document warehouses and dedicated web sites. Computational Linguistics 30(2):151–179

Nakashole N, Weikum G and Suchanek FM (2012) PATTY: A Taxonomy of Relational Patterns with Semantic Types. In EMNLP-CoNLL, pages 1135–1145

Nastase V, Strube M (2013) Transforming Wikipedia into a Large Scale Multilingual Concept Network. Artif Intell 194:62–85

Ng H-T, Goh W-B, Low K-L (1997) Feature selection, perceptron learning and a usability case study for text categorization. In: Belkin NJ, Narasimhalu AD, Willett P (eds) Proceedings of the 20th annual international ACM/SIGIR conference on research and development in information retrieval: Philadelphia, pp 67–73

Noraset T, Chen Liang, Larry Birnbaum, Doug Downey (2017) Definition Modeling: Learning to Define Word Embeddings in Natural Language. AAAI

Ourioupina O and Galitsky B (2001) Application of default reasoning to semantic processing under question-answering. DIMACS Technical Report 2001–16, Rutgers University

Pascu A, Carpentier F-G (2002) object determination logic—a categorization system. In: FLAIRS conference. AAAI Press, pp 178–180

Piaget J, Cook MT (1952) The origins of intelligence in children. International University Press, New York, NY

Poggi A, Lembo D, Calvanese D, De Giacomo G, Lenzerini M, Rosati R (2008) Linking data to ontologies. In: Journal on data semantics X, pp 133–173. Springer Verlag

Ponzetto SP, Strube M (2011) Taxonomy induction based on a collaboratively built knowledge repository. Artif Intell 175(9–10):1737–1756

Raza M, Gulwani S, Milic-Frayling N (2015) Compositional program synthesis from natural language and examples. IJCAI

Reinberger ML, Spyns P (2005) Generating and evaluating triples for modelling a virtual environment. OTM workshops, pp 1205–1214

Reiter R (1978) On Closed World Data Bases. In: Gallaire, H, Minker J (eds) Logic and data bases. Plenum Press, pp 119–140

Silva VS, Freitas A, Handschuh S (2018) Building a knowledge graph from natural language definitions for interpretable text entailment recognition. arXiv:1806.07731v1

Song D, Schilder F, Smiley C, Brew C, Zielund T, Bretz H, Martin, R., Dale C, Duprey J, Miller T (2015) TR discover: a natural language interface for querying and analyzing interlinked datasets. In: The Semantic Web-ISWC 2015. Springer

Tellex S, Kollar T, Dickerson S, Walter MR, Banerjee AG, Teller SJ, Roy N (2011) Understanding natural language commands for robotic navigation and mobile manipulation. In: AAAI

Thomason R (1990) Accommodation, meaning, and implicature: Interdisciplinary foundations for pragmatics. In: Cohen PR, Morgan J, Pollack M (eds) Intentions in communication. MIT Press, Cambridge, Massachusetts, pp 326–363

Thomason R (1991) Logicism, artificial intelligence, and common sense: John Mc-Carthy's program in philosophical perspective. In: Lifschitz V (ed) Artificial intelligence and mathematical theory of computation. Academic Press, San Diego, pp 449–466

Unger C, Bühmann L, Lehmann J, Ngonga Ngomo A-C, Gerber D, Cimiano P (2012) Template-based question answering over RDF data. In: Proceedings of the 21st WWW, ACM, pp 639–648

Volker J, Hitzler P, Cimiano P (2007) Acquisition of OWL DL axioms from lexical resources. In: ESWC. Springer, pp 670–685

Webscope (2017) Yahoo! answers dataset. https://webscope.sandbox.yahoo.com/catalog.php?

Wieting J, Gimpel K (2018) ParaNMT-50M: Pushing the limits of paraphrastic sentence embeddings with millions of machine translations. In: Proceedings of ACL

Weizenbaum (1976). Computer power and human reason: from judgment to calculation. W. H. Freeman Publishing

Wilks Y, Slator B, Guthrie L (1996) Electric words-dictionaries, computers and meanings. The MIT Press, Cambrdge, MA, London, England

Zettlemoyer LS, Collins M (2012) Learning to map sentences to logical form: structured classification with probabilistic categorial grammars. arXiv preprint arXiv:1207.1420

Zhang WV, He X, Rey B, Jones R (2007) Query rewriting using active learning for sponsored search. In: Proceedings of SIGIR

Zhang WV, Jones R (2007) Comparing click logs and editorial labels for training query rewriting. In: WWW 2007 workshop on query log analysis: social and technological challenges

Chapter 7
Inferring Logical Clauses for Answering Complex Multi-hop Open Domain Questions

Abstract We enable a conventional Question Answering (Q/A) system with formal reasoning that relies on clauses learned from texts and also on the complex question decomposition into simple queries that can run against various sources, from local index to intranet to the web. We integrate the reasoning, multi-hop querying and machine reading comprehension (MRC) so that a value can be extracted from a search result of one simple query and substituted into another simple query, till the answer is obtained via the recomposition of simple queries. The integrated approach boosts the Q/A performance in a number of domains and approaches the state-of-the-art for some of them, designed to train a deep learning (DL) Q/A system to answer complex, multi-hop queries. We assess the contribution of two reasoning components: ontology building from text, and entity association, as well as multi-hop query decomposer and MRC and observe that these components are necessary and complement each other answering complex questions. We apply a similar multi-hop framework to the problem of a natural language (NL) access to a database. The conclusion is that the proposed architecture with the focus on formal reasoning is well suited for industrial applications where performance is guaranteed in cases of no or limited training sets.

7.1 Introduction

In many cases, answering questions require some kind of reasoning. This is the most difficult case of question answering (Q/A), because no answer prepared in advance exists in a search index. Solving a search relevance problem, difficult on its own for complex queries and large indexes (Harel et al. 2019), targets the case where candidate answers need to be shortlisted based on a score, a rule or a machine-learned model. Neither exists where an answer needs to be inferred from unstructured, textual documents. The Reading Comprehension problem that is focused on extracting a passage does not help either where a required answer is not stored anywhere.

Answering complex questions is a time-consuming activity for humans that requires navigation through, reasoning about and integration of various pieces of

© Springer Nature Switzerland AG 2020   265
B. Galitsky, *Artificial Intelligence for Customer Relationship Management*,
Human–Computer Interaction Series,
https://doi.org/10.1007/978-3-030-52167-7_7

information. A recent work on machine reading comprehension (MRC) succeeded in answering simple questions within a document of a limited size, but answering complex questions is still an ongoing research challenge. Conversely, semantic parsers have been successful at handling compositionality in questions, but only when the information is structured and encoded in integrated knowledge resources (Galitsky 2001; Galitsky and Kovalerchuk 2014).

In this section, we focus on the Q/A setting where the only way to obtain an answer is to derive some knowledge from data, by means of induction (generalization from knowledge extracted from text) or deduction (applying reasoning rules to a chunk of knowledge extracted from text and formalized). Induction is also referred to as learning clauses from data, that should not be confused with learning associations between questions and answers which are expected to be applied to existing answers. We also present a framework for answering broad and complex questions, both factoid and non-factoid. This framework is based on the assumption that answering simple questions is possible using a search engine API and/or an MRC. We propose to decompose a complex, compound question into a sequence of simpler questions, and compute the final answer from the sequence of answers.

Answering questions which require reasoning is one of the long-term goals of AI. To track the progress toward this goal, several challenges have been recently proposed that employ a Q/A-based strategy to test an agent's understanding. We mention such challenges as *Allen Institute for AI*'s flagship project ARISTO, (Richardson et al. 2013)'s MCTest, the Winograd Schema Challenge (Levesque et al. 2012) and Facebook bAbI dataset where solving each task develops a new skill set by an agent. According to (Weston et al. 2015), even though these tasks are promising and provide some approximation of the real-world challenges, successfully answering their questions require competence on many logical and linguistic sub-tasks such as deduction, use of common-sense, abduction and coreference. Often the state-of-the-art systems are highly domain-specific and rely heavily on the prior knowledge.

7.1.1   Related Work

Open-domain Q/A has been inspired, in particular, by the series of TREC QA competitions (Trek 2017). As neural Q/A models appeared for individual documents, there was an interest to extend them toward the open-domain setting. A typical hybrid architecture is to shortlist candidates by a TF*IDF and then to apply a deep learning (DL) model to zoom into the exact answer. Recent work on open-domain question answering largely follows this approach where retrieval is followed by MRC, and focuses on improving the former component (Nishida et al. 2018; Kratzwald and Feuerriegel 2018; Nogueira et al. 2019). However, these two-step retrieve-and-MRC approaches are limited to simpler factoid questions. The disadvantage of these fixed two steps is that they do not accommodate multi-hop reasoning well, especially when the necessary facts and values have not been retrieved at the first step.

At a broader level, the need for multi-step searches, query task decomposition, and subtask extraction has been clearly recognized in the information retrieval and NL access to a database communities (Galitsky 2005; Awadallah et al. 2014; Mehrotra and Yilmaz 2017; Galitsky 2019d), but multi-hop Q/A has only recently been studied thoroughly with the release of large-scale datasets. Much research has focused on enabling multi-hop reasoning in Q/A models in the few-document setting, e.g., by modeling entity graphs (De Cao et al. 2019) or scoring answer candidates against the context (Zhong et al. 2019). These approaches, however, suffer from scalability issues when the number of supporting documents and/or answer candidates grow beyond a hundred. In the entity graph modeling in HotpotQA dataset, Ding et al. (2019) expand a small entity graph starting from the Q to arrive at the A for the Q/A model. The limitation of this model is its focus around entity names, potentially missing purely descriptive clues in the Q.

Qi et al. (2019) build an open-domain multi-hop Q/A that auto generates NL queries for each step of search session. The system is more interpretable to humans compared to neural retrieval approaches described above and assures better understanding and verification of model behavior. Similar to our approach, instead of using opaque and computationally expensive neural retrieval models, the system generates NL search queries given the question and available context, and leverages a third party information retrieval systems to search for missing entities.

A substantial work on Q/A through semantic parsing has focused primarily on compositionality where questions are translated into compositional programs that encode a sequence of actions for finding the answer in a knowledge-base, database or ontology (Kwiatkowski et al. 2013; Liang et al. 2011; Galitsky et al. 2011). However, this reliance on a manually curated KB has limited the coverage and applicability of semantic parsers.

As to the Facebook Q/A challenge, (Weston et al. 2015) formulates the Q/A task as a search procedure over the set of narratives. Their DL model takes as input the Q/A samples and the set of facts required to answer each question and learns to find the supporting facts for a given question as well as set of words from the supporting facts which are given as answer. Given a Q, the DL system iterates through the narratives in the reverse order of time and finds the most relevant hypothesis. It then tries to find the next most relevant narrative and the process continues until a special marker narrative is chosen as the most relevant.

Kumar et al. (2015) also models the Q/A task as a search procedure over the set of narratives. The algorithm first identifies a set of useful narratives conditioning on the question and updates the agent's current state. The process then iterates and in each iterations it finds more useful facts that were thought to be irrelevant in the previous iterations. After several passes, the module finally summarizes its knowledge and provides the answer (Fig. 7.1). The examples of an input set of sentences and the attention gates are triggered by a given question from the bAbI tasks (Weston et al. 2015). The gates change with each search over inputs.

These DL-based systems successfully handle simple tasks which were designed to measure various skills of an agent, such as: fact-based question-answering, simple induction, the ability to find paths, co-reference resolution and many more. Their

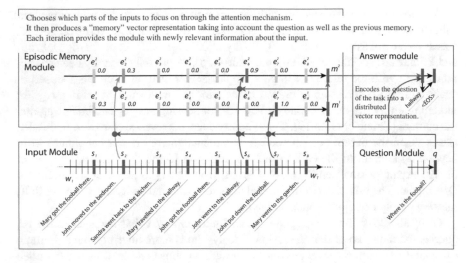

Fig. 7.1 Example of (Kumar et al. 2015) module solving (Weston et al. 2015) problem

goal is to aid in the development of systems that can learn to solve such tasks and to allow a proper evaluation of such systems. These systems cannot fully solve many of these toy tasks.

Both these systems take into account only the given narratives to answer a question. However, many Q/A tasks (such as task of Path finding) require additional world knowledge that is not present in the text or a training dataset to successfully answer a question. Both these models suffer in this case; at the same time, the clause inference method being proposed can efficiently combine knowledge learned from various tasks to handle more complex Q/A tasks. Unlike these DL system, a traditional AI Reasoning system of (Mitra and Baral 2016) excels at all Facebook dataset tasks except one, so we employ the Answer Set programming (Baral et al. 2004) and Inductive Logic Program following these authors to solve a real-world complex Q/A tasks.

In this work, we develop a technique from these simple reasoning problems and apply it to a number of Q/A datasets, some of which were designed for a combination of DL and IR approaches. These complex multi-hop questions require much more sophisticated reasoning than simple factoid questions for finding an attribute of an entity, such as the majority of questions in such question databases as SQuAD. Our reasoning varies on the level of abstraction (Galitsky et al. 2010), from informal to formal, and also varies in the cognitive type of required reasoning, from induction to deduction (Galitsky 2006).

For non-factoid complex questions, where an answer is expected to contain a recommendation, an advice, a recipe or a problem resolution strategy, a totally different technique to the one developed in this chapter is required. This technique is based on discourse analysis of Q and A and enforces what is called rhetorical agreement (Galitsky 2017b, 2019b).

7.1.2 Multihop Q/A Datasets

Table 7.1 compares several existing datasets along five key dimensions (Khot et al. 2020), which we believe are necessary for effectively developing retrieval and reasoning models for knowledge composition. Available datasets for the science domain require different reasoning techniques for each question (Clark et al. 2016). Instead, QASC dataset clearly identifies two facts which are decided by Mechanical Turkers to be sufficient to answer a question. These facts exist in an associated corpus and are provided for model development.

Multi-hop datasets from the Web domain use complex questions that bridge multiple sentences. We discuss the following datasets:

(1) WikiHop (Welbl et al. 2018) contains questions in the tuple form $(e, r, ?)$ based on edges in a knowledge graph. However, WikiHop lacks questions with natural text or annotations on the passages that could be used to answer these questions;

(2) ComplexWebQuestions (Talmor and Berant 2018) is derived by converting multi-hop paths in a knowledge-base into a text query. By construction, the questions can be decomposed into simpler queries reflecting the edges in the path of the knowledge graph;

(3) HotPotQA (Yang et al. 2018) contains a mix of multi-hop questions authored by crowd workers using a pair of Wikipedia pages. While these questions are authored in a similar way, due to their domain and task setup, they can be decomposed well;

(4) DROP (Dua et al. 2019) is based on reasoning and aggregate operations over text (such as counting or addition). Most queries perform mathematical operations on chunks of texts. Multiple approaches answer science questions by composing multiple facts from partially-structured and unstructured knowledge sources;

Table 7.1 Comparison between Q/A multihop datasets

Property	CompWebQ	DROP	HotPotQA	MultiRC	OpenBookQA	WikiHop	QASC
Supporting facts are available	N	Y	Y	Y	N	N	Y
Supporting facts are annotated	N	N	Y	Y	N	N	Y
Decomposition is not evident	N	N/A	N	Y	Y	Y	Y
Multi-document inference	Y	N	N	N	Y	N	Y
Requires knowledge retrieval	Y	N	Y	N	Y	N	Y

(5) OpenBookQA (Mihaylov et al. 2018) includes multiple-choice questions and a corpus of science facts. These are the sources for question generation. Each question requires combining the seed core fact with additional knowledge. However, it is unclear how many additional facts are needed, or whether these facts can even be retrieved from any existing knowledge sources;

(6) MultiRC (Khashabi et al. 2019) uses passages to create multi-hop questions. However, MultiRC and other single-passage datasets (Mishra et al. 2018; Weston et al. 2015) have a stronger emphasis on passage discourse and entity tracking, rather than relation composition.

(7) In QASC (Khot et al. 2020), each question is built by combining a pair of facts from a text corpus. Instead of forming compositional questions from scratch, the authors give Mechanical Turkers a single seed fact. Then Mechanical Turkers randomly identify other relevant facts from an extensive corpus; these facts are then composed with this seed fact. This approaches assists in finding other facts that fit naturally with the seed fact that has already been introduced. In QASC, it is hard to rely on simple syntactic signals to determine how to decompose a question into simpler queries.

We will not use all these datasets in our evaluation, only the selected ones.

7.1.3 Contribution

We intend to clearly differentiate from the competitive approaches to multi-hop querying that are based on MRC + data-driven question decomposition. Our goal is to explore how various kinds of formal reasoning can help offline and online Q/A components, experimenting with respective architectures:

- Rather than relying on learning query execution planning, we employ a rule-based and clause-based reasoning system to decide on where to look for answers and/or values next.
- The system employs deduction to infer new clause attempting to associate existing answers with the question. If it fails, inductive reasoning yields new clauses which can in turn be employed by deduction.
- Relying on inductive reasoning, we automatically build an ontology as sets of clauses from documents. This ontology then supports answering complex questions lacking explicit information or direct answers (Galitsky 2004).
- We rely on a search engine API to answer intermediate decomposed queries if necessary. At the same time, we improve these API searches, demonstrating superior performance answering complex multi-hop open-domain questions (Galitsky 2017c) in comparison to major web search engines.
- Most authors train their Q/A systems of Wikipedia, that are well structured around entities which correspond to the Wiki page titles. Instead, we focus on the whole web deploying search engine API and an arbitrary corpus of documents.

- Multi-hop Q/A is typically adjusted to a specific dataset, such as HotpotQA with a limited number of options. Most current multi-hop Q/A systems only handle complex factoid questions. In this chapter we take a broader look at various classes of multi-hop queries including recommendations, problem resolution, handling difficult situations, etc. Query decomposition occurs in a metalanguage, whereas query itself is formulated in a language-object (Galitsky 2017b)
- In the recent literature on Q/A, *reasoning* is used in a very broad sense: it is an operation with data that is not covered by *learning* (something not purely data driven) such as query decomposition. Here we treat reasoning within the traditions of logical AI. Proposed Q/A setting not only relies on substituting identified values into sub-queries (as we outlined above), but also employing logical clauses as well. These clauses can be automatically obtained from a corpus of texts, in advance or on demand, in real time.
- We develop a unified framework approaching text search in NL and database querying in NL (NL2SQL). We propose the same query decomposition method for a web search, an internal index search and a database querying in NL.
- In a number of academic systems described in this subsection, the architectures are selected to tackle a specific training dataset. Most of the authors build their own dataset to illustrate the idea behind the chosen architecture. This is especially true for the case of complex questions: each author attaches her own meaning to the choice of question complexity and the necessity of multi-hop search sessions. On the contrary, in this chapter, we build a universal Q/A architecture for an arbitrary information access.

7.2 Building a Logical Ontology from Texts

Ontology Builder takes tagged texts as an input and produces the rules formed from data in the form of clauses. A dataset of texts needs to include a target feature, a positive set of texts and a negative set of texts. Ontology Builder composes rules to infer this target feature, based on the hypotheses of logical induction: common features D shared by the positive set imply this target feature, and common feature shared by the negative set must be excluded from D. The value of an ontology that includes clauses in addition to just relations between entities is that it can perform deductive as well as inductive reasoning (Galitsky 2006, 2019c) that is essential for Q/A.

7.2.1 Simple Reasoning Tasks and Formalisms

We provide some examples of the tasks from (Weston et al. 2015) that require deductive reasoning (Figs. 7.2 and 7.3). A detailed description of all the tasks can be found

> 'Mary grabbed the expense report.'
> 'Mary traveled to the accountant office.'
> 'Mary took the application form there.'
> Q: 'What is Mary carrying?' A: 'expense report' & 'application form'
> 'Mary left the expense report.'
> 'Daniel went back to the invoice department.'
> Q: 'What is Mary carrying?' A: 'application form'
> Narrative:
> happensAt(grab(mary, expense_r),1). happensAt(travel(mary,office),2).
> happensAt(take(mary,app_form),3). happensAt(leave(mary, expense_r),5).
> happensAt(go back(daniel, invoice_dept),6).
> Annotation:
> holdsAt(carry(mary, expense_r),4). holdsAt(carry(mary,),3). happensAt(leave(mary, expense_r),5).
> happensAt(go   back(daniel,   invoice_dept),4).   holdsAt(carry(mary,   app_form),7).   not
> holdsAt(carry(mary, expense_r),7).

Fig. 7.2   Example of a task on lists/sets and its representation in Situation Calculus

> Being a college candidate, to get accepted to the preparatory_math_tutorial1 you need to file form
> for pt1
> Once pt1 is filed it needs to pass the approval2
> To get accepted to theor_physics_module3 once pt1 is approved, you need to write an application4
> To get accepted to the preparatory_math_tutorial1
> preparatory_math_tutorial1 needs to be successfully passed to proceed to theor_physics_module3
> Knowledge of basic physics is required for theor_physics_module3
>
> Q: Once you have pt1 filed, what do you need to do to enroll in theor_physics_module3?
> A: pass the approval, write an application

Fig. 7.3   Another example concerning reasoning about actions and states. The steps from the answer
are highlighted

there. Each task is noiseless, provides a set of training and test data and a human can
potentially achieve 100% accuracy.

There is a number of tasks that may have clear reasoning behind their actions. For
example, the knowledge needed to answer the previous question "*Which report does
Mary need to submit?*" is clear and can be described formally. We now proceed to a
required formalization (Table 7.2).

The narratives in Fig. 7.2 describe that the event of *grabbing an expense_r by Mary*
has happened at time point 1, then another event named *travel* has happened at time
point 2 and so on. The first two annotations state that both the fluents specifying Mary
is carrying an *app_form* and Mary is carrying an *expense_r* holds at time point 3. The
not holdsAt annotation states that at time point 7 Mary is not carrying a *expense_r*.
Given such a set of narratives and annotations, the reasoning module employs an
Inductive Logic Programming algorithm to derive a hypothesis H, that can explain
all the annotations. Given more examples, it updates the existing H incrementally to
remain consistent with the data.

Table 7.2 The basic predicates and axioms of simple event calculus

Predicate	Meaning
happensAt(F,T)	Event E occurs at time T
initiatedAt(F,T)	At time T a period of time for which fluent F holds is Initiated
terminatedAt(F,T)	At time T a period of time for which fluent F holds is terminated
holdsAt(F,T)	Fluent F holds at time T
Axioms	

holdsAt(F, T + 1) ← initiatedAt(F, T)
holdsAt(F, T), not terminatedAt(F, T)

7.2.2 Generalization and Answer Set Programming

We first introduce generalization. It is a fundamental method in relational and inductive learning (Plotkin 1970). Given a finite number of positive examples, one seeks a description in a logical language that encompasses all examples and in this sense provides a generalization. To ensure that the description is as informative as possible, we intend to obtain a least general generalizations. It is a generalization that cannot be made more specific without losing at least one example. Note that computing least general generalizations is a form of supervised learning in which only positive, but no negative examples are given. The least general generalizations can be studied in the context of description logics, a widely known family of ontology languages that is a web ontology language OWL (Baader et al. 2017). In description logics, concepts are the building blocks of an ontology that are learned through generalization.

There is a number of applications in which building an ontology through generalization is useful, including ontology design by domain experts who are not experts in logical formalization. Other applications include supporting the improvement and restructuring of an ontology (Cohen et al. 1992), and creative discovery of novel concepts through conceptual blending (Eppe et al. 2018). Description logics are natural choices for generalization without overfitting due to their limited expressive power. We want to avoid generalization by disjunctively combining descriptions of each single example so that we can find a true generalization (Jung et al. 2020).

When the examples are given in the form of concepts extracted from text, the desired generalization is the least common subsumer, the least general concept that subsumes all examples. A natural alternative is to give examples using relational data. Traditionally, one uses only a single example, which takes the form of an individual in the data, and then asks for the most specific concept (the least general concept that this individual is an instance of (Nebel 1990).

An answer set program (ASP) is a collection of rules of the form,
$L_0 \leftarrow L_1,...,L_m, \text{not } L_{m+1},...,\text{not } L_n$ where each of the L_i's is a literal in the sense of classical logic. Intuitively, the above rule means that if $L_1,...,L_m$ are true and if $L_{m+1},...,L_n$ can be safely assumed to be false then L_0 must be true (Baral 2003).

The left-hand side of an ASP rule, L_0 is called the *head* and the right-hand side is called the *body*. The semantics of ASP is based on the stable model (answer set) semantics of logic programming (Gelfond and Lifschitz 1988). For example, *initiatedAt(carry(A,O),T) ← happensAt(take(A,O),T)*.

The above rule represents the knowledge that the fluent *carry(A,O)*, denoting *A* is carrying *O*, gets initiated at time point *T* if the event *take(A,O)* occurs at *T*. Following Prolog's convention, throughout this paper, predicates and ground terms in logical formulae start with a lower case letter, while variable terms start with a capital letter. A rule with no *head* is often referred to as a *constraint*. A rule with empty *body* is referred to as a *fact*. An answer set program P containing the above rule (Rule 1) and the axioms of Event calculus (from Table 7.2) along with the fact *happensAt(take(mary,expense_r),1)* logically entails (I =) that *mary* is *carrying a expense_r* at time point 2 i.e. *holdsAt(carry(mary,expense_r),2)*. Since it can be safely assumed that *mary* is not *carrying a expense_r* at time point 1, P I = *holdsAt(carry(mary,expense_r),1)*.

It should be noted that it is also true that *P I = holdsAt(carry(mary,expense_r),3)*, due to the axioms in Table 7.2. However, if we add the following two rules in the program P:

$$terminatedAt(carry(A, O), T) \leftarrow happensAt(drop(A, O), T).$$

$$happensAt(drop(marry, expense\_r), 2).$$

then the new program *P* will no longer entail *holdsAt(carry(mary,expense_r),3)* due the axioms of Event calculus. This is an example of non-monotonic reasoning when adding more knowledge changes one's previous beliefs and such thing is omnipresent in human reasoning. First Order Logic does not allow non-monotonic reasoning and this is one of the reasons why we have used the ASP language as the formal reasoning language.

7.2.3 Inductive Logic Programming

Inductive Logic Programming (ILP) (Muggleton 1991) is a subfield of Machine learning that is focused on learning logic programs. Given a set of positive examples E^+, negative examples E^- and some background knowledge B, an ILP algorithm finds a Hypothesis H (answer set program) such that $B \cup H$I $= E^+$ and not $(B \cup H$I $= E^-)$.

The possible hypothesis space is often restricted with a language bias that is specified by a series of mode declarations M (Muggleton 1995). A *head(s)* declaration denotes a literal *s* that can appear as the head of a rule. A *body(s)* declaration denotes a literal *s* that can appear in the body of a rule. The argument *s* is called *schema* and comprises of two parts:

(1) An identifier for the literal
(2) A signature of a literal (a list of *placemakers* for each argument). A *placemaker* is either *+type* (input), *-type* (output) or *#type* (constant), where *type* denotes the type of the argument. An answer set rule is in the hypothesis space defined by L (call it $L(M)$) iff its head (resp. each of its body literals) is constructed from the schema s in a *head(s)* (resp. in a *body(s)*) in $L(M)$) as follows:

By replacing an output $(-)$ placemaker by a new variable.

By replacing an input $(+)$ placemaker by a variable that appears in the head or in a previous body literal.

By replacing a ground (#) placemaker by a ground term.

$head(initiatedAt(carrying(+arg_1, +arg_3), +time))$
$head(terminatedAt(carrying(+arg_1, +arg_3), +time))$
$body(happensAt(grab(+arg_1, +arg_2), +time))$
$body(happensAt(take(+arg_1, +arg_3), +time))$
$body(happensAt(go\_back(+arg_1, +arg_2), +time))$ $body(happensAt(leave(+arg_1, +arg_3), +time))$

The Rule 1 of the previous section is in this $L(M)$ and so is the fact, $initiated(carrying(A, O), T)$.

However the following rule is not in $L(M)$): $initiated(carrying(A, O), T) \leftarrow happensAt(take(A, O), T^0)$.

The set E^- is required to restrain H from being over-generalized. Informally, given a ILP task, an ILP algorithm finds a hypothesis H that is general enough to cover all the examples in E^+ and also specific enough so that it does not cover any example in E^-. Without E^-, the learned H will contain only facts. In this case study, negative examples are automatically generated from the positive examples by assuming the answers are complete, i.e. if a Q/A pair says that at a certain time point *mary* is carrying an *expense_r* we assume that *mary* is not carrying anything else at that timestamp.

7.2.4 Learning Answer Set Programs for QA

In this section, we illustrate the formulation of an ILP task for a Q/A task and the way the answer set programs are learned. We explain our approach with the XHAIL (Ray 2009) algorithm and specify why ILED (Katzouris et al. 2015) algorithm is needed.

Given an ILP task $ILP(B,E) = \{E^+ \cup E^-\}, M)$, XHAIL derives the hypothesis in a three-step process. In our example, B contains both the axioms of Event Calculus and the narratives from Table 7.2. The set E comprises of the annotations from Table 7.2 which contains three positive and one negative examples. M is the set of mode declarations above.

Step 1. In the first step the XHAIL algorithm finds a set of ground (variable free) atoms $\Delta = \cup_{i=1}^{n} \alpha_i$ such that $B \cup \Delta \models E$ where each α_i is a ground instance of the *head(s)* declaration atoms. For our example ILP problem there are two *head* declarations. Thus the set Δ can contain ground instances of only those two atoms described in two *head* declarations. In the following, we demonstrate one possible Δ that meets these requirements for the ILP task for our example:

$$\Delta = \{initiatedAt(carry(mary, expense\_r)), 1),$$
$$initiatedAt(carry(mary, app\_form)), 3),$$
$$terminatedAt(carry(mary, expense\_r)), 5)\}.$$

Step 2. In the second step, XHAIL computes a clause $\alpha_i \leftarrow \delta_i^{1.} \ldots \delta_i^{mi}$ for each α_i in Δ, where $B \cup \Delta| = \delta_i^j, 1 \leq i \leq n, 1 \leq j \leq m_i$, $B \cup \Delta| = \delta_i^j, 1 \leq i \leq n,$ $1 \leq j \leq m_i$, and each clause $\alpha_i \leftarrow \delta_i^{1.} \ldots \delta_i^{mi}$ is a ground instance of a rule in $L(M)$. In the running example, Δ contains three atoms that each must lead to a clause k_i, $i = 1,2,3$. The first atom $\alpha_1 = initiatedAt(carry(mary, expense\_r),1)$ is initialized to the head of the clause k_1. The body of k_1 is saturated by adding all possible ground instances of the literals in *body(s)* declarations that satisfy the constraints mentioned above. There are six ground instances (all the narratives) of the literals in the *body(s)* declarations; however only one of them, i.e. *happensAt(grab(mary, expense_r),1)* can be added to the body due to restrictions enforced by $L(M)$. In the following, we enumerate the set of all the ground clauses K constructed in this step and their variabilized (uninstantiated) version K_v that is obtained by replacing all input and output terms by variables.

K:

initiatedAt(carry(mary, expense_r),1 ← happensAt(grab(mary, expense_r), 1).
initiatedAt(carry(mary, app_form), 3) ← happensAt(take(mary, app_form), 3).
terminatedAt(carry(mary, expense_r), 6) ← happensAt(leave(mary, app_form), 6).

K_v:

initiatedAt(carry(X, Y), T) ← happensAt(grab(X, Y), T).
initiatedAt(carry(X, Y), T) ← happensAt(take(X, Y), T).
terminatedAt(carry(X, Y), T) ← happensAt(leave(X, Y), T).

Step 3 In this step, XHAIL tries to find a "compressed" theory H by deleting from K_v as many literals (and clauses) as possible while ensuring that $B \cup H| = E$. In the running example, working out this problem will lead to $H = K_v$.

We now comment on the scalability of the learning algorithm. The discovery of a hypothesis H depends on the choice of Δ. Since the value of Δ that satisfies the constraints described in Step 1 is not unique, we employ an iterative deepening strategy (Meissner and Brzykcy 2011) to select Δ of progressively increasing size until a solution is found. Furthermore, in Step 2 of XHAIL, we restricted the algorithm to consider only those ground instances of *body* declarations that are not from the future time points. This method works when the size of the example is small. However, when a dataset contains thousands examples each comprising a set of narrative and annotations, versions of Δ grow extremely fast. It is handled by learning rules from each example and then using the learned rules to learn new rules from yet unsolved examples. A recent incremental learning algorithm, ILED (Katzouris et al. 2015) can be used to address the scalability issue. The first step of the ILED algorithm is the XHAIL algorithm. After finding an initial hypothesis H_1 by XHAIL, the ILED algorithm incrementally revises the current hypothesis H_i when subjected to a new example E_i so that the revised hypothesis H_{i+1} is consistent with the current example E_i and all the previous ones $E_0,...,E_{i-1}$. It is natural to assume that ILED can scale up to this dataset.

7.2.5 Navigating Through States

In the task of Fig. 7.4, each example first describes the relative positions of several places and then asks a question about moving from one place to another. The answer to the question is then a sequence of directions. For the question *"How do you go from the state of an school applicant to the graduation of theoretical physics course?"* the answer enumerates the actions needed to be committed.

Given such an example, an agent learns how navigating through states toward a desired state with respect to the particular transition between these states occurs. A natural language text is first translated from AMR to the syntax of ASP. However, in this task, the background knowledge B also contains the rules learned from the situational representation.

Input

Narrative

holdsAt(move(college_candidate, file(pt), ready_for_approval(pt)),1).

holdsAt(move(ready_for_approval(pt), approved(pt)&approval(pt), prep_math_tutorial1),2).

holdsAt(move(approved(pt), write(application), theor_physics_module),3).

holdsAt(move(start(prep_math_tutorial1), complete(prep_math_tutorial),
start(theor_physics_module3)),4).

holdsAt(move(knowledge_of_basic_physics, complete(theor_physics_module),5). holdsAt(stage(you,
college_candidate),6).

happensAt(agent_in_state(you, file(pt)),6).

happensAt(agent_in_state(you, approved(pt)),7).

Annotation

not holdsAt(stage(you, complete(theor_physics_module3),6).

holdsAt(stage(you, college_candidate),8).

not holdsAt(stage(you, prep_math_tutorial),8).

Mode declarations

head(initiatedAt(stage(+arg₁,+arg₂),+time)) head(terminatedAt(stage(+arg₁,+arg₂),+time))

body(happensAt(agent_in_state (+arg₁,+ arg₂),+time))

body(holdsAt(stage(+arg₁,+arg₂),+time))

body(holdsAt(move(+arg_state₁, +action, +arg_state₂),+time))

Background Knowledge: axioms of Event Calculus

Output: learned clauses

initiatedAt(stage(X, Y), T) ← happensAt(stage(X, D), T), holdsAt(move(Y, Z, D), T), holdsAt(stage(X,
Z), T).

terminatedAt(agent_in_state(X, Y), T) ← happensAt(stage(X, D), T).

Fig. 7.4 Hypothesis generation for path finding

Figure 7.4 shows the corresponding ILP task for the example of pathfinding and the hypothesis generated by the XHAIL algorithm. This example illustrates how the task of path finding can be easily learned when a formal representation is used. Notice that while the state-of-the-art neural network-based systems (Weston et al. 2015) have achieved only 36% accuracy on this task with an average of 93% on all tasks, the system of (Mitra and Baral 2016) and was able to achieve 100% with the two compact rules shown in Fig. 7.4.

7.2.6   Implementation of Ontology Builder

The architecture of Ontology Builder is shown in Fig. 7.5. Ontology Builder takes tagged texts and attempts to generalize from them to build clauses, which will be a basis of inductive and deductive reasoning (Galitsky et al. 2005) in the course of a Q/A session.

On the left, there is an Abstract Meaning Representation Parser (AMR) pipeline (Banarescu et al. 2013; Flanigan et al. 2014).

The Formal Reasoning Layer (in the middle and on the right) uses the Answer Set Programming (ASP, Gelfond and Lifschitz 1988) language as the knowledge representation and reasoning language. The knowledge required for reasoning is learned with a modified version of the Inductive Logic Programming algorithm XHAIL (Ray 2009). The reasoning module takes sentences represented in the logical language of Event Calculus that is a temporal logic for reasoning about the events (Galitsky and Botros 2012) and their efforts. The ontology of the Event Calculus comprises of *time points, fluent* (i.e., properties which have certain values in time) and *event* (i.e.,

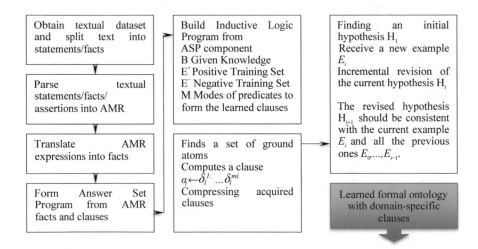

Fig. 7.5 The architecture of clause acquisition component by means of formal reasoning about AMR representations obtained from text

occurrences in time that may affect fluents and alter their value). The formalism also contains two domain-independent axioms to incorporate the commonsense *law of inertia*, according to which fluents persist over time unless they are affected by an event. The building blocks of Event Calculus and its domain-independent axioms were presented in Table 7.2.

7.2.7 Error Analysis in Ontology Building Component

Let us consider an example where the acquired rule does not work 100%.

> Lily is a frog. Lily is grey.
> Julius is a swan. Julius is green.
> Greg is a swan.
> Q: What color is Greg? green

The learning algorithm could not find a hypothesis that can assign proper labels to the entire training data with the given set of available predicated. Since it is impossible to form a hypothesis that explains all the data, we chose the one that partially explains the data. It is implemented by ignoring the examples in the training data which let to a failure. The resulted hypothesis is as follows:

$holdsAt(color(X,C),T) \leftarrow holdsAt(domain(Z,D),T), holdsAt(color(Z,C),T), holdsAt(domain(X,D),T).$

This rule states that X has color C at time T if there exists a Z that is of type D and has color C at time point T, where X is also of type D. This rule covers more than 96% of test set cases. However, it does not cover the examples of the following kind where there are two different entity of type D having two different colors (Table 7.3).

For the error sample A, the acquired clause will produce two answers stating that *Bernhard* has the color *grey* and *yellow*. Since, the most *frogs* are *grey*, one may

Table 7.3 Failure cases for induction

Error sample A	Error sample B
Lily is a frog.	Lily is a rhino.
Brian is a frog.	Lily is yellow.
Greg is frog.	Bernhard is a frog.
Lily is yellow.	Bernhard is white.
Julius is a frog.	Brian is a rhino.
Brian is grey.	Greg is a rhino.
Julius is grey.	Greg is yellow.
Greg is grey.	Julius is a rhino.
Bernhard is a frog.	Julius is green.
Q: *What color is Bernhard?* **A**:*grey*	**Q**: What color is Brian? A:green

assume that the correct clause should produce the color that has appeared maximum number of times for that type (here, *frog*). However, error case B contradicts this hypothesis. There are two *yellow rhino* and one *grey rhino* and the color of *Brian* which is a rhino is *grey*. The actual derived clause is the one that determines the color on the basis of the latest evidence.

7.3 Answering Compound Multi-hop Questions Through Iterative Query Decomposition

Although modern search engines can provide exact and thorough answers for simple factoid questions, they experience difficulties in processing multiple attributes or parameters constraining the answer. It is hard for current one-step retrieve-and-read Q/A systems to answer questions like *"Which novel written in 1990 was adapted as a feature film by Steven Spielberg?"* because questions like that usually do not include explicit clues about the missing entity (here, the novel author name). Answering such a question requires multi-step iterative reasoning where it is necessary to manage information about the missing entities and facts at each iteration to proceed with further reasoning.

Given a complex questions q, we decompose the question to a sequence of simple questions q_1, q_2, . . ., using a search engine and a Q/A model to answer the simple questions, from which we compute the final answer A. Notice that the third simple question relies on a clause that can be learned from textual description of a financial product (Fig. 7.6).

We now show how question decomposition may occur on the basis of semantic representation such as AMR (Fig. 7.7, Chap. 3).

Three red circles show three simple queries the main question needs to be decomposed into. The main entity of this question is *product*; its node is shown in pink.

---

q : *'What is Annual Yield of the financial product that is available for CA residents, has 401K-type tax restrictions and require direct deposit from your employer?'*
Decompose:
q_1 : 'financial product available for CA residents?' $\Rightarrow$ {Annuity1, Annuity3_MoneyMarket}
q_2 : 'financial product 401K-type tax restrictions?' $\Rightarrow$ {Annuity1, Annuity2CD, Annuity3_MoneyMarket}
q_3 : 'financial product require direct deposit from your employer' $\Rightarrow$ {
//need associated checking
associated(Annuity2CD, Checking2), associated(Annuity1, Checking1), ...
deposit(employer, Checking2)
product(Account) :- deposit(Employer, AccountAssoc), associated(AccountAssoc, Account),
saving(Account). }
Recompose: ({ *Annuity1, Annuity3_MoneyMarket* } $\cap$ { *Annuity1, Annuity2CD,*
Annuity3_MoneyMarket } $\cap$ { *Annuity1*}={ *Annuity1* }
A: 'Annual Yield of [Recompose $(q_1 \cap q_2 \cap q_3)$] = 1.4%

Fig. 7.6 Question decomposition chart

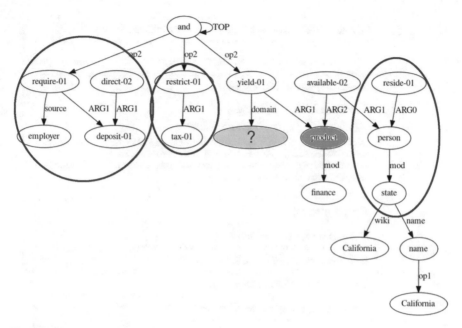

Fig. 7.7 Abstract meaning representation for the complex question

The attribute of product in question is shown in yellow with the question mark. One can observe that an AMR graph can help with question decomposition here.

Modern state-of-the-art web search engines can provide an exact answer for an attribute of an entity. For example, Google gives an exact answer as a list of composers for the question *"music composer of movie titanic 1997"*. In addition to this exact answer, Google provides a path in its knowledge graph, from the entity to its attribute *"Titanic/Music by/Movies/Music composed by"*. The list of composers starts from *James Horner*. If we then formulate a question *"how many children does musician James Horner have"*, the search engine provides an exact answer "2". However, if we combine these two steps and formulate the same question in one shot, we will not get this exact answer. Once there are two entities *composer* and *children,* Google switches from a factoid answer to a general web search (Fig. 7.8).

We now proceed to the second example. For the second example, we get Google search result and subject it to MRC:

Q: Which team explored the deepest cave in the world.

Google search result finds the result with "deepest cave in the world" and gives a number of entity parameters, but does not extract the value for "the team" (The top of Fig. 7.9). Then MRC system (on the bottom) finds out that "team" corresponds to "association" and provides a complete, exact answer. MRC system did it by word2vec similarity between "team" and "association", iterating through phrases of the type <noun-phrase> -verb.

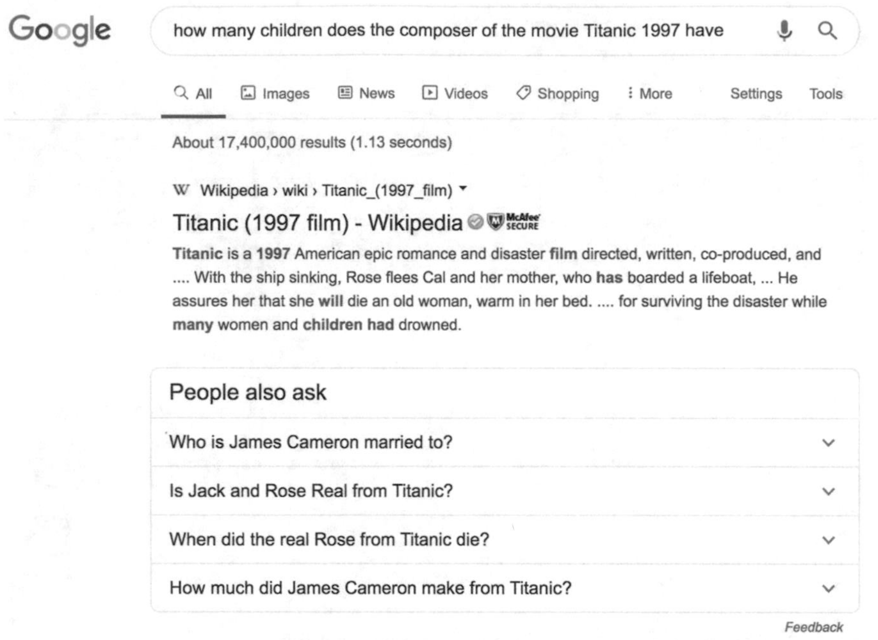

Google | how many children does the composer of the movie Titanic 1997 have   🎤 🔍 |

Q All   🖾 Images   📰 News   ▶ Videos   🛇 Shopping   ⋮ More   Settings   Tools

About 17,400,000 results (1.13 seconds)

W Wikipedia › wiki › Titanic_(1997_film) ▾
Titanic (1997 film) - Wikipedia ⊘ 🛡️ McAfee SECURE

Titanic is a **1997** American epic romance and disaster **film** directed, written, co-produced, and
.... With the ship sinking, Rose flees Cal and her mother, who **has** boarded a lifeboat, ... He
assures her that she **will** die an old woman, warm in her bed. .... for surviving the disaster while
many women and **children had** drowned.

People also ask

Who is James Cameron married to?   ⌄

Is Jack and Rose Real from Titanic?   ⌄

When did the real Rose from Titanic die?   ⌄

How much did James Cameron make from Titanic?   ⌄

Feedback

Fig. 7.8 Google search result for a multi-hop question where an exact answer is absent

7.3.1 Implementation of Decomposition

The following scenarios are applied at multi-hop queries:

In Table 7.3, we enumerate Types of multi-hop reasoning required to answer questions in the HotpotQA set. We show the bridge entities in red and in green the answer in the paragraph or following the question.

Building a discourse tree (DT) of a query is a good source of splitting the query into simple ones according to EDUs. A DT can be mapped into a query execution tree (Fig. 7.10).

We assign each rhetorical relation a representation hop subquery. Some of them are void. This DT does not always specify an order the sub-queries run but provides a good means to split into sub-queries.

Formally, question decomposition is represented in meta-functions (or metapredicates). This is relative to language-object predicates which represent the queries themselves. Here are the cases for question decomposition:

- *simpleQA(·)* meta-function is used for answering simple questions. It takes a string argument and yields a set of strings or numbers as answer.
- *comparison(·, ·)* meta-function takes a string containing one unique variable VAR, and a set of answers. The metapredicate replaces the variable with each answer string representation and yields their union. Formally, *comparison* $(q, A) = \cup_a$

Fig. 7.9 Combining Google search with MRC system takes the user to exact answer span

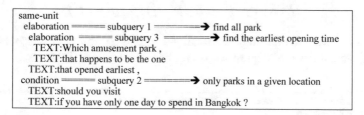

Fig. 7.10 A discourse tree showing how a question can be decomposed into sub-queries

simpleQA(q_a), where *q_a* is the string produced when replacing VAR in *q* with *a*.

- *conjunction(·, ·)* meta-function takes two sets and produces their intersection. Other set operations can be defined analogously. *conjunction* (·) can also take strings as input, which means that *simpleQA(·)* is initiated to obtain a set and then perform intersection.

- *add(·, ·)* meta-function takes two singleton sets of numbers and returns a set with their addition. Similar functions can be defined analogously.

Superlative and comparative questions like *"What is the deepest lake in Asia?"* or *"Which South American mountains are higher than Elbrus?"* are answered by joining the set of mountains located in X with their elevation. Answering such questions from the web is cumbersome: we would have to extract a list of entities and a numerical value for each. Instead, one can rely on *simpleQA* metapredicate.

In many cases, simple syntactic cues are insufficient to determine how to decompose the question into simpler queries. Figure 7.11 gives an example, where the question is answered by decomposing its main relation *"leveraged for"* (in f_C) into a similar relation "used for" (in f_L) and a newly introduced relation *generates* (in f_S), and then composing these back to infer f_C. While this question can be answered by composing the two facts f_S and f_L, that this is the case is unclear based solely on the question. This property of relation decomposition not being evident from reading the question pushes reasoning models toward focusing on learning to compose new pieces of knowledge, a key challenge in language understanding. Further, f_L has no overlap with the question, making it difficult to retrieve it in the first place.

Training data includes the associated facts f_S and f_L, as well as their composition f_C. The term *current* connects f_S and f_L, but appears neither in f_C nor in the question. Further, decomposing the question relation "leveraged by" into f_S and f_L requires introducing the new relation *"produces"* in f_S. The question can be answered by using broad knowledge to compose these facts together and infer f_C.

A key challenge in multi-hop Q/A is that syntactic cues in the question are insufficient to determine how one should decompose the question relation, r_Q, into two sub-relations, r_S and r_L, corresponding to the associated facts f_S and f_L. At an abstract level, 2-hop questions in is in the following form:

$$Q : R_S^?(x_q,\ y^?) \wedge R_L^?\left(y^?, z_a^?\right) \Rightarrow r_Q\left(x_q,\ z_a^?\right)$$

$y^?$—unknowns: the decomposed relations R_S and R_L and the bridge concept y. Also, $z_a^?$, an answer to the question, is an obvious unknown. To check if R_Q holds

---

Question: How a source of water at an altitude can be leveraged?
(A) electricity generation
(B) transportation of goods
(C) water-needed production plant
(D) transfer of electrons . . .
Annotated facts:
f_s: *A source of water at an altitude produces current* .
f_l: *Current can be used to generate electricity* .
Composed fact f_c : *A source of water at an altitude can be leveraged for electricity generation* .

Fig. 7.11 A multiple-choice question

Q: *How are caves formed by penetrating into the rock and dissolving karst?*
As: (A) *carbon dioxide in snow water*
(B) *oxygen in water*
(C) *pure oxygen*
(D) *salt in water*
f_s: *A cave is formed by carbonic acid in groundwater seeping through rock and dissolving karst*
f_L: *When carbon dioxide is in water, it creates carbonic acid*
$f_s + f_L => R_Q =$ *carbonic acid dissolves karst*

Fig. 7.12 Solving multiple choice questions

between some concept x_q in the question and some concept z_a in an answer candidate, we need to find the missing or implicit relations and also the bridge concept. In our example, $R_Q =$ "*leveraged for*", $x_q =$ "*source of water at an altitude*", $y =$ "*current*", $R_S =$ "*produces*", and $R_L =$ "*used for*".

In contrast, less difficult multi-hop questions in many existing datasets which are syntactically decomposable often explicitly contain both R_S and R_L: $Q = R_S$ $(x_q, y^?) \wedge R_L (y^?, z_a^?)$. The example "*Which government position was held by the CEO of X?*", could be stated in this notation as: $ceo(X, y^?) \wedge held\text{-}gov\text{-}pos(y^?, z_a^?)$. This difference in how a multi-hop question is presented makes it challenging to both retrieve relevant facts and reason with them via knowledge composition. This difficulty is further extended by the property that a single relation r_Q can often be decomposed in multiple ways into R_S and R_L.

IR system (Clark et al. 2016) is designed for science Q/A with its associated corpora of web and science text. It retrieves sentences for each question and answer choice from the associated corpora, and returns the answer choice with the highest scoring sentence (based on the retrieval score). Standard IR approaches for Q/A retrieve facts using *question + answer* as their query, which can be effective for lookup questions, but would miss important facts needed for multi-hop questions (Fig. 7.12). Neural retrieval methods that use distributional representations attempt to attack the brittleness of word overlap measures.

7.4 Learning Associating Clauses for Phrases in Q and A

One of the major bottlenecks for finding relevant answers in MRC is associating phrases in context. For example, can an answer with the phrase "*pay for a tuition*" be relevant for a question with a phrase "*draw a check*". How to establish similarity between these phrases online in the context of a Q and an A? This is usually considered a reasoning problem: this is not about a similarity between two phrases but rather concerning if one can imply another (Galitsky 2002).

To learn if such the implication exists, one can try to check if *a* the first phrase can be implied by the second phrase in a document that would contain a cue that there is an implication between these phrases. One way to find such a document for an arbitrary pair of phrases is to rely on web mining.

Failing to do this association dramatically drops the search recall, reducing a successful search to the cases where a phrase in Q is syntactically similar to a phrase in A. When major search engines learn from user choice of correct answers, they can solve this phrase association problem directly, without tackling the meanings of these phrases. However, in the majority of Q/A setting such as a chatbots, user search data is not available.

A DL approach to MRC where the association between phrases is established based on word2vec similarity has a limited value since it is based on a similarity score and assists with a selection of a correct answer only among a very small number of candidates. Instead, a robust search needs a systematic way to accept/reject an implication between two phrases, so that a proper association between a Q and an A can be made.

To establish a logical association between two phrases such as *"explore a cave"* and *"go down a pit"*, we form a conjunction query of these exact phrases (in double quotes) and analyze search results (Fig. 7.13).

Multiple search requests need to be issued varying articles and prepositions. Once we identify the text that includes both of these phrases, we need to establish an implication. To do that, one needs to perform a discourse analysis and identify a rhetorical relation between the text fragments containing these phrases. This rhetorical relation should express the logical continuity between these text fragments. This is a necessary condition for these phrases to be associated with implication.

The pair of sentences below naturally follow one another, and the verb phrases of interest are the only verb phrases, so we can observe that the former phrase can naturally follow the latter phrase. In the discourse tree for this text, there is a default relation of Elaboration, or Joint, or temporal sequence between the text fragments (here, sentences). Hence if one of them occurs in a question, it is natural to assume that its meaning is associated with the meaning of the second phrase in an answer.

*"The next day, I joined up with John Doe and others to **explore a cave** at the resurgence just upstream from camp. No one would **go down the pit** before the rescue system was ready".*

Another example of phrases is *"many children"* vs *"one son and one daughter"* from the question *"How many children does a father have"* from text *"… father of*

Fig. 7.13 Mining for association between two phrases

> "many children" "one son and one daughter"   🎤 🔍
>
> 🔍 All   🖼 Images   ▶ Videos   🗐 News   🗺 Maps   ⋮ More   Settings   Tools
>
> ---
>
> **[PDF] The House (A1) - Text in English - Lingua.com**
> https://lingua.com › pdf › english-text-house ▾
> Mr. and Mrs. Smith have **one son and one daughter**. The son's name is John. ... Did you
> understand the text? 1) How **many children** do Mr. and Mrs. Smith have?

Fig. 7.14 Association mining for a commonsense fact

one son and one daughter …". Figure 7.14 shows how a clause for a commonsense phrase association can be confirmed.

What do we do here in comparison with distributional semantics models? We take a single sample instead of thousands of co-occurrences. The disadvantage of doing this is a sensitivity to a noisy example that does not fit with common sense. However, this is very rare in web search results. The strong point of learning from individual examples is that we can acquire an exact meaning of a phrase and make an exact decision about how this phrase is associated with another phrase.

Even if the context of text where phrases are associated does not coincide with the content of an answer, such association is expected to be applicable since it is *meaningful*. On the contrary, a fuzzy association learned from the averaged occurrences of words can be *meaningless*. If we compute an averaged meaning of *go down the pit*, averaging through multiple, incompatible meanings of *go* and *pit* (*a large hole in the ground, or a hollow or indentation in a surface*), this averaged meaning as an action related to an object would be meaningless.

Therefore, we do not want to combine the meaning of averaged *go* with the meaning of averaged *pit*, as distributional semantic analysis does. Instead, one wants to consider a manifold of meanings of *go* only with compatible meanings of *pit*, as far as a set of available samples allows.

We now proceed to an example of questions (Fig. 7.15) the MRC community refuses to tackle (Qi et al. 2019; Min et al. 2019).

We need to compute similarity between the Q and the first question in the A. To do that, we need to assess weather *"English Victorian"* and *"Charles Dickens"* are at least closely related, and at most one (the person) is the instance of the other. Searching the web for *"Charles Dickens"* is *"English Victorian"* we obtain a confirmation of the latter case (Fig. 7.15).

To conclude this subsection, we comment on a difference between web mining and distributional semantics training approaches. The former is implemented in the on-demand mode, where an association between phrases is done searching billions of documents on the web or a corpus of a domain-specific documents in an intranet or a cloud. The latter is based on advance training on a significantly smaller fixed dataset and only the statistics of individual words co-occurrences is extracted and stored.

Q: *The papers of which famous English Victorian author are collected in the library?*

A: *Writers whose papers are in the library are as diverse as Charles Dickens and Beatrix Potter. Illuminated manuscripts in the library dating from the 12th to 16th centuries include: the Eadwine Psalter, Canterbury; Pocket Book of Hours, Reims; Missal from the Royal Abbey of Saint Denis, Paris; the Simon Marmion Book of Hours, Bruges; 1524 Charter illuminated by Lucas Horenbout, London; the Armagnac manuscript of the trial and rehabilitation of Joan of Arc, Rouen. Also, the Victorian period is represented by William Morris.*

Charles Dickens and his work depicting the Industrial Revolution

westerncivguides.umwblogs.org › 2012/04/28 › charles-dickens-and-his-w... ⊘ ▾

Apr 28, 2012 - **Charles Dickens** was an **English Victorian** era author who wrote about the hard
labor and living situations during the Industrial Revolution.

Fig. 7.15 The Q/A pair which is a bottleneck for MRC systems (on the top). A web search result that associates "Charles Dickens" and "*English Victorian*" (on the bottom)

In most cases, it is a one-serves-all domain dataset such as Wikipedia. Hence the accuracy of the former is expected to significantly exceed that of the latter (Chap. 2).

7.4.1   Implementation of Phrase Association

Web mining-based phrase association method requires multiple search engine API calls for each Q/A pair to verify relevance. Hence this method is applicable when the keyword-based and linguistic-based components have been produced as a shortlist of plausible Q/A pairs and the web mining needs to select a final answer.

Given a Q and a candidate A, we need to select a single phrase in Q and a single phrase in A to verify an association between them (Fig. 7.16). Both phrases can be named entities, where we attempt to associate them as a different way of referring to the same entity. If one is a named entity and another is not, we mine for *is-a*, *instance-of* and other kinds of entity type/name-instance association. If neither phrase is a named entity, then an association can have a fuzzy shape and relate an action to a state, a cause to a conclusion and so forth.

7.5   Designing NL2SQL Based on Recursive Clause Building and Acquired Clauses

We will briefly describe the special case of Q/A where queries need to be translated from NL to SQL to be run against a database.

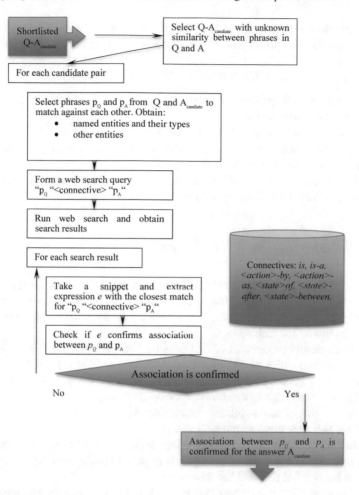

Fig. 7.16 Architecture of the phrase association system

7.5.1 *Selecting Deterministic Approach*

An extensive corpus of work in NL2SQL showed that it is rather difficult to convert all user queries into SQL mostly due to ambiguity of database field names and a complex structure of real-world databases, in addition to a query understanding difficulty. Also, it is hard for NL2SQL problem to communicate with the user which NL queries are acceptable and which are not. Even if 80% of user NL queries are properly translated to SQL, which is hard to achieve, the usability is questionable.

To address this problem, we proposed to implement NL2SQL as a chatbot (Galitsky 2019d), so that the system can clarify every encountered ambiguity with the user right away. If a confidence score for a given NL2SQL component is low, the chatbot asks the user to confirm/clarify whether the interpretation of a query focus or a given clause is correct. For example, interpreting a phrase *movie actor name,* the chatbot requests user clarification if *name* refers to the actor's last name, first name or film title.

The main highlights of the selected approach are as follows:

(1) We extract a linguistic representation for a SQL clause in the form of *table.column* assignment;
(2) We build the sequence of SQL clauses in an iterative way;
(3) We rely on an ontology and other cues to build a mapping from NL representation for a clause into table and column names;
(4) We resolve all kinds of ambiguities in NL query interpretation as a clarification request via chatbot (Chap. 1 Volume 2).

7.5.2   Interpreting Table.Field Clause

The input of *Table.Field* clause recognizer is a phrase that includes a reference to a table and/or its field. Each word may refer to a field of one table and a name of another table, only to a field, or only to a table, hence the query understanding problem is associated with rather high ambiguity.

The fundamental problem in NL2SQL is that interpreting NL is hard in general and understanding which words refer to which database field is ambiguous in nature (Galitsky 2003). People may use slang words, technical terms, and dialect-specific phrasing, none of which may be known to the NL2SQL system. Regretfully, even with appropriate choice of words, NL is inherently ambiguous. Even in human-to-human interaction, there are miscommunications.

One of the difficulties is substituting values for attributes of similar semantic types, such as *first* and *last name.* For example, it is hard to build the following mapping unless we know what first and last names are.

There is a need for transformations beyond mapping *phrase2table.field*, such as a lookup of English first names and knowledge that first and last name can be in a single field, can be in various formats and orders, or belong to distinct fields, like in the case of Sakila database (Oracle 2018).

When a user is saying "*film name*" the system can interpret it as a table with field = "*name*" when *film.name* does not exist. Although "name" is a synonym of "title", the phrase "name" can be mapped into totally foreign table such as category.name instead of *actor.first_name.* If a phrase includes "*word1 word2*" it is usually ambiguous since *word2* can be *Table1.field* and also *Table2.word2* can be a field (or a part of a field, as a single word) in another table. Hence we need a hypothesis management system that proceeds from most likely to least likely cases, but is deterministic so that the rule system can be extended.

We start with the rule that identifies a single table name and makes sure there are no other table names mentioned (Fig. 7.17). Also, we need to confirm that no field name is mentioned in the string to be mapped into a table name. Once the table is

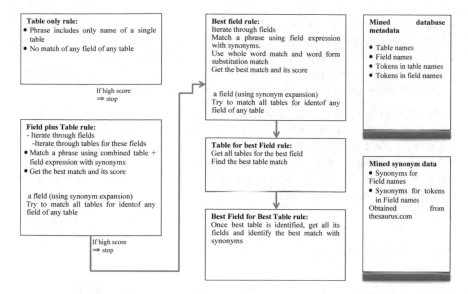

Fig. 7.17 *Phrase2Table.Field* Unit

confirmed, we select its default field such as 'title' or any other field with the name of entity represented by this table.

If a pure table rule is not applicable, we proceed to the *table + its field* rule. The system identifies a table and its field together. We iterate through all table-field words and select the table-field combination when the highest number of words are matched against the phrase. If we do not find a good match for a table-filed set of keywords against the phrase, we proceed to matching a field only (the third step). At this step, we use ontology to expand a list of keywords for a field with synonyms. Once we find a match for a field, we get a list of table this field can possibly belong to.

In the second step, we try to find words in the phrase correlated with this table name. In this step, for each of these tables, we in turn obtain a list of their fields and verify that the original field from the step one of this unit is identified, not another one. If the second step fails we stop on the first one, and if the verification of the third step fails, we stop on the second step. The higher is the number of steps, the higher is the confidence level.

7.5.3 Collecting Information on a Database and Ontology for NL2SQL

The NL2SQL system is designed to automatically adjust to an arbitrary database where table and column names are meaningful and interpretable (Galitsky 2020). The following data structures are used by *Phrase2Table.Field* and other algorithms

- Set *fieldsForMatching*: A set of fields;
- Map *tablesFieldsForMatching* gives a list of fields for a table;
- Map *fieldsTableListsForMatching* gives a list of tables for a field;
- Map *fieldsTablesForMatching* gives a selected table for a field. For some fields such as entity name, there is just a single table for this entity.

Since terms in a user query can deviate from field names in a database, it is necessary to mine for synonyms offline from sources like thesaurus.com or use trained synonym models such as word2vec (Mikolov et al. 2013). Lists of synonyms or similarity function are then used in *phrase2table.field* component of Query understanding pipeline. The arrow in the right-middle shows communication with the *Phrase2Table.Field* Unit of Fig. 7.18.

7.5.4   Iterative Clause Formation

Once a focus clause is identified, we consider the remainder of the NL query as a *Where* clause (Fig. 7.19; Galitsky et al. 2013). It is hard to determine boundaries of clauses; instead, we try to identify the assignment/comparison word (anchor) such as *is, equals, more, before, as,* which indicates the "center anchor" of a phrase to be converted into SQL clause. Once we find the leftmost anchor, we attempt to build the left side (attribute) and the right side (value).

To find the boundary of an attribute, we iterate toward the beginning the NL query to the start of the current phrase. It is usually indicated by the prepositions *with* or *of*, connective *and*, or a Wh-word. The value part is noun and/or a number, possibly with an adjective. The same words mark the end of value part as the beginning of next attribute part.

Once the clause is built, we subject the remaining part of the NL query to the same clause identification algorithm, which starts with finding the anchor. If a structure of phrase follows Fig. 7.20, it is processed by the middle-left component *Clause builder from phrase* in Fig. 7.18 chart. Otherwise, there is no anchor word and it is hard to establish where the phrases for attribute and values are, we apply *the Clause builder by matching the phrase with indexed row* approach.

7.5.5   Clause Building by Matching the Phrase with Indexed Row

We also refer to this alternative approach to building SQL query clauses as NL2SQL via *search engineering*: it involves building a special index (not to confuse with database own index) and executing a search of a part of user NL query against it. At indexing time, we index each row of each table in the following format (top-right of Fig. 7.18):

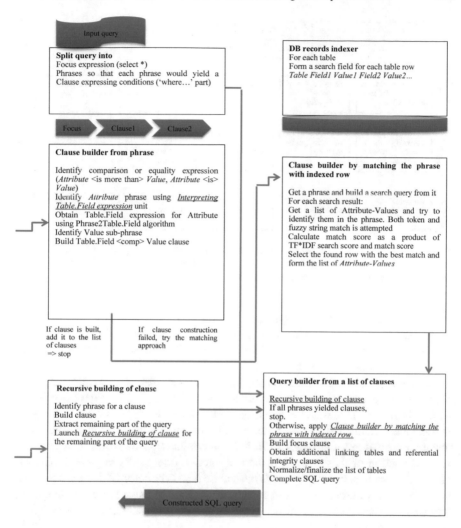

Fig. 7.18   A high-level view of NL2SQL system. Integration of *Phrase2Table.Field* and *Recursive building of clause* units is shown by step-arrows on the left

Beginning of a clause (*where, and, with*)	Attribute (to be converted into *table.field*)	Anchor (*is, equals, more, less, as*)	Value (to be converted into *table.field >= **)	end of a clause (beginning of the next one)

Fig. 7.19   A structure of a clause to be converted into *table.field [=/</ >/like] value*

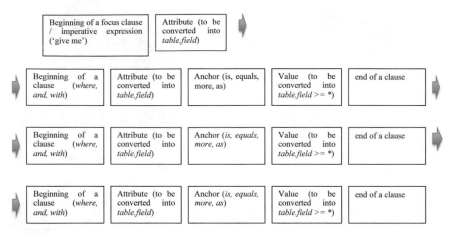

Fig. 7.20 User query as a sequence of clauses: some of them follow the template on the top and are processed by *Clause builder from phrase*, and some of them do not and are handled by *Clause builder by matching the phrase with indexed row*

Table field1 value1 field2 value2 ...

Associative tables and other ones which do not contain data for entities such as customer of address are not indexed for matching. The index includes the fields for search and for storing the values.

Once an NL query is obtained and *Clause builder from phrase* failed to build a clause from a phrase expected to contain a *Where* clause, a search expression is built from this phrase. This search expression includes the words which are expected to match tables, fields and values. Since we do not know what is what before search results are obtained, the query is formed as conjunction of words first and then as a disjunction of these words, if the conjunction query fails to give results. In a disjunction queries, not all keywords have to be matched: some of them are just used by the NL query author but do not exist in table data. To make search more precise, we also form span-AND queries from entities identified in the phrase to be converted, such as "*Bank of America*".

Once search results are obtained, we iterate through them to find the most likely record. Although the default TF*IDF relevance is usually right, we compute our own score based on the number of attribute-value pairs which occur in both the query and a candidate search result. Our own score also takes into account individual values without attribute occurrence in both the query and the record. String-level similarity and multiword deviations between occurrences in the query and the record are also taken into account (whether some words in a multiword are missing or occur in a different form, such as plural for a noun or a tense for a verb).

Depending on the type of string for the value (numeric or string), we chose the operation "=" or "like" when the *table.field* <*assignment*> *value* clause is built. Obviously, when this clause building method is employed, we do not need to call the *phrase2Table.Field* component.

We refer to text which is converted into "select *" statement as *focus clause*. We start with *Wh* word and then extract the phrase that follows it. This phrase must be the shortest one among those, which follow the *Wh* word. Noun, verb, prepositional, and other kinds of phrases are acceptable. From this phrase, a clause will be built applying *phrase2table.field* component. This clause will not have an assignment but will possibly have a grouping term instead, such as *"give me the maximum temperature of water … "*

7.5.6 A Sample Database Enabled with NL2SQL

To build an industrial-strength NL2SQL, we select a default database Sakila (Oracle 2018) that demonstrates a variety of MySQL capabilities. It is intended to provide a standard schema that can be used for examples in tutorials and samples, and also serves to highlight the latest features of MySQL such as Views, Stored Procedures, and Triggers. The Sakila sample database was designed as a replacement to the *world* sample database, which provides a set of tables containing information on the countries and cities of the world and is useful for basic queries, but lacks structures for testing MySQL-specific functionality and new features found in MySQL 5.

Notice that for NL2SQL we selected a fairly feature-rich database with a complicated structure of relations (Fig. 7.21). The database structure is much more complex than the ones used in academic studies to evaluate NL2SQL (Galitsky 2019d).

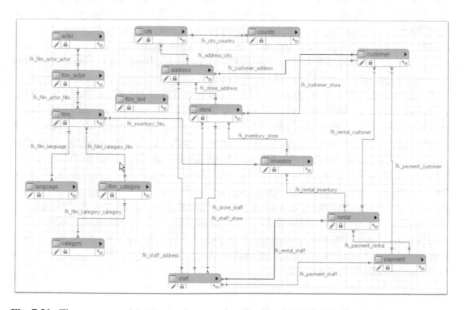

Fig. 7.21 The structure of Sakila database as visualized by MySQL Workbench

These are the examples of NL query, logs for intermediate step, resultant SQL representation and query results (Fig. 7.22).

Notice that we do not require the user to highlight the parameter values versus parameter names.

For the last, fourth example, the query could have been formulated as *"What is a category of film…"* but it would make it harder for NL2SQL system to determine the fields of the tables referred to by the words *category* and *film*.

In many cases, when a reference to a table name is not mentioned in an NL query, we attempt to identify it based on a column name. If multiple tables have this extracted column name, the chatbot mode is initiated and the user needs to pick up a single table from the list of ones with this column name.

7.6   Implementation and Evaluation of Multi-hop Q/A with Formal Reasoning

7.6.1   System Architecture

The integrated Q/A system architecture is shown in Fig. 7.23. On the left, we show the main processing steps. In the middle, we show search engines and *Answer value extraction* components. On the right, we depict the most complex components which make this architecture unique and ensure complex reasoning-intense questions can be answered: *Ontology Builder from Text* (top-right, Fig. 7.23), *Entity Association* (middle-right, Fig. 7.23) and *Machine Reading Comprehension* (bottom-right). The first two components produce domain-specific clauses from available sources such as a corpus of text and the web offline and also in search time. The third component is a third-party one from Allen AI (Peters et al. 2018).

Firstly, the query is subject to decomposition in a rule-based manner employing a discourse tree or AMR analysis (Chap. 3, Galitsky 2019c). As a result, we obtain multiple simple queries each of which delivers a set of values. Multiple search engines are available: local, based on ElasticSearch (in the top-middle, Gormley and Tong 2015) and web/intranet (Bing Azure, Microsoft Cognitive Services, in the bottom-middle) search engine API. We take search results and extract value from them based on pattern-matching or applying the MRC technique. Once the values for search results of simple, the intermediate queries are obtained, *Substitution of obtained values* happens, followed by *Recomposition*. These two components also send the queries to the *Reasoning* module (middle-bottom) if searching has failed. Reasoning in turn relies on clauses obtained by *Ontology Builder* from *Text and Entity Association* components.

Query: *'what is staff first name when her movie return date is after 2005-06-02 01:02:05'*
looking for table.field for '[staff, first, name]'
found table.field = staff.first_name
looking for table.field for '[movie, return, date]'
found table.field = rental.return_date
Results: Mike
```
SQL:   select   staff.first_name   from   staff,   rental   where
rental.return_date > '2005-06-02 01:02:05' and rental.staff_id =
staff.staff_id
```

Query: *'what film title has actor's first name as Christian and category Documentary'*
looking for table.field for '[film, title]'
found table.field = film.title
looking for table.field for '[actor, first, name]'
found table.field = actor.first_name
Results: ACADEMY DINOSAUR |
CUPBOARD SINNERS |
MOD SECRETARY |
PRINCESS GIANT |
```
SQL: select film.title from film_category, film_actor, film, actor,
category   where   actor.first_name   like   '%Christian%'   and
category.name = 'documentary' and film_actor.film_id = film.film_id
and film_actor.actor_id = actor.actor_id and film_actor.film_id =
film.film_id   and   film_actor.actor_id   =   actor.actor_id   and
film_category.film_id = film.film_id and film_category.category_id =
category.category_id and film_category.film_id = film.film_id and
film_category.category_id = category.category_id.
```

Query: *'What is actor fist name when movie category is Documentary and special features are Behind the Scenes'*
looking for table.field for '[actor]'
found table.field = actor.first_name
looking for table.field for '[movie, category]'
found by table ONLY = category.name
Results: PENELOPE |
CHRISTIAN |
LUCILLE |
SANDRA |
```
SQL: select actor.first_name from film_category, film_actor, film, actor,
category where category.name  like '%Documentary%' and
film.special_features  like '%behind%the%scenes%'  and film_actor.film_id =
film.film_id and film_actor.actor_id = actor.actor_id and film_actor.film_id
= film.film_id and film_actor.actor_id = actor.actor_id and
film_category.film_id = film.film_id and film_category.category_id =
category.category_id and film_category.film_id = film.film_id and
film_category.category_id = category.category_id.
```

Query: *'What is a film category when film title is Ace Goldfinger'*
looking for table.field for '[film, category]'
found table.field = category.name
looking for table.field for '[film, title]'
found table.field = film.title
Results:
Horror |
```
SQL: select category.name from film_category, film, category where
film.title  like '%ACE GOLDFINGER%' and film_category.film_id = film.film_id
and film_category.category_id = category.category_id
```

Fig. 7.22 Logs for selected queries in NL and SQL, as well as their results

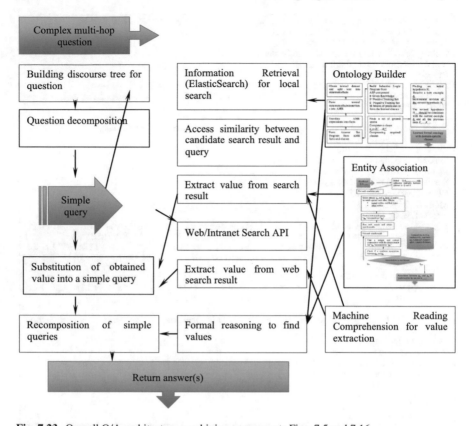

Fig. 7.23 Overall Q/A architecture combining components Figs. 7.5 and 7.16

7.6.2 Overall Evaluation

We now evaluate the integrated Q/A system, relying on multiple datasets and also performing the ablation study, varying the sources of clauses. In Fig. 7.23, we analyze the contribution of components shown in bolded frame.

Evaluation of the integrated Q/A system is shown in Table 7.4. There is a high variability of results for distinct Q/A domains and datasets. The baseline F1 for these domains vary from 28.3 for *Complex Web Questions* designed for multi-hop answer search, to 81.9 for SQuAD, where the features designed in this chapter are not essential but nevertheless help. Facebook bAbl and HotpotQA have also fairly low baseline performance.

As we add multi-hop feature without reasoning, the largest gainers of about 10% are Facebook bAbl and free-form complex questions of Car Repair, Fidelity and Auto-generated. When we proceed to reasoning, *Acquired Clauses* are mostly leveraged by Facebook, Car Repair and Auto-generated domains. The highest value of *Association Clauses* component is Facebook and Car Repair. Hence adding each

Table 7.4 Types of multi-hop questions

Informal reasoning identifying the bridge entity to complete the 2nd-hop question	Q: Which rocket was used to launch the first human in space P1: The USSR launched the first human in space, Yuri Gagarin … P2: Yuri Gagarin was launched into a single orbit on a Vostok 3KA rocket, on 12 April 1961
Comparing two entities (comparison)	Q: What is a comparative number of components in sand and glass. P1: The most common component of sand is silicon dioxide in the form of quartz P2: Silica sand is the main component of glass as glass contains about 70% silica by weight. Soda is added during the glassmaking process
Locating the answer entity by checking multiple properties	Q: Which former member of the Pittsburgh Pirates was nicknamed "The Cobra"? P1: Several current and former members of the Pittsburgh Pirates … John Milner, Dave Parker, and Rod Scurry… P2: David Gene Parker, nicknamed "The Cobra", is an American former player in Major League Baseball…
Informal reasoning about the property of an entity in question through a bridge entity	Q: Near what city is the deepest cave in the world located P1: The deepest cave in the world, Veryovkina cave, is located in the Arabika mountain ridged with Karst thickness exceeding … P2: Arabika massif is north from the Abkhazian city of Gagra
Informal reasoning that require more than two supporting facts	Q: Other than Yodobashi, what other towns were merged into the ward which gave the major Japanese retail chain specializing in electronics, PCs, cameras, and photographic equipment its name? P1: … the towns of Yodobashi, Okubo, Totsuka, and Ochiai town were merged into Yodobashi ward. … Yodobashi Camera is a store with its name taken from the town and ward P2: Yodobashi Camera Co., Ltd. is a major Japanese retail chain specializing in electronics, PCs, cameras and photographic equipment
Formal reasoning involving clauses	Q: How does John qualify for exemptions from the fee for not having coverage? P1: You had a financial hardship or other circumstances that prevented you from getting health insurance P2: You lived in a state that didn't expand its Medicaid program and your household income was below 138% of the federal poverty level Clause1: *exemption(P, not(insured(P)) :- hardship(P, financial), prevent(hardship(P, financial), P, insured(P)).* Facts: *hardship(john, financial), prevent(hardship(john, financial), john, insured(john))*

multi-hop or reasoning component boosts the performance by 2–10% depending on the question complexity of its domain, but mostly on the availability of an answer in the corpus (Table 7.5).

Pure data-driven systems attempt to explain their search results by enumerating the documents they use to obtain their answer. As we integrate our Q/A from multiple

Table 7.5 Evaluation of the overall Q/A

	IR/web + MRC + single hop	IR/web + MRC + multi-hop	IR/web + MRC + multi-hop + acquired clauses	IR/web + MRC + multi-hop + association clauses	IR/web + MRC + multi-hop + acquired clauses + association clauses
Facebook's bAbl dataset	34.1	43.6	57.9	55.4	69.3
SQuAD	81.9	82.7	83.1	84.7	84.9
HotpotQA (Yang et al. 2018)	32.7	36.1	43.5	39.7	46.2
ComplexWebQuestions (Talmor and Berant 2018)	28.3	31.8	37.1	34.8	38.7
Car Repair domain (Galitsky 2019a)	60.9	67.2	78.9	77.2	81.3
Fidelity financial domain (Galitsky 2019a)	65.4	76.8	81.8	79.8	83.0
Auto-generated questions (Galitsky 2019a)	63.0	73.6	78.3	75.2	79.4

components with their specific functions and can easily log the output of each, explainability of the overall system is naturally achieved. We do not assess auxiliary parameters like *Supported Texts* since they are only available for the dataset specifically designed to imitate Q/A explainability.

We show the comparative results of systems designed to handle complex, multi-hop questions which require reasoning, in Table 7.6. We denote with "X" the cells where we believe a given system is not applicable to this search domain, and leave the cell blank if there is no available performance data. We show in bold the values of the top performance in the respective settings and domains.

Whereas the performance of the proposed system does not exceed the performances of individual systems tuned for specific datasets, it demonstrates the universal Q/A skills in a broad variety of domains. This universality is achieved without a dataset-specific training: only general MRC model and automated clause-building skills are reused from domain to domain. Therefore, we can expect the F1 performance of our integrated system to approach 80% in an arbitrary multi-hop Q/A domain that require reasoning in a broad sense.

Lagging by 2–3% behind the specialized system, the developed reasoning support assures that where there is no direct answer (for the terms being searched for) in the local index, the web search would try to find it on the web. Furthermore, clause-building components would try to associate the original question or decomposed queries with an information available locally or on the web.

Table 7.6 Comparison of Q/A accuracy (F1-Measure) for a number of Q/A systems. Empty cells denote the cases where evaluation data is not available

	(Qi et al. 2019)	(Yang et al. 2018)	(Talmor and Berant 2018)	(Mitra & Baral 2016)	MRC of Peters et al. 2018) +IR	Bing (searching specific domain)	Google (searching specific domain)	This work
Facebook's bAbl dataset (Weston et al. 2015)	X	X		**100% for all tasks, (93% for induction)**		75.2	74.2	69.3
SQuAD				X		85.3	87.0	84.9
HotpotQA (Yang et al. 2018)	**48.6**	34.40		X		34.9	32.8	46.2
ComplexWeb Questions (Talmor and Berant 2018)			**40.9**	X		28.6	30.7	38.7
Car Repair domain					72.1			**81.3**
Fidelity Financial domain					74.9			**83.0**
Auto-generated questions					75.6			**79.4**

Notice that the proposed architecture handles well the cases where there is no answer, unlike a conventional DL-based MRC system that needs a specific training dataset with no-answer tags to function properly. In the case of our integrated system, there is an iterative deterministic procedure consulting the sources one-by-one, when a current source provides no answer.

As we integrate MRC (Peters et al. 2018) in our overall architecture, we evaluate how MRC + our IR only (without multi-hop and reasoning) performs in comparison to our complete integration system (column 6).

7.7   Conclusions

We proposed a new framework for answering complex questions that is based on question decomposition, interaction with the web and applying a number of reasoning methods. We developed a model under this framework and demonstrate that it maintains a Q/A performance close to the state-of-the-art on a broad range of question datasets, from a toy one designed to imitate simple reasoning patterns, to the real-word one of complex financial advice and recommendation (Galitsky 2016).

One such dataset is Facebook's bAbl, proposed by a group of researchers from Facebook (Weston et al. 2015). It includes a set of 20 question-answering tasks as a challenge for the natural language understanding ability of an intelligent agent. These tasks are designed to measure various skills of an agent, such as: fact-based question-answering, simple induction, the ability to find paths, co-reference resolution and many more. Their goal is to aid in the development of systems that can learn to solve such tasks and to allow a proper evaluation of such systems. They show existing systems cannot fully solve many of those toy tasks.

We targeted Q/A datasets of various natures that require logical, formal reasoning in one way or another. Deep learning approach can approximate this reasoning task by induction, generalizing through available samples, which allows solving a problem and answering a question in a significant portion of cases. In this Chapter, we employed a systematic approach where logical clauses are built from data inductively offline or online and then deductively employed to answer a question. As a result, we obtained a universal problem solver / Q/A engine that did not need to be trained offline for each domain but instead learned necessary clauses on demand to answer a question. In addition to reasoning, to tackle complex questions, we employed question decomposition for multi-hop querying which integrates well with reasoning components.

We used the Answer Set Programming (ASP) language as the primary knowledge representation and reasoning language along with the standard statistical Natural Language Processing (NLP) models. Given a training dataset containing a set of narrations, questions and their answers, the agent jointly uses a translation system, an Inductive Logic Programming algorithm and Statistical NLP methods to learn the knowledge needed to answer similar questions. Our results demonstrated that the introduction of a reasoning module improves the Q/A performance by at least 6%, depending on the domain and a nature of the question.

This chapter presented an integrated learning + reasoning approach for the task of Q/A that benefits from the field of knowledge representation and reasoning, inductive logic programming and statistical NLP. We have shown that the addition of a formal reasoning layer significantly increases the Q/A performance. This chapter is an example of an architecture that has been anticipated by (Mitra and Baral 2016) work as a starting point for more sophisticated architectures of agents that combine statistical NLP methods with formal reasoning methods.

It is well known that current MRC are still far from true language understanding. Recent analysis shows that models can do well at SQuAD by learning context and type-matching heuristics (Weissenborn et al. 2017), and that success on SQuAD does not ensure robustness to distracting sentences (Jia and Liang, 2017). One root cause of these problems is SQuAD's focus on questions for which a correct answer is guaranteed to exist in the context document. Therefore, models only need to select the span that seems most related to the question, instead of checking that the answer is actually entailed by the text. On the contrary, the system described in this chapter is well aware if a sought answer exists or not in each source.

This is what we frequently hear about DL bots (Fig. 7.24, on the left). As DL is prone to overfitting, it is hard to guarantee how well a given model is performed. An artificial or natural trained subject may perform well or may fail a task he has been trained (on the right). Another controversy associated with DL is how MRC beats the humans. As the DL NLP community claims that MRC exceeds human

Fig. 7.24 Illustration for overfitting

Fig. 7.25 Illustration for a strategy to select the team of annotators so that they would be outperformed by an existing MRC system

performance, it is time to start selecting human annotators properly to substantiate this claim (Fig. 7.25).

Figure 7.25 (on the bottom and on the right) depicts a team of annotators for a hypothetical Wikipedia article on impeachment.

We conducted an evaluation of the contribution of two reasoning components: ontology building from text, and entity association, as well as multi-hop query decomposer and MRC. We ran into conclusions that these components are all required and complement each other well for answering complex multi-hop questions. A similar multi-hop framework was successfully applied to the problem of NL access to a database. The overall conclusion is that the proposed architecture with the focus on formal reasoning is a good fit for industrial applications where performance is guaranteed in the environments where a data -driven approach lacks training sets.

References

Awadallah AH, White RW, Pantel P, Dumais ST and Wang Y-M (2014) Supporting complex search tasks. In: Proceedings of the 23rd ACM international conference on conference on information and knowledge management. ACM, pp 829–838

Baader F, Horrocks I, Lutz C, Sattler U (2017) An introduction to description logic. Cambridge University Press

Banarescu L, Bonial C, Cai S, Georgescu M, Griffitt K, Hermjakob U, Knight K, Koehn P, Palmer M, Schneider N (2013) Abstract meaning representation for sembanking. In: Proceedings of the 7th linguistic annotation workshop and interoperability with discourse, pp 178–186

Baral C, Gelfond M, Scherl R (2004) Using answer set programming to answer complex queries. In: Workshop on pragmatics of question answering at HLT-NAAC2004

Baral C (2003) Knowledge representation, reasoning and declarative problem solving. Cambridge University Press

Clark P, Etzioni O, Khot T, Sabharwal A, Tafjord O, Turney PD and Khashabi D (2016) Combining retrieval, statistics, and inference to answer elementary science questions. In: AAAI

Mihaylov T, Clark P, Khot T, Sabharwal A (2018) Can a suit of armor conduct electricity?. A new dataset for open book question answering, In EMNLP

Cohen WW, Borgida A, Hirsh H (1992) Computing least common subsumers in description logics. In: Proceeding of the AAAI. pp 754–76

De Cao N, Wilker Aziz, and Ivan Titov (2019) Question answering by reasoning across documents with graph convolutional networks. In: Proceedings of the conference of the North American Chapter of the Association for Computational Linguistics (NAACL).

Dua D, Wang Y, Dasigi P, Stanovsky G, Singh S, Gardner M (2019) DROP: a reading comprehension benchmark requiring discrete reasoning over paragraphs. arXiv:1903.00161

Eppe M, Maclean E, Confalonieri R, Kutz O, Schorlemmer M, Plaza E, Kuhnberger K (2018) A computational framework for conceptual blending. Artif. Intell. 256:105–129

Flanigan J, Thomson S, Carbonell J, Dyer C, Smith NA (2014) A discriminative graph-based parser for the abstract meaning representation from Minimal Context over Documents. ACL 1725–1735.

Galitsky B (2001) A natural language question answering system for human genome domain. In: Proceedings of the 2nd IEEE international symposium on bioinformatics and bioengineering

Galitsky B (2002) A tool for extension and restructuring natural language question answering domains. In: International conference on industrial, engineering and other applications of applied intelligent systems. Springer, Berlin, Heidelberg, pp 482–492

Galitsky B (2003) Natural language question answering system: technique of semantic headers. Advance Knowledge International, Australia

Galitsky B (2005) Natural language front-end for a database. Encyclopedia of database technologies and applications. IGI Global Pennsylvania, USA, p 5

Galitsky B, Kuznetsov SO, Vinogradov DV (2005) Applying hybrid reasoning to mine for associative features in biological data. J Biomed Inform 40(3):203–220

Galitsky B (2006) Merging deductive and inductive reasoning for processing textual descriptions of inter-human conflicts. J Intell Inf Syst 27(1):21–48

Galitsky B, Dobrocsi G, de la Rosa JL, Kuznetsov SO (2010) From generalization of syntactic parse trees to conceptual graphs. In: Croitoru M, Ferré S, Lukose D (eds) Conceptual structures: from information to intelligence, 18th international conference on conceptual structures, ICCS 2010. Lecture notes in artificial intelligence, vol 6208, pp 185–190

Galitsky B, Dobrocsi G, de la Rosa JL, Kuznetsov Sergei O (2011) Using generalization of syntactic parse trees for taxonomy capture on the web. 19th international conference on conceptual structures. ICCS 2011:104–117

Galitsky B, S Botros (2012) Searching for associated events in log data. US Patent 8,306,967

Galitsky B, Kovalerchuk B (2014) Improving web search relevance with learning structure of domain concepts. Clusters, orders, and trees: methods and applications, pp 341–376

Galitsky B (2016) Providing personalized recommendation for attending events based on individual interest profiles. Artif. Intell. Research 5(1):1–13

Galitsky B (2017a) Matching parse thickets for open domain question answering. Data Knowl Eng 107:24–50

Galitsky B(2017b) Using extended tree Kernel to recognize metalanguage in text. Uncertainty Modeling, pp 71–96

Galitsky B (2017b) Discovering rhetorical agreement between a request and response. Dialogue Discourse 8(2):167–205

Galitsky (2019a) Automated building of expanded datasets for training of autonomous agents. US Patent App. 16/426,878, 2019.

Galitsky B (2019b) Rhetorical Agreement: Maintaining Cohesive Conversations. In: Developing enterprise chatbots. Springer, Cham, pp 327–363

Galitsky B (2019c) Semantic skeleton thesauri for question answering bots. In: Developing enterprise chatbots. Springer, Cham, pp 327–363

Galitsky B (2019d) Developing Conversational Natural Language Interface to a Database. In Developing Enterprise Chatbots, Springer, Cham 85-120.

Galitsky B (2020) Natural language interfaces for databases using autonomous agents and thesauri. US Patent 10,592,505

Gelfond M, Lifschitz V (1988) The stable model semantics for logic programming. ICLP/SLP 88:1070–1080

Gormley C, Tong Z (2015) Elasticsearch: The definitive guide: a distributed real-time search and analytics engine. O'Reilly Media, Inc.

Harel S, Albo S, Agichtein E, Radinsky K (2019) Learning novelty-aware ranking of answers to complex questions. The World Wide Web Conference

Jia R, Liang P (2017) Adversarial examples for evaluating reading comprehension systems. In: Empirical methods in natural language processing (EMNLP)

Jung JC, Lutz C, Wolter F (2020) Least general generalizations in description logic: verification and existence. AAAI, New York NY

Katzouris N, Artikis A, Paliouras G (2015) Incremental learning of event definitions with inductive logic programming. Machine Learning 100(2–3):555–585

Khashabi D, Azer ES, Khot T, Sabharwal A, Roth D (2019) On the capabilities and limitations of reasoning for natural language understanding. CoRR abs/1901.02522

Khot T, Clark P, Guerquin M, Jansen PE, Sabharwal A (2020). QASC: A dataset for question answering via sentence composition. In: AAAI

Kratzwald B, Feuerriegel S (2018) Adaptive document retrieval for deep question answering. In: Proceedings of the conference on empirical methods in natural language processing (EMNLP).

Kwiatkowski T, Choi E, Artzi Y, Zettlemoyer L (2013) Scaling semantic parsers with on-the-fly ontology matching. In: Empirical methods in natural language processing (EMNLP)

Levesque HJ, Davis, E, Morgenstern L (2012) The winograd schema challenge. In: KR

Liang P, Jordan MI, Klein D (2011) Learning dependency-based compositional semantics. In: Association for computational linguistics (ACL), pp 590–599

Mehrotra R, Yilmaz E (2017) Extracting hierarchies of search tasks & subtasks via a bayesian nonparametric approach. In: Proceedings of the 40th international ACM SIGIR conference on research and development in information retrieval. ACM, pp 285–294

Meissner A, Brzykcy G (2011) Reasoning with the depth-first iterative deepening strategy in the DLog system. LNAI 7046:504–513

Mikolov T, Chen K, Corrado G, Dean J (2013) Efficient estimation of word representations in vector space. In: Proceedings of Workshop at ICLR

Min S, Zhong V, Zettlemoyer L, Hajishirzi H (2019) Multi-hop reading comprehension through question decomposition and rescoring. ACL

Min S, Zhong V, Socher R, Xiong C (2018) Efficient and robust question answering from minimal context over documents. ACL, pp 1725–1735

Mitra A, Baral C (2016) Addressing a Question Answering Challenge by Combining Statistical Methods with Inductive Rule Learning and Reasoning. AAAI.

Muggleton S (1991) Inductive logic programming. New generation computing 8(4):295–318

Muggleton S (1995) Inverse entailment and progol. New generation computing 13(3–4):245–286

Nebel B (1990) Reasoning and revision in hybrid representation systems. Springer

Nishida K, Saito I, Otsuka A, Asano H, Tomita J (2018) Retrieve-and read: multi-task learning of information retrieval and reading comprehension. In: Proceedings of the 27th ACM international conference on information and knowledge management. ACM, pp 647–656

Oracle (2018) Sakila Database. https://docs.oracle.com/cd/E17952_01/workbench-en/wb-docume nting-sakila.html

Peters ME, Neumann M, Iyyer M, Gardner M, Clark C, Lee K, Zettlemoyer L (2018) Deep contextualized word representations. NAACL

Qi P, Xiaowen L, Leo M, Zijian W, Manning C (2019) Answering complex open-domain questions Through Iterative Query Generation

Plotkin G (1970) A note on inductive generalizations. Edinburgh University Press

Ray O (2009) Nonmonotonic abductive inductive learning. Journal of Applied Logic 7(3):329–340

Richardson M, Burges CJ, Renshaw E (2013) MCtest: A challenge dataset for the open-domain machine comprehension of text. In EMNLP

Talmor A, Berant J (2018) The web as a knowledge-base for answering complex questions. Proceedings of NAACL

Trek (2017) Question Answering Track. https://trec.nist.gov/data/qamain.html

Welbl J, Stenetorp P, Riedel S (2018) Constructing datasets for multi-hop reading comprehension across documents. Transactions of the Association for Computational Linguistics 6:287–302

Weissenborn D, Wiese G, Seiffe L (2017) Making neural QA as simple as possible but not simpler. In: Computational natural language learning (CoNLL)

Weston J, Bordes A, Chopra S, Mikolov T (2015) Towards ai-complete question answering: a set of prerequisite toy tasks. arXiv preprint arXiv:1502.05698

Yang Z, Qi P, Zhang S, Bengio Y, Cohen W, Salakhutdinov R, Manning C (2018) HotpotQA: a dataset for diverse, explainable multi-hop question answering. 2369–2380

Chapter 8
Managing Customer Relations in an Explainable Way

Abstract We explore how to validate the soundness of textual explanations in a domain-independent manner. We further assess how people perceive explanations of their opponents and what are the factors determining whether explanations are acceptable or not. We discover that what we call a *hybrid discourse tree* (hybrid DT) determines the acceptability of explanation. A complete DT is a sum of a traditional DT for a paragraph of actual text and an imaginary DT for a text about entities used in but not explicitly defined in the actual text. Logical validation of explanation is evaluated: we confirm that a representation of an explanation chain via complete DTs is an adequate tool to validate the explanation soundness. We then proceed to a Decision Support scenario where a human expert and a machine learning (ML) system need to make decision together, explaining how they used the parameters for their decisions. We refer to this scenario as bi-directional since the involved decision-makers need to negotiate the decision providing explanations. We also address the explanations in behavioral scenarios that involve conflicting agents. In these scenarios, implicit or explicit conflict can be caused by contradictory agents' interests, as communicated in their explanations for why they behaved in a particular way, by a lack of knowledge of the situation, or by a mixture of explanations of multiple factors. We argue that in many cases to assess the plausibility of explanations, we must analyze two following components and their interrelations: (1) explanation at the actual object level (explanation itself) and (2) explanation at the higher level (meta-explanation). Comparative analysis of the roles of both is conducted to assess the plausibility of how agents explain the scenarios of their interactions. Object-level explanation assesses the plausibility of individual claims by using a traditional approach to handle an argumentative structure of a dialogue (Galitsky and Kuznetsov in International Conference on Conceptual Structures, pp. 282–296, 2008a). Meta-explanation links the structure of a current scenario with that of previously learned scenarios of multi-agent interaction. The scenario structure includes agents' communicative actions and argumentation defeat relations between the subjects of these actions. We also define a ratio between object-level and meta-explanation as the relative accuracy of plausibility assessment based on the former and latter sources. We then observe that groups of scenarios can be clustered based on this ratio; hence, such a ratio is an important parameter of human behavior associated with explaining something to other humans.

© Springer Nature Switzerland AG 2020   309
B. Galitsky, *Artificial Intelligence for Customer Relationship Management*,
Human–Computer Interaction Series,
https://doi.org/10.1007/978-3-030-52167-7_8

8.1 Introduction

Providing explanations of decisions for human users, and understanding how human agents explain their decisions, are important features of intelligent systems. A number of complex forms of human behavior is associated with attempts to provide acceptable and convincing explanations. In this paper, we propose a computational framework for treating what we believe constitutes two major explanation sources: factual explanations and structural explanations. The former source (level) is more traditional and deals with the feasibility of individual claims. The latter source (level) of explanation, meta-explanation, is introduced in this chapter to formalize the explanation patterns based on structural similarity: "*I did it because people behave like this in a conflict dialogue with similar structure*".

This chapter is written in an environment when the notion of explanation is becoming fairly diluted. Any response to the *Why* question other than "*…Just because*" is considered as an explanation in the Deep Learning (DL) community where an explanation is defined as something similar in some sense to a text tagged as an explanation by an annotator (Bowman et al. 2015; Camburu et al. 2018). Conversely, in this chapter, we treat explanations as perceived by a competent adult, from a commonsense reasoning perspective, as a chain to link a premise with a hypothesis, so that a *Why* question regarding the hypothesis is answered completely by the explanation chain.

Importance of the explanation-aware computing has been demonstrated in multiple studies and systems (Wheeldon 2007; Ma et al. 2008; Elizalde et al. 2008; Dey 2009). Also, (Walton 2007) argued that the older model of explanations as a chain of inferences with a pragmatic and communicative model that structures an explanation as an exchange of utterances in a dialog. The field of argumentation is now actively contributing to such areas as legal reasoning, natural language processing and also multi-agent systems (Chesñevar and Maguitman 2004; Dunne and Bench-Capon 2006). It has been shown (Walton 2008) how the argumentation methodology implements the concept of explanation by transforming an example of an explanation into a formal dialog structure. In this chapter, we differentiate between explaining as a chain of inference of facts mentioned in dialogue, and meta-explaining as dealing with formal dialog structure represented as a graph. Both levels of explanations are implemented as argumentation: explanation operates with individual claims communicated in a dialogue, and meta-explanation relies on the overall argumentation structure of scenarios (Galitsky and Kuznetsov 2008b).

The main reasons for AI systems to be explainable are as follows:

- Improve human readability;
- Determine the justifiability of the decision made by the machine;
- Help in deciding accountability, liability leading to good policy-making;
- Avoid discrimination;
- Reduce societal bias.

Understanding, simulating and explaining the behavior of human agents, as presented in text or other media, is an important problem to be solved in a number of decision-making and decision support tasks (e.g. Fum et al. 2007). One class of the solutions to this problem involves learning argument structures from previous experience with these agents, from previous scenarios of interaction between similar agents (Galitsky et al. 2008). Another class of the solutions for this problem, based on the assessment of quality and consistency of argumentation of agents, has been attracting the attention of the behavior simulation community as well (Chesñevar et al. 2000).

In the context of agent-based decision support systems, the study of dynamics of *argumentation* (Prakken and Vreeswijk 2002) has proven to be a major feature for analyzing the course of interaction between conflicting agents (e.g., in argument-based negotiation or multiagent dialogues (Weigand and de Moor 2004). The issue of argumentation semantics of communicative models has also been addressed in the literature (eg Parsons et al. 2002). Case-based reasoning has been applied to learn interaction scenarios as well (Aleven 2003).

However, when there is a lack of background domain-dependent information to obtain a full object-level explanation, the evolution of *dialogues* where human agents try to explain their decisions should be taken into account in addition to the communicative actions these arguments are attached to. We are concerned with the emerging *structure* of such dialogues in conflict scenarios, based on inter-human interaction and refer to such structure as *meta-explanation*. Meta-explanation is implemented as a comparison of a given structure with similar structures for other cases to mine for relevant ones for assessing its truthfulness and a verification whether agents provide proper explanations.

In our earlier studies, we proposed a concept learning technique for scenario graphs, which encode information on the sequence of communicative actions, the subjects of communicative actions, the causal links (Galitsky et al. 2005), and argumentation attack relationships between these subjects (Galitsky et al. 2008). Scenario knowledge representation and learning techniques were employed in such problems as predicting an outcome of international conflicts, assessment of an attitude of a security clearance candidate, mining emails for suspicious emotional profiles, and mining wireless location data for suspicious behavior (Galitsky and Miller 2005; Galitsky et al. 2007a).

Providing explanations of decisions for human users, and understanding how human agents explain their decisions, are important features of intelligent decision making and decision support systems. A number of complex forms of human behavior are associated with attempts to provide acceptable and convincing explanations. In this chapter, we propose a computational framework for assessing the soundness of explanations and explore how such soundness is correlated with discourse-level analysis.

Importance of explanation-aware computing has been demonstrated in multiple studies and systems. Also, (Walton 2007) argued that the older model of explanations as a chain of inferences with a pragmatic and communicative model can structure an explanation as a dialog exchange. The field of explanation-aware computing is now actively contributing to such areas as legal reasoning, natural language processing and also multi-agent systems (Dunne and Bench-Capon 2006). It has been shown (Walton et al. 2008) how the argumentation methodology implements the concept of explanation by transforming an example of an explanation into a formal dialog structure. Galitsky (2008) differentiated between explaining as a chain of inference of facts mentioned in dialogue, and meta-explaining as dealing with formal dialog structure represented as a graph. Both levels of explanations are implemented as argumentation: explanation operates with individual claims communicated in a dialogue, and meta-explanation relies on the overall argumentation structure of scenarios.

8.1.1   Example-Based Explanations

An example-based explanation method selects particular instances of the dataset to explain the behavior of a machine learning (ML) model or to explain the underlying data distribution. Example-based explanations are mostly model-agnostic because they make any ML model more interpretable. The example-based methods explain a model by selecting the elements of the training set instead of building summaries of features (such as feature importance or partial dependence). Example-based explanations are meaningful in cases when an ML developer can represent elements of the training set in a form understood by a customer in such an environment as CRM. Example-based explanations perform well in the domains such as music, speech, images and videos recommendation because a human user can perceive the examples directly (Fig. 8.1).

Fig. 8.1 A convincing explanation (Cartoonbank 2020)

Usually, example-based methods are suitable to the domains where the feature values of an element of a training set possess substantial context (such as text or image with a structure) and not an abstract feature space. It is more challenging to represent table or analytical data in a meaningful way because a data point is described by hundreds or thousands of features where a possible structure is implicit. Formal concept analysis can be valuable here (Ganter and Kuznetsov 2003; Galitsky and de la Rosa 2011), as listing all feature values to describe an instance is usually not useful. It works well if there are only a handful of features or if we have a way to summarize an instance.

Example-based explanations help humans construct mental models (Galitsky 2016a, b) of the ML and the data the ML model has been trained on. Example-based explanations help to understand complex data distributions. As an example (Aamodt and Plaza 1994), let us imagine a physician seeing a patient with an unusual cough and a mild fever. The patient's symptoms remind her of another patient she had years ago with similar symptoms. She suspects that her current patient could have the same disease and she takes a blood sample to test for this specific disease (Sect. 8.3).

Counterfactual explanations tell us how an instance has to change to significantly update its prediction. By creating counterfactual instances, we learn about how the model makes its predictions and can explain individual predictions. Adversarial questions are counterfactuals used to trick machine learning models. The idea is to flip the prediction instead of explaining it. The prototypes are a selection of representative instances from the data and the adversarial set includes instances that are not well represented by those prototypes (Kim et al. 2016).

8.1.2 Causal Explanations

The notion of causal explanations has been introduced by philosophers and psychologists of reasoning; causal explanations exist in the form of a conversation. Causal explanations are selected by questions and are thus governed by the general rules of discourse. A conversational model of causal explanation is introduced that develops social aspects of the explanation process in detail by claiming that a good explanation should be relevant to the focus of a *Why* question, as well as being true (Molnar 2019). Relevance of the conversational perspective for research on causal networks, the social context of explanation, and intra-psychic explanation has been addressed by (Hilton 1988). A causal explanation of an event is a result of a chain of events (Botros et al. 2013), according to a mental model of a certain individual. For example, to discover influencing factors in product selection by a buyer, one needs to identify possible previous conditions that led to the particular product selection. Causal links (not necessarily explainable) can be mined from data deploying a hybrid deductive + inductive + abductive system (Galitsky et al. 2007b).

The interpersonal nature of explanation is overlooked in most contemporary theories of causal attribution. The preferred view is the one associated with the *man-the-scientist* analogy first proposed by (Heider 1958; Nisbett and Ross 1980). In this view, a layperson is pictured as arriving at explanations by observing the covariation of putative causes and effects and using procedures analogous to the scientific analysis of variance to attribute causality. The *man-the-scientist* model describes the process of causal attribution as being essentially intra-psychic in nature. It does not explicitly concern itself with interpersonal and functional factors that might constrain the attribution, such as who is doing the explaining, to whom the explanation is being given, or why an explanation is needed.

Psychological theories of causal reasoning make a distinction between two stages of causal judgment:

(1) Diagnosis. It is an event that is attributed (traced back) to its source. The problem is to identify a causal connection between two events;

(2) Explanation. In explaining a tram crash, one may start by considering the key hypotheses such as accident and sabotage and collect evidence to evaluate these hypotheses. This stage of hypothesis evaluation is a judgment under uncertainty, and one can speak of judging the probable cause of the event. If investigations reveal that the tram crash was most probably due to an accident, one would cite the accident as the "best" explanation, as it is the most probable cause.

In the stage (2) of interpersonal explanation, one may speculate about certainty in the explainer's mind about the causes of the event. We refer to this speculation activity as *meta-explanation.*

The explainer's causal diagnosis can possibly reveal that the tram crash occurred because of a combination of several necessary conditions that are jointly sufficient: a bent rail in the track and the speed and weight of the tram. Rather, the problem is how to resolve a puzzle in the explainee's mind about why the event happened by building an explanation chain (closing a gap in her knowledge (Turnbull 1986)).

If one knows that the explainee knew about the speed and weight of the tram but did not know that there was a bent rail in the track, the solid and informative answer to the *Why* question would be to refer to the bent rail track as the main cause. It would be the best explanation because it is the most relevant answer to the question posed, not because it is a more probable cause of the accident than the speed and weight of the tram.

On the other hand, the explainee might have obtained knowledge that there was a bent rail track and assume that the tram was obeying special speed restrictions. However, if in fact the train driver had failed to see the special speed restrictions and traveled at normal speed over the bent rail, thus producing the accident, then the most valid explanation would refer to the speed of the tram. In this case, it is the fact that the train traveled at its normal speed that makes the difference to the accident from the viewpoint of the question author. Consequently, abnormal conditions such as a bent rail should only constitute an explanation in the context of the specific knowledge of the question author.

8.1.3 Questions Requesting Counterfactual Explanations

A question requesting counterfactual explanation describes a causal situation in the form: "*If X had not occurred, Y would not have occurred*". The question can be formulated as "*If X had not occurred, would Y still has occurred?*" "*If I had my bank account for 10 years, would my current mortgage application be approved?*"

For example: "*If he hadn't taken a sip of this hot coffee, he would not have burned his tongue*". Event Y is that he burned his tongue; cause X is that he had a hot coffee. Reasoning in counterfactual way requires imagining a hypothetical world that is inconsistent with the observed facts (e.g., a world in which I have not drunk the hot coffee), hence the name "counterfactual". The ability to think in counterfactuals makes us humans so smart compared to other animals.

In interpretable ML, counterfactual explanations can be used to explain predictions of individual data set elements. The "causes" are the particular feature values of an element that were input to the model and *caused* a certain prediction. Displayed as a graph, the relationship between the inputs and the prediction is very simple: the feature values cause the prediction.

The causal relationships hold between inputs of an ML model and the predictions, when the model is merely seen as a black box. The inputs cause the prediction (not necessarily reflecting the real causal relation of the data, Fig. 8.2).

Even if in the real life the relationship between the inputs and the outcome to be predicted might not be causal, one can perceive the inputs of a model as the cause of the prediction. Given this simple graph, it is easy to see how we can simulate counterfactuals for predictions of ML models. One needs to update the feature values of an instance before making the predictions and we analyze how the prediction changes. We are interested in scenarios in which the prediction changes in a relevant way, like a flip in predicted class (e.g., credit application accepted or rejected) or in which the prediction reaches a certain threshold (e.g., the probability for cancer reaches 10%). A counterfactual explanation of a prediction describes the smallest change to the feature values that changes the prediction to a predefined output.

The counterfactual explanation method is model-agnostic, since it only works with the model inputs and output. The interpretation can be expressed as a summary of the differences in feature values ("*change features A and B to change the prediction*"). Unlike prototypes, counterfactuals do not have to be actual instances from the training data, but can be a new combination of feature values.

Use cases for counterfactuals are as follows.

Fig. 8.2 The causal relationships between inputs of an ML model and the predictions

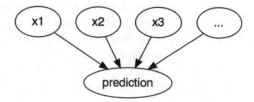

(1) Peter applies for a mortgage and gets rejected by an ML-based banking software. He wonders why his application was rejected and how he might improve his chances to get a loan. The question of "why" can be formulated as a counterfactual: What is the smallest change to my features (*income, number of credit cards, age, credit score*) that would change the outcome from *rejected* to *approved*? One possible answer could be: If Peter gets a second job and earns \$40,000 more per year, he would qualify for the loan. Or if Peter had fewer credit cards and had not defaulted on a loan 5 years ago, he would get the loan. Peter will never know the reasons for the rejection (as, regretfully, the bank has no interest in transparency);

(2) We want to explain a model that predicts a continuous outcome with counterfactual explanations. Mary wants to rent out her house, but she is not sure how much to charge for it, so she decides to train an ML model to predict the rent. Naturally, since Mary is an office worker, that is how she solves her problems. Having specified all the parameters including size, location and pets, the model tells her that she can charge \$770. She expected \$880 or above, but she trusts her model and decides to play with the feature values of the house to see how she can improve the lease value of the house. She finds out that the house could be rented out for over \$830, if it were 3 m^2 larger. Interesting, but useless knowledge, because she cannot enlarge her apartment. Finally, by adjusting only the feature values under her control (*built-in kitchen yes/no, pets allowed yes/no, type of floor*, etc.), she finds out that if she allows pets and installs windows with better insulation, she can charge \$870. Mary applied counterfactuals reasoning to actually change the outcome.

Counterfactuals are human-friendly explanations, because they are revisions of the current instance and because they are selective, meaning they usually focus on a small number of feature changes. But the flaw of counterfactuals stems from multiple different counterfactual explanations. Each counterfactual tells a different scenario of how a certain outcome is achieved. One counterfactual might say to change feature X, the other counterfactual might say to leave X intact but instead update feature Y, which is a contradiction. This issue of multiple truths can be addressed either by reporting all counterfactual explanations or by having a criterion to assess contradicting counterfactuals and select the best one.

How to define a *good* counterfactual explanation? First, a customer of a system that employs counterfactual explanations defines a relevant change in the prediction of an instance. An obvious first requirement is that a counterfactual instance should produce a prediction that is the closest to the predefined one. It is not always possible to have an exact match with the predefined outputs. In a classification setting with two classes, an infrequent class and a frequent class, an ML model can just always classify an instance as the frequent class. It is not always plausible to change the feature values so that the predicted label would switch from the frequent class to the infrequent class. This requirement needs to be attenuated accordingly so that the predicted ML output of the counterfactual must correspond exactly to the defined outcome.

In the classification example, we could look for a counterfactual where the predicted probability of the rare class is increased to 20% instead of the current 1%. One needs to determine the minimum changes to the features so that the predicted probability changes from 1 to 20%. Also, a counterfactual should be as similar as possible to the instance in terms of feature values. This requires a similarity measure between two instances. The counterfactual should not only be close to the original instance, but should also change as few features as possible. This can be achieved by selecting an appropriate similarity measure, such as syntactic generalization (Galitsky 2017).

8.1.4 Google Explainable AI Tool

The tool helps the developers to build interpretable and inclusive ML models and deploy them with confidence. The explainable AI Tool assists in understanding feature attributions by means of such components as AutoML Tables and AI Platform, as well as to visually investigate model behavior using the What-If Tool. It also further simplifies model governance through continuous evaluation of models managed using the AI Platform. Explainable AI tool is intended to help detect and resolve bias, drift, and other issues in data, model architectures and model performance. *AI Explanations* provide a score explaining how each factor contributed to the final result of the model predictions, and a continuous evaluation feature.

One of the things that challenge Google AI engineers is that they often build really accurate ML models, but experience difficulty understanding why these models are doing what they are doing. And in many of the large systems they built for Android smartphones or for their search-ranking systems, or question-answering systems, they have worked hard to understand what was going on.

Introducing the Google What-If Tool, the CEO of Google Cloud Thomas Kurian, said: "If you're using AI for credit scoring, you want to be able to understand why the model rejected a particular model and accepted another one. Explainable AI allows you, as a customer, who is using AI in an enterprise business process, to understand why the AI infrastructure generated a particular outcome". In some fields, like healthcare, improving the transparency of AI would be particularly useful. In the case of an algorithm programmed to diagnose certain illnesses, for example, it would let physicians visualize the symptoms picked up by the model to make its decision, and verify that those symptoms are not false positives or signs of different ailments.

Google announced that it was launching a new concept of what it calls "model cards"—short documents that provide snap information about particular algorithms. The documents are essentially an ID card for machine learning, including practical details about a model's performance and limitations. The cards will help developers make better decisions about what models to use for what purpose and how to deploy them responsibly. Examples are a face detection algorithm (Fig. 8.3) and an object detection algorithm.

Fig. 8.3 Google face detection with explainability

8.2 Validating Correctness of Textual Explanation with Hybrid Discourse Trees

In this section, we explore how a *good* explanation in a text can be computationally differentiated from bad explanation. Intuitively, a good explanation convinces
the addressee that a communicated claim is right, and it involves valid argumentation patterns, logical, complete and thorough. A bad explanation is unconvincing,
detached from the beliefs of the addressee, includes flawed argumentation patterns
and omits necessary entities. In this Section, we differentiate between good and bad
explanations based on a *human response* to such an explanation. Whereas users are
satisfied with a good explanation produced by an automated system or a human, bad
explanations usually lead to dissatisfaction, embarrassment and complaints (Galitsky
2006b).

To systematically treat the classes of explanation, we select an environment where customers receive explanations from customer service regarding certain dissatisfactions these customers encountered. If these customers are not satisfied with explanations, they frequently submit detailed complaints to consumer advocacy sites (Cho et al. 2002). In some of these complaints, these customers explain why they are right and why the company's explanation is wrong (Galitsky and Tumarkina 2004). From these training sets, we select the *good/bad* explanation pairs and define respective explanation classes via learning to recognize them. Another way to consider a bad explanation is what we call an *explanation attempt*: a logical chain is built but it has some omissions and inconsistencies so that the explanation is bad. An absence of a logical chain means the absence of explanation; otherwise, if such the chain obeys certain logical properties it can be interpreted as another logical structure such as argumentation, clarification, confirmation (or another mental or epistemic state).

8.2.1 Explanation and Argumentation

Explanations are correlated with argumentation and sentiments. A request to explain is usually associated with certain arguments and a negative sentiment. For an arbitrary statement S a person may have little or no prior reason for believing this statement to be true. In this case, a cognitive response is a doubt, which is articulated with a request for evidence. Evidence is a kind of reason, and the attempt to provide evidence in support of a conclusion is normally called an *argument*. Argument reasoning is represented on the top of Fig. 8.4.

On the other hand, a person may already know S and require no further evidence for the truth of S. But she still may not understand why S holds (*occurred, happened*), etc. In this case, she would request a cause. Explanation is defined as an attempt to provide a cause in support of a conclusion. Explanation-based reasoning is represented at the bottom of Fig. 8.4.

Fig. 8.4 Relationship between argumentation and explanation

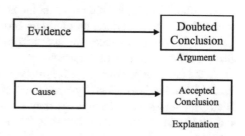

8.2.2 Hybrid Discourse Trees

We assume the reader is familiar with the notion of a discourse tree (DT) and a communicative discourse tree (CDT, Galitsky et al. 2018) from the previous chapters. In the banking domain, *nonsufficient fund fee* (NSF) is a major problem that banks have difficulties communicating with customers. An example of a brief, informal explanation follows:

> It's not always easy to understand overdraft fees. When a transaction drops your checking account balance below zero, what happens next is up to your bank. A bank or credit union might pay for the transaction or decline it and, either way, could charge you a fee.

The concept of *transaction* is not tackled in this text explaining nonsufficient fee. An ontology could specify that transaction = {*wiring, purchasing, sending money*} but it is hard to be complete (Al-Fedaghi 2016). Instead, one can complement the notion of transaction via additional text that will elaborate on transaction, providing more details on it.

Hence *Elaboration* relation for nucleus *transaction* is not in actual DT but is assumed by a recipient of this explanation text. We refer to such rhetorical relations (RRs) as *Imaginary*: they are not produced from text but are instead induced by the context of explanation. Such multiple imaginary RRs form additional nodes of an actual DT for a text being communicated. We refer to the extended DT as *hybrid*: it combines the actual DT and its imaginary parts. Naturally, the latter can be dependent on the recipient: different people keep in mind distinct instances of *transactions*.

We formalize this intuition by using discourse structure of the text expressed by DTs. Arcs of this tree correspond to rhetorical relations (RR), connecting text blocks called Elementary Discourse Units (EDU). We rely on the Rhetorical Structure Theory (Mann and Thompson 1988) when construct and describe discourse structure of text.

When people explain stuff, they do not have to enumerate all premises: some of them implicitly occurring in the explanation chain and are assumed by the person providing explanation to be known or believed by an addressee. However, a DT for a text containing explanation only includes EDUs from the actual text. At the same time, the assumed, implicit part with its entities and phrases (which are supposed to enter explanation sequence) are absent from the actual (*real*) DT. How can we cover these implicit entities and phrases?

In the considered example, *Elaboration* relation for nucleus *transaction* is not in actual CDT but is assumed by a recipient of this explanation text. We refer to such rhetorical relations as *imaginary*: they are not produced from text but are instead induced by the context of explanation. Such multiple imaginary RRs form additional nodes of a real DT for a text being communicated. We refer to the combined CDTs as *hybrid*: it combines the actual CDT and its imaginary parts. Naturally, the latter can be dependent on the recipient: different people keep in mind distinct instances of *transactions*. The hybrid discourse tree for this example is shown in Fig. 8.5. Hybrid discourse trees also have communicative actions attached to their edges in the form of VerbNet verb signatures (Galitsky and Parnis 2018).

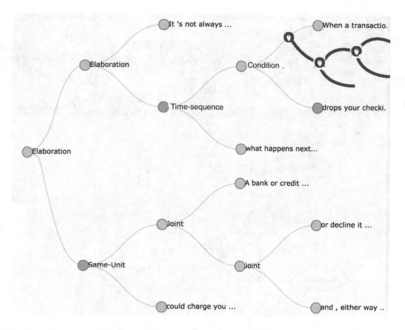

Fig. 8.5 The discourse tree of explanation text with the imaginary part shown in the top-right for nucleus "*transaction*"

8.2.3 Semantics for Explanations

Notice the difference between the discourse and the semantic representation (Fig. 8.6). They complement each other: the former is domain independent and essentially an abstract logic of how thoughts are organized. The latter expresses the meaning of words and phrases and can be abstract as well. Unlike the structure of the discourse level, there is nothing very specific in the semantics of explanation versus semantics of a regular information-sharing activity (Fig. 8.6 on the bottom). Abstract Meaning Representation attempts to abstract away from the lexical details and shows an interconnection between concepts for words. Notice an abstraction and generalization from *checking account – drop* into drop-out (the family of verbs related to *drop*, the root of the semantic tree): *check – balance – account.* Regretfully, some meaning of involved entities such as "*checking account*" is lost in this abstraction. '*happens*' is lost as well as uninformative. However, it does not affect our explanation chain as we need to logically link *balance – drops => bank – next.*

A frame semantic parse for the same text is shown in Fig. 8.6 on the top. The reader observes that it is hard to tag entities and determine the context properly. *Bank* is tagged as Placing (not disambiguated properly) and "*credit union might*" is determined as a hypothetical event since *union* is represented literally, as an *organization*, separately from *credit*. Overall, the main expression being explained, "*transaction drops your checking account balance below zero*", is not represented as a cause

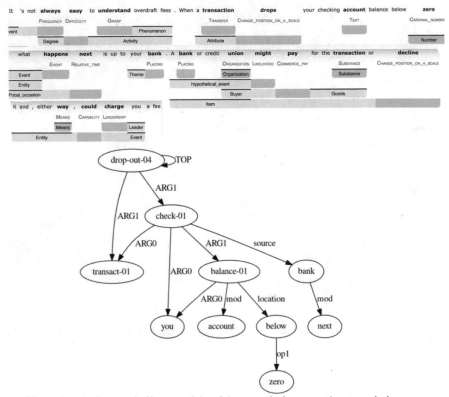

Fig. 8.6 Frame semantic parse for a 3-sentence explanation (on the top). Abstract Meaning Representation for the second sentence is on the bottom (Chap. 3)

of a problem by semantic analysis, since a higher level considerations involving a banking-related ontology would be required.

The discourse-level machinery allows including the explanation structure beyond the ones from explanation text but also from the accompanying texts mined from various sources to obtain a complete logical structure of the entities involved in explanation.

8.2.4 Discourse Tree of Explanations

A valid explanation in text follows certain rhetoric patterns. In addition to default relations of *Elaboration*, valid explanation relies on *Cause*, *Condition* and domain-specific *Comparison* (Fig. 8.7). As an example, we provide an explanation for why *thunder sound comes after lightning*:

```
joint
  elaboration
    cause
      temporal
        TEXT:We see the lightning
        TEXT:before we hear the thunder . [we need to associate lightning with light and thunder with sound]
        TEXT:This is because light travels faster than sound .
      elaboration
        TEXT:The light from the lightning travels to our eyes much quicker than the sound from the lightning .
        comparison    [ we need to associate quicker with later ]
          TEXT:so we hear it later
          TEXT:than we see it .
```

```
joint
  elaboration
    cause
      temporal
        TEXT:We see the lightning
        TEXT:before we hear the thunder .
        elaboration /joint
          TEXT... lightning....
          TEXT ... light ...
        elaboration /joint
          TEXT... thunder....
          TEXT ... sound ...
      TEXT:This is because light travels faster than sound .
        elaboration
          TEXT:The light from the lightning travels to our eyes much quicker than the sound from the lightning .
          comparison    [ we need to associate quicker with later ]
            TEXT:so we hear it later
            TEXT:than we see it .
          elaboration/contrast/restatement/condition
            TEXT... quicker....
            TEXT ... later ...
```

Fig. 8.7 A real part of the discourse tree for an explanation of lightning (on the top). Indentation for each line shows the tree hierarchy. Notes about missing associations between entities are shown in italic in square brackets. A complete discourse tree with imagery part highlighted in green is shown on the bottom

We see the lightning before we hear the thunder. This is because light travels faster than sound. The light from the lightning comes to our eyes much quicker than the sound from the lightning. So we hear it later than we see it.

The clause we need to obtain for implication in the explanation chain is verb-group-for-moving {*moves, travels, comes*} *faster* → *verb-group-for-moving-result* {*earlier*}. This clause can be easily obtained by web mining, searching for expression '*if noun verb-group-for-moving faster* than *noun verb-group-for-moving-result earlier*'.

How to determine which entities need to be linked by imaginary DTs? It needs to be done for all entities Y in the explanation chain which does not occur in expression "Z *because of* Y, Y *because of* X". If either of these text fragments are missing, they need to be acquired via an imaginary DT. Phrases can be formed as "... *because* ..." or in an analogous way.

Let us consider an explanation of text S as a chain of premises $P_1, ...,P_m$ which imply S. Each P_i contains just a single entity. This can be represented as a sequence of text fragments.

"P_m because of $P_{m=1}$, ..., P_{i+1} because of P_i, P_i because of P_{i-1}, ...,P_{i-2} because of P_{i-1}".

For each missing text fragment in text P_{k+1} *because of* P_k, we need to obtain an imaginary DT for P_{k+1} and P_k. In Fig. 8.7 we show which entity pairs are missing in *[italic]* on the right of the DT.

What would make this DT look like a one for an invalid explanation? If any RR under top-level *Elaboration* turns into *Joint*, it would mean that the explanation chain is interrupted.

We explore argumentation structure example of (Toulmin 1958; Kennedy et al. 2006). We show two visualizations of the discourse tree and the explanation chain (in the middle) in Fig. 8.8.

The phrase *"Harry was born in Bermuda"* is the Datum. The Datum is further **elaborated** on. This is evidence to support the Claim. The Claim (under RR of **condition**) is *"Harry must is a British subject"*. The Warrant is under **attribution**: *"A man born in Bermuda will be a British subject"*. It is not necessary to state the Warrant in a sentence. Usually, one explains the warrant in the following sentences. Other times, the speaker of the sentence assumes the listener already knows the fact that *"all people born in Bermuda are British subjects"*. An author usually will not bother to explain the warrant because it is too obvious. It is usually an assumption or

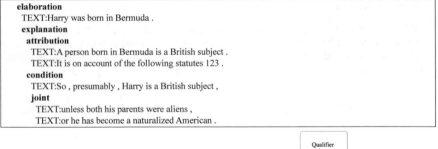

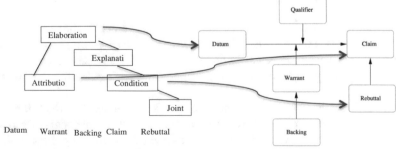

Fig. 8.8 A discourse tree representation (on the top), Toulmin's argument structure (in the bottom-right) and a simplified discourse tree showing only non-terminal nodes with rhetorical relations, as they are mapped into Toulmin's argument structure

a generalization. However, the author must make sure the warrant is clear because the reader must understand the author's assumptions and why the author assumes these opinions. Notice that the argumentation component of Rebuttal occurs in the discourse tree under **condition**. In this particular case, this condition is a disjunction (two possibilities), so they are linked via **joint**.

An interesting application of Toulmin model is the argumentative grammar by Lo Cascio (1991). This paper introduced associative rules for argumentative acts which were naturally applicable to the analysis of discourse structure in the pre-DT times.

8.2.5   *Imaginary Discourse Trees for Linking Entities*

Linking entities are required to build an explanation chain. Let us build an explanation chain between information in texts A and B. Augmenting a discourse tree of an entity e in text A with imaginary DT fragments obtained from a corpus of supporting documents, we derive a canonical discourse representation of A that is independent of a thought structure of an author. This mechanism is critical for linking entities in A with themselves and other entities in B. We need to assure these entities are not only relevant in terms of a topic, but are also suitable in terms of interrelations between these entities in an explanation.

When DTs are used to coordinate entities in different texts, we would want to obtain an "ideal" DT for text A, where all rhetorical relations between involved entities occur (Galitsky 2014). To do that, we need to augment a real DT of A with a certain rhetorical relations which are missing in A instance but can be mined from text corpora or from the web. Hence to verify that text A is good for explaining text B, we first verify that their DTs (*DT-A* and *DT-B*) agree and after that we usually need to augment the *DT-A* with fragments of other DTs to make sure all entities in B are communicated (addressed) in augmented *DT-A*. Hence, instead of relying on an ontology, which would have definitions of entities missing in a candidate answer, we mine for rhetorical relations between these entities online. This procedure allows us to avoid an offline building of bulky and costly ontologies.

The baseline requirement for A to be linked (relevant) to B is that entities (En) of A cover the entities of B: $E\text{-}B \subseteq E\text{-}A$. Naturally, some $E\text{-}A$ are not explicitly mentioned in B but are needed to provide a recipe-type A. The next step is to follow the logical flow of B by A. Since it is hard to establish relations between En, being domain dependent, we try to approximate them by logical flow of B and A, expressible in domain-independent terms $EnDT\text{-}B \sim EnDT\text{-}A$.

However, a common case is that some entities E are not explicitly mentioned in B but instead are assumed. Moreover, some entities in A used to be associated with B do not occur in A but instead more specific or general entities do. How would we know that these more specific entities are indeed addressing issues from B? We need some external, additional source that we call *imaginary EnDT-A* to establish these relationships. This source contains the information on inter-relationships between

En which is omitted in *B* and/or *A* but is assumed to be known by the peer. We intend to obtain this knowledge at the discourse level:

EnDT-B ~ EnDT-A + imaginary EnDT-A.

We start with a simple example:

B: What is an advantage of electric car?

A: No need to for gas.

How can one figure out that *A* is a good association for *B*? We have an abstract general-sense entity *advantage* and a regular noun entity *car*. We need to link explicit entities in *A* {*need, gas*}. Fragments of a possible *imaginary EnDT-A* are shown: [*…No need… –Elaborate –Advantage*] … [*gas –Enablement –engine*] … [*engine –Enablement –car*]. We do not need to know the details how this *Enablement* occurs; we just need an evidence that these rhetorical links exist. We could have used semantic links between entities but for that we would need a domain-specific ontology.

We now present to the second example to demonstrate how imaginary DT component would improve a web search (Fig. 8.9). Currently, search engines show certain keywords they do not identify in a given search result. However, it is possible to indicate how these keywords are relevant to this search result by finding documents where these unidentified keywords are rhetorically connected with the ones occurring in the query for *B*. This feature would naturally improve the linking relevance.

Now we proceed to the third example. Let us explain how a match between a *B* and an *A* is facilitated by DTs (Fig. 8.10).

A: [A faulty brake switch can effect the cruise control.] [If it is,] [there should be a code] [stored in the engine control module.] [Since it is not an emissions fault,] [the check engine light will not illuminate.] [First of all, watch the tachometer] [to

Fig. 8.9 How imaginary DTs would enable Google search to explain missing keywords in the search results. In the default search, *munro* is missing. However, by trying to rhetorically connect *munro* with the entities in the question, the Imaginary DT system finds out that *Munro* is a person who is an inventor of automatic transmission. DT fragment is shown with rhetorical relation Attribution, as well as the Wikipedia source for Imaginary DT

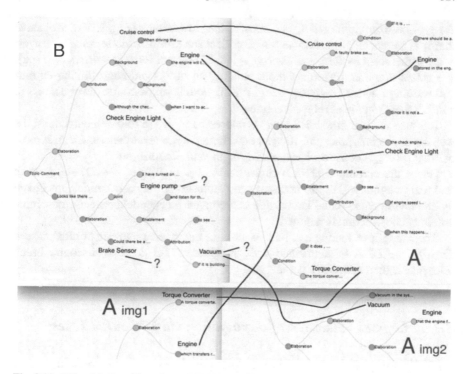

Fig. 8.10 DTs of A, B and imaginary $DT\text{-}A_{img1}$ and $DT\text{-}A_{img2}$

see] [if engine speed increases 200 rpm][when this happens.] [If it does,] [the torque converter is unlocking transmission.]

B: [When driving the cruise control][the engine will turn off] [when I want to accelerate,] [although the check engine light was off.] [I have turned on the ignition] [and listen for the engine pump running] [to see] [if it is building up vacuum.] [Could there be a problem with the brake sensor under the dash?] [Looks like there could be a little play in the plug.]

A explains a situation and also offer some interpretation, as well as recommends a certain course of action. A introduces extra entities which are not in B and needs to involve background knowledge to communicate how they are related to $E\text{-}B$. We do it by setting a correspondence between $E\text{-}B$ and $E\text{-}A$, shown by the horizontal curly (red) arcs.

Notice that some entities E_0 in B are *unaddressed*: they are not mentioned in A. $E_0\text{-}B$ includes {*Engine pump*, *Brake sensor* and *Vacuum*}. It means that either A is not fully relevant to B omitting some of its entities E_0 or it uses some other entities instead. Are $E_0\text{-}B$ ignored in A? To verify the latter possibility, we need to apply some form of background knowledge finding entities E_{img} which are linked to both $E_0\text{-}B$ and $E\text{-}A$.

It is unclear how $En\text{-}A = Torque\ Convertor$ is connected to B. To verify this connection, we obtain a fragment of text from Wikipedia (or another source) about

Torque Convertor, build *DT-A$_{img1}$* (shown on the left-bottom of Fig. 8.10) and observe that it is connected with *Engine* via rhetorical relation of *Elaboration*. Hence we confirm that *En-A = Torque Convertor* is indeed relevant for *B* (*a vertical blue arc*). We obtain this confirmation without building an offline ontology linking entities and learning relations between then: instead, we rely on discourse-level context to confirm that A includes relevant entities.

It is also unclear how *En-B pump* is addressed in *A*. We find a document on the web about *Engine Pump* and *Vacuum* and attempt to connect them to *En-A*. It turns out that *DT-A$_{img2}$* connects *Vacuum* and *Engine* via *Elaboration*.

Hence the combined *DT-A* includes real *DT-A* + *DT-A$_{img1}$* + *DT-A$_{img2}$*. Both real and imaginary DTs are necessary to demonstrate that two entities are linked by employing background knowledge in a domain independent manner: no offline ontology construction is required.

The strength of linking can be measured as the inverse number of unaddressed *En$_0$–B* once *DT-A* is augmented with imaginary *DT-A$_{img}$*. This discourse-based relevance is then added to a default one.

8.2.6 Logical Validation of Explanation via Discourse Trees

Logically, explanation of text S is a chain of premises P_1, ...,P_m which imply S. S is frequently referred to as a subject of explanation. For this chain P_1, ..., P_m each element P_i is implied by its predecessors: P_1, ...$P_{i-1} \Rightarrow P_i$. In terms of a discourse tree, there should be a path in it where these implications are realized via rhetorical relations. We intend to define a mapping between EDUs of a DT and entities P_i occurring in these EDUs which form the explanation chain. In terms of underlying text, P_i are entities or phrases which can be represented as logical atoms or terms.

These implication-focused rhetorical relations *RR* are:

(1) *elaboration*: P_i can be an elaboration of P_{i-1};
(2) *attribution*: P_i can be attributed to P_{i-1};
(3) *cause*: this is a most straightforward case.

Hence $P_i \Rightarrow P_j$ if $RR(\text{EDU}_i, \text{EDU}_j)$ where $P_i \in \text{EDU}_i$ and $P_j \in \text{EDU}_j$. We refer to this condition as "*explainability*" *via Discourse Tree*.

Actual sequence P_1, ...,P_m for S is not known, but for each S we have a set of good explanations P_{g1}, ...,P_{gm} and a set of bad explanations P_{b1}, ...,P_{b2}.

Good explanation sequences obey *explainability via DT* condition and bad do not (Galitsky 2018). Bad explanation sequences might obey *explainability via DT* condition for some P_{bi}. If a DT for a text is such that *explainability via DT* condition does not hold for any P_{bi} then this DT does not include any explanation at all.

The reader can observe that to define a good and a bad explanation via a DT one needs a training set covering all involved entities and phrasing Pi occurring in both positive and negative training sets.

By our definition, imaginary DTs are the ones not obtained from actual text but instead built on demand to augment the actual ones. For a given chain $P_1, ..., P_i', ..., P_m$ let P_i' be the entity which is not explicitly mentioned in a text but instead is assumed to be known to the addressee. This P_i' should occur in other texts in a training dataset. To make the *explainability via DT* condition applicable, we need to augment actual DT_{actual} with imaginary $DT_{imaginary}$ such that $P_i' \in$ EDU of this $DT_{imaginary}$. We denote $DT_{actual} + DT_{imaginary}$ as DT_{hybrid}.

If we have two textual explanations in the positive set of good explanations for the same S, T_1 and T_2:

$T_1: P_1, ..., P_m \Rightarrow S$

$T_2: P_1, P_i', ..., P_m \Rightarrow S$

then we can assume that P_i' should occur in a complete explanation for S and since it does not occur in T_1 then $DT(T_1)$ should be augmented with $DT_{imaginary}$ such that $P_i' \in$ EDU of this $DT_{imaginary}$.

8.2.7 Learning Framework and Evaluation

In this Section, we automate our validation of text convincingness including a description of a training dataset and learning framework.

We conduct our evaluation in two steps. Firstly, we try to distinguish between texts with explanations and without explanation. This task can be accomplished without the involvement of virtual DTs. Secondly, once we confirm that that can be done reasonably well, we drill into more specific tasks of differentiating between good and bad explanation chains within the dataset of the first task.

We form the positive explanation dataset from the following sources:

1. Customer complaints;
2. Paragraphs from physics and biology textbook;
3. Yahoo! Answers for *Why/How-to* questions.

The negative training dataset includes the sources of a totally different nature:

1. Definition/factoid paragraphs from Wikipedia, usually, first paragraphs;
2. First paragraphs of news articles introducing new events;
3. Political news from Functional Text Dimension dataset.

We formed the balanced components of the positive and negative dataset for both tasks: each component includes 240 short texts 5–8 sentences (250–400 words).

We now comment on each source. The purpose of the customer complaint dataset is to collect texts where authors do their best to explain their points across by employing all means to show that they are right and their opponents are wrong. Complaints are emotionally charged texts providing an explanation of problems they encountered with a financial service, how they tried to explain their viewpoint to a company and also a description of how these customers attempted to solve it (Galitsky et al. 2007a; Galitsky and Kuznetsov 2008a, b; GitHub Customer Complaints dataset 2019).

Also, to select types of text with and without explanation, we adopt the genre system and the corpora from (Lee 2001). The genre system is constructed relying on the Functional Text Dimensions. These are genre annotations that reflect judgments as to what extent a text can be interpreted as belonging to a generalized functional category. A genre is a combination of several dimensions. For the positive dataset, we select the genre with the highest density of explanation such as a scientific textbook. For the negative dataset, we focus on the genres which are least likely to contain explanations, such as advertisement, fiction-prose, instruction manuals and political news. The last one is chosen since it has the least likelihood to contain an explanation.

For the positive dataset for the second task, as good explanation chains, we rely on the following sources:

1. Customer complaints with *valid* argumentation patterns;
2. Paragraphs from phisics textbook explaining certain phenomena, which are neither factoid nor definitional;
3. Yahoo! Answers for *Why/How-to* questions.

We form the negative dataset from the following sources:

1. Customer complaints with *invalid* argumentation patterns; these complaints are inconsistent, illogical and rely on emotions to bring their points across;
2. Paragraphs from phisics textbook formulating longer questions and problems;
3. Yahoo! Answers for *Why* (not *How-to*) questions which are reduced to break the explanation flow. Sentences are deleted or re-shuffled to produce an incohesive, non-systematic explanation.

Imaginary DTs can be found by employing background knowledge in a domain-independent manner: no offline ontology construction is required. Documents that were found on the web can be the basis of constructing imaginary DTs following the algorithm described in the Sects. 8.2.2–8.2.4.

Given an actual part of the text A, we outline a top-level search strategy for finding a source for imaginary DTs (background knowledge) K.

---

(1) Build DT for A;
(2) Obtain pairs of entities from A that are not linked in DT (e.g. *thunder, eye*);
(3) Obtain a set of search queries based on provided pairs of entities
(4) For each query:
    (a) Find a short list of candidate text fragments on the web using search engine API (such as Bing) searching K;
    (b) Build DT for the text fragments;
    (c) Select fragments which contain rhetoric relation (*Elaboration, Attribution, Cause*) linking this pair of entities;
    (d) Choose the fragment with the highest relevance score

The *entity* mentioned in the algorithm can be interpreted in a few possible ways. It can be named entity, head of a noun phrase or a keyword extracted from a dataset.

Relevance score can be based on the score provided by the search engine. Another option is computing the score based on structural discourse and syntactic similarity (Galitsky 2017).

Discourse Tree Construction. A number of RST parsers constructing discourse tree of the text are available at the moments. For instance, in our previous studies we used the tool provided by Surdeanu et al. (2015) and Joty and Moschitti (2014).

Nearest Neighbor learning. To predict the label of the text, once the complete DT is built, one needs to compute its similarity with DTs for the positive class and verify that it is lower than similarity to the set of DTs for its negative class (Galitsky 2014). Similarity between CDTs is defined by means of maximal common sub-DTs. Formal definitions of labeled graphs and domination relation on them used for construction of this operation can be found, e.g., in Ganter and Kuznetsov (2001).

SVM Tree Kernel learning. A DT can be represented by a vector of integer counts of each sub-tree type (without taking into account its ancestors). For Elementary Discourse Units (EDUs) as labels for terminal nodes only the phrase structure is retained: we suppose to label the terminal nodes with the sequence of phrase types instead of parse tree fragments. For the evaluation purpose, Tree Kernel builder tool (Moschitti 2006) can be used.

8.2.7.1 Detecting Explanations and Valid Explanation Chains

We start with the first task, detecting paragraphs of text which contain explanation, and estimate the detection rate in Table 8.1. We apply two different learning techniques, nearest neighbor (in the middle, greyed) and SVM TK, applied to the same discourse-level and syntactic data. We evaluate the recognition into positive and negative classes of the same nature (complaints, physics, Yahoo! Answers) first and then the hybrid positive set versus the hybrid negative set.

The highest recognition accuracy, reaching 80%, is achieved for the first pair of the dataset components, complaints versus wikipedia factoids, most distinct 'intense' explanation versus enumeration of facts, with least explanations. The other datasets deliver 2–3% drop in recognition performance. These accuracies are comparable with various tasks in genre classification (one-against-all setting in Galitsky and Shpitsberg 2016).

Table 8.1 Explanation detection rate

Source	P_{KNN}	R_{KNN}	$F1_{KNN}$	P_{SVM}	R_{SVM}	$F1_{SVM}$
1^+ versus 1^-	77.3	80.8	79.0	80.9	82.0	81.4
2^+ versus 2^-	78.6	76.4	77.5	74.6	74.8	74.7
3^+ versus 3^-	75.0	77.6	76.3	76.6	77.1	76.8
$1..3^+$ versus $1..3^-$	76.8	78.9	77.8	74.9	75.4	75.1

Table 8.2 Recognizing good and bad explanation chains

Source	P-virtual	R-virtual	F1-virtual	P	R	F1
1^+ versus 1^-	64.3	60.8	62.5	72.9	74.0	73.4
2^+ versus 2^-	68.2	65.9	67.0	74.6	74.8	74.7
3^+ versus 3^-	63.7	67.4	65.5	76.6	77.1	76.8
$1..3^+$ versus $1..3^-$	66.4	64.6	65.5	74.9	75.4	75.1

Table 8.2 shows the results of differentiation between good and bad explanation. The accuracy is about 12% lower than for the first task, since the difference between the good and bad explanation in text is fairly subtle. As an ablation study, we removed the imaginary DT component that leads to 10% loss of F1 (the second to fouth column).

The achieved accuracy of explanation chain validation is not that high, in mid-70%. However, validation of explanation chain is an important task in a decision support. A low accuracy can still be leveraged by processing a large number of documents and detecting a birst in problematic explanation in a corpus of documents or emails.

8.3   A Bi-Directional Explainability for Decision Support

In the previous sections, a human user was receiving a decision with an explanation, and an ML system was producing this decision with an explanation. In this section, we consider a bi-directional explanation case: both sides, the human user who is now a domain expert, and the ML produce decisions with explanations and exchange them in the course of a negotiation process to come to the final mutually agreed decision.

This is an active learning framework for a decision support since each agent selects his own training set to rely on for making his decision and forming his explanation. A user expert presents her decision first in an explicit manner. Our framework allows the ML to leverage the explainable decision presented by the human expert and then to produce an explainable decision comparable with the one provided by the human expert. This type of active learning framework is expected to improve the quality of the resultant, hybrid decision and constantly maintain a solid level of decision-making skills of the human user.

As the usability of ML in a broad range of domains grows, some implications of these advances for the skills of human decision makers are causing concerns. As human experts increasingly rely on ML and automation systems, their sense of responsibility for decisions and outcomes is decreasing. In spite of the high success of the existing decision support systems (DSS) (Newman et al. 2000; Hartono et al. 2007; Galitsky et al. 2009), their expert users rely on them more and more, obtain and use a DSS result and become detached from a decision process itself. As a demand for human expertise diminishes, the skill set of human experts might be reduced as well. It can affect situations where human experts intervene and do not make correct decisions. In such a domain as aviation, it is well known that auto-pilots reduce the skill set of human pilots flying in different conditions, which has led to accidents.

Current ML and DSS techniques for addressing these issues focus on improving the explainability of decisions generated by ML algorithms and by requiring that humans confirm or approve such decisions (Goodman and Flaxman 2017; Gilpin et al. 2018). These measures are indeed very helpful, but explainability remains challenging, particularly for complex ML models, on one hand, and maintains the human experts in passive mode, on the other hand. As a result, human experts exercise less in their decision making, and their skills might deteriorate. Additionally, the better ML systems become, the more likely the users will stop putting much effort into analyzing or critically evaluating their decisions, especially if ML-produced explanations are convincing.

The issue here is a lack of responsibility of these expert users for the final decision, as well as the accuracy of future decisions (Goldberg et al. 2008). It is well known that a drop in accuracy of a DSS system is caused by domain evolution, where the training occurred on the original, old data and the current, new data may significantly deviate. The rate of this domain evolution, concept drift (Krawczyk et al. 2017), can be much higher than the self re-training capabilities of the DSS. Hence it is fairly important that this DSS produces an adequate explanation of its decision so that the human expert can assess this decision with respect to recent data (Shklovsky-Kordi et al. 2005b).

In this section, we build a decision-support meta-agent that controls the interaction between the human expert-agent and ML-agent in the course of their mutual decision-making. One task of this meta-agent is to mitigate the potential loss of expertise of a human agent and restore a fuller sense of responsibility to her. The DSS requires the user to first make an unassisted decision and provide this as an input to the ML before the ML generates its own automated decision. The DSS is trying to find weaknesses in the decision of the user, which may be, in particular, a result of the user's "cognitive bias" (Plous 1993). If the user's decision continues to differ from the decision of the ML, the DSS helps the user identify the reasons for it. Figure 8.11 shows the schematic diagram of the DSS.

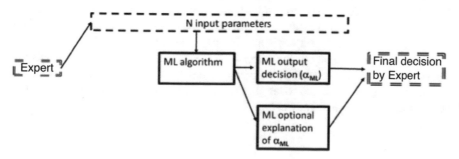

Fig. 8.11   Traditional interaction between the expert user and ML

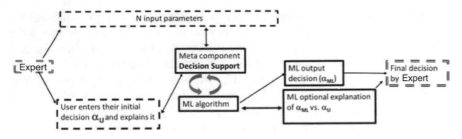

Fig. 8.12 Proposed interaction between an expert and ML

In the traditional ML setting, a user specifies a set of input parameters. The ML algorithms use a training set of "similar" inputs to derive its decision. The user does not know that a slight change in any of these inputs could result in a different decision.

On the contrary, when using the DSS, the expert user is given an ML decision along with its explanation (Fig. 8.12). The DSS finds the values of input parameters that might force the human expert to revise her original decision. Informing the expert user by the DSS about these critical values is important as it alerts the user to pay more attention to these parameters.

We focus on interactions between an ML and a human expert, mediated by DSS. A DSS session starts with a human expert's delivery of her decision to the DSS, given a set $m \ll N$ of features this human expert relied her decision upon. Then the ML would have to explain disagreement of its own decision with the human experts' prior decision, presenting the set d of employed features.

There are two reasons decision agents including human experts and machines make mistakes:

(1)   A recognition model;
(2)   A distortion of parameter values due to measurement errors and cognitive bias (Galitsky and Shpitsberg 2016).

In most cases, on top of that, humans are subject to errors associated with their sentiments.

Both machines and humans learn and generalize from data and both make errors. Goldberg et al. (2007) has been investigating this in a medical decision support domain. However, unlike machines, humans possess ontologies and are capable of applying them to assess their decisions. Humans usually learn from a smaller set of examples but the accuracy of their decisions is achieved by applying ontologies on top of generalizations. Even when a machine has an ontology, we assume that it is limited in scope and cannot cover all cases. For humans, all cases are covered by some kind of ontological knowledge.

As an example, we use a case of visual recognition of images of dogs and wolves. Generalizing from available data, machines build a model where if there is snow in the background, it is a wolf. Although this turns out to cover the training set well, the human ontology hints that this generalization is prone to errors since dog images can have snow in background as well.

The DSS does not have its own model of a phenomenon; instead, it controls the information exchange between the ML and human expert in the form of a decision and its explanation as a set of parameters and their values.

8.3.1 Example of a Decision Support Session

We present a classification problem for three animals: a wolf, a greyhound and a coyote, relying on the following parameters: animal length, skin color, height, speed, tail length and tail direction (Table 8.3).

Imagine a Zoo CRM environment where a human visitor saw an animal at a distance and wants to know whether it is a wolf, a greyhound or a coyote. Image recognition algorithms are unlikely to be helpful for Zoo CRM in this case since dogs, wolves and coyotes are similar, especially when seen from far away in a cage. Imagine the user can enter key features such as size, fur color, etc into the CRM DSS and iteratively converge to a solution. In total, there are 6 features describing the animal (length, color, height, speed, tail length and tail direction. In our example, 4 features (length, color, speed and tail length) are numerical and the other 2 features (color and tail direction) are categorical.

Human agent and DSS have different models of a phenomenon such as an animal. They cannot exchange model parameters but instead they can encourage each other to pay attention to particular parameters they think are important for recognition.

As a start, given some input values, the user makes an initial decision that the animal is a wolf. Let us assume that this decision was based on *length, color, height, tail direction* and that these features are most important for our expert. The DSS

Table 8.3 Classification features

	Wolf	Coyote	Greyhound
Length, sm	100–160	75–100	100–120
Height, sm	80–85	45–55	68–76
Color	Gray	Light gray	Any
Speed, km/h	Up to 60	Up to 70	70
Tail length, sm	Long	Average	Long
Tail direction	Down	Down	Not down

might agree with such a decision. However, a small change in these parameters (at the level of measurement errors) could cause the ML system to change its decision.

The DSS would then look for the most critical parameters that determine such a change. In our example, these parameters could be *speed* or *tail direction*. The DSS would then ask the user how reliable these parameters are. As long as the user and ML decisions are different, the DSS would be tracking the difference and encourage both party to come to an agreement backed up by the value-by-value explanations. Each party may agree or disagree with such an explanation and make its final decision.

We now present this session more precisely on a step-by-step basis:

Step 1. A human expert takes a sample and attempts to solve a problem. Let us imagine the following parameters as identified by her:
Length = 115 sm with the range of possible errors [100 – 130]
Color = '*light grey*' with the range [*white … grey*]
Height = 70 sm with the range [55 – 85]
Speed = 40 km/h with the range [35 – 45]
Tail.length = *long* with the range [*average*]
Tail.direction = *down* with range [*straight*]

Step 2. Expert decides that it is a wolf, since
Length = 115
Color = *light grey*
Height = 70 sm
Tail.direction = *down*

Step 3.
Selected features are Length, Color, Height, Tail.direction

Step 4. DSS: If turn length = 115sm into 100sm and height = 70sm into 55 ⇒ *coyote*
If Tail.direction = *straight* ⇒*dog*
If without correction ⇒ *wolf*
DSS is asking human about the tail:
Tail.direction = *straight* and Tail.length = *average*, nevertheless ⇒ wolf.
Now the new set of feature values:
Tail.length = *average* with the range [*short…long*]
Tail.direction = *straight* with range [*down…up*]

Step 5. DSS ⇒ *dog* since (Step 6)
Tail.direction = *straight*
Speed = 40 km/Ec

(Explanation only for *dog* vs. *wolf*)
Expert: <u>what if</u> Tail.direction = down?
DSS: <u>still *dog*</u> since can only be *wolf*, not *coyote*
Speed = 40 km/h
Tail.length = *average*
Expert: What if both Tail.direction = *down* and speed = 35 km/h?
DSS: then it becomes *wolf*
Expert: What if Tail.direction = *down* and tail.length = *long*?
DSS: *wolf*

Step 7. Now the human expert can do the final judgment.

Table 8.4 Symptoms of *cold, flu and allergy*

Symptoms	Cold	Flu	Airborne Allergy
Fever	Rare	Usual, high (100–102 °F), sometimes higher, especially in young children); lasts 3–4 days	Never
Headache	Uncommon	Common	Uncommon
General Aches, Pains	Slight	Usual; often severe	Never
Fatigue, Weakness	Sometimes	Usual, can last up to 3 weeks	Sometimes
Extreme Exhaustion	Never	Usual, at the beginning of the illness	Never
Stuffy, Runny Nose	Common	Sometimes	Common
Sneezing	Usual	Sometimes	Usual

8.3.2 An Example in a Medical Domain

We now consider a special case of CRM in a health domain. A physician ("expert user") needs to make a diagnosis for a patient and has to differentiate between *cold, flu and allergy* (Table 8.4).

Let us assume that this physician describes patient symptoms to the ML, provides his preliminary diagnosis as *flu* and notes that this decision was made based on "*high* temperature of 38.1 °C", "a *strong* headache" and "a *strong* chest discomfort". The DSS asks to confirm "*strong chest discomfort*" and additional symptoms of "*stuffy*" and "*sore*" throat. Now imagine the physician revises the symptom from "*strong* chest discomfort" to "*mild* chest discomfort" and leaves the other two symptoms, "stuffy and sore throat" unchanged, and does not change the initial diagnosis. The DSS outputs the decision *cold* and reports that for the diagnosis "flu" it lacks "higher temperature like 38.5". The physician now decides that such the revision is insignificant and maintains the initial diagnosis, or accepts this argument and changes the diagnosis to "cold".

8.3.3 Computing Decisions with Explanations

Let $x = (x_1, x_2, \ldots, x_n)$ be a vector of the n input parameters to the algorithm. x_i can be continuous (numerical) or categorical (Boolean) variable. Let X be a set of x. Let $v = (v_1, \ldots, v_n)$ be the particular input values entered by the user. Let us represent the example from the previous section as v = (*temperature(38.1), headache(strong), stuffy_nose(strong), sore_throat("moderate"), chest discomfort("strong")*).

Let $D = \{\alpha_j\}, j = 1, \ldots, k$ be the set of k possible decisions or output classes.

Let $\alpha_U \in D$ be the initial unassisted decision of the user.

Additionally, we allow the user to mark a subset of input parameters $(v_1, \ldots, v_m)$ $m \leq n$ as being particularly important to their decision α_U

We define the decision function f which maps an input vector $\mathbf{v}$ and a class $\alpha \in D$ to confidence $c \in [0, 1]$:

$f(\alpha, \mathbf{x}): \alpha, \mathbf{x} \to [0, 1]$.

Let α_{ml} be the algorithm decision based on the user-provided input values v.

$f(\alpha_{ml}, \mathbf{v}) = \max(f(\alpha, \mathbf{x}))$ for all $\alpha \in D$.

For any parameter of x, its value x_i may have bias or error. Therefore, we define $\Omega(x_i)$ such that $\Omega(x_i) > (\Omega(x_i)^-$ and $\Omega(x_i) < \Omega(x_i)^+$ as the set of values which are considered within the error bounds for x_i. The bias includes the uncertainty of an object and uncertainty of the assessor. When there is an uncertainty in assessing a feature, we have the phenomena of "confirmation bias" and "selective perception" (Plous 1993; Lee et al. 2013).

We introduce a feature normalization x_i^{new} for each i-th dimension, set based on the following four thresholds: $a_{0i}, a_{1i}, a_{2i}, a_{3i}, a_{4i}$ (Shklovsky-Kordi et al. 2005a):

$x_i < a_{0i}$: strong_deviation: $x_i^{new} = 0 + x_i/a_{0i}$

$a_{1i} < x_i < a_{2i}$: abnormal: $x_i^{new} = 1 + (x_i - a_{1i})/(a_{2i} - a_{1i})$

$a_{2i} < x_i < a_{3i}$: normal: $x_i^{new} = 2 + (x_i - a_{2j})/(a_{3i} - a_{2i})$

$a_{3i} < x_i < a_{4i}$: abnormal: $x_i^{new} = 3 + (x_i - a_{3j})/(a_{4i} - a_{3i})$

$a_{4i} < x_i$: strong_deviation: $x_i^{new} = 3 + x_i/(a_{4ii})$

Thus, normalized parameters will belong to five intervals: $[0, 1], [1, 2], [2, 3], [3, 4], [4, \infty]$.

Based on this definition, we compute $X \to X^{new}$ and $X^{new} \to X$. Now we define the similarity between the object x and y as a vector distance $\|x - y\|$.

A division of the measured value by the accepted average value accomplishes the normalization. The calculation is executed separately for *normal, abnormal* and *strong_deviation* values. To define a range of sub-normal values, a team of experts empirically establishes the score of acceptable parameters. They are determined for certain combination of features and certain objects. If a parameter stays within the defined abnormal or normal range, no special action is required. The *strong_deviation* range covers the whole area of possible values beyond the abnormal values.

For example, in medicine, the standard scale for *fever* is as follows: if the body temperature is less than 35.0 °C, then it is a strong deviation. If it is in the range 35.0–36.0 °C, then it is considered abnormal. If it is in the range 36.10–37.5, then it is normal. If the range is 37.6–38.3, then it is abnormal, and if it is greater than 38.30, then it is a strong deviation. However, the norm for a flue is 38.1–39.0, the norm for a cold is 37.6–38.3, the norm for allergy is 36.1–37.5 and any higher fever is a strong deviation.

The normalization can be defined for categorical parameters also. For example, for *allergy* any *general aches, pain* >2 and only *No General Aches, Pains* is *normal* or 2. We expect that, when implementing a DSS based on this approach, the thresholds are provided by domain experts using empirically established knowledge of what values of the input parameters are normal or abnormal for a given decision class α.

Based on this definition, we can define a mapping between the input parameters X and the normalized parameters:

$X^{norm}: X \rightarrow X^{norm}$ and $X^{norm} \rightarrow X$. Using this normalization we substitute $[x_1, ..., x_n]$ for $[x_1^{norm}, ..., x_1^{norm}]$. Now we can define the distance between strings x and y in a standard way as $\|x - y\| = \sqrt{(x_1 - y_1)^2 + \cdots + (x_n - y_n)^2}$.

8.3.4 An Overall Step-by-Step DS

Here is the user interaction flow (Fig. 8.13):

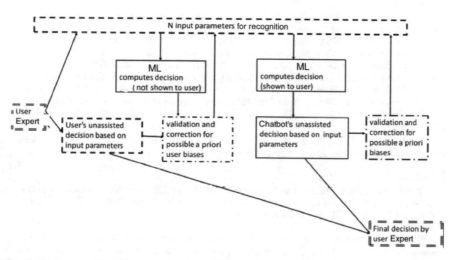

Fig. 8.13 An overall architecture of a bi-directional explanation DSS

Step 1:
Expert user input : $v = [v_1, ..., v_n] \in X$.

Step 2:
Initial unassisted decision α_U of the user. For example, *flu.*

Step 3:
Expert user indicates m out of n input values as being particularly important to his decision α_U $[v_{1,...} v_m]$ $m << n$
For example, *(Fever =38.1 , strong Headache, strong Chest Discomfort).*

Step 4:
Now DSS verified the decisions of user α_U without sharing α_{ml}.
In order to determine how stable α_U is relatively to perturbations of v within error bounds Ω, we compute α_{ml} by means of *Stability Assessment* Algorithm.
If α_{ml} does not match α_U , go to Step 5.
If α_{ml} matches α_U, then α_U is selected as a preliminary solution, and we proceed to Step 6.
Example: if we have *(Fever =38.1 , strong Headache, strong Chest Discomfort Fever, strong Stuffy, moderate Sore Throat 38.1)*, as user noted, $\alpha_{ML} = flu$, but if we have *(moderate Headache, moderate Chest Discomfort, strong Stuffy, strong Sore Throat)* as obtain from $\Omega(v)$ $\alpha_{ml} = cold$).

Step 5:
Since $\alpha_U \neq \alpha_{ml}$, we iteratively work with the user to see if we can converge on a stable decision. We apply *Discovering Abnormal Parameters* Algorithm.
We could, at this point, just show α_{ml} to the user, but we avoid doing this in order to prevent the user from unthinkingly changing their decision to α_{ml}. Instead, we use a more nuanced, indirect approach where we try to find the parameter whose value v_i from the ones indicated by the user to be in the set proving α_U. v_i is such that its possible deviation affects α_U in the highest degree.
After finding this parameter, we report to the user that the value she provided for this parameter is to some degree inconsistent with α_U. We then give the user the option to change their initial α_U.
If the user maintains the same decision α_U, α_U is set as a preliminary decision and we proceed to Step 6.
If user changes their decision, go to Step 2 (unless this point is reached a third time, in which case go to Step 6 to avoid an overly long interaction loop).

Step 6:
Compute decision α_{ml} based on unchanged input values $f(\alpha_{ml}, v)$. α_{ml} is set as a decision of DSS and is shown to the human expert along with the set of key features which has yielded α_{ml} instead of α_U. Explainability of DSS algorithm is in use here.
Step 7:
The human expert can modify v and observe respective decisions of DSS. DSS can in turn change its decision, and provide an updated explanation. Once the human expert obtained DSS decision for all cases of interest, she obtains the final decision.
Hence in the 3rd step, the human expert explains her decision, and in the 6th step the ML explains its decision. In the 5th step, DSS assesses the stability of human experts' decision with respect to selected features. In the 7th step, the human expert does the same with DSS decisions. So the 6th step is inverse to the 3rd and the 7th is inverse to the 5th.

For a DSS to handle explainable decision support, explanation format should be simple and have a natural representation, as well as match the intuition of a human expert. Also, it should be easy to assess DSS explanation stability with respect to deviation of decision features. It is worth mentioning that the available methods such as (Baehrens et al. 2010) where DSS is a black box, similar to the current setting, do not obey all of these requirements.

We show the overall architecture of bi-directional explainable DSS in Fig. 8.13.

8.3.5 Three Bi-Directional DSS Algorithms

8.3.5.1 Algorithm for Step 4: Stability Assessment

In this step, the DSS checks whether α_{ml} is stable when the input parameters are perturbed within the error bounds $[\Omega^{\text{lower}}(v_i); \Omega^{\text{upper}}(v_i)]$. If, when entering the input values, the user also markes a subset of input parameters $(v_1, \ldots, v_m)$ as particularly important to his decision α_U, then the DSS only adds noise to this subset. This is because, given the user expert's focus on these parameters, they are the ones more likely to contain user bias.

Let us consider a n-dimensional space $\Omega(v_1), \ldots, \Omega(v_m), v_{m+1}, \ldots, v_n$. In the dimensions 1 to m it is a parallelepiped, and in dimension $m+1 \ldots n$ it is a plane.

Let $\Omega(\mathbf{v})$ be a set of points where for each dimension $\Omega(v_i)^- < \Omega(v_i) < \Omega(v_i)^+$ for $I < m + 1$ and v_i for $I > m$.

Let α be the decision of DSS where $f(\alpha, \mathbf{x}) - f(\alpha_U, \mathbf{x}) > 0$ with $\mathbf{x} \in \Omega(\mathbf{v})$ and $\alpha \in D$. Out of these pairs, let us select the pair $(\alpha_{ml}, \mathbf{y})$ which relies on a minimum number of *important* dimensions $1 \ldots m$.

In our example, the precise specification of initial parameters gives the same result by the expert and by the ML. However, in the vicinity of these parameters, it is possible to find both *cold* and *allergy* diagnoses. For the *cold* diagnosis, it may be enough to just *lower temperature* or *not severe headache* or *strong chest discomfort*, whereas for *allergy* we would need changes in at least 5 parameters. Therefore, the ML diagnosis α_{ml} is chosen to be *cold*.

8.3.5.2 Algorithm for Steps 5: Discovering Abnormal Parameters and Deviations in Parameters for α_U

The DSS asks the expert to reconsider the input values of the input parameters for which v' deviates from v. The expert user may then realize that these input values imply a different α_U and change her initial α_U to a different α_U'. Alternatively, if the input values have a subjective component or contain errors or bias, the user may adjust the input values. In either case, if changes are made, the DSS goes back to Step 4 with the new values but does this no more than 3 times to avoid endless iteration.

Let us imagine an expert is presented with a "suspicious" parameter for α_U to support her/his decision.

From the explanation of an expert we obtain point at which we have the minimum $\min f(\alpha_U, [v'_j]), j = 1, \ldots, m, v'_i \in \Omega(v_i)$.

And the most important parameter for α_{ML}, $\Omega(\mathbf{v})$, we have the maximum $\max f(\alpha_U, [v'_j]), j = 1, \ldots, n, v'_i \in \Omega(v_i)$.

If $\alpha_U = \alpha_{ML}$ at point v, but $\alpha_U \neq \alpha_{ML}$ in $\Omega(v)$ then we would like to indicate more important parameters whose change would lead to decision α_{ML}. To that end, we need to look for the direction where the distance from v to α_{ML} is minimal (Fig. 8.14).

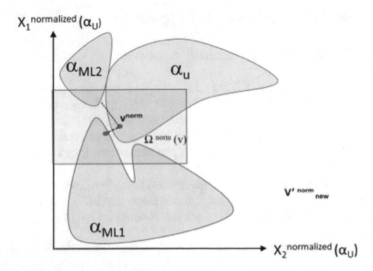

Fig. 8.14 DSS is finding a closer point in the normalized n-dimensional space from $v^{normalized}$ in the area where α_U turns into α_{ML}

In this case, there is no need to get an explanation from an expert for decision α_U. However, our task in the 5th step of the algorithm also consists of mainatining a conflict between the choice of an expert and the ML. Our experiments show that this usually creates the prerequisites for the expert user to make the optimal decision. Therefore, the choice of a clarifying question as shown above, taking into account the expert's explanation of his decision, is a preferred way.

The user expert is then suggested to consult parameter i delivering maximum value $(y_i^{new} - v_i^{new})$, $I = 1, \ldots, m$, y_i – i-th dimension of vector y, when feature normalization procedure is fixed. If human decision deviates from the DSS decision in initial data, meta-agent needs to focus on a single parameter value from $\{v_1, \ldots, v_n,\}$ that would direct the human expert toward the DSS decision. This is how to find this parameter.

What is the *worst* feature dimension for a human decision? To find it, we first identify the best feature value (we call it *typical*) for α_U for all i:

$v_i^{typ}(\alpha_U) = \max_j f(\alpha_U, [v_1, \ldots, v_{i-1}, x_j, v_{i+1}, \ldots, v_n])$ over all values x_j of i-th dimension. For example, $x_1 =$ "white", $x_2 =$ "light grey",

$x_3 =$ "grey", $x_4 =$ "dark grey", $x_5 =$ "black", $j = 1, \ldots, 5$.

$v_i^{typ}(\alpha_U)$: color = "grey" when $\alpha_U =$ "wolf".

We do it for all dimensions i.

Now we proceed to the dimension i that is best for the DSS decision

$\max_i (f(\alpha_{ml}, [v_1, \ldots, v_{i-1}, v_i, v_{i+1}, \ldots, v_n]) - f(\alpha_{ml}, [v_1, \ldots, v_{i-1}, v_i^{typ}(\alpha_U), v_{i+1}, \ldots, v_n])$

Here, the feature could be as follows

v_i: color = "light grey", $v_i^{typ}(\alpha_U)$: color = "grey" when $\alpha_U =$ "wolf".

8.3.5.3 Algorithm for Step 6: Explainability of ML

This algorithm attempts to explain the DSS decision for human expert in the same way as has been done by the human expert. The DSS delivers most important features for its decision.

If at this point the user's decision still differs from the ML's decision, the DSS attempts to explain the difference between the ML decision α_{ml} and the user decision α_U in a way that is intuitive for a human user rather than a way that is based on the ML's internal representation. To do that, the DSS determines what input parameters were most important for the ML's decision. This can be done by finding the input vector z which is closest to the expert's input values v and which leads the ML to change its decision from α_{ml} to α_U. A crucial part of this step is that the distance between points v and z' is computed in normalized parameter space ($X^{norm}(\alpha_{ML})$). The DSS can use a grid search in normalized parameter space to find points on the boundary between α_{ML} and α_U (Fig. 8.15). Once z is found, the parameters that have the largest one-dimensional distance between z' and v are taken as the parameters that are most important for explaining the difference between α_{ml} and α_U.

Let us use a random generator with v^{new} as average value and $(1, \ldots, 1)$-vector as standard deviation to select in X^{new}, where

$$-\varepsilon < f(\alpha_{ml}, x) - f(\alpha_U, x) < 0$$

Then we take a point z delivering the minimum $\| z^{new} - v^{new} \|$. Then in the cube, we randomly select a point z' around z in where $-\varepsilon < f(\alpha_{ml}, x) - f(\alpha_U, x) < 0$ such that z' gives us a minimum of $\| z'^{new} - v^{new} \|$. We iteratively set $z = z'$ and do the above iteratively till the distance $\| z'^{new} - v^{new} \|$ stops decreasing.

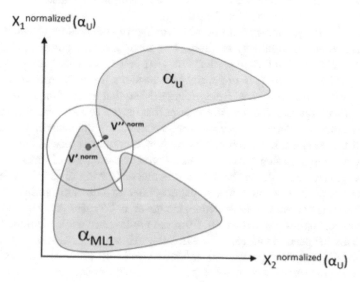

Fig. 8.15 DSS is finding a closer point in a normalized

The feature i which do not belong to $\Omega(z'_i)$ are important for decision making of DSS to obtain the decision α_{ml} that different from α_U. Most important features i are those where $(z_i{}^{new} - v_i{}^{new}) >= 1$.

As shown, the normalization "normal versus abnormal" is performed according to the opinion of an expert. If we have a few points v''^{norm} where the ML decision coincides with the expert's and is equally close to our point v''^{norm}, then from these points we choose the closest point under normalization. It is possible that during the search for such minimal points, the decision of an expert coincides with the ML decision but the point itself may not exist. We assume that an expert can specify conditions for the search to avoid such a situation.

8.3.6 Evaluation with Human Experts

We experiment with how humans revise their decisions when they encounter the one produced by a machine. Participants (college students) were asked to make judgments in the area in which they had some relevant knowledge. Specifically, they were presented with tens of fragments of songs of popular music groups and were asked to identify the group associated with that song (from a set of four options, each representing a different music group). After participants made their decision ("initial choice"), they were presented with the machine's decision about the same song ("machine choice"). They were told that the machine is not always accurate but were not given any specific information about the machine's accuracy. After being presented with the machine choice, participants were asked to make a final decision from the same set of options ("final choice").

Prior to the study, a survey was conducted to identify music groups with which the college students were relatively familiar. Four music groups identified in the survey as most popular and familiar to participants were selected for the present chapter.

Each participant took part in several test sessions. In each session, they were presented with 10–12 test items (song fragments) so that none of the items included the same song fragment. The key difference across the test sessions was the base accuracy of the machine choice, which was predetermined by the authors. For example, in one of the sessions, the machine was making a correct choice in 75% of items, whereas in another session it was making a correct choice 90% of times.

Frequently, there is a doubt about the correctness of the initial decisions versus the final decision of the test. As a rule, an expert either abandons his initial decision or makes the same decision as the machine. However, in 76 cases (2.82% of all cases), the final expert opinion was different from the preliminary choice and the machine choice. This happened in 45 (6.64%) when the ML was wrong, and in 31 (1.54%) when the ML was right ($p < 0.0001$). Moreover, in 40 (88.9%) cases out of 45, when the machine was not right, the expert indicated the correct solution ($p < 0.0001$ compared to 50% of random assumptions). Even the doubts about the correctness of the initial decision had a positive impact on the final decision of the examination.

The question was as follows: "Is it possible that your final decision was different from your initial decision and the decision of the machine? (check all that apply)". A survey of 67 students produced the following results:

(1) This never happened: (40.3%);
(2) I was not sure of my initial decision and did not agree with the machine solution, so I chose the third option (59.7%);
(3) Random selection of remaining opportunities (10.8%);
(4) I thought about the most likely solution and chose the third option without a machine solution (43.2%);
(5) I tried to understand why the computer chose such a solution, and based on this, I chose the third option (57.1%);
(6) 2 students did not indicate reasons (1)–(3) and some of the 38 others used more than one reason.

8.3.7 Discussion of Bi-Directional Explainability

There are a number of benefits and opportunities associated with the proposed bi-directional DSS architecture. Requiring the user expert to first form her own decision serves to counteract the loss of user experts' knowledge and sense of responsibility that often occurs when users delegate decisions to an ML. It prevents the user experts from being complacent and motivates them to give more thoughts to their initial decision. The bi-directional decision support provides a continued possibility for user experts to revisit and refresh their domain knowledge. When the user and the algorithm do not agree, DSS forces the user to reconsider their decision in light of the parameters highlighted by the algorithm. As a result, it makes more likely that the user will critically evaluate the machine's decision. In applications domains where the algorithm is more accurate than human experts, this even allows the human users to challenge themselves to anticipate the ML decision—either on their own, or explicitly, by adding game-playing elements to the DSS interaction (Galitsky and Parnis 2017).

Explaining an ML classifier's decision in general while treating the classifier as a black box has been proposed before, for example. However, the fundamental point in the current approach is that instead of answering broad, abstract questions like: "Why is α_{ml}?" an expert asks more specific questions: "Why is α_{ml} and not α_U?" In medicine, this approach is called "Differential Diagnostics".

Since our question is addressed to a machine, its formulation can be more detailed: "Which minimal changes are needed for the inputs to change the machine decision from a to b? The ML's reply to this question would not only give the standard answer "I understand *why* and I agree or disagree with the machine decision" but also suggest a correction in inputs. If changes in inputs are sufficient to change decisions and are within the measurement errors then the ML decision agrees with that of an expert. To adequately explain the machine decision, we need an adequate concept of minimal changes. Therefore, all computations are done in normed spaces. Furthermore, the overall data analysis is done in normed spaces as well. As shown, this "normal-abnormal" normalization is made from the point of view of the solutions chosen by an expert.

8.4 ML Transparency and Explainability for Customers' Retention

Accuracy Versus Explainability

Machine learning (ML) has been successfully applied to a wide variety of fields ranging from information retrieval, data mining, and speech recognition, to computer graphics, visualization, and human-computer interaction. However, most users often treat an ML model as a black box because of its incomprehensible functions and unclear working mechanism (Liu et al. 2017). Without a clear understanding of how and why a model works, the development of high-performance models typically relies on a time-consuming trial-and-error process. As a result, academic and industrial ML scientists are facing challenges that demand more transparent and explainable systems for better understanding and analyzing ML models, especially their inner working mechanisms (Tsiakmaki et al. 2020).

The question of whether accuracy or explainability prevails in an industrial machine learning systems is fairly important. The best classification accuracy is typically achieved by black-box ML models such as Support Vector Machine, neural networks or random forests, or complicated ensembles of all of these. These systems are referred to as black boxes and their drawbacks are frequently cited since their inner workings are really hard to understand. They do not usually provide a clear explanation of the reasons they made a certain decision or prediction; instead, they just output a probability associated with a prediction. The major problem here is that these methods typically require extensive training sets.

On the other hand, ML methods whose predictions are easy to understand and interpret frequently have a limited predictive capacity (inductive inference, linear regression, a single decision tree) or are inflexible and computationally cumbersome, such as explicit graphical models. These methods usually require less data to train from.

Our claim in this chapter for industrial applications of ML is as follows. Whereas companies need to increase an overall performance for the totality of users, individual users mostly prefer explainability (Galitsky 2018, Fig. 8.16). Users can tolerate wrong decisions made by the companies' ML systems as long as they understand why these decisions were made. Customers understand that any system is prone to errors, and they can be positively or negatively impressed by how a company rectifies these errors. In case an error is made without an explanation, and could not be fixed reasonably well and communicated properly, customers frequently want to leave the business.

We will back up this observation, automatically analyzing customer complaints. To do that, we develop a machinery to automatically classify customer complaints

Fig. 8.16 Customers request an explanation and react to it

with respect to whether explanation was demanded or not. This is a nontrivial problem since complaint authors do not always explicitly write about their intent to request explanation. We then compare the numbers of customers complaining about problems associated with products and services and estimate the proportion of those complaints, which require explanations.

8.4.1 Use Cases for the ML System Lacking Explainability

Although ML is actively deployed and used in industry, user satisfaction is still not very high in most domains. We will present three use cases where explainability and interpretability of machine learning decisions is lacking and users experience dissatisfaction with certain cases.

A customer of financial services are appalled when they travel and their credit cards are canceled without an obvious reason (Fig. 8.17). The customer explains what had happened in detail and his Facebook friends strongly support his case again the bank. Not only the bank made an error in its decision, according to what the friends write, but also it is unable to rectify it and communicate it properly.

If this bank used a decision-making system with explainability, there would be a given cause of its decision. Once it is established that this cause does not hold, the bank is expected to be capable of reverting its decision efficiently and retaining the customer.

An example of a popular machine learning system is shown in Fig. 8.18, on the left. The system translates the term *coil spring* (in Russian) into *spring spring*. This example shows a problem in the simplest case of translation where the meaning of two words needs to be combined. A simple meta-reasoning system, a basic grammar checking component or an entity lookup would prevent this translation error under

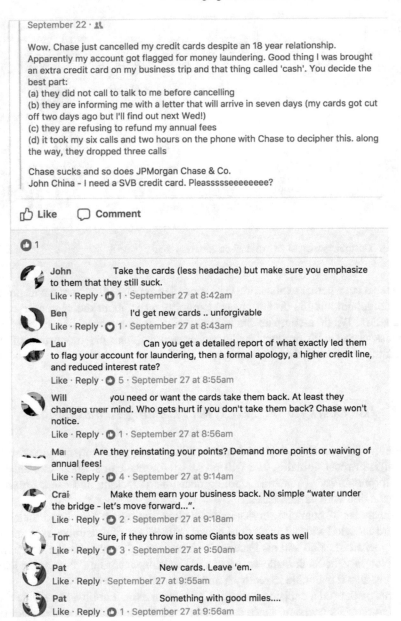

September 22 ·

Wow. Chase just cancelled my credit cards despite an 18 year relationship.
Apparently my account got flagged for money laundering. Good thing I was brought
an extra credit card on my business trip and that thing called 'cash'. You decide the
best part:
(a) they did not call to talk to me before cancelling
(b) they are informing me with a letter that will arrive in seven days (my cards got cut
off two days ago but I'll find out next Wed!)
(c) they are refusing to refund my annual fees
(d) it took my six calls and two hours on the phone with Chase to decipher this. along
the way, they dropped three calls

Chase sucks and so does JPMorgan Chase & Co.
John China - I need a SVB credit card. Pleassssseeeeeeee?

👍 Like   💬 Comment

👍 1

John   Take the cards (less headache) but make sure you emphasize
to them that they still suck.
Like · Reply · 👍 1 · September 27 at 8:42am

Ben   I'd get new cards .. unforgivable
Like · Reply · 👍 1 · September 27 at 8:43am

Lau   Can you get a detailed report of what exactly led them
to flag your account for laundering, then a formal apology, a higher credit line,
and reduced interest rate?
Like · Reply · 👍 5 · September 27 at 8:55am

Will   you need or want the cards take them back. At least they
changed their mind. Who gets hurt if you don't take them back? Chase won't
notice.
Like · Reply · 👍 1 · September 27 at 8:56am

Mai   Are they reinstating your points? Demand more points or waiving of
annual fees!
Like · Reply · 👍 4 · September 27 at 9:14am

Crai   Make them earn your business back. No simple "water under
the bridge - let's move forward...".
Like · Reply · 👍 2 · September 27 at 9:18am

Tom   Sure, if they throw in some Giants box seats as well
Like · Reply · 👍 3 · September 27 at 9:50am

Pat   New cards. Leave 'em.
Like · Reply · September 27 at 9:55am

Pat   Something with good miles....
Like · Reply · 👍 1 · September 27 at 9:56am

Fig. 8.17 A customer is confused and his peers are upset when his credit card is canceled but no
explanation is provided

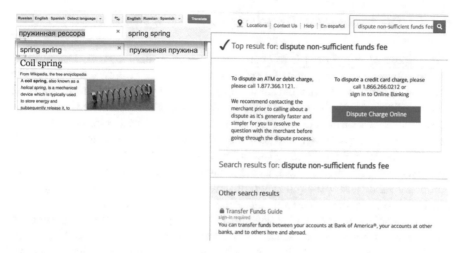

Fig. 8.18 On the left: Google translation results for a simple phrase shows the problems in handling context (as of March 2020). On the right: A search engine shows results very far from what a user is asking and do not attempt to explain how they were obtained

appropriate compartmental ML architecture with explainability. However, a black-box implementation of machine translation breaks even in simple cases like this. Inverse translation is obviously flawed as well (in the middle-left of Fig. 8.18). The bottom shows the fragment of a Wikipedia page for the entity.

Search engine is another application area for ML where relevance score is a major criterion to show certain search results (Fig. 8.18 on the right). Having a highest relevance score does not provide an explanation that the results are indeed relevant. Typical relevance score such as TF*IDF (Trstenjak et al. 2013) is hardly interpretable; search highlighting features are helpful but the search engine needs to be able to explain *why* it ignored certain keywords like *non-sufficient funds*. A better phrase handling would also help: the system should recognize the whole expression *non-sufficient funds fee* and if it does not occur in search results, explain it.

To investigate how important it is for a customer to have a company's decision explained, to have a decision associated with financial service *interpretable and compatible with common sense*, we need the following. A high number of scenarios of financial service failure have to be accumulated and a proportion of those requiring explanation from the company in one form or another have to be assessed. To do that, we form a dataset of customer complaint scenarios and build an automated assessment framework to detect the cases where explainability is requested.

8.4.2 The Dataset for Tracking Explainability Intent

The purpose of this dataset is to obtain texts where authors do their best to bring their points across by employing all means to show that they (as customers) are right and their opponents (companies) are wrong (Galitsky et al. 2009). Complainants are emotionally charged writers who describe problems they encountered with a financial service, lack of clarity and transparency as this problem was communicated with customer support personnel, and how they attempted to solve it. Raw complaints are collected from PlanetFeedback.com for a number of banks submitted over last few years. Four hundred complaints are manually tagged with respect to perceived complaint validity, proper argumentation, detectable misrepresentation, and whether request for explanation concerning the company's decision occurred.

Most people who complain are appalled at a company because of a strong deviation between what they expected from a service, what they received, how this deviation was explained and how the problem was communicated by a customer support. Most complainants report incompetence (Chaps. 7–9, Volume 2), deficient company policies, ignorance, a lack of a proper judgment, inability to understand the reason behind the company's decision, indifference to customer needs from the customer service personnel. The complaint authors are frequently confused, looking for company's explanation, seeking recommendation from other users and advise others on avoiding particular financial service. The focus of a complaint is a proof that the proponent is right and her opponent is wrong, suggested explanation for why the company decides to act in a certain way, a resolution proposal and a desired outcome.

Multiple argumentation patterns are used in complaints. We are interested in argumentation patterns associated with explainability: *I can explain (communicate why I did) it but my opponent (the company) cannot*. The most frequent is a deviation from what has happened from what was expected, according to common sense. This pattern covers both valid and invalid argumentation. The second in popularity argumentation patterns cites the difference between what has been promised (advertised, communicated) and what has been received or actually occurred. This pattern also mentions that the opponent does not play by the rules (valid pattern).

A high number of complaints are explicitly saying that bank representatives are lying. Lying includes inconsistencies between the information provided by different bank agents, factual misrepresentation and careless promises (valid pattern).

Complainants cite their needs as reasons bank should behave in certain ways. A popular argument is that since the government via taxpayers bailed out the banks, they should now favor the customers (invalid pattern).

For most frequent topics of complaints such as insufficient funds fee or unexpected interest rate rise on a credit card, this dataset provides many distinct ways of argumentation that this fee is unfair. Therefore, this dataset allows for systematic exploration of the peculiar topic-independent clusters of argumentation patterns such as a request to explain why certain decision was made. Unlike professional writing in legal and political domains, authentic writing of complaining users have a simple motivational structure, a transparency of their purpose and occurs in a fixed domain and context. Arguments play a critical rule for the well-being of the authors, subject to an unfair charge of a large amount of money or eviction from home. Therefore, the authors attempt to provide as strong argumentation as possible to back up their claims and strengthen their case.

The tag in this dataset used in the current chapter, request for explanation, is related to the whole text of complaint, not a paragraph. Three annotators worked with this dataset, and inter-annotator agreement exceeds 80%. The set of tagged customer complaints about financial services is available at https://github.com/bgalitsky/rel evance-based-on-parse-trees/blob/master/examples/opinionsFinanceTags.xls.

8.4.3 Automated Detection of a Request to Explain

Obviously, just relying on keywords, using keyword rules is insufficient to detect implicit request to explain. Hence an ML approach is required with the training dataset with texts including a request to explain and with texts not including one. Not just the syntax level but also discourse-level features are required when a request to explain is not explicitly mentioned. As in other chapters, we select the Rhetoric Structure Theory (Mann and Thompson 1988) as a means to represent discourse features associated with a request to explain.

We use an example of a request to recommend and explain to demonstrate a linguistic structure for explainability (Fig. 8.5). This text (from a collection of odd questions to Yahoo! Answers) is a question that expects not just a brief answer "do this and do that" but instead a full recommendation with explanation:

> *I just had a baby and it looks more like the husband I had my baby with. However it does not look like me at all and I am scared that he was cheating on me with another lady and I had her kid. This child is the best thing that has ever happened to me and I cannot imagine giving my baby to the real mom.*

The chain of rhetorical relations *Elaboration* (default), *Sequence* and *Contrast* indicate that a question is not just enumeration of topics and constraints for an expected answer (that can be done by *Eaboration* only). Instead, this chain indicates that a conflict (an expression that something occurs in contrast to something else) is outlined in a question, so an answer should necessarily include an explanation (Galitsky 2006a).

We combine parse trees for sentences with pragmatic and discourse-level relationships between words and parts of the sentence in one graph, called parse thicket (Fig. 8.19, Galitsky 2012). We complement the edges for syntactic relations obtained and visualized with the Stanford NLP system (Manning et al. 2014). For corefer ences, (Recasens et al. 2013 and Lee et al. 2013) was used. The arcs for pragmatic and discourse relations, such as anaphora, same entity, sub-entity, rhetorical relation and communicative actions are manually drawn in red. Labels embedded into arcs

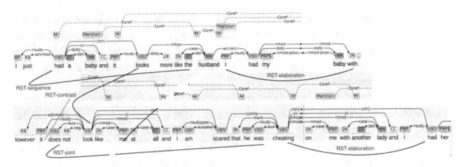

Fig. 8.19 Linguistic representation for text which contains a request to explain

denote the syntactic relations. Lemmas are written below the boxes for the nodes, and parts-of-speech are written inside the boxes.

This graph includes much richer information than just a combination of parse trees for individual sentences would. Navigation through this graph along the edges for syntactic relations as well as arcs for discourse relations allows us to transform a given parse thicket into semantically equivalent forms to cover a broader spectrum of possibilities to express a request to explain.

To form a complete formal representation of a paragraph, we attempt to express as many links as possible: each of the discourse arcs produces a pair of thicket phrases that can be a potential match with an expression for explainability request. Further details on using nearest neighbor learning (Tan 2005) via maximal common sub-parse thicket are available in (Galitsky 2012).

8.4.4 Evaluation of Recognition Accuracy and Assessment of the Proportion of Request to Explain

Once we developed our algorithm for explanation request detection, we want to train it, test it and verify how consistent its results are across the domains. We also test how the recognition accuracy varies for cases of different complexity.

Detection accuracy for explanation request for different types of evidence is shown in Table 8.5. We consider simpler cases where the detection occurs based on phrases, in the top row. Typical expressions here have an imperative form such as *please explain/clarify/motivate/comment*. Also, there are templates here such as you *did this but I expected that … you told me this but I received that*.

The middle row contains the data on higher evidence implicit explanation request case, where multiple fragments of DTs indicate the class. Finally, in the bottom row, we present the case of the lower confidence for a single occurrence of a DT associated with an explanation request. The second column shows the counts of complaints per case. The third column gives examples of expressions (which include keywords and phrase types) and rhetorical relations which serve as criteria for implicit

Table 8.5 Cases of explanation requests and detection accuracies for model development and evaluation

Evidence	#	Criteria	P	R	F1
Imperative expression with communicative action *explain*	44	Keywords Explain Clarify Make clear Why did they act-VP Why was it	92	94	93.0
Double, triple + implicit mention	67	Multiple rhetoric relation of *contrast, attribution, sequence, cause*	86	83	84.5
Single implicit mention	115	A pair of rhetoric relation chains for *contrast* and *cause*	76	80	77.9

explanation request. Fourth, fifth and sixth columns present the detection rates where the complaints for a given case is mixed with a hundred of complaints without explanation request.

Recognition accuracies, bank-specific topics of complaints and an overall proportion of the complaints with explanation request are shown in Table 8.6. We used 200 complaints for each bank to assess the recognition accuracies for explanation request. One can observe that 82% is a reasonable estimate for recognition accuracy for an explanation request. The last column shows that taking into account <20% error rate in explanation request recognition, 25% is an adequate estimate of complaints requiring explainability in implicit or explicit form, given the initial set of 800 complaints to assess the detection accuracy.

Finally, we ran our explanation request detection engine against the set of 10,000 complaints scraped from PlanetFeedback.com and observed that 23% of complainants explicitly or implicitly require explainability from companies for their decisions. Our observation is that since almost a quarter of customers strongly demand and rely on explainability of the companies' decisions, these customers are strongly affected by the lack of explainability and may want to switch to another service (Galitsky 2017). Hence the companies need to employ explainable ML algorithms. A very small number of customers complained about errors in decisions irrespectively of how these errors were communicated (a manual analysis). Hence

Table 8.6 Discovering explanation request rates for four banks

Source	#	Main topics of complaints	P	R	F1	ER rate
Bank1	320	NSF, credit card interest rate raise, low CD rates	84.1	84.2	84.1	24.5
Bank2	200	NSF, unexpected card cancellation, transactions shuffled	82.3	83.1	82.7	22.7
Bank3	200	Foreclosure, mortgage application, refinancing,	81.7	82.8	82.2	22.0
Bank4	200	Card application, NSF, late payment, unexpected card cancellation	82.9	83.0	82.9	24.1

we conjecture that customers are affected by a lack of explainability in a much higher degree than by an error rate (such as extra 10%, based on anecdotal evidence) of a company's decision-making system.

We updated our explainability request rate in comparison with our previous study (Galitsky and Goldberg 2019) and obtained a lower number by about 3%. This is due to improved rhetorical parsing, a richer set of linguistic templates and more accurate explanation representation means developed in Sect. 8.2.

This explainability feature is more important than the recognition accuracy for the customers, who understand that all businesses make errors. Typically, when a company makes a wrong decision via ML but then rectifies it efficiently, a complaint does not arise. The most important means for customer retention is then properly communicating with them both correct and possibly erroneous customer decisions (not quantitatively evaluated in this chapter).

We demonstrated that customers are strongly dissatisfied when decisions strongly affecting them are made by ML systems lacking explainability and interpretability features. Popularity of deep learning approaches, which make these features harder to implement, further increase customer dissatisfaction and negatively affect their retention. Whereas deep learning and big data approaches decrease the development costs for companies, especially when sufficient data is available, customer satisfaction drops.

8.5   Explainability and Meta-Explainability

In the corpus of research on explanations and explainability, the subjects of studies are usually object-level explanations. Object-level explanations link facts and clauses, such as an explanation chain connected a *rain* with *wet ground*. However, in explanations occurring in the form of a dialogue, we can frequently observe *explanations about explanations*. A simple example here is "*I explained him that what he explained to the teacher was wrong*". A meta-explanation (Explanation on Wikipedia 2018) is an essential notion to properly formalize certain mental states which appear in interactions between customers and customer support agents (CSAs).

A semantic representation of object-level and meta-level explainability is shown in Fig. 8.20 on the top. One explanation action serves as an argument for another: this is similar to logical representation: *explain(I, he, explain(he, teacher, wrong(teacher, ...)))*.

The most basic decision in classical meta-reasoning is whether an agent should act physically or continue to communicate, to reason, to explain (Fig. 8.20 on the bottom). An agent is expected to be able to explain its own decision and also its own resource management. For example, an agent's planner always has a current best plan produced by the object level reasoning. Given that the passage of time itself has a cost, the meta-reasoner must decide whether the expected benefit gained by planning further outweighs the cost of not doing a new physical action but instead explaining its previous actions to peers. If a new physical action is preferred, the agent produces

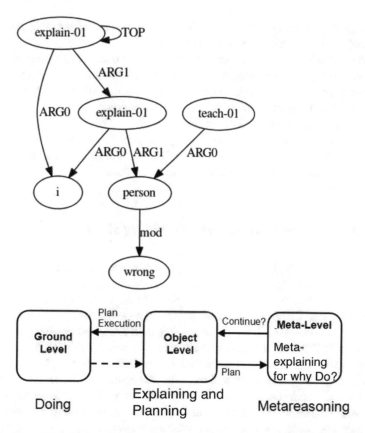

Fig. 8.20 A semantic representation for a simple sentence with meta-level explanation (on the top). A cognitive diagram for ground, object and meta-levels for agent's planning with explanation (on the bottom)

another plan; otherwise, it executes the actions in the plan it already has. Note that this simple decision can be performed without reference to any perception of the ground level. Naturally, many more sophisticated meta-level control policies exist which are related to explanation.

We have performed a comparative analysis of the *two levels* of explanation-related information to assess the plausibility of scenarios of interaction between agents (Galitsky et al. 2011). The *meta-level* of explanation is expressed via an overall structure of a scenario, which includes communicative actions and argumentation attack relations. This scenario explains something, such as implication of facts, in a conversational mode. This explanation is learned from previous experience of multi-agent interactions. Scenarios are represented by directed graphs with labeled vertices (for communicative actions) and arcs (for temporal and causal relationships between these actions and their parameters) (Galitsky et al. 2005). The *object-level* explanation is expressed via argumentative structure of a dialogue, assessing the plausibility of individual claims, which has been a subject of multiple applied and theoretical AI studies (Galitsky and Ilvovsky 2019).

To observe which forms of explanations humans use in dialogues, we use the domain of customer complaints, where relevant explanation of problems is a main communication means to obtain customer satisfaction. We used this domain to evaluate how combination of both explanation sources contribute to complaint plausibility assessment (Galitsky et al. 2011).

To treat explanations at each level computationally, we perform *classification* of complaint scenarios into the classes of plausible and implausible scenarios and observe how each explanation level allows us to do that.

8.5.1   *Explaining* **Why** *Versus Explaining* **How**

We start with a non-dialogue example of explanations and demonstrate that they refer to object-level and meta-level of explanation in various degrees.

Consider a situation where a teacher explains to the student how to build a house. Let us assume that we have a 2nd grade student. The satisfactory explanation will be as follows: first, somebody builds a foundation, then walls and finishes with building a roof. This is a natural reasoning chain with the relationship *to be on top*. The next case is when the student is in the 7nd grade. The previous explanation will not be satisfactory. The explanation will have the same structure but will include more objects such as windows, doors, etc. Now let us assume that the student is a college student who studies a civil engineering course. The previous explanations are not satisfactory any more, because the construction student needs to learn how he can actually make a project and build a house himself.

These simple examples show that the concept of explanation is context-specific. In these examples, it was easy for us to understand that first two explanations are not satisfactory for the construction student. Often students complain that they did not get hands-on experience. This is another was to say that the explanation is not satisfactory, or not an explanation at all. In this section, we attempt to represent such context as two-level explanation system.

The explanation has two aspects: (1) explain how to build, and (2) explain why to build in a particular way. In many cases, a student cannot judge whether the explanation is satisfactory if he still did not try to build a house using obtained explanations. The explanation may miss critical details ("know-how"). However, if she is asked if she has got a satisfactory explanation, she may say "yes" because she simply does not know that the explanation is incomplete. We call this situation *illusion of explanation*. Even mathematical proof can be faulty. History tells us that it may take time to discover that the proof was incomplete. The issue is that the person who understands, that the construction explanation is not satisfactory, often does not need the explanation. He poses the construction knowledge already; there is no need for reasoning chains here.

In some sense, this is a meta-knowledge about the explanation. The fact that *illusion of explanation* can happen is exploited in social communications such as advertisement. The customer believes that he has got a satisfactory explanation while in fact he was manipulated. The interesting research issue is how to recognize and separate real and illusory explanations for applications such as recommender systems. The key idea here is in the concept of trust. If the agent, who receives the explanation, trusts the agent who provides the explanation, then the illusion of the explanation can happen. The lack of trust leads to the opposite conclusion—a perfect logical explanation can be rejected. In the case of high trust, if the receiving agent has a very limited knowledge base in the domain then it will increase chances for the illusion of the explanation. In the same way, the agent with the low trust and a very limited knowledge base in the domain will likely reject a legitimate explanation. These observations will be treated at meta-explanation level.

Explaining *why* usually requires object-level explanation, whereas *how* may rely on meta-explanation level only. We will further consider *why*—kind of explanation, analyzing how agents in a conflict scenario attempt to explain *why* they are right and their opponent are not.

If one takes a fresh look at the above examples, she can see that various cases are specific combination of object-level and meta-explanation. In the further sections, we define each level formally and outline the means to calculate the *ratio* between the "roles" of object-level and meta-explanation in meeting the objective of an agent trying to communicate his explanation.

8.5.2 Explaining a Scenario: Which Levels Are Used?

We first introduce a scenario as described in a blog (Rase-dezert.com 2008, Fig. 8.21) and give the reader a chance to reconstruct what might have happened. This is a simple example, where one can observe how both sources of argumentation data help to make sense of the scenario, classifying it with respect of the roles of involved agent. Our first example does not include an explicit dialogue/conflict between agents.

Tragedy on the Baja 1000

> A helicopter that was flying over the Baja 1000 race route came down today, leaving a death toll of two. Apparently, the craft came in contact with some high voltage cables. The helicopter was rented in the city of Tijuana with the intention of filming the race from the air and reporting its progress.
>
> However it seems that its mission wasn't as innocent as it seemed at first sight…Armed men burst into Ensenada's morgue Wednesday night and took the body of one of the men who died in the helicopter crash. The commando took two state social workers hostage as they grabbed the body. The commando then left the morgue carrying their macabre cargo. As they retreated, a group of law enforcement officers pursued the assailants, and in the ensuing shootout two Mexican policemen were killed.
>
> The dead man taken from the morgue was identified as Pablo González. It was unclear whether that is his real name and why such measures were taken to recover the body. Mexican media reported he was believed to be a member of the region's Arellano Félix drug cartel.

Fig. 8.21 An introductory scenario where both sources of argumentation are required to find plausible interpretation

Trying to understand whether González is a prominent criminal, a witness of a crime, or a well-known auto race enthusiast, the reader employs two levels to explain her interpretation of this scenario:

- Meta-explain: observe typical most familiar scenarios which are similar to our scenarios with respect to expected logic of events (which we call argumentation patterns in this chapter). These include: a *helicopter crash* and accident handling, an *attack by criminals* to eliminate witnesses or help gang members escape, and a criminal run-away. A number of features of our scenario are hard to match by common/typical scenarios, such as *attack of a morgue, appearance of a criminal at a public event, attack of a police car* by a large group of criminals.
- Explain: take into account relevant commonsense knowledge, assess whether the main involved agent is a *criminal* or a *crime witness*, because his body was hijacked by a criminal gang, and/or an *auto enthusiast*, because he rented a helicopter to report the auto race.

We now show the "official" explanation in the press:

We now show the 'official' explanation in the press:

"Maybe it was sentimental reasons," said David A. Shirk, director of the Trans-Border Institute at the University of San Diego. The attackers, said Shirk and others, may have wanted to ensure that the man's funeral was attended by his friends. "If he was buried by authorities, they would expose themselves by coming out for any kind of public funeral," Shirk said.

Federal authorities had initially pointed that the son of Alicia Arellano was participating in a vehicle registered with the number 113, but later the authorities presented a new version where it is presumed that a member of the Arellano Felix family was actually aboard the helicopter that crashed.

On one hand, the most plausible explanation of events comes from the scenario *funeral of a criminal, where friends attend without exposure to public*, which is not very frequent. On the other hand, such explanation might be derived in an attempt to find an argument that attacks the statement "*hijack a crime witness*" and supports the argument "*release a member of criminal gang*" without attacking the assertion that this member is dead at the time of release. Hence the reader observes that both meta-explaining by learning links between events from familiar scenarios (1), and finding plausible explanation (as we illustrated by defeating relationships for individual statements (2)) contribute to understanding this scenario and assessing its truthfulness. Hence in this example, both levels of explanation are required to come up with a plausible scenario interpretation.

In this Section, we estimate a relative importance of these levels of explanation for the overall assessment of scenario plausibility. To do that, we build both representations, classify scenarios based on these representations, and evaluate which representation improves the classification accuracy to a higher degree.

Then we will explore the correlation between overall semantic characteristics of scenarios (such as level of competence, truthfulness, motivation of the agent being explaining, and possible attitudes of agents being explained to) and the *ratio* between the above degrees of how each level contributes to classification accuracy.

8.5.3 *Explanation Phase Space*

Having discussed two levels of explanation, we now intend to explore how the explanation style of individual agent and multi-agent system can be characterized in terms of **degrees** each of these two levels are used. Our intention here is to characterize explanation behavior by a numerical parameter. Since one can 'measure' contribution of object-level and meta-explanation to scenario plausibility as **relative accuracy**, we believe this measure can serve as explanation behavior parameters, which is invariant with respect to subjects of dialogue and even individual attitudes of particular scenario agents. Hence, we depict a scenario with explanation behavior as a point of two-dimensional space (which we call *explanation phase space*).

We demonstrate that using explanation phase space (Fig. 8.22), one can visualize the phenomenology of various forms of multi-agent behavior associated with explanation. Less plausible explanation scenarios are shown in the left-bottom corner, and fully valid ones are shown in the top-right corner. A number of epistemic states are

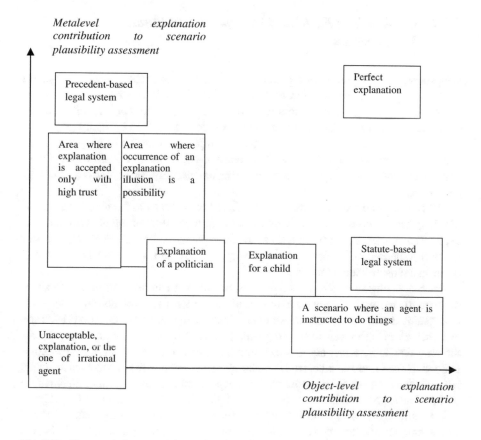

Fig. 8.22 Characteristic areas at the explanation phase space

shown in the phase space and their object-level and meta-explanations are described. When the trust is high, detailed causal links in explanation do not have to be provided. When object level explanation is very incomplete and meta-explanation is somewhat complete, illusion of explanation (discussed above in example 1) may occur. An adult can say a child about somebody: "*He is happy because he is always friendly. Be friendly too*". This explanation may not be true but if the child trusts this adult, it will be accepted. This explanation has a structure close to the explanations by politicians: "*These people do good things because they are friendly, Let's be friendly people, and lets elect people who look friendly*".

The incompleteness at the object-level can be augmented by an agent receiving explanation by accepting meta-explanation. In English, precedent-based legal system, meta-level explanations prevail over continental statute-based legal system. A change in the behavior of agent system (demonstrated as a set of scenarios) can be shown as a trajectory in the explanation phase space.

8.5.4   Application: Explanation Type-Based Email Inbox Visualization

We proceed to an example of a practical application visualizing explanation phase space. We consider the problem of visualization of email inbox content. Usually, emails are sorted by date, authors and conversations. If, for each email, one can assess the levels of explanation (a *trust* view), communicated by email authors, a novel way of clustered email view in explanation phase space can be proposed. Such trust-based view would facilitate an efficiency of email communication and relieve a user from some of the burden of trust management replying a manifold of emails (Fig. 8.23).

When emails are clustered by what email authors *want* from the recipient, it turns out that each group of email authors correspond to clusters of emails with specific explanation patterns (a specific ratio between explanation levels). Each such cluster relies on a specific logic of explanation, so replying to emails from each cluster would occur in a cluster-specific manner.

Each such cluster also reflects a *trust* associated with authors: authors who know they are trusted well, do not have to provide as a thorough explanation as the ones unacquainted with the recipient. An email from an unknown person should contain explanation on both levels to be acceptable (top-right corner of the phase space). As the trust develops, email authors can simplify and decrease the strength of explanations. Hence there is a common tendency in the explanation phase space for an inbox: when the trust for a given email correspondent increases in time, the location on the phase space might move toward top-right (shown by an arrow in Fig. 8.23).

Implementation of the inbox clustering would rely on rather advanced NLP and ML techniques of automated extraction of explanation patterns (Sect. 8.4). Obviously, the email clustering problem does not provide statistical significance to calculate the

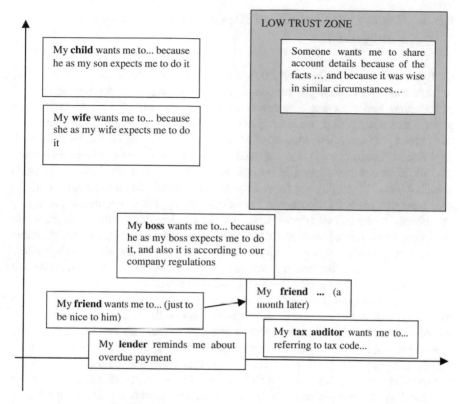

Fig. 8.23 Explanation phase space showing clusters of emails with similar explanation pattern (ratio between object-level and meta-explanation)

ratio of level1/level0 recognition accuracy, but the representation via the explanation phase space is still relevant.

The novelty of this section is three-fold.

(1) We split the general notion of explanation into two levels;
(2) We propose a level-specific learning method which allowed to treat these levels computationally;
(3) We propose a representation technique for explanation patterns that allows a computational treatment and visualization in a practical domain of customer complaints and mentioned other relevant domains.

We have not found any study concerned with matching the structured representation of explanation patterns or argumentation patterns as a source of "global" structural information about scenarios; therefore, we believe the current chapter is a pioneering one in this respect.

8.5.5 Dealing with Validity of Explanations in Complaint Management

Complaint processing (Davidow 2003) has become an important issue for CRM in large companies and organizations. Complaint management is a formal process of recording and resolving a customer complaint. Even though CRM systems in general and complaint processing systems in particular are expensive, companies can extract priceless knowledge from an appropriate handling of a complaint, with significant effects on customer retention rates and word-of-mouth recommendations. If complaints are transformed into knowledge about customers, they can provide valuable business intelligence for enterprises. To exploit this intelligence, companies must design, build, operate and continuously upgrade systems for managing complaints. In the last two decades, several approaches have emerged to automate complaint management such as (Yuan and Chang 2001), among others. Retailers and service providers may profit from such software services because they allow complaints to be handled faster, providing the possibility of feedback analysis and data mining capabilities on the basis of a complaint database.

A typical complaint is an *explanation* of a failure of a product or service, followed by a narrative on the customer's attempts to resolve the issue. These complaints include both a description of the product or service failure as well as a description of the resulting interaction process (negotiation, conflict, etc.) between the customer and the company representatives. Because it is almost impossible for CRM personnel to verify the actual occurrence of such failures, company representatives must judge the adequacy of a complaint on the basis of the communicative actions provided by the customers in their explanation. Customers usually do their best to bring their points across, so the consistency of communicative actions of an explanation and the appropriateness of their arguments (represented as parameters of these actions) are major clues for the validity of their complaints. Indeed, a complaint narrative usually describes a conflict between an unsatisfied customer and a CRM personnel, in which communicated claims need to be rationally justifiable by sound arguments.

In contrast with the almost unlimited number of possible details regarding product failures, the emerging argumentative dialogues between customer and company can be subject to a systematic computational study (Galitsky et al. 2009). In this context, a major challenge in complaint processing involves distinguishing those customer complaints which are rationally acceptable from those which are not, so that the whole procedure of complaint handling can be better supported. Currently, most CRM solutions are limited to the use of keyword processing to relate a complaint to a certain domain-specific class (e.g., banking and travel complaints, as reported in this chapter), or to the application of knowledge management techniques in software platforms for workflow. To the best of our knowledge, existing industrial complaint management platforms do not make use of natural language processing nor machine learning techniques for quicker performance, quality assurance and lower sustainability costs; most complaint handling functionalities remain manual. In particular, no automated solutions have been developed to assess the validity of a customer complaint on the basis of the emerging dialogue between a customer and the company representatives, with the goal of better supporting the procedure of complaint handling as a part of CRM. Hence we believe a complaint validity assessment of a CRM system is expected to leverage the representations formalisms and algorithms introduced in this chapter.

8.6 Discussion and Conclusions

8.6.1 Enabling Deep Learning with Explainability

A hybrid AI, combing Deep Learning (DL) and a rule-based system, enables the former with explainability (Young et al. 2018). End-to-end DL models can solve fascinating problems, but the accuracy and complexity comes at a price of not knowing exactly what happens in the black box. However, the programming instructions output by a hybrid system can be traced and debugged step by step, giving developers and engineers a clear picture of how the hybrid system is solving the problem. If the model delivers a wrong answer, a developer can see why it did so and where it got confused. If it got the right answer, the system developer can consult the log and observe if there is a right reason for the right answer.

A hybrid system can be used in most applications where we are currently using DL. Furthermore, one can also use hybrid models in settings where we are not using DL because we do not have enough data and there are concerns about adversarial attacks or explainability.

An architecture of a visual question answering is shown in Fig. 8.24. A logical component is needed when the problem is fundamentally compositional, if the domain has a structure that needs to be leveraged and has a symbolic quality to it. The problem needs to be attacked with the skeleton of that symbolic processing, and one can get by with dramatically less data.

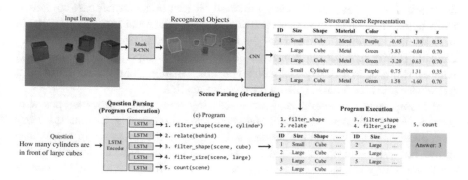

Fig. 8.24 An architecture of a hybrid DL + rules visual Q/A system

A convolutional neural network processes an image and forms a list of objects and their characteristics such as color, location and size. This is the kind of symbolic representation of the image that a rule-based AI model can easily work on. A second sequence-to-sequence neural network performs NLP, processing a user question and parsing it into a list of pre-defined programming functions (that can be run on the objects list). The result is a rule-based program that expresses and solves the problem symbolically, in an explainable way (Mao et al. 2019).

8.6.2 Discourse Analysis for Explainability

What we confirmed in this chapter is that explanation does not occur in the level of words or syntactic relations on them and neither it lives in the level of semantics. Instead, explanation is a discourse level feature: the structure of how text authors organized their thoughts to explain something to an addressee. An explanation chain can include knowledge explicitly contained in text, referred to in text and also implicitly cited in text. For the third source of knowledge for explanation, to systematically treat it at the discourse level, we introduced the notion of *imaginary discourse tree*. We also introduced the notion of a *hybrid discourse tree* that includes real and imaginary parts. Imaginary DT is constructed for the text about entities used but not explicitly defined in the actual text.

In this Chapter, we considered a new approach to validating the convincingness of textual explanations. We outlined an algorithm for building an imaginary discourse tree. We described a possible strategy for crawling background knowledge which is the source of the imaginary part of a DT. We also introduced the new dataset of good and bad explanations made by complainants in the financial domain. Finally, we outlined the learning framework used for automated detection of good and bad explanations. It is based on RST parsing and learning of hybrid discourse trees provided by the parser.

Both professional and non-professional writers provide explanations in texts but detection of invalid explanations is significantly harder in the former case compared to the latter. Professional writers in such domains as politics and business are capable of explaining "anything", and in user-generated content explanation errors are visible. Detecting faulty explanations in user-generated content is important in CRM systems where a response to user requests with a *valid* explanation should be different from a response to a user request with an *invalid* explanation.

It is important to combine rule-based learning frameworks with the ones with implicit feature engineering such as statistical and deep learning. The latest history of applications of statistical technique sheds a light on the limitation of these techniques for systematic exploration of a given domain. Once statistical learning delivered satisfactory results for discourse parsing, the interest to automated discourse analysis faded away. Since the researches in statistical ML for discourse parsing were mainly interested in recognition accuracies and not the interpretability of obtained DTs, no further attempts at leveraging these DTs were made. However, a number of studies including the given one demonstrate that DTs provide essential insights in the domains where keyword statistics does not help.

We observed how humans provide explanation of their problems in such conflict environments as customer complaints. We suggested how to split explanation-related behavior presented in a human language into two levels, using reasoning chains (deduction) and similarity between explanation structures (inductive learning). Relative to the former level (explanation), the latter level is an explanation of explanation structure, which we refer to as meta-explanation (explanation of explanation). Hence, we split the explanation in multi-agent behavior into a deductive object-level and an inductive meta-level. For the first level, we use an interactive form to obtain a defeasible logic program to verify plausibility of individual claims used in explanation. For the meta-level, we represented scenarios as graphs and used graph-based nearest neighbor techniques to determine whether the given scenario is similar to plausible or implausible scenarios.

Marcus and Davies (2019) defines robust AI as an intelligence that, while not necessarily superhuman or self-improving, can be counted on to apply what it knows to a wide range of problems in a systematic and reliable way. This intelligence should be capable of synthesizing knowledge from a variety of sources such that it can reason flexibly and dynamically about the world, transferring what it learns in one context to another, in the way that we would expect of an ordinary adult. To assure robustness, systematicity, reliability, transferability of context and the flexibility of reasoning, AI has to be explainable.

8.6.3 Comparison with other Approaches to Assessment of Customer Opinions

Since we are not aware of computational studies addressing plausibility of explanations in customer complaints, we generalize our domain and compare our results with the state-of-the-art results in communicating and explaining opinions. This domain is usually referred to as *opinion mining* and assesses positive and negative sentiments as communicated by the authors of reviews, which can be viewed as a more general forms of communication of customers.

Evaluation studies of customer feedback mostly arise out of academia; we outline the main differences between the industrial opinion mining settings and the ones used in most academic studies on sentiment classification and opinion mining. In industrial settings, attempt to improve the accuracy of opinion mining is conducted in a test-driven development environment, where the goal of the system is to properly extract polarity and sentiment of a manually constructed dataset. This dataset and system settings are adjusted so that the accuracy approaches 100%, so that the system provides the "bug free" code that is expected by quality assurance personnel. The resultant accuracy is therefore lower than academic-style evaluations which target maximum accuracy on the testing dataset, something that is frequently not even measured in industrial applications. In order to suit the quality assurance procedures of an industrial environment, the deterministic approaches are preferred over statistical ones because they provide more control over individual cases, which confirm that topic and polarity extraction can be carried out on the entire dataset.

Although most approaches to opinion mining focus on the overall assessment of customer reviews (Liu et al. 2005), it is necessary for commercial recommendation applications to extract and determine the individual sentiment expression, its topicality and its polarity properly so that a particular user's needs or concerns are addressed. Hence, we evaluated the accuracy of the extraction of individual reviews that are quoted to support a user decision. Obviously, assessing a group of opinion expressions as a single opinion in a given review is more accurate than assessing an individual opinion expression.

We also compare our work to the somewhat similar domain of U.S. Congressional floor debates (Pang and Lee 2008). The investigation addressed the possibility of determining from the transcripts whether the speeches were in support of or opposed to proposed legislation. The authors leveraged the observation that these speeches occur as part of a discussion and are backed by arguments; this fact allows them to use sources of information regarding relationships between discourse segments, such as whether a given utterance indicates agreement with the opinion expressed by another, similar to our procedure for complaints. The authors found that the incorporation of the information on discourse structures yields substantial improvements over classifying speeches in isolation; an accuracy of 84% on the training dataset and 81% on the testing dataset is achieved.

Chaovalit and Zhou (2005) conducted a comparison between supervised and unsupervised sentiment and topicality classification approaches using movie reviews. Their supervised machine learning accuracy is 85.5%. The semantic orientation approach, because it is unsupervised, required extracting phrases containing adjectives or adverbs from the review data. Five patterns of phrases were extracted to find their semantic orientation values based on a selected part-of-speech tagger, and 77% classification accuracy on 100 movie reviews from Movie Vault was achieved after adjusting the dividing baseline. Turney (2002) obtained 65.8% accuracy in mining 120 movie reviews from the Epinions website. Pang et al. (2002) mined movie reviews using various ML techniques to determine whether they are as effective as other sentiment classification methods like movie review mining. They obtained the best classification accuracies ranging from 77 to 83% by varying input features (i.e., unigrams, bigrams, unigrams + bigrams).

On the basis of work by Austin, Searle, Grice and Lorenzen, such discipline as pragmadialectics provides a comprehensive analysis of argumentative dialogues which sometimes include explanations (Grasso 1999). This discipline combines the study on the formalism to represent data, from modern logic, and empirical observations, from descriptive linguistics, for the analysis of argumentative dialogues, modeled by dialectics, seen as sets of linguistic speech. The model proposes rule-base argumentative dialogues, but does not help with a dialogue generation algorithm.

8.6.4 Skepticism About Explainable AI

Some skeptics believe that whenever humans make up a convenient, oversimplified story that fits the inputs and outputs in hindsight, that is an easy case (Kozyrkov 2018). The skeptics of explainable AI believe that ML developers always have access to the same level of explainability for any model; it can even be model-agnostic. Developers can look at input and output data and attempt to interpret the data and produce analytics' results, and explainability of this analytics is not required. This viewpoint is defeated by at least classical or nonmonotonic reasoning system that is a foundation for generation of an explanation: a lack of explainability is always a loss of information, and the question always remains whether this lost information is valuable or not. Hence once the explainability is removed there is a loss of information that is frequently valuable.

An ML algorithm can remember (store in a disk) a billion examples perfectly unlike a human being, and process them one by one or in parallel, in contrast to a human. As a result, AI algorithms make solutions that are more complicated than the code human developers can potentially write. A statistical learning system can write a million of lines of instructions. Explainable AI opponents believe that such complicated representations are always better than simpler representations which human cognition can handle. It is hard to agree with that.

Voting for explainability, one needs to choose from:

- *Interpretability*: you do understand it but it does not work well.
- *Performance*: you do not understand it but it does work well.

If something already works well for a majority of real-world scenario (not a limited test dataset), the interpretability requirement can be reduced. But, in the real world, most systems trained on a limited dataset do not work well, so to be trusted, they always need to explain what they do.

In the past few years, the public sees that ML raises novel challenges for ensuring non-discrimination, due process, understandability and explainability in decision-making. Policy makes, regulators and advocates have expressed concerns that ML can be discriminatory against certain members of public. Many call for further technical research into a possibility of inadvertently encoding bias into decisions by statistical or deep ML systems. Also, there is an increasing fear that the complexity of ML may reduce the justification for consequential decisions to "I did it because an ML algorithm told me so".

We conclude this subsection that although explainable AI is associated with technical difficulties, it is a must for a modern consumer.

8.6.5   *Explainability and an Overall Success Rate*

At the beginning of 2020, Geoffrey Hinton posted this provocative question on twitter: *"Suppose you have cancer and you have to choose between a black box AI surgeon that cannot explain how it works but has a 90% cure rate and a human surgeon with an 80% cure rate. Do you want the AI surgeon to be illegal?"* (Fig. 8.25).

- Opinion (1) Many times it is difficult or even impossible to explain to a lay person how a medical result is achieved anyway. Because of that, I think the AI is an emotional red herring here. You should go with a higher success rate. Human beings often have difficulty making such rational decisions. One way to help in that regard is to push the argument to the extreme. Let's say the AI achieved 100% success rate (defined as survival past 5 years, with no decrease in quality of life). Let's say human surgeons reach about 50%. Which surgeon would you choose?
- Opinion (2) Depends if explainability showed my risk was higher.
- Opinion (3) But isn't that 90% gonna stick? That 90% figure is usually reported from a train/test and always goes down in real-world settings. Secondly, humans improve. They draw correlations from the mistakes they make and try to avoid those. Current AI algorithms don't. Now comparison becomes 'we don't care about the 10% at all' versus 'next time I will try that won't happen'. Which would you choose now?
- Opinion (4) I would pick the black box AI since the human physician themselves are black box to people who don't understand medicine. As a lay person, I am never going to fully understand why the physician decided to treat me one way and not the other. Considered another way, in general, we already don't understand how exactly the medicine that the doctor prescribed to us works when ingested so in that sense it is already a black box. Better take chances with the AI that has statistically higher chances of working. This is assuming that the % success is reported on similar data set size for both human and AI.

Fig. 8.25 A discussion is initiated about an unexplainable AI in medicine

- Opinion (5) I would definitely be suspicious of anything that "cannot be explained".
- (Healthcare expert opinion) Success rate is for a totality of patients. Each individual case is unique, and ML/doctor rate could be 70% versus 95% or 95% versus 75%. There are multiple reasons an ML error is much more dangerous than a human doctor error. The best possibility is to *combine* the 80% rate doctor with 90% rate black box ML, per evaluation of bi-directional DSS. A conflict of decisions improves the outcome of a multiagent DSS with 80–90% decision success rate.
- (Author opinion) What is given is that 90% might mean a success rate for an average patient, and human explainable doctor treats an average person with 80%. However, a particular patient can have a much higher success rate because the human doctor might adjust treatment. For an individual a chance of success varies and deviates from an average. So I vote for a human explainable doctor who would know the patient. Whereas a human doctor has an overall success rate of 80%, he can cure a given patient with a success rate higher than a black-box ML that has overall rate of 90% but since it is unexplainable, we don't know what happens with a given patient.

Computer scientists feel busy arguing with each other concerning the necessity and various forms of explainability. At the same time, as we investigated in Sect. 8.4, customers demand explainability explicitly together with accountability, transparency and other desired features of the intelligence employed in the modern society.

Handling a Lack of Explainability

To tackle the challenges associated with the lack of explainability of most popular modern ML algorithms, there are some initial efforts on interactive model analysis. These efforts have shown that interactive visualization plays a critical role in understanding and analyzing a variety of machine learning models. DARPA I2O has released Explainable Artificial Intelligence proposal to encourage research on this topic. The main goal of explainable AI is to create a suite of ML techniques that produce explainable models to enable users to understand, trust, and manage the emerging generation of AI systems.

There have been attempts to augment the learning models intrinsically lacking explainability with this feature. ML models can be trained to automatically map documents into abstract concepts such as semantic category, writing style, or sentiment, allowing to categorize a large corpus. Besides predicting the text's category, it is essential to trace how the categorization process arrived to a certain value. Arras et al. (2017) demonstrated that it can be achieved by tracing the classification decision back to individual words using layer-wise relevance propagation, a recently developed technique for explaining predictions of complex non-linear classifiers. The authors trained two word-based ML models, a CNN and a bag-of-words SVM classifier, on a topic categorization task and applied the layer-wise relevance propagation method to decompose the predictions of these models onto words. Resulting scores indicate how much individual words contribute to the overall classification decision. This enables one to distill relevant information from text documents without an explicit semantic information extraction step. The authors further used the word pair-wise relevance scores for generating novel vector-based document representations which capture semantic information. Based on these document vectors, a measure of model explanatory power was introduced and showed that, although the SVM and CNN models perform similarly in terms of classification accuracy, the latter exhibits a higher level of explainability which makes it more comprehensible for humans and potentially more useful for other applications.

Although ML models are widely used in many applications due to high accuracy, they fail to explain their decisions and actions to users. Without a clear understanding, it may be hard for users to leverage their knowledge by their learning process and achieve a better prediction accuracy. As a result, it is desirable to develop more explainable machine learning models, which have the ability to explain their rationale and convey an understanding of how they behave in the learning process. The key challenge here is to design an explanation mechanism that is tightly integrated into the ML model. Accordingly, one interesting future work is to discover which parts in an ML model structure explains its different functions and plays a major role in the performance improvement or decline at each iteration. One possibility is to better back up both the model and the decisions made. In particular, (Lake et al. 2015) proposed a probabilistic program induction algorithm, having developed a stochastic program to represent concepts, which are formed compositionally from parts and spatial relations. Lake et al. (2015) showed that their algorithm achieved human-level performance on a one-shot classification task, However, for the tasks that have abundant training data, such as object and speech recognition, CNN approaches still outperform (Lake et al. 2015) algorithm. There is still a long path to proceed toward more explainable DL decisions.

Following the recent progress in deep learning, ML scientists are recognizing the importance of understanding and interpreting what goes on inside these black box models. RNN have recently improved speech recognition and translation, and these powerful models would be very useful in other applications involving sequential data. However, adoption has been slow in domains such as jurists, finance, legal and health, where current specialists are reluctant to let an explanation-less engine make crucial decisions. Krakovna and Doshi-Velez (2016) suggested making the inner workings of RNNs more interpretable so that more applications can benefit from their power.

CNNs have achieved breakthrough performance in many pattern recognition tasks such as image classification. However, the development of high-quality deep models typically relies on a substantial amount of trial-and-error, as there is still no clear understanding of when and why a deep model works. Liu et al. (2017) presents a visual analytics approach for better understanding, diagnosing, and refining deep CNNs. The authors simulated CNN as a directed acyclic graph. Based on this formulation, a hybrid visualization is developed to visualize the multiple facets of each neuron and the interactions between them. The authors also introduced a hierarchical rectangle-packing algorithm and a matrix re-shuffling method to show the derived features of a neuron cluster. They also proposed a bi-clustering-based edge merging algorithm to minimize visual distortion caused by a large number of connections between neurons.

8.6.6 Logical Issues of Meta-Explanations

From the ML standpoint, our approach to meta-explanation is induction. In terms of its deterministic methodology of prediction and implementation via logic programming, meta-explanation as learning is close to Explanation-Based Learning (EBL), (Ellman 1989) class of methods which are intended to derive as general expressions as possible from available data. EBL has been deployed in forming rules while observing a human expert, decision-making and advising systems in rather compact domains. One of the motivations for this project is to deploy the power of EBL, expressiveness of its representations and delivery of explanation (which is essential for understanding the underlying mechanisms) for more extensive and less structured domains such as scenarios of inter-human interactions. Therefore, the proposed ML mechanism is able to accommodate such noisy and scarce date as customer complaints, where a lack of an adequate domain theory and other deficiencies such as problems with completeness, correctness and tractability occur. To achieve this, we use more cautious prediction settings to decrease the number of false negatives and iterative application of induction-abduction procedure on the one hand, and provide an interactive environment to visualize explanations on the other hand. Furthermore, unlike the EBL approach, we used negative examples to falsify hypotheses that have counter-examples.

In our previous studies of argumentation in complaint scenarios (Galitsky et al. 2007a, 2008), we verified that using attack relationship in addition to communicative actions as a way to express dialogue discourse indeed increases the accuracy of scenario plausibility assessment (in a similar setting to the current chapter). Having showed the importance of both explanation levels, we proceeded to defining such characteristic parameter of scenarios with explanation behavior as a *ratio* between contributions of each level to the overall scenario assessment. We then demonstrated that using such measure as the phase space can visualize scenarios with various forms of explanation activities by agents. We also showed that a number of various behaviors can be represented via the explanation phase space.

We formed a generic methodology based on learning and reasoning to detect specific attitudes of human agents and patterns of their interactions (Galitsky et al. 2007a). Human attitudes are determined in terms of communicative actions of agents; models of machine learning are used when it is rather hard to identify attitudes in a rule-based form directly. We employed scenario knowledge representation and learning techniques in such problems as predicting an outcome of international conflicts, assessment of an attitude of a security clearance candidate, mining emails for suspicious emotional profiles, mining wireless location data for suspicious behavior, and classification of textual customer complaints. A performance evaluation was carried out in the above domains which are fairly distinct. A successful use of this methodology demonstrated its adequacy for mining human attitude-related data in a wide range of applications.

Ma et al. (2008) introduced an inferential framework for deriving logical explanations from partial temporal information. Based on a graphical representation which allows expression of both absolute and relative temporal knowledge in incomplete forms, the system can deliver a verdict to the question if a given set of statements is temporally consistent or not, and provide understandable logical explanation rule-based reasoning. The scenario graph representation proposed in this paper is a particular way to encode such "absolute" and "relative" relationships between actions.

Elizalde et al. (2008) selected statistical approach to the problem of explaining the recommendations generated by a Markov decision process. The authors proposed an automatic explanation generation that includes, firstly, the most *relevant variable* given the current state is obtained, based on a factored representation (the relevant variable is defined as the factor that has the greatest impact on the utility given certain state and action). Secondly, an explanation is generated by *combining* the information obtained from the Markov decision process with domain knowledge represented as a frame system. The state and action are used as pointers to the knowledge base to extract the relevant information and fill-in the explanation template. In this way, explanations of the recommendations can be generated online and incorporated to an intelligent assistant. In terms of the current chapter, this can be viewed as an automated building of the explanation scenarios in two levels by learning.

We observed how two levels of explanation, overall argumentation pattern of a scenario and explanations for individual claims, compliment each other. Comparative computational analysis of scenario classification with respect to plausibility showed that assessment of both levels of explanation is essential to determine whether a scenario is plausible or not (contains misrepresentation or self-contradiction). Hence, we believe a practical explanation management system where an explanation procedure is implemented via argumentation should include scenario-oriented machine learning capability, in addition to handling argumentation for individual claims.

There are examples in AI where quantitative characterization of computational complexity is rather complex and notion of phase transitions is introduced (see, e.g., Selman 1995). In this Chapter, we demonstrated that changing a ratio between explanation levels can visualize a wide range of behavior patterns related to explanations activity, which is an important part of overall activity of communicating agents. In future studies, we plan to extend our evaluation from the domain of customer complaint to a wide domain of customer relationship management (Galitsky and de la Rosa 2011), formalizing an extensive list of explanation-related behavior. We have built a commercial recommendation system for attending events, based on social network profile (Galitsky 2016a, b). The system developed in 2012 (Zvents.com acquired by Stabhub.com, an eBay company) provides explanation for why a given event is recommended based on users' Facebook profile "*likes*" (object-level explanations), and also based on choices of similar users and Facebook friends (meta-level explanation, involving "*users like you*").

Acknowledgement I am grateful to my colleague **Saveli Goldberg** for help in preparation of this chapter.

References

Aamodt A, Plaza E (1994) Case-based reasoning: foundational issues, methodological variations, and system approaches. AI Commun 7(1):39–59

Al-Fedaghi S. (2016) Toward flow-based ontology. In: Lee R (eds) Software engineering, artificial intelligence, networking and parallel/distributed computing. Studies in computational intelligence, vol 653. Springer, Cham

Aleven V (2003) Using background knowledge in case-based legal reasoning: a computational model and an intelligent learning environment. Artif Intell 150:183–237

Arras L, Horn F, Montavon G, Müller K-R, Samek W (2017) What is relevant in a text document?: An interpretable machine learning approach. PLoS ONE. https://doi.org/10.1371/journal.pone.0181142

Baehrens D, Schroeter T, Harmeling S, Kawanabe M, Hansen K, Müller K-R (2010) How to explain individual classification decisions. 11(Jun):1803–1831

Botros S, Zhen JL, Liu M, Galitsky B (2013) Customized reporting and mining of event data. US Patent 8,380,752

Bowman SR, Angeli G, Potts C, Manning CD (2015) A large annotated corpus for learning natural language inference. In: EMNLP

Braines D, Preece A, Harborne D (2019) Achieving useful AI explanations in a high-tempo complex environment. A conference on Artificial Intelligence and Machine Learning for Multi-Domain Operations Applications. v11006. International Society for Optics and Photonics

Camburu OM, Rocktäschel T, Lukasiewicz T, Blunsom P (2018) E-SNLI: Natural language inference with natural language explanations. In: Neural information processing systems, vol 31

Cartoonbank (2020). https://cartoonbank.ru/?page_id=29&color=all&offset=140

Chaovalit P, Zhou L (2005) Movie review mining: a comparison between supervised and unsupervised classification approaches. In: Proceedings of the Hawaii international conference on system sciences (HICSS)

Chesñevar C, Maguitman A (2004) An argumentative approach for assessing natural language usage based on the web corpus. In: Proceedings of the ECAI 2004 conference Valencia, Spain, pp 581–585

Chesñevar C, Maguitman A, Loui R (2000) Logical models of argument. ACM Comput Surv 32(4):337–383

Cho Y Im II, Hiltz SR, Fjermestad J (2002) An analysis of online customer complaints: implications for web complaint management. In: Proceedings of the 35th annual Hawaii international conference on system sciences (HICSS'02), vol 7, pp 2308–2317

DARPA (2016) Explainable artificial intelligence (XAI). https://www.darpa.mil/program/explainable-artificial-intelligence. Last downloaded November 2018

Davidow M (2003) Organizational responses to customer complaints: what works and what doesn't. J Serv Res 5(3):225–250

Dey A (2009) Explanations in context-aware systems. In: IJCAI Workshop on explanation-aware computing 2009

Dunne PE, Bench-Capon TJM (2006) Computational models of argument: proceedings of COMMA. IOS Press

Elizalde F, Sucar LE, Noguez J, Reyes A (2008) Integrating probabilistic and knowledge-based systems for explanation generation. In: ECAI workshop on explanation-aware computing

Ellman T (1989) Explanation-based learning: a survey of programs and perspectives. ACM Comput Surv 21(2)

Explanation on Wikipedia (2018) https://en.wikipedia.org/wiki/Explanation#Meta-explanation

Fum D, Missiera FD, Stoccob A (2007) The cognitive modeling of human behavior: why a model is (sometimes) better than 10,000 words. Cogn Syst Res 8(3):135–142

Galitsky B, Tumarkina I (2004) Justification of customer complaints using emotional states and mental actions. FLAIRS conference, Miami, Florida

Galitsky B, Miller A (2005) Determining possible criminal behavior of mobile phone users by means of analyzing the location tracking data. In: AAAI Spring symposium: AI technologies for homeland security, pp 120–122

Galitsky B (2006a) Reasoning about mental attitudes of complaining customers. Knowl Based Syst (Elsevier) 19(7):592–615

Galitsky B (2006b) Merging deductive and inductive reasoning for processing textual descriptions of inter-human conflicts. J Intell Info Syst 27(1):21–48

Galitsky B, Kovalerchuk B, Kuznetsov SO (2007a) Learning common outcomes of communicative actions represented by Labeled graphs. ICCS, pp 387–400

Galitsky B, Kuznetsov SO, Vinogradov DV (2007b) Applying hybrid reasoning to mine for associative features in biological data. J Biomed Inform 40(3):203–220

Galitsky B, Kuznetsov SO (2008a) Scenario argument structure vs individual claim defeasibility: what is more important for validity assessment? In: International conference on conceptual structures, pp 282–296

Galitsky B, Kuznetsov SO (2008b) Learning communicative actions of conflicting human agents. J Exp Theor Artif Intell 20(4):277–317

Galitsky B, González MP, Chesñevar CI (2009) A novel approach for classifying customer complaints through graphs similarities in argumentative dialogue. Decis Support Syst 46–3:717–729

Galitsky B, de la Rosa JL, (2011) Concept-based learning of human behavior for customer relationship management. Inf Sci 181(10):2016–2035

Galitsky B (2012) Machine learning of syntactic parse trees for search and classfication of text. Eng Appl AI 26(3):1072–1091

Galitsky B, Kovalerchuk B, de la Rosa JL (2011) Assessing plausibility of explanation and meta-explanation in inter-human conflicts. A special issue on semantic-based information and engineering systems. Eng Appl Artif Intell 24(8):1472–1486

Galitsky B (2014) Learning parse structure of paragraphs and its applications in search. Eng Appl Artif Intell 32:160–184

Galitsky B (2016a) Providing personalized recommendation for attending events based on individual interest profiles. Artif Intell Res 5(1):1–13

Galitsky B (2016b) Theory of mind engine. In: Computational autism, Springer

Galitsky B (2017) Matching parse thickets for open domain question answering. Data Knowl Eng 107:24–50

Galitsky B (2018) Customers' retention requires an explainability feature in machine learning systems they use. In: AAAI Spring symposium series

Galitsky B, Shpitsberg I (2016) Autistic learning and cognition. Computational autism. Springer, Cham, Switzerland, pp 245–293

Galitsky B, Parnis A (2017) How children with autism and machines learn to interact. In: Autonomy and artificial intelligence: a threat or savior? Springer, Cham, Switzerland

Galitsky B, Parnis A (2018) Accessing validity of argumentation of agents of the internet of everything. Artificial intelligence for the internet of everything, pp 187–216

Galitsky B, Goldberg S (2019) Explainable machine learning for chatbots. In developing enterprise chatbots. Springer, Cham Switzerland

Galitsky B, Kuznetsov SO, Samokhin MV (2005) Analyzing conflicts with concept-based learning International conference on conceptual structures. 307–322

Galitsky B, Kuznetsov SO, Kovalerchuk B (2008) Argumentation vs Meta-argumentation for the Assessment of Multi-agent Conflict. Proceedings of the Workshop on Metareasoning (colocated with the 23rd AAAI)

Galitsky B, Ilvovsky D, Kuznetsov SO (2018) Detecting logical argumentation in text via communicative discourse tree. J Exp Theor Artif Intell 30(5):637–663

Galitsky B, Ilvovsky D (2019) A demo of a chatbot for a virtual persuasive dialogue. In Persuasive technologies 14th international conference, Limassol, Cyprus, April 9–11

Ganter B, Kuznetsov SO (2001) Pattern structures and their projections. In: Stumme G, Delugach H (ed) Proceedings of the 9th international conference on conceptual structures, ICCS'01. Lecture notes in artificial intelligence, vol 2120, pp 129–142

Ganter B, Kuznetsov SO (2003) Hypotheses and version spaces. In: Proceedings of the 10th international conference on conceptual structures, ICCS'03. Lecture notes in artificial intelligence, vol 2746, pp 83–95

Gilpin LH, Bau D, Yuan BZ, Bajwa A, Specter M, Kagal L (2018) Explaining explanations: an approach to evaluating interpretability of machine learning. https://arxiv.org/pdf/1806.00069.pdf

GitHub Customer Complaints dataset (2019) https://github.com/bgalitsky/relevancebased-on-parse-trees/blob/master/examples/opinionsFinanceTags.xls

Goldberg S, Niemierko A, Turchin A (2008) Analysis of data errors in clinical research databases. In: AMIA symposium, vol 242–6

Goldberg S, Shklovsky-Kordi N, Zingerman B (2007) Time-oriented multi-image case history—way to the "disease image" analysis. VISAPP (Special Sessions), pp 200–203

Goodman B, Flaxman S (2017) European Union regulations on algorithmic decision-making and a "right to explanation" AI Magazine, vol 38, No 3

Grasso F (1999) Playing with RST: two algorithms for the automated manipulation of discourse trees. In: Matousek V, Mautner P, Ocelíková J, Sojka P (eds) Text, speech and dialogue. TSD 1999. Lecture notes in computer science, vol 1692. Springer, Berlin/Heidelberg

Hartono E, Santhanam R, Holsapple CW (2007) Factors that contribute to management support system success: an analysis of field studies. Decis Support Syst 43(1):256–268

Heider F (1958) The psychology of interpersonal relations. Wiley, New York

Hilton DJ (1988) Logic and causal attribution. In: Hilton DJ (ed) Contemporary science and natural explanation: commonsense conceptions of causality. Harvester Press, Brighton, England, pp 33–65

Joty S, Moschitti A (2014) Discriminative reranking of discourse parses using tree kernels. EMNLP

Kennedy XJ, Kennedy DM, Aaron JE (2006) Reasoning. In: The Bedford reader, 9th ed. Bedford/St. Martin's, New York, pp 519–522

Kim B, Khanna R, Koyejo OO (2016) Examples are not enough, learn to criticize! Criticism for interpretability. Adv Neural Inform Proc Syst

Kozyrkov C (2018) Explainable AI won't deliver. Here's why. https://hackernoon.com/explainable-ai-wont-deliver-here-s-why-6738f54216be

Krakovna V, Doshi-Velez F (2016) Increasing the interpretability of recurrent neural networks using hidden Markov models. CoRR. https://arxiv.org/abs/1606.05320

Krawczyk B, Minku LL, Gama J, Stefanowski J, Wozniak M (2017) Ensemble learning for data stream analysis: a survey. Inf Fusion 37:132–156

Lake BM, Salakhutdinov R, Tenenbaum JB (2015) Human-level concept learning through probabilistic program induction. Science 350(6266):1332–1338

Lee CJ, Sugimoto CR, Zhang G, Cronin B (2013) Bias in peer review. J Am Soc Inf Sci Tech 64:2–17

Lee DYW (2001) Genres, registers, text types, domains and styles: clarifying the concepts and navigating a path through the BNC jungle

Liu B, Hu M, Cheng J (2005) Opinion observer: analyzing and comparing opinions on the Web. In: 14th WWW conference, pp 342–351

Liu M, Shi J, Li Z, Li C, Zhu J, Liu S (2017) Towards better analysis of deep convolutional neural networks. IEEE Trans Visual Comput Graph 23(1):91–100

Lo Cascio V (1991) Grammatica dell'Argomentare: strategie e strutture [A grammar of Arguing: strategies and structures]. La Nuova Italia, Firenze

Ma J, Knight B, Petridis M (2008) Deriving explanations from partial temporal information. In: ECAI workshop on explanation-aware computing 2008

Mann W, Thompson S (1988) Rhetorical structure theory: towards a functional theory of text organization. Text-Interdiscip J Study Discourse 8(3):243–281

Mao J, Gan C, Kohli P, Tenenbaum JB, Wu J (2019) The neuro-symbolic concept learner: interpreting scenes words and sentences from natural supervision. abs/1904.12584

Marcus G, Davies E (2019) Rebooting AI. Pantheon Publishing, New York, NY

Molnar C (2019) Interpretable machine learning. A guide for making black box models explainable. https://christophm.github.io/interpretable-ml-book/

Moschitti A (2006) Efficient convolution kernels for dependency and constituent syntactic trees. In: Proceedings of the 17th European conference on machine learning, Berlin, Germany

Newman S, Lynch T, Plummer AA (2000) Success and failure of decision support systems: learning as we go. J Anim Sci 77

Nisbett RE, Ross L (1980) Human inference: strategies and shortcomings of social judgment. PrenticeHall, Englewood Cliffs, NJ

Pang B, Lee L (2008) Opinion mining and sentiment analysis. Found Trends Inf Retr 2(1–2):1–135

Pang B, Lee L, Vaithyanathan S (2002) Thumbs up?: sentiment classification using machine learning techniques. EMNLP 79–86

Parsons S, Wooldridge M, Amgoud L (2002) An analysis of formal inter-agent dialogues. In: Proceedings of the international conference on autonomous agents and multi-agent systems, Bologna

Plous S (1993) The psychology of judgment and decision making, McGraw-Hill, p 233

Prakken H, Vreeswijk G (2002) Logical systems for defeasible argumentation. In: Gabbay D, Guenther F (eds) Handbook of Phil. Kluwer, Logic, pp 219–318

Selman B (1995) Stochastic search and phase transitions: AI Meets physics. IJCAI 1:998–1002

Shklovsky-Kordi N, Shakin VV, Ptashko GO, Surin M, Zingerman B, Goldberg S, Krol M (2005a) Decision support system using multimedia case history quantitative comparison and multivariate statistical analysis. CBMS, pp 128–133

Shklovsky-Kordi N, Zingerman B, Rivkind N, Goldberg S, Davis S, Varticovski L, Krol M, Kremenetzkaia AM, Vorobiev A, Serebriyskiy I (2005b) Computerized case history—an effective tool for management of patients and clinical trials. In: Engelbrecht R et al (eds) Connecting medical informatics and bio-informatics. ENMI, pp 53–57

Surdeanu M, Hicks T, Valenzuela-Escarcega MA (2015) Two practical rhetorical structure theory parsers. In: Proceedings of the conference of the North American chapter of the association for computational linguistics—human language technologies: software demonstrations (NAACL HLT)

Tan S (2005) Neighbor-weighted K-nearest neighbor for unbalanced text corpus. Expert Syst Appl 28:667–671

Toulmin S (1958) The uses of argument. Cambridge at the University Press

Tsiakmaki M, Kostopoulos G, Kotsiantis S, Ragos O (2020) Implementing AutoML in educational data mining for prediction tasks. Appl Sci 10:90

Trstenjak B, Sasa M, Donko D (2013) KNN with TF-IDF based framework for text categorization. Procedia Eng 69

Turnbull WM (1986) Everyday explanation: the pragmatics of puzzle resolution. J Theory Soc Behav 16:141160

Turney PD (2002) Thumbs up or thumbs down? Semantic orientation applied to unsupervised classification of reviews. In: 40th ACL, New Brunswick, N.J.

Walton D (2007) Dialogical models of explanation' explanation-aware computing. In: Papers from the AAAI workshop, association for the advancement of artificial intelligence. Technical Report WS-07-06, AAAI Press, pp 1–9

Walton D (2008) Can argumentation help AI to understand explanation? Kunstliche Intelligenz 22(2):8–12

Walton D, Reed C, Macagno F (2008) Argumentation schemes. Cambridge University Press, Cambridge MA

Weigand H, Moor A (2004) Argumentation semantics of communicative action. In: Proceedings of the 9th international working conference on the language-action perspective on communication modeling, Rutgers University, New Jersey

Wheeldon A (2007) Generating explanations using a classical planner and modelling reasoning processes, skills and knowledge. In: AAAI workshop on explanation-aware computing, Vancouver, BC, Canada

Young T, Hazarika D, Poria S, Cambria E (2018) Recent trends in deep learning based natural language processing. https://arxiv.org/pdf/1708.02709.pdf

Yuan ST, WL Chang (2001) Mixed-initiative synthesized learning approach for web-based CRM. Expert Syst Appl 20(2):187–200(14)

Chapter 9
Recognizing Abstract Classes of Text Based on Discourse

Abstract The problem of classifying shorter and longer texts into abstract classes is formulated and its application areas for CRM are proposed. These classes include reasoning patterns expressed in text such as object-level versus metalanguage, document styles such as public versus containing sensitive information, containing a description of a problem versus a solution for a problem, instructions on how to solve it. The commonality between the tasks of classification into such classes is that keyword analysis is insufficient and an accent to higher-level (discourse) representation is necessary. To do that, we define thicket kernels as an extension of parse tree kernels from the level of individual sentences toward the level of paragraphs to classify texts at a high level of abstraction (Galitsky et al. in Graph structures for knowledge representation and reasoning, pp 39–57, 2014). We build a set of extended trees for a paragraph of text from the individual parse trees for sentences. It is performed based on anaphora and rhetorical structure relations between the phrases in different sentences. Tree kernel learning is applied to extended trees to take advantage of additional discourse-related information. We evaluate our approach in the security-related domain of the design documents. These are the documents which contain a formal well-structured presentation on how a system is built. Design documents need to be differentiated from product requirements, architectural, general design notes, templates, research results and other types of documents, which can share the same keywords. We also evaluate classification in the literature domain, classifying text in Kafka's novel "The Trial" as metalanguage versus novel's description in scholarly studies (a mixture of metalanguage and language-object).

9.1 Introduction

In the majority of text classification problems, keywords statistics is sufficient to determine a class. Keywords and n-grams form a feature set to determine a topic of a text or a document, such as *finance* versus *legal*, or *apple* versus *banana*. However, there are classification problems where distinct classes share the same keywords and their distributions in both domains are similar. In these cases, specific writing

© Springer Nature Switzerland AG 2020
B. Galitsky, *Artificial Intelligence for Customer Relationship Management*,
Human–Computer Interaction Series,
https://doi.org/10.1007/978-3-030-52167-7_9

styles of document, the way they are organized and other kinds of text structure information need to be taken into account. To perform text classification in such a domain, discourse information including rhetorical relations needs to be involved.

We are interested in classifying a text with respect to being *metalanguage or language object*. If a text tells us how to do things, or how something has been done, we relate this text to a language object. If a text is saying how to write a document that explains how to do things, we related it to metalanguage. Metalanguage is a language or symbolic system used to discuss, describe, or analyze another language or symbolic system. In theorem proving, metalanguage is a language in which proofs are manipulated and tactics are programmed, as opposed to the logic itself (the "object language"). In logic, it is a language in which the truth of statements in another language is being discussed.

Obviously, using just keyword information would be insufficient to differentiate between texts in a metalanguage and a language-object. A use of parse trees would give us specific phrases employed by texts in metalanguage, but still will not be sufficient for systematic exploration of metalanguage-related linguistic features. It is hard to identify them, unless one can analyze a discourse structure, including anaphora, rhetorical relations, and interaction scenarios by means of communicative language (Searle 1969; Galitsky and Kuznetsov 2008). Furthermore, to systematically learn these discourse features associated with metalanguage, we need a unified approach to classify graph structures at the level of paragraphs (Galitsky 2013).

The design of syntactic features for automated learning of syntactic structures for classification is still an art nowadays. One of the approaches to systematically treat these syntactic features is the *set kernels* built over syntactic parse trees. Convolution tree kernel (Collins and Duffy 2002) defines a feature space consisting of all subtree types of parse trees and counts the number of common subtrees as the syntactic similarity between two parse trees. They have found a number of applications in a series of NLP tasks, including syntactic parsing re-ranking, relation extraction, named entity recognition (Cumby and Roth 2003), Semantic Role Labeling (Moschitti 2006; Zhang et al. 2008), relation extraction, pronoun resolution (Kong and Zhou 2011), question classification (Zhang and Lee 2003) and machine translation (Sun et al. 2010, 2011).

The kernel's ability to generate large feature sets is useful to assure we have enough linguistic features to differentiate between the classes, to quickly model new and not well understood linguistic phenomena in learning machines. However, it is often possible to manually design features for linear kernels that produce high accuracy and fast computation time whereas the complexity of tree kernels may prevent their application in real scenarios. SVM (Vapnik 1995) can work directly with kernels by replacing the dot product with a particular kernel function. This useful property of kernel methods, that implicitly calculates the dot product in a high-dimensional space over the original representations of objects such as sentences, has made kernel methods an effective solution to modeling sentence-level structures in NLP.

An approach to build a kernel based on more than a single parse tree has been proposed, however for a different purpose than treating multi-sentence portions of text. To perform classification based on additional discourse features, we form a single tree from a tree forest for a sequence of sentences in a paragraph of text. Currently, kernel methods tackle individual sentences. For example, in question answering, when a query is a single sentence and an answer is a single sentence, these methods work fairly well. However, in learning settings where texts include multiple sentences, we need to represent structures which include paragraph-level information such as discourse.

A number of NLP tasks including classification require computing of semantic features over paragraphs of text containing multiple sentences (Galitsky 2003). Doing it at the level of individual sentences and then summing up the score for sentences will not always work. In the complex classification tasks where classes are defined in an abstract way, the difference between them may lay at the paragraph level and not at the level of individual sentences. In the case where classes are defined not via topics but instead via writing style, discourse structure signals become essential. Moreover, some information about entities can be distributed across sentences, and classification approach needs to be independent of this distribution. We will demonstrate the contribution of paragraph-level approach versus the sentence level in our evaluation.

9.2   Classification Domains

9.2.1   Design Documents Versus Design Meta-documents

We define design document as a document which contains a thorough and well-structured description of how to build a particular engineering system. In this respect a design document according to our model follows the reproducibility criteria of a patent or research publication; however, its format is different from them. What we exclude is a document that contains meta-level information relatively to the design of engineering system, such as *how to write design documents* manuals, standards design documents should adhere to, tutorials on how to improve design documents, and others.

We need to differentiate design documents from the classes of documents which can be viewed as ones containing meta-language, whereas the genuine design document is expected to consist from the language-object only. Below we enumerate such classed of *meta-documents*:

- design requirements, project requirement document, requirement analysis, operational requirements
- construction documentation, project planning, technical services review
- design guidelines, design guides, tutorials
- design templates (template for technical design document)
- research papers on system design
- general design-related notes
- educational materials on system design

- the description of the company, which owns design documents
- of a design professional
- specifications for civil engineering
- functional specifications
- "best design practices" description
- project proposals

Naturally, design documents are different from similar kinds of documents on the same topic in terms of style and phrasing. To extract these features, rhetorical relations are essential.

Notice that meta-documents can contain object-level text, such as design examples. Object level documents (genuine design docs) can contain some author reflections on the system design process (which are written in metalanguage). Hence the boundary between classes does not strictly separate metalanguage and language object. We use statistical language learning to optimize such the boundary, having supplied it with a rich set of linguistic features up to the discourse structures. In the design document domain, we will differentiate between texts in mostly meta-language and the ones mostly in language-object.

9.2.2 Text in Metalanguage Versus Text in Language-Object

A mixture of object-language and metalanguage descriptions can be found in literature. Describing the nature, a historical event, an encounter between people, an author uses a language object. Describing thoughts, beliefs, desires and knowledge of characters about the nature, events and interactions between people, an author uses a metalanguage. The entities/relations of such metalanguage range over the expressions (phrases) of the language-object. In other words, the physical world is usually described in language-object, and the mental world (theory of mind, the world of thoughts) typically combines both levels.

One of the purest examples of use of metalanguage in literature is Franz Kafka's novel "The Trial". According to our model, the whole plot is described in metalanguage, and object-level representation is absent. This is unlike a typical work of literature, where both levels are employed. In "The Trial", a reader learns that the main character Joseph K. is being prosecuted, his thoughts are described, and meeting with various people related to the trial are presented. However, no information is available about a reason for the trial, the charge, the circumstances of the investigation. The novel is a pure example of the presence of a meta-theory and absence of an object-level theory, from the standpoint of logic. The reader is expected to form the object–level theory herself to avoid ambiguity in interpretation of the novel.

Exploration of "The Trial" would help to understand the linguistic properties of metalanguage and language-object. For example, it is easy to differentiate between a mental and a physical words, just relying on keywords. However, to distinguish meta-language from language object in text, one need to consider different discourse structures, which we will automatically learn from text.

The following paragraph of text can be viewed as a fragment of an algorithm for how to solve an abstract problem of acquittal. Since it suggests a domain-independent approach (it does not matter what an accused did), it can be considered as a meta-algorithm.

> There are three possibilities: absolute acquittal, apparent acquittal and deferment. Absolute acquittal is the best, but there is nothing I could do to get that sort of outcome. I don't think there's anyone at all who could do anything to get an absolute acquittal. Probably the only thing that could do that is if the accused is innocent. As you are innocent it could actually be possible and you could depend on your innocence alone. In that case you will not need me or any other kind of help.

In some sense this algorithm follows along the lines of a simple Prolog interpreter, a typical example of a meta-program:

achieve_acquittal(true).
achieve_acquittal ((A,B)) :- achieve_acquittal (A), achieve_acquittal (B).
achieve_acquittal (A) :- clause(A,B), achieve_acquittal(B).

where the novel enumerates various *clauses*, but never ground terms expressing the details of a hypothetical crime. We hypothesize that a text expressing such a meta-program, Kafka's text, should have specific sequences of rhetorical relation, infrequent in other texts. We will attempt to find distinct discourse patterns associated with metalanguage and differentiate it with other texts.

In the literature domain, we will attempt to draw a boundary between the pure metalanguage (peculiar works of literature) and a mixed level text (a typical work of literature).

9.3 Extending Tree Kernel Toward Discourse

Why can sentence-level tree kernels be insufficient for classification? Important phrases can be distributed through different sentences. So we want to combine/merge parse trees to make sure we cover the phrase of interest.

For the following text:

> This document describes the design of back end processor. Its requirements are enumerated below.

from the first sentence, it looks like we got the design document. To process the second sentence, we need to disambiguate the preposition "its". As a result, we conclude from the second sentence that it is a requirements document (not a design document).

9.3.1 Leveraging Structural Information for Classification

How can a sentence structural information be indicative of the class?

The idea of measuring similarity between the question–answer pairs for question answering instead of the question–answer similarity turned out to be fruitful (Moschitti and Quarteroni 2011). The classifier for correct versus incorrect answers processes two pairs at a time, $<q_1, a_1>$ and $<q_2, a_2>$, and compare q_1 with q_2 and a_1 with a_2, producing a combined similarity score. Such a comparison allows to determine whether an unknown question/answer pair contains a correct answer or not by assessing its distance from another question/answer pair with a known label. In particular, an unlabeled pair $<q_2, a_2>$ will be processed so that rather than "guessing correctness" (Galitsky and Ilovsky 2019) based on words or structures shared by q_2 and a_2, both q_2 and a_2 will be compared to their correspondent components q_1 and a_1 of the labeled pair $<q_2, a_2>$ on the grounds of such words or structures. Since this approach targets a domain-independent classification of answer, only the structural cohesiveness between a question and answer is leveraged, not "meanings" of answers.

We follow along the lines of this idea and consider an arbitrary sequence of sentences instead of question-sentence and answer-sentence pair for text classification. Our positive training paragraphs are "plausible" sequences of sentences for our class, and our negative training paragraphs are "implausible" sequences, irrespectively of the domain specific keywords in these sentences.

In our opinion, for candidate answer selection task, such structural information is important but insufficient. At the same time, for the text classification tasks just structure analysis can suffice for proper classification.

Given a positive sequence and its parse trees linked by RST relations:

A hardware system contains classes such as GUI for user interface, IO for importing and exporting data between the emulator and environment, and Emulator for the actual process control. Furthermore, a class Modules is required which contains all instances of modules in use by emulation process. (Fig. 9.1)

and a negative sequence and its linked parse trees:

A socio-technical system is a social system sitting upon a technical base. Email is a simple example of such system. The term socio-technical was introduced in the 1950s by the Tavistok Institute. (Fig. 9.2)

We want to classify the paragraph

A social network-based software ticket reservation system includes the following components. They are the Database for storing transactions, Web Forms for user data input, and Business rule processor for handling the web forms. Additionally, the backend email processing includes the components for nightly transaction execution". (Fig. 9.3)

One can see that it follows the rhetorical structure of the top (positive) training set element, although it shares more common keywords with the bottom (negative)

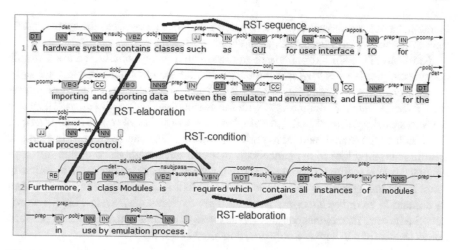

Fig. 9.1 A sequence of parse trees and RST relations for a positive example

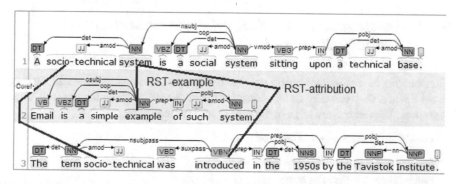

Fig. 9.2 A sequence of parse trees and RST relations for a negative example

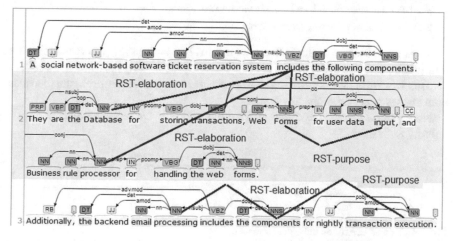

Fig. 9.3 A sequence of parse trees and RST relations for a text to be classified

element. Hence we classify it as a design doc text, since it describes the system rather than introduces a term (as the negative element does).

To illustrate the similar point in the question answering domain, we use a simple query example. If q_1 is *"What is plutocracy?"* and the candidate answers are $a_1 =$ *"Plutocracy may be defined as a state where ..."* versus $a_0 =$ *'Plutocracy affects the wills of people ...'*, comparison with the correct pair formed by $q_2 =$ *"What is a source control software?"* and $a_2 =$ *"A source control software can be defined as a ... "* will induce the kernel method to prefer a_1 over a_0. One can see that a_1 has similar wording and structure to a_2, hence $<q_1, a_1>$ will get a higher score than $<q_1, a_0>$ using the kernel method. In contrast, the opposite case would occur using a similarity score matching q_1 with a_1 as compared with matching q_1 with a_0, since both a_1 and a_0 contain keywords *plutocracy* from q_1. This explains why even a bag-of-words kernel adjusting its weights on question/answer pairs has a better chance to produce better results than a bag-of-words question/answer similarity.

9.3.2 Anaphora and Rhetorical Relations for Sentiments Topicality Classification

For example, in sentiment analysis, we classify sentences and documents with respect to sentiments they contain. Let us consider the sentiment classes for the following sentences. We are interested in both polarity and topicality classes:

I would not let my dog stay in this hotel (Fig. 9.4)

Our dog would have never stayed in this hotel

Filthy dirty hotel, like a dog house

They would not let my dog stay in this hotel

The hotel management did not let me in when I was with my dog

We were not allowed to stay there with our dog

What one observes is that polarity = negative in both cases, whereas topics are totally different. Topic1 = *"hotel is dirty"*, and topic2 = *"dogs are not allowed"*.

This is a difficult task for keyword-based text classification problems because both classes share the same keywords.

Notice these classes are different from the topic3 = *"hotels intended for dogs"*, polarity = *"neutral"*

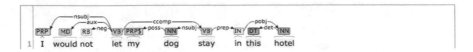

Fig. 9.4 A parse tree for an individual sentence

If you have never been to a dog hotel, now is the time. It is even harder to perform a classification, where the information about *staying in a hotel* and *having a dog* is spread through different sentences. An easier case is anaphora:

I arrived to the hotel. It was too bad even for a dog. (Fig. 9.5)

The hardest case is when a rhetorical structure is needed to link information about a *hotel* and a *dog*:

I was traveling for business. My partner invited me to stay at his place, however it looked like a house for dogs.

I was traveling with my dog for business. I was not going to stay at a hotel but at my partner's place, however he turned out to be allergic to dogs. Sadly, the hotel did not let us in. (Fig. 9.6)

In the above cases, the parts of the parse trees (sub-trees) essential to determine the meanings occur in different sentences, so need to be connected. An anaphora is a natural way to do that, but is not always sufficient. Hence we need rhetorical relations to link "*travel, dog owner, hotel*" and hotel permission relationships.

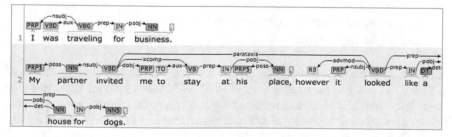

Fig. 9.5   A fragment of text with a coreference relation

Coreference:

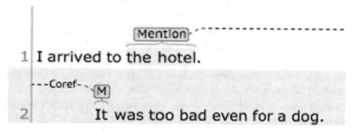

Basic dependencies:

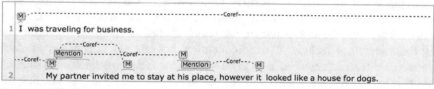

Fig. 9.6   The parse tree and respective coreference arcs for two sentences

9.3.3   *Anaphora and Rhetorical Relations for Classification Tasks*

We introduce a domain where a pair-wise comparison of sentences is insufficient to properly learn certain semantic features of texts. This is due to the variability of the ways an information can be communicated in multiple sentences, and variations in possible discourse structures of text which needs to be taken into account.

We consider an example of text classification problem (Chap. 6 in Volume 1), where short portions of text belong to two classes:

(1)   Tax liability of a landlord renting office to a business;
(2)   Tax liability of a business owner renting an office from landlord.

> I rent an office space. This office is for my business. I can deduct office rental expense from my business profit to calculate net income.

> To run my business, I have to rent an office. The net business profit is calculated as follows. Rental expense needs to be subtracted from revenue.

> To store goods for my retail business I rent some space. When I calculate the net income, I take revenue and subtract business expenses such as office rent.

> I rent out a first floor unit of my house to a travel business. I need to add the rental income to my profit. However, when I repair my house, I can deduct the repair expense from my rental income.

> I receive rental income from my office. I have to claim it as a profit in my tax forms. I need to add my rental income to my profits, but subtract rental expenses such as repair from it.

> I advertised my property as a business rental. Advertisement and repair expenses can be subtracted from the rental income. Remaining rental income needs to be added to my profit and be reported as taxable profit.

Note that keyword-based analysis does not help to separate the first three paragraph and the second three paragraphs. They all share the same keywords *rental/office/income/profit/add/subtract*. Phrase-based analysis does not help, since both sets of paragraphs share similar phrases. Secondly, pair-wise sentence comparison does not solve the problem either. Anaphora resolution is helpful but insufficient. All these sentences include "I" and its mention, but other links between words or phrases in different sentences need to be used. Rhetorical structures need to come into play to provide additional links between sentences. The structure to distinguish between

> renting for yourself and deducting from total income and
> renting to someone and adding to income

embraces multiple sentences. The second clause about "*adding/subtracting incomes*" is linked by means of the rhetorical relation of *Elaboration* with the first clause for *landlord/tenant*. This rhetorical relation may link discourse units within a sentence, between consecutive sentences and even between first and third sentences in a paragraph. Other rhetorical relations can play similar role for forming essential links for text classification.

Coreference:

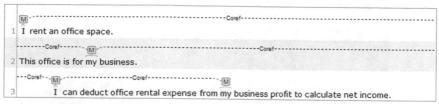

Basic dependencies:

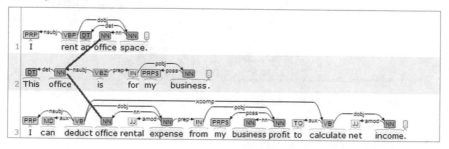

Fig. 9.7 Coreferences and the set of dependency trees for the first text

Which representations for these paragraphs of text would produce such common sub-structure between the structures of these paragraphs? We believe that extended trees, which include the first, second, and third sentence for each paragraph together can serve as a structure to differentiate the two above classes.

The dependency parse trees for the first text in our set and its coreferences are shown in Fig. 9.7. There are multiple ways the nodes from parse trees of different sentences can be connected: we choose the rhetorical relation of elaboration which links the same entity office and helps us to form the structure *rent-office-space—for-my-business—deduct-rental-expense* which is the base for our classification. We used Stanford Core NLP, coreferences resolution (Lee et al. 2013) and its visualization to form Figs. 9.1, 9.2, 9.3, 9.4, 9.5, 9.6 and 9.7.

Figure 9.8 shows the resultant extended tree with the root "I" from the first sentence. It includes the whole first sentence, a verb phrase from the second sentence and a verb phrase from the third sentence according to rhetorical relation of *Elaboration*. Notice that this extended tree can be intuitively viewed as representing the "main idea" of this text compared to other texts in our set. All extended trees need to be formed for a text and then compared with that of the other texts, since we do not know in advance which extended tree is essential. From the standpoint of tree kernel learning, extended trees are learned the same way as regular parse trees.

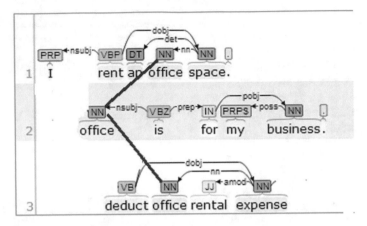

Fig. 9.8 Extended tree which includes 3 sentences

9.4   Building Extended Trees

For every arc which connects two parse trees, we derive the extension of these trees, extending branches according to the arc (Fig. 9.9). In this approach, for a given parse tree, we will obtain a set of its extensions, so the elements of the kernel will be computed for many extensions, instead of just a single tree. The problem here is that we need to find common sub-trees for a much higher number of trees than the number of sentences in text; however, by subsumption (sub-tree relation) the number of common sub-trees will be substantially reduced.

If we have two parse trees P_1 and P_2 for two sentences in a paragraph, and a relation R_{12}: $P_{1i} \rightarrow P_{2j}$ between the nodes P_{1i} and P_{2j}, we form the pair of extended trees $P1 * P2$:

$$\ldots, P_{1i-2}, P_{1i-1}, P_{1i}, P_{2j}, P_{2j+1}, P_{2j+2}, \ldots$$
$$\ldots, P_{2j-2}, P_{2j-1}, P_{2j}, P_{1i}, P_{1i+1}, P_{2i+2}, \ldots,$$

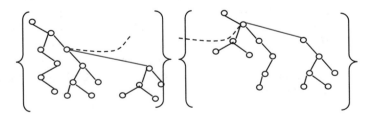

Fig. 9.9 An arc which connects two parse trees for two sentences in a text (on the top) and the derived set of extended trees (on the bottom)

which would form the feature set for tree kernel learning in addition to the original trees P_1 and P_2. Notice that the original order of nodes of parse trees are retained under operation "*".

The algorithm for building an extended tree for a set of parse trees T is presented below:

Input:
1) Set of parse trees T.
2) Set of relations R, which includes relations R_{ijk} between the nodes of T_i and T_j: $T_i \in T$, $T_j \in T$, $R_{ijk} \in R$. We use index k to range over multiple relations between the nodes of parse tree for a pair of sentences.

Output: the exhaustive set of extended trees E.

Set $E = \varnothing$;
For each tree $i=1:|T|$
  For each relation R_{ijk}, $k= 1: |R|$
   Obtain T_j
   Form the pair of extended trees $T_i * T_j$;
   Verify that each of the extended trees do not have a super-tree in E
    If verified, add to E;
Return E.

Notice that the resultant trees are not the proper parse trees for a sentence, but nevertheless form an adequate feature space for tree kernel learning.

To obtain the inter-sentence links, we employed conferences from Stanford NLP (Recasens et al. 2013; Lee et al. 2013). Rhetorical relation extractor is based on our rule-based approach to finding relations between elementary discourse units (Galitsky et al. 2013a, b). We combined manual rules with automatically learned rules derived from the available discourse corpus by means of syntactic generalization (Galitsky 2012).

Rhetorical Structure Theory (RST) (Mann et al. 1992) is one of the most popular approach to model extra-sentence as well as intra-sentence discourse. RST represents texts by labeled hierarchical structures, called Discourse Trees (DTs). The leaves of a DT correspond to contiguous Elementary Discourse Units (EDUs). Adjacent EDUs are connected by rhetorical relations (e.g., Elaboration, Contrast), forming larger discourse units (represented by internal nodes), which in turn are also subject to this relation linking. Discourse units linked by a rhetorical relation are further distinguished based on their relative importance in the text: nucleus being the central part, whereas satellite being the peripheral one. Discourse analysis in RST involves two subtasks: discourse segmentation is the task of identifying the EDUs, and discourse parsing is the task of linking the discourse units into a labeled tree.

9.4.1   Kernel Methods for Parse Trees

Kernel methods are a large class of learning algorithms based on inner product vector spaces. Support vector machines (SVMs) are mostly well-known algorithms. The main idea behind SVMs is to learn a hyperplane,

$$H(\vec{x}) = \vec{w} \cdot \vec{x} + b = 0, \tag{9.1}$$

where $\vec{x}$ is the representation of a classifying object o as a feature vector, while $\vec{w} \in \Re^n$ (indicating that $\vec{w}$ belongs to a vector space of n dimensions built on real numbers) and $b \in \Re$ are parameters learned from training examples by applying the Structural Risk Minimization principle (Vapnik 1995). Object o is mapped into $\vec{x}$ via a feature function

$$\phi : \mathcal{O} \rightarrow \Re^n,$$

where $\mathcal{O}$ is the set of objects; o is categorized in the target class only if $H(\vec{x}) \geq 0$.
The decision hyperplane can be rewritten as:

$$H(\vec{x}) = \left(\sum_{i=1,\dots l} y_i \alpha_i \vec{x}_i \right) \cdot \vec{x} + b = \sum_{i=1,\dots l} y_i \alpha_i \vec{x}_i \cdot \vec{x} + b = \sum_{i=1,\dots l} y_i \alpha_i \phi(o_i) \cdot \phi(o_i) + b, \tag{9.2}$$

where y_i is equal to 1 for positive examples and to -1 for negative examples $\alpha_i \in \Re$ with $\alpha_i \geq 0, o_i \forall i \in \{1, \dots, l\})$.

are the training instances and

$$K(o_i, o) = \langle \phi(o_i) \cdot \phi(o) \rangle$$

is the kernel function associated with the mapping ϕ.

Convolution kernels as a measure of similarity between trees compute the common sub-trees between two trees T_1 and T_2. Convolution kernel does not have to compute the whole space of tree fragments. Let the set $\mathcal{T} = \{t_1, t_2, \dots, t_{|\mathcal{T}|}\}$ be the set of sub-trees of an extended parse tree, and $\chi_i(n)$ be an indicator function which is equal to 1 if the subtree t_i is rooted at a node n, and is equal to 0 otherwise. A tree kernel function over trees T_1 and T_2 is

$$TK(T_1, T_2) = \sum_{n_1 \in N_{T_1}} \sum_{n_1 \in N_{T_2}} \Delta(n_1, n_2), \tag{9.3}$$

where N_{T1} and N_{T2} are the sets of T_1's and T_2's nodes, respectively and

$$\Delta(n_1, n_2) = \sum_{i=1}^{|\mathcal{T}|} \chi_i(n_1) \chi_i(n_2). \tag{9.4}$$

Equation (9.4) calculates the number of common fragments with the roots in n_1 and n_2 nodes.

9.4.2 The Chart of Tree Kernel Learning

The architecture of the classification system is shown in Fig. 9.10. Once Stanford NLP performs parsing and identifies coreferences, VerbNet components obtains verb signatures, and Stanford NLP builds anaphora relations, we proceed to finding the same-entity and sub-entity links. After that, we perform segmentation into elementary discourse units and find RST relations, using our own templates (also, third party RST parsers can be incorporated).

As a result, we obtain parse thicket for a text as a sequence of parse trees with additional discourse level arcs linking parse trees for different sentences. For a parse thicket, we form the set of all phrases and then derive the set of extended phrases according to inter-sentence arcs. Once we build the totality of extended phrases, we form a representation for SVM tree kernel learning, which inputs the set of extended parse trees.

9.5 Metalanguage and Works of Literature

For the example use of metalanguage we consider Frantz Kafka's (1883–1924) novel "The Trial" (Fig. 9.11). This novel, written in 1915, has been puzzling many generations of literature critics. Kafka's novels belong to the modernist trends in the literature, which uses various philosophical concepts and new ways of depicting reality. In his works, Franz Kafka went largely beyond other modernists, since his novel structure and language feature very sophisticated artistic expression. The language

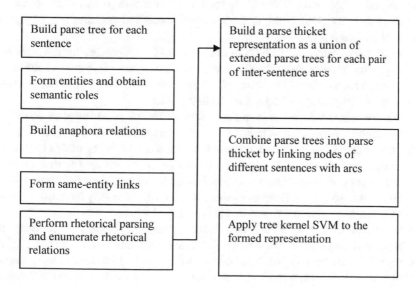

Fig. 9.10 The architecture of learning system

Fig. 9.11 Various designs of the book cover

of Kafka, apparently devoid of any revelations and interpretations, contains an inexhaustible material for linguistic theories. Through scientific analysis of the novel "The Trial", one can see that the writer's use of language is a pointer to an understanding of the underlying aspects of his work. Novel "The Trial" consists of sixteen chapters and an appendix "Dream". In the course of his life,Franz Kafka could not complete this work. Max Brod, Kafka's closest friend and executor helped publish this novel and gave it the title.

Undoubtedly, many unfinished manuscripts of Kafka makes treating his work with an even greater interest, since the absence of ties and open ending always contribute to the construction of the set of inconsistent theories. "The Trial" does not represent a complex, multi-passage structure, at the first glance.

The story presented by Kafka is fairly simple. Joseph K. is the alter ego of the writer. Joseph K. from the first lines of the novel became involved in a lawsuit. The reader does not get any information about the reason and meaning of this trial, given the common description of its flow and the suspects' encounters with a series of law enforcement officials. It turns out that Joseph K. himself does not know why he ended up in this situation. There are no clues and hints as to why the hero suddenly became defendants and for what crime is he charged with.

Incomprehensibility of what is happening in the novel makes us scrutinize the peculiarities of language used by Franz Kafka to describe the events in "The Trial". To comprehend the meaning of the novel as a whole, we need to ascend to the certain level of abstraction. To systematically treat the plot, we consider the text of the novel as written in meta-language, and the remaining part about the reason and the subject of the trial as hypothetically represented in the language-object. Hence what seems to be most interesting and informative to the reader is the theory-object (which is absent), and what is available is the meta-theory (what is explicitly described in the novel).

A metalanguage includes the relations over the expressions of language object, such as the features of the trial flow. On the contrary, a traditional literature style relies on language-object only, which includes the relations between subjects such as objects of physical and mental world. In most works of literature, a metalanguage might be present but its role is secondary and its purpose is to present some generalizations of characters and observations of a writer. However, in "The Trial" language-object level is minimal.

Hence Kafka describes all events in metalanguage only, relatively to the subject of the trial. It is easy to verify this statement, having taken an arbitrary paragraph. It describes some discussions of details of the trial with some individuals involved in law enforcement, such as the following:

> If you want an apparent acquittal I'll write down an assertion of your innocence on a piece of paper. The text for an assertion of this sort was passed down to me from my father and it's quite unassailable. I take this assertion round to the judges I know. So I'll start off with the one I'm currently painting, and put the assertion to him when he comes for his sitting this evening. I'll lay the assertion in front of him, explain that you're innocent and give him my personal guarantee of it. And that's not just a superficial guarantee, it's a real one and it's binding.

We attempt to represent the novel "The Trial" at the meta-level only. One can observe that the key character meets with other characters to discuss the details of the trial. All these characters are aware of what is happening, the plot is fully focused on the trial procedures, but the knowledge of the process itself (the object-level) is absent.

Franz Kafka naturally used his peculiar writing style and way of narration working on a novel. Many of Kafka's novels are full with mystery and deep analysis of characters' mental states, and the author often uses meta-language as a means of expression. What are the reasons for it?

In the novel, the use of metalanguage symbolizes the impossibility to come up with a term for the whole trial. The authors are so appalled by what is describing that he is unable to name it (this name would belong to language-object). Possibly, the described trial is not correlated with the socio-historical context of 1910s.

Metalanguage describes all the specific information about Joseph K., for example, the reader learns from the first pages where Joseph K. lives and what he receives for breakfast and when. But we can not say for sure that Kafka describes the physical reality, not a human condition between sleeping and waking. In other words, the writer may be using a meta-language to enhance the effect of involvement of the reader in the phantasmagoric and absurd world with the blurred boundaries between dream and reality.

For Franz Kafka's representation of sleep and awakening, it is an inexhaustible source for the exploration of the world and its characters. It was after a restless sleep (troubled dreams) that Gregor Samsa has turned into an insect in the novel "The

Metamorphosis" of 1912. On the contrary, a partial detachment from the real world and the abundance of household items in "The Trial" gives the author an opportunity to create a completely different reader perception, subject to human comprehension in even smaller degree.

Kafka's scholars consider his biography for better comprehension of his novel. It is important for "The Trial" since the details of Kafka's life are similar to Joseph K.'s. They both occupy an office position (Joseph K. was a bank's vice president). Kafka is familiar with bureaucratic structures. All venues in the novel change as if theater decorations, dwellings are instantly turned into a courtroom. Other characters also belong to the same common bureaucratic/mechanical system, as its indispensable parts. Many characters in the novel are not bright personalities at all, for example, the officers who arrested Joseph K. The writer aims to convincingly capture the whole bureaucratic world, relying on the expressiveness of metalanguage instead of satirical motifs. Apparently, the elements of satire in "The Trial" were deliberately rejected by the author to make the novel sound as a parable.

Creating a novel in which the metalanguage is the only means of descriptions of what is happening, Kafka continues the tradition of historical writings and legends. "The Trial" is a novel where ancient cultural traditions are deeply intertwined with the subconscious mind of the author. In the story of Josef K., described in the metalanguage, there is a lot of social terms: the court, the law, the judge, the arrest, the process of accusation. These terms could have been used from ancient times to the modern era of social development. For example, the process of Joseph K. may well be a reference to the Last Judgment and his sentence denotes the divine punishment. In the novel "The Trial" with its metalanguage much can be seen from the perspective of theology and spirituality.

For sure, Franz Kafka believed in an idea, not a reality, being a modernist. His idea came from his own subconscious, which can be described by metalanguage means only (Aurora 2001; Ricoeur 1975). All moral reflection of the author, his spiritual studies and innermost thoughts showed his special method of expression.

To some extent, the novel can be attributed to the detective genre (Galitsky et al. 2016). The events occur in the environment Joseph K. is familiar with, and all the characters are described by the author in a fairly routine manner. Yet "The Trial" does not belong to the classical detective because its logical constructions cannot be assessed as a truth. This is because the facts are represented in metalanguage and the object-level facts are missing, so a reader cannot appreciate a solution to a problem, an inherent part of a detective novel. Initiation of "The Trial" occurs in the object level outside of text and cannot be used to accuse the main character.

Kafka's use of metalanguage has a significant impact on the perception of the whole process as something absurd, not subject to any expected rules. All the actions of Joseph K. cannot be viewed from the standpoint of a legal system and are deliberately fairly generic in nature. The writer presents the Court as an omnipotent organization, but in fact this court makes no investigation of the main character, at least from what we know from the novel. The investigation itself cannot exist in this novel, given the style of the description of the whole process to the metalanguage.

The lack of investigation and disclosure of secrets do not prevent Kafka from maintaining the suspense until the last pages of the novel. One gets the impression that the final sentence of Joseph K. in all circumstances of the case may not be an acquittal. The very first cause of any judicial process lies in the fact of charges being brought. The metalanguage only emphasizes the bureaucratic proceedings, which is the foundation and skeleton of the novel.

Endless absurdity of the described process reminds us about the famous novel by Charles Dickens "Bleak House". Completed in 1853, "Bleak House" was forerunner of a new narrative paradigm. It is important to note that the plot of a Dickens novel in many respects anticipates the history of "The Trial". All events of "Bleak House" take place during an endless litigation process in which the Court of Chancery determines the fate of the characters of the novel.

Dickens conducted a certain extent artistic experiment, outlining the events in a very detached way, but not depriving them of a secret meaning. Kafka and Dickens are united in their desire to express in new linguistic forms the meaninglessness and injustice of what is happening in the courts. Both writers were looking for the truth, which is mired in unpleasant courtrooms and stuffy offices. Franz Kafka, perfectly familiar with the works of Dickens, partially enriched "The Trial" by the narrative technique of "Bleak House". But the metalanguage of Kafka does not express deep personal experiences of the character. Instead, it is limited to the dis-attached vision of the distant events.

Commenting and clarification of events by the author are absent in "The Trial". Interestingly, the nature of the novel is close to the authors' perception of what is happening in the society. However, the writer expresses his attitude to the society implicitly, in the metalanguage. The absence of any background information and causes of the trial makes the reader focus primarily on the fate of Josef K. Perhaps Kafka strongly felt connection with his main character and considered supplementing the text with his subjective emotions unnecessary. In addition to the above, Kafka's metalanguage hides his deep personal alienation from the system of justice. By the very use of metalanguage the author emphasizes that any litigation is senseless a priory. Also, any man is doomed to become a victim of the system, where bureaucratic principles dominate.

"The Trial" is both illogical and systematic through the use of metalanguage. Joseph K. was not ready for the trial, but at the same time it is clear that without the involvement of a trial this character would be no longer interesting for the reader. Kafka carefully hides mentions of the past of the main character, and also does not give us any opinion about him by the other novel characters. It becomes difficult for the reader to determine whether Josef K. guilty or not guilty. Metalanguage does not provide any clues about previously occurred events in the novel. The metalanguage of "The Trial" prevents its unequivocal interpretation and leaves the ending of the novel open and ambiguous.

The expectation of the novel's outcome is rather strong in the novel. The metalanguage expressive means reinforces the impression of the reader from the seemingly meaningless wandering of the main character through the courtrooms. Here the author attempts to create a hostile atmosphere, where the usual course of time is replaced by eternal awaiting of sentencing. The conflict is manifested not in the struggle of the main character for his honor and dignity, but in the endless discussion of details. Having ruled out by the use of the metalanguage, any information about the reasons for the charges of Josef K., the writer depicts the stages of the judicial process in detail. Even the passage of time in the novel is completely subordinated to the trial. Any decision depends on the unknown higher powers, and the activity of the main character cannot affect the situation.

Metalanguage of "The Trial" is not only a way to describe events, but it also gives this novel an artistic value, independent of the historical and philosophical concepts of the era. Undoubtedly, Franz Kafka does not give any answer in the novel, it only raises questions. Writer's method manifests itself in the complete absence of any reasons and plot ties, so that the boundaries of the reader's imagination are unlimited. Thanks to the metalanguage, the writer creates an artistic world where thoughts and speculations become the only possible form of the perception of the novel. Through the analysis of "The Trial", it becomes clear that any conclusions on the product may not be final. Metalanguage creates a paradoxical situation where the lack of basic information makes it possible for any interpretations of the text. Applying the metalanguage in the novel, Franz Kafka included it in the list of works of literature appealing for new generations of readers.

9.6   Documents Versus Meta-documents for CRM Data Loss Prevention

An ever-increasing amount of sensitive data and confidential information is being stored as electronic documents, and the amount of transmission of such data is increasing. Accordingly, there is a need to ensure that only the authorized parties have access to the data. Various techniques have been used to attempt to prevent unauthorized access to data, such as through the use of data encryption and secure communication channels. Frequently, available techniques are not flexible enough to enable users with multiple security permissions to concurrently access data with different security levels. Moreover, there is difficulty in controlling what a given individual does with a secure document once that information is accessed (Roth et al. 2015).

Automated understanding and categorizing of documents has a high value in document processing systems. One class of such system in the cyber security domain is data loss prevention (DLP), a mechanism that prevents leaking sensitive documents from an organization. In recent years companies intensively use data sharing, cloud-based services which led to an increasing number of data breaches, i.e., malicious or inadvertent disclosures of confidential and sensitive information, such as person identifying information, medical records, trade secrets, and enterprise financial information, to unintended parties. These data breaches may have severe consequences, such as violation of customers' privacy, loss of competitive advantage, loss of customers and reputation, punitive fines, and tangible monetary loss. In 2009 the cost of a data breach was estimated as $6–10 million for an organization (Poneman Institute 2009; Hackett 2015; Fortune 2015).

Company employees often have access to documents including information concerning various significant business operations of this company. This information may include sensitive data on clients and patients, contracts, agreements, supplies, employees, production details, etc. Conventional DLP techniques typically scan data as it is departing from an endpoint system, and apply a set of DLP rules based on static policies to prevent disclosure of sensitive information. In conventional DLP techniques, for a given set of employees, article of information and attempted user operation, the same predetermined actions are applied over and over again. This requires a sysadmin to make a decision concerning whether to have highly restrictive DLP policies or less restrictive DLP policies. This is done at the time that the security system is tuned. Highly restrictive policies make sensitive data safer on one hand, but incur the cost of consuming large amounts of system resources on the other hand (Barile 2013). False positive rate of such systems is fairly high, regretfully. Also, restrictive policies frequently prevent users from performing legitimate operations. Less restrictive policies use fewer resources and cause fewer false positives, but provide a less secure environment. Conventional security techniques are not able to dynamically change actions and DLP policies, increasing or decreasing protection based on the document content (Galitsky 2019). Hence DLP can leverage document analysis in a high degree.

Sony's November 2014 hacking led to the disclosure of unreleased movies, embarrassing internal emails, and personal data—including Social Security numbers—of 47,000 celebrities and employees. It was so traumatic and disruptive to the company that it delayed its 10-K filing. Sony estimates its breach's financial impact has been just $15 million to date in investigation and remediation costs, which represent from 0.9 to 2% of Sony's total projected sales for 2014.

Security companies distribute a number of DLP systems designed to help businesses avoid data breaches (McAfee 2016; Symantec 2016; TrendMicro 2016; RSA 2016). DLP software detect confidential and sensitive data on storage servers, in the cloud, process network. DLP systems share their results by either enforcing data control policies or generating reports for system administrators to investigate potential cases of data leaks.

Currently available DLP systems are fairly good at detecting the structure of information distribution. However, their features to recognize sensitive information is rather limited. Document analysis systems mostly rely on keywords and regular expressions, but they are insufficient to solve the problem. Judging by keywords only, it is hard to recognize documents which should not be leaked since they can be written in a way without the keywords explicitly indicating its class, such as "confidential" or "sensitive financial report". Over last few years, security exports became aware of the need of the DLP systems to automatically learn and recognize sensitive material. A limited number of keyword-based statistical classification algorithms for sensitive documents (Wüchner and Pretschner 2012; Hart et al. 2013) have been proposed to distinguish public and private documents.

Using an ML approach, system administrators do not have to develop and maintain keyword lists, and the classifier can recognize private information, even in documents that do not have a substantial overlap with previously observed private documents. However, statistical keyword-based classifiers have a strong limitation since private and public documents frequently have the same keywords, the difference between them being the writing style.

In this Chapter, we describe a DLP document classification system that leverages a discourse-level analysis in addition to syntactic one to recognize a grammar and discourse style inherent to private versus public documents. The main advantage of such the system over the keyword-based one is that the recognition engine is style-dependent instead of domain-dependent and therefore requires neither advanced keywords nor extensive training set from a system administrator. Instead, it uses a training set prepared in advance in the key domains such as sensitive financial, legal, health and technical document.

Let us compare the rhetorical structures of engineering system description text (such as the last paragraph of the next section, shown in blue) and a scientific text outlining an state of knowledge in a given domain. The former rhetorical structure includes relations of *Sequence, Purpose* and *Elaboration* (Fig. 9.12). Describing a

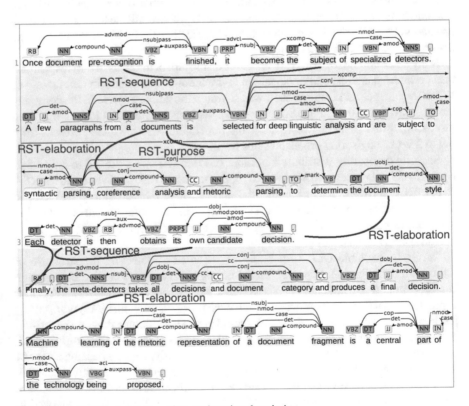

Fig. 9.12 A rhetorical structure of an engineering description

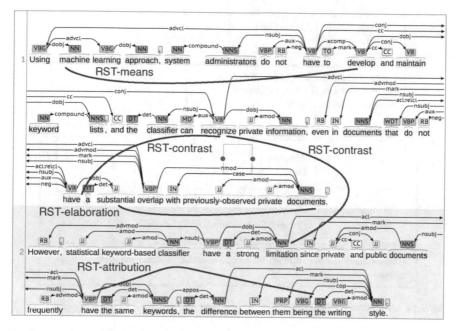

Fig. 9.13 Rhetorical structure of a scientific description

system, authors usually do not express their thoughts via *Contrast* or *Attribution*, which is typical for a scientific discourse. The latter rhetorical structure includes the relations of *Means, Contrast, Attribution* and also *Elaboration* (Fig. 9.13).

9.6.1   Architecture of the DLP System

DLPs are designed to protect the following types of data:

(1)   Static data stored in document management systems, email servers, file servers, networked-attached storages, personal computers, and cloud storages.
(2)   Outbound network traffic such as emails, instant messages and web traffic.

In different enterprises, a definition of sensitive data varies, but personally identifiable information, health records under HIPAA and educational records under FERPA are supposed to be always protected. Trade secrets and internal communications are almost always sensitive. A secret information is the one generated within a company that is not generally known, unlike the facts that can be found in an encyclopedia or industry magazines or contained in public materials from the company. A DLP system is intended to identify sensitive information in one or more of the above kinds.

The DLP system architecture being proposed is depicted in chart Fig. 9.14. Once a document is obtained, it is subject to (Apache 2020) extraction that recognizes

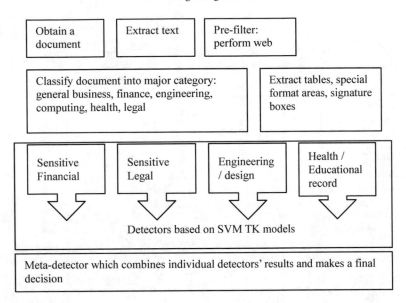

Fig. 9.14 DLP system architecture

document format, extracts metadata and text. Certain features of the document format are extracted as well, including image captions, headers and footers, signature boxes and form-specific elements.

To quickly recognize if the document is public, a phrase search engine query is formed and submitted to Bing Azure search engine API. This query is extracted from multiple sections of a document. If a returned result is not very frequent (such as "this is private and confidential") and very similar (in terms of string distance) to some sentences in the document, then we conclude that the document is public and should be classified as such. To get a broad category of a document, we classify it into six major classes that cover the totality of all documents. This is done by an efficient coarse method such as nearest neighbor and implemented via Apache Lucene search of the phrases extracted from this document. The most probable class is defined via the majority vote algorithm.

Once document pre-recognition is finished, it becomes the subject of specialized detectors. A few paragraphs from a documents is selected for deep linguistic analysis and are subject to syntactic parsing, coreference analysis and rhetorical parsing, to determine the document style. Each detector then obtains its own candidate decision. Finally, the meta-detectors takes all decisions and document category and produces a final decision. Meta-detector also selects the threshold values to assure the best position on the ROC curve for the optimal value of the false-positive rate. Machine learning of the rhetorical representation of a document fragment is a central part of the technology being proposed.

The paragraph above is used to illustrate an engineering description (Fig. 9.12) that can be a sensitive document with a limited access.

9.6.2   Rule Post-processing to Reduce False Alerts

So far, the Data Loss Prevention system has been treating data loss of a given document as of equal risk value, regardless of who is sending the document or where it is going to. When deploying this system for different clients, they would want to configure it differently based on their company policies and procedures. For certain job roles, people are expected to communicate with known external organizations. The external organizations can be identified with their email domain names. For example:

- Public relations is expected to give press releases, new product designs, new financial disclosures to a fixed list of external news organizations.
- Human resources and Payroll to communicate with ADP for managing payroll, deductions for benefits, insurance enrollments and so on.
- The legal department and executives will be involved in confidential legal contracts for mergers and acquisitions.
- Technical security professionals may be communicating with offsite backup vendors, external data centers for roll over in cases of disaster.
- Banks with an investment division and a retail bank division will by Federal law have a "Chinese wall" or specified limitations on communications and data sharing, even though the email domain may be the same.

The way role-based computer systems can control view/edit/delete data access inside a company (Ferraiolo and Kuhn 1992), role-based tags can control which people are allowed what kinds of communications outside of the company. This is a natural extension of existing management processes.

Given a table of all employees, with their emails, a system administrator can add attributes for roles such as: *public relations, health insurance, payroll, contracts, secure tech, retail banking, investment banking*. The role attributes may have 0/1 values (1 = true) or represent a security degree level, such as *confidential, classified, highly classified* (specific to that role).

To ease the configuration of this DLP software system, to more easily get a list of employees in their departments, large companies typically have existing LDAP (Zeilenga, 2006) access controls already defined. This DLP system can start by reading any existing LDAP files.

A table of email domains would contain the company name and attributes indicating the suitability for communication with employees acting in a given role (one column per role), with true/false or security level values. Some organizations may be listed here with all false values—in effect creating black list enforcement—such as with primary competitors or news leak concerns.

Using the DLP subject detectors, the employee roles and email domain roles, the company policy rules can be specified with clauses, such as the following:

```
IF (financialServices_DLP) and
   ((alert_confidential) or (alert_signature)) and
   (undesired_person_co_communication) THEN
       ALERT confidential_financialServicesDoc
IF (healthcare_DLP) and
   ((alert_confidential) or (alert_signature)) and
   (undesired_person_co_communication) THEN
       ALERT confidential_healthcareDoc
IF (legalDoc_DLP) and
   ((alert_confidential) or (alert_signature)) and
   (undesired_person_co_communication) THEN
       ALERT confidential_legalDoc
IF (designDoc_DLP) and
   (undesired_person_co_communication) THEN
       ALERT confidential_designDoc
```

Alternatively, alert counter aggregation may be incremented in the above rules, if the policy is to detect a certain number of alerts over a certain time period.

The job and company role related rules, to reduce false alerts would be placed after the other rules, to "turn off" alerts on expected behavior.

For Marketing, Public Relations and related job functions:

```
For Marketing, Public relations and related job functions:
IF (employee.is_PublicRelations) AND
   (email.sendToDomain_vettedNews) THEN
       ALERT = FALSE
For HR, any internal personal trainer or nurse
IF (employee. is_healthCare) AND
   (email.sendToDomain_vettedHealthCare) THEN
       ALERT = FALSE
For Finance, Mergers and Acquisitions, Sales, Purchasing, Legal
IF (employee. is_contracts) AND
   (email.sendToDomain_vettedContracts) THEN
       ALERT = FALSE
For IT employee involved in DevOps or SOC or other high security
IF (employee. is_secureTech) AND
   (email.sendToDomain_vettedTechSecure) THEN
       ALERT = FALSE
For ALWAYS ALERT, or High Alert (if there is different severity)
IF (email.sendToDomain_is_competitor) OR
   (email.sendToDomain_is_avoidNews) THEN
       ALERT = TRUE
       HIGH_ALERT = TRUE.
```

9.7   Evaluation

9.7.1   Baseline Classification Approaches

TF*IDF Nearest Neighbor approach finds a document in the training set which is the closest to the given one being recognized. Nearest Neighbor feature is implemented via the search in inverse index of Lucene (Croft, Metzler and Strohman 2009) where the search result score is computed based on TF*IDF model (Salton and Buckley 1988). The query is formed from each sentence of the documents being classified as a disjunctive query including all words except stop-words. The resultant classes along with their TF*IDF scores are weighted and aggregated on the basis of a majority vote algorithm such as (Moore and Boyer 1991).

A *Naive Bayes classifier* is a simple probabilistic classifier based on applying Bayes' theorem (from Bayesian statistics) with strong (naive) independence assumptions. This classifier assumes that the presence (or absence) of a particular feature of a class is unrelated to the presence (or absence) of any other feature. For example, a fruit may be considered to be an apple if it is red, round, and about 4″ in diameter. Even if these features depend on each other or upon the existence of the other features, a naive Bayes classifier considers all of these properties to independently contribute to the probability that this fruit is an apple. Depending on the precise nature of the probability model, a naive Bayes classifier can be trained very efficiently in a supervised learning setting. In many practical applications, parameter estimation for naive Bayes models uses the method of maximum likelihood. WEKA classifier is based on (John and Langley 1995).

Since the available datasets for classification into abstract classes are rather limited in size, we did not conduct deep learning-based classification we would apply to discourse-level data. We believe for larger size training sets, the classification accuracy would increase without using more complex learning system, so for an industrial system SVM TK is a good balance between an ease of deployment and performance.

9.7.2 Forming Training Datasets

For design documents, we built a web mining utility that searched for public design documents on the web in a number of engineering and science domains. This utility is based on Microsoft Cognitive Services API (Bing search) that provides an extensive set of search results for a query. The documents identified by keywords as related to "design documents" are then downloaded and are subject to verification. Manual confirmation that a given document is a design document and not the one belonging to the negative class was performed by Amazon Mechanical Turk workers.

We used the following keywords to add to a query for *design document*: *material, technical, software, pharmaceutical, bio, biotech, civil engineering. construction, microprocessor, c++, python, java, hardware, processor, architectural, creative, web.* As a result a set of 1235 documents was formed, but only about 10% of those were confirmed to be genuine design documents. It turned out we had almost 90% of non-design engineering documents of the classes we want to exclude (meta-documents).

For the financial domain, we collected 350 private communication emails related to corporate finance from the ENRON dataset (Cohen 2016). We automatically selected emails related to finance by relying on financial keywords. We also collected common answers from Fidelity (2018) dataset. The former dataset is an example of meta-documents, and the latter belongs to object-level documents.

For the literature domain, we formed 200 paragraphs from Kafka's novel "The Trial" describing interaction with people related to the court, as a training set of meta-documents. As a set of object-level documents, we manually selected 100 paragraphs of text in the same domain (scholarly articles about "The Trial").

We also classify a chatbot utterance with respect to being an information query or a request to fulfill a transaction, such as a banking account transfer (Chap. 1 Volume 2). As the texts are short, we do not apply discourse analysis and instead rely on syntactic features. We use this evaluation domain to draw a comparison between classification domains of different natures. For the query classification task, we formed two datasets:

(1) Request dataset was obtained from multiple set of requests for Alexa, Api.ai, Microrsoft QnA maker, IBM Watson chatbot development environment, available at chatbot developers' github project pages such as (Watson-Github 2017). Another set of source of requests includes banking websites such as (ICICI Bank FAQ 2017). We collected 1860 requests from finance,
(2) The dataset of question requiring answers includes 1600 frequently asked questions in the financial domain scraped from banks websites, such as (CitiBank 2017), Fidelity, Bank of America, and others.

In all four domains, we split the data into 5 sub-sets for training/evaluation portions (Kohavi 1995; Ben-David 2008). For the design documents, finance/legal and query type, evaluation results were assessed by quality assurance personnel and interns. For the literature domain, it was done by the author.

9.7.3   Evaluation Results

Table 9.1 shows evaluation results for all four domains selected for this study to evaluate text and document classification. Each row contains the results of a particular classification method.

The baseline approaches are shown in the first and second rows. The keyword statistic-based methods, including Nearest-Neighbor classification and Naïve Bayes, produce rather poor results in all four domains. For short texts such as user requests, the classification accuracy is not as low as for documents. For the literature domain, a keyword-based Nearest-Neighbor classification is almost as bad as random, since the texts are fairly diverse in keywords (in comparison with *Design/Financial/Legal* domains) and the training dataset is relatively small.

The third and fourth rows contain recognition results obtained for the same rich set of linguistic features including syntax and discourse, but a simple machine learning algorithm. Instead of using SVM for tree-based features, this approach computes maximal common substructures, such as parse trees and parse thickets. A parse thicket is a graph that represents the syntactic structure of a paragraph of text and includes parse tree for each sentence for this paragraph plus some arcs for discourse

Table 9.1 Classifying documents and texts in four domains of this study

Method	Design document (%)				Literature (%)			
	P	R	F1	Std dev	P	R	F1	Std dev
Nearest neighbor classifier, BoW (TF*IDF based)	55.8	61.4	58.47	2.1	51.7	54.0	52.82	2.9
Naive Bayesian classifier, BoW (WEKA)	57.4	59.2	58.29	3.2	52.4	50.4	51.38	3.0
Maximum common sub-parse trees	76.1	77.5	76.79	4.3	68.5	65.3	66.86	4.3
Maximum common sub-parse thickets	78.7	77.8	78.25	3.2	70.1	68.4	69.24	3.2
Tree kernel—regular parse trees	73.4	77.6	75.44	2.8	65.7	67.3	66.49	3.9
Tree kernel SVM—extended trees for anaphora	77.0	79.3	78.13	3.1	67.1	67.8	67.45	3.4
Tree kernel SVM—extended trees for RST	78.3	81.5	79.87	2.6	69.3	72.4	70.82	3.6
Tree kernel SVM—extended trees for both anaphora and RST	82.1	85.2	83.62	2.7	70.8	73.0	71.88	4.2

Method	Financial and Legal (%)				Query type (%)			
	P	R	F1	Std dev	P	R	F1	Std dev
Nearest neighbor classifier, BoW (TF*IDF based)	56.7	53.4	55.00	3.3	58.3	60.1	59.19	3.1
Naive Bayesian classifier, BoW (WEKA)	52.4	50.4	51.38	3.4	60.2	59.6	59.90	2.7
Maximum common sub-parse trees	78.1	77.8	77.95	2.3	76.3	74.7	75.49	3.3
Maximum common sub-parse thickets	78.9	79.1	79.00	3.2	79.3	80.9	80.09	4.6

(continued)

Table 9.1 (continued)

Method	Financial and Legal (%)				Query type (%)			
	P	R	F1	Std dev	P	R	F1	Std dev
Tree kernel—regular parse trees	71.7	73.4	72.54	2.8	79.2	80.4	79.80	3.0
Tree kernel SVM—extended trees for anaphora	73.1	74.8	73.94	4.4	78.2	76.9	77.54	2.8
Tree kernel SVM—extended trees for RST	76.3	73.4	74.82	3.7	81.2	79.4	80.29	3.3
Tree kernel SVM—extended trees for both anaphora and RST	80.8	83.1	81.93	4.2	83.7	82.5	83.10	2.9

relations between words other than syntactic (Galitsky 2017). The maximal common sub-graph approach outperforms the baseline by about 20%.

The rows from fifth to eight show the performance of SVM TK approaches applied to a range of linguistic features. The performance of tree kernel-based methods improves as the sources of linguistic features expand. For all four domains, there is a few percent improvement by using RST relations compared with the pure syntactic-based tree kernel SVM which relies on parse trees only. For the literature domain, the role of anaphora was rather low. Overall, one can achieve recognition accuracy above 80% for both document and short text domains. For the peculiar literature domain, the recognition accuracy is limited to 70%.

When either type of discourse information (RST or anaphora) is missing, the performance of SVM TK is comparable with the maximal common sub-graph approach employing both of these sources of discourse information. The trade-off is explicit: either a richer set of linguistic features or more sophisticated learning is required to achieve 80% accuracy.

9.7.4 Implications for Industrial Implementation

For industrial implementation, the classification settings need to be altered, and the results of detectors are subject to Receiver operating characteristic (ROC) curve optimization (Ben-David 2008). For a user of DLP system, the false positive rate is critical. The following additional considerations are applied:

- Sensitive document needs to be pre-categorized into major classes. To be a sensitive financial report, a document first needs to be categorized as financial, for example.

- Only *bursts* of sensitive documents trigger an alert, not an individual one. Usually, if leaks are intentional, multiple documents are attempted to be shared.
- Aggregate detection results are wrongly associated with a certain company's department. In case of unintentional leaks, the category of document will usually stand out, such as engineering document shared by a human resources department or finance document shared by engineering.

Also, an increase in accuracy by a few percent can be achieved in design/legal/financial documents by using human comprehension of which expressions are used in metalanguage and style in meta-documents. These rules also included regular expressions relying on specific document formatting including a table of content and structure of sections. In the literature domain, that was not possible.

As a result of applying these considerations, having above 80% style recognition rate, we achieve:

(1) Detection rate of above 90%
(2) False positive rate of below 0.1%.

Hence using deep linguistic analysis to recognize style in a document, in addition to traditional machine learning of keyword statistics, is a key to successful DLP system.

9.8 Conclusions

In our previous works, it was observed how employing a richer set of linguistic information such as syntactic relations between words assists relevance tasks (Galitsky et al. 2012, 2013a, b). To take advantage of linguistic discourse information, we introduced the parse thicket representation and proposed the way to compute similarity between texts based on generalization of parse thickets (Galitsky 2014, 2016). We built the framework for generalizing PTs as sets of phrases on one hand, and generalizing PTs as graphs via maximal common subgraphs, on the other hand.

In this Chapter we focused on how discourse information can help with a fairly abstract text classification tasks by means of statistical learning. We selected the domain where the only difference between classes lays in phrasing and discourse structures and demonstrated that both are learnable. We compared two sets of linguistic features:

- The baseline, parse trees for individual sentences,
- Parse trees and discourse information,

and demonstrated that the enriched set of features indeed improves the classification accuracy, having the learning framework fixed. We demonstrated that the baseline text classification approaches perform rather poorly in the chosen classification domain. Also, kernel-based learning was unable to reach the performance

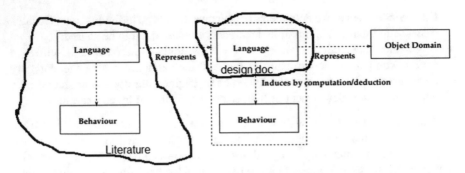

Fig. 9.15 Meta-reasoning chart: mutual relationships between major classes of our interest

of manually structure-based rules, and we hypothesize that a noticeable amount of discourse-related information is not employed in the proposed learning framework.

Meta-reasoning addresses a question of how to give a system its own representation to manipulate. Meta-reasoning needs both levels for both languages and domain behavior. We depict out two main classes of interest in Fig. 9.15.

Russel et al. (1991) outline a general approach to meta-reasoning in the sense of providing a basis for selecting and justifying computational actions. Addressing the problem of resource-bounded rationality, the authors provide a means for analyzing and generating optimal computational strategies. Because reasoning about a computation without doing it necessarily involves uncertainty as to its outcome, probability and decision theory were selected as main tools.

A system needs to implement metalanguage to impress peers with being human-like and intelligent and also must be capable of thinking about one's own thinking. Traditionally within cognitive science and artificial intelligence, thinking or reasoning has been cast as a decision cycle within an action-perception loop (Cox and Raja 2008). An intelligent agent perceives some stimuli from the environment and behaves rationally to achieve its goals by selecting some action from its set of competencies. The result of these actions at the ground level is subsequently perceived at the object level and the cycle continues. Meta-reasoning is the process of reasoning about this reasoning cycle. It consists of both the meta-level control of computational activities and the introspective monitoring of reasoning. In this study, we focused on linguistic issues of text which describes such cognitive architecture. It turns out that there is a correlation between a cognitive architecture and a discourse structure used to express it in text. Relying on this correlation, it is possible to automatically classify texts with respect to metalanguage they contain.

Traditionally, ML of linguistic structures is limited to keyword forms and frequencies. At the same time, most theories of discourse are not computational, they model a particular set of relations between consecutive states. In this work, we attempted to achieve the best of both worlds: learn complete parse tree information augmented with an adjustment of discourse theory allowing computational treatment.

9.8.1 Detecting Private Documents

Hart et al. (2013) classifier had a false negative rate of less than 3.0% and a false discovery rate of less than 1.0% on all tests. It means that the overall detector in a real-world environment can identify more than 97% of information leaks while raising at most 1 false alarm every 100th time. In our case, F-measure of our classifier in a vertical domain such as finance is about 15% higher. As a result, using additional criteria other than document style, we achieve comparable false negative rate and substantially lower false positive rate. This improved performance is the key for adoption of the style-based document classification DLP component by system administrators.

In our previous studies, we considered the following sources of relations between words in sentences: coreferences, taxonomic relations such as sub-entity, partial case, predicate for subject, etc., rhetorical structure relations and speech acts (Galitsky 2013). We demonstrated that a number of NLP tasks including search relevance could be improved if search results are subject to confirmation by parse thicket generalization, when answers occur in multiple sentences (Galitsky 2018). In this study, we employed coreferences and rhetorical relation only to identify correlation with the occurrence of general style for "how to write" in text. Although the phrase-level analysis allows extraction of weak correlation with the presence of sensitive data in texts, an ascend to discourse structures makes this correlation more explicit (Galitsky and Lebedeva 2015).

In this chapter, we used extended parse trees instead of regular ones, leveraging available discourse information, for text classification. This work describes one of the first applications of tree kernel to industrial scale NLP tasks. The advantage of this approach is that the manual thorough analysis of text can be avoided for complex document and text classification tasks where the classes are fairly abstract. The feasibility of suggested approach to classification lays in the robustness of statistical learning algorithms to noisy and unreliable features inherent in NLP.

The experimental environment, the classifier into abstract classes and the evaluation framework is available at https://code.google.com/p/relevance-based-on-parse-trees.

References

Apache T (2020) https://tika.apache.org/. Accessed 12 Oct 12 2020

Aurora V (2001) Freudian metaphor and Surrealist metalanguage. In: Michel Leiris: the unconscious and the sea LittéRéalité, vol XIII

Barile I (2013) Adaptive data loss prevention policies. US Patent 8,613,040

Ben-David A (2008) About the relationship between ROC curves and Cohen's kappa. Eng Appl Artif Intell 21(6):874–882

Citibank FAQ (2017) https://www.online.citibank.co.in/customerservice/cs-faq.htm. Accessed 19 June 2017

Cohen W (2016) Enron email dataset. https://www.cs.cmu.edu/~/enron/. Accessed 10 July 2016

Collins M, Duffy N (2002) Convolution kernels for natural language. In: Proceedings of NIPS, pp 625–632

Cox M, Raja A (2008) Metareasoning: a manifesto. AAAI Workshop - Technical Report

Croft B, Metzler D, Strohman T (2009) Search engines—information retrieval in practice. Pearson Education, North America

Cumby C, Roth D (2003) On kernel methods for relational learning. In: ICML, pp 107–114

Ferraiolo DF, Kuhn DR (1992) Role-based access control. In: 15th national computer security conference, vol 554–563

Fidelity   (2018)   https://github.com/bgalitsky/relevance-based-on-parse-trees/blob/master/exa mples/Fidelity_FAQs_AnswerAnatomyDataset1.csv.zip

Fortune (2015) Target will pay $10 million to settle lawsuit from data breach. https://fortune.com/ 2015/03/19/target-10-million-settle-data-breach/

Galitsky B (2003) Natural language question answering system: technique of semantic headers. Advanced Knowledge International, Adelaide, Australia

Galitsky B, Kuznetsov S (2008) Learning communicative actions of conflicting human agents. J Exp Theor Artif Intell 20(4):277–317

Galitsky B (2012) Machine learning of syntactic parse trees for search and classification of text. Eng Appl Artif Intell 26(3):1072–1091

Galitsky B, de la Rosa JL, Dobrocsi G (2012) Inferring the semantic properties of sentences by mining syntactic parse trees. Data Knowl Eng 81–82:21–45

Galitsky B, Usikov D, Kuznetsov SO (2013a) Parse thicket representations for answering multi-sentence questions. In: 20th international conference on conceptual structures, ICCS 2013

Galitsky B, Ilvovsky D, Kuznetsov SO, Strok F (2013b) Improving text retrieval efficiency with pattern structures on parse thickets. In: Workshop formal concept analysis meets information retrieval at ECIR 2013, Moscow, Russia

Galitsky B (2013) Machine learning of syntactic parse trees for search and classification of text. Eng Appl Artif Intell 26(3):1072–1091

Galitsky B (2014) Learning parse structure of paragraphs and its applications in search. Eng Appl Artif Intell 32:160–184

Galitsky B, Ilvovsky D, Kuznetsov SO, Strok F (2014) Finding maximal common sub-parse thickets for multi-sentence search. In: Graph structures for knowledge representation and reasoning, pp 39–57

Galitsky B, Lebedeva N (2015) Recognizing documents versus meta-documents by tree kernel learning. In: FLAIRS conference, pp 540–545

Galitsky B (2016) Generalization of parse trees for iterative taxonomy learning. Inf Sci 329:125–143

Galitsky B, Ilvovsky D, Kuznetsov SO (2016) Style and genre classification by means of deep textual parsing. Computational Linguistics and Intellectual Technologies, CICLING

Galitsky B (2017) Matching parse thickets for open domain question answering. Data Knowl Eng 107:24–50

Galitsky B (2018) Data loss prevention system for cloud security based on document discourse analysis. US Patent App 20180365593

Galitsky B (2019) A content management system for chatbots. In: Developing enterprise chatbots. Springer, Cham, pp 253–326

Galitsky B, Ilvovsky D (2019) Validating correctness of textual explanation with complete discourse tree. In: FCA4AI@IJCAI2019

Hackett R (2015) How much do data breaches cost big companies? Shockingly little. https://for tune.com/2015/03/27/how-much-do-data-breaches-actually-cost-big-companies-shockingly-lit tle/Fortune

Hart M, Manadhata P, Johnson R (2013) Text classification for data loss prevention. In: SPIN 2013—Stony Brook privacy enhancing technologies. Lecture Notes in Computer Science, vol 6794, pp 18–37

ICICI Bank FAQ (2017) https://www.icicibank.com/personal-banking/insta-banking/internet-ban king/list-of-service-requests.page. Accessed 19 June 2017

John GH, Langley P (1995) Estimating continuous distributions in Bayesian classifiers. In: Eleventh conference on uncertainty in artificial intelligence, San Mateo, pp 338–345

Kohavi R (1995) A study of cross-validation and bootstrap for accuracy estimation and model selection. In: International joint conference on artificial intelligence, pp 1137–1143

Kong F, Zhou G (2011) Improve tree kernel-based event pronoun resolution with competitive information. In: Proceedings of the twenty-second international joint conference on artificial intelligence, vol 3, pp 1814–1819

Lee H, Chang A, Peirsman Y, Chambers N, Surdeanu M, Jurafsky D (2013) Deterministic coreference resolution based on entity-centric, precision-ranked rules. Comput Linguist 39(4):885–916

Mann W, Matthiessen C, Thompson S (1992) Rhetorical structure theory and text analysis. In: Mann W, Thompson S (eds) Discourse description: diverse linguistic analyses of a fund-raising text. John Benjamins, Amsterdam, pp 39–78

McAfee (2016) Data loss prevention. https://www.mcafee.com/us/enterprise/products/data_loss_prevention/. Accessed 10 Oct 2016

Moore JS, Boyer RS (1991) MJRTY—a fast majority vote algorithm. In: Boyer RS (ed) Automated reasoning: essays in honor of Woody Bledsoe. Automated reasoning series. Kluwer Academic Publishers, Dordrecht, The Netherlands, pp 105–117

Moschitti A (2006) Efficient convolution kernels for dependency and constituent syntactic trees. In: Proceedings of the 17th European conference on machine learning, Berlin, Germany,

Moschitti A, Quarteroni S (2011) Linguistic kernels for answer re-ranking in question answering systems. Inf Process Manag 47(6):825–842

Poneman Institute (2009) Fourth annual us cost of data breach study. https://www.poncmon.org/local/upload/fckjail/generalcontent/18/file/2008-2009USCostofDataBreachReportFinal.pdf, Jan 2009. Accessed 10 Oct 2016

Recasens M, de Marneffe M-C, Potts C (2013) The life and death of discourse entities: identifying singleton mentions. In: Proceedings of NAACL

Ricoeur P (1975) The rule of metaphor: the creation of meaning in language. University of Toronto Press, Toronto

RSA (2016) Data Loss Prevention. https://www.rsa.com/node.aspx?id=1130. Accessed 10 Oct 2016

Roth GB, Brandwine EJ, Baer GD (2015) Dynamic data loss prevention in a multi-tenant environment. US Patent 8,938,775

Russell S, Wefald E, Karnaugh M, Karp R, McAllester D, Subramanian D, Wellman M (1991) Principles of metareasoning. In: Artificial intelligence. Morgan Kaufmann, pp 400–411

Salton G, Buckley C (1988) Term-weighting approaches in automatic text retrieval. Inf Process Manag 24(5):513–523

Searle J (1969) Speech acts: an essay in the philosophy of language. Cambridge University, Cambridge, England

Sun J, Zhang M, Tan C (2010) Exploring syntactic structural features for sub-tree alignment using bilingual tree kernels. In: Proceedings of ACL, pp 306–315

Sun J, Zhang M, Tan C (2011) Tree sequence kernel for natural language. In: AAAI-25.

Symantec. Data Loss Prevention Products & Services (2016) https://www.symantec.com/business/theme.jsp?themeid=vontu. Accessed 10 Oct 2019

Trend Micro (2016) Trend micro data loss prevention. https://us.trendmicro.com/us/products/enterprise/data-loss-prevention/. Accessed 10 Oct 2016

Vapnik V (1995) The nature of statistical learning theory. Springer

Watson-GitHub (2017) https://github.com/watson-developer-cloud/conversation-with-discovery. Accessed 19 June 2017

Wüchner T, Pretschner A (2012) Data loss prevention based on data-driven usage control. In: IEEE 23rd International Symposium on Software Reliability Engineering.

Zeilenga K (2006) Lightweight Directory Access Protocol (LDAP) read entry controls. IETF. RFC 4527:2006

Zhang D, Lee WS (2003) Question classification using support vector machines. SIGIR. 26–32

Zhang M, Che W, Zhou G, Aw A, Tan C, Liu T, Li S (2008) Semantic role labeling using a grammar-driven convolution tree kernel. IEEE Trans Audio Speech Lang Process 16(7):1315–1329

Chapter 10
Conversational Explainability

Abstract In this Chapter, we focus on an interface that makes explainability of a machine learning (ML) system convincing and effective. We propose a conversational interface to the decision log of an abstract ML system that enumerates the decision steps and features employed to arrive at a given decision. Conversational content augments the decision log with background knowledge to better handle questions and provide complete answers. As a result, the users who can chat with the decision-making system (such as a loan application approval) develop a substantially higher trust in it than in a black-box ML or conventional report-based explanation. Conversational explainability (CE) allows the users to get into as much details as they wish concerning the decision process. The proposed CE system delivers meaningful explanation in 65% cases, whereas a conventional, report-based explanations in 49% of cases (for the same decision sessions).

10.1 Introduction

Machine learning has great potential for improving products, processes and research. But computers usually do not explain their predictions, which is a barrier to the adoption of machine learning (Molnar 2019). Explanations are widely considered as an essential component of scientific progress. The fact that many recent AI systems operate mostly as a black box has led to some serious concerns (see Došilovic et al. 2018, for a recent survey). Despite widespread adoption, machine learning (ML) models remain mostly unexplainable. Understanding the reasons behind predictions is, however, quite important in assessing trust, which is fundamental if one plans to take action based on a prediction, or when choosing whether to deploy a new model. Such understanding also provides insights into the model, which can be used to transform an untrustworthy model or prediction into a trustworthy one (Galitsky et al. 2019b).

Whether humans are directly using machine learning classifiers as tools, or are deploying models within other products, a vital concern remains: if the users do not

© Springer Nature Switzerland AG 2020   415
B. Galitsky, *Artificial Intelligence for Customer Relationship Management*,
Human–Computer Interaction Series,
https://doi.org/10.1007/978-3-030-52167-7_10

trust a model or a prediction, they will not use it. It is important to distinguish two different ML components trust (Ribeiro et al. 2016):

(1) Trusting a prediction, i.e., whether a user trusts an individual prediction sufficiently to take some action based on it;
(2) Trusting a model, i.e., whether the user trusts a model to behave in reasonable ways if deployed. Both are directly impacted by how much the human understands a model's behavior, as opposed to seeing it as a black box.

In this Chapter, we provide an *explanation* for a decision of an abstract ML system in the form of a *conversation*, to improve the user's trust in that this decision is fair and reasonable, even if this decision does not favor the goal of this user. The main value of a conversational explanation versus a static explanation in the form of a report is that it can provide as many details as user wants and as are available. The conversational explanation does not overload a user with details outside of her interest. The value of conversation instead of just a single-step search is a user capability of drilling in/drilling out of factors determined as essential when the decision has been made. Therefore, we believe an explanation in a conversational form is an efficient way to increase users' trust of both a particular decision and an overall ML model.

If an ML model performs well, why do not we just trust the model and ignore why it made a certain decision? The problem is that a single metric, such as classification accuracy, is an incomplete description of most real-world ML tasks" (Doshi-Velez and Kim 2017). Therefore, beyond supporting a trust by a user, an explainability is a measure of an ML system's own performance irrespectively of its interpretation by an observer.

A number of application domains of explainability select free-form NL explanations, instead of the ones in a formal language, for a series of reasons:

(1) NL is readily comprehensible to an end-user who needs to assert a model's reliability;
(2) NL is the easiest for humans to provide free-form language, eliminating the additional effort of learning to produce formal language;
(3) NL justifications might eventually be mined from existing large-scale free-form text. We take this direction one step further and proceed from free-form NL report to a conversational mode.

The value of conversational explanation is to combine the best of both worlds to achieve trust: a conversational mode allows for a broad range of decision exploration scenarios, brings flexibility, drilling in/out, comprehensive information acquisition and tellability. At the same time, explainability brings in trust, assuring fairness, accountability and transparency (Galitsky 2018).

We now describe a range of possible conversational explanation types. A CRM in a financial domain is used as an example (Table 10.1):

(1) *Transparent*. Since the classification (such as customer application approved/denied) is created by a rule-based system, it is possible to offer a transparent explanation. In this case, it is a simple statement of the premises

Table 10.1 Examples for the types of explanations in a dialogue

(1)	User: Would application (1) be accepted? CE: No I am confident it will not User: Why? CE: *Param1 = value ... Param5 = value*
(2)	User: Would application (2) be accepted? CE: I am **not** confident but it will accepted User: Why? CE: These are available parameter values *Param1 = value ... Param7 = value* and I am 73% confident it will be accepted
(3)	User: Would application (3) be accepted? CE: I cannot be confident but it will accepted User: Why? CE: Parameter values for (3) are not available These are parameter values for an available similar case *Param1 = value ... Param4 = value* and I am 61% confident it will be accepted
(4)	User: Would application (4) be accepted? CE: I cannot be confident either way User: Why? CE: Parameter values *Param1 = value ... Param4 = value* vote for acceptance and parameter values *Param7 = value ... Param9 = value* vote for not acceptance

that led to the conclusion. This is a deliberately simple example but many real rule-based systems have rich rule base and long transparent explanations which may be harder to communicate via simple text techniques;

(2) *Post-hoc by saliency.* Many classifiers are unable to provide transparent explanations in a form that is suitable for human consumption. Explanation mechanisms are therefore post-hoc and take the form of an explanation based on the output or the input rather than the internal processing. This is the case with ML algorithms and new techniques to achieve explainability for these types of algorithms is an active area of research;

(3) *Post-hoc by example.* This is a very similar case to the previous example, but with an important restriction. The user cannot have an access to a full list of features and transactions. This is most likely to be due to security restrictions but it could also be for more mundane reasons such as the original list of transactions not being available, or being too expensive to request from a remote server. In this case, the user is shown a similar anonymized application of a real or an abstract applicant. This is less informative than the previous case but does provide an analogous example for the user to observe, learn and understand.

(4) *Disagreement within services.* In a composite system, it is possible for different techniques for determining the status of applications to run into a conflict in their assessments. In this example, we simply show the disagreement to the user, delegating the decision-making as to the correct interpretation to them. In a real system, it is likely that additional contextual information would be taken into account to try to reliably choose the correct classification even with service

disagreements. In all of these examples, the user is not only trying to find out the decision on whether a particular application is accepted or denied but to also determine some insight into how the ML component is making this decision.

We use simple two-step dialogues to illustrate each case (Table 10.1).

10.2   Conversational Explanations in Personal Finance

We consider the domain of personal finance, where customers are applying for a loan from a financial institution such as a bank. As is typically the case in many deployed applications, we assume here that the bank has a complex existing process based on a combination of data-driven approaches and business rules to arrive at the final loan approval decision, which they would like to preserve as much as possible. A loan officer has an option to validate the approval or denial recommendations of an AI model. Every customer is naturally interested in the reasoning behind the decisions, in particular, when a loan application is denied. They may want to know about a few factors that could be changed to improve their profile for possible approval in the future. Also, a data science executive needs some assurance that in most cases the recommendations made by the model are reasonable.

A Bank Customer wants to get answers to the following questions:

Why was my application rejected?

What can I improve to increase the likelihood my application is accepted?

The Bank Customer wants to know how and why the decision was made to accept or reject their mortgage application. The explanation given will help them understand if they have been treated fairly, and also provide an insight into what (if their application was rejected) they can improve in order to increase the likelihood it will be accepted in the future. An explainability algorithm wraps existing ML component and helps to detect both the features that a bank customer could improve (e.g., amount of time since last credit inquiry, average age of accounts), and also further detects the features that will increase the likelihood of approval and those that are within reach for the customer. See examples in Fig. 10.1.

Under the CE support, this bank response occurs in a conversational form (Fig. 10.2).

Interpretability might enable people or programs to trick an ML system. Problems with users who deceive a system result in a mismatch between the goals of the creator of an ML decision system and the goals of the end users of a model (loan applicants). Credit scoring is such a system since financial institutions want to make sure that loans are only given to people who are likely to return them, and applicants aim to get the loan irrespectively of the bank wanting to give them one or not. This conflict between the goals of involved parties introduces incentives for applicants to trick the ML system to increase their chances of getting a loan. For example, if an applicant knows that having more than two credit cards negatively affects his score, he simply returns his third credit card to improve his score, and organizes a new card after the

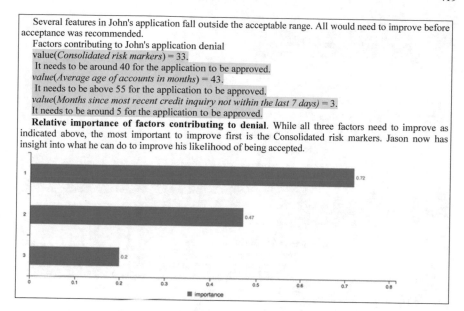

Several features in John's application fall outside the acceptable range. All would need to improve before acceptance was recommended.
Factors contributing to John's application denial
value(*Consolidated risk markers*) = 33.
It needs to be around 40 for the application to be approved.
value(*Average age of accounts in months*) = 43.
It needs to be above 55 for the application to be approved.
value(*Months since most recent credit inquiry not within the last 7 days*) = 3.
It needs to be around 5 for the application to be approved.
Relative importance of factors contributing to denial. While all three factors need to improve as indicated above, the most important to improve first is the Consolidated risk markers. Jason now has insight into what he can do to improve his likelihood of being accepted.

Fig. 10.1 An example of a static explanation in the form of a report

loan has been approved. While her score is improved, the probability of her repaying the loan stays the same. The system can only be gamed if the inputs are proxies for a causal feature, but do not actually cause the outcome. Whenever possible, such proxy features should be avoided from being employed by ML as they make models prone to be tricked by some users.

10.3 A Taxonomy of Explanation Types and Conversational Explanations

It is important to understand the diverse forms of explanations that are available and the questions that each can address (Arya et al. 2019). A proper structuring of the explanation space is important not just in academia researchers who design and build new algorithms, but also in industry practitioners who want to select technologies most suitable for their application and might be lost otherwise.

In Fig. 10.3, we visualize the taxonomy of explanation types in the form of a small decision tree. Each node in this decision tree poses a question to the user concerning the expected type of explanation. We rely on the following definitions:

(1) A *static explanation* is the one that does not change in response to feedback from the user, while an interactive explanation allows consumers to drill down or ask for different types of explanations (e.g., through CE) until they are satisfied. Static explanation is a default explanation type;

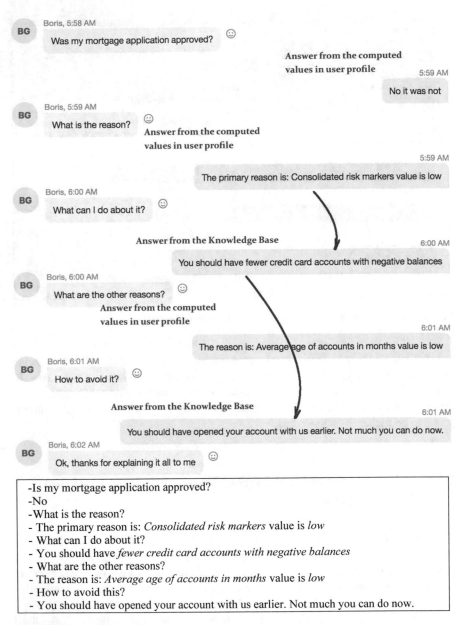

BG Boris, 5:58 AM
Was my mortgage application approved? ☺

Answer from the computed
values in user profile   5:59 AM

No it was not

BG Boris, 5:59 AM
What is the reason? ☺   Answer from the computed
values in user profile

5:59 AM

The primary reason is: Consolidated risk markers value is low

BG Boris, 6:00 AM
What can I do about it? ☺

Answer from the Knowledge Base   6:00 AM

You should have fewer credit card accounts with negative balances

BG Boris, 6:00 AM
What are the other reasons? ☺
Answer from the computed
values in user profile

6:01 AM

The reason is: Average age of accounts in months value is low

BG Boris, 6:01 AM
How to avoid it? ☺

Answer from the Knowledge Base   6:01 AM

You should have opened your account with us earlier. Not much you can do now.

BG Boris, 6:02 AM
Ok, thanks for explaining it all to me ☺

-Is my mortgage application approved?
-No
-What is the reason?
- The primary reason is: *Consolidated risk markers* value is *low*
- What can I do about it?
- You should have *fewer credit card accounts with negative balances*
- What are the other reasons?
- The reason is: *Average age of accounts in months* value is *low*
- How to avoid this?
- You should have opened your account with us earlier. Not much you can do now.

Fig. 10.2 A conversational explanation. On the top: The origin of answers is written in red. Also, blue arrows show the source of the current answer (multiple previous utterances can be used). On the bottom: a CE dialogue in plain text

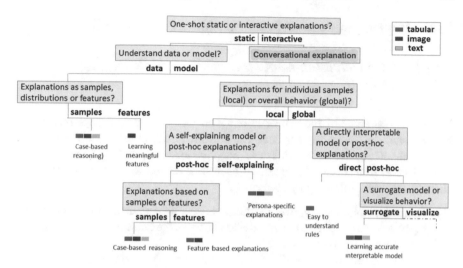

Fig. 10.3 A Decision Tree for Explanation Type. Notice the node for the CE

(2) A *local explanation* is for a single prediction, whereas a global explanation describes the behavior of the entire model;

(3) A *directly interpretable model* is understandable by most consumers due to its intrinsic transparent nature. A typical example here is a small decision tree. At the same time, a *post-hoc explanation* involves auxiliary methods to explain a model after it has been trained. One could also have a *self-explaining model* that itself generates local explanations, but may not necessarily be directly interpretable (e.g., rationale generation in text).

(4) A hybrid model is a second, usually directly interpretable model that approximates a more complex model, while a visualization of a model may focus on parts of it and is not itself a full-fledged model.

Post-hoc explainability targets models that are not readily interpretable (by design) by resorting to diverse means to enhance their interpretability, such as text explanations, visual explanations, local explanations, explanations by example, explanations by simplification and feature relevance explanations techniques (Arrieta et al. 2019).

The proposed decision tree is based on questions about what is explained (e.g., data or model), how it is explained (e.g., direct/post-hoc, static/interactive) and at what level (i.e., local/global). The decision tree leaves indicate the methods currently available through the toolkit along with the modalities they can work with.

10.4   Implementation of Conversational Explainability

10.4.1   A Conversation About a Decision and Reasoning About It

We reconstruct some of the conversations from our Customer Complaints dataset in the domain of Non-sufficient Fund Fee and Interest Rate Increase. The users are notified about the decision (in this case, negative for them) and start a conversation trying to sort things out. The question users ask related to explainability can be classified into the following five types:

(1)   General factoid/banking rule question: "Is my interest rate up due to slow down in the economy?", "Am I charged a fee because the bank has to borrow money to cover my negative balance?";

(2)   Features of customers (FoC) affecting decision: "Am I charged NSF because my paycheck was delayed?", "Did my interest rate go up due to a high number of my credit card accounts?";

(3)   Other kinds of personalized questions such as account balance;

(4)   "Why" associated with FoC: "Why was I charged NSF when my paycheck was greater than what I paid for?";

(5)   Request to perform a transaction.

The first case is straight-forward in terms of Q/A, and the second case requires a special treatment of two distinct parts of the search index, Domain Knowledge and the Decision Log (Fig. 10.10). On top of that, the third question type requires answers which are suitable for Why questions, plus FoC. More query types can occur in a CE dialogue.

10.4.2   Associating Entities in Decision Log and User Queries

Things look different and are verbalized differently in decision logs and in user questions. Respective entities need to be associated, which require a commonsense reasoning and/or learning from sources where these associations can be mined. For example, *How many?* in a user questions should be associated with "a number of". This task is done by learning, in particular, in machine reading comprehension tasks, if respective training pairs of questions and answers are available (Chap. 3). Alternatively, fragments of training set can be mined from the web or an intranet source (Chap. 7). Table 10.2 shows some examples of association between how an entity occurs in a user query and in a decision log.

For example, Table 10.2 data can answer the following questions. Required associations are written below each example, multiple options are shown in []:

What is my current balance for [travel/free currency conversion] card ?
"free currency conversion" → *"travel"*

Table 10.2 Phrases in questions against domain knowledge and entries from the decision log

User query and domain knowledge	Entry in decision log
Too many credit card account ...	# accounts
High balance on your credit card ...	$ amount balance
Missed payment ...	Due date delay
Paid with one credit card the balance for another card	Irregular payment pattern
Insufficient/Non-sufficient fund fee	NSF
Credit card type	Visa, AmEx, ...
Checking account	chck, checking
Move funds from	Amount is decreased
Move funds to	Amount is increased

What Is My [Due Date/Transfer Deadline/Payment Due] On My Visa Card?
"transfer deadline" → "due"
Did my [target/goal/achievement/account purpose] affect the denial of my application?
"target" → "goals"
Is it ok to miss [alerts/notifications/updates]?
"notifications" → "alerts"

Associations between account names and activities are shown in Fig. 10.4. Relying on BERT or on search engine API, one can associate '*Chkg*' with '*checking*' (Fig. 10.5).

Accounts Overview		
CHECKING - 312	$ 230.11	Statements & Documents
Adv Tiered Interest Chkg - 170	$ 1230.18	Spending & Budgeting
Advantage Savings - 172	$ 301.78	Goals Boost credit rating
Advantage Savings - 651	$ 1201.55	Alerts Credit card statement 2-27
Bank of America Travel... - 395	$ 201.15 Due 2/23/20	My Portfolio
BankAmericard Visa... - 184	$ 20.65 Due 2/21/20	Manage card settings Paperless
		6-month CD
		Open an account 1.65%APR

Fig. 10.4 A bank account overview that can be a part of a decision log to verify association between entities

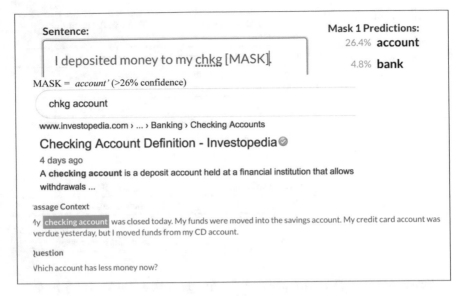

Fig. 10.5 Associating entities and answering questions about them

On the bottom of Fig. 10.5 a machine reading comprehension system is attempting to associate the notions of "*less money*" with three instances in text: "closed", "moved into" and "moved funds from". This trained system was supposed to associate the notion with the third option, "*moved funds from*", but it did not. Hence entity association task required for CE is beyond the skill set of most machine reading comprehension systems as of today. As the web accessible via a search engine API has much richer set of entities, it is expected to be able to associate a broader set of entities. This entity association is a part of the overall answering questions about the decision log that is evaluated in this Chapter.

The main problem here is to associate entities from logs with entities from customers' descriptions of their issues. The association problem is non-trivial and ambiguous (Fig. 10.6). An association between phrases is based on mining the web of a domain-specific corpus and is described in detail in Chap. 7 as a part of multi-component reasoning-based Q/A system.

10.4.2.1   CE Dialogue Manager

The dialogue manager needs to rely on the type of previous utterance to determine the type of the current utterance. The utterances of the CE are shown with indentation.

As we see in Fig. 10.7, the utterances are dependent, and the Dialogue Manager needs to acquire rules on how to answer the following utterance given the previous ones.

For example,

Fig. 10.6 Establishing association between entities. A mapping is being established between the entities on the top and those on the bottom (on the left). Association between entities is context-dependent (on the right, cartoonbank 2020)

User	Bot
- *Factoid Question*	
	- *Factoid Answer*
- *FoC1 Question 1*	
	- *confirmation and Factoid + FoC Answer*
- *FoC2 Question*	
	- *negation of FoC2 + Factoid*
- *Why.Decision_Log.FoC1 Question*	
	- *Why.Decision_Log.FoC1 Answer + Why.Decision_Log.FoC2 Answer + temporal_sequence(Why.Decision_Log.FoC1)*

- *When am I getting NSF?*
    - *You are charged NSF when your balance goes below zero*
- *Did my balance go below zero?*
    - *Your balance was -$24.43 on Mon Jan 7, 2019*
- *Was my pay check used against my payments?*
    - *No. Your balance was -$24.43. Only available funds in a checking account can be used for your debit transaction*
- *Why was not my paycheck used?*
    - *Your paycheck was debited in ATM on Sun Jan 6, 2019 and processed by the end of day Mon Jan 7, 2019*

Fig. 10.7 A conversational dialogue template and a dialogue example which is covered by this template

– *FoC2 Question*
– *negation of FoC2 + Factoid*
– *Why.Decision_Log.FoC1 Question*

10.4.3   Query Type Recognizer

One of the essential skills of CE is to discriminate between a question to obtain some general information versus specific personalized customer information versus a request to commit a transaction associated with a decision (Galitsky and Ilvovsky 2017). Usually, these forms of user activity follow each other (Galitsky 2019b).

Before a user wants to request a particular personal financial information from CE or performs an action (such as opening a new bank account), she would want to know the rules and conditions for this account. Once the user knowledge request is satisfied, she makes a decision and orders a transaction. Once this transaction is completed, the user might want to know her list of options available and asks a question (such as *"How to avoid the fees for this XYZ account in the future?"*). Hence user questions and transactional requests are intermittent and need to be recognized reliably.

A request for general information, personal, specific information, or a transaction can be formulated explicitly or implicitly. *"Could you do this"* may mean both a question about the access control as well as an implicit request to do this. Even a simple question *"When is my payment due? Pay now"* may be a factoid question or a transactional request to select an account and execute a database query. Another way to express a request is via mentioning of a desired state instead of an explicit action to achieve it. For example, utterance *"I am short of funds in my checking account #2"* indicates not a question but a desired state that can be achieved by transferring funds (to *account #2*). To handle this ambiguity in a domain-independent manner, we differentiate between the types of questions and requests linguistically, not pragmatically.

Although a vast training dataset for each class is available, it turns out that a rule-based approach provides an adequate performance. For an utterance, classification into a request or question is done by a rule-based system on two levels:

1.   Keyword level;
2.   Linguistic analysis of phrases level.

The algorithm chart includes four major components (Fig. 10.8):

- Data, vocabularies, configuration
- Rule engine
- Linguistic Processor
- Decision Former

Data, vocabularies, configuration components included leading verbs indicating that an utterance is a request. It also includes expressions used by an utterance author to indicate he wants a customer support agent (CSA) to do something, such as *"Please do … for me"*. These expressions also refer to information request such as "Give me MY …" (for example, current account yield). For a question, this vocabulary includes the ways people address questions, such as *"please tell me…"*.

Rule engine employs a set of rules, including the keyword-based, vocabulary-based and linguistic ones. The rules are applied in certain order, oriented to find

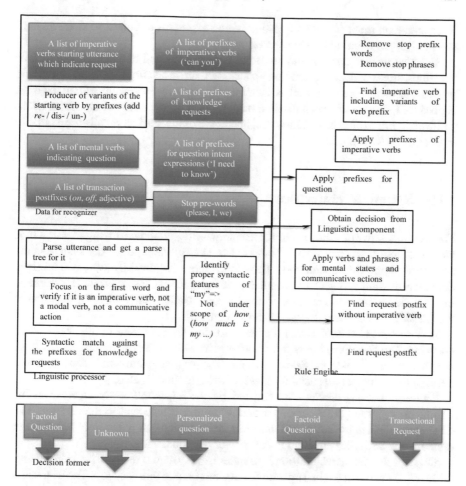

Fig. 10.8 Architecture of query type recognizer

indication of a transaction. If main cases of *transactions* are not identified, only then the rule engine applies *question* rules. Finally, if question rules did not fire, we classify the utterance as *unknown,* but nevertheless treat it as default, a *question.* Most rules are specific to the class of requests: if none of them fire then the decision is also a *question.*

Linguistic processor is designed to work with two templates: imperative leading verb and a reference to *MY* object. Once parsing is done, the first word should be a regular verb in present tense, active voice, neither modal, mental or a form of *"be"*. These constraints assure this verb is in the imperative form *"Drop the temperature in the room"*. The second case addresses utterance related to an object the author owns or is associated too, such as *"my account balance"* and *"my car"*. These utterances are connected with an intent to perform an action with these objects or request for an information on them (versus a question which expresses a request to share general knowledge, not about this particular, *my* object).

Decision former takes an output of the Rule Engine and outputs one out of four decisions, along with an explanation for each of them. Each fired keyword-based rule provides an explanation, as well as each linguistic rule. So when a resultant decision is produced, there is always a detailed back up of it. If any of the components failed while applying a rule, the resultant decision is *unknown*. Further details are available in (Galitsky 2019b).

10.5   System Architecture

The Architecture for Conversational Explainability is shown in Fig. 10.9. CE is wrapped around an abstract ML component. The offline input of the system is the corpus of supporting documents. The online input for the ML system is a given document or another object to recognize or detect, and for CE system is ML's decision log. The output is provided in the form of a conversation concerning the decision of the classifier or detector processing this document.

A document is classified and the classification features used in the decision are provided. The final decision with its back-up, as well as intermediate decision logs, are provided and sent to the *Search Indexer*. The original document is converted into a form where the features used for classification are highlighted.

The explanations chains are extracted by the *Explanation Manager* from the corpus of supported documents, verified, filtered and also sent to the *Indexer*. The *Explanation Manager* indexes all text fragments which can potentially be useful in combination with the decision logs to answer user questions.

Once the document recognition is complete, the system is ready to provide the user with a decision result backed up with the reasons behind this decision. The user starts the conversation with a question concerning the decision, followed by questions to the decision log. The questions are recognized with respect to the question type and sent to the *Question Answering* component and also to the *Dialogue Manager* along with the recognized question type. *Question Answering* forms a query (Galitsky 2015) and issues a search request to the *Index* together with the *Dialogue Manager* that forms the query constraints. The returned text fragment with attributes is processed by the *Dialogue Manager* (Galitsky 2019a) and sent back to the user as a reply.

Hence there are three stages of how this architecture functions:

(1) The *offline* stage processes the corpus of supporting documents;
(2) The *online classification* stage performs classification of the input document, obtains intermediate and final decisions and puts the classification log into the search index;
(3) The *online conversational explanation* stage processes the user query and replies to it.

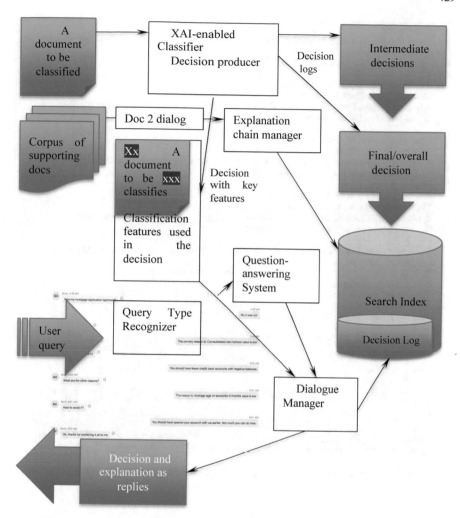

Fig. 10.9 Overall architecture of the CE system

This architecture can access an arbitrary classifier hosted outside of the conversational explanation framework.

10.6 Decision Log and User Questions

One can see from this classification decision log (Fig. 10.10) that three negative matches with the training set elements *"compensation is **not** required"* outvote a single match with the positive set *"compensation **is** required"*. Therefore, the final

Decision log
The following customer communication is classified with respect to: should this customer be compensated
Decision: compensation is not required

Similar assessment of customer situation:
This text: "The balance is high because"
A relevant fragment from the Training set text # 2182 tagged as "compensation **is not required**"
"...because of ... I owed a lot of money..."

Similar assessment of customer decision:
This text: "I opted out of all my XYZ Bank credit cards"
A relevant fragment from the Training set text # 790 tagged as "compensation **is not required**"
"...requested to cancel my credit card accounts"

Similar assessment of customer sentiment:
This text: "I took advantage of a good deal"
A relevant fragment from the Training set text # 127 tagged as "compensation **is not required**"
"...I enjoyed the promotion ... on financial products"

Similar assessment of customer adherence to regulations (www.livemint.com › money › personal-finance › what-is-minimum-amount...):
This text: "now will pay them to the penny ONLY the minimum amount due"
A fragment from a regulation document tagged as "compensation **is required**"
"...minimum amount you are required to pay on or before the payment due date to maintain your card account. It is only a small portion of the principal outstanding every month. Typically, the minimum amount due is calculated as 5% of your outstanding balance..."

I have been a customer with a Platinum card for a number of years. I always pay my bill on time, usually pay much more than the minimum due and have a high balance but still way below my credit limit. The balance is high because XYZ Bank called me due to my fantastic credit rating and history and offered me a great rate for balance transfers. So being a savvy individual I took advantage of a good deal for cash advance and always kept up my part of the bargain.
*   Well because XYZ Bank was greedy when the economy was good and can't run a sound business without needing a bailout from the American people, they decided to try to screw me by upping my interest rate substantially for no reason (my credit score, income and debt/savings ratio have not changed at all despite this lousy economy). They are worth a class suite, as it is unclear how they that much interest! Well I opted out of all my Bank of America credit cards and now will pay them to the penny ONLY the minimum amount due, so it will now take these greedy idiots much longer to get their money.*

Fig. 10.10 A customer message and its Decision log for classifying as *compensation is required* versus *is not required*

decision is *"compensation is not required"*. This is the nearest neighbor classification by means of identifying tagged cases.

Each log entry has the following format:

(1)   Assessment type;
(2)   Fragment from the customer communication being classified;
(3)   Matching fragment from the element of the training dataset + the **assigned class.**

We show an example on how questions for evaluation can be generated from a similar text (Fig. 10.11). We split the text into sentences and propose one-two questions from each with the answers from the text and Decision Log of Fig. 10.10. Some answers (highlighted in gray) for the question formed from this text are obtained from the text (Fig. 10.10 on the bottom) and some from the respective Decision Log.

We now proceed to an example of a dialogue facilitated by the CE (Fig. 10.12).

I've a AAA gas rebate XYZ Bank Visa credit card and while I was looking at recent monthly statements, I found how XYZ Bank grossly misleads customers and collects interest through devious methods.
Formed Q: *How does XYZ Bank collect interest?*
Expected A: *It is unclear how they collect that much interest!*

Formed Q: *What are devious [sentiment -] methods of interest collection?*
Expected A from Decision Log:
    Similar assessment of customer sentiment:
    This text: *... interest is collected via [method]*

Here is what happened in my case and same must be true for all customers, therefore good cause for class action suit, and request all customers to look closely your statements if you took cash advances any time.
Formed Q: Is XYZ Bank a good cause for class action suit?
Expected A: *They are worth a class suite, as it is unclear how they collect that much interest!*

Formed Q: *Was I requested to look closely into my statement?*
Expected A from Decision Log: ...
    Similar assessment of customer compliance with regulations:
    This text: *... customers are required to verify their statements...*

Initially AAA card was offered to me with low interest rate balance transfer. After the initial offer period, interest rate on my balance transfers and purchases gone up to 13.99% and now I've cash advance interest rate of 19.99%.
Formed Q: *What happened after the initial offer period?*

Fig. 10.11   A text of a similar complaint that is a good source of questions to assess the CE system

- Why did XYZ Bank raise interest rate?
- With banks limiting home equity lines, gas and food bills on the rise, and homeowners struggling to make their mortgage payments, some Americans are turning to credit cards to make ends meet. Many, however, are finding their cards more expensive to use as credit card companies increasingly raise interest rates, lower credit limits and cancel inactive accounts. It's all happening, some industry watchers say, for a good reason: The companies are trying to avert a crisis. In the first three months of the year 2008, commercial banks in the U.S. took losses on 4.7 percent of their credit card loans, up from 3.9 percent the year before, according to the Federal Reserve.

- What kind of credit card rate can I expect?
- The inflation rate in 2016 was just 1.26%, quite low by historical standards. What economists refer to as the "real" interest rate is the nominal rate minus the rate of inflation. So the average real credit card rate in 2016 was 12.30%. In 2008, by contrast, inflation was 3.85%, so the real credit card rate that year was 9.72%, the lowest since 1981.

- Why cannot I be compensated for the higher interest rates?
- YOU opted out of all YOUR XYZ Bank credit cards"

Fig. 10.12   A CE-based dialogue

10.7   Evaluation

To evaluate the performance of the Conversational Explainability system, we need to choose an explainable learning framework, obtain a number of classification sessions, possess a set of user queries concerning these sessions and assess the set of conversations the CE is capable of producing. We select customer complaints and its nearest-neighbor classification as a domain for CE evaluation. The recognition engine with its data and recognition sessions are genuine, and real-time user questions will be generated from *similar* customer complaints, the ones on the same topic. We will be forming the initial question, as well as the consecutive information-seeking questions from this similar complaint, converting opinionated sentences such as the ones expressing disagreement or a lack of understanding into these questions. As to non-information seeking questions, they will be generated by the same dialogue manager acting for CE but now also acting on behalf of a hypothetical customer. This way we will be generating CE sessions for an assessment automatically, but the assessment of these sessions is manual.

One of the evaluation subtasks is to generate a user question from sentences. This technique is explained in detail in Chap. 1 Volume 2. In Table 10.3, we show the classification domains and the nature of classes. The same nearest neighbor learning is used in each class for the sake of improved explainability and not necessarily the highest recognition rate.

We aim at an automated evaluation of CE performance. To achieve it, we try to design an automated assessment algorithm and evaluate the quality of the assessment manually. The assessment algorithm should be different from the recognition algorithm for a given component. We separately estimate the accuracy of the assessment algorithm and of the CE component itself.

The assessment algorithm is estimated manually with respect to how accurately it is assessing the system component. The assessment measurement error $\varepsilon = 1 - F1_{\text{assessment algorithm}}$. We consider the assessment algorithm satisfactory for most evaluations if $\varepsilon < 20\%$. Hence ε is estimated manually but allows for an automated assessment of a system component with certain measurement error. Once this manual assessment is done, we can apply the assessment algorithm to the system component, measuring its accuracy as $F1_{\text{component}} \pm \varepsilon$. We usually just denote it as $F1$ of a component or an overall system.

For the query type recognizer, we collect 320 queries of the known type (information request and transactional, Galitsky (2019b)) and confirm that this query type is determined correctly (the second column).

Cohesiveness of conversation is assessed based on the rhetorical agreement measure (Chap. 4 Volume 2), applied to utterances longer than 20 words. Rhetorical agreement is based on coordination of communicative discourse trees for the current and preceding utterances, such as a question and its answer. The percentages of proper rhetorical agreement are shown in the third column.

We evaluate the search components (Table 10.4) with respect to two tasks: searching the decision log with personalized questions and searching the background knowledge. In addition to search F1 measure, we use a normalized Discounted Cumulative Gain (NDCG, Wang et al. 2013), measuring the top five search results (the second column from the right).

Achieved query type recognition of almost 80% is 10% above the assessed conversation cohesiveness. Naturally, when the query type is recognized incorrectly, the logic of conversation breaks; however, there are other reasons for flaws in the logic of conversation not explicitly measured. Search accuracy for the background information (open domain, Galitsky 2017a) is 5% lower than that of the decision logs

Table 10.3 Characteristics for each classification domain in CE evaluation

Source name	# in the dataset	Recognition classes	Origin of data	Source of recommendations
Finance	1600	Needs compensation versus does not need it	my3cents.com bankrate.com	Web search of Bloomberg, Fidelity, Bankrate for financial products
Auto repair	6750	A genuine failure of a product versus an attempt to get compensation	2carpros.com	Web search for services
Sports shopping	1890	A sports equipment led to a genuine accident versus not a reason for an accident	REI, Big5Sports and L.L.Bean data from RichRelevance.com	Internal API for product search
Home products shopping	2350	Led to a genuine problem of usability versus not a reason for a failure	Walmart, HD Supply, OfficeDepot data from RichRelevance.com	eBay product search API
Home-related services	740	A service is completed satisfactorily versus not satisfactorily	Yelp reviews	Yelp API
Travel	1860	A genuine problem while traveling because of an operator versus a different kind of travel problem	www.zicasso.com/travel-reviews www.tripadvisor.com reviews Airline forums on tripadvisor.com	Tripadvisor.com
Genuine human dialogues	2000	Plausible dialogue versus unrealistic dialogue	(Li et al. 2018) ENRON email thread Reddit discourse dataset (Logacheva et al. 2018)	Yelp API, eBay product search API, Bing Forum search, Bing Web search

(which is a closed domain, however, requiring entity association). All issues of relevance and logical errors end up affecting the overall meaningfulness of conversation, which is 15–20% lower than the achieved search relevance. At the same time, this overall meaningfulness is only 3% lower than the achieved cohesiveness of conversation: in some cases the conversation logic is broken but overall conversation is nevertheless meaningful.

We also evaluate a comparative performance of a conventional, report-based explainability for the same sources and decision logs (Table 10.5). Average

Table 10.4 Evaluation of CE, %

Source name	Query type recognition	Cohesiveness of conversation	Access to decision log			Access to the background documents				Overall *meaningful* explanation
			P	R	F1	P	R	F1	NDCG	
Finance	81	69	82	80	81.0	87	85	86.0	0.352	67.1
Auto repair	73	73	76	79	77.5	81	83	82.0	0.341	65.3
Sports shopping	80	65	86	84	85.0	88	88	88.0	0.360	69.0
Home products shopping	78	63	80	81	80.5	90	89	89.5	0.359	66.2
Home-related services	83	73	77	74	75.5	80	83	81.5	0.330	63.9
Travel	81	70	81	82	81.5	86	84	85.0	0.347	64.7
Genuine human dialogues	77	64	74	75	74.5	79	80	79.5	0.312	60.1
avg	79.0	68.1	79.4	79.2	79.3	84.4	84.6	84.5	0.340	65.2

Table 10.5 A comparison between CE and report-based explainability

Source name	Overall *meaningful* explanation for CE	Overall *meaningful* explanation by a report that contain the decision log
Finance	67.1	53.1
Auto repair	65.3	50.5
Sports shopping	69.0	47.9
Home products shopping	66.2	44.3
Home-related services	63.9	52.8
Travel	64.7	50.3
Genuine human dialogues	60.1	46.0
avg	65.2	49.3

percentage of meaningful explanation as received via dialogue is 15.9% higher than that of the conventional, report-based explanations which were assessed by human judges (on Amazon Mechanical Turk) as meaningful.

We do not evaluate the performance of the classifier itself but instead the overall quality of how its decision is communicated via conversation.

10.8   Logical Foundation

10.8.1   *Textual Entailment*

The task of recognizing textual entailment is a critical NL understanding task. Given a pair of sentences, called the premise and hypothesis, the task consists of classifying their relation as either.

(a)   entailment, if the premise entails or *explains* the hypothesis,
(b)   contradiction, if the hypothesis contradicts the premise, or
(c)   neutral, if neither entailment nor contradiction hold.

The Stanford NL Interface dataset (SNLI, Bowman et al. 2015), containing more than a half-million samples of human-generated triples < premise, hypothesis, label >, has driven the development of a large number of neural network models. Conneau et al. (2017) demonstrated that training universal sentence representations on SNLI is both more efficient and more accurate than the traditional training approaches of orders of magnitude larger, but unsupervised, datasets. Camburu et al. (2018) advances this research toward an additional layer of explanations on top of the label supervision and bring in further improvements.

Gururangan et al. (2018) cast doubt on whether models trained on SNLI are learning to "understand" language, and claims that these models are largely fixating on spurious correlations also called artifacts. For example, specific words in the hypothesis tend to be strong indicators of the label, e.g., *friends, old* appear very often in neutral hypotheses, *animal, outdoors* appear most of the time in entailment hypotheses, while *nobody, sleeping* appear mostly in contradiction hypothesis. They show that a premise-agnostic model, i.e., a model that only takes as input the hypothesis and outputs the label, obtains 67% test accuracy. Camburu et al. (2018) show that it is much more difficult to rely on artifacts to generate explanations than to generate labels.

In the dataset of Camburu et al. (2018), in the large majority of cases, one can easily detect for which label an explanation has been provided. We state that this is not the case in general, as the same explanation can be correctly arguing for different labels, depending on the premise and hypothesis. For example, the explanation "*A woman is a person*" would be a correct explanation for the entailment pair ("*A woman is in the park*", "*A person is in the park*") as well for the contradiction pair ("*A woman is in the park*", "*There is no person in the park*"). However, there are multiple ways of formulating an explanation. In our example, for the contradiction pair, one could also explain that "*There cannot be no person in the park if a woman is in the park*". If this sentence is read in a stand-alone mode, one would infer that the pair is a contradiction.

There has been little work on incorporating and outputting NL free-form explanations, mostly due to the lack of appropriate datasets. A recent work by Park et al. (2018) follows along these lines; the authors introduce two datasets of natural language explanations for the tasks of visual question-answering and activity recognition. Another work in this direction is that of (Ling et al. 2017), who introduced a dataset of textual justifications for solving math problems and formulated the task in terms of program execution. Nonetheless, their setup is specific to the task of solving math problems, and thus hard to transfer to more general natural understanding tasks. Jansen et al. (2018) provided a dataset of NL explanation graphs for elementary science questions. However, with only 1, 680 pairs of questions and explanations, their corpus is orders of magnitude smaller than e-SNLI.

Dasgupta et al. (2018) assembled a dataset to test whether inference models actually capture compositionality beyond word level. They showed that the sentence embeddings of (Conneau et al. 2017) indeed do not exhibit significant compositionality and that downstream models using these sentence representations largely rely on simple heuristics that are ecologically valid in the SNLI corpus. For example, high overlap in words between premise and hypothesis usually predicts entailment, while most contradictory sentence pairs have no or very little overlap of words. Negation words would also strongly indicate a contradiction.

Ontology-supported Q/A is an extensively studied approach in the logical AI community. This approach targets improving Q/A with the use of a logical theory. As a form of logical entailment, ontology-supported Q/A is fully interpretable, which makes it possible to derive explanations for query answers. Ontology languages are mostly fragments of first-order logic (FOL), selected to maintain the expressivity of the language on one hand, and to limit its computational complexity of reasoning in the language on the other hand. As a form of first-order entailment, ontology-supported query answering is fully interpretable, which makes it possible to derive explanations for query answers.

10.8.2 Learned Explanations Versus True Explanations

There is a confusion between what deep learning (DL) community calls *reasoning, explanation, argumentation,* etc., and what these notions use to mean for the last few decades of AI, especially a logical AI. The DL community refers to a reasoning result, explanation or argumentation (Galitsky et al. 2018) as abstract object, or textual objects which are similar in some metric to the objects tagged by a training set annotators as a reasoning result, explanation, or argumentation. Hence, although these *similar to manually tagged* objects possess some features of a reasoning result, explanation, or argumentation, the completeness of this feature is relative and is determined by the definition of similarity metric and the accuracy of annotation. Therefore, learned reasoning result, reasoning process, explanation or argumentation *deviate* from those defined logically, within a formal framework with defined syntax and semantics of a formal language. Furthermore, learned explanations and other objects are not those obtained by approximate reasoning means, but instead those similar to them in the sense of NL similarity of words and sentences, not a logical similarity that can be defined deductively.

When a DL system build a wrong "explanation", it can potentially be corrected by extending a dataset, but cannot be "repaired" by involving new facts and clauses. A *true explanation* can be deduced, linked to other facts and explanations and be reflected in as much thoroughness as needed. If there is an error in a true explanation, it can be rectified involving new facts. A true explanation, when having broken links, does not fail miserably: involving additional chunks of knowledge can repair it.

DL explanations are learned by generalization:

(1) Formally, not an explanation: counter-examples which were removed while generalization to avoid overfitting, would break it;
(2) Cannot be repaired;
(3) Is a result of inductive generalization (Galitsky et al. 2006) between similar decisions and similar explanations.

On the contrary, true explanations:

(1) Constitutes a deduction link between a decision and its explanation;
(2) Genuine explanation errors: missing links;
(3) An explanation is provided in an interactive, conversational format. A user can drill into each member of an explanation chain;
(4) Exists in the form of an explanation chain. If a given step is broken, it can be repaired;

(5) If a given explanation chain encounters an inconsistency, the true explanation system can try again to form a different chain of premises for a given hypothesis.

Although high recognition and generalization accuracy is achieved by DL methods, the DL community should tone down its claims since in the cases the classification and generation is erroneous, it does not fail gracefully.

One of the leading mathematician of the twentieth century, Israel Gelfand expressed his skepticism (personal communication, 1996) about the neural network approaches in both simulating brain and solving recognition problem. His thoughts were that the underlying formalism is neither rich enough nor sufficiently expressive. Back then, a computing power was too limited to scale a neural network up to a real data-rich problem.

Recent attempts to push DL toward explainability have focused, among others, on learning symbolic operations which are interpretable. This idea was biologically inspired and formulated, in particular, in (Galitsky 1992), where a concept of symbol solver and its neural network implementation was introduced. A capability of the mind to provide an explanation of the behavior it produces and controls is an essential Theory-of-Mind skill (Galitsky 2016).

10.8.3 Existential Rules and Ontology-Supported Q/A

The semantics of First-Order Logic (FOL) is given by means of interpretations $I = (\Delta^I, \cdot^I)$, where Δ^I is a possibly infinite domain, and $\cdot_I$ is an interpretation function that maps every constant a to a domain element $a^I \in \Delta^I$, every predicate p with arity n to a relation $p^I \subseteq ((\Delta^I)^n$. A sentence Φ is satisfied by an interpretation I, if $I \models \Phi$, where "$\models$" is the standard first-order entailment relation.

A (first-order) theory Σ is a (finite) set of first-order formulas. An interpretation I is a model of a theory Σ, denoted $I \models \Sigma$, if I satisfies all $\Phi \in \Sigma$. Σ entails a sentence Φ, written $\Sigma \models \Phi$, if all models of Σ are also models of Φ.

A tuple-generating dependency (TGD) is a first-order formula of the form $\forall X$ $\Phi(X) \rightarrow \exists Y \, \Psi(X, Y)$,

where $\Phi(X)$ is a conjunction of atoms, called the body of the TGD, and $\Psi(X, Y)$ is a conjunction of atoms, called the head of the TGD. Classes of TGDs are also known as existential rules; an ontology is a finite set Σ of TGDs. TGDs can express the inclusion and join dependencies of databases. In its general form, however, reasoning with TGDs is undecidable (can always construct a corresponding algorithm that can answer the problem correctly), but a decidable fragment is used for industrial applications. We follow the presentation of Ceylan et al. (2019).

A database D is a finite set of facts over a (finite) relational vocabulary. A conjunctive query (CQ) is an existentially quantified formula $\exists X \, \Phi(X, Y)$, where $\Phi(X, Y)$, is a conjunction of atoms over the set of variables X and Y; a union of conjunctive queries (UCQ) is a disjunction of CQs (over the same free variables).

The paradigm of ontology-supported query answering generalizes a query answering over databases by incorporating additional background knowledge expressed in an ontology. Formally, a query is a pair (Q, Σ), where Q is a Boolean query, and Σ is an ontology. Given a database D and a pair (Q, Σ), we say that D entails the pair (Q, Σ), denoted D $\models (Q, \Sigma)$, if for all models I $\models \Sigma \cup$ D it holds that I $\models Q$, where $\models$ is first-order entailment. Ontology–supported Q/A is the task of deciding whether $D \models (Q, \Sigma)$ for a given database D and a pair (Q, Σ).

10.8.4 Explainability with an Ontology

Definition. For a database D and an query-ontology pair (Q, Σ), where Σ is a set of existential rules, and Q is a query, an explanation for (Q, Σ) in D is a *subset* $E \subseteq D$ of facts such that $E \models (Q, \Sigma)$. A *minimal* explanation E for (Q, Σ) in D is an explanation for (Q, Σ) in D such that it is *subset-minimal*. It means that there is no proper subset $E' \not\subseteq E$ that is an explanation for (Q, Σ) in D.

When the ontology-supported query (Q, Σ) and the database D are clear from the context, we simply speak about a minimality of explanation without explicitly mentioning (Q, Σ) or D.

Let us consider a customer support expertise allocation scenario illustrated in Fig. 10.13. In this example, we are interested in identifying customer support agents (CSA) $p_1, ..., p_6$ in relation to their expertise domains c_1, c_2, and c_3. We want to find a minimal subset of CSAs that covers all knowledge domains, i.e., a minimal subset of CSA that has at least one representative from each knowledge domain.

We can express this problem as an ontology-supported query in a way that every answer to this problem is in bijection with a minimal explanation E as follows. We define the database:

$D_p = \{CSA(p_i) \mid 1 \leq i \leq 6\}$, which encodes the set of proteins, and the pair $\{Q_p, \Sigma_p\}$:

$$\Sigma_p = \{CSA(p_i) \rightarrow \bigwedge_{p_i \ in \ c_j} covered(\ c_j) \mid 1 \leq i \leq 6\},$$
$$Q_p = covered(c_1) \wedge covered(c_2) \wedge covered(c_3).$$

Fig. 10.13 Illustration for six customer support agents and three knowledge domain: expertise allocation

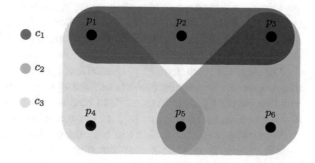

Our ontology encodes the relation between CSAs and their knowledge domains, and the query asks whether the knowledge domains c_1, c_2 and c_3 are covered.

Consider now a subset $E \subseteq D_p$. Then, it is easy to verify that a subset $E \subseteq D_p$, $E \models (Q_p, \Sigma_p)$ iff.

$E \models \{covered(c_i), \Sigma_p\}$, for every c_i. Thus, the minimum explanation for $\{Q_p, \Sigma_p\}$ in D_p are in bijection with minimal covers.

10.8.5   Deciding Whether a Given Subset of a Database is a Minimal Explanation

Given a database D, a pair (Q, Σ), where Q is a UCQ and Σ is TGDs, and a set of facts $E \subseteq D$, we formulate a question if E is a minimum explanation for (Q, Σ) in D.

Let us illustrate this problem by the CSA example. The subsets.

$E_1 = \{CSA(p_1), CSA(p_3)\}$,

$E_2 = \{CSA(p_2), pCSA(p_5)\}$,

$E_3 = \{CSA(p_2), CSA(p_4), CSA(p_6)\}$.

of the database D_p are minimum explanations for the pair (Q_p, Σ_p), and give the minimal covers by CSAs of their total domain knowledge. However, $\{CSA(p_4), CSA(p_5), CSA(p_6)\}$ is not a minimum explanation, as it does not cover all domains and thus does not entail (Q_p, Σ_p). The set $\{CSA(p_1), CSA(p_2), CSA(p_3)\}$ does entail (Q_p, Σ_p), but it is not a minimum explanation, since $CSA(p_2)$ could be removed and the formula satisfaction would not change.

We proceed to the problem of deciding whether a given set of subsets of a database is the set of all minimal explanations. Similarly to above, we have a database D and a pair (Q, Σ), but now our focus is on the set of $E \subseteq$ subsets of D. The question is whether E is set of all minimal explanations for (Q, Σ) in D.

Consider the set E provided as:

$\{CSA(p_1), CSA(p_3)\}$, $\{CSA(p_1), CSA(p_5)\}$,

$\{CSA(p_1), CSA(p_6)\}$, $\{CSA(p_2), CSA(p_5)\}$, $\{CSA(p_3), CSA(p_4)\}$, $\{CSA(p_3), CSA(p_5)\}$,

$\{CSA(p_2), CSA(p_4), CSA(p_6)\}$.

One can verify that E is precisely the set of all minimal explanations for (Q_p, Σ_p), in D_p. Given a set E of subsets of the database, to decide if it is the set of all minimal explanations, we can proceed as follows. We perform a polynomial number of C checks to decide whether all sets in E entail (Q, Σ). Then, we need to decide whether all sets in E are minimal, and there is no minimal explanation that is not in E. This holds if there is no $\varepsilon' \subseteq D$ entailing (Q, Σ) such that $\varepsilon' \subseteq \varepsilon$ for all $\varepsilon \in E$. There is an accompanying problem of finding a set ε' such that $\varepsilon' \subseteq \varepsilon$ for all $\varepsilon \in E$ and that entails (Q, Σ). What needs to be done now is checking whether all sets in E are minimal, and there is no minimal explanation that is not included in E.

We now focus on the problem of building explanations excluding *forbidden* sets. This is about finding a minimal explanation that does not include a given set of facts.

Let F be a set of subsets of a database D, which intuitively encodes a set of invalid facts in D: elements of F may be known to be erroneous, or we may want to avoid them for some other reason, depending on the application. The objective is to find an explanation that is not a superset of any of the sets in F, if possible.

Let us imagine that the set of CSA agents $F = \{ \{CSA(p_1)\}, \{ CSA(p_3), CSA(p_5)\}, \{ CSA(p_2), CSA(p_4), CSA(p_6)\}\}$ encodes a group of CSA agents that are not allowed to be in a cover of a certain domain knowledge (for example, due to a certain conflict of interests). In this case, $\{CSA(p_3), CSA(p_4)\}$ is a minimum explanation, being a cover that does not contain any configuration from F.

To decide the existence of a minimum explanation not including the forbidden sets, it is sufficient to randomly select such a subset of a database and then check whether it entails the ontology-supported query. There is no need to check minimality as, if there is a subset E of a database that does not contain any of "forbidden" sets and entails the ontology-supported query, then E has a minimal subset with these properties (due to monotonicity of the entailment relation).

10.9 Conclusions

It is known that human students do not learn only from available examples supplied and annotated by their trainers (as typical DL systems do). In addition, they attempt to form a conceptual understanding of a task to be completed by means of both demonstrations and explanations. ML models trained simply to obtain high accuracy on fixed datasets often end up learning to rely heavily on shallow input statistics, resulting in brittle models susceptible to adversarial attacks (Galitsky and de la Rosa 2011). For example, Ribeiro et al. (2017) present a document classifier that distinguishes between two religion-related classes with an accuracy of 94%. However, on a close inspection, the model spuriously separates classes based on words contained in the headers, such as *Posting, Host* and *Re*.

Neither extractive nor attention-based techniques can provide full-sentence explanations of a model's decisions. Moreover, they cannot capture fine-grained relations and asymmetries, especially in a task like recognizing textual entailment. For example, if the words *person, woman, mountain, outdoors* are extracted as justification, one may not know whether the model correctly learned that *A woman is a person* and not that *A person is a woman*, let alone that the model correctly paired (*woman, person*) and (*mountain, outside*).

It is well known that humans are reluctant to rely on interfaces that are not directly interpretable, tractable and trustworthy (Galitsky et al. 2014; Zhu et al. 2018). Explainability is one of the main barriers AI is facing nowadays in regards to its practical implementation. It is customary to think that by addressing performance first, the systems will be increasingly opaque. This is true in the sense that there is a trade-off between the performance of a model and its transparency (Došilovic 2018, Fig. 10.14). However, an improvement in the understanding of a system can lead to the correction of its deficiencies. When developing a ML model, the consideration

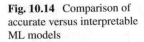

Fig. 10.14 Comparison of accurate versus interpretable ML models

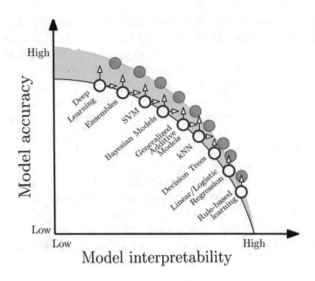

of interpretability as an additional design motivation can improve the implementation, testing and deployment efficiency of ML in CRM due to the following. Interpretability helps ensure impartiality in decision-making. As a result, interpretability allows avoiding a bias in the training dataset. Also, interpretability improves a robustness of a CRM ML system by highlighting potential adversarial perturbations that could potentially alter the decision. Finally, interpretability can assure that only meaningful variables infer the output with proper causal links. That provides that an underlying truthful causality exists in the model reasoning.

Whereas conventional explainable AI relies on plain text, images and other media, the conversation mode makes explainability complete and further improves the trust. Users can ask *Why* questions as much as they need to understand a decision. Interactivity is tightly associated with explainability and transparency (Harbers et al. 2010; Chander et al. 2018).

One of the examples of an ML system missing explainability, in particular, highlighting causal links, is Google Flu Trends. Google developed it to predict flu outbreaks. The system correlated Google searches with flu outbreaks, and it ended up performing poorly (Lazer and Kennedy 2015). The distribution of search queries changed and Google Flu Trends missed many flu outbreaks. Google searches do not cause the flu. When people search for symptoms like "fever" it is merely a correlation with actual flu outbreaks, not a causal link from search to actual occurrence but rather the other way around. Ideally, models would only use causal features because they would not be tricked. An assent to the meta-explanation level is sometimes fruitful to identify causal links in the meta-language, when it is hard to find them in the language-object (Galitsky et al. 2011, Galitsky 2017b).

Fig. 10.15 Constructing an explanation report

In this Chapter, we assessed a step forward from a report-based explanation to the conversational explanation framework. Not only CE's success rate (of being a meaningful explanation) exceeds that of the report-based by almost 16%, but CE does not involve a costly process of designing a report format (Fig. 10.15). The achieved success rate of 65% should be compared with that of a conventional decision system that frequently does not provide explanations at all (0% success rate). CRM is the domain where a high successful explainability rate is essential: customers tend not to trust a decision that not only does not favor them (reject their application) but also does so without a proper explanation.

References

Arrieta AB, D'iaz-Rodr'iguez N, Ser JD, Bennetot A, Tabik S, Barbado A, Garc'ia S, Gil-Lopez S, Molina D, Benjamins R, Chatila R, Herrera F (2019) Explainable Artificial Intelligence (XAI): concepts, taxonomies, opportunities and challenges toward responsible AI. ArXiv, abs/1910.10045

Arya V, Bellamy RK, Chen PY, Dhurandhar A, Hind M, Hoffman SC, Houde S, Liao QV, Luss R, Mojsilović A, Mourad S (2019) One explanation does not fit all: a toolkit and taxonomy of AI explainability techniques. arXiv preprint arXiv:1909.03012

Bowman SR, Angeli G, Potts C, Manning CD (2015) A large annotated corpus for learning natural language inference. In EMNLP

Camburu OM, Rocktäschel T, Lukasiewicz T, Blunsom P (2018) E-SNLI: natural language inference with natural language explanations. In Neural Information Processing Systems 2018 V 31

Ceylan İ, Lukasiewicz T, Malizia E, Vaicenavičius A (2019) Explanations for query answers under existential rules. IJCAI, 1639–1646

Chander A, Srinivasan R, Chelian S, Wang J, Uchino K (2018) Working with beliefs: AI transparency in the enterprise. In: Workshops of the ACM Conference on Intelligent User Interfaces

Conneau A, Kiela D, Schwenk H, Barrault L, Bordes A (2017) Supervised learning of universal sentence representations from natural language inference data. CoRR, abs/1705.02364

Cartoonbank (2020) https://cartoonbank.ru/?page_id=29&offset=29320

Dasgupta I, Guo D, Stuhlmüller A, Gershman SJ, Goodman ND (2018) Evaluating compositionality in sentence embeddings. ArXiv, abs/1802.04302

Došilovic FK, Brc M and Hlupic N (2018) Explainable artificial intelligence: A survey. In Proc. MIPRO, 210–215

Galitsky B (1992) Symbol solver in single neuron and in network. RNNS/IEEE Symposium on Neuroinformatics and Neurocomputers

Galitsky B, González MP, Chesñevar CI (2006) Inductive learning of dispute scenarios for online resolution of customer complaints. 3rd International IEEE Conference Intelligent Systems, 103–108

Galitsky B, JL De la Rosa B (2011) Learning adversarial reasoning patterns in customer complaints. Workshop at AAAI

Galitsky B, Kovalerchuk B, de la Rosa JL (2011) Assessing plausibility of explanation and meta-explanation in inter-human conflicts. Eng Appl Artif Intell 24(8):1472–1486

Galitsky B (2014) Learning parse structure of paragraphs and its applications in search. Eng Appl Artif Intell 32:160–184

Galitsky B, Ilvovsky D, Lebedeva N, Usikov D (2014) Improving trust in automation of social promotion. AAAI Spring Symposium Series

Galitsky B (2015) Finding a lattice of needles in a haystack: forming a query from a set of items of interest. FCA4AI@ IJCAI, pp 99–106

Galitsky B (2016) Theory of mind engine. In: Computational Autism. Springer, Cham

Galitsky B (2017) Matching parse thickets for open domain question answering. Data Knowl Eng 107:24–50

Galitsky B (2017b) Using Extended tree kernel to recognize metalanguage in text. In Uncertainty Modeling, Studies in Computational Intelligence 683, 71–96

Galitsky B, de la Rosa JL (2011) Concept-based learning of human behavior for customer relationship management. Inf Sci 181(10):2016–2035

Galitsky B, Ilvovsky D (2017) Chatbot with a discourse structure-driven dialogue management. EACL Demo E17–3022. Valencia

Galitsky B (2018) Customers' retention requires an explainability feature in machine learning systems they use. AAAI Spring Symposium Series

Galitsky B, Ilvovsky D, Pisarevskaya D (2018) Argumentation in text: discourse structure matters. CICLing

Galitsky B (2019a) Chatbot components and architectures. In Developing Enterprise Chatbots. Springer, Cham, Switzerland

Galitsky B (2019b) Explainable machine learning for chatbots. In Developing Enterprise Chatbots, 53–83, Springer, Cham, Switzerland

Galitsky B (2019c) Chatbot components and architectures. In Developing Enterprise Chatbots, 365–426, Springer, Cham, Switzerland

Gururangan S, Swayamdipta S, Levy O, Schwartz R, Bowman S, Smith NA (2018) Annotation artifacts in natural language inference data. In Proc. of NAACL

Gustavo Polleti, Hugo Neri, Fabio Cozman (2020) Explanations within conversational recommendation systems: improving coverage through knowledge graph embedding

Harbers M, van den Bosch K, Meyer J-J (2010) Design and evaluation of explainable BDI agents, in: IEEE/WIC/ACM International Conference on Web Intelligence and Intelligent Agent Technology, Vol. 2, IEEE, pp. 125–132

Jansen PA, Wainwright E, Marmorstein S, Morrison CT (2018) Worldtree: a corpus of explanation graphs for elementary science questions supporting multi-hop inference. CoRR, abs/1802.03052

Lazer D, Kennedy R (2015) What we can learn from the epic failure of google flu trends. https://www.wired.com/2015/10/can-learn-epic-failure-google-flu-trends/

learning natural language inference

Ling W, Yogatama D, Dyer C and Blunsom P (2017) Program induction by rationale generation: Learning to solve and explain algebraic word problems. CoRR, abs/1705.04146

Molnar C (2019) Interpretable machine learning. a guide for making black box models explainable. https://christophm.github.io/interpretable-ml-book/

Park DH, Hendricks LA, Akata Z, Rohrbach A, Schiele B, Darrell T, Rohrbach M (2018). Multimodal explanations: justifying decisions and pointing to the evidence. CoRR, abs/1802.08129

Ribeiro MT, Singh S, Guestrin C (2016). "Why should I trust you?": Explaining the predictions of any classifier. CoRR, abs/1602.04938

Sixun Ouyang, Aonghus Lawlor (2020) Improving recommendation by deep latent factor-based explanation

Wang Y, Liwei Wang, Yuanzhi Li, Di He, Wei Chen, Tie-Yan Liu (2013) A theoretical analysis of normalized discounted cumulative gain (NDCG) ranking measures. In Proceedings of the 26th Annual Conference on Learning Theory (COLT 2013)

Zhu J, Liapis A, Risi S, Bidarra R, Youngblood GM (2018) Explainable AI for designers: a human-centered perspective on mixed-initiative co-creation, 2018 IEEE Conference on Computational Intelligence and Games (CIG) 1–8

Printed in the United States
by Baker & Taylor Publisher Services